Mission-Critical Active Directory

Architecting a Secure and Scalable Infrastructure

Micky Balladelli
Jan De Clercq

Digital Press
An imprint of Butterworth-Heinemann

Boston • Oxford • Auckland • Johannesburg • Melbourne • New Delhi

Mission-Critical Active Directory

Architecting a Secure and Scalable Infrastructure for Windows 2000

Micky Balladelli
Jan De Clercq

Digital Press
An imprint of Butterworth-Heinemann

Boston • Oxford • Auckland • Johannesburg • Melbourne • New Delhi

Library of Congress Cataloging-in-Publication Data

Balladelli, Micky.
   Mission-critical active directory : architecting a secure and scalable infrastructure / by Micky Balladelli and Jan De Clercq.
      p. cm.
      ISBN 1-55558-240-0 (alk. paper)
   1. Directory services (Computer network technology) I. De Clercq, Jan. II. Title.
   TK5105.595 .B35 2000
   005.7'1369--dc21

                                        00-047510

British Library Cataloging-in-Publication Data

A catalogue record for this book is available from the British Library.

The publisher offers special discounts on bulk orders of this book.
For information, please contact:

Manager of Special Sales
Butterworth–Heinemann
225 Wildwood Avenue
Woburn, MA 01801-2041
Tel: 781-904-2500
Fax: 781-904-2620

For information on all Butterworth–Heinemann publications available, contact our World Wide Web home page at: http://www.bh.com.

10 9 8 7 6 5 4 3 2 1

Printed in the United States of America

To my father.

—Micky Balladelli

To my wife, Katrien, for the many hours and days
I could not spend with her, and for her continuous support
and loving care while I was writing this book.

—Jan De Clercq

Contents

Foreword

In comparison to Windows 2000, Windows NT seems remarkably straightforward and easy to deploy. Yet administrators still struggle to deal with the challenges of corporate deployments as they figure out interdomain trust relationships, set up and manage resource domains, determine how best to secure resources, and keep their systems up and running. The improvements and enhanced features in Windows 2000 address many of the challenges in Windows NT and provide a true platform for enterprise applications such as those now being introduced in the Microsoft .NET initiative. While it might not get the same recognition as some of the headline features in Windows 2000, such as Intellimirror, the Active Directory is the key to making Windows 2000 servers work.

Compaq is Microsoft's Prime Integrator for Windows 2000. We've had the chance to get a unique insight into how the Active Directory really works through our partnership with Microsoft, hard experience gained through many large customer projects, and the Windows 2000 deployment at Compaq. There's certainly a huge difference in the issues faced by different deployments, from those that span the world and involve a multidomain forest to others that confine themselves to a single domain within one country. Networks, applications, hardware, and project team competence all add to the mix, but our experience gained to date leaves no doubt that successful deployment of servers and applications is only possible if a solid infrastructure is established first, and that means getting the Active Directory right.

Micky and Jan have set themselves an onerous task in this book. They have to cover the Active Directory in technical detail and explain its complexities clearly. At the same time, they can't afford to descend to the level where detail obscures the truly important information. Achieving the balance between a practical approach to Active Directory design and implementation while incorporating many background tips that allow you to tune and tweak the directory isn't easy, but I think they have done a good job.

If you read and understand everything here, you'll be in good shape to put your knowledge into practice. After a couple of deployments you might even become a true master of the black art of the Active Directory.

Enjoy!

Tony Redmond
Vice President and Chief Technology Officer
Compaq Professional Services

The first time I met Micky Balladelli and Jan De Clercq was in January 1998 when we had dinner with several Compaq Windows 2000 experts. Micky told me that he took a small Compaq Proliant server home for the holidays to test Active Directory scalability. His plan was to create more than 5 million users. I was really amused by their passion for and fascination with technology, and I couldn't believe that they could really do it. "Wait," Micky said, "in two years, we will put together a directory with all the phone numbers of all U.S. households."

Of course, I did not believe them, and, of course, they pulled it off. When Windows 2000 launched in February, they demonstrated their Active Directory with more than 100 million users. This is only one example of how professional and knowledgeable Jan and Micky are. Their book is the best reference on Active Directory that can be written from outside building 40 on the Microsoft campus. It's probably even better, because, in addition to their passion for knowing everything about Active Directory architecture, they also have the opportunity to work with the biggest customers Compaq and Microsoft have in common and to collect experiences from large, real-life deployments.

Andreas Luther
Program Manager
Microsoft

Preface

When I attended the very first Microsoft Windows NT 5.0[1] Rapid Deployment Program[2] meeting in Seattle almost three years ago, I was sitting among three hundred other early adopters and was not expecting such a dramatic change in the new version of the operating system. I knew that something called the Active Directory was going to remove the limitations of the NT SAM database, and I knew about some of the cool new features concerning the networking elements, but I did not yet see all the implications of Windows 2000 from the perspective of large enterprise deployments.

As the various Microsoft program managers were introducing the new features provided by their components in the product, it became clear that the approach of designing operating system infrastructures was going to change radically. Windows 2000 and Active Directory did change a lot:

- A new design methodology is required with a strong focus on political, business, and security requirements. This methodology also needs to take into account how the big picture evolves as new applications are integrated with a Windows 2000 infrastructure over time. This becomes even more important as the Microsoft software is evolving into the .NET world.

- A stronger cooperation between IT department groups that had little in common in the past must be put in place. An Active Directory design cannot happen effectively without a good communication between the directory, networking, and security groups.

---

1. Windows NT 5.0 was the previous name of Windows 2000.
2. The Windows 2000 Rapid Deployment Program, also know as the Joint Development Program, allowed selected large corporations to provide input to the Windows 2000 development team. The pioneers that took part in this program met regularly, exchanged experiences, and received copies of the new operating system for testing and to check that it contained all the features they needed to meet their enterprise requirements.

- A Windows 2000-Active Directory architect needs to master a broad spectrum of technologies. Windows 2000 incorporates many more technologies and features than its predecessor.

- Practice is key. A small lab with a few systems cannot provide the necessary skills to understand large deployments. For big organizations it's worth setting up a multisite lab that includes a simulation of the physical network.

- Roles may be inverted. In the past, the NT people owned the data, and the Exchange group owned the directory. Now with the Web store in Exchange 2000 the inverse will happen: the messaging group will own the data, and the NT people will own the directory. Furthermore, the NT group will also provide the necessary services for e-business in terms of security, interoperability, and availability.

- Interoperability is more important then ever. Since the rise of the Internet and Linux, Microsoft cannot afford to implement proprietary solutions anymore. What's more, many organizations are no longer building their complete IT environment on a single operating system platform.

Once back from the RDP meeting, Dung Hoang Khac and I decided to put together a training session for our internal consulting organization. We ran a few of these sessions with an audience of about 15 to 20 people with the goal of designing Windows NT 4.0 infrastructures with Windows 2000 in mind. This is when I first met Jan De Clercq. Jan was already focusing on IT security in Windows NT, and he was particularly interested in the security aspects of Windows 2000—especially since Windows 2000 embraces so many open standards, such as Kerberos, PKI, and VPN standards.

Tony Redmond, who at the time was the Technical Director for the Enterprise NT and Mail & Messaging practice at Compaq Professional Services, had the vision of a new type of training where consultants would teach other consultants. The Windows 2000 Academy concept was born.

Jan, Dung, Mike Dransfield, Ian Burgess, and myself ended up being the instructors for the academy, traveling around the world to train more than 1,000 consultants and more than 500 Compaq customers. What was unique about the academy concept was that it was a course given by consultants for consultants. In other words, it involved peer-to-peer knowledge transfer; the instructors were not professional trainers but field consultants working on customer projects. The Academy consisted of sessions as well as hands-on labs and design workshop exercises. The labs consisted of a number of exercises with more than 50 systems connected together to simulate a common enterprise. The workshop was a real customer case study. We wanted to make sure that everyone attending was able to see the important aspects of Windows 2000 designs. This made it a difficult course but at the same time very enriching and challenging.

Since the success of the Windows 2000 Academy, Compaq has run two more Academy programs: one on Exchange 2000 and another on .NET technology.

This is not all. Over the years, Compaq-Digital has built an organization of very curious and talented individuals who like to try out new technology by themselves. These folks will never believe a white paper unless they have personally tried the concepts and seen the results with their own eyes. Some of these consultants created their own underground infrastructures of Windows 2000 servers using the early beta kits when the product was still called Windows NT 5.0. As everyone became eager to learn more, some of the leaders of these underground infrastructures met during one of the Microsoft RDP meetings, and the idea of building a worldwide Windows 2000 laboratory emerged. Our corporate IT folks in charge of the design of Compaq's own Windows 2000 infrastructure also attended the RDP and agreed to let us create our worldwide forest. Using this forest we were able to push the limits of the Active Directory and work directly with the Windows 2000 development team on some of the scalability issues. In other words, we were able to gain invaluable experience with worldwide deployments. Our forest is called QTEST and is composed of more than 100 servers deployed on all continents. This unique lab environment allowed us to collect the necessary hands-on experience required to write this book. We will refer to QTEST throughout the different chapters of this book.

Since the Academy program, Jan and I have been working with many international companies on the design of their Windows 2000 infrastructure. Many of the lessons learned with these companies are reflected in this book.

The audience of this book is solutions architects and technical consultants involved in large Windows 2000 projects.

I wrote Chapters 1, 3, 4, and 10. Jan wrote Chapters 2, 5, 6, 7, 8, and 9. If have you any comments, questions, or suggestions concerning this book, please send us e-mail: *micky.balladelli@compaq.com* and *jan.declercq@compaq.com*.

Windows 2000 provides a solid foundation and the ability to evolve with new business requirements. This level of flexibility is required by large enterprises that need to react quickly to reorganizations and mergers.

Windows 2000 also provides the basic building block for the next generation of Microsoft applications that will be using Microsoft's .NET framework. Although we were very impressed by the capabilities of Windows 2000 and Active Directory, there are some features on which Microsoft could have done a better job. This book talks about all of them: the good, the bad, and the ugly.

We hope that this book will be a useful guide in understanding the many complexities of the Windows 2000 product. Let's start our journey. Have fun!

October 2000
Micky Balladelli
Jan De Clercq

Acknowledgments

We would like to thank the following people for helping us create this book.

Tony Redmond for his mentorship and leadership, for his support in bootstrapping this book project, and for his efforts in getting the Windows 2000 Academy running.

The drivers on the Digital Press side: Pam Chester for keeping us rolling in hard times, Theron R. Shreve and Phil Sutherland for convincing us of the value of writing this book.

The technical reviewers: David Cross (Microsoft), Roland Schoenauen (Fortis ebanking), Alain Lissoir (Compaq), Rudy Schockaert (Compaq), Ian Burgess (Compaq), Mike Dransfield (Compaq), Janusz Gebusia (Compaq), Aric Bernard (Compaq), and Andreas Luther (Microsoft).

The members of the Applied Microsoft Technologies Group: Don Vickers, Donald Livengood, Kieran McCorry, Kevin Laahs, Aric Bernard, Emer McKenna, John Featherly, Steve Atkins, Pierre Bijaoui, Jean-Pierre Julaude, Dung Hoang Khac, Pat Baxter, Olivier D'Hose, Barb Moatz, and Jerry Cochran for their technical and other advice (and for the "Kool-Aid").

Compaq's technical community of consultants, always willing to learn and share: Gary Olsen, Stephen Craike, Kim Mikkelsen, Neal Condon, Alain Lissoir, Ken Punshon, Mike Dransfield, Lasse Jokinen, and many others.

The Compaq Windows 2000 Academy team: Ian Burgess, Mike Dransfield, and Dung Hoang Khac for all the fun and for being great colleagues. John Moore, Karen Eber, Joanne Sterling for their great instructional advice. Kathryn MacDonald for the nice graphics (some of which are used in this book).

We would particularly like to thank the following people.

Andreas Luther (Microsoft) for the long discussions on migrations and various aspects of Windows 2000 and Whistler.

James Raquepau and Michael Craig from the Bellevue Compaq Expertise Center for helping to achieve the 100-million object Active Directory.

Jeff Parham of Microsoft for insights on Active Directory replication.

Pierre Bijaoui and Jerry Backlin for I/O performance and storage explanations and for helping to tune the SAN used in the 100-million object database.

—Micky Balladelli

John Brezak, for his great insights into the Microsoft Kerberos implementation; Greg Baribault, Cameron Stillion, and Vic Heller, for their help on the PKI chapters; Andreas Luther and Markus Vilcinskas, for providing excellent technical feedback; Sanjay Anand for his great insights into the AD access control model.

Yvan Moriamé of the Belgian Army, Paul Van Goethem of Dolmen, Pierre Hubaut of TotalFina, Rudy Schockaert of Compaq, and Alain Lissoir of Compaq for showing me what a passion for IT really means.

The Belgian Compaq Global Services messaging team, for being great colleagues and for being one of the best teams I ever worked with: Marc Van Hooste, Els Thonnon, Rudy Schockaert, Alain Lissoir, René Haentjens, Herman De Vloed, Susan McDonald, Jo Saels, and Francis Van Bever.

Gemplus (especially Eric Vandermeersch), for offering free hardware and software support; and FullArmor, for their free FAZAM software. Pauli Hopea of Tieturi Knowledgepool, Finland, for his interesting insights into Microsoft's SCA.

My parents, my wife's parents, and the whole family (especially my little nieces and nephew, Johanna, Lucas, Charlotte, Clara, Astrid, and Kato), for the time I could not spend with them, for their interest in my writing this book, and for being a great family!

—Jan De Clercq

Introduction to Active Directory

1.1 Introduction

When the Windows NT operating system first shipped in 1993 it was mainly used as a departmental file and print server. Corporations still relied on OpenVMS, UNIX, and other operating systems to run their business applications.

The evolution of back office applications and, more specifically, Microsoft Exchange was the major driver that made Microsoft enhance Windows NT to meet the requirements of the enterprise. Over the last few years, the Windows NT operating system has evolved from a small workgroup to a large enterprise server. Some limitations remain in Windows NT that prevent true scalability in terms of user accounts.

The Windows NT 4.0 account database (also known as the Security Account Manager [SAM] database) contains information about users, groups, and computers. The SAM database is limited in size to approximately 60 MB. This is not an architectural limitation but rather a Microsoft recommendation that it is unwise to exceed this size. In some circumstances, large corporate deployments have encountered the limit. For example, the DIGITAL1 account domain in Compaq contains 33,000 user accounts. The limited size of the SAM database impacts on large deployments that must accommodate tens of thousands of accounts. If a single account domain can't host the required number of accounts, the accounts must be divided across multiple domains. Trust relationships must then be created between the different account domains to allow roaming users to benefit from passthrough authentication and access resources in all the domains. Creating trust relationships is not a difficult task, provided that the number of trusted domains is limited. It's a best practice to limit the number of outgoing trust relationships to 1,024 per domain. In addition to account domains, resource domains are often created to delegate resource management. For example, all of the Exchange or SQL servers might be placed in a separate resource domain, which can then be managed by a restricted group of administrators. In many cases, the number of resource domains grows to exceed the limit of recommended trust relationships. Inside Compaq, over 1,000 resource domains were deployed to support different applications, but trust relationships are seldom granted between resource domains (unless required by a specific application) because it is easy to reach the limit. Many of the resource domains were not created by design and have come about as a result of deploying many different applications, which operate at the level of the workgroup within enterprise Windows NT 4.0 infrastructures.

Scaling Windows NT 4.0 through the deployment of multiple domains makes it difficult to match the naming scheme of the infrastructure with the business organizational or geographical model of the enterprise. Replication of account information can also pose scalability problems for distributed Windows NT 4.0 deployments. The Windows NT Server 4.0 replication model is based on a single master server, which is the owner and writer of the account database. The single master, also called the Primary Domain Controller, or PDC, replicates the content of the database to secondary read-only servers called Backup Domain Controllers, or BDCs. Replication can be either full or partial. Full replication means that the entire content of the SAM database is replicated from the PDC to the various BDCs. Partial replication means that individual objects are replicated between controllers. For example, when a user changes his or her password, only the specific user object is replicated in its entirety. Except for scheduling when replication takes place, large corporations are limited in the number of steps they can take to control Windows NT Server 4.0 SAM replication. Another limitation of Windows NT Server 4.0 is the lack of a common Directory Service (DS). For example, Windows NT Server 4.0 has its SAM database and Exchange Server V5.5 has its directory. Both store information about NT accounts, but neither leverages the other. Not having a common DS for the enterprise forces applications to deploy their own, resulting in independent islands of information that are difficult to manage and keep up-to-date.

Windows 2000 is a complete redesign of the operating system that aims to meet the requirements of enterprise deployments. The Active Directory is a scalable and robust DS, which is embedded into the operating system. This chapter describes how the Active Directory is integrated into Windows 2000.

1.2   Directory Services

A Directory Service is a way to look up and retrieve information from any-where within a distributed environment.

A DS provides storage for data, a schema to define what the data are, methods to access these data, and it is capable of organizing these data in a hierarchical way.

Enterprise information requires certain characteristics from a DS. These include the following:

- Scalability

- Availability

- Manageability

- Security

- Accessibility

1.2.1   Scalability

The DS must be scalable before it can be deployed in large enterprises. A DS in a large enterprise may contain multiple gigabytes of data. In case of mergers or acquisitions, the DS of two or more enterprises may merge to form an even bigger DS. Often, the term *scalability* is misused. In this con-text, the term is used to define an implementation that can sustain a defined growth rate without requiring to be redesigned. When two companies merge, if the directory service doesn't require a redesign for the addition of the new objects and the new concurrent connections, then it is scalable.

1.2.2   Availability

A DS must make information available from anywhere in the enterprise. Searching and retrieving information from the DS must be done within acceptable response times, usually determined in a few seconds. Meeting the requirement for fast and available access means either that the directory must be distributed and replicated so that it is closer to the users or that fast connectivity must be provided to reach a remote DS. Distributing informa-tion has impacts in terms of manageability.

1.2.3   Manageability

Different companies may require different management structures; some require a centralized management infrastructure with, for example, all the administrators physically located at the same site. Some other companies may prefer administrators disseminated to multiple sites. These requirements are mainly due to the organizational, geographical, or political structure of the company.

In all cases a DS must be flexible enough to accommodate all needs.

1.2.4   Security

The DS holds sensitive information, which must be secured. A security model must be implemented to preserve data integrity and control different levels of access. Delegation of management is another aspect of security that must be accommodated in a distributed management model.

1.2.5   Accessibility

A DS must support different protocols, allowing various clients based on different operating systems and interfaces to access the information stored in the directory.

1.3   What is the Active Directory?

The Active Directory is the Directory Service for Windows 2000 servers. It is deeply embedded into the operating system. Many other components of Windows 2000 depend on data held in the directory. These facts mean that careful thought must be given to the deployment of the Active Directory before any implementation of Windows 2000 can begin.

The Active Directory provides the storage, the access methods, and the security for both the OS and applications that use its services. It is extensible and shareable, and it provides the scalability and manageability required by large enterprises. These aspects of the directory are described in later chapters.

Many different objects can be stored in the Active Directory, including the following:

- All the objects necessary for running a Windows 2000–based infrastructure, such as:

  - Users and groups.
  - Security credentials such as certificates.
  - System resources such as computers (or servers) and resources.
  - Replication components and settings are themselves objects in the Active Directory.
  - COM components, which, in previous versions of Windows NT Server 4.0 required storing in the registry information about their location, are now stored in the Class Store in the Active Directory.
  - Rules and policies to control the working environment.

- Active Directory–enabled applications can extend the schema of the AD to define their own objects. The release of Microsoft Exchange Server 2000 is the first AD-enabled application. This version of Exchange uses the Active Directory to store information about servers, mailboxes, recipients, and distribution lists in the Active Directory.

Figure 1.1
*The Active
Directory*

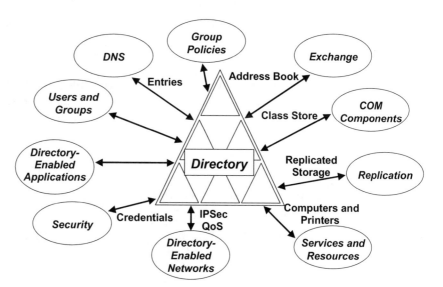

■ Directory-Enabled Networks use the Active Directory to retrieve security rules and user and computer settings to set the networking environment. Quality of Service (QoS) will be among the first areas to use DEN and Active Directory. QoS allows applications to reserve bandwidth on the network.

■ Domain Naming Service (DNS) can store its data in the Active Directory and take advantage of its replication features as well as secure dynamic updates.

Figure 1.1 illustrates the Active Directory.

1.4   Active Directory namespaces

Windows NT Server 4.0 uses a flat namespace, meaning that the name of domains does not reflect a hierarchical naming structure representing the geographical or business organization of the company. The names of domains in Windows NT Server 4.0 are based on the NetBIOS convention and can be up to 15 alphanumeric characters. Windows NT Server 4.0 uses Windows Naming Service (WINS) to resolve NetBIOS names into IP addresses. NetBIOS names can also be used to refer to services on the network, such as directory shares or printer shares.

While WINS is the primary name resolution service in Windows NT Server 4.0, DNS is used to resolve IP-based host names for applications such as FTP or Telnet.

DNS today is configured via static files, which contain information about server or host computers. Administrators are required to manually create or update details about the hosts in the domain that they manage.

Figure 1.2
Namespaces

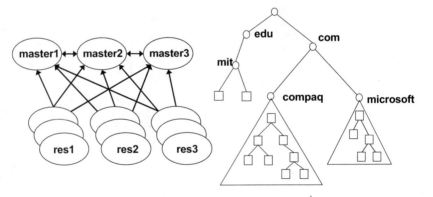

On the other hand, WINS is updated automatically at system boot. The only requirement imposed by WINS is that the NetBIOS name requested by the system is unique on the network.

The Windows 2000 namespace is hierarchical. This fact has a tremendous impact on the roles of services such as DNS and WINS. DNS becomes the primary name service for Windows 2000, which implements a new version of DNS called Dynamic DNS, or DDNS, to overcome the management limitations of classic DNS. Dynamic DNS also takes advantage of a new feature (SRV records, discussed later in this book), which allows Windows 2000 to resolve the names of services and locate computers that provide those services. Figure 1.2 illustrates namespaces.

While DNS is used to find servers and services in the Active Directory, the Lightweight Directory Access Protocol (LDAP) is also used to access objects in the Directory.

1.4.1   The role of DNS

Today, largely because of its role as the naming service used by the Internet, DNS is the largest naming service in general use. In addition to the Internet, any company that uses an IP-based network depends on DNS to resolve "friendly" names (those given to computers) into 32-bit IP addresses (and vice versa).

DNS overcomes the limitations of the static host table (HOST.TXT), a file mapping host names and IP addresses. The most notable limitations imposed by the static host table are as follows:

- Scalability. Due to its inherent distributed nature, DNS is very scalable. A simple list of server to IP address translations maintained in a text file scales with difficulty.

- Dissemination of updated information. Every host is required to regularly retrieve updated information about other host computers in the network. DNS servers receive updates about other servers via an automated replication mechanism, which ensures that each server maintains a fully synchronized database containing information about the computers in the network.

DNS has two roles in Windows 2000, as follows:

1.   Windows 2000 uses DNS domain names as its basic naming scheme. This means that the same name can used to find com-

puters across the Internet and within a Windows 2000 infrastructure. For example, *compaq.com* is the DNS domain name registered by Compaq with the Internet's Network Information Center (NIC). The NIC manages the names of all the registered systems on the Internet to ensure that computers from different companies can be easily located. After Compaq has completed its Windows 2000 deployment, *compaq.com* could also be a Windows 2000 domain name. Using the same name for different purposes can result in some confusion as to what a domain is. In this document, the term *domain* is used to refer to Windows 2000 domains, and the term *DNS domain* is used to refer to DNS domains. We will come back to Windows 2000 domains in a later section.

2.   Dynamic DNS, an updated version of DNS, supports records that point to network services. The new records are called SRV records and are specified in the Internet Engineering Task Force (IETF) Request For Comments (RFC) number RFC 2052.

Windows 2000 implements Dynamic DNS (IETF RFC 2136). Dynamic DNS allows servers and workstations to automatically update the DNS database when they boot, removing the administrative burden of previous versions, which required manual modifications of the database. In addition, Dynamic DNS can be configured to control which servers and workstations are allowed to update the database during boot time.

Windows 2000 is not the only system to provide Dynamic DNS support. For example, Berkeley Internet Name Domain (BIND) version 8.1.2 (BIND-8) implements Dynamic DNS. BIND can be used with Windows 2000 since it also supports SRV records.

Microsoft DNS has one major advantage over BIND for Windows 2000 networks in that the Microsoft implementation of DNS can be integrated in the Active Directory. This means that DNS uses the Active Directory for data storage and replication, and no separate effort is required to design and maintain a DNS network. Integrating DNS in the Active Directory also provides the advantage of record scavenging and secure dynamic updates. These benefits are discussed in more details in a later chapter.

1.4.2   The role of LDAP

LDAP is an IETF standard described in RFC 1777. The latest version (LDAP V3.0) is described in RFC 2251.

In essence, LDAP is a lightweight version of DAP, the X.500 Directory Access Protocol. Over the past few years, LDAP has become the most commonly accepted directory access protocol and is supported in implementations of X.500, the NetWare DS, and the Microsoft Exchange (5.0 and 5.5) directories. DSLDAP V3 is implemented in Windows 2000 and is used by applications to access the hierarchically organized objects in the Active Directory.

1.4.3   Combining two protocols

As we've seen, two separate protocols (DNS and LDAP) are used by Windows 2000 to access data in the Active Directory. Some explanation is required to outline why two protocols are required and when they are used.

DNS is a very effective and well-proven protocol for locating host computers. Windows 2000 uses DNS to find LDAP servers within its network. In fact, the LDAP servers are Domain Controllers (DCs), and, once they are located, Windows 2000 then uses LDAP to access the data managed by the DCs. LDAP is most efficient at retrieving information organized in finely grained attributes, such as the properties maintained for objects in the Active Directory. DNS is therefore used to locate the LDAP servers, and all further access to directory information is accomplished with LDAP. Accessing information via LDAP means performing one of four operations: read, write, modify, or delete.

1.4.4   WINS

WINS provides the primary naming service in Windows NT Server 4.0 networks. Due to the adoption of DNS and LDAP, Windows 2000 does not use WINS as a naming service. However, an improved version of WINS is still supported for backward compatibility. WINS is required during the migration phase to ensure that servers and clients that depend on WINS can continue to access Windows NT Server 4.0 resources even though these resources are being migrated to Windows 2000.

The improved version of WINS incorporates the following changes:

- Manual tombstoning (indicating records marked for deletion)
- Improved management tool (MMC, multithread support)
- Enhanced filtering and record searching
- Dynamic record deletion and multiselect

- Record verification and version number validation

- Consistency checking (intensive with bandwidth!)

- Export function (use Excel to produce reports)

- Increased fault tolerance (clients to define 12 servers)

- Dynamic reregistration

1.5   Domains

Similar to Windows NT Server 4.0, a Windows 2000 domain is a security boundary. What this means is that a domain boundary limits the scope of access control and policy rules implemented within the domain.

A domain is also a partition of the Active Directory. In this respect, a domain is a partition of the data and the namespace held in the Active Directory. In fact, the Active Directory is the sum of all domains within an enterprise. In other words, the Active Directory is composed of one or more domains linked together. As the namespace within the Active Directory is hierarchical, the domain structure in Windows 2000 is made up of a series of parent/child relationships between the different domains. This is very different from the trust relationships that connected domains in earlier versions of Windows NT Server 4.0. Figure 1.3 illustrates a Windows 2000 domain.

Windows NT 4.0 uses a single master replication model. In this model, all changes are made at a single primary domain controller and then replicated out to the backup domain controllers. The Active Directory allows Windows 2000 to use a multimaster replication model. This means that an administrator can use any Domain Controller in a Windows 2000 domain to manage resources. The need to connect to the primary domain controller is therefore eliminated. As previously noted, the Windows NT SAM data-

Figure 1.3
Windows 2000
domain

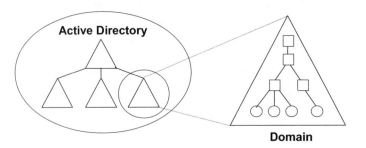

base is limited to a size of approximately 60 MB, in turn limiting the size of a domain to the number of accounts that can be stored in the SAM. By comparison, the Active Directory can grow to store millions of objects, so Windows 2000 domains can contain millions of accounts. The theoretical limitation of objects that can be hosted in the Active Directory is 2 to the 32nd power, or some 4 billion objects. Chapter 4 discusses large Active Directory implementations.

1.6   Organizational units and objects

The Active Directory is built from a collection of organizational units (OUs) and containers, which forms the base of the hierarchical representation of objects within a domain. An OU is a generic object container. It can contain any object in the domain, including other OUs.

OUs can be used to delegate administration control to a particular group of users without allowing them to have administrative permissions for other objects in the domain. Delegation of administration must not however be confused with access control. OUs are not groups and must not be used to control access to resources within the domain. We will discuss groups and access control in a later chapter.

Active Directory objects include users, groups, computers, and printers to name but a few. Objects can be organized hierarchically using organizational units.

Every object in the Active Directory has a unique name referenced by an LDAP Distinguished Name (DN). Distinguished names are the fully qualified LDAP representation of an object and are composed of a sequence of Relative Distinguished Names (RDNs). RDNs are a portion of a DN identifying all the ancestors or containers of the object and the object itself.

Figure 1.4 illustrates a domain composed of a number of organizational units. The user Jack is referenced by the RDN CN=Jack. User Jack belongs to a tree of organizational units. Each OU is identified by its own RDN and in the hierarchical order in which it was created. The OUs belong to the *compaq.com* domain, which is referenced by the domain DC RDN. The full representation of the distinguished name is the sum of all the RDNs composing it, which results in CN = JACK; OU = SALES; OU = USERS; DC = COMPAQ; DC = COM. To retrieve the full description of distinguished names, refer to RFC 2247.

Figure 1.4
Distinguished
names

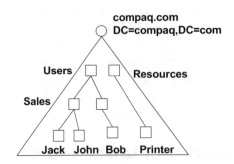

CN=Jack, OU=Sales, OU=Users, DC=compaq, DC=com

1.7   Active Directory schema

The schema contains the definition of all the objects in the Active Directory. Every object has its own class and a set of attributes (also called properties) associated with it. A class is the unit of storage in the Active Directory. This means that for an object to be stored in the Active Directory it must first have a class, which defines how it is stored and what attributes it may have.

Attributes hold the value of a particular property in the object. Attributes are typed, which means that their value is stored as a string, octet, numeric, and so on. Attributes may be multivalued, which means that an attribute may be stored using multiple values. For example, a user can have multiple telephone numbers.

The internal structure of the Active Directory can be compared with a relational database. Objects are stored in a large table. Each object is stored in a row within the table, and the different attributes for objects are stored in the columns in the table.

When an attribute is not used, it doesn't occupy any space within the database. For example, if the telephone number attribute for a user object is not filled, the column will be empty and no space will be allocated to store the attribute inside the database. This feature is necessary since the number of attributes associated with an object may be considerable. For example, the class *user* went from a few attributes in Windows NT 4.0 to more than 100 in Windows 2000.

Attributes may be associated with multiple classes, which means that they are created independently of classes. Attributes have their own ID (described later) and their own characteristics.

The Active Directory schema is object oriented. This means that classes can derive from other classes to inherit their characteristics.

Let us take, for example, the class *user*, which, as its name implies, describes the user object. The class *user* is associated with a number of attributes related to the user account, such as principalName, logonHours, groupMembership and many more.

The class *user* derives from the class *organizationalPerson*. The class *organizationalPerson* defines a person with attributes such as homePostalAddress, homeNumber, mobile, EmployeeID, and more.

Now, *organizationalPerson* derives from *person*, which simply defines five attributes: cn, seeAlso, sn, userPassword, and telephoneNumber.

The class *contact* also inherits from the characteristics of *organizationalPerson* and *person*, its parent classes (superclasses in object-oriented terms), which means that the instance of a *contact* may also have any of the attributes associated with *organizationalPerson* and *person*. A contact is a lightweight object containing information about a person. It is generally used to store a mail recipient in the Active Directory. Looking carefully at the *person* class, we can see that cn, which stands for common name, is a mandatory attribute.

There are two types of attributes: mandatory and optional. Mandatory attributes must be provided with a value to allow the object to be created. Given that cn is the only mandatory attribute of class *user* and its parents, to create an object of class user we must define its common name, or cn. Optional attributes may be filled after the object has been created and are not required to create the object.

Classes and attributes have a unique ID, as mentioned previously. This ID is called, wrongly, the Object ID (OID). I say wrongly because in object-oriented terms an object is the instance of a class, so the term should really have been Class ID. Given that OID comes from the X.500 world and can be found in other DS implementations such as Exchange, Microsoft decided to use the same term in the Active Directory.

There may be multiple instances of the class *user*: users Joe and Jack may be those instances. The OID identifies the class *user*, whereas the Globally Unique Identifier (GUID) identifies the instances of the objects. GUIDs are generated by the operating system when the object is created. They are 128-bit numbers computed to be unique. Various "issuing authorities," such as the ISO, issue OIDs; enterprises can then extend them to add their own class extensions.

Objects are identified by their GUID, not by their name. This allows objects to be always referenced when they are moved or are renamed. This behavior is an improvement over how Exchange Server V5.5 references the objects it manages. Exchange uses a DN for every object—not the object GUID. This implies that when an object has to be moved in Exchange, it must first be deleted and then be re-created. Using GUIDs, objects can be moved anywhere in the domain but also within the forest.

The schema itself is stored in the Active Directory as a partition and is replicated to all DCs in the Active Directory. This is very important, because it allows Active Directory–enabled applications to programmatically browse the Directory, learn how objects (or classes) are defined, and adapt a user interface accordingly. These schema-driven applications automatically adapt to meet the requirements of different companies. These applications are able to view and manage Active Directory objects that have been implemented in different ways at different companies. For example, a company may require a particular set of attributes to identify the organization in which users belong. At Compaq, we use user badge numbers and cost centers. Another company may have a totally different identification system based on some other business rules. A schema-driven application could browse the Directory for the definition of a user. When the application needs to display a UI for a user, it does it following the schema definition, and, in our example, the cost center and badge number would be part of the list of displayed attributes.

Applications can extend the Active Directory with their own class definitions or extend the definition of an existing class. For example, Microsoft Exchange Server extends the user object to allow it to store information about mailboxes on an Exchange server. One of the most important features introduced in Windows 2000 is that different levels of access control can be defined to allow users to view different portions of an object. For example, we might want to have different levels of administrative access to user objects. We can define a set of administrators who are allowed to modify user passwords and modify logon hours. We can then define a different set of administrators, which might come from the HR department, who can manage sensitive user information, such as home addresses, personal telephone numbers, and so on. The goal is to permit different views of information held in a common directory, allowing administrators to access the information they need to do their jobs, while restricting access to data that shouldn't be generally available.

1.8   Linking domains to form trees and forests

Windows NT 4.0 links domains together through trust relationships. The collection of Windows NT 4.0 domains that are linked together form the enterprise Windows NT 4.0 infrastructure. Domains can also be linked together in Windows 2000, in this case to form the enterprise namespace. However, the link set by a trust relationship in Windows NT 4.0 establishes a very loose connection between the participating domains. Connecting Windows 2000 domains together within an enterprise namespace forms a far more coherent and well-connected infrastructure.

1.9   Trust relationships

As illustrated in the left portion of Figure 1.5, trust relationships link Windows NT 4.0 domains together. Trusts allow users in trusted domains to access resources in the trusting domain.

In Windows NT 4.0 trust relationships must be explicitly defined. As we've already seen, there are a number of limitations that must be considered when setting up trust relationships in large enterprise deployments.

Trust relationships also exist in Windows 2000, but the trusts take on a very different nature because they are based on Kerberos and can be transitive. The right portion of Figure 1.5 illustrates how Windows 2000 trusts might be used to connect Windows 2000 domains together. In this instance, the U.S. domain trusts the Compaq domain, which in turn trusts the Europe domain. In Windows NT 4.0, no trust would exist between the U.S. and Europe domains because no formal trust relationship has been established to connect the two. However, in Windows 2000, the Kerberos-

Figure 1.5
Kerberos trusts
versus NTLM
trusts

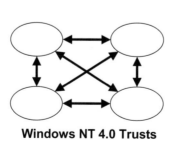

Windows NT 4.0 Trusts

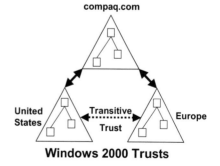

Windows 2000 Trusts

based trust means that the U.S. and Europe domains trust each other through the transitive trust relationship established through the Compaq domain. Trust relationships are transitive and use Kerberos within the same forest only. Administrators can also create explicit trusts within a forest. These trusts are called *shortcut* and are transitive. Trusts created between Windows 2000 forests are not transitive, since they are based on the NTLM protocol; however, trusts created with non-Windows 2000 Kerberos realms can be transitive.

1.9.1   Trees

Trees are hierarchies of domains linked by trust relationships. Each tree shares a contiguous namespace. Figure 1.6 illustrates a tree formed by the Compaq, U.S., and Sales domains. The names of the three domains are *compaq*, *us.Compaq*, and *sales.us.compaq*. The names are contiguous, since the child domains inherit from the names of the parent domains. Hence, the U.S. domain inherits part of its name from its parent, Compaq domain, and in turn provides the root of the name for its child, Sales domain. When generating the tree, you must start with the root of the tree. You cannot create a domain and later decide to create the parent of this domain. The parent domain must be there before any child domain can be created.

New subtrees can be created within a tree. So, for example, we could create a new subtree under the *compaq* domain, *europe*. This new subtree would then be called *europe.compaq*. The *europe* portion of the name is contiguous to the *compaq* name but is disjointed from the *us* name. This is why we have two separate subtrees, the *europe* subtree and the *us* subtree.

Figure 1.6
A tree of domains

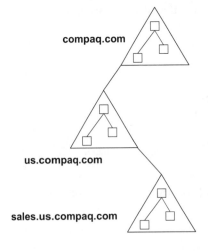

compaq.com

us.compaq.com

sales.us.compaq.com

1.9.2   Forests

A forest is a set of trees linked together via trust relationships. The trees that are joined together at the top level of the forest do not necessarily have to share the same namespace.

Figure 1.7 illustrates a forest formed by two trees. The trees are formed from domains called *compaq* and *digital*. After the forest is formed, each domain remains unchanged, and each domain remains at the head of its own tree. A forest is sometimes referred to as the Active Directory. Earlier we defined a domain to be a portion of the Active Directory, and we defined the Active Directory as the sum of all the domains that are connected together. A forest is exactly this: the sum of all trees, which are composed of domains connected together via transitive Kerberos trusts. A forest and the Active Directory are the same thing.

The trees within the same forest share the following characteristics:

- A common configuration. The topology of the domains within the forest is known by all domains and is replicated immediately whenever a new domain joins the forest. The topology includes objects such as connection objects, sites, IP subnets, site links, site link bridges, and so on. These objects are discussed later.

- A common schema. The schema defines all the objects in the forest and is composed of classes and attributes.

- A common Global Catalog (GC). Global catalogs are discussed in a later chapter.

Figure 1.7
A forest

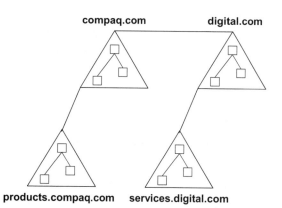

compaq.com   digital.com

products.compaq.com   services.digital.com

1.9.3   Flexible, single-master operation roles

Windows 2000 supports multimaster replication of Directory data. This means that any DC in the domain can be used to modify the values of an object. Replication then occurs between DCs to update all the DCs with the latest data for the object. Inevitably, some potential for update conflicts exists in a multimaster replication model. The replication process is covered in more detail later on, but for now it is enough to say that when a replication conflict occurs, the time stamps of each modification are evaluated, and the last writer wins.

Some objects in the Directory, such as the schema itself, cannot be resolved with such methods, because two versions of the schema may generate instances of objects using different properties. It would be hard to resolve such conflicts without losing data. To avoid schema conflicts, a single-master replication mechanism is performed by a special DC, called the Schema Master. This is one of five flexible, single-master operation (FSMO, pronounced "fizmo") roles implemented in a single-master replication model. FSMO roles are also known as Operation Masters.

Schema Master

The Schema Master is unique in the entire forest. New classes or attributes can only be created by the Schema Master. Updates are then replicated to all domains in the forest. Note: A Schema Master must also be set to allow schema updates before the schema can actually be modified.

Domain Naming Master

The Domain Naming Master manages the names of every domain in the forest. It is unique in the forest. Only the Domain Naming Master can add and remove domains in the tree or forest to avoid having naming conflicts occur. In future releases, the Domain Naming Master will allow domain moves within the forest.

PDC Emulator

The PDC Emulator is unique in the domain and provides backward compatibility to down-level clients and servers in the following ways:

- Provides down-level clients support for password updates
- Performs replication to down level BDCs (NT 4.0)

- Acts as the Master Domain Browser, if the Windows NT 4.0 browser service is enabled

- Verifies password uniqueness. Windows 2000 DCs attempt to replicate password changes to the PDC first. Each time a DC fails to authenticate a password it contacts the PDC to see whether the password can be authenticated there, perhaps as a result of a change that has not yet been replicated down to the particular DC.

- Synchronizes time. The PDC emulator synchronizes time for the computers in the domain. The PDC emulator of the first domain in the forest (the root domain) also synchronizes time with the PDC emulators of the other domains in the forest.

RID Master

The RID Master is unique in the domain. When a security principal (e.g., user, group) is created, it receives a domain-wide Security ID (SID) and a domain-wide unique Relative ID (RID).

Every Windows 2000 DC receives a pool of RIDs it can use. The RID Master ensures that these IDs remain unique on every DC by assigning different pools.

Infrastructure Master

The Infrastructure Master is unique in the domain. When an object from another domain is referenced, this reference contains the GUID, the SID, and the DN of that object. If the referenced object moves, the following happens:

- The object GUID does not change (it is issued when the object is created and never changes).

- The object SID changes if the move is cross-domain (to receive an SID from the new domain).

- The object DN always changes.

A DC holding the infrastructure master role in a domain is responsible for updating the SIDs and DNs in cross-domain object references in that domain. An example of such objects is groups. Groups can contain members from other domains and the Infrastructure Master is responsible for updating and maintaining the reference.

1.10   Naming contexts

Naming contexts (NCs) are portions of the Active Directory that follow different replication rules—they are boundaries for Active Directory replication.

The domain NC contains all the data within a domain. The schema NC contains all the classes and attributes and is replicated throughout the forest. The configuration NC contains the topology of the forest and is replicated throughout the forest.

The three naming contexts are replicated to the global catalog either entirely or partially. Chapter 2 describes this in more detail.

All naming contexts have a location in the Directory. The root of a domain namespace is its DNS name, and all objects within the domain are children of this root.

When the first domain is created, the first DC in the domain generates the configuration NC. This NC is then replicated to all DCs joining the forest.

1.11   Global Catalog

The Global Catalog (GC) is a special type of domain controller. As a domain controller it contains all the objects and attributes of its own domain. It is a full replica of the other DCs in the same domain. However, in addition to the objects of its own domain, a GC contains a subset of the attributes of all the other domain NC objects in the forest as well as the schema NC and the configuration NC. The GC contains all the objects in the Active Directory. The role of the GC is to provide the Active Directory with a search engine. By containing an indexed partial replica of all the objects in the forest, GCs become extremely fast search engines.

The subset of the attributes is defined and modifiable in the schema and is by default the attributes most commonly searched, such as name, e-mail address, and phone number for a user.

Any DC can be configured to become a GC. A GC incurs more overhead than a DC because it performs more replication and requires more disk space for its database. However, because users and applications connect to the GC to search for objects in the Active Directory, it is recommended to deploy enough GCs to ensure that clients can make a high-quality connection. Normally, this implies a LAN-quality connection established by locating a GC close to each major user community.

In order to understand how a search works against a GC, let's imagine that we are looking for a color printer located on the same floor in a building. We only know a subset of the characteristics of the printer we wish to use. We know that it supports color and we have a rough idea of its location, but we don't know its network name, so we can't connect to it and print our documents. We can use LDAP to search the indexes maintained by the GC for all matching printer objects using the known characteristics. The search will return all matching objects, hopefully including the printer we want to use.

Without the GC, we would have to conduct a search against a domain controller and drill down through the entire forest. Such a search would take too much time, and the response time would be unacceptable.

In order to provide the ability of GC queries, at least one GC must be defined in a domain. That GC will accept LDAP requests to both port 389 and port 3268. The Domain Naming Master role must be hosted on a GC. By containing all the objects of the Active Directory, including the accounts for the domains in the forest, GCs provide the necessary visibility to allow the Domain Naming Master to know if a domain name is currently in use.

On the other hand, it is not recommended to place the Infrastructure master on GCs. This is due to phantom records. These records are created on DCs when a referenced object does not exist in the same domain. For example, a user object may reference another user residing in another domain using an attribute such as manager. The role of the Infrastructure Master in this case is to update the phantom object if the remote object is removed or deleted. The infrastructure master would not be able to perform this operation on a GC. GCs do not create phantom records since they have a copy of the real object.

1.12 Groups

Windows NT 4.0 supports groups, literally a convenient way to bring one or more users together under a common heading. Windows 2000 introduces two types of general-purpose groups: security and distribution list.

Security groups contain security principals and are used for access control. Conceptually, security groups are similar in use and function to Windows NT 4.0 groups. Distribution lists are similar to the distribution lists currently in use by Exchange Server. Windows 2000 also introduces four group scopes with special behavior: universal groups, global groups, domain local groups, and local groups.

1.12.1   Universal groups

Universal groups are available throughout the forest. They may contain other universal or global groups or users from the current domain or any trusted domain. Because this type of group may contain objects located anywhere in the forest, they are expensive to use in terms of performance when used in ACLs. Authorization still requires authentication performed by the domain in which the user belongs.

Universal groups are published in GCs. However, when used as distribution lists, replicating them locally to users via GCs provides applications such as Exchange with a convenient, powerful, and simple way to implement global address list.

The implication of publishing universal groups in GCs affects the authentication process. During the authentication process a DC will contact a GC to verify the membership of the user in the universal groups. This means that DCs require GCs to add the SID of universal groups in the token or ticket of the authenticating security principal.

Placement of GCs is usually desired in remote sites in order to improve performance in user logon time, searches, and other actions requiring communication with GCs, as well as reducing WAN traffic. However, in some instances, it may be desirable not to locate a GC at a remote site to reduce administrative intervention, hardware requirements, and replication overhead—in short, duplicating the functions of the BDC in the Windows NT 4.0 environment.

It is possible to remove the need to involve GCs during the authentication process; however, careful consideration must be applied, since it may introduce a security breach.

Administrators can use regedit to modify a key for the LSA process that allows it to ignore GCs during the authentication process. The key is \\HKLM\System\CurrentControlSet\Control\Lsa\IgnoreGCFailures. If this key is set, administrators must not use universal groups to deny access to resources. The key will prevent the authentication process from adding the SIDs of the universal groups to the user's token; therefore, the access control cannot verify that the user is denied access to the resource. Use this key very cautiously.

1.12.2   Global groups

Global groups are available throughout the forest. They can contain other global groups, computers, and users from the same domain, but they cannot contain security principals from other domains.

1.12.3   Domain local groups

Domain local groups cannot be exported to other domains. They can be applied only to resources in the domain in which they are created. Domain local groups may contain references to universal groups, global groups, computers, and users from any domain, as well as domain local groups, computers, and users from its own domain.

1.12.4   Local groups

Local groups are available only on the local computer but may contain objects from anywhere in the forest just like Windows NT 4.0.

1.13   Domain modes

There are two domain modes: mixed mode and native mode.

Mixed mode is the default mode and is used when a new domain is created or when a Windows NT 4.0 PDC is upgraded to Windows 2000. Mixed mode implies that there are NT 4.0 backup domain controllers in the domain. One of the Windows 2000 DCs takes the FSMO role of PDC emulator and acts as a Windows 2000 PDC in the eyes of the down-level clients and BDCs. This is quite important, because it allows Windows NT 4.0 operations to be maintained while the domain is migrated to Windows 2000. It is important to remember that in a mixed-mode environment there may be down-level backup domain controllers. These BDCs have a SAM database with the same limitations of a Windows NT 4.0: 65 MB in size. Therefore, it's important to remember that in an effort to reduce domains and consolidate resources the limitation of the SAM database still exists in a Windows 2000 mixed-mode domain. This is discussed in more detail later in the book.

The groups in the domain use Windows NT 4.0 behavior when operating in mixed mode, This means that groups cannot be nested. In addition, security universal groups are not available in mixed mode.

When all the down-level clients and BDCs have been upgraded to Windows 2000, the domain can be switched over to native mode. This is a one-shot operation, which cannot be undone.

Once in native mode the groups can be nested and universal groups are available. In native mode it is also possible to have Windows NT 4.0 member servers; however, Windows NT 4.0 BDCs are no longer accepted in the domain. It's worth noting that once in native mode, the PDC emulator is still available. It performs other unique tasks in the domain, such as ensuring that passwords remain unique and synchronizing time.

1.14   Sites

A site is a collection of IP subnets that share Local Area Network (LAN)–type connectivity. In fact, the best way to think of a site is to compare it to a LAN. Sites reflect locality—all the systems that belong to the same site are close to each other and benefit from good bandwidth.

When a Windows 2000 server creates a new domain, the Active Directory creates the site Default-First-Site-Name and stores the DC there. All the DCs joining the domain are added to the default site. Systems continue to be added to the default site until a new site is explicitly created.

A domain may span multiple sites, as seen in Figure 1.8; however, multiple domains may belong to the same site. Sites are independent from the domains they belong to.

Sites are used for the following two roles:

1.   During workstation logon to determine the closest DC. We will get into how workstations discover their closest DC in the next section.

2.   During Active Directory data replication to optimize the route and transport of replicated data depending on the DC sites.

In order to achieve these two roles, all DCs in the forest know about all the sites. Sites are stored in the configuration naming context.

Finding the closest DC

At boot time or, more precisely, when the netlogon service starts, DCs publish information about the domain and site they belong to in DNS using SRV records. As previously mentioned, they cache information about all sites locally. When a workstation boots, it either receives its IP address from a DHCP server or the network administrator statically assigned this address

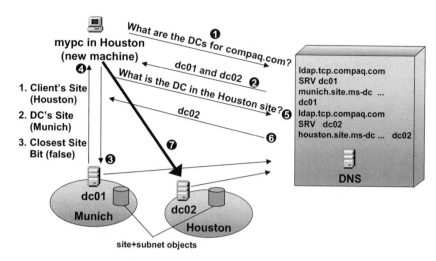

Figure 1.8
*Steps for finding
the closest site*

to it. DHCP may also provide the DNS server address unless this information was entered manually.

During the logon process, the workstation is attempting to locate the closest DC to improve logon performance. The workstation does not have information about sites so it must perform five steps to receive it. These steps are as follows:

1.   The workstation asks DNS for DCs in the domain it is trying to log on to. In our example, for the domain *compaq.com*, DNS returns two names: DC01 and DC02.

2.   The workstation then performs the logon on the DC01 DC. When the workstation receives multiple servers in response to a DNS query, it will use an internal algorithm to choose a DC. This allows for spreading the load when multiple clients are performing the same operation. DC01 accepts the logon and returns information about the site the workstation belongs to. This is possible since the workstation provided its own IP address, and the DC was able to match that IP address with one of the IP subnets forming a site.

3.   DC01 returns the fact that the workstation does not belong to the Munich site, but it belongs to the Houston site, which is not the closest DC available.

4.   With information about the site it belongs to, the workstation can make a much more specific request to DNS and ask for the

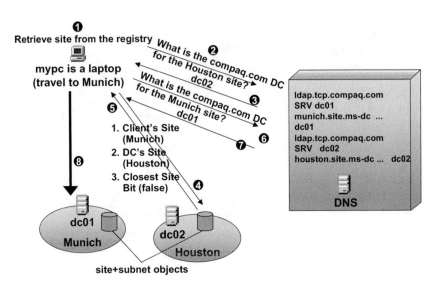

Figure 1.9
Mobile user finding closest site

DC in the domain that belongs to the Houston site. DNS returns DC02.

5.   The workstation can then log on to DC02, which is in the same site, and can store site information in its own registry.

Let's now imagine that the workstation isn't really a workstation—it's a laptop—and this laptop travels to Munich. Let's assume that the Munich DHCP provides a new IP address. As shown in Figure 1.9, the following steps now occur:

1.   The laptop retrieves the site information that it previously stored in the registry and very naturally attempts to retrieve from DNS information about the DC in that site.

2.   The laptop goes back to DNS simply because the DC that it used previously may have been shut down or have been replaced with a different one, and if that were the case the SRV records in DNS would have been updated. The laptop asks DNS for a DC in the Houston site. DNS returns DC02.

3.   Upon logon, the DC02 updates the laptop about the new site it belongs to, it mentions that it is no longer the closest site, and that it now must log on to a DC in the Munich site.

4.   The workstation goes back to DNS and asks for the DC in the Munich site and DNS returns DC01. Now the laptop performs logons on DC01.

What is important to see in this example is that the discovery of the closest site was done automatically without administrator intervention.

Workstations can be set to contact the DCs that match their own IP subnet first. This can considerably reduce the time required by contacting remote DCs. However, a site can be composed of a number of IP subnets, and even if a DC and a client are in the same site they could still belong to different subnets. In this case the above scenario would still apply.

Sites play a major role in replication of data. Chapter 3 covers replication in more detail.

1.15 Protocols and APIs

The Active Directory supports both LDAP V2 and LDAP V3 protocols (RFC 1777 and 2251) and HTTP. LDAP is essential for interoperability reasons, since most of the DS implementations are supporting it.

The supported APIs are as follows:

- Active Directory Service Interface (ADSI), a set of COM interfaces for searching and managing various directory services

- LDAP API, a low-level C interface (RFC 1823). However, access to the Active Directory via this interface is not recommended, since ADSI is available.

- MAPI, the Windows Open Services Architecture (WOSA) Messaging API. MAPI is supported for backward compatibility, largely to support access from MAPI clients such as Outlook 98 and Outlook 2000. Other messaging clients (e.g., Outlook Express) use LDAP.

1.16 Naming conventions

The Active Directory supports a number of naming conventions that are already widely used either in the Internet or in various DS implementations. These include the following:

- RFC 822 names are in the form of *JohnS@compaq.com*. Anyone using the Internet or an IP-based network are familiar with these names, since they serve as e-mail addresses.

    In Windows 2000, these names can be used to log on, as they allow concatenating the username and the logon domain. In a Windows 2000 implementation of a forest containing multiple trees and domains, it may be interesting to use a single logon name instead of having to remember the exact authentication domain. To provide this functionality, Windows 2000 has the concept of a User Principal Name (UPN). UPNs are suffixes that are appended to the logon name of a user. These suffixes have a forest-wide scope. For example, we may have a forest with 12 different domains, with many users disseminated in those domains. We can create a UPN suffix called *compaq.com*. This suffix allows any user in the forest to authenticate using the RFC 822 convention, where the user name is followed by the chosen suffix, in this case, by *@compaq.com*. This has the benefit of reducing complexity and hiding long names and prompting users to use a well-known domain name. It is also possible to add multiple UPN suffixes in the same forest.

- HTTP URL names allow accessing Active Directory data using Web browsers: *HTTP://SomeServer.compaq.com/Product/Sales/JohnS*.

- LDAP URLs. The Active Directory supports access via the LDAP protocol from any LDAP-enabled client: *LDAP://SomeServer.compaq.com/CN=JohnS, OU=Sales, OU=Product, DC=compaq, DC=com*.

- Universal Naming Convention (UNC) names were the norm in Windows NT 4.0 and are still supported in Windows 2000: *\\compaq.com\product\sales\john\public\budget.xls*.

1.17   Administration tools

Windows 2000 uses the Microsoft Management Console (MMC) as the common infrastructure for management tools. The management tools designed for the MMC are snap-ins or COM-based applications, which snap into the MMC. Snap-ins are easy to use, since they are based on a graphical user interface.

All the Windows NT 4.0 management tools have been migrated to snap-ins. The MMC allows a customization of the loaded snap-ins and allows saving the console with the snap-ins loaded. This way, administrators can create custom management consoles dedicated to particular tasks. The console in Figure 1.10 shows four snap-ins loaded, as follows:

- Active Directory Domains and Trusts, managing the trust relationships between domains

- Active Directory Schema Manager, which is the snap-in used to modify the content of the schema

Figure 1.10
*Microsoft
Management
Console with four
snap-ins loaded*

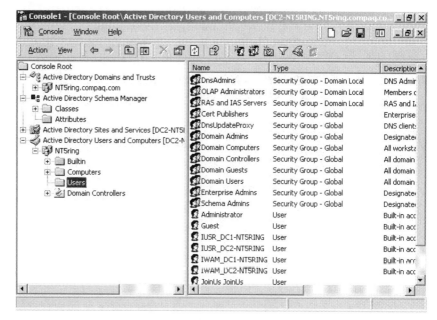

- Active Directory Sites and Services, used to manage the replication topology and connectivity between DCs and sites

- Active Directory Users and Groups, the replacement of User Manager for Domains, managing users, groups, and the hierarchical organization of a domain

Many more snap-ins exist and applications will provide add-ins to manage objects that are added to the Active Directory. Tools provided in Visual Studio V6.0 allow programmers to write additional add-ins, if required.

1.18   Summary

Windows 2000 is a lot more than a major upgrade—it's a whole new operating system that was designed clearly with the enterprise in mind. The Active Directory is the most important technology introduced in Windows 2000. It provides the foundation for the enterprise infrastructure.

Before attempting to design a Windows 2000-based infrastructure, one should carefully understand the replication topology required for effectively disseminating data throughout the enterprise so that these data remain available at a reasonable cost. Understanding how the schema must evolve, what objects should be published in the Directory, and who needs to have access to what are prerequisites for a successful Windows 2000 design. Always keep in mind that designing a Windows 2000 infrastructure involves designing the DNS namespace, the domain, the organizational unit structures, and, possibly, the Exchange Server and other Active Directory–enabled application infrastructures. All these concepts are reviewed in more detail in the following chapters.

Understanding and Designing the Windows 2000 Domain Name System

The Domain Name System (DNS) is Windows 2000 primary locator and name resolution service. The planning and design of an Active Directory infrastructure requires a solid understanding of the internals of this critical service, which is heavily used by the Active Directory and the Windows 2000 operating system. In this chapter we will also explore the critical steps you need to consider when planning and designing an AD DNS namespace and infrastructure for your organization.

2.1   An introduction to the domain name system

This section includes a general introduction to the Domain Name System (DNS). Because DNS is one of the most critical services in Windows 2000, every administrator and architect needs a thorough understanding of how this name resolution service works. To be able to look at the nuts and bolts of DNS we will first look at why we need DNS and explain some key DNS concepts such as DNS domains, DNS namespace, resource records, DNS servers, resolvers.

If you want to read another excellent introduction to DNS, read the book by Paul Albitz and Cricket Liu, *DNS and BIND*.

2.1.1   Why do we need DNS?

DNS provides an easy way to locate computers and services on a TCP/IP network. On a TCP/IP network, every entity is identified by an IP address. In DNS terminology, any network entity that can be linked to an IP address is known as a *host*. A host can be a computer, a router, a service, and so on.

IP addresses are just numbers (e.g., 124.34.3.23). For most people numbers are hard to remember. Using DNS a user can name a host by its friendly name (e.g., mymachine). In DNS terminology this friendly name is called the *hostname*.

The hostname to IP address translation service offered by DNS is also known as a name resolution service. To find out which IP address corresponds to a particular hostname, a DNS client sends out a query to a DNS server. The DNS server then tries to resolve the hostname to the host's IP address. Resolving means that the DNS server will query its database for a mapping between the hostname and an IP address, and return the IP address to the user. In DNS terminology these types of queries are called *forward lookups*. DNS can also resolve IP addresses to friendly names; these are called *reverse lookups*.

Before DNS was introduced on the Internet, a static file, called the *hosts file*, was used to provide name to IP mapping services. This file was administered from a single server and shared between all computers that required name resolution services. The more hosts were added, the bigger the hosts file became. It's clear that this method would never scale to the level of the Internet as we know it today. The hosts file is still supported in Windows 2000 and is still a viable alternative for name resolution in small environments. The hosts file is located in the %systemroot%\System32\Drivers\etc folder.

2.1.2   DNS characteristics

DNS provides a scalable alternative to the hosts file: It is based on a client server application and uses a replicated, partitioned, and hierarchical database, as follows:

- DNS is a client-server application: DNS clients and servers work together to resolve hostnames to IP addresses and vice versa.

- The DNS database is partitioned: The database is spread across different servers. No DNS server will ever store the complete DNS database. Also, not every computer will host a partition of the DNS database: only a set of special servers, the ones that are running a DNS service. All the other computers will resolve a hostname or an IP address by sending queries to the DNS servers.

- The DNS database is replicated: The same DNS database partition can be hosted on more than one DNS server. The DNS specification defines replication protocols that can synchronize DNS partitions between different DNS servers.

- The DNS database and the associated namespace are organized in a hierarchical manner. DNS uses a tree-like structure, more particularly a tree turned upside-down.

Besides scalability, the DNS architecture described above also provides other advantages, as follows:

- Reduced name resolution network traffic. DNS database partitions are only replicated between DNS servers. Also, partitions will always be smaller than a single hosts file. Regular computers and DNS servers will exchange tiny name resolution messages.

- Distributed administration. The administration of the DNS database can be distributed among different administrators, who are responsible for a particular DNS server. In DNS this is known as delegation.

- Name resolution server load balancing. In DNS name resolution processing is spread across different servers. Since the DNS database is distributed, multiple servers can serve the same request.

Another major advantage of DNS over the hosts file is that the DNS database can deal with more than just name to IP mappings (forward lookups). As explained previously, DNS can also handle IP to hostname mappings (reverse lookups). This is because the DNS database can contain other types of information than just hostname to IP mappings. DNS database entries are known as resource records. We will discuss the different types of resource records later in this chapter.

2.1.3   DNS concepts

To fully understand DNS one has to speak the DNS language. DNS uses quite a few specific terms and concepts which are too often confused or misunderstood. To clearly differentiate between them we will categorize the DNS concepts as follows:

- We consider DNS namespace, DNS domain names, and DNS hostnames as logical concepts. All of them are primarily DNS-client oriented: they help the user by providing users with friendly names which are easy to remember, and by grouping hostnames together into logical units.

- We consider DNS zones, resource records, DNS server and DNS client, as physical concepts. All of them are primarily DNS infrastructure oriented: They enable DNS delegation and DNS database replication, lay out the schema for the DNS database, and enable an application or user to query the DNS database.

Figure 2.1
*Internet DNS
namespace*

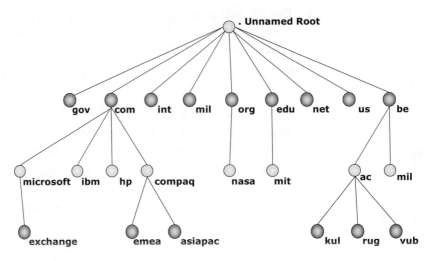

Logical concepts

The DNS namespace

DNS deals with names, many names. It deals with two basic types of names: domain names and hostnames. To put a logical order in the huge collection of DNS hostnames, DNS uses the concept of domains. To put order in the huge collection of DNS domain names, DNS uses the concept of a DNS namespace.

The DNS namespace is organized in a hierarchical manner. It is a tree, consisting of several nodes, that is turned upside-down. In the DNS namespace domain names are linked to subtrees or branches of the tree; hostnames are linked to leaf entities (known as hosts).

Figure 2.1 shows the best-known DNS namespace: the one that is used on the Internet. A company can also build its own internal DNS namespace, which is completely independent of the Internet namespace.

DNS domains

A DNS domain is a subtree or branch of the DNS namespace tree, starting at a node in the tree. As such, it is a logical grouping of hosts and other domains located underneath it. These domains are called *subdomains*. Figure 2.2 shows a company's private namespace, starting at the private root *mycorp.net*. This namespace contains multiple examples of domains: for example, everything beneath the europe node is part of the *europe.mycorp.net* domain; everything beneath the sales node is part of the *sales.Europe.mycorp.net* domain.

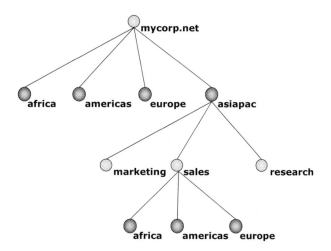

Figure 2.2
Private namespace for the mycorp *organization*

A domain's name has to be unique on its level of the DNS namespace. In Figure 2.2 there can only be a single americas domain beneath the *mycorp.net* node. There could be another americas domain beneath the sales node.

To uniquely identify a domain in the DNS namespace DNS uses the concept of a Fully Qualified Domain Name (FQDN). An FQDN consists of a domain's name and all the domain names located on the path between the domain's node and the root of the DNS namespace tree. The different parts of an FQDN are separated by dots. An example of an FQDN is *whitehouse.usa.gov.*

As with domains a host's FQDN consists of its hostname and all the domain names that are located higher up in the DNS namespace, for example: *mymachine.compaq.com.* As with domain names, in order to avoid ambiguous name resolution, an entity's hostname (in the previous example mymachine) has to be unique within a domain. The same hostname could, however, be reused in different DNS domains.

Let's look in detail at the domains in the Internet DNS namespace. DNS domains in the Internet namespace can be classified based on their location in the DNS tree, as follows:

- The root domain. The DNS namespace consists of a single root domain. This domain is also known as the null domain, because it doesn't have a real DNS name. It is represented by a simple dot.

- Top-level domains. Top-level domains are registered and administered by an Internet name registration authority. Their names consist of two or three characters. For forward lookups: the Internic (*http://rs.internic.net*) and the Internet Corporation for Assigned Names and Numbers (ICANN) (*http://www.icann.org*); for reverse lookups: the American Registry for Internet numbers (*http://www.arin.net*). Top-level domains can be further classified as follows:

- Geography-based top-level domains are used to hold the DNS data of a specific country or region (e.g., "be" for Belgium, "fr" for France, "us" for the United States, "uk" for the United Kingdom, and so on).
- Organization-based top-level domains hold DNS data of a set of organizations that are of the same type (e.g., "mil" for military organizations, "gov" for government organizations, "com" for commercial organizations, and so on).
- A very special top-level domain known as *in-addr.arpa* is the reverse lookup domain, used for DNS reverse lookups and holding IP address to name mappings. A separate reverse lookup domain exists for IP version 6 addresses (known as *IP6.INT*).

- Second-level domains. Second-level domains are linked to specific organizations or individuals (e.g., *compaq.com*, *mit.edu*, *nasa.org*). As with top-level domains, second-level domains are registered by an Internet name registration authority. Unlike top-level domains, their name, however, is not limited to two or three characters. Also the administrative responsibilities of a second-level domain are given to the administrators of the domain, not to some Internet authority. Consequently, an organization can create its own hosts and subdomains within its domain.

- Subdomains. Subdomains are additional domains underneath the registered second-level domains that are created by the organization the domain belongs to (e.g., *exchange.microsoft.com*, *emea.compaq.com*). In most cases organizations create them to better reflect the organizational structure into the DNS namespace. Subdomains are not registered and administered by an Internet name registration authority.

Physical concepts

DNS zones

A DNS zone is a physical concept directly linked to the DNS database. It is often confused with a DNS domain. A domain is a subtree in the logical DNS namespace tree. A zone is a physical partition of the DNS database, starting from a particular domain node in the DNS namespace.

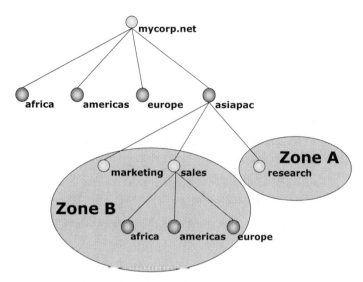

Figure 2.3
DNS domains and DNS zones

Another way to put it is that hostnames are logically partitioned using DNS domains and that the resource records in the DNS database are physically partitioned using DNS zones. Nevertheless, the two concepts are closely related: Resource records (physically contained in zones) can link hostnames (logically partitioned in domains) to IP addresses (or vice versa).

A zone can contain resource records pointing to hosts that are part of the same domain or different domains. In Figure 2.3, zone A only contains records of hosts belonging to the research domain; zone B contains records of hosts belonging to the sales domain and also those belonging to the marketing domain. Figure 2.3 also shows how hosts belonging to single domain asiapac can be split across multiple zones: Part of the hosts in asiapac is in zone A, another part is in zone B.

When discussing zones we must introduce the concept of a DNS server that is called authoritative for a particular zone. A DNS server is authoritative for a DNS zone if it has loaded the corresponding zone file. If a DNS server has loaded a particular zone file, the server can manage the resource records in it. There's no one-on-one mapping between DNS zones and DNS servers: A single DNS server can host multiple zone files and be authoritative for multiple zones.

Since forward lookup domains and reverse lookup domains are clearly separated from one another in the DNS tree, the zone files linked to them are different and clearly separated. In DNS speak we call them forward lookup zones and reverse lookup zones.

In classic DNS implementations zones are stored as files in the file system of a DNS server. (In NT and Windows 2000: %systemdrive%/winnt/system32/dns.) In Windows 2000 DNS zone files can also be stored in the Active Directory. We will discuss this later in this chapter. Windows 2000-NT DNS uses the following naming conventions for zone files (BIND DNS typically uses *db.<domain name>* and *db.<IP address>* to name its zone files):

- *<domain name>.dns* represents a forward lookup zone—for example, *compaq.com.dns.*

- *<IP address>.dns* represents a reverse lookup zone—for example, *0.0.10.in-addr.arpa.dns.*

Note that the syntax of the name differs, depending on whether it is used for forward lookups or for reverse lookups.

So far so good. We know now that DNS zones are the key to the partitioning of the DNS database. They tell us what portion of the DNS namespace a particular DNS server can manage. Next, we will look at what we can do with those partitions. DNS zones are used for DNS database replication and delegation.

Using zones for replication   DNS allows for multiple copies of the same portion of the DNS namespace on different servers. To stay synchronized the zone files are replicated between different DNS servers. DNS replication brings up two other important DNS concepts: primary and secondary zone. To explain the difference between the two, one has to understand the single-master replication model which is used in classical DNS implementations for the replication of zone files between different servers.

In DNS, the basic unit of replication is the zone file. In a single-master model, only one DNS server, authoritative for a particular zone, holds a read-write copy of the zone's data; all the other authoritative DNS servers hold read-only copies of the zone data. A primary zone is a one that holds the read/write copy of the zone data; in other words, it's the zone on which the updates occur. A secondary zone is a zone that holds a read only copy of the zone data. A secondary zone gets its updates from a primary zone. Note that a DNS server can hold multiple primary and secondary zone files. A DNS server hosting a primary zone is referred to as a primary name server for that particular zone; a DNS server hosting a secondary zone is referred to as a secondary name server for the zone.

To enable a reliable replication of the zone data between different servers every zone contains a special resource record known as the *SOA record*. It is the first resource record listed in a zone file. We will discuss the content of the SOA record later in the chapter. One of the important things contained in the SOA is the name of the DNS server hosting the primary zone file.

The replication of DNS zone data between DNS servers is known in DNS terminology as *zone transfer*. A zone transfer can occur between a primary and a secondary zone but also between a secondary and another secondary zone. The DNS server from which other DNS servers receive secondary zone updates is also known as the master server. A zone transfer takes place when the following occurs:

- The master server sends a notification to the secondary zone DNS server.

- A DNS service on a server hosting a secondary zone starts up. At startup DNS automatically queries the master server.

- A DNS zone's refresh interval expires. (The refresh interval is mentioned in a zone file's SOA; by default, it is set to 15 minutes.) This is another event that causes a DNS service to automatically query the master server.

To perform zone transfers DNS supports several replication protocols. In classical DNS these are known as full zone transfers (AXFR) and incremental zone transfers (IXFR). Windows 2000 DNS supports three DNS replication protocols: full zone transfers, incremental zone transfers, and Active Directory replication. AD replication is explained extensively in Chapter 3. Full zone transfers replicate the entire zone file; incremental zone transfers (IXFR) replicate only the changes that occurred since the last update. Some DNS systems provide full zone transfers that support the transmission of only a single record per packet; others support multiple records per packet. We will discuss DNS replication protocols later in this chapter. Windows 2000 DNS includes important replication protocol changes compared with its NT4 predecessor.

Using zones for delegation In DNS terminology delegation is the process of assigning the administrative authority over a portion of the DNS namespace to another DNS server. Whereas zones tell the DNS server which resource records it is responsible for, delegation tells the DNS server which resource records it is not responsible for and for which it should call on other DNS servers.

For example, as shown in Figure 2.4, the domain *compaq.com* is delegated from the *.com* domain. The domain *compaq.com* is then made up of a number of zones. These may include other delegations to geographical loca-

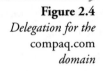

Figure 2.4
Delegation for the
compaq.com
domain

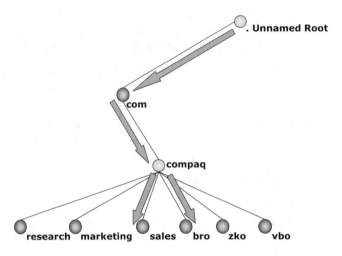

tions, such as *bro.compaq.com* or to functions, such as *sales.compaq.com* (for your information, "bro" is the internal Compaq location code for the Brussels office, Belgium). Since delegation includes updates to the zone data, only the administrator of the DNS server hosting the primary zone compaq can delegate a portion of the zone's content to another DNS server.

Besides administrative delegation, delegation also allows for the load of the DNS database to be distributed across different DNS servers. This improves name resolution performance and can provide a certain amount of name resolution fault tolerance.

In the DNS database, delegation is represented by Name Server (NS) resource records. An NS resource record links a domain name to a DNS server responsible for that domain. NS records appear in forward as well as in reverse lookup zones. Multiple NS records can appear in the same zone file, because multiple DNS servers can host the same zone file. The NS resource record example below points to a DNS server named *qemea-dc16.qemea.qtest.cpqcorp.net*, which is authoritative for the *qemea.qtest.cpqcorp.net* domain:

```
qemea.qtest.cpqcorp.net IN NS qemea-dc16.qemea.qtest.cpqcorp.net
```

NS records play a major role in the name resolution process. To find the IP address linked to a particular hostname a DNS server must navigate through the DNS hierarchy. This can be done by starting at the root of the namespace and then descending the namespace hierarchy, following name server delegations. This only occurs if insufficient information is available in the resolver and server cache.

Table 2.1   *DNA Resource Record Fields*

Field Name	Field Meaning
Owner	Contains the name of the host to which the record belongs.
TTL	Contains the record's Time-to-Live. The TTL specifies the amount of time a record remains in a DNS client or server DNS cache.
Class	Contains the record class; in Windows NT and Windows 2000 this is always the Internet class (IN).
Type	Indicates the resource record type (the main types will be explained later in the chapter).
RDATA	Contains the resource record's data.

DNS resource records

Resource records are the entries that are contained in DNS zone files. In most cases a resource record is represented on a single line; if it spans multiple lines, the lines are linked together using parentheses. They are used by a DNS server to respond to the DNS queries it gets from DNS clients (resolvers or other DNS servers). In general, a DNS resource record consists of owner, TTL, class, type, and RDATA fields; the fields are explained in Table 2.1.

In the following text we will explain the meaning and the syntax of the most important DNS resource records: A, CNAME, PTR, SOA, NS, MX, and SRV records. For an overview of all existing resource records take a look at RFCs 1035, 1183, and 1886, available from *http://www.ietf.org*.

A, CNAME, and PTR records   An A (Address) record maps an FQDN to an IP address. A PTR (Pointer) record does the opposite: it maps an IP address to an FQDN. A records are used for forward lookups; PTR records are used for reverse lookups.

A CNAME (Canonical Name) record creates an alias for an FQDN. One of the most common uses of a CNAME is to hide changes to application servers for the users of the applications. In the following example, you could easily move your intranet application from *oldserver.qemea.qtest.cpqcorp.net* to a new server without interrupting your users. You would do this by simply adding a CNAME record to your DNS database, pointing to the new server *newserver.qemea.qtest.cpqcorp.net* and using the same alias *intraweb*.

Forward lookup zone:

```
Oldserver   IN   A   16.195.84.41
Newserver   IN   A   16.195.84.42
intraweb.qemea.qtest.cpqcorp.net.   IN   CNAME   oldserver.qemea.qtest.cpqcorp.net.
intraweb.qemea.qtest.cpqcorp.net.   IN   CNAME   newserver.qemea.qtest.cpqcorp.net.
```

Reverse lookup zone:

```
41.84.195.16.in-addr.arpa.   IN   PTR   oldserver.qemea.qtest.cpqcorp.net.
42.84.195.16.in-addr.arpa.   IN   PTR   newserver.qemea.qtest.cpqcorp.net.
```

Note in the example above that the IP address appears to be noted backwards in the PTR record; this is not a typo: An IP address gets more specific from left to right, whereas an FQDN gets more specific from right to left.

NS and SOA records   Every DNS zone has an SOA (Start of Authority) record and contains at least one NS (Name Server) record (pointing to the DNS server hosting the primary zone).

An NS record points to servers that are authoritative for a particular zone. NS records are also used in delegation: when a partition of the DNS namespace is delegated to another server, an NS record for that server will be added to the DNS zone.

An SOA record contains vital DNS information mainly used for DNS replication. A good example is the SOA's serial number. To decide which data need to be replicated between primary and secondary DNS zones, DNS

Figure 2.5
Properties of an SOA record as displayed in the Windows 2000 DNS MMC snap-in

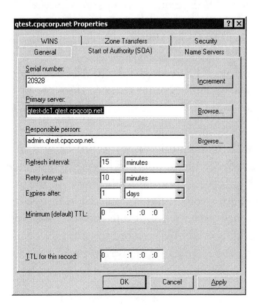

Table 2.2 *DNS SOA Resource Record Fields*

Field	Meaning—Content
Owner, TTL, class, type	See Table 2.1
Authoritative Server	Name of DNS server hosting primary zone
Responsible Administrator	E-mail address of zone administrator
Serial Number	Number of updates performed on zone; this is used to determine whether a zone transfer is needed
Refresh	Number of times a secondary server checks for zone changes
Retry	Amount of time a secondary server will wait for a response from the primary server before retrying
Expire	Amount of time after a zone transfer a secondary server considers its proper zone data valid
Minimum TTL	TTL added to replies containing resource records that do not have a proper TTL field

will compare the serial number of the secondary zone file to the one of the primary zone file each time a zone transfer is triggered. The SOA record also contains a pointer to the DNS server hosting the primary zone. In classical DNS this pointer is the same in all primary and secondary zones. This is not true in Windows 2000 if the zone is Active Directory–integrated: In this case, the pointer is different in every AD-integrated zone. It points to the local DNS server hosting an AD-integrated copy of the zone. All the SOA fields are listed in Table 2.2. Figure 2.5 shows the properties of an SOA record as displayed in the Windows 2000 DNS MMC snap-in.

Here's an example of NS and SOA records extracted from a zone file for the *qtest.cpqcorp.net* domain (the items following the semicolon explain the different fields of the record).

```
qtest.cpqcorp.net.    IN   NS    qtest-dc2.qtest.cpqcorp.net.
qtest.cpqcorp.net.    IN   NS    qtest-dc1.qtest.cpqcorp.net.
qtest.cpqcorp.net. IN SOA (
    qtest-dc1.qtest.cpqcorp.net.    ;name of DNS server hosting primary zone
    administrator.qtest.cpqcorp.net. ;e-mail address of zone administrator
    18907                           ;serial number
    900                             ;refresh
    600                             ;retry
    86400                           ;expire
    60  )                           ;minimum TTL
```

In this example, server qtest-dc1 hosts the primary zone linked to the *qtest.cpqcorp.net* domain, qtest-dc2 hosts a secondary zone for the same zone. Note that the zone for the *qtest.cpqcorp.net* domain contains both an SOA and an NS record pointing to the qtest-dc1 DNS server.

SRV and MX records   A Service Resource Record (SRV) enables a DNS client to locate a particular service. These records are the Windows 2000 DNS equivalent for NetBIOS advertisements. SRV records have been defined recently (in the experimental RFC 2052) and are supported in Windows 2000. Long before SRV records the IETF already defined MX, or Mail Exchange, records. MX records enable a DNS client to locate an SMTP service that can handle the mail messages of a particular domain.

An MX record has the following format: `DomainName Class MX Priority Target`. The MX record field contents are described in the Table 2.3.

An SRV resource record has the following format:

`_Service._Protocol.Name TTL Class SRV Priority Weight Port Target`

The SRV field contents are described Table 2.4.

Below are examples of an MX and a Windows 2000 SRV record:

`*.compaq.com.  IN  MX  0  mailserver1.compaq.com.`

`_ldap._tcp.compaq.com IN SRV  0 100 389 win2kdc1.compaq.com.`

The MX record points to an SMTP server for the *compaq.com* domain. The SRV record points to an LDAP service (domain controller) for the *compaq.com* domain. Figure 2.6 shows how the properties of a Kerberos KDC service SRV record are displayed in the Windows 2000 DNS MMC snap-in.

Table 2.3   *DNS MX Resource Record Fields*

Field	Meaning—Content
DomainName	The name of the service.
Class	See Table 2.1.
Priority	Fault Tolerance mechanism. The priority lists the preference that is given to an MX record. The lower the number, the higher the priority.
Target	FQDN of the machine hosting the SMTP service.

Table 2.4   *DNS SRV Resource Record Fields*

Field	Meaning—Content
_Service	Name of the service
_Protocol	Protocol used to access the service (TCP, UDP, etc.)
Name	Domain name of the resource record
TTL, Class	See Table 2.1
Priority	Load balancing mechanism: Clients contact host with lowest priority
Weight	Load balancing mechanism: clients contact host with lowest weight
Port	Service port
Target	FQDN of the machine hosting the service

DNS clients and servers

A DNS client (also known as a DNS resolver) is a service that tries to resolve DNS names or IP addresses by querying its local cache or by sending query messages to a DNS server. A DNS client can run on any machine, including a DNS server. Most DNS clients also provide programmatic

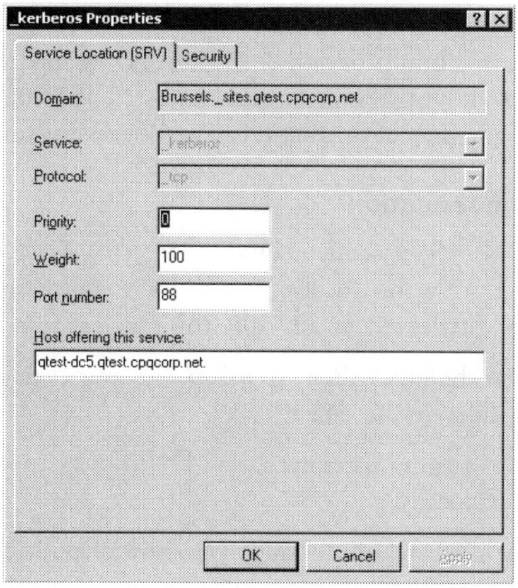

Figure 2.6

Properties of a Kerberos KDC SRV record as displayed in the Windows 2000 DNS MMC snap-in

interfaces to let programmers call on name resolution services from their code.

A DNS server is a server running a DNS service. It is queried by DNS clients to help with name resolution tasks (IP address to name or name to IP address). When queried by a client, a DNS server can either return a positive or negative answer or refer the client to another DNS server. Different types of DNS servers exist, based on their role in the name resolution process, as follows:

- A caching-only server is not authoritative for any DNS domains; it just caches information. Initially, when its starts up, a caching-only server knows nothing; over time as it resolves names by sending queries to other authoritative DNS server, it will gather knowledge.

- Forwarders and Slaves. A DNS server that is configured to forward all its recursive queries to a set of preconfigured DNS servers is known as a slave; the servers that receive the queries in this scenario are known as forwarders. The use of forwarders and slaves is an interesting option to limit the number of queries that are sent across a slow link and to share the results of the queries locally.

2.1.4   How DNS name resolution works

Now that we have introduced the basic DNS concepts, we can look at how DNS name resolution works: what happens when a DNS client needs to resolve a DNS name? How do DNS servers interact to resolve a DNS name? DNS name resolution consists of two distinct phases: the local name resolution phase and the DNS server query phase. The second phase will not take place if the outcome of the first phase is a successful name resolution.

Local name resolution

Before a DNS client sends a DNS query to a DNS server, it will try to resolve the DNS name locally. Local DNS name resolution uses the local DNS cache. Entries can be added to this cache in two ways, as follows:

1.   When the DNS client starts up, the entries in the local hosts file are loaded in the cache.

2.   When a name is resolved by a DNS query to a DNS server, it is cached locally.

DNS caching includes both the caching of positive and negative DNS query responses. This last one is also known as *negative caching*. Negative

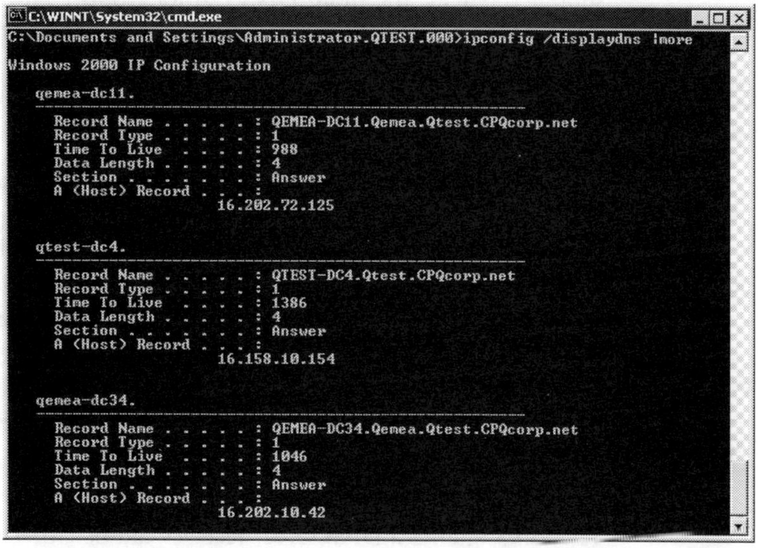

Figure 2.7
Looking at the DNS client cache using ipconfig

```
C:\WINNT\System32\cmd.exe                                              _ □ ×

C:\Documents and Settings\Administrator.QTEST.000>ipconfig /displaydns |more

Windows 2000 IP Configuration

    qemea-dc11.
    ------------------------------------------
        Record Name . . . . . : QEMEA-DC11.Qemea.Qtest.CPQcorp.net
        Record Type . . . . . : 1
        Time To Live  . . . . : 988
        Data Length . . . . . : 4
        Section . . . . . . . : Answer
        A (Host) Record . . . :
                                16.202.72.125

    qtest-dc4.
    ------------------------------------------
        Record Name . . . . . : QTEST-DC4.Qtest.CPQcorp.net
        Record Type . . . . . : 1
        Time To Live  . . . . : 1386
        Data Length . . . . . : 4
        Section . . . . . . . : Answer
        A (Host) Record . . . :
                                16.158.10.154

    qemea-dc34.
    ------------------------------------------
        Record Name . . . . . : QEMEA-DC34.Qemea.Qtest.CPQcorp.net
        Record Type . . . . . : 1
        Time To Live  . . . . : 1046
        Data Length . . . . . : 4
        Section . . . . . . . : Answer
        A (Host) Record . . . :
                                16.202.10.42
```

caching is defined in RFCs 1034 and 2308. The caching of both response types can greatly reduce the overall DNS server and resolver response time.

To look at the content of a Windows 2000 DNS client's cache, use the ipconfig command prompt tool with the /displaydns switch (as illustrated in Figure 2.7).

The amount of time an entry stays in a client's DNS cache depends on the Time-To-Live (TTL) property of the entry. The TTL is always expressed in seconds. In Windows 2000 it can be configured on the DNS server and client side, as follows:

- On the server side, it can be set per zone file (using the minimum TTL field of the SOA resource record). Individual records inherit the zone's default TTL set in the SOA.

- On the client side, a MaxCacheEntryTtlLimit and DefaultRegistrationTTL can be set. The MaxCacheEntryTtlLimit setting determines how long resource records are kept in the client-side cache (it is set in HKLM\system\currentcontrolset\services\dnscache\parameters). The DefaultRegistrationTTL specifies the TTL that is sent with Dynamic DNS update requests (it is set in HKLM\system\currentcontrolset\services\tcpip\parameters).

When setting TTL parameters you'll have to balance DNS information accuracy (the shorter the TTL the better the accuracy) and DNS traffic (the shorter the TTL the more DNS traffic). Your TTL choice should also be related to the DHCP lease renewal intervals: Short TTLs are advisable if your DHCP leases have a short lifetime.

DNS server query

If local name resolution is unsuccessful, the DNS client will send a DNS query to a DNS server. In the following text we will explore the DNS query types and the DNS query process. The concepts and processes explained here are valid for both forward and reverse lookup. They are not valid for a special type of lookup known as inverse lookups. During an inverse lookup a DNS server does not call on other DNS servers to resolve a query, but tries to resolve the query using its local zone files. The use of this type of query is very limited.

Query types

The DNS queries a DNS server receives can be either recursive or iterative. A query sent out by a DNS resolver mostly results in both recursive and iterative queries. The two types are illustrated in Figure 2.8. In Figure 2.8, a DNS resolver tries to resolve the FQDN *webserver.nasa.org*.

When a DNS server receives a recursive query it means that it must return either a matching resource record or an error message. It cannot return a referral to another DNS server. If the DNS server cannot resolve the query using its local cache, it will call on other DNS servers to resolve the recursive query until the name gets resolved or the name query fails.

When are recursive queries used? Queries sent out by a DNS resolver are always recursive (in Figure 2.8, query 1) as are the queries sent out by DNS servers that are configured as forwarders.

In order for recursive queries to work, DNS uses a feature called *root hints*. Root hints are special resource records in the DNS cache that point to the DNS servers that are authoritative for the DNS top-level domains. In case you're dealing with a private network (not connected to the Internet), update your root hints to point to your internal top-level domain DNS servers (the private root). Without root hints a DNS server would never be able to respond to DNS queries for FQDNs that are part of domains located at a higher layer of the DNS namespace. Of course this is only needed if the DNS server cache does not contain any relevant information. Root hints are contained in a special file named cache.dns (located in %SystemRoot%\System32\Dns—in BIND DNS this file is named db.cache); the latest version of the Internet DNS namespace root hints file can be downloaded from *ftp://rs.internic.net/domain/named.cache*.

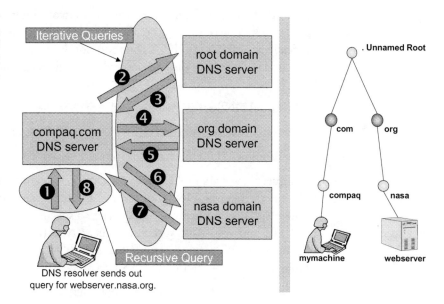

Figure 2.8
Recursive and iterative DNS queries

DNS resolver sends out query for webserver.nasa.org.

Iterative means that the DNS server receiving the query can return either a matching resource record or a referral to another DNS server, which is located at a lower level of the DNS tree and authoritative for a particular DNS domain.

When are iterative queries used? Queries sent out by a DNS server to another DNS server in response to a recursive query of a DNS client are always iterative (in Figure 2.8, queries 2, 4, and 6). Also, when a client sends a recursive query to a DNS server on which recursive queries are disabled, the server will respond to the query as if it got an iterative query.

The difference between the two query types can be explained as follows:

- In a recursive query, a DNS server acts on behalf of the client. While the client waits, the DNS server tries to resolve the query. In a recursive query the responsibility for driving the name resolution process is at the server side.

- In an iterative query, a DNS server returns the best possible answer based on locally available information. In an iterative query the responsibility for driving the name resolution process is at the client side.

Query process

If local name resolution is unsuccessful, the DNS client will send a DNS query to one of the servers on its DNS server list. This list contains both the preferred and alternate DNS servers of all network interfaces. Preferred and alternate DNS servers can be configured manually or can be obtained automatically as part of the DHCP configuration information. The DNS server list is updated dynamically and ordered and maintained using the following rules:

- Preferred DNS servers have precedence over alternate DNS servers.
- Unresponsive servers are removed temporarily from the list.

In Windows 2000 this happens for each network adapter.

A query sent by a DNS client to a DNS server contains the DNS name to be resolved (an FQDN), a query and a domain name class specification. A query specification narrows the query to a specific type of resource record (A, PTR, and so on) or specifies a query type (iterative, recursive). The domain name class specification that is sent to a Windows DNS server should always be of the Internet (IN) class.

When a DNS server receives a DNS query (either from a client or from another server) it will try to resolve the name using one of the two following methods (listed in the order in which they are tried):

1. Query the locally available primary or secondary DNS zone files.

2. Query the local DNS cache.

If none of these methods is successful the DNS server will forward the query to an authoritative DNS server (in case of an iterative query) or send a negative response back to the requester (in case of a recursive query). If a DNS zone contains multiple NS records (servers authoritative for a particular zone), a server will be selected based on the measurement of the round-trip delay.

The answers returned by a DNS server to a DNS query can be a combination of positive, negative, authoritative, and referral answers. To illustrate an answer that is a combination of two types: a positive answer returned by an authoritative DNS server will be both a positive and an authoritative answer. The following list defines these four answers:

1. A positive answer consists of a resource record or a set of resource records.

2. A negative answer tells the requester that "No authoritative DNS servers exist for this domain in the DNS namespace" or that "An authoritative DNS server exists, but no resource record matching the request could be found."

Figure 2.9
DNS name resolution process

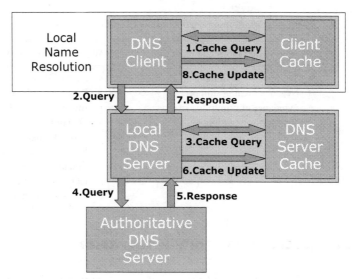

3.   An authoritative answer tells the requester that the answer was returned by a DNS server authoritative for a particular DNS domain.

4.   A referral answer is an answer that contains information other than the information that was initially requested in the DNS query. This information can be a referral to another DNS server or type of resource record other than the one initially requested (e.g., returning a CNAME record when an A record was requested).

Figure 2.9 brings together the major steps used during DNS name resolution: from local name resolution to the different steps involved in a DNS query sent to a DNS server. Notice the importance of caching—both on the client side and the DNS server side.

2.2   The power of Windows 2000 DNS

In the following text we will introduce the new features of Windows 2000 DNS. Table 2.5 shows the most important new features of Windows 2000 DNS on both the client and the server side.

Windows 2000 DNS has more new features than just the ones listed in Table 2.5. Two other key features are the enhanced DNS server performance and the support for clustering.

Table 2.5   *Features of the Windows 2000 DNS Client and Server*

Windows 2000 DNS Client	Windows 2000 DNS Server
▓ System-wide caching	▓ Active Directory integration
▓ Negative caching support	▓ Windows 2000 service localization
▓ Avoidance of unresponsive servers	▓ Incremental zone transfer support
▓ Subnet prioritization	▓ Dynamic update protocol
	▓ Unicode character support
	▓ Enhanced domain locator
	▓ Enhanced caching resolver service
	▓ RFC compliancy
	▓ Improved administration tools

2.2.1   Active directory integration

At the beginning of this chapter we mentioned the importance of DNS in Windows 2000: DNS is the Windows 2000 core naming service. In the following text we will elaborate on the way AD and DNS are and can be integrated and on the tight interdependencies between the Windows 2000 directory and naming service.

Locating and naming AD domains and objects

AD uses DNS to name and locate AD domains and objects. Every Windows 2000 domain is identified by its DNS domain name. Remember that although an AD domain is identified by its DNS domain name, an AD domain and a DNS domain are completely different concepts: An AD domain stores objects; a DNS domain stores resource records. Consequently, every object member of the domain wears the domain name in its distinguished name (DN). The DNS parts of an object's distinguished name are known as domain components and start with dc=. To illustrate this look at the DN of the user object jdc member of the *emea.nt.compaq.com* domain (see also Figure 2.10):

```
cn=jdc,cn=consultants,cn=users,dc=emea,dc=nt,dc=compaq,dc=com
```

The cn= components of the object's DN reflect the container and OU structure of the *emea.nt.compaq.com* domain. In the above example user jdc is part of the consultants OU, located in the users container. These common name (CN) components are not DNS-based but follow the LDAP naming standards. Every Windows 2000 object's DN is thus a combination of DNS and LDAP names.

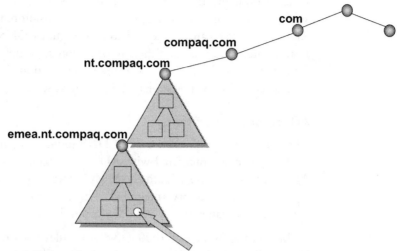

Figure 2.10
Locating objects in AD using DNS and LDAP

LDAP://cn=jdc,cn=consultants,cn=users,dc=emea,dc=nt,dc=compaq,dc=com

The domain example in Figure 2.10 clearly shows what an AD domain tree is all about: it's a hierarchical collection of domains that share a contiguous DNS namespace. Contiguous in this context means that they all originate from the same AD domain tree root domain. For example, the *emea.nt.compaq.com* and the *asiapac.nt.compaq.com* domain would be in the same domain tree, because they are both child domains of the *compaq.com* domain. *Emea.nt.compaq.com* (root domain *compaq.com*) and *asiapac.nt.cpqcorp.net* (root domain *cpqcorp.net*) could never be a member of the same domain tree because they both originate from a different AD domain tree root domain. Both *emea.nt.compaq.com* and *asiapac.nt.cpqcorp.net* could, however, be part of the same AD forest—a forest can contain multiple noncontiguous or disjointed DNS namespaces.

DNS can also be used to locate AD domains, AD objects and core Windows 2000 services, such as a Kerberos KDC, a global catalog, and so on. DNS contains specific resource records pointing to AD domains or to the dc= portions of an AD object's DN. These records are simple A records linking domain names to Windows 2000 DCs. Once you know the DC, you can query it for a particular domain object using LDAP. Every DC hosts the AD domain NC of a particular domain. You can easily test whether the DNS name of a particular domain is present in the DNS database by pinging the domain name.

All of this shows the tight integration of the Windows 2000 AD namespace and the DNS namespace; in fact, the AD namespace is contained within the DNS namespace. Every AD forest can be mapped to a single contiguous namespace or to multiple disjointed namespaces; every AD domain tree can be mapped to a contiguous DNS domain hierarchy. Both namespaces can store their information separately (in the DNS zone files or in the AD database) or in the same location (in the AD database). The latter option will be explained in the next section.

AD storage integration

The zone files of a Windows 2000 DNS service running on a DC can be configured to be integrated with AD. To integrate a DNS zone file with AD, open up its properties in the MMC DNS snap-in and change its zone type to Active Directory Integrated. This AD integration is an option; if you want, you can still run DNS like you did in NT4.

Integrating Windows 2000 DNS zone files with the Active Directory has two important consequences. DNS zone file data are stored in AD as AD objects and are replicated using AD replication mechanisms.

The AD schema includes a set of generic objects that can be used to store DNS-specific information, such as zones, domain nodes, resource records and general DNS configuration information in the Active Directory. Table 2.6 shows the principal attributes of the DnsZone and the DnsNode object classes.

Table 2.6   *Attributes of the DnsZone and the DnsNode AD Object Classes*

Object Class (Object Type) Attributes	Meaning
DnsZone (Container object)	Represents an AD integrated zone
ManagedBy	Administrator of DNS zone
DnsProperty	Stores configuration information
DnsNotifySecondaries	Support for notify messages
DnsAllowXFR	Support for incremental zone transfer
DnsAllowDynamic	Support for dynamic update
DnsNode (Leaf object)	Represents a host (a host can be a machine, a service, a subdomain, etc.)
DnsRecord	Stores resource records linked to a particular host
DnsProperty	Stores configuration information linked to a particular host

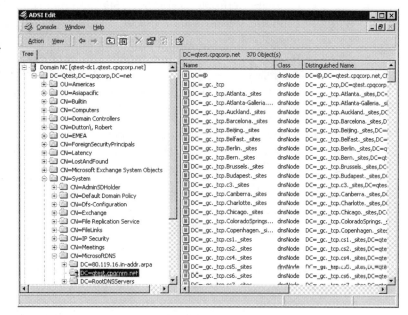

Figure 2.11
Looking at the storage location of an AD integrated zone using adsiedit

An AD integrated zone is stored in the AD domain NC, underneath the System\MicrosoftDNS container. This is a very important detail: It means that DNS zones are not replicated forest-wide but domain-wide

The MicrosoftDNS container can hold three types of DnsZone container objects: forward lookup zones, reverse lookup zones, and root hints. You can look at the AD integrated DNS data using the users and computers MMC snap-in or using adsiedit (as shown in Figure 2.11).

All DnsZone containers contain multiple DnsNode leaf objects, representing the different hosts within the zone. A special DnsNode is the one represented by the "@" symbol; this represents a node having the same name as the DnsZone object.

AD Replication Integration

From a replication point of view integrating DNS zones with AD offers the following advantages:

- AD integrated DNS uses the same replication mechanism as Active Directory. Unlike NT4 there's no need to set up other DNS replication mechanisms. The same is true for the replication topology; DNS can use the same replication topology as the one used for AD replication.

- Contrary to the classical DNS replication model, AD replication uses
  a multimaster replication model. A major advantage of a multimaster
  model is that it eliminates a possible single point of failure: the primary zone server. AD integrated DNS does not use the concept of
  secondary zones; all zones are considered primary zones (at least on
  Windows 2000 DCs; a member server running a DNS server can still
  host a secondary copy of an AD integrated zone).

- AD replication provides per-property replication granularity. Classical
  DNS replication mechanisms had, in the best case (when using incremental zone transfers), per-object (resource record) granularity.

- AD replication is secure. It can take place across RPC or SMTP; both
  protocols can be secured and provide adequate authentication, confidentiality, and integrity services for the replicated AD data.

Obviously AD replication integration positively impacts the amount of
resources that are needed for the design of a DNS namespace and for
administering and maintaining the DNS servers. You can leverage the
efforts done for the design of your AD infrastructure, and your AD administrators can manage the DNS services as well.

Relying on AD replication for DNS data replication clearly has numerous advantages. In Chapter 3 we will explain why one of the negative consequences of the AD replication model is the AD's constant state of loose
consistency. In DNS terminology this means that at any given moment in
time different DNS servers hosting the same zone could return different
answers to the same DNS query. After all, this is nothing new. This can also
happen in a classic DNS replication model using primary and secondary
zones.

The concept of a multimaster DNS also raises some other interesting
challenges: Some operations such as object deletion require a single authoritative server. How does DNS deal with the deletion of resource records?
Which DNS server is authoritative to delete a record and to replicate it to
the other servers? We will discuss this later in this chapter.

2.2.2 Service localization

Windows 2000 uses DNS not just to name and locate domain and AD
objects but also to locate Windows 2000 services such as the Kerberos KDC
or a GC. DNS service localization is based on support for a special type
of resource records: service records; in the DNS database they are marked
as SRV records. Two important features of the way SRV records are implemented in Windows 2000 are the support for dynamic SRV record

Table 2.7 *Key Windows 2000 Services and Corresponding SRV Records*

SRV Record*	Meaning—Service
_gc	Points to a server hosting a GC
_kerberos	Points to a server running the Kerberos KDC
_kpasswd	Points to a server that can accept and handle Kerberos password change request
_ldap	Points to a server hosting an LDAP service (AD)

* Notice that all Windows 2000 SRV resource records and some of the DNS zone containers (service and protocol identifiers) start with an underscore. This naming convention is based on an update (defined in Internet draft *draft-ietf-dnsind-rfc2052bis-05.txt*) to RFC 2052. The use of underscores is not accepted by some older DNS BIND implementations. To get around this problem you can set the name checking configuration of your BIND server to not reject records starting with an underscore.

updating and the site awareness of the service localization system. Table 2.7 lists some of the key Windows 2000 services and the SRV records used to register them in DNS.

When you look at these records using the DNS MMC snap-in, you'll notice that the same record occurs several times in different DNS containers within a zone file. A query for a _gc SRV record, for example, will return all _gc records within a zone. You can observe this behavior from the command prompt using the nslookup tool. The default DNS zone containers are listed in Table 2.8.

From a DNS point of view it's very confusing to call all the entries in Table 2.8 containers; in fact, they are kinds of logical DNS subdomains. Table 2.8 would contain even more rows if the AD held the definition of multiple sites. Every row containing Default-First-Site-Name would be repeated for every site defined in AD. Figure 2.12 shows how these containers are displayed in the MMC DNS snap-in.

Microsoft included these containers to enable a DNS client to query DNS for services (SRV resource records) by site, by protocol, or by GUID. A GUID is a 128-bit automatically generated unique identifier used to reference AD objects.

The reflection of sites in the DNS namespace allows a client to connect to the service closest to or within its proper site.

The reflection of protocols in the DNS namespace allows a client to find out the protocols supported by a particular service and to connect to the service using the protocol of its choice.

Table 2.8   *Default Windows 2000 DNS Zone Containers*

DNS Zone Container	Meaning
_msdcs	Microsoft DC services
_msdcs.dc	DC
_msdcs.dc._sites	Sites
_msdcs.dc._sites.Default-First-Site-Name	Default First Site
_msdcs.dc._sites.Default-First-Site-Name._tcp	TCP protocol
_msdcs.dc._tcp	TCP protocol
_msdcs.domains	Windows 2000 domain
_msdcs.domains.<domain GUID>	Windows 2000 domain GUID
_msdcs.domains.<domain GUID>._tcp	TCP protocol
_msdcs.gc	GC
_msdcs.gc._sites	Sites
_msdcs.gc._sites.Default-First-Site-Name	Default first site
_msdcs.gc._sites.Default-First-Site-Name._tcp	TCP protocol
_msdcs.gc._tcp	TCP protocol
_msdcs.pdc	Primary DC
_msdcs.pdc._tcp	TCP protocol
_sites	Sites
_sites.Default-First-Site-Name	Default first site
_sites.Default-First-Site-Name._tcp	TCP protocol
_tcp	TCP protocol
_udp	UDP protocol

The inclusion of domain GUIDs in the DNS namespace allows a client to query for a DC in a particular domain using the domain GUID.

Let's look at some combinations of SRV records and Windows 2000 DNS-specific containers, what type of DC registers them, and what wisdom they can bring to a DNS resolver (see Table 2.9).

Figure 2.12
DNS containers in the MMC DNS snap-in

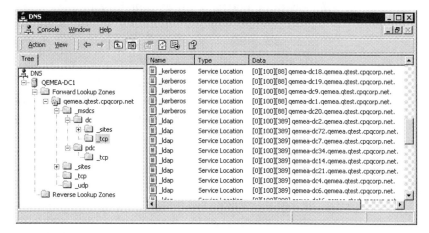

Table 2.9 *Windows 2000 SRV Records*

Resource Record	Meaning	Registered By
_ldap._tcp.<DnsDomainName>	Allows a client to find a Windows 2000 DC in the AD domain named <DnsDomainName>.	Each DC
_ldap._tcp.<SiteName>._sites.<DnsDomainName>	Allows a client to find a Windows 2000 DC in the domain named by <DnsDomainName> and in the site named by <SiteName>.	Each DC
_ldap._tcp.pdc._msdcs.<DnsDomainName>	This record allows a client to find the PDC emulator named by <DnsDomainName>.	The PDC emulator of the domain
_ldap._tcp.gc._msdcs.<DnsTreeName>	This record allows a client to find a (GC) server.	DCs serving as GCs for the tree named by <DnsTreeName>
_ldap._tcp.<SiteName>._sites.gc._msdcs.<DnsTreeName>	This record allows a client to find a GC server that is in the site named by <SiteName>.	DCs serving as GCs for the tree named by <DnsTreeName>
_ldap._tcp.<domain GUID>.domains._msdcs.<DnsTreeName>	This record allows a client to find a DC in a domain based on its GUID.	Each DC

Because a domain usually contains multiple DCs, a DNS zone linked to an AD domain will contain multiple service records of the same type in the same subcontainers (e.g., _tcp, _udp, etc.). What will a DNS resolver base its choice on when it receives multiple records?

To facilitate the resolver's decision making an SRV resource record contains two special numeric fields: the weight and the priority field. How does this work? The first thing the resolver looks at when it receives multiple similar SRV records is the priority value of the records; the rule that counts for priority is: the smaller the value, the higher the priority. If all records' priorities are equal, the resolver will look at the weight field. The rule that counts for the weight field is the larger the value, the heavier the weight. If all records' weights are equal, the resolver will select a record in a round-robin fashion. Later on, if the client fails to connect to the service on the selected DC using the selected resource record, it will try the next record in the list (the list is built in the same way: priority, weight, and, if necessary round-robin). Note that this decision making process provides some degree of load balancing and fault tolerance.

2.2.3   DNS-specific replication protocols

DNS-specific replication protocols deal with the replication of DNS data between primary and secondary zones. In Windows 2000 they are used between non–AD-integrated DNS zones. For a detailed discussion of how AD replication works for AD integrated zones, have a look at Chapter 3. Windows 2000 includes two major changes on the level of the DNS-specific replication protocols. Windows 2000 DNS supports NOTIFY requests and the incremental zone transfer (IXFR) protocol.

NOTIFY extension

To limit the replication latency of DNS database changes Windows 2000 supports the DNS NOTIFY extension. A NOTIFY message is sent by a DNS master server (the DNS server hosting the primary zone) to inform secondary servers that changes have taken place to the DNS database. Secondary servers can then check the master server and initiate a zone transfer to download the DNS database changes.

The NOTIFY message is not enabled by default in Windows 2000 DNS. To configure a Windows 2000 primary zone to send NOTIFY messages, enter the addresses of the secondary zone servers using the Notify pushbutton in the Zone Transfer tab of the zone properties (as illustrated in Figure 2.13).

Figure 2.13
*Setting up
NOTIFY messages
in the zone
properties*

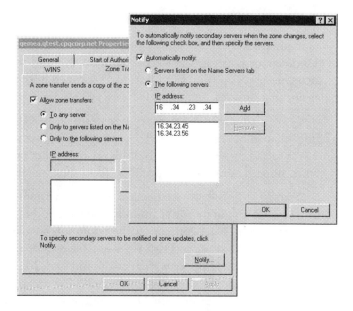

Incremental zone transfers

Windows 2000 secondary DNS servers can send requests for incremental zone transfers (IXFR) to their master server. IXFR is based on a special protocol in which the message sent by the secondary server contains the SOA serial number of the secondary server's copy of a zone. The master server receiving the request will compare the serial number with the one on its local copy; what is sent back to the secondary server are just the changes since the last update. A consequence of this is that the master server has to maintain all the changes occurring per serial number update.

Windows 2000 includes some special cases where a full zone transfer (AXFR) will take place, as follows:

- If the number of changes is bigger than the amount of data in the DNS zone file.

- Since the number of serial numbers for which the DNS server maintains a change list is limited, clients having serial numbers that are lower than the oldest entry in the DNS server's list will get a full zone transfer.

- If the DNS server responding to the IXFR initialization does not support IXFR, it will be automatically switched to a full update (AXFR).

2.2.4   DNS update

Windows 2000 DNS includes two major changes related to the way the DNS database can be updated: dynamic DNS and the support for secure dynamic DNS updates. Both features, explained in the following text, are a major step forward compared with NT4 DNS.

NT4 used static DNS: Every update to the DNS database had to be done manually. Also, in NT4, DNS authentication and access control were not enforced on the resource record level, but rather on the zone level: only an authorized administrator could perform zone updates.

Static DNS is hard to manage in an environment where machines receive IP configuration dynamically from DHCP servers. This is one of the reasons why NT4's primary name resolution service was WINS and not DNS. In addition, static DNS does not scale to provide name resolution services in big environments such as the Internet. Microsoft's implementation of dynamic DNS for Windows 2000 was mainly driven by the increased importance of both DNS naming and DHCP in the Windows 2000 operating system.

Dynamic DNS

Dynamic DNS enables a Windows 2000 service to request the update of a machine's resource records to the authoritative DNS server on behalf of the machine (workstation or server). Network services enabled to request a dynamic update are the DHCP client and server, the netlogon service, and clustering services. In this chapter we will discuss dynamic update by the DHCP client, the DHCP server, and the netlogon service. Dynamic DNS in Windows 2000 is based on a special DNS update message, as defined in RFC 2136.

Dynamic DNS update is a Windows 2000 feature only: It is not supported on any other Windows platform (Windows 95, 98, or NT4). Windows 2000 supports dynamic DNS updates on primary DNS zones, independently of whether they are Active Directory integrated or non–AD-integrated zones. A DNS zone does not support dynamic updates by default; it must be configured to do so. Figure 2.14 illustrates how to do this: Select Yes for the *Allow dynamic updates?* zone property.

Windows 2000 clients and dynamic DNS

On a Windows 2000 client machine (workstation or server) dynamic DNS update requests are sent by a machine's DHCP client service. Because every Windows 2000 machine runs the DHCP client, every machine can per-

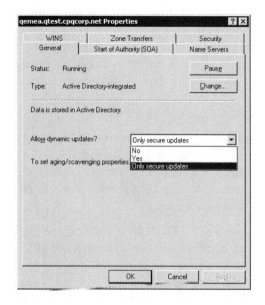

Figure 2.14

Setting up a zone to allow dynamic DNS updates

form dynamic updates, independently of whether the machine's network adapters are configured to use DHCP or not. The Windows 2000 DHCP client can send update requests for different types of network adapters: adapters configured using DHCP, statically configured adapters, and logical remote access adapters.

By default a Windows 2000 machine's DHCP client sends a dynamic update request every 24 hours and whenever one of the following events occur (this happens for every network adapter):

- The computer starts up or a dial-up connection is established.

- An adapter's TCP/IP configuration is changed manually.

- An adapter's DHCP TCP/IP configuration is renewed or gets a new lease.

- A network adapter is added to a machine and triggers a plug and play event.

- The client launches ipconfig /registerdns from the command prompt.

- Stopping and restarting the network interface from the computer's network and dial up connections container.

Dynamic updating by the client can be disabled by clearing the Register this connection's address in DNS check box in the advanced TCP/IP properties. The Microsoft Knowledge Base article Q246804, "How to Enable/ Disable Windows 2000 Dynamic DNS Registrations," explains all the details on enabling and disabling dynamic DNS update. In this case, dynamic update may still occur if the client got its TCP/IP configuration from a DHCP server, and this one is configured to perform dynamic updates on behalf of the client. We will discuss the relationship between a DHCP server and dynamic DNS update later in this chapter.

Windows 2000 DCs and dynamic DNS

Another major service that uses dynamic update is the Windows 2000 DC's netlogon service. The netlogon service uses dynamic update to register and keep a server's A, PTR, and SRV records up-to-date. Thanks to dynamic DNS, netlogon can dynamically register services. In NT4 this was done using NetBIOS advertisements.

On a Windows 2000 DC the netlogon service performs a dynamic update every hour. To force netlogon to register the SRV records stop and start the service. You can do this from the command prompt using **net stop netlogon** and **net start netlogon**. Netlogon dynamic update can be disabled by setting the following registry key to 0: HKLM\System\CurrentControlSet\ Services\Netlogon\Parameters\UseDynamicDns. A list of the records registered for a Windows 2000 DC can be found in the netlogon.dns file (located in the %SystemRoot%\System32\Config folder).

Behind the scenes

Behind dynamic update in Windows 2000 is a two-step process (as illustrated in Figure 2.15). The dynamic update process takes place for every network interface; in Windows 2000, every interface has a proper set of TCP/IP configuration settings. Every interface can be configured to register its DNS hostname in a particular DNS domain. The two-step process is as follows:

1.   Before a DNS client can request an authoritative server of its DNS zone to update its resource records, it must first find out where those authoritative servers are actually located. Windows 2000 DNS clients query not just for authoritative servers (NS records) but for the DNS server mentioned in the SOA record of the zone. In the first step the DNS client will send a DNS query to the DNS servers configured in the TCP/IP configuration of the client's network interface. The query contains the DNS domain name configured in the TCP/IP configuration of a particular network interface (the DNS domain name is configured as the DNS suffix in the network interface's advanced TCP/IP properties).

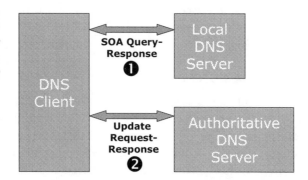

Figure 2.15
DNS dynamic update process in Windows 2000

2.   The second step includes the sending of the actual update request. This request is based on the update message. The update message will be sent to the SOA DNS server returned from the query in the first step.

Dynamic DNS updates, as defined in RFC 2136, include a third step. This is because the client machine queries for NS records, not SOA records. In this case, the DNS server serving the update request may be a primary, but also a secondary, server for the zone. When the message is received by a secondary server, it will be forwarded to the primary server of the zone. The primary server of the zone will then make the actual update to the zone and notify the secondary servers that a change has occurred. Finally, the secondary servers will pull the change to their local zone copy.

The update request can include certain prerequisites, which must be fulfilled before an update can be done. These prerequisites can be based upon whether the resource record already existed prior to the update request, whether it was in use prior to the update, or whether the requester has permission to do an update on a particular resource record.

Windows 2000 uses some of these prerequisite extensions: an update will not happen when the record is still up-to-date. Also, an update will fail if the requester does not have sufficient permissions to do the update. The Windows 2000 implementation of dynamic DNS includes even more intelligence. If the update fails, the system will retry after 5-, then 10-, and then 50-minute wait intervals.

Updating of the DNS database covers the addition, deletion, or modification of a single resource record or a set of resource records. A good example of this is the following. When a Windows 2000 machine is shut down properly, it will automatically perform a deregistration of the resource records linked to every statically configured network interface. Dynamic deregistration even works for dial-up interfaces. If the resource records of a dial-up network interface cannot be deregistered within four seconds, the connection will be closed. Later on, the RRAS server will launch another attempt to deregister the dial-up network interface's PTR record.

Secure dynamic DNS update

Secure DNS update is closely related to dynamic update. Besides allowing network entities to update DNS records, Windows 2000 also allows this to be done in a secure manner. Because of the increased importance of DNS in Windows 2000, this secure dynamic DNS update is an important feature. You don't want just anyone to change or even add DNS records to one of your DNS zones. Without secure dynamic update, hackers, for example, could add or change records to redirect users to their bogus server. Later on in this chapter we will explain other DNS security configuration options.

Secure dynamic DNS update means that before a DNS update is allowed the updating entity's identity is validated and checked against the access control settings set on the dnszone or dnsnode object that needs to be updated. Secure DNS update is based on the ability of Windows 2000 to integrate DNS zones and records into the Active Directory, as well as on the built-in support for the Kerberos authentication protocol. The Kerberos authentication protocol is explained in detail in Chapter 6.

Secure DNS update can be configured on the zone and the resource-record level. To set secure update on a DNS zone, select *Only secure updates* in its general properties (as illustrated in Figure 2.14). To view the access control settings on a resource record, select its security properties from the advanced view of the AD users and computers MMC snap-in (System\ MicrosoftDNS subcontainer) or from the DNS MMC snap-in. When setting ACLs on resource records, remember that in the AD resource records are attributes of Dnsnode objects. Access control settings are set on the Dnsnode object level; in other words, if the same Dnsnode object has two different resource record attributes, they will both have the same ACLs.

Although Windows 2000 Secure DNS update is not based on the DNS security extensions and the secure DNS dynamic update (known as DNS-SEC and defined in RFCs 2535 and 2137), it uses open IETF standards. It is built upon the secure negotiation and message exchange mechanism (specified in a set of IETF-drafts). BIND version 8.2 has limited support for DNSSEC. At the time of this writing, Microsoft was evaluating DNS-SEC for a future release. The drafts are the following: "GSS Algorithm for TSIG (GSS-TSIG)," "Secret Key Establishment for DNS (TKEY RR)," and "Secret Key Transaction Signatures for DNS (TSIG)." The Windows 2000 secure dynamic DNS update mechanism uses the GSS-API program-

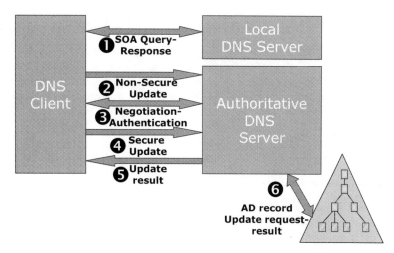

Figure 2.16
Secure dynamic DNS update process

ming interface (defined in RFC 2078) and involves a set of specific resource records: the TKEY and the TSIG records. TKEY is used during the negotiation phase to establish secret keys; TSIG is used after the negotiation phase to exchange digitally signed messages.

A complete secure dynamic DNS update sequence consists of the following steps (as illustrated in Figure 2.16):

- The DNS client finds out the SOA server for a particular DNS zone (as set in a network interface's TCP/IP configuration): This involves a query to the DNS server.

- The DNS client tries out a non secure update for the machine's resource record; since the zone has Only secure updates set, this will fail.

- In the negotiation phase, both the DNS client and server decide upon which security protocol to use (this involves the use of the TKEY resource record). Once the Kerberos protocol has been agreed upon, a Kerberos authentication takes place between the DNS client and server.

- The DNS client and server then exchange digitally signed DNS messages (this involves the use of the TSIG resource record) containing the DNS information that needs to be updated.

- The DNS server impersonates the client and requests an LDAP update for the client's resource records to the AD LDAP provider.

- The DNS server returns the outcome of the operation to the client.

Table 2.10   *Windows 2000 DNS Dynamic Update Registry Configuration Parameters*

UpdateSecurityLevel

By default a Windows 2000 client will first try out an unsecure update; if this fails it will switch to a secure update. You can configure this by setting the registry key: 256 specifies secure update only, 16 insecure update only, and 0 specifies the default behavior.

DefaultRegistrationTTL

Specifies the default TTL with which a DNS client registers its A and PTR record (the default is 20 minutes)

DisableReplaceAddressesInConflicts

In zones that are not configured with secure dynamic DNS update, a client that detects an already existing resource record with an equal FQDN, can replace the IP address of the RR with its proper address. This behavior can be disabled by setting the parameter to 1; in this case conflicting addresses will not be replaced but logged in the event viewer, (overwriting [0] is the default).

Configuring dynamic update

Table 2.10 lists some dynamic update-related registry hacks. All of them are located in HKEY_LOCAL_MACHINE\SYSTEM\CurrentControlSet\ Services\Tcpip\Parameters.

2.2.5   Scavenging

In Windows 2000 DNS scavenging is used to remove obsolete DNS resource records from the DNS database. Obsolete records may fill up the DNS database and the server disk space. Obsolete records can occur frequently in dynamic environments where all clients rely on DHCP for their TCP/IP configuration.

To determine which resource records can be scavenged DNS uses a time stamp and a set of parameters that can be set through the DNS administration interface. A time stamp is added to the DNS database for each dynamically created record written to a zone with scavenging enabled and each time such record is updated. Note that scavenging changes the default DNS database format. This format cannot be used by non–Windows 2000 DNS servers. The word *dynamic* in the previous sentence is very important. Scavenging applies only to records that are updated dynamically. Static records can never be scavenged. This is the reason why a static record has a timestamp 0.

When setting up aging and scavenging you'll have to consider two important parameters: the no-refresh and the refresh interval. Before we explain these concepts you need to understand the difference between a refresh and an update. A dynamic update is considered a refresh if it includes no changes to the record; it is considered an update if it includes changes to the record, as follows:

- The no-refresh interval determines the period of time during which the DNS server accepts no refreshes to the DNS records. The reason Microsoft added this parameter is to limit unnecessary replication traffic.

- The refresh interval determines the period of time during which the DNS server accepts refreshes to the DNS records; it starts after the no-refresh interval ends. The refresh interval also determines the period of time during which the record cannot be scavenged. When the refresh interval has expired, the DNS server can start scavenging obsolete DNS records (or records that have not received a refresh during the refresh interval).

Both the no-refresh and the refresh interval apply only to refreshing; in other words during the no-refresh interval a record can still receive an update. Following an update the resource records time stamp will be changed and the no-refresh interval, followed by the refresh interval, will both start over again.

When setting the refresh and no-refresh interval, always consider making them bigger than the refresh period of the different Windows 2000 services performing DNS updates: netlogon refreshes every hour, the DNS

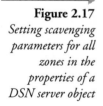

Figure 2.17

Setting scavenging parameters for all zones in the properties of a DSN server object

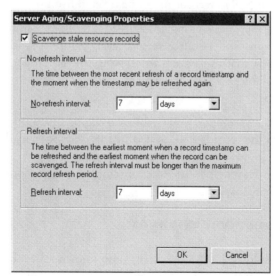

Table 2.11 *Scavenging Properties and Configuration Tools*

Tool	Property	Default
DNS MMC snap-in (DNS server) Dnscmd tool	Default no-refresh interval (days)	7 days
DNS MMC snap-in (DNS server) Dnscmd tool	Default refresh interval (days)	7 days
DNS MMC snap-in (DNS server) Dnscmd tool	Default enable scavenging	Disabled
DNS MMC snap-in (DNS server) Dnscmd tool	Scavenging period (days)	7 days
DNS MMC snap-in (DNS zone) Dnscmd tool	No-refresh interval (days)	7 days
DNS MMC snap-in (DNS server) Dnscmd tool	Refresh interval (days)	7 days
DNS MMC snap-in (DNS server) Dnscmd tool	Enable scavenging	Disabled
Dnscmd tool	Scavenging	Servers

client every 24 hours, and a DHCP server at every new lease. If you fail to do so, valid DNS records might be deleted from the DNS database.

By default scavenging is disabled. It can be configured on the DNS server, zone, and resource record level. Figure 2.17 shows the scavenging parameters that can be set for all zones in the properties of a DNS server object. Table 2.11 shows which scavenging properties can be set using which tool.

A final warning: If you enable scavenging on an existing zone, it will not apply to the records that existed in the zone prior to the enabling of scavenging. To set scavenging for all records, including the ones existing prior to enabling scavenging, use the dnscmd command prompt tool with the ageallrecords switch.

2.2.6 DNS resolver changes

The Windows 2000 DNS client (also known as the DNS resolver) is very different from its NT4 predecessor. It includes some major enhancements over its NT4 predecessor. The main changes are as follows:

- DNS-centric name resolution

- Enhanced DNS query string configuration

- Support for negative caching

- Support for subnet prioritization

DNS-centric name resolution

The first resolution method a Windows 2000 client tries out when it needs to resolve a name is querying the local name caches. A Windows 2000 client has two name caches: one for NetBIOS names and another one for DNS names (called the DNS resolver cache). To find out the content of your NetBIOS name cache, type nbtstat –n at the command prompt; to find out the content of your DNS name cache, type ipconfig /displaydns.

If this fails, the Windows 2000 client will try to resolve the name using classic NetBIOS or DNS name resolution. NetBIOS name resolution is only tried if *NetBIOS over TCP/IP* is enabled; on a Windows 2000 system it is enabled by default. By default, the Windows 2000 client tries out both resolution methods in parallel. The NetBIOS track is not tried if the name to be resolved cannot possibly be a NetBIOS name (i.e., if it is an FQDN or longer than 15 bytes).

We will now look in more detail at the way DNS name resolution works and, in particular, how DNS queries sent out to DNS servers work: What is the order in which DNS servers are tried out and how does the resolver deal with unqualified names? Note that before the DNS resolver sends out any DNS query, it will first try to resolve the name using the local DNS resolver cache.

Windows 2000 also allows multiple DNS servers to be configured per network interface. In NT4 a single list of DNS servers was specified per machine. During name resolution the DNS resolver tries out these servers in the following order:

- First DNS server on preferred adapter—wait for response for one second

- First DNS server on all adapters—wait for response for two seconds

- All DNS servers on all adapters—wait for response for two seconds

- All DNS servers on all adapters—wait for response for four seconds

- All DNS servers on all adapters—wait for response for eight seconds

If none of an adapter's configured DNS servers replies, all queries on that adapter will fail for a time interval of 30 seconds.

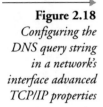

Figure 2.18
Configuring the DNS query string in a network's interface advanced TCP/IP properties

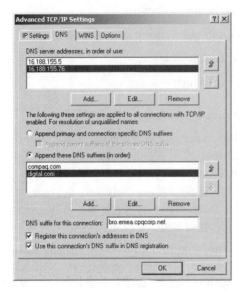

Name resolution using DNS is simple if the user enters a fully qualified DNS name (FQDN); it gets more complex if an unqualified name is entered. An unqualified name can be multiple or single label. An example of a multiple label is *mymachine.qemea*; an example of single label is *mymachine*; an example of a fully qualified name is *mymachine.qemea.cpqcorp.net.* (notice the dot at the end of the FQDN). The way the DNS resolver attaches DNS suffixes to an unqualified name and sends out the query string to a DNS server depends on the way DNS suffixes are configured in the DNS tab of the advanced TCP/IP configuration (as shown in Figure 2.18). Windows 2000 allows far more query string configuration then NT4.

The dialog box shown in Figure 2.18 holds two basic choices: *Append primary and connection-specific DNS suffixes* and *Append these DNS suffixes (in order)*, as follows:

- If *Append these DNS suffixes (in order)* is selected, the DNS resolver will rely solely on the specified suffixes to create the query string. As illustrated in Figure 2.18, first *compaq.com* and then *digital.com.*

- If *Append primary and connection-specific DNS suffixes* is selected, the query string is generated as follows (ordered following their try out order):

  - DNS suffix in the Network Identification tab of the system properties

* *DNS suffix for this connection* in the DNS tab of advanced TCP/IP configuration
* DNS suffix returned by connection's DHCP server

* If *Append parent suffixes of the primary DNS suffix* has been enabled, the resolver appends all the suffixes (one by one) resulting from the name devolution of the suffix specified in *DNS suffix for this connection*. As illustrated in Figure 2.18, *bro.emea.cpqcorp.net* results in *emea.cpqcorp.net*, then *cpqcorp.net*, then *net*.

An interesting name resolution security feature is that the Windows 2000 DNS resolver can be configured to reject DNS responses it gets from DNS servers it did not query. By default the Windows 2000 resolver accepts them. To disable them set QueryIpMatching in the HKEY_LO-CAL_MACHINE\SYSTEM\CurrentControlSet\Services\DnsCache\Parameters registry folder to 1.

DNS resolver cache

The Windows 2000 DNS resolver caches both positive and negative DNS server responses. The DNS resolver cache is different from the DNS server cache; a server running a DNS service has two caches. One for its resolver and one for the DNS server. Caching can have an important impact on the amount of network traffic. To look at the content of the DNS resolver cache, type ipconfig /displayDNS at the command prompt. To flush the content of the cache, type ipconfig /flushDNS.

The amount of time a record (resulting out of positive response) is cached depends on its TTL and on the content of the MaxCacheEntry-TtlLimit registry setting in the HKEY_LOCAL_MACHINE\SYSTEM\CurrentControlSet\Services\DNSCache\Parameters registry folder. The default value is 86,400 seconds or 1,440 minutes or 24 hours. The caching time will never exceed this value independently of the record's TTL.

Windows 2000 supports negative caching as defined in RFC 2308. The amount of time a negative response is cached depends on the registry key NegativeCacheTime in the HKEY_LOCAL_MACHINE\SYSTEM\CurrentControlSet\Services\DNSCache\Parameters registry folder. The default value is 300 seconds or 5 minutes. Setting this key to 0 disables negative caching.

Subnet prioritization

Subnet prioritization affects the DNS resolver's behavior when it receives multiple A records from a DNS server in response to a name query.

Table 2.12 *Resource Record Return Order Following Setting of Enable Round Robin and LocalNetPriority Parameters*

Enable Round Robin	LocalNetPriority	Behavior
Selected	1	Rotation + Records ordered with ones similar to client's subnet first
Deselected	1	No Rotation + Records ordered with ones similar to client's subnet first
Selected	0	Rotation + Records ordered following order records added to database
Deselected	0	No Rotation + Records ordered following order records added to database

Through subnet prioritization the DNS resolver will prioritize the A records that are part of its own subnet. The goal of this feature is to reduce cross-subnet IP traffic. Notice that this feature also ignores the round robin sequence (round-robin DNS is defined in RFC 1794) of the records returned by a DNS server. A DNS client that has subnet prioritization enabled will always reorder the records and choose the ones that are part of his or her own subnet first. In some case you may not want this; to disable subnet prioritization set PrioritizeRecordData to 0 in the HKEY_LO-CAL_MACHINE\SYSTEM\CurrentControlSet\Services\DnsCache\Parameters registry folder.

The order in which records are returned to the DNS resolver also depends on the way subnet prioritization is set up on the DNS server side. Two settings determine the server's behavior: the *Enable Round Robin* option in the advanced properties of the DNS server and the LocalNet-Priority parameter in the HKEY_LOCAL_MACHINE\SYSTEM\Current-ControlSet\Services\DNS\Parameters registry folder. Table 2.12 summarizes the order in which the records are returned following the setting of these two parameters.

2.2.7 Unicode character support

Classic DNS supports only a very limited character set (defined in RFCs 1123 and 952). This applies only to hostnames and domain names. For SRV records, classic DNS supports a more extended character set. To cope with this and to ease the migration from NetBIOS naming, Windows 2000 DNS supports unicode encoding or UTF-8 (as defined in RFC 2044).

| **Table 2.13** | *NetBIOS, Classic DNS and Windows 2000 DNS Supported Character Set and Name Length* |

	Supported Characters	**Supported Length**
NetBIOS	Unicode characters, numbers, white space, symbols: ! @ # $ % ^ & ') (. - _ { } ~	15 bytes
Classic DNS	A to Z, a to z, 0 to 9, and the hyphen (-) (as defined in RFC 1123).	63 bytes per label and 255 bytes for an FQDN
Windows 2000 DNS	xxxx	63 bytes per label and 255 bytes for an FQDN (limited to 64 bytes)

Table 2.13 compares classic DNS, Windows 2000, and NetBIOS naming. Note that NetBIOS supports a broader character set than classic DNS.

The Windows 2000, DNS unicode support can cause interoperability problems with other DNS implementations. This is why administrators can allow or disallow UTF-8 support on a per-server basis. To configure unicode support, go to the advanced properties of the DNS server object; the name checking dropdown box offers several options (as illustrated in Figure 2.19 and listed in Table 2.14).

Notice in Table 2.14 that the configuration options are cumulative. Strict RFC supports the smallest character set, All Names the biggest one.

Figure 2.19
Configuring Unicode support in the DNS server properties

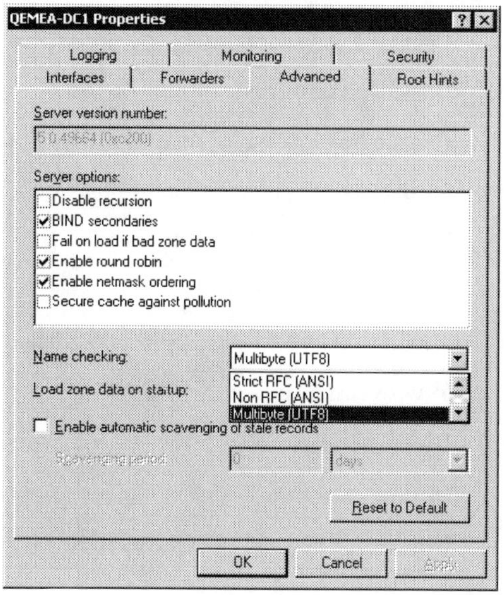

Table 2.14   *Windows 2000 DNS Name Checking Configuration Options*

Configuration Option	Supported Characters	Meaning—Supported RFCs
Strict RFC (ANSI)	Allows A to Z, a to z, the hyphen (-), the asterisk (*) as a first label, and the underscore (_) as the first character in a label	Strict name checking according to RFC 1123
Non-RFC (ANSI)	Allows all characters supported in Strict RFC and also the underscore anywhere in a name	Allows for names noncompliant with RFC 1123
Multibyte (UTF-8)	Allows all characters supported in Non-RFC and also the UTF-8 characters	Support for ANSI and Unicode characters
All Names	Allows for any character	

2.2.8   Support for open standards

Throughout this chapter we referred to the open standards supported in Windows 2000 DNS. Open standards are key for interoperability between DNS implementations on different platforms and by different vendors. Table 2.15 gives an overview of the RFCs the Windows 2000 DNS implementation is based upon. All RFCs can be downloaded from the Web site of the IETF: *http://www.ietf.org*.

Table 2.15   *Open Standards Supported in Windows 2000 DNS*

RFC Number	Content
1034	Domain Names—concepts and facilities
1035	Domain Names—implementation and specification
1123	Requirements for Internet Hosts—application and support
1886	DNS Extensions to Support IP version 6
1995	Incremental Zone Transfer in DNS
1996	A Mechanism for Prompt DNS Notification of Zone Changes
2052	SRV Records
2136	Dynamic Updates in the Domain Name System (DNS update)
2181	Clarifications to the DNS Specification
2308	Negative Caching of DNS Queries (DNS NCACHE)

Figure 2.20
DNS MMC snap-in and delegation wizard

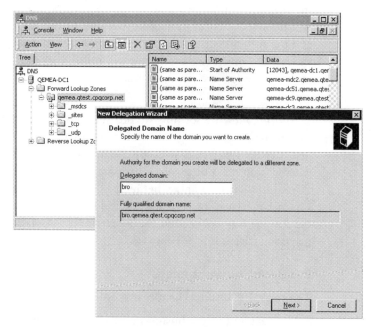

2.2.9 Enhanced administration tools

Windows 2000 comes with a brand new DNS administration interface, which is based on an MMC snap-in. Accompanying the snap-in is a set of wizards that simplifies a set of common administrator tasks, such as setting up delegation for a particular zone (as illustrated in Figure 2.20). The Windows 2000 support tools contains an interesting command prompt DNS administration tool: dnscmd.exe. We will discuss this tool later in the chapter.

2.3 Planning and designing Windows 2000 DNS

The planning and design of the Windows 2000 DNS can be split into two subtasks: the namespace design and the design of a DNS server infrastructure.

2.3.1 Namespace design

The reason the DNS chapter is the second chapter of this book is not just by accident. The book was structured with planning and designing an AD infrastructure in mind. The design of a DNS namespace is one of the AD architect's first crucial tasks. Because of the tight integration of DNS and the AD infrastructure, the namespace design will go hand in hand with the Active Directory design. You will notice that both DNS and AD infrastructure design are iterative processes, which will influence one another continually.

In the following sections we provide some guidelines that may help you in your namespace design. First, it's important that you examine your business needs. Two main decision points in the namespace design will be whether you need or plan to integrate Windows 2000 DNS with a legacy DNS infrastructure and whether you need to consider the impact of an Internet presence for your corporate DNS namespace design. Throughout the design you may need to choose new DNS domain names; although this may look trivial, it is not easy task.

Evaluating business needs

The following business factors may influence your DNS namespace design:

- Current and future business needs. The DNS design must cover both current and future DNS naming business needs. If your organization is planning acquisitions or mergers, provide as much flexibility as possible in your current DNS namespace design. DNS names are there to remain unchanged for a long time.

- The need for an Internet presence. Consider whether parts of your AD infrastructure will ever be exposed to the Internet. If they do, you'll have to involve an official Internet name registration authority in your namespace design discussions.

- Organization type and size. The size and type of your organization will have an impact on the scope of the AD infrastructure. The AD infrastructure scope will obviously affect DNS namespace design. Depending on the size and type of your organization you may want to include your core organization, subsidiaries, external partners, or even customers in your AD infrastructure design.

- Legal and organizational constraints. When choosing DNS names be sure that they are in accordance with the legal environment in which your organization is operating. For example, in the case of an Internet presence make sure that the name is not already registered by another organization. Also make sure that you have complete approval from the top-level management of your organization.

Choosing a DNS domain name

The choice of a DNS name is critical. If you plan to reuse your existing legacy DNS domain names, you may not need to do this as part of your Windows 2000 DNS namespace design. The following are some general guidelines that may help you in choosing a good DNS domain name:

- DNS domain names must be unique in the DNS namespace. If your domain will be exposed on the Internet, its name should be unique in the Internet namespace. If it isn't, its name should be unique within your private DNS namespace. As will be explained later on in this chapter, most organizations prefer a separate external (Internet namespace) and internal DNS domain name (intranet-extranet namespace).

- DNS domains also should be stable. This is even more critical when you think about the integration of DNS with the AD infrastructure: A name change after the installation of a domain will impact your complete AD infrastructure.

- DNS domain names should be meaningful. Remember that DNS is a name resolution service, so it doesn't make sense to choose a domain name that's hard to remember.

- The name should represent your entire organization or should at least be accepted by your entire organization. This may not be the case in organizations resulting from a merger: they may require several DNS names, each one representing part of the organization.

- The choice of the DNS name of the root domain of a domain tree is critical. The root domain's DNS name impacts the DNS name of all the child domains in the same tree; also, once the root domain has been installed, it cannot be renamed without removing and reinstalling the AD.

Integration with legacy DNS systems

Many organizations already have a DNS infrastructure in place prior to the installation of an AD infrastructure. This may be an NT4 DNS or a BIND DNS (mostly UNIX-based) infrastructure. More information on Berkeley Internet Name Domain (BIND) can be found on the Internet Software Consortium (ISC) Web site: *http://www.isc.org/products/BIND/*. In the NT4 DNS case, it's advisable to upgrade to Windows 2000 DNS, given the new functionalities.

Different scenarios exist for how to integrate an existing BIND DNS infrastructure with an AD infrastructure. These include the following:

- Rely completely on BIND DNS.

- Rely completely on Windows 2000 DNS.

- Coexistence between BIND DNS and Windows 2000 DNS. This scenario contains three other scenarios:

  - Delegated subdomains from BIND to Windows 2000 DNS with namespace overlap
  - Delegated subdomains from BIND to Windows 2000 DNS without namespace overlap
  - Separate namespaces

The different scenarios are explained in the following sections. The discussion focuses on the configuration of forward lookup integration. We have also added a section discussing reverse lookup integration.

BIND DNS Windows 2000 compliancy

The first scenario (relying completely on BIND DNS) is an option when your BIND DNS is Windows 2000 DNS compliant. The compliancy requirements are the following:

- The BIND DNS version must support RFC 2052 (SRV records). SRV records are supported in BIND versions 4.9.6 and higher.

- The BIND DNS version should support RFC 2136 (dynamic update) and RFC 1995 (IXFR). Dynamic update is supported in BIND versions 8.1.2 and higher. To see whether your BIND version supports dynamic update use the nsupdate tool accompanying BIND. Although dynamic update is not an absolute requirement, not supporting it will cause a lot of administrative overhead.

In a Windows 2000 environment, Microsoft recommends using BIND 8.2.1 or higher. This version supports SRV records, dynamic update, IXFR, and negative caching. If you don't want to upgrade to a higher BIND version and prefer to go with Windows 2000 DNS, read the following section on how to migrate (this brings us to scenario 2).

Migration of BIND DNS to Windows 2000 DNS

The second scenario can be used when your BIND DNS is not compliant, and your organization is prepared to migrate to Windows 2000 DNS. Migration from BIND DNS to Windows 2000 DNS involves the following steps:

1.   Install a Windows 2000 server machine, and add the DNS service.

2.   Copy the forward and reverse lookup zone files from the BIND server to the %systemdrive%\winnt\system32\dns directory on the Windows 2000 server. To find out where the zone files are located on the BIND server check out the named.boot (for BIND 4.x) or named.conf (for BIND 8.x) file in the /etc directory.

3.   Start the new zone wizard from the DNS MMC snap-in and choose the use this existing file option. Point to the zone files that you copied over from the BIND server.

4.   Install Active Directory (using DCPROMO).

As with any DNS server migration, don't forget to point the DNS resolver's of static machines to the IP address of the new DNS server and to change your DHCP DNS configuration information. Likewise, if the migrated servers were Internet name servers, contact the internic to change your Internet registration to point to the new DNS servers for forward lookup, and contact the American Registry for Internet Numbers (ARIN) to point to the new DNS servers for reverse lookup. (Find more information about internic at *http://rs.internic.net.* and about ARIN at *http://www.arin.net.*)

Coexistence scenarios

The third scenario contains three other scenarios. They can be used when your BIND DNS is not compliant with Windows 2000 DNS and your organization is not prepared to upgrade the legacy DNS to Windows 2000 DNS. Remember: Not compliant means does not support SRV records, IXFR, and dynamic updates.

Delegation with namespace overlap   In this scenario (illustrated in Figure 2.21) the Windows 2000 domain uses the same DNS domain name *cpqcorp.net* as the one hosted on the legacy BIND DNS. The scenario is set up by delegating the Windows 2000–specific subdomains from the BIND DNS server to a Windows 2000 DNS server, a member of the *cpqcorp.net* Windows 2000 root domain. The delegated Windows 2000–specific subdomains are *_msdcs.cpqcorp.net, _sites.cpqcorp.net, _tcp, cpqcorp.net,* and *_udp.cpqcorp.net.* As Figure 2.21 shows, the DNS subdomains of the AD child domains (*americas, europe,* and *asiapac*) are also delegated from the BIND DNS *cpqcorp.net zone.*

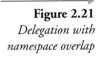

Figure 2.21
*Delegation with
namespace overlap*

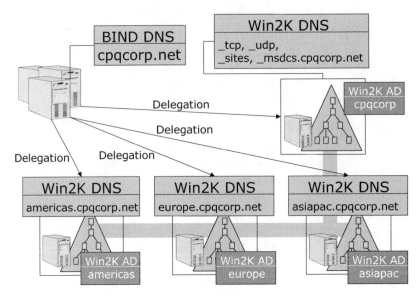

In this scenario the netlogon service on Windows 2000 DCs should be disabled to send dynamic DNS updates to the BIND domain. By default netlogon will try to update an A record in the DNS domain identical to its AD domain. To disable this set DnsRegisterARecords (DWORD) to 0 in the HKLM\SYSTEM\CurrentControlSet\Services\NetLogon\Parameters registry path.

Delegation without namespace overlap   In this scenario (illustrated in Figure 2.22) the Windows 2000 domain infrastructure uses a DNS domain name, *win2k.cpqcorp.net* different from the one hosted on the legacy BIND DNS. The way this scenario is implemented is by delegating the *win2k.cpq-corp.net* subdomain from the BIND DNS server to the Windows 2000 DNS server. In this scenario the name of the AD domain can be identical to the name of the delegated DNS subdomain. The Windows 2000 server running the Windows 2000 DNS service will be a member of the *win2k.cpqcorp.net* Windows 2000 domain (not the *cpqcorp.net* domain as in the previous scenario). As Figure 2.22 shows, the DNS subdomains of the AD child domains (*americas, europe,* and *asiapac*) are now delegated from the Windows 2000 DNS *win2k.cpqcorp.net zone.*

Separate namespaces without delegation   As in the previous scenario, this scenario (illustrated in Figure 2.23) also uses a different DNS domain name for the Windows 2000 domain infrastructure: *compaq.com* on the BIND side and *cpqcorp.net* on the Windows 2000 side. Contrary to the previous

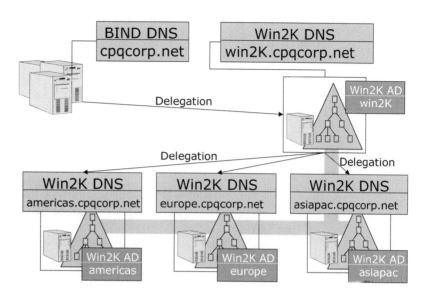

Figure 2.22
*Delegation without
namespace overlap*

scenario, this one is not implemented at the top level using delegation, but using separate namespaces. As Figure 2.23 shows, the DNS subdomains of the AD child domains (americas, europe and asiapac) are, as in the previous scenario, delegated from the Windows 2000 DNS *win2k.cpqcorp.net* zone

Handle with care Coexistence between Windows 2000 DNS and legacy DNS is nice but should be handled with care. Never implement it in a production environment without serious testing. Small details related to, for

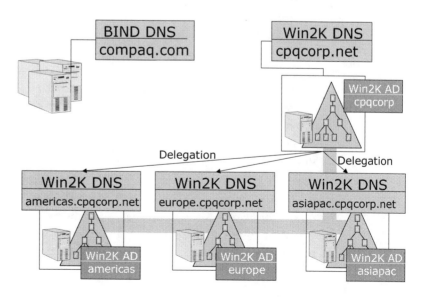

Figure 2.23
*Separate
namespaces
without delegation*

example, the zone transfer between Windows 2000 and BIND DNS zones might corrupt your DNS database, as follows:

- Some Windows 2000 DNS resource records are not supported by BIND (and vice versa)—for example, WINS and WINS-R or the A records used for global catalog DCs. Replication of these records can be disabled; this is discussed later in the chapter.

- Windows 2000 DNS is the only DNS supporting unicode UTF-8 encoding. Unicode encoding can be disabled; this was discussed in Section 2.2.7.

- Windows 2000 supports fast zone transfers. Fast zone transfers can be disabled in the advanced DNS server properties by checking BIND secondaries.

Integrating reverse lookup with legacy DNS

Before starting the discussion about reverse lookup integration, we want to stress the following facts:

- The Windows 2000 operating system itself does not require reverse lookup. Reverse lookup might be a requirement for applications running on top of the Windows 2000 platform.

- The configuration of reverse lookup is totally independent of the Windows 2000 domain infrastructure. Contrary to the hostnames used in forward lookup, the IP addresses used in reverse lookup are not bound to a Windows 2000 domain, but to a range of IP addresses.

The solution for reverse lookup integration is simple if your organization's Windows 2000 machines and non–Windows 2000 machines reside in separate subnets; in this scenario you can create reverse lookup zones for the Windows 2000 machines on a Windows 2000 DNS server and another reverse lookup for the non–Windows 2000 machines on a legacy DNS server. You shouldn't be concerned about whether your legacy DNS system supports dynamic updates or not. Remember, Windows 2000 dynamic updates also register reverse lookup PTR records. PTR records can be updated by both Windows 2000 resolvers and DHCP servers.

Things get more complicated if both Windows 2000 and non–Windows 200 machines reside on the same subnets. An issue will come up if you want to use dynamic update. Older legacy DNS systems do not support dynamic update. To resolve this problem there are two choices:

upgrade legacy DNS to a version supporting dynamic update or upgrade to Windows 2000 DNS.

Internet and intranet DNS namespace

Many companies have a separate Internet and intranet DNS infrastructure. Most even split their DNS namespace into private and a public portion.s The public portion is visible from the Internet; the private portion isn't. A DNS name that's part of of the public portion is known as an *external name*; a private portion name is known as an *internal name*. The main reason for setting up DNS this way is to secure internal DNS hostnames and zones; this means hiding internal hostnames from the Internet and protecting internal zones against unauthorized modifications coming from the Internet. The protection is usually provided by a firewall or set of firewalls located between the intranet and extranet portion of the DNS infrastructure. Also, in most cases the choice for hidden internal hostnames and zones is coupled with the choice of the private IP addressing scheme.

Digital, for example, gave machines outside the firewall a name ending in *.digital.com*; the ones on the inside firewall had a name ending in *dec.com*. Digital used global IP addresses and allowed DNS queries to go through the firewall. After the merger Compaq reorganized both its own and the Digital namespace. The internal namespace of both merged companies was converted gradually to *cpqcorp.net*. Similar to the Digital example, Compaq machines are known externally by the *compaq.com* domain name and internally using the *cpqcorp.net* domain name. Contrary to Digital, Compaq uses a hidden internal DNS system: DNS queries coming from the Internet are not allowed to go through the firewall.

In the following text, we will discuss the different ways to set up the Internet and intranet DNS namespace. A company can use separate namespaces, a single namespace, or a hybrid model. By the end of this discussion you'll understand why the first model, separate namespaces, is the best way to go.

Separate namespaces

When using separate namespace (illustrated in Figure 2.24) the internal and the external DNS domain, have a different DNS name (in Figure 2.24 *compaq.com* and *cpqcorp.net*). If the internal namespace is meant to be visible only internally, we talk about a private root. A private root scenario may require some special configuration to enable your internal clients to resolve both internal and external hostnames. The easiest way is to configure your

Figure 2.24
Separate
namespaces

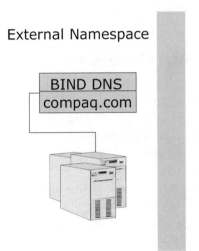

External Namespace

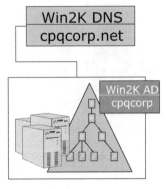

Internal Namespace

internal DNS servers as forwarders to Internet DNS servers. The alternative is to provide smart clients that can decide whether a given host is located internally or externallly—in other words, whether they should send a DNS query to the internal DNS servers or the Internet DNS servers. Smart clients are the ones having installed WinSock Proxy (shipped with MS Proxy Server) or Internet Explorer. This software can provide name exclusion lists or proxy autoconfiguration.

In this setup the internal *cpqcorp.net* DNS domain can be mapped to the root of the Windows 2000 forest. The standard separate namespaces setup will require a Windows 2000 user to use a different Windows 2000 logon name and external mail address. Thanks to the UPN suffix feature of Windows 2000 you can align both, and let a user use a single DNS name for both logon and mail. You may not want to do this for security reasons. Using the same UPN for mail and logon could give away half of the domain logon credentials if a malicious person learns the mail address from sniffing SMTP traffic.

From a DNS infrastructure point of view, separate namespaces can be set up as follows:

- Install an Internet DNS server and create primary zones for the internal and external DNS domains (*compaq.com* and *cpqcorp.net*). Doing so requires both names to be registered with the Internic or the ICANN. More information is available at *http://www.icann.org* or *http://www.networksolutions.com*. The external DNS zone will contain all the hostnames that should be visible from the Internet and the

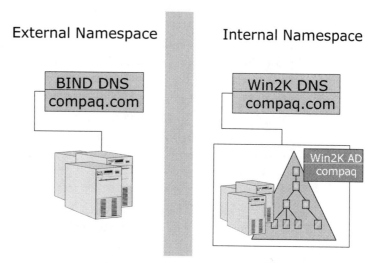

Figure 2.25
Single namespace

SOA record for the external domain. The internal DNS zone will contain an SOA record for the internal domain.

- Install an intranet DNS server and create another primary zone, *cpq-corp.net*, for the internal DNS domain. This zone will contain all the hostnames that should be visible from the intranet and the SOA record for the internal domain.

Single namespace

When using a single namespace (illustrated in Figure 2.25), both the internal and the external DNS domain have the same DNS name (in Figure 2.25, *compaq.com*). This scenario will create a lot of administrative overhead if you want your external resources also to be available to your internal users (which is something most companies normally want). You'll have to duplicate your external DNS zone and your external servers internally and keep the duplicates one way or the other in sync with the real servers and zone.

In this setup the internal *compaq.com* DNS domain can be mapped to the root of the Windows 2000 forest. A nice end-user feature of this setup is that the user will be able to log on to the Windows 2000 domain using the same DNS extension as the one that was used for his or her e-mail address.

From a DNS infrastructure point of view a single namespace can be set up as follows:

- Install both an Internet and intranet DNS server and create a primary zone on both for the DNS domain *compaq.com*. Since it's visible from the Internet, the *compaq.com* name will need to be registered with the internic or the ICANN. The external DNS zone will contain all the hostnames that should be visible from the Internet and the SOA record for the external domain. The internal DNS zone will contain an SOA record for the internal domain and all the hostnames that are part of the intranet and should be hidden from the Internet.

■ To ensure that the internal DNS server can answer queries for Internet resources, configure the external DNS server as forwarder on the internal DNS server.

Hybrid model

In a hybrid model (illustrated in Figure 2.26) the internal and the external DNS domains have a different DNS name (in Figure 2.26, *compaq.com* and *europe.compaq.com*), but the domains are part of the same namespace. In this setup one or more DNS subdomains are delegated from the external DNS zone to the internal DNS server(s).

In this setup the external *compaq.com* DNS domain can be mapped to the root of the Windows 2000 forest. In this case the domain will, for security reasons, not hold any user accounts; it's a kind of a placeholder domain. To align the mail address with the user account for your Windows 2000 users, you can also the UPN suffix feature.

You could also map the Windows 2000 domain one level below the top-level external DNS domain (as illustrated in Figure 2.26). Advantages of

Figure 2.26
Hybrid model

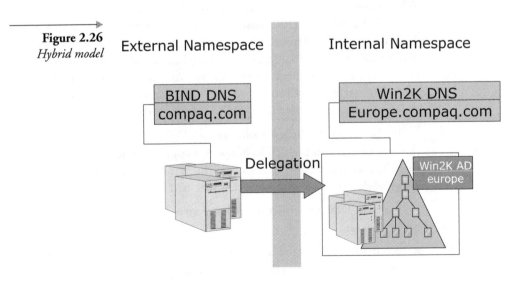

this method are that a legacy external DNS system can remain in place and the AD infrastructure can be completely isolated from the external world.

From a DNS infrastructure point of view the hybrid model can be set up as follows:

- Install an external and one or more internal DNS server(s). Create a primary zone, *compaq.com* on the external DNS server. The external DNS zone will contain all the hostnames that should be visible from the Internet and the SOA record for the external domain *compaq.com*. This name should be registered on the Internet.

- Create the primary zones *europe.compaq.com* and *americas.compaq.com* on the internal DNS server(s). Delegate the *europe* and the *americas* domains from the external DNS server. To optimize query performance create secondary zones for *compaq.com* on the internal DNS servers. The internal DNS zones will contain the SOA record for the internal domains and all the hostnames that are part of the intranet and should be hidden from the Internet.

- To ensure that the internal DNS server can answer queries for Internet resources, configure the external DNS server as a forwarder on the internal DNS server.

- Make sure that zone transfers between the primary and secondary zones of the *compaq.com* domain are allowed from the Internet to the intranet, but not the other way around.

Advantages and disadvantages

Table 2.16 lists the advantages and disadvantages of the different intranet and Internet namespace design choices.

Table 2.16 *Advantages and Disadvantages of intranet and Internet Namespace Design Choices*

	Advantage	Disadvantage
Separate Namespaces	▓ Easier management ▓ Best security if set up correctly	▓ More complex to use for the end user ▓ Complex setup and configuration ▓ Need to register extra domain names
Single Namespace	▓ Ease of use for the end user	▓ No need to register extra domain names ▓ Complex administration and maintenance ▓ Need to duplicate data
Hybrid Model	▓ Contiguous namespace ▓ Ease of use for the end user	▓ Longer FQDNs

2.3.2   Designing the DNS server infrastructure

A DNS server infrastructure must be fault tolerant, highly available, and easily accessible, and it must provide minimal latency for the replication of DNS database changes.

Fault tolerance, high availability, and easy access can partially be provided using the built-in DNS database replication and partitioning features. A higher level of fault tolerance and high availability can be obtained by implementing a clustered DNS service. Support for clustering is one of the new features of Windows 2000 DNS.

To obtain minimal latency it's advisable to rely on dynamic updates and AD integrated DNS zones. If your organization does not choose AD integrated zones, it should at least implement NOTIFY messages and incremental zone transfers.

In general it's recommended to have at least two DNS servers in every AD domain and to provide one DNS server at every AD site. To speed up DNS queries it's a good idea to create secondary zones of the complete DNS zone or just the _msdcs_ zone of the root AD domain on all DNS servers in the child domains of the AD forest.

2.3.3   Securing DNS

Besides secure dynamic update, Windows 2000 DNS also offers other security options, such as zone transfer restrictions and denial of service attack protection.

To restrict zone transfers, configure the Zone Transfers tab in a primary zone's properties: set allow zone transfers to only to servers listed on the Name Servers tab or to only to the following servers (as illustrated in Figure 2.27).

To protect against denial of service attacks you can turn off your DNS server's recursive query capabilities, secure the cache against pollution, or disable DNS on one of your server's network interfaces.

Recursive queries are disabled in the Advanced tab of the server properties by selecting *Turn off recursion*. This is not the only reason why you'd want to turn off recursive queries: You can also do it to limit the name resolution depth to the level of a particular DNS server or a particular namespace (e.g., only to the level of your intranet namepace but not beyond) or to redirect your resolvers to another DNS server for name reso-

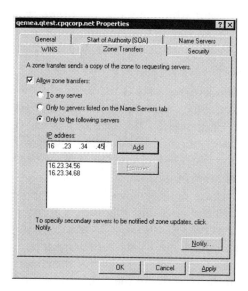

Figure 2.27
*Configuring zone
transfer restrictions
in the zone
properties*

lution in another namespace (e.g., the Internet namespace). If recursive queries are disabled, the DNS server will always answer a resolver's query using referrals. The same Advanced tab lets you set secure cache against pollution. If this option is enabled, the DNS server will not cache entries that are unrelated to the initial recursive query. For example, if the DNS server launches a query for *compaq.com* and the query returns *microsoft.com*, the return will not be stored in the DNS server cache. Also in the server properties, in the Interfaces tab you can restrict the interfaces on which the DNS server listens for DNS queries; this can be an interesting option for a dual-homed DNS server that has one network interface connected to the Internet.

2.3.4   **Integration with other core networking services**

In this section we will discuss the integration between Windows 2000 DNS and the Dynamic Host Configuration Protocol (DHCP) and between Windows 2000 DNS and the Windows Internet Name Service (WINS).

DHCP

One of the important new features of the Windows 2000 DHCP server is its support for dynamic DNS update. This enables the DHCP server to register A and PTR records on behalf of Windows 2000 clients, or more importantly, on behalf of down-level clients (NT4, Windows 98, etc.) that do not support the dynamic DNS update protocol. A DHCP server sends out a dynamic update request every time a lease is renewed. Deregistration is done only by a Windows 2000 client. Its DHCP client will automatically deregister a resource record when the DHCP lease expires.

The way DHCP dynamic update works between the DHCP client and server is based on some extra information that's added to the messages used during the DHCP protocol. (The DHCP protocol consists of four phases: discover, offer, request, and acknowledge.) Doing so lets the DHCP client negotiate whether the DHCP server should do a DNS update on the client's behalf and how it should do it. The client and server set a special flag in the DHCP request and acknowledge messages; this flag can have one of the following values: 0, meaning that the client requests to set the A record itself and the server the PTR record, 1, meaning that the client requests the server to set both the A and PTR records, or 3, meaning that the server sets both the A and PTR records regardless of the client's request. By default a Windows 2000 client sends out the 1 flag. Depending on its configuration, the server can change this flag to 3. Depending on the way the DHCP server and client are configured, the DHCP server can register just the PTR record, both A and PTR records, or nothing at all. By default a Windows 2000 client registers its A record, and the DHCP server registers the PTR record. This is because the client is considered to own its proper hostname, while the DHCP server is considered to own IP addresses. Table 2.17 gives an overview of how the client type and the client and server configuration affect the way dynamic DNS update will occur.

Note in Table 2.17 that an identical dynamic update behavior can be obtained for a Windows 2000 client as for a down level client by disabling the *Register this connection's address in DNS* option in the advanced TCP/IP properties of the Windows 2000 network interface.

The Windows 2000 DHCP configuration settings mentioned in Table 2.17 are set in the DNS tab of a DHCP scope's properties. To enable or disable DHCP server dynamic DNS update, check or uncheck *Automatically update DHCP client information in DNS* (by default this option is set). To set the DHCP server to update depending on the client's request, set *Update DNS only if DNS client requests*. To perform a complete update (A and PTR records) in any scenario, select *Always update DNS*; to do a complete update only if the request comes from a down-level client or a Windows 2000 client with dynamic update disabled, choose *Enable updates for DNS clients that do not support dynamic update*. You may want to let the DHCP server do all the work (always update both records) for down-level clients and for RAS clients.

Table 2.17 *Effect of Client Platform and DHCP Server Configuration on Dynamic DNS Update Behavior*

Client Platform	Windows 2000 DHCP Server Configuration	Dynamic DNS Update Behavior
Windows 2000 client: *Register this connection's address in DNS* selected (default)*	Not supporting dynamic update or not configured to do so	Client tries dynamic update for both A and PTR record
	Update depending on client request	Client tries dynamic update for A record, DHCP server tries for PTR record
	Always update both records	DHCP server tries update for both records
Windows 2000 client: *Register this connection's address in DNS* not selected	Not supporting dynamic update or not configured to do so	No dynamic update
	Update depending on client request	No dynamic update
	Always update both records	DHCP server tries update for both records
Windows NT4, Windows 95, Windows 98 client	Not supporting dynamic update or not configured to do so	No dynamic update
	Update depending on client request	No dynamic update
	Always update both records	DHCP server tries update for both records

*If the *Use this connection's DNS suffix in DNS registration* check box is also checked, the client will not only attempt to register its primary DNS suffix but also the specified connection-specific DNS suffix. *Note:* the primary DNS suffix is the one specified in the Network Identification tab of the system properties; the connection-specific DNS suffix is the one specified in the advanced settings of the TCP/IP configuration.

To end this discussion on DHCP-DNS integration, here's an important note related to secure dynamic DNS update. You don't want a DHCP server to perform a secure update on behalf of a down-level client. Why? When the DHCP server performs the secure update of a record, it becomes the owner of the record, meaning that nobody else can touch (modify) the record anymore. This may cause problems when another DHCP server takes over and wants to update a record previously securely registered by the first DHCP server. To get around this problem, Microsoft introduced the DNSupdateproxy group. A DCHP server that's added to this group will make no changes to the security settings of the resource record objects it creates in AD. Never do this for a DHCP server that's also a DC; doing so gives any user full access to the DC-specific resource records (including service records).

WINS

The Windows Internet Name Service (WINS) is the dynamic NetBIOS name resolution service. Because of the importance of NetBIOS naming WINS was a critical service in NT4. Windows 2000 relies primarily on DNS for name resolution; nevertheless, WINS may still be required, though for backward compatibility.

Windows 2000 DNS still supports WINS lookup. This feature (introduced in NT4) enables a DNS server to call on WINS if DNS name resolution fails. The way WINS lookup works is based on two special resource records (WINS and WINS-R), which are added to the forward and reverse lookup zone files. To set it up configure the WINS and WINS-R properties in your Windows 2000 forward and reverse lookup zone files.

When an authoritative DNS server cannot resolve a forward lookup and it is configured for WINS lookup, it will strip the DNS domain off the hostname, and forward the hostname to the WINS server. The IP address returned from the WINS to the DNS server is then passed by the DNS server to the DNS resolver. To the resolver it will appear as if the DNS server resolved the query.

Things look a little bit different in the case of a reverse lookup combined with WINS lookup. The problem in this scenario is that the WINS database is not ordered using IP addresses (as is a DNS reverse lookup zone) but is ordered using NetBIOS names. In fact, it's very misleading to talk about WINS lookup in this scenario. DNS will not call on WINS at all; it will use a node adapter status request. This is a special message the DNS server sends to the IP address to be resolved; if the machine is online, it can return its NetBIOS name to the DNS server. The DNS name will append the configured DNS domain name and forward this all together to the DNS resolver. *Domain to append to returned name* is an option that can be set in the WINS-R properties of a reverse lookup zone.

Windows 2000 allows an administrator to set up multiple WINS servers per zone and to configure different WINS servers for primary and secondary zones. Your organization may have different WINS servers depending on geographical sites. To do this check the *Do not replicate this record* in the WINS or WINS-R properties of the forward or reverse lookup zones. This will mark the resource record as local and exclude it from zone replication.

You may also want to do this if you're using non–Windows 2000 DNS servers; WINS lookup is a proprietary mechanism only supported by Windows 2000 DNS.

2.4 Administering and troubleshooting Windows 2000 DNS

The continuity of the DNS infrastructure you planned, designed, and implemented for your organization largely depends on the quality of the administration, troubleshooting, and the monitoring tools you use. This section contains an overview of the Windows 2000 tools we think are very useful to the average DNS administrator.

If these tools do not fill in the DNS administration and configuration needs of your organization, you can look at third-party tools or develop custom administration scripts using the Windows Management Instrumentation (WMI) DNS provider. The WMI DNS provider can be downloaded from *ftp://ftp.microsoft.com/reskit/win2000/dnsprov.zip.* A list of interesting third-party tools can be found at *http://www.dns.net/dnsrd/mark/wintools.html.*

2.4.1 Administration and troubleshooting tools

As with every service in Windows 2000 the main administration interface for DNS is an MMC snap-in. For administration and troubleshooting Microsoft has provided some interesting command prompt tools: classic ipconfig and nslookup and the dnscmd tool shipping with the support tools.

Before using any of the troubleshooting tools it's advisable to test the normal and recursive query capabilities of your DNS server. Microsoft has included a testing tool in the DNS MMC snap-in interface. The Monitoring tab of the server properties allows you to launch simple and recursive queries manually or at a specified interval. The tool displays the outcome of the tests in the same dialog box.

Ipconfig includes some interesting new switches to flush the DNS resolver's cache (/flushDNS), to force a dynamic update of DNS (/registerDNS), and to display the contents of the DNS resolver's cache (/displayDNS).

An indispensable tool to query the DNS zone files is nslookup. Nslookup can be used in interactive and non interactive mode. You get to interactive

Table 2.18   *Nslookup Tool Switches*

Nslookup (interactive mode)	Meaning
server <DNS server name>	Switch to DNS server <DNS server name>
ls –t <resource record type> <DNS domain name>	List all resource records of type <resource record type> in the zone file for domain <DNS domain name>
set querytype=<resource record type> or set type=<resource record type>	Limit the scope of a query to a particular resource record type
exit	Quit the nslookup program

mode by launching the tool from the command prompt without parameters. Typing a question mark in interactive mode will bring up a list of all possible commands. Table 2.18 shows some important nslookup commands for interactive mode.

An interesting alternative to nslookup is the dig tool, which comes with BIND. One of the features of dig is that allows the display of complete DNS messages sent back from a DNS server to a DNS resolver.

Dnscmd is a very powerful command prompt tool, which is shipping with the Windows 2000 support tools. It can be used to look at the configuration of DNS servers, zones, and resource records and to modify their properties. Table 2.19 shows some interesting dnscmd commands.

2.4.2   Monitoring DNS

In Windows 2000 the DNS monitoring capabilities have been extended; we will discuss event monitoring and performance monitoring in the following text.

Event monitoring

The most important DNS events are written by default to a special DNS folder in the Windows 2000 Event Viewer. Additional events (queries, NOTIFY and update messages, number of UDP-TCP requests, etc.) can be monitored by setting the appropriate options in the Logging tab of the DNS server properties (as illustrated in Figure 2.28). These additional events are not written to the Event Viewer but to the Dns.log stored in the %systemroot%\System32\Dns folder. A complete overview can be found in the Windows 2000 DNS online help.

Table 2.19 *Dnscmd Tool Switches*

Dnscmd (Support Tools)	Meaning
Dnscmd <DNS server name> /info	Gives an overview of a DNS server's configuration. <DNS server name> can be a DNS, NetBIOS name, or IP address; specifiying "." means the local computer.
Dnscmd <DNS server name> /statistics	Gives DNS statistics of the DNS server <DNS server name> (including number of queries and responses, WINS referrals, zone transfers, etc.).
Dnscmd <DNS server name> /zonedelete <zone name>	Deletes zone <zone name> from the DNS server <DNS server name>.
Dnscmd <DNS server name> /zoneadd <zone name>	Adds zone <zone name> on the DNS server located on <DNS server name>.
Dnscmd <DNS server name> /clearcache	Clears the DNS server cache of the DNS server <DNS server name>.
Dnscmd <DNS server name> /ZoneResetType <zone name> <zone type>	Changes the zone type (choices are /Primary, /Secondary, or /DSPrimary) of <zone name> on DNS server <DNS server name>.
Dnscmd <DNS server name> /RecordAdd <zone name> <resource record>	Adds resource record <resource record> to the zone <zone name> located on DNS server <DNS server name>.
Dnscmd <DNS server name> /restart	Restarts the DNS server <DNS server name>.

Figure 2.28
Configuring DNS server logging options

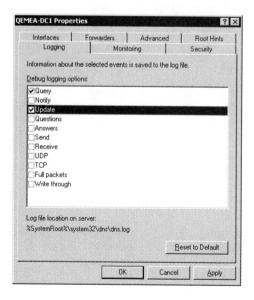

An interesting third-party monitoring tool is Netpro's Directory Analyzer. Among the many things you can do with this tool is DNS monitoring: You can monitor the status of the DNS service, the status of DC SRV records, and DNS response time. More information can be found at *http://www.net-pro.com/directoryanalyzer/default.asp*.

Performance monitoring

As for any Windows service the primary performance monitoring for DNS is the performance monitor. The Windows 2000 version of performance monitor (also known as system monitor) has a brand-new MMC-based interface and includes a new DNS object containing several interesting DNS-specific counters. They are related to zone transfer, incremental zone transfer, memory usage, dynamic update, secure dynamic update, WINS lookup, zone transfer, and so on. Probably the most important function of the performance monitor is its ability to send or log alerts when a particular setting reaches a certain predefined limit.

2.5   Summary

This chapter provided an overview of the basics of DNS and the power of Windows 2000 DNS. It also introduced the critical steps involved when planning and designing a domain name system namespace for Windows 2000 AD. What you certainly should remember from this chapter is the important role of DNS in Windows 2000 and the impact it has on the overall health of your AD infrastructure.

3

Site Topology Design

3.1 Introduction

This chapter reviews various aspects of Active Directory replication. We will introduce the terminology that describes the replication technology used in Windows 2000 and explain how data are replicated between Windows 2000 servers. We will also look at how replication topologies are generated within a Windows 2000 site and between sites. Finally, we will review some possible designs for a replication topology and provide recommendations.

We will be doing a technical drill-down of the replication features implemented by the Active Directory and review some of the design options that should be considered during a deployment project.

Active Directory replication is an important step to master when dealing with large corporate deployments. Many new applications will be relying on the consistency of the Active Directory. Many will also store their own objects and attributes in the Active Directory. An Active Directory–enabled application will not worry about the replication aspects of the data it stores in the Active Directory. Once the data are defined in the schema and instances of objects created in the Active Directory, the application will attempt to access these objects, potentially in a distributed manner, but will not be involved in the replication of these data between Domain Controllers. An example of such application is Exchange 2000. The Global Address List (GAL) in Exchange V5.5 is integrated in the Active Directory in the Exchange 2000 release. This means that the directory portion of Exchange is stored in the Active Directory, and, therefore, it is important to design a replication topology and avoid inconsistencies, failing which Exchange will be highly affected.

Replication in Windows 2000 has changed drastically from previous versions of Windows NT. For Windows NT, replication was a simple matter of copying information from the Primary Domain Controller (PDC) system to the other computers that act as Backup Domain Controllers (BDCs). Windows 2000 uses a multimaster, store-and-forward replication mechanism to allow changes to be made at any controller within an organization and have those changes successfully copied to all other domain controllers.

Replication is the mechanism that ensures that data are copied in a robust and reliable manner so that domain controllers are updated in the most efficient and controlled way, no matter how distributed the organization. One of the design goals of Windows 2000 is to accommodate the requirements of large enterprises.

Windows NT replication was too simple to be able to match the scalability issues that are addressed in Windows 2000. The extensibility of the Active Directory and the number of objects it can support far surpass the capabilities of the single-master replication model used in previous versions of Windows NT.

A new replication strategy with the ability to sustain a large number of objects in an environment where domains are grouped together to form a global namespace had to be defined.

During the design phase of the site topology, architects must ask themselves the following questions:

- How many partitions (or domains) are composing the Active Directory?

- What kind and how much data must be replicated?

- How fast must replication be executed within the Active Directory between two end-points?

- What is the size of the user base and how distributed is it?

- How frequently are the data stored in the Active Directory is modified?

- What is the network connectivity between the physical locations where the users reside? Keep in mind that network bandwidth is not necessarily available all the time. Net available bandwidth and schedules for peak usage should be considered here.

This is the information that provides the base for the site topology design. When dealing with namespace and domain designs, a number of domain models may be produced. Some of these models are due to political constraints. Some, however, are due to the business model in which the company operates. In other cases domain models are the result of security and law constraints. The site topology will help identify how the different domain models are affecting the replication traffic. In some cases a particular domain model, which looked interesting at the early phases of the design, may not be implemented due to the low network bandwidth available or unreliability or latency of the network. We will review these challenges and see how they can be addressed.

3.2   Replication basics

3.2.1   What is replication?

Windows 2000 Domain Controllers (DCs) hold a replica of all the objects belonging to their domain and have full read/write access to these objects. Administrators can perform management operations using any DC in a domain. These operations affect the state of the value of an object and must therefore be replicated to the other DCs. Replication is the process of propagating object updates between DCs.

The goal of replication is to allow all controllers to receive updates and to maintain their copies of the Active Directory database in a consistent state. Replication is not triggered immediately when an object has been modified, since this could trigger a flood of replication operations if the directory is being manipulated by programs that insert or update many records in a short period of time, such as directory synchronization procedures. Instead, replication is triggered after a period of time, gathering all changes and providing them to other controllers in collections. Replication can be scheduled to control when these changes are disseminated to other DCs. Therefore, since replication is not instantaneous, in normal operation the Active Directory on any controller can be regarded as always being in a state of loose consistency, since replication changes may be on the way from other controllers. Eventually the changes arrive and DCs synchronize with each other. However, when performing a management operation, an administrator does not know if another user or another administrator is performing the same operation on another DC. This could lead to a replication collision, which must be resolved. We will see how these collisions are resolved in a later section.

The goal of the replication topology is to mirror the data stored in the Active Directory so that these data are close to the users. The larger the user community, and the more distributed, the harder it is to design and implement a replication topology that fulfills the requirements of corporate enterprises. Because of this it is important to understand how replication works in detail.

3.2.2 Domain controllers

Windows NT 4.0 uses a single-master replication model. This means that operations can only be performed on the Primary Domain Controller (PDC), since it is the only DC with read/write access to the database. Operations performed on the PDC are then replicated to Backup Domain Controllers (BDCs). BDCs maintain a read-only copy of the database and are designed to provide a replica of the domain information closer to the users. This allows faster authentication, because users are not required to connect to distant DCs over a potentially slow link.

In Windows NT 4.0, the replication granularity is coarse. If a user or an administrator modifies a password, the entire user object with all its attributes has to be replicated to all BDCs in the domain. In other words, NT 4.0 uses object-level replication. The replication topology is simple and consists of linking the PDC to all the BDCs in the same domain.

In a Windows 2000 infrastructure every Domain Controller (DC) maintains a copy of the Active Directory database with full read/write access to all of the objects belonging to the domain. This implies that if an operation is performed on one of the DCs, it must then be replicated to all other DCs in the domain. If domains are linked together to form a forest, some of the data from each domain must be replicated to the other domains to form a collective view of the forest. Windows 2000 introduces a multimaster replication model to support copying of data within the domain and, indeed, between domains. At the same time, Active Directory replication is optimized, because only the data that are actually changed are replicated. In other words, if a user updates his or her password, then only the updated password is replicated to other controllers, instead of the complete object. Active Directory uses attribute-level replication.

Domain Controllers are responsible for initiating and performing replication operations. Each DC serves as a replication partner for other DCs. Replication is always performed between DCs. Member servers do not play a role in the replication process (they don't hold Active Directory information).

Internally, DCs reference other DCs or replication partners using Globally Unique Identifiers (GUIDs). GUIDs are unique numbers, which can be used to identify objects. A GUID is a 16-byte (128-bit) number introduced by the Open Software Foundation (OSF) to uniquely identify the application interfaces of the Distributed Computing Environment (DCE). The OSF called them Universally Unique Identifiers, or UUIDs. Microsoft COM used the term *globally unique identifiers*; however, the underlying algorithm for generating them didn't change. Microsoft used them to identify COM interfaces, and GUIDs prevent two programs from defining the same API, even if the functions and callable routines have the same name. GUIDs are by definition unique. This implies that they are generated using an algorithm that ensures their uniqueness even if they are generated at the same time on the same system.

There are two GUIDs used internally by Windows 2000 to reference a DC, as follows:

1.   Server GUID. Replication partners use this GUID to reference a specific DC. The GUID for each DC is saved in the DNS database as SRV resource records and is used by replication partners to locate the IP address of available DCs.

2.   Database GUID. Initially, this GUID is the same as the Server GUID and is used to identify the database during replication calls. In the event of an authoritative restore, this GUID is changed to allow other DCs to realize that the database was restored and therefore the state of the DC was changed.

GUIDs are more reliable than names, because their values remain constant even if systems are renamed. This ensures a safe rename environment. In other words, an object can be moved from one part of the Active Directory to another without requiring the object to be deleted and then recreated in its new location.

It's important to note, however, that in Windows 2000, a DC cannot be renamed. Once a member server becomes a DC in a domain, its name cannot be changed. To change the name of a DC, administrators must use the Domain Controller Wizard (DCPROMO) to demote the DC back to a member server first, and then change the name. Finally DCPROMO can be run again to promote the renamed member server back to a DC. This can be a tedious operation if a number of DCs must be renamed or if the Active Directory partition that they managed is large. Demoting a DC means getting rid of all Active Directory information and generating a SAM database for built-in security principals. Promoting the member server means replicating an entire domain to the local Active Directory database. This could take days if the domain is really big. So it's important to define the naming conventions during the planning and design phase of the Windows 2000 project.

3.2.3 **Replication operations**

A number of operations trigger replication between DCs. Depending on permissions, an Administrator or a user performs these operations on objects stored in the Active Directory.

The operations that trigger replication are the following:

- Object creation—the creation of a new object in the database, for example, a new user.

- Attribute modification—the modification of an object attribute, for example, a user changes his or her password

- Object move—moving an object from one container to another. Organizational units are special containers to help organize objects within the Active Directory and often use the same names as departments within a company, for example, "Sales" or "Marketing." A move from the Sales organizational unit (OU) to the Marketing OU is an example of an object move that might happen as a result of reorganization within a company. Object move operations are very similar to attribute modification, in that an object move implies the modification of an attribute, the distinguished name of the object.

- Object deletion—this operation deletes objects from the database. This operation doesn't actually delete the object immediately but transforms it into a tombstone. See the following section for more information about tombstones.

3.2.4 **Tombstones**

A tombstone is a state of the object, or a flag, meaning that the object has been deleted and is no longer accessible. If, for example, we create a large number of objects in the database, and then we delete them, the database doesn't shrink. This is because all objects in the database have been transformed into tombstones. Inside the Active Directory, when an object is transformed into a tombstone its isDeleted attribute is set to "true" and the object is moved to a special container, the Deleted Objects container. Tombstones have the size of the original objects. However, when objects are transformed into tombstones, most of their attributes are removed. The role of tombstones is to replicate throughout the domain the fact that an object has been deleted. Tombstones have a configurable lifetime of 60 days. After 60 days, the object is really removed from the database. However, amending the following attribute in the Active Directory can change the lifetime of a tombstone:

```
cn=DirectoryServices,cn=WindowsNT,cn=Services,
cn=Configuration,dc=DomainName with the name
tombstonelifetime.
```

The minimum lifetime of a tombstone is two days. If set to a lower value, the lifetime defaults back to 60 days.

The lifetime of tombstones dictates how long backups are valid. This is because if restore is performed with objects stored in the backup that were deleted by other domain controllers, a replication partner of the restored DC will not be able to replicate the deletion event of these objects. Its tombstones will have expired and the garbage collection will have removed them. This means that the restored DC will have objects that were removed in other DCs and the Active Directory would be inconsistent.

Tombstones cannot be viewed in the Active Directory. The management console snap-ins as well as the ADSI edit tool will not be able to show these objects. To view a tombstone, an administrator must institute a specific search with a dedicated LDAP control. A tool capable of using LDAP controls to define the scope of the search is LDP. LDP ships with the resource kit. The LDAP control used to search tombstones has the following OID: 1.2.840.113556.1.4.417.

3.2.5 Update types

When performing write operations, there is a distinction based on whether the operation was performed locally on a DC or whether the operation was performed on a remote DC and replicated locally. As shown in Figure 3.1, the two update types are as follows:

- The originating write is an operation that was originally performed on the same system. The originating write is one of the four operations (add, modify, move, delete) performed on a DC. It's called originating write because this operation originated on the current DC. For example if we create a user on the current DC, we are performing an originating write.

Figure 3.1
Active Directory database write operations

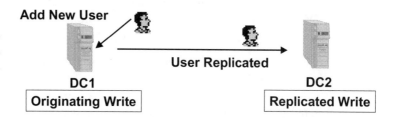

- The replicated write is an operation that was performed on another system and was replicated locally. A replicated write is a database modification issued from an operation that originated from another DC and was replicated to the current DC. For example if we create a user on DC1 and the operation gets replicated to DC2, we refer to the modification of the DC2 database as a replicated write.

3.2.6 Naming contexts

Naming contexts are a new concept introduced in Windows 2000. The scope of replication within a Windows NT domain is only domain-wide and therefore this concept did not exist previously.

A Naming Context (NC) is a tree of objects stored in the Active Directory. There are three NCs, as follows:

- Configuration NC—contains all the objects that represent the structure of the Active Directory in terms of domains, DCs, sites, enterprise CAs, and other configuration type objects.

- Schema NC—contains all the classes and attributes that define the objects and their attributes that are stored in the Active Directory.

- Domain NC—contains all the other objects of the Active Directory: the users, the groups, the OUs, the computers, and so on.

Domains act as partitions for the Active Directory, but they are not the boundary of replication. Naming Contexts define the boundary of replication and define the replication scope. The boundary of replication indicates how far management operations performed on DCs are replicated to other DCs in the same domain or to other DCs in the forest. In other words, NCs define how far Active Directory changes are replicated in an organization. (See Figure 3.2.)

There are two scopes of replication for NCs: forest-wide and domain-wide.

The configuration and schema are unique in the entire forest and form a unit in the forest. This means that their NCs must be replicated to all the DCs in every domain comprising the forest. The configuration NC and schema NC are therefore said to have a forest-wide scope.

Domain objects are replicated only within the domain to which they currently belong. The domain NC has a domain-wide scope. In other words, information stored in a domain is confined to an NC and is replicated in the domain itself. There is one exception to this rule: When the

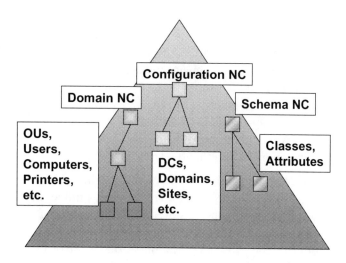

Figure 3.2
Naming contexts

domain NC is replicated to a GC, its scope becomes forest-wide. This is because GCs are available in multiple domains and therefore domain NCs need the forest-wide scope to reach them. We will see later how the replication topologies will allow a domain NC to reach GCs in other domains.

Naming Contexts contain all the objects of the Active Directory and are obviously held in the Active Directory. The characteristic of objects in the Active Directory is that they always have a parent. Objects are contained in other objects, such as organizational units, computers, and domains. The parents of these top-level objects are the NCs. Some NCs are a child of other NCs. This is the case of the schema NC that is a child of the configuration NC. The parent of child domains is their parent domain. This means that the child domain NC is a child of the parent domain NC. The parent of the top-level NCs is the RootDSE. The RootDSE is a virtual container. It contains all the objects in the domain. It's the only object in the entire Active Directory that doesn't have a parent object. The RootDSE object doesn't get replicated and doesn't hold any space. It is simply a virtual parent for the top-level NCs stored in the Active Directory. The RootDSE could be viewed as the summit of the Active Directory and is often used by applications to discover the NCs available at a particular DC.

3.2.7 Update sequence number

DCs maintain a sequence number to keep track of the operations that have been performed on objects stored in the Active Directory. This number is called the Update Sequence Number (USN).

The USN is a number associated with an operation performed on a DC. Every time an operation is performed the sequence number is increased by one and updated within the object. The operation may succeed or fail. However, the USN remains updated. This is due to the LSASS process (the name of the process that is executing the Active Directory), which is multi-threaded, and multiple threads may perform operations affecting the database concurrently. Each operation requires a distinct USN. USNs are increased and assigned atomically to every committed operation. This transaction ensures that the USN can uniquely reference an operation.

USNs are 64-bit numbers that begin at 1 and increase sequentially, which allows a USN to reach a 20-digit number before the capacity of 64 bits overflows. If such an overflow condition occurred, the replication process would request all changes since USN 1 from the other DCs in the domain and cause a replication storm. While it is theoretically possible to overflow a USN, in practical terms this is unlikely, since a Windows 2000 infrastructure would need to be operational for centuries to accumulate enough object changes to reach such a large number. Every DC maintains its own USN independently from other DCs in the domain. This means that USNs change on each DC regardless of the USNs of other DCs.

So far it might appear that an object carries a single USN to track changes to the object. However, two different USNs are maintained for every object in the Active Directory. The first USN is called "usnCreated," and its value is set when the object is first created. The second USN is called "usnChanged," and this value is updated each time the object is changed. Every attribute for each object also carries two USNs. One is associated with the operation when the attribute is changed. The second USN is associated with the originating write operation performed on the originating DC. Attributes carry USNs because Windows 2000 supports attribute-level replication. Without attribute USNs, it would be impossible to track attribute-level replication operations across a distributed infrastructure.

3.2.8   The replication process

In this section we will look closely at the role of USNs and originating writes versus replicated writes in the replication process.

Creation of an object

We have a DC in a domain named DC1. Let's assume that a number of operations have been performed on the DC and the current USN is 110.

We create a user. The creation operation is automatically allocated the next USN in sequence, that is, 111. Note that the create operation may fail; however, the USN will nevertheless remain associated with this operation. The following operation will be allocated as USN 112.

Every Active Directory object maintains a table called Replication Metadata. This table is stored in the replMetaData attribute of every object, and it contains the following replication data concerning the object:

- Name of the attribute

- Value of the attribute

- Version number for the attribute. This number is increased everytime the attribute is modified.

- Time stamp of the originating write operation

- USN for the operation

- Orginating USN number

- Originating DC GUID

If we look at the replication metadata table in the Active Directory database on DC1 after the create operation is performed (see Table 3.1), we can see the following:

- The usnCreated and usnChanged attributes for the new object have been assigned the same USN because the user has just been created.

- Various attributes (we assume that only four have been filled: name, address, phone, and password) have received a value.

- Each attribute has the current USN (111) associated with it.

- The version is set to 1, because this is a new user and we have set the values for each attribute once. The version number will be used to resolve a conflict. We will see this in a later section.

- The time stamp of the operation is saved. Time stamps are also used to resolve replication conflicts.

- The originating write DC GUID is saved. We have created the user on DC1. So DC1 is the originating DC and its GUID is saved in the table (see Table 3.1). The originating USN, in this case 111, is also saved in the table.

Table 3.1　*Replication Metadata at User Creation*

Attribute	Value	USN	Version	Time Stamp	Originating DC GUID	Originating USN
Name	Joe	111	1	TS	DC1 GUID	111
Address	Compaq Valbonne	111	1	TS	DC1 GUID	111
Phone	+33 4 92 95 1111	111	1	TS	DC1 GUID	111
Password	********	111	1	TS	DC1 GUID	111

Replication to a second DC

Now let's replicate this user to a second DC named DC2. DC2 is a replica of DC1—that is, they are both DCs of the same domain. DC2 has its own USN sequence, which happens to be at 520. This means that there have been 520 operations on DC2, either originating writes or replicated writes. When the replication operation occurs to add the new user object, the USN value goes up to 521.

If we look at the replication metadata table (see Table 3.2) on DC2 after the object is replicated, we can ascertain the following:

- This is a new object creation; therefore, the object USNs, usnCreated and usnChanged, received the value of the current USN for the DC, or 521.

- The values for the object's attributes have been replicated.

Table 3.2　*Replication Metadata When User is Replicated to the Second DC*

Attribute	Value	USN	Version	Time Stamp	Originating DC GUID	Originating USN
Name	Joe	521	1	TS	DC1 GUID	111
Address	Compaq Valbonne	521	1	TS	DC1 GUID	111
Phone	+33 4 92 95 1111	521	1	TS	DC1 GUID	111
Password	********	521	1	TS	DC1 GUID	111

- The USN value associated with the replication operation (521) is saved for each attribute.

- The time of the originating write operation is saved in the time stamp column. This time stamp can be used to resolve conflicts.

- The originating write DB GUID and originating write USN are saved. This operation was originally performed on DC1; therefore, it's the DC1 GUID and USN that are saved.

Object manipulation on the second DC

We now modify one of the attributes for this user: the address. For this operation, the USN value on DC2 goes from 521 to 522. The user's address is modified. When the operation is performed, we can see in the table for this user (Table 3.3) the following:

- The usnChanged attribute is updated with the USN value associated with the operation.

- The address value has been changed.

- The USN for the operation (522) is saved for the address attribute.

- The version number went up by one. We will see how version numbers are useful later.

- The time stamp for the operation is saved.

- This operation was originally performed on DC2, which means that this is an originating write. The GUID for the DC2 database and the originating USN (522) are saved.

Table 3.3   *Attribute Modification*

Attribute	Value	USN	Version	Time Stamp	Originating DC GUID	Originating USN
Name	Joe	521	1	TS	DC1 GUID	111
Address	Compaq Sophia Antipolis	522	2	TS	DC2 GUID	522
Phone	+33 4 92 95 1111	521	1	TS	DC1 GUID	111
Password	********	521	1	TS	DC1 GUID	111

Replication back to DC1

Given that we are in a multimaster replication model, the operations performed on DC2 must replicate to DC1 to keep all replicas consistent and equal. When the data are replicated, the following occurs:

- The USN on DC1 goes from 111 to 112. If we look at the table for the user on DC1 (Table 3.4), we can see that the usnChanged property has been updated with the USN for the operation, 112. Note that usnCreated property is not modified.

- The value for the address attribute has been replicated.

- The USN for the operation is saved at the attribute level.

- The version number is increased to 2.

- The time stamp for the originating write operation on DC2 has been saved.

- This operation was originally performed on DC2; therefore, this is a replicated write. The DC GUID and USN (522) of the originating DC are saved.

Making a distinction between originating writes and replicated writes and saving USNs at the attribute level is very important because of the following:

- Given that Active Directory replication is performed at the attribute level we need to distinguish between object creation, which affects all attributes, and attribute modifications. This allows the value of the attribute to be replicated instead of the entire object.

- Originating USNs are used for propagation dampening, or the ability to detect that a DC has already been updated. We will discuss this mechanism in more detail later in the next section.

Table 3.4   *Attribute-Level Replication*

Attribute	Value	USN	Version	Time Stamp	Originating DC GUID	Originating USN
Name	Joe	111	1	TS	DC1 GUID	111
Address	Compaq Sophia Antipolis	112	2	TS	DC2 GUID	522
Phone	+33 4 92 95 1111	111	1	TS	DC1 GUID	111
Password	********	111	1	TS	DC1 GUID	111

3.3   Understanding propagation dampening

Propagation dampening is the ability to detect that a replication operation has already happened at a replication partner. The goal of propagation dampening is to avoid replicating the same information twice to the same DC.

This is a very important feature of Active Directory replication and is key in a multimaster replication environment where DCs may have multiple replication partners, which may use different paths to replicate data back to the target DC. The first replication instruction to arrive at the target DC will update the Active Directory, so it's important to detect that all DCs know that the replication operation has already happened in order to reduce the amount of traffic and cut unnecessary duplicate operations.

To understand propagation dampening and how replications are triggered, we need to look at the roles of two tables maintained by the Active Directory: the high-watermark vector table and the up-to-date vector table.

3.3.1   High-watermark vector table

The high-water mark vector is a table stored on every DC. It contains the list of all the replication partners and their highest known USN values. The high-watermark vector table is used to detect changes performed at other DCs that are replication partners. The table also allows a DC to determine and request only those changes that haven't been replicated yet. For example, in a domain with two DCs (DC1 and DC2), the two systems are replication partners. DC1 stores the highest USN from DC2 in its high-watermark vector table. Let's assume that this USN is set to 100. On DC2, the USN is currently at 120. This means that 20 operations are outstanding and need to be replicated to DC1. Without this table, DC2 would have no choice but to replicate all operations. That would be an enormous waste of bandwidth and time.

Replication partners exchange their highest known USNs through notification messages. If no update has occurred within one hour, replication partners will notify each other with their highest USN. This is done in case a DC has been offline and just restored a connection to its replication partners and has missed a number of notifications. For example, let's assume that we have a domain with four DCs: DC1, DC2, DC3, and DC4. Each DC has two replication partners forming a ring. If we look at Figure 3.3 and examine the high-watermark vector table for DC4, we can see data for its two replication partners, including the highest known USN for each. If DC4 ever detects that the number held in the table is smaller than the actual number on the partner DC, then DC4 knows that it is not up-to-date and needs to initiate a replication cycle to request data from its partner.

3.3.2 Up-to-date vector table

In an enterprise Windows 2000 network, there may be a large number of DCs. Replication may follow multiple paths, in turn incurring the risk that attempts might be made to update an object multiple times on the same DC.

In order to avoid unnecessary replication, the Active Directory uses a table of up-to-date vectors also called the *state vector table*. This table contains the list of domain controllers that performed originating writes and the highest originating write USN. All DCs that perform an orginating write operation are listed in this table. Even DCs that are not direct replication partners. Each DC has its own up-to-date vector table, which is sent to the replication partners to filter out unwanted data that are up-to-date. The replication partner matches the USN in the up-to-date vector table with its high-watermark vector table to identify which attributes need to be updated. This operation implements replication dampening, since all DCs know which replication partners are up-to-date and can avoid unnecessary replication.

If we use the previous example of a domain containing four DCs to illustrate the up-to-date vector table and we assume that DC1 and DC2 were the only two DCs on which an originating write was performed, then the GUIDs of these two DCs will be stored in the up-to-date vector table of DC4, as shown in Figure 3.3. In a synchronized environment, the up-to-date vector table is the same on all DCs.

How replication activity is triggered and dampened

It's important to understand how the high-watermark vector table and up-to-date vector table are used to trigger and dampen replication. As we have seen, DCs may have two or more replication partners. This means that operations may potentially be replicated multiple times by the various DCs that want to replicate the same data with a common replication partner. We are now going see in more detail how Active Directory replication supports dampening. To illustrate how the high-watermark vector table and up-to-date vector table are used during replication, we will go through the process of replicating data within our sample domain and review the roles of each DC. Once again, we have four DCs in a domain: DC1, DC2, DC3, and DC4. The high-watermark vector table on each DC tells us which control-

Figure 3.3
Up-to-date and high-watermark vector tables

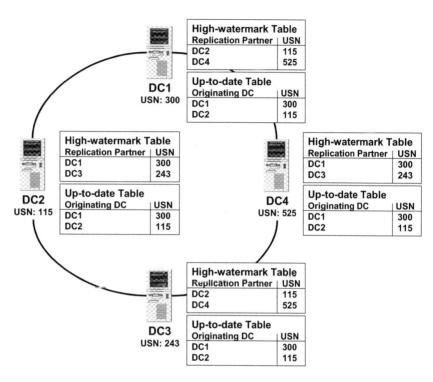

lers are its replication partners. Referring to Figure 3.3, we see that every DC has its two adjacent DCs as its replication partners. The data in the table also tell us whether each DC is fully synchronized with its replication partners. For example, if we look at the high-watermark vector table of DC4, we can see that it has DC1 and DC3 as replication partners and that it is currently synchronized. This is because the USNs stored in the table are the same as the current USNs on DC1 and DC3.

When DCs are fully synchronized, the up-to-date vector table is the same on every DC. If we look at DC4, its up-to-date vector table shows that DC1 and DC2 have performed originating writes—that is, administrators or users performed tasks on those DCs that trigger replication. Let's now examine what happens when a new user object is created on DC2.

Step 1: Creation of a user and replication to immediate partners

We create a user on DC2. The USN on DC2 associated with this operation is 116, an increment of 1 from the previous USN (115). (See Figure 3.4.)

After a period of time, DC2 notifies its replication partners that a change has occurred and sends its own highest USN. The replication part-

Figure 3.4
Creation of a user

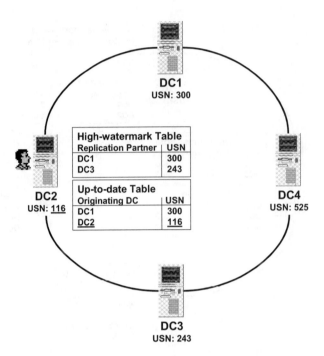

High-watermark Table	
Replication Partner	USN
DC1	300
DC3	243

Up-to-date Table	
Originating DC	USN
DC1	300
DC2	116

ners for DC2 are DC1 and DC3. These DCs will check the high-water-mark table for the highest USN they have for DC2 and realize that a change has occurred. The two DCs will trigger a replication cycle and request (pull) the information from DC2. Let's start with the operations performed by the first controller, DC1.

To request an update, DC1 sends the following information to DC2:

- Each replication operation is associated with a particular NC, so DC1 must specify which NC it wants. In this case we are replicating a created user, which belongs to the domain NC.

- The highest known USN value for this NC allows DC2 to determine what changes must be replicated. DC1 tells DC2 that its highest known USN is 115, so DC2 is able to determine that it must provide data for USN 116.

- The number of replicated objects and their values. By default, this value is set to 100, but it can be changed in the registry and is dependent on the memory size of the system. The goal here is to avoid congesting the network and swamping the replication partners with changes. So replication is performed using chunks of 100 objects. A

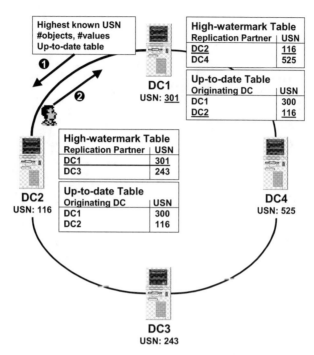

Figure 3.5
Replication to immediate replication partner

total of 100 objects are transferred and then some time is allowed to process the values. After a period of time another 100 objects are sent.

- The up-to-date vector table. This allows DC2 to know which originating write operations have already been replicated to DC1.

With this information, DC2 knows exactly which operation must be replicated. The data are provided from DC2 to DC1, and the new user object is created in the Active Directory on DC1, forcing the USN to increase from 300 to 301 on DC1, as shown in Figure 3.5.

Step 2: Replication to the second level partners

DC1 has two replication partners: DC2, from which it replicated the user, and DC4. It's now the turn of DC1 to notify DC4 that information has to be replicated. DC1 notifies DC4 that its USN has been increased.

When DC4 is informed that the current USN on DC1 has changed, it can compare the notified USN value against the value held in its high-watermark vector table and detect that replication must occur. The information necessary to initiate the replication operation is then sent from DC4 to DC1, and DC4 can then pull the information from DC1.

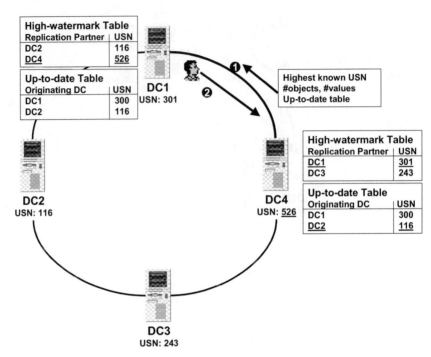

Figure 3.6
Replication to
transitive partners

These operations demonstrate that Active Directory replication is performed at multiple tiers. In other words, DCs contact DCs that in turn contact other DCs. This is quite important, because it allows a distributed implementation to create information once and spread it like a multitiered tree. This is one of the key features of Active Directory replication. Windows NT had a very simple replication model where all information could only be replicated from the PDC. This means that the bandwidth required in NT4 was dependent on the number of BDCs in the domain. In Windows 2000, the bandwidth requirements are dependent only on the amount of information that must be replicated from one DC to other DCs. Bandwidth requirements are heavily dependent on the replication topology used within a Windows 2000 domain.

Now, if we look at the tables for DC4 (Figure 3.6) we see the following:

- The up-to-date vector table has been updated with the originating write information. The user object was originally created on DC2; therefore, the GUID of DC2 and its highest USN is stored there.

- The high-watermark vector table is updated with the information concerning DC1, which is DC4's replication partner. DC1's highest USN is stored there.

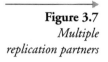

Figure 3.7
Multiple replication partners

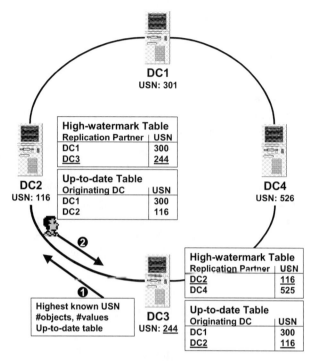

Step 3: Multiple Replication partners

So far a new user object was created on DC2 replicated to DC1. The object was then replicated to DC4.

DC2 has a second replication partner: DC3. When DC2 notifies its partners that its USN has changed, all replication partners receive the highest USN of DC2 and react accordingly. DC3, similar to DC1, detects that a change must be replicated and initiates replication with DC2.

Figure 3.7 shows the result of the replication from DC2 to DC3.

Step 4: Propagation dampening

This step is key in understanding how propagation dampening works and brings the whole concept together.

DC3 has two replication partners: DC2 and DC4. The user object has been replicated from DC2 to DC3. DC3 will now want to replicate it to DC4, since DC4 is a replication partner. However, DC4 has already replicated data for the new user object from DC1 and is now up-to-date. However, DC3 is not aware that DC4 is up-to-date and will attempt to replicate the data again unless the propagation process is dampened.

As part of the replication process, DC4 sends a number of parameters that will allow DC3 to determine the exact data to be replicated. One of those parameters is the up-to-date vector table, which contains the originating writes in the domain.

The up-to-date vector table controls propagation dampening, since it enables DC3 to realize that DC4 is already up-to-date. The up-to-date vector contains the originating write DC GUID and the USN for that operation and allows DC3 to detect that the user originally created on DC2 has already been replicated to DC4 using an alternate path. When DC3 receives the up-to-date vector table, it finds that DC4 knows about all changes made on DC2 up to USN 116. The highest USN for DC2 known to DC3 is also 116, so the two values match, meaning that DC3 does not need to replicate the user to DC4, dampening propagation. It will instead only send its own highest USN so that DC4 will be able to update the high-watermark vector table and be up-to-date with this replication partner. (See Figure 3.8.)

This is a small example with just a few DCs. Imagine a network with an enterprise Windows 2000 infrastructure and hundreds of DCs. Propagation

Figure 3.8
Propagation
dampening

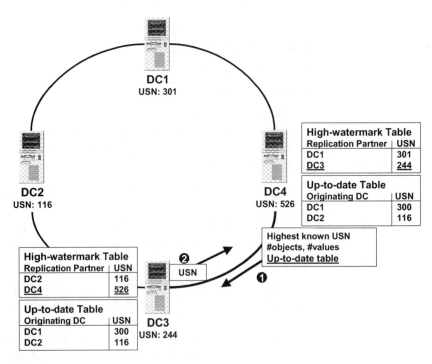

dampening is key in a model where a DC may have multiple replication partners, because it avoids the same information replicating multiple times, thus saving network bandwidth and time.

3.3.3 Sites

A Windows 2000 site is a collection of IP subnets with good connectivity. In fact, the best way to think of a site is to compare it to a LAN. Sites reflect locality, insofar as all the systems belonging to the same site can be considered to be physically close to each other and benefit, ideally, from LAN-quality network connectivity. In other words, each of the servers within a Windows 2000 site should be connected with links of 512 Kb/s or greater of net available bandwidth. True LAN-type bandwidth (10 Mb/s or greater) is preferable and recommended. The LAN-quality connectivity requirement for the subnets within a site is largely due to how intrasite replication is performed.

The concept of locality is extended to workstations, since workstations always attempt to connect to a DC in the same site. The Active Directory contains information about sites and their underlying IP subnets and is able to associate a workstation with a site by comparing the workstation's IP address with the site definitions. As servers and clients are added to a domain, their IP address will allow them to find the closest Active Directory DC.

When a Windows 2000 server creates a new domain, the Active Directory creates the site Default-First-Site-Name and places the DC there. All the DCs joining the domain are added to the default site. Systems continue to be added to the default site until a new site is explicitly created.

A domain can span multiple sites, as seen in Figure 3.9. Multiple domains may also belong to a single site, because sites are independent from the domains they belong to. Sites are objects stored in the Configuration Naming Context (CNC) and therefore site information is replicated to all DCs in the forest.

Sites are used for the following two roles:

1. To define locality. For example a site is used during a client's logon to determine the closest DC. Chapter 1 reviews how workstations discover the closest DC.

2. Active Directory replication. This is used to optimize the route and transport of replicated data between sites.

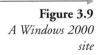

Figure 3.9
A Windows 2000
site

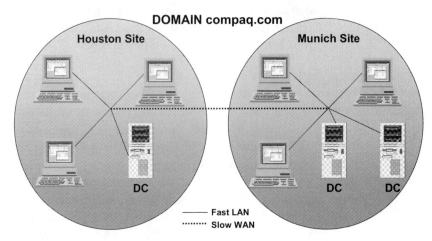

In order to achieve these two roles, all DCs in a forest know about all the sites.

3.3.4   Replication transports

Replication occurs between DCs at the same site and between DCs located at different sites. Intrasite replication is performed through standard Windows 2000 Remote Procedure Calls (RPCs). However, different transports can be used to replicate data between DCs at different sites. The Active Directory holds information about the DCs at each site, the connectivity that exists between each site, and the best route to take to replicate information. Network links between sites vary greatly. To support varying types of connections the Active Directory supports two major replication transports, as follows:

1.   DS-RPC (Directory Services RPC)

2.   ISM-SMTP (Intersite Messaging—Simple Mail Transport Protocol)

A general assumption is made that replication must occur quickly within a site and that there is a low tolerance for inconsistencies within the Directory across all controllers in a site. For this reason, intrasite replication is always RPC-based. Intersite replication can be performed through RPCs or via special forms of SMTP messages sent between DCs. RPC replication is always synchronous, whereas message-based replication is asynchronous. Intrasite replication cannot be scheduled. Each DC sends update notifications to its replication partners after updates have occurred. Normally this happens within five minutes. This interval is configurable through the system registry. Even if no changes have occurred and replication has not taken place, DCs "ping" each other every hour by exchanging details of the latest USN value held on the controller to ensure that an update has not been missed. This communication between DCs can be scheduled. We will discuss scheduling later. After a DC receives a notification that an update is available, it makes a connection to the DC where the change has occurred to initiate replication. Data are not compressed during intrasite replication.

Intersite replication uses compressed data when the data are bigger than 50 KB regardless of the replication transport. The data are compressed to 10 to 15 percent of their original volume before they are sent. This means that the compression is very efficient. CPU cycles are required to compress and expand the replication data, but the overhead required in CPU cycles is more than compensated for by the reduction in data that passes across the network. Intersite replication can also be scheduled to occur at a particular time.

Connectivity between sites is usually not as good as with intrasite, and replication can take advantage of compression and scheduling. Scheduling can be defined to force replication to take place at specific times. Replication topologies are normally automatically generated. Table 3.5 describes intrasite versus intersite replication.

A number of important differences exist between intersite replication and intrasite replication.

The intrasite replication model has the following characteristics:

- Transport can only be RPC over IP.

- The generated replication topology is a ring between DCs with additional connections between DCs depending on the number of replication partners in the site and the presence of GC servers in the site

Table 3.5   *Intrasite versus Intersite Replication*

	Intrasite	Intersite
Transport	RPC	RPC or SMTP
Topology	Ring	Spanning tree
Schedule	Pull schedule	Availability and frequency schedule
Replication model	Notify and pull	Optional notification and pull
Compression	None	Full beyond 50 KB

(GC replication is discussed later). If a DC cannot reach another DC in the same site within three hops, then it will generate additional connection objects. This means that if there are seven DCs in a site, then a simple ring connecting all DCs will be generated because all DCs can reach all the other DCs within the three-hop limit. If there are more than seven DCs, additional connection objects will be created and the topology will look like a ring containing a star.

- The replication period uses a default interval of every five minutes configurable in the registry.

- Replication is based on a notify and pull model.

- Data are never compressed. This is because within a site bandwidth is by definition available.

The intersite replication model has the following characteristics:

- The transport can be either RPC or SMTP. Note, however, that SMTP transport can only be used when replicating the configuration and schema NCs, or when replicating from a DC to a GC that belongs to a different domain. This is due to Group Policy Objects. While GPO use File Replication Service (FRS), FRS under the hood uses DS-RPC and relies on the topology generated by the Active Directory. If no RPC connectivity is allowed, then GPOs cannot replicate to remote DCs.

- The topology generated will be a spanning tree, which, by definition, avoids creating any loop.

- Replication is based on a scheduled pull; however, notification can be enabled.

- The availability schedule controls when data are replicated between sites. By default intersite replication occurs every three hours; the minimum is every 15 minutes and the maximum is 10,080 minutes (or one week).

- Compression is enabled when data are bigger than 50 KB.

3.4 Replication topologies

The replication topology is a map of how information replicates between DCs. The topology is generated and maintained by a service running on every DC.

The replication topology allows DCs to find other replication partners. If a DC becomes unavailable—for example, because it is shut down—its replication partners will change the topology to allow replication to happen using an alternate route.

There is a replication topology per domain NC. The schema and configuration NCs, which have a forest-wide scope, share the same topology. For example, if we assume we have three domains in a forest, four replication topologies will be created, as follows:

- One each per domain NC

- One for the configuration and schema NCs

3.4.1 Knowledge Consistency Checker

The Knowledge Consistency Checker (KCC) is a service running on every DC. The role of the KCC is to generate and optimize the replication topology by creating connection objects between DCs.

By default, the KCC runs every 15 minutes. Administrators can trigger the KCC manually via the Active Directory Sites and Services snap-in. Administrators can customize the frequency for triggering the KCC in the registry.

3.4.2 Connection objects

A connection object is an authenticated communication channel used to replicate information from one DC to another DC. The properties of a connection object include the replication partner and the site it belongs to. The properties also define the transport that the connection object will use (RPC or SMTP) and a schedule that will be used for replication if the notification message is not received (we discuss replication schedules in more detail later). (See Figure 3.10.)

A connection object is a unidirectional connection from a replication partner. This means that there are always two connection objects between DCs in a site. Connection Objects are normally created by the KCC, but an administrator can also create them manually. If necessary, administrators can force replication to occur immediately over a specific connection object.

Replication can be forced by right-clicking a connection object in the Active Directory Sites and Services snap-in and clicking on the Replicate Now button.

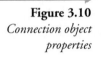

Figure 3.10
Connection object
properties

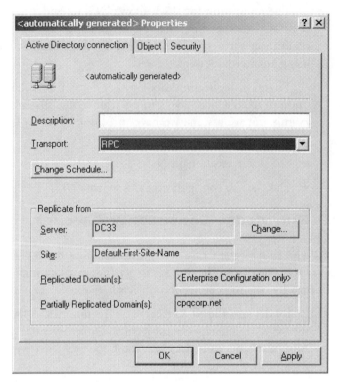

Another way to force replication is to use the resource kit tool Replication Monitor. Using this tool, it is possible to synchronize an entire NC. By doing this, Replication Monitor will trigger replication between all DCs containing the selected NC.

The connection object shown in Figure 3.10 was generated by the KCC. We can also see that DC is a GC and that it replicates the configuration and schema NCs as well as the partial information from domain cpqcorp.net.

If you create a connection object, the KCC will not manage it; you will need to delete it. This connection object is said to be explicit. The KCC only manages connection objects that it has generated, and it will not override manually created connection objects.

Connection objects are the most important components in a replication topology, because they enable information transfer from a DC to its replication partners. Connection objects show when replication happens (storing this information in the replication schedule) and they regulate the consistency of the Active Directory.

3.4.3 Connection object schedules

The process of replication within a site involves a notification from the source DC to its replication partners. This triggers the replication process. In the event of a missing notification, DCs will use a schedule to trigger replication by themselves. This schedule is defined at the level of the site and can be set to specify any hour in a week to replicate once per hour, twice per hour, or four times per hour, or it can be turned off. All the connection objects within a site will reflect the schedule defined for the site. This means that if you modify the site schedule, you are affecting all the schedules of connection objects managed by the KCC at the site. If you modify the schedule for a connection object that was generated by the KCC, then the KCC will no longer manage the connection object and you will need to manage it. If that is the case, the schedule of connection object, will take precedence over the site schedule.

3.4.4 Intrasite replication topology generation

When a new Windows 2000 domain is created and there is only one DC in the domain, no replication is necessary and none occurs. As soon as a second DC joins the network, the KCC generates the replication topology between the two DCs.

If the two DCs are in the same site, two unidirectional connection objects are created, as shown in Figure 3.11. These connection objects are mutually authenticated channels between the two DCs that allow them to replicate information. The replicated objects depend on the NC in which they belong. When two DCs connect for the first time, all NCs are replicated: the configuration, the schema and the domain to which the DCs

Figure 3.11
Joining a domain

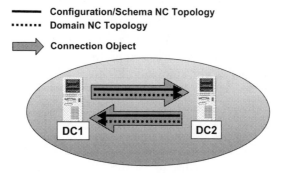

— Configuration/Schema NC Topology
······ Domain NC Topology
⇨ Connection Object

belong. Between DCs of different domains, only the configuration and schema NCs are replicated. In the case of a DC that is also a GC, the three NCs will be replicated. However, only a subset of the domain NC is replicated to a GC.

When additional DCs join the domain in the same site, the KCC service running on every DC will automatically create the required connection objects and avoid duplicate replication paths. In order to optimize the number of connections created, the KCC on each DC attempts to compute the required number of connections required for every DC at the site so that the number of hops between itself and any other DC at the site is three at the most.

Rings of replication

Let's assume we have a domain, *compaq.com*, and a site with one DC called DC1.

We run DCPROMO on a second server, DC2. DCPROMO is a wizard-based application, which allows the promotion of the standalone server to a DC. Using DCPROMO we configure DC2 as a replica of the *compaq.com* domain.

During the DCPROMO process, the KCC on DC2 creates a connection object and generates two replication topologies, one per scope (forest-wide and domain-wide). In Figure 3.11, the top line shows the configuration NC and schema NC replication topology, while the dotted line shows the domain NC replication topology. DC2 replicates the configuration, schema, and domain objects from DC1. Once the DCPROMO process is completed DC1 then generates connection objects from DC2 to replicate any operation performed on that DC.

We then boot a third server, DC3, and run DCPROMO to allow it to join the *compaq.com* domain as a replica.

As shown in Figure 3.12, DC3 then joins the domain after connecting to DC2. A question we may ask ourselves is why the initial connection for a new controller is not automatically made with the first controller in the domain? The DCPROMO utility is used to promote a server to be a DC. It is during the promotion process that the decision is made to contact a particular controller to retrieve information about the domain.

When DCPROMO runs on DC3, a query is performed against DNS. DNS then returns a list of all the DCs that belong to the *compaq.com* domain. After reviewing the SRV records for the *compaq.com* domain, DNS

Figure 3.12
*A third DC joins
the domain*

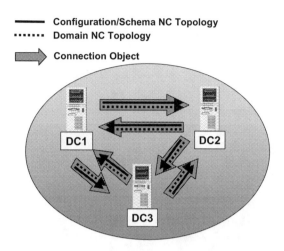

returns DC1 and DC2. DC3 will then contact the two DCs to find out which one is currently available. In our example we assume that DC2 responds faster.

DC3 then contacts DC2 and creates the connection object for the two topologies required for the schema/configuration and domain NCs. Replication is then performed and DC3 joins the domain.

DC2 will then create its own replication topologies using the updated information from DC3 and will notify DC1 that a new DC has joined the domain. DC1 learns about the new DC in the site (DC3) by replicating the configuration NC from DC2. DC1 and DC3 then create the connection objects necessary for replication to happen between each other.

Figure 3.13 illustrates what happens when a fourth DC is added to the domain. Essentially DC2 and DC3 now create connection objects to DC4.

The KCC service running on each DC constantly tries to optimize replication topologies. One rule is that if a DC cannot be accessed within three hops, an additional connection object will be created to reach that DC. This means that Active Directory replication uses a store-and-forward mechanism to disseminate information from DCs to other DCs. Replication partners will pull information from a particular DC and treat it locally, and then another DC (or hop) will replicate the same information and will be ready to disseminate it further. If, for example, we have eight DCs belonging to the same site, a DC in that configuration will not be able to reach all the other DCs within three hops and must create an additional connection object to each controller that it cannot reach.

Figure 3.13
*Additional
connection objects*

Configuration/Schema NC Topology
········· Domain NC Topology

Connection Object

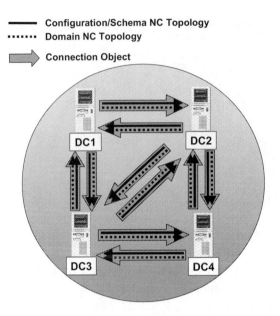

In our example (Figure 3.13), we have only four DCs, which means that any DC can reach any other DC within three hops. Therefore, when the KCC reviews the replication topology, it will conclude that the connection objects between DC3 and DC2 are not necessary, because sufficient replication paths exist without these connections. The KCC always attempts to create a ring of replication paths within a site. This implies that the KCCs on DC3 and DC2 will remove the connection objects pointing at each other, since there are other valid replication routes. This leaves us with two replication topologies forming a ring.

There will always be a maximum of two generated connection objects between two DCs—one per direction—additional connection objects could, however, be manually created by administrators. Multiple replication topologies will share the connection objects for replication purposes. (See Figure 3.14.)

We now create a child domain for the *compaq.com* domain, called *sales.compaq.com*, shown in Figure 3.15. We install a DC (DCA) of the child domain in the same sites as the other DCs belonging to the *compaq.com* domain. Once again, during the DCPROMO process, the new controller (DCA) queries DNS to find all the DCs belonging to the *compaq.com* domain and then contacts them to discover which one is available. Let's assume that DC2 from the *compaq.com* domain responds faster again.

Figure 3.14
*Optimized
connection objects*

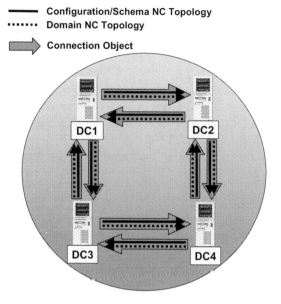

Figure 3.15
*Second domain
joins the forest*

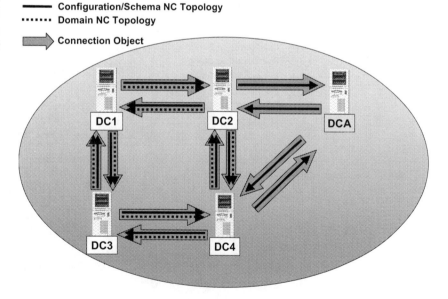

During the DCPROMO process, DCA creates a connection object for both the configuration and schema NCs. Note that the *compaq.com* domain NC connection is not created (Figure 3.15). This is due to the fact that a domain NC is replicated only within its own domain. DCA does not belong to the *compaq.com* domain; therefore, only a connection object for the forest-wide topology is created. DCA joins the forest and DC2 informs all the other DCs that a new child domain exists with a DC in the same site. The other DCs, or, more accurately, the KCCs running on the DCs, evaluate the situation and DC4 closes the loop by creating a connection object with DCA. DCA will do the same and create a connection object with DC4.

To complicate matters even further, we add a second DC in the *sales.compaq.com* child domain, DCB (Figure 3.16). During the DCPROMO process, DCB communicates with DCA and replicates the *sales.compaq.com* domain NC as well as the configuration and schema NC. DCA informs the rest of the forest that a new DC (DCB) has joined its domain. The KCCs once again evaluate the situation and optimize the topologies. Connection objects are created from and to DC4 and DCB.

During the optimization process, DCA and DC4 remove the connection objects between them. This is because the rings are available on an

Figure 3.16
*Multiple DCs in
child domain*

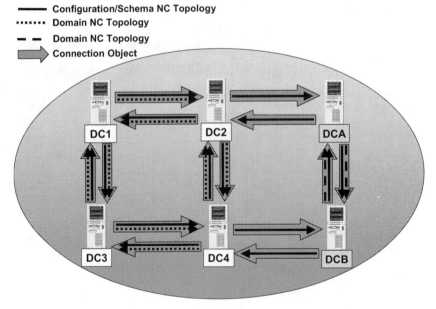

━━━ **Configuration/Schema NC Topology**
••••••• **Domain NC Topology**
━ ━ **Domain NC Topology**
▨▷ **Connection Object**

alternate route. As a result, we have created two domains, with three rings of replication, as follows:

1. One domain NC for *compaq.com*

2. One domain NC for *sales.compaq.com*

3. One schema/configuration NC for the entire forest

Global catalog replication

A global catalog (GC) is a special form of DC that holds read-only subsets of information about objects from all domains in the forest. Replication to form GCs implies that the domain NC is replicated within the forest; this is because GCs can belong to different domains. When generating a brand-new forest, the first DC in the root domain (the first domain in the forest) will be by default a GC. Administrators can, however, transform other DCs, even those belonging to other domains in the same forest, to GCs. In our example, DC1 is the default GC when creating the *compaq.com* domain.

If we take the example we have just been reviewing and assume that DC4 and DCA are GCs in their respective domains (instead of DC1), then we can see that the KCCs will extend the *compaq.com* and *sales.compaq.com* domain NC replication topologies to reach those GCs and replicate domain information across the domain boundaries. Domain NC information replication to GCs in the forest occurs in the same manner as between DCs of the same domain, except that the domain NCs are outbound to GCs in other domains and never inbound. This means that a DC can replicate information from the domain NC to a GC belonging to another domain; however, it cannot replicate *from* that GC for the same information. In our example, the result of the replication topology shows additional connection objects; these are created to be able to close the ring. In Figure 3.17, it's important to note the inbound connection objects created toward GCs and the replication topologies they contain. As shown in Figure 3.17, domain NCs reach GCs, but if the GCs have multiple replication partners, then other DCs belonging to a domain different from the GC (e.g., DC2) will not replicate their own domain NC from that GC.

For replication, the relationship between a DC and a GC is as follows:

- A DC replicates three NCs (the domain NC in which it belongs, the schema, and the configuration NCs); therefore, replication for a DC is the sum of the three NCs. The following equation shows that the

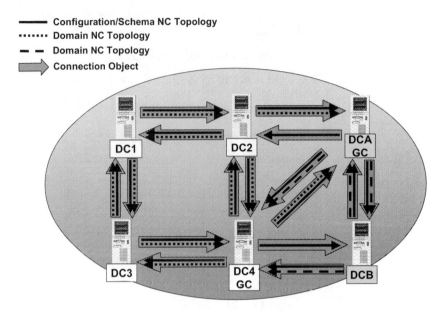

Figure 3.17
GC replication

replication involving a DC is affected by changes in any of its three NCs:

$$R_{dc} = NC_{domain} + NC_{schema} + NC_{configuration}$$

- Global catalog replication is equal to the replication of a normal DC if the two servers belong to the same domain and if there is only one domain in the forest. This is because a GC is also a DC in its own domain and as such has read/write access to the forest-wide NCs as well as the domain NC of its own domain. However, if the forest contains multiple domains, then each GC also replicates partial domain NCs from all other domains in the forest. A partial domain NC contains all the objects in the domain NC but only covers a subset of the attributes for each object. The decision whether to replicate an attribute to a GC is governed by the isMemberOfPartialAttributeSet property, which is set in the schema. If the property is set, the attribute is published to all GCs. Therefore, the difference between GC replication and DC replication can be represented as follows:

$$R_{gc} = R_{dc} + NC_{partial\ domain} * (n - 1)$$

where n = the number of domains in the forest

In the case of a forest with only one domain, there is no increased traffic generated by setting all DCs as GCs, because each controller in a domain replicates the full set of attributes for all objects and is demonstrated by the GC formula above, which would equate to $R_{gc} = R_{dc}$ when *n* equals 1.

If a site contains a GC, then it is most likely that it will be used for inter-site replication (and become the bridgehead server; BHS is discussed later). If that is the case, then all the DCs belonging to the same domain as the GC in that site can also be GCs. This is because there will always be one bridgehead server replicating information for one domain NC from a server at a different site, meaning that only one GC will perform intersite replication. The other controllers in the same site will use intrasite replication. GC replication with all GCs in the same site is always performed over RPCs, because a site is composed of a well-connected subset.

DCs cannot replicate domain NC data from GCs belonging to other domains. This is because GCs contain read-only replicas from all domains and are not authorities on these objects. Administrators cannot use GCs to modify the read-only replicas and therefore DCs cannot use GCs in the replication topology generation to replicate data from them.

3.4.5 Site topology

Fundamentals of site topology design

For Windows 2000, a site topology is a logical model layered on top of a physical network. Windows 2000 does not communicate with network routers to retrieve information from the OSPF tables about the network and its characteristics. This means that Windows 2000 does not attempt to detect the physical network and relies on the site topology for information about network availability and the cost of replication. The site topology is used by the KCC to generate the optimal path for information to replicate between DCs. (See Figure 3.18.)

The role of the Windows 2000 infrastructure architect is to model the site topology to accurately reflect the underlying network topology. As shown in Figure 3.18, there are three layers to consider when you design Windows 2000 sites, as follows:

1.   The physical network forms the bottom layer.

2.   The middle layer is the Windows 2000 site topology, which reflects the physical network.

3.   The Windows 2000 domain structure forms the top layer. Domains rely on the site topology for replication and should be designed to conform to that model. Replication restrictions may

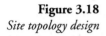

Figure 3.18
Site topology design

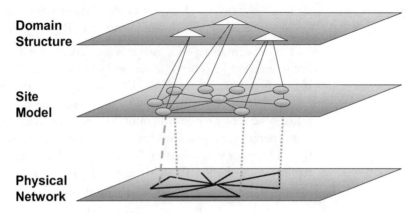

be a reason for splitting domains. In turn, the physical network may be responsible for imposing some restrictions on how replication is possible.

It's important to make a distinction between domain structure design and site topology design. Sites reflect the location of user communities, whereas domains contain objects. A domain is mapped to a site by placing a replica of the domain within the site. A site does not contain a portion of a domain. It contains the entire domain. Sites contain DCs and these are entire replicas of a domain. If a GC is placed in a site, then the entire Active Directory becomes available to the site. From a different perspective, if a site does not contain a DC or a GC it is essentially useless, since no objects are available within the site.

The site topology may affect the domain structure due to the available bandwidth required to perform replication. Ideally, given the scalability of the Active Directory, most companies could deploy just one domain in their enterprise. However, there are usually a number of reasons for a company to split domains. The network bandwidth used for Active Directory replication is one such reason. This could be the case if the number of objects in the Active Directory and the rate at which these objects change generate a lot of traffic. A fine-tuned site topology can help reduce the network traffic required for performing replication.

Site links

Intersite replication requires an explicit site link to be created. As the name indicates, a site link links two sites together. A site link represents a network connection between two sites.

A site link has a cost associated with it. The cost is used to determine how easily data can be replicated between sites. When multiple sites are linked together using site links, the KCC will use the cost and the site link availability schedule to determine which connection objects must be created between DCs to enable replication.

The KCC creates a spanning tree of connection objects between DCs at different sites. Spanning trees avoid loops being created between the sites.

A site is a collection of IP subnets with good connectivity, and a site link is a logical connection between sites. Site links must mimic the network and should be viewed as possessing similar characteristics to the underlying connection between the sites. In other words, a Site Link represents a WAN link.

It's important to make the distinction between connection objects and site links. Connection objects connect DCs and are generated by the KCC, or they can be created manually by administrators. Site links must be created by administrators and are used by the KCC to determine the cost and availability of a network for performing replication between two sites. If there is no site link between two sites, the KCC will not be able to generate the connection objects between the DCs belonging to the two sites. This will actually result in a number of error messages (error number 1311) logged in the event log.

Figure 3.19 illustrates the properties of a site link. The complete list of available sites appears on the left side. Administrators can select which sites are connected using this site link. In the illustration, the two available sites are selected.

A site link has an associated cost and an availability schedule, which are used as inputs for the KCC to generate or optimize the replication topology. Figure 3.20 shows the site link replication availability schedule.

The cost factor is a number between 1 and 32,767, which indicates the cost of replicating data from one site to another. The default value is 100 and the smaller the value, the better the network connectivity and the easier it is to replicate information across the link. The KCC uses the cost factor to generate and optimize replication topologies. Referring to Figure 3.19, we see that there are two sites: Valbonne and Seattle. The cost of replication is 100, and the link is scheduled to replicate every 15 minutes. The default replication frequency for a site link is 180 minutes; the minimum is 15 minutes and the maximum is 10,080 minutes (or one week).

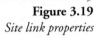

Figure 3.19

Site link properties

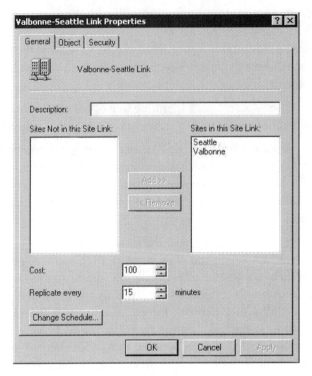

Figure 3.21 shows how the KCC computes the replication costs between sites. Basically the cost of every site link is added between two distant sites and the total cost is used to determine the best (cheapest) route.

In this example, given that it costs 1 for replication to go from the New York site to the Chicago site and it costs 8 to go from the Chicago site to Atlanta, replication from DC1 to DC3 costs 9, whereas replication between DC1 to DC4 has a cost of 10.

Using the store-and-forward mechanism, data are replicated from DC1 to DC2. However, on DC2 there are two possible paths to reach DC4: DC3 and DC5. The KCC on DC2 will opt for DC3 because the cost value is smaller. If DC3 becomes unavailable, then the KCC on DC2 will generate a connection object directly to DC4; this is because the sum of the cost of site link B and site link C is still cheaper than the sum of the cost of site link D and E. Cost is used to provide hints to the KCC about the speed of a network link. Bandwidth could be a factor, however, given that Windows 2000 doesn't see the underlying network and will not see firewalls. Cost can be used to avoid paths or to prefer a particular path versus another one.

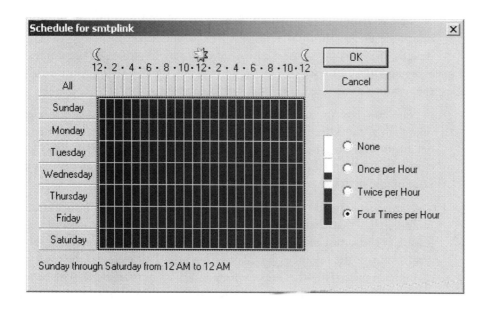

Figure 3.20   *Site link schedule*

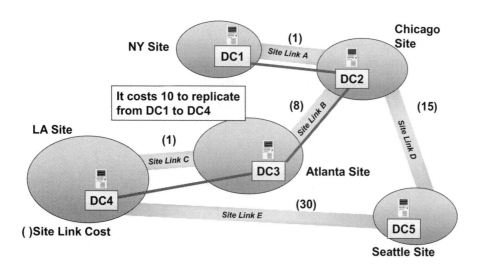

Figure 3.21   *Site link cost*

Cost is a number that by itself doesn't mean anything. The site topology design designates the different cost values and their meaning. In some designs, it is possible to use a cost structure to highlight leased lines, unreliable networks, or firewalls. The site topology designer will judge the state of the network to choose the right cost structure.

The cost has an additional role. When all the DCs in a site become unavailable, the DCs in the remaining sites will use the cost structure to determine the closest site for clients to connect. This feature is called site coverage. Without this feature, clients would connect randomly to remote DCs on the network.

It is possible to add multiple sites in a site link. What this means is that multiple sites that share the same cost and same availability schedule can belong to the same site link. The KCC will then treat these sites equally and create/manage the resource objects consequently. This could be the case, for example, between sites that are connected to the same backbone. The bandwidth will be the same between all sites and so will the connectivity. If the backbone becomes unavailable, then all sites will be affected. At Compaq, two distinct companies are providing the network forming the main ATM backbone, which means that if one network becomes unavailable, replication is still possible via the second one. In order to simplify management of replication between all the sites connected to the same backbone, it's simpler to put them in the same site link. The replication schedule will then be the same and any changes will affect all sites in the site link.

When adding multiple sites to the same site link, the KCC will create a virtual hub in the site link. The oldest site (or the site with the oldest GUID) will be selected to be that hub. The KCC will then generate a spanning tree from the hub to the spokes in the same site link.

Creating sites, site links, and defining IP subnets

To create a site topology there are a number of configuration objects that must be defined in a specific order. These management functions can be performed using the AD Sites and Services MMC snap-in. Figure 3.22 illustrates this snap-in and displays the site topology of Compaq's internal test forest:QTest.

To create a site, right click on the Sites container displayed in the AD Sites and Services snap-in and select the New Site button. A dialog box, shown in Figure 3.23, pops up. Sites must always be associated with a site link; however, when creating a site links, as shown in Figure 3.24, two sites are required. This looks like a chicken and the egg problem, but it's not.

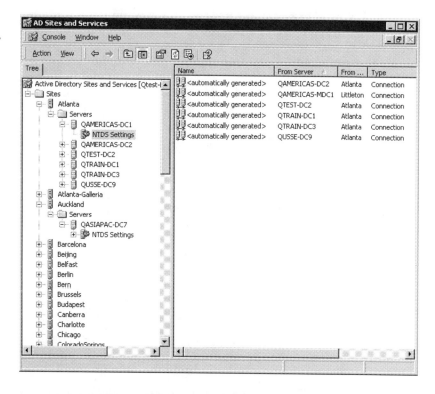

Figure 3.22
AD Sites and Services snap-in

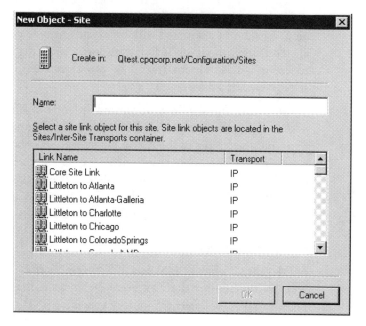

Figure 3.23
New Object – Site dialog box

Figure 3.24
New site link

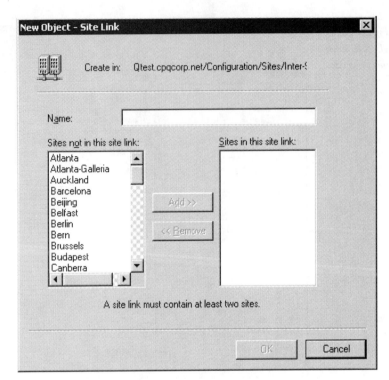

When creating a site for the first time, it can be associated with a built-in site link called DEFAULTIPSITELINK. Once multiple sites have been created, they can be associated with other site links. To create a site link, right-click on either the IP or SMTP transport, depending on whether you want to create a synchronous (RPC) or asynchronous (SMTP) site link, and select New Site Link.

Once sites and site links are created, in order to allow servers and clients to determine the site in which they belong, the IP subnets used by these systems must be created in the Active Directory and associated with the appropriate site. These subnets are created by right-clicking on the Subnets container and clicking on New Subnet. The Subnets container can be found in the Sites container in the Active Directory Sites and Services snap-in. Figure 3.25 shows the New Subnet dialog box.

Bridgehead servers

A bridgehead server (BHS) is a DC that performs replication operations with DCs in another site. Not every DC in a site is a BHS. Each site has a DC that takes the intersite topology generator (ISTG) role. The ISTG role

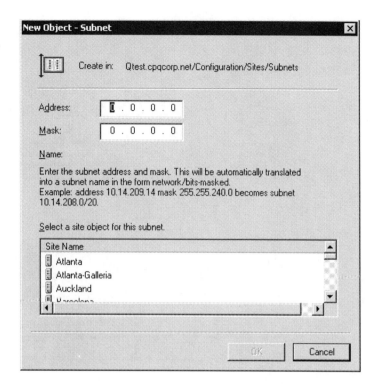

Figure 3.25
New subnet

reviews the list of available DCs in the site and determines the BHS. The ISTG role cannot be transferred like other operation master roles using management tools; however, administrators can use ADSI Edit to modify the interSiteTopologyGenerator attribute on the NTDS settings of the DC. All DCs in a site are eligible for this role.

The algorithm used by the DCs to determine which DC will be the ISTG role owner is that every DC evaluates the list of DCs present in the site, as defined in the configuration NC, removes any DCs that are not currently available, and orders the remaining DCs in the list by GUID. The DCs then select the first DC in ascending order of that list. In other words, the oldest DC in a site becomes the ISTG. Because every DC follows the same algorithm, all will agree on which machine is the ISTG role owner. The ISTG has the responsibility to communicate to the other DCs in the site about its role. Failing that, the other DCs will elect a new ISTG.

The ISTG will assign one BHS per transport per site and per domain NC. You can, however, create explicit connection objects between DCs located at different sites. By doing this you are implicitly adding more BHSs to the site. If a site contains two DCs belonging to two domains, the ISTG

Figure 3.26
DC properties

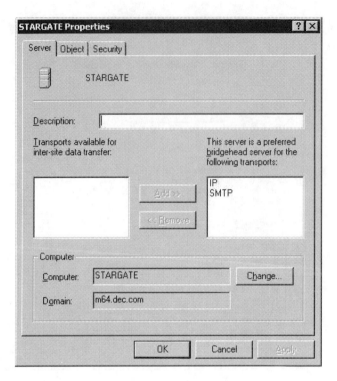

Figure 3.26
DC properties

will designate both of them as BHSs. A DC cannot replicate information belonging to another domain, so the two DCs will be assigned to replicate information to DCs in other sites belonging to their respective domains.

You can only have one BHS per transport per site. Therefore, you could designate one BHS for RPC and/or one BHS for SMTP. Figure 3.26 shows the properties of a DC in a domain. These can be found by right-clicking on a DC in the Active Directory Sites and Services snap-in, under the default site and servers folder.

Selecting RPC over IP and/or SMTP as transport for this DC means that it is enabled as a preferred BHS.

If you designate a set of DCs as preferred BHSs, the ISTG will not assign DCs that are not part of the preferred list. If, for example, a site has five DCs, and two of them are designated as preferred BHSs, the ISTG will use only those two DCs. If both of them are shut down, the ISTG will not use any of the remaining DCs because they are not part of the preferred list. In other words, by defining a preferred list of DCs, you are informing the ISTG that you want intersite replication to only occur using the DCs in that list.

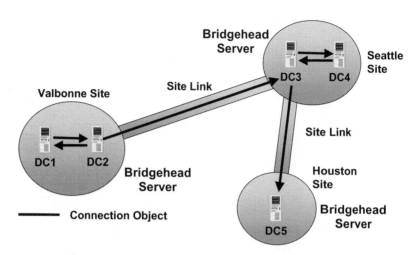

Figure 3.27
Intersite replication and bridgehead servers

Figure 3.27 is an illustration of bridgehead servers. We have three sites: Valbonne, Seattle, and Houston. In the Valbonne site we have two DCs: DC1 and DC2. These two DCs have created a ring of replication between them. DC2 is the BHS for the site. This means that an Administrator has defined the transport on this server for intersite replication.

At the Seattle site we have a similar configuration with two controllers: DC3 and DC4. DC3 is the BHS. Note that there is a connection object between DC2 and DC3 only. If one of these two servers happens to be unavailable, then replication to the Seattle site would fall back to use the remaining DC as a BHS. If the remaining server (DC4) is shut down, replication could still be working to the Houston site, since by default site links are transitive. This means that a connection object between DC2 and DC5 could be generated automatically if these BHSs couldn't find a suitable DC running at the Seattle site. Let's examine how this happens in more detail.

Site links implementation

Figure 3.28 illustrates four sites containing two domains. The controllers that belong to the *compaq.com* domain are indicated by shading, while those belonging to the *sales.compaq.com* domain are not shaded.

Connection objects are created by the various KCCs as site links become available between sites. Replication is working for the *sales.compaq.com* domain. A DC is available on every site, and a spanning tree replication topology is generated. If we focus on the *compaq.com* domain, we can see that replication is only working between DC2 and DC3. There are a number of reasons for this: The DC2 server in *compaq.com* cannot transport rep-

Figure 3.28
Site link
transitivity

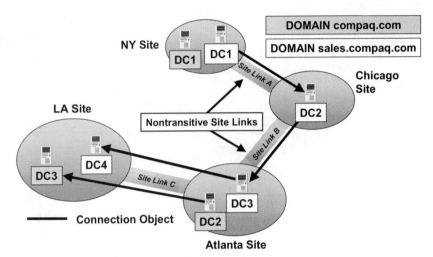

lication information for a domain other than its own. There are no direct site links between the NY and LA sites. The site links between NY and Chicago and Chicago and Atlanta are not transitive. In this case DC1 from the *compaq.com* domain cannot communicate to DC2 in the same domain.

There are three ways to fix the replication topology, as follows:

1. Place a DC for the *compaq.com* domain at the Chicago site. However, if there aren't any users for this domain, this would be an expensive operation and it wouldn't be worth it.

2. Change the setting of the site links to make them transitive.

3. Create an explicit site link bridge between site link A and site link B.

Let's see in more detail what a site link bridge is.

Site link bridges

A site link bridge connects two site links to form a bridge. Think of site link bridges as routers that connect two networks together. In replication terms, these networks are site links. A site link bridge connects site links together and creates a transitive and logical link between two sites that don't have an explicit site link between them. (See Figure 3.29.)

In the previous example, we have four sites. The NY site does not have an explicit site link to the Atlanta site. Using a site link bridge to connect those two site links enables the DC in the Atlanta site to generate the connection objects from the DC in the NY site and replication can be performed.

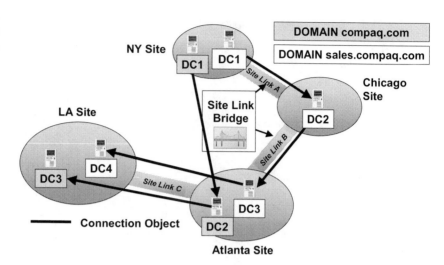

Figure 3.29
Site link bridge

In Windows 2000 site links transitivity is enabled by default, which means that site link bridges are not necessary in most cases. Site link transitivity can be disabled by selecting the properties of a replication transport. Transitivity affects all site links, which means that when it is turned off none of them is a transitive, and explicit site link bridges must created.

Site link transitivity is turned on by default in Windows 2000, because for most small to medium deployments of Windows 2000 it is acceptable and recommended to allow the KCC to find an alternate DC on any available site. On larger deployments, on the other hand, it is recommended to turn transitivity off. This may be the case when, for example, there is a firewall in the network and the generation of the replication topology must be controlled to avoid it. The replication topology, in this case, must be fine-tuned by creating explicit site link bridges to control the creation of the connection objects between sites.

Figure 3.30 shows the properties of the IP replication transport. Administrators can turn on site link transitivity by clicking on the *Bridge all site links* check box. This operation can also be performed for other transports.

Creating replication topologies

The following approaches can be used to create a replication topology:

- One option is to turn off the KCC entirely or partially (e.g., between sites) and manually create the connection objects between the various DCs. You can certainly attain total control, but if a server goes down, the KCC will not try to find an alternate route and an administrator would have to create a replacement connection object. In a large

Figure 3.30
*Bridging all site
links*

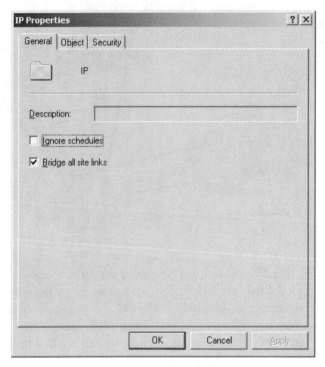

implementation the cost of managing the explicit connection objects
and monitoring all the DCs would be too high, so this solution is not
practical.

- Another option is to give the KCC information about the underlying
  network by creating a set of sites—site links with associated costs and
  availability schedule. The goal here is to reflect the constraints of the
  physical network and avoid replication during peak working hours.
  This is the most flexible and powerful scenario, because it allows
  administrators to fine-tune and optimize replication. Further tuning
  in this scenario could be achieved by turning off site link transitivity
  and creating specific site link bridges to allow transitivity and create
  redundant site links in specific cases. This scenario involves a careful
  design of the site topology.

3.5   Network topologies and site design

In this section we will review different network topologies and analyze the
consequences of different site designs. We will also look at redundant topologies and see how site link bridges can contribute to site designs.

3.5.1   **Hub and spoke topology**

A hub and spoke topology is composed of sites organized in multiple tiers, similar to a tree of sites. Figure 3.31 illustrates a typical hub and spoke topology, where the first tier contains one or more central sites connected to the sites in the second tier. The second-tier sites may be connected to a third tier and so on. Generally bandwidth becomes smaller as we descend to lower tiers. The goal of a hub and spoke topology is to centralize management. Replicated information should flow from one tier to another but not between tiers on the same level, except at the first level because this is where most bandwidth is available.

To achieve this, site links can be created between sites of different tiers. Site link transitivity can be turned on; however, the cost of every site link will dictate the generation of the connection objects. The cost is low between the site links of the top-level sites. The cost will then gradually become more important between the sites of the lower tiers. The result is that the KCC will always generate a connection object with the adjacent sites in the above tier. If, for example, the DC5 in the middle tier becomes unavailable, then the KCC on DC1 will generate a connection object directly from DC7; this is because the sum of the site links will always be lower between these two DCs.

Figure 3.31
Hub and spoke topology

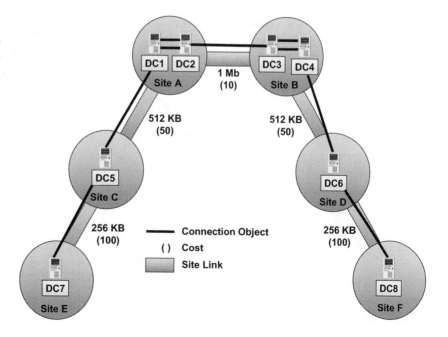

Replication will always flow from the lower tiers toward the top tiers and from there down again to other tiers. This configuration will work best when there is a central backbone with high bandwidth and multiple sites connected to it through slower links.

If, instead of creating a cost structure, we leave the costs to their defaults (100), we could achieve the same results using site link bridges. This is not the best solution; however, it helps understanding the role of site link bridges. In that case a site link bridge should be created between sites links at different levels. This will ensure that if a site in a middle tier doesn't have a DC capable of storing and forwarding the replicated information, the KCC will attempt to contact a site at the next level. Because the site link bridges will limit the visibility from the lower tier to the top tier, connection objects will never be generated between two sites of the same tier (except the first tier).

3.5.2   Ring topology

In the case of a ring topology, each site is connected to other sites forming a loop or ring, as shown in Figure 3.32. The advantage of a ring topology is that DCs in different sites are allowed to store and forward replicated infor-

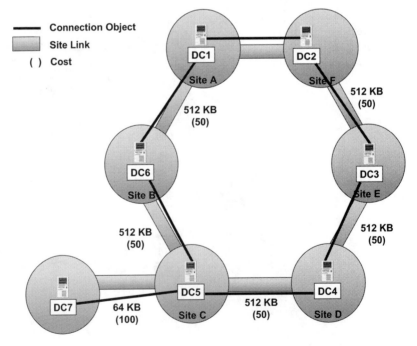

Figure 3.32
Ring topology

mation to the adjacent site. The information is routed around the ring simultaneously to reduce replication latency.

Generally a ring topology can be found when multiple sites are connected to the same backbone, such as multiple data centers connected to a corporate ATM link. The cost will be a constant since the connectivity is the same for all sites.

If a number of spokes are attached to the sites in the ring, then the cost of the links between the ring sites should be lower than the cost of the links between the ring sites and the spokes. In Figure 3.32, the cost of the ring site links is 50, while the cost of a spoke is 100. By maintaining a low cost for the site links connecting the ring sites, if the DCs of a site become unavailable, the DCs in the other sites will fall back using the next adjacent site in the ring. This is because the cost of reaching those sites will still be lower than reaching the spokes.

3.6   Replication challenges

3.6.1   Urgent replication

Even though priority cannot be assigned to the replication of different Active Directory objects, some objects replicate without considering the schedule. For example, when an account is disabled or locked out, this change must be replicated as quickly as possible to all DCs for obvious security reasons.

Another case of urgent replication is the assignment of RID pools, without which a DC cannot assign a SID when a new security principal is created.

LSA secrets such as computer passwords will also take advantage of urgent replication.

Urgent replication is available by default only between the DCs running in the same site. Urgent replication relies on notification to initialize replication.

Between sites, this mechanism can be enabled. In that case the replication process between sites follows the process used within a site: A notification is sent to a domain controller, which, in turn provides the NC, USN, up-to-date vector table, number of objects, and number of values. The information is prepared by the DC initiating the replication and pulled by the replication partner.

3.6.2 Password uniqueness

A management operation involving a password modification does not take advantage of urgent replication. However, this operation uses its own mechanism to ensure that passwords remain unique within a domain.

Windows 2000 DCs replicate password changes preferably to the Operation Master that owns the PDC emulator. Each time a DC fails to authenticate a password it contacts the PDC emulator to see whether the password can be authenticated there, perhaps as a result of a change that has not yet been replicated down to the particular DC.

3.6.3 Collisions

In a multimaster replication model, there is a possibility that a concurrent attempt might be made to update the same attribute at two different DCs. Such an update will result in the USN advancing on both DCs. When replication occurs, the changed data are sent to replication partners, which then have to deal with a replication collision. The attribute has been updated multiple times, but which update is most valid and what should the attribute contain after the collision is resolved?

The Active Directory resolves the conflict by comparing the version numbers for the two replication operations and the highest one wins. In case the version numbers are the same, the time stamps for the operation are evaluated and the latest time stamp found is used to determine the update that will be applied; any update with an earlier time stamp is discarded. All DCs in a domain have their times synchronized. In the unlikely event that the operation happened at two DCs at the exact same time, the GUIDs of the DCs are evaluated and the latest-generated GUID wins. This is, however, very unlikely. Generally, the last writer wins.

Another possible collision is the creation of an object in a particular OU on one DC. On a different DC an administrator could delete the very same object. In this case the object is created under a deleted OU. How is the collision handled? The delete operation on the OU is replicated throughout the domain and the object is moved to the Lost & Found container. Enabling the advanced features of the Active Directory Users and Computers snap-in will make this special container visible.

One more case of conflict can be generated for the creation of an object. An object creation name conflict resolution occurs when two administrators create two different user objects that have the same relative distinguished name (RDN) on two different DCs at the same time. Again, the time stamps and DC GUIDs are evaluated to resolve the conflict. However, in the case of a user, instead of deleting the oldest object, the RID associated with the user's SID is appended to the name of the object and both objects causing the conflict are kept.

When a collision happens in a network with a large number of DCs the two originating DCs will replicate their conflicting changes to every DC. Every DC will receive the conflicting replication request and will need to resolve it individually by evaluating the data of the originating DCs. All the DCs will follow the same resolution algorithm and will store the result of the conflict in the event log.

3.6.4 Replication topologies for a large number of sites

Large corporations have a large number of physical locations. Companies such as banks, financial institutions, and large conglomerates may have many branch offices. The KCC will need to evaluate the topology for all the NCs and take into consideration the number of sites where the DCs reside.

$$(D + 1) * \text{sites}^2 > 100,000$$

where D is the number of domains in the forest.

This formula deserves a bit of explanation. D is the number of domains in the forest. Each domain will have its own replication topology. In addition to that there is a topology for the schema and configuration NCs. The sites are squared, because each site will see every other site via site link transitivity.

If the above formula is true, then special considerations must be applied during the site topology design. For example, let's assume that we have a tree with four domains and an infrastructure with 200 sites. Applying the formula shows a result of 200,000. This is twice as much as the allowed configuration for the KCC to run in an optimum fashion. The site topology in this case must apply the following quidelines.

Reducing the visibility of the KCC

To reduce the visibility of the KCC and therefore reduce the number of sites that will take place in the formula, site link transitivity must be turned off. Specific site links bridges can be created to automate the replication topology generation for chunks of sites. The formula will apply within those site link bridges.

This technique works well in a multitiered hub and spoke environment where the second-level spokes are the hubs of the third-level spokes. Each level can be seen as a ring of sites. Site link bridges can be created to limit the visibility of the spokes to their closest hub.

Manual generation of topology

Another workaround is to turn off the KCC for intersite topology generation. You will then be responsible for generating and maintaining the BHSs and their connection objects. Generating redundant connection objects will be essential in this case. It's also important to understand that there is only one thread performing inbound replication, and DCs are configured by default to sustain ten concurrent connections to replication partners.

3.7   SMTP replication process

Basic SMTP functionality is included in Windows 2000 to allow servers to send information to each other across this transport. In terms of replication, SMTP can be used as a transport for replicating the schema and configuration NCs and for replicating a domain NC to global catalogs. A layer called intersite messaging (ISM) is used to load the asynchronous transport. The transport is defined as a property of the connection object between two replication partners. The connection object is created by either the KCC or by an administrator and relies on the transport defined in the site link. A connection object cannot use a transport different from than the one defined in the site link.

Transports are provided to Windows 2000 in the form of loadable DLLs. The only asynchronous transport shipping in Windows 2000 is SMTP, but vendors could write their own transport DLL and provide it in the following location in the Active Directory:

```
CN=Inter-Site Transports,CN=Sites,CN=Configuration,
DC=domain-name
```

The SMTP transport DLL uses Collaborative Data Objects (CDO), a collection of COM interfaces used to create and send SMTP messages. When Exchange 2000 is installed on a Windows 2000 server, the CDO library is updated to allow SMTP transport between mailboxes as well as servers, and interpersonal messaging is enabled. Any DC that wishes to use the SMTP transport must have IIS installed in order to activate the CDO library.

The SMTP transport requires that a certificate be issued to all DCs using SMTP. This is because SMTP uses certificates to mutually authenticate two replication partners. Certificates contain the public key assigned to the DC. A Certificate Server issues keys in pairs: the private and the public key.

The private key is used by its owner to sign a message. The recipient of the message can then use the public key stored in the certificate to authenticate the message. The mathematical relationship between the key pair ensures that only one private key can be associated to a public key. The recipient of the message must rely on a trusted Certificate Server to validate the public key as a key belonging to the owner. We will discuss public key infrastructures in a later chapter.

Once two DCs decide that they must replicate information, they perform a mutual authentication using certificates. Certificates are stored in global catalogs, and this allows DCs in different domains to locate the necessary certificates.

The sender DC prepares the data that must be sent to the target DC. It compresses the data if they are larger than 50 KB and requests the ISM layer to load the SMTP transport DLL. This DLL will sign the compressed data using the public key of the DC and will then use CDO to create and send the message to the target DC.

Figure 3.33
SMTP replication

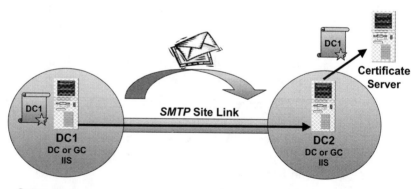

❶ **DC compresses data**

❷ **Passes data to ISM**

❸ **ISM loads CDO**

❹ **CDO loads SMTP transport**

❺ **SMTP signs data using DC private key and sends message**

❻ **Message is received by SMTP server**

❼ **SMTP contacts Certificate Server to verify authenticity of public key associated with certificate**

❽ **If OK, data are passed to ISM**

❾ **ISM passes data to DC to process**

The target DC receives the message and uses the Certificate Server to verify the validity of the signature. This is done by checking with the Certificate Server that the public key in the certificate is really the one issued to the sender DC. If this is the case, the target DC will process the message and the data will be replicated locally.

SMTP is designed to operate over extended and slow network links if required, which means that this transport can be used to replicate over slow and unpredictable network links. In fact, implementations could use public Internet links to transport messages from one intranet to another intranet.

Figure 3.33 shows the steps performed by the DCs using SMTP replication.

3.7.1   RPC versus SMTP replication

Choosing between RPC and SMTP

In a configuration where both the SMTP and RPC site links are available, the KCC will always prefer RPC replication to SMTP. For example, let's assume that we have two sites, each containing a GC. The two GCs belong to two distinct domains within the same forest. Replication between these GCs can use the SMTP transport for the schema/configuration NC as well as the partial domain NC.

If we create two site links, one using SMTP and one using the RPC transport, the KCC will generate a connection object for the RPC transport. This is the case even if the cost defined in the SMTP site is lower than the one defined in the RPC link. This is because the KCC will always attempt to use RPC if available.

To create an SMTP site link, explicit connection objects must be created between sites that are not connected with an RPC site link. If an RPC link is added between two sites that are already replicating using the SMTP transport, then the DC will stop using the SMTP connection and generate an RPC connection.

SMTP replication should be used only in specific environments where bandwidth is scarce or connectivity is unpredictable.

Security differences

While SMTP replication takes advantage of digital signatures for protecting the messages and avoiding the possibility of tampering with them, RPC replication does not use digital signatures. Connection objects are authenticated channels; however, if you need to improve further the replication confidentiality and integrity you can consider using IPSec. IPSec provides transport security between systems. The IP packets transmitted between DCs are then encrypted and authenticated.

One of the advantages of SMTP replication is that is can be used through firewalls, because e-mail messages are usually allowed to use a specific open port. RPC, on the other hand, is using a range of ports to perform replication. Going through a firewall then becomes problematic, because network administrators are very hesitant to open ports on a firewall.

IPSec can be a solution to allow replication to be performed through a firewall. A tunnel mode IPSec rule can be defined between the two DCs that are separated by a firewall. The tunnel will use a specific port and will encapsulate the original packets (and their destination ports) in other packets. This allows replication to be secure and control the ports used in a firewall. Using IPSec, the two DCs can be authenticated using a certificate, therefore achieving the same level of security provided by SMTP replication.

3.8 File Replication Services

The File Replication Service (FRS) is the Windows 2000 replacement for the NT4 LM replication service. FRS is used to replicate files and folders between domain controllers and member servers. It enables clients to download critical files from multiple locations. The file system folder dedicated to FRS is called the System Volume (SYSVOL); it is located in %systemdrive%\winnt\sysvol. As with NT4 LM replication, FRS runs as a separate system service, it is started by default on domain controllers, and it has to be started manually on member servers.

FRS is fundamentally different from LM replication.

- FRS uses, like Active Directory, a multimaster replication model; LM replication used a single-master replication model.

- FRS is network topology–aware or, in Windows 2000 terminology, site-aware. LM replication was not network topology–aware. For SYSVOL replication, FRS uses the same replication topology as Active Directory. It also reuses Active Directory's replication topology generator, the KCC. As a consequence, FRS uses the same concepts: sites, site links, site bridges, and connection objects provided by the site topology design. This also means that FRS replication between sites can be scheduled. Contrary to Active Directory replication, FRS information replicated between sites cannot be compressed.

- FRS uses a different replication model, where only the changes (the unit of change is a file) are replicated. LM replication used a plain push-pull model that replicated everything at each replication cycle, from one side to the other.

- FRS replicates not only files and folders, but also the file and folder attributes (such as ACLs). LM replication replicated only the stripped version of files and folders.

- FRS is a multithreaded application; LM replication was single-threaded. Overall, multithreaded applications have higher performance.

Some of the Windows 2000 key technologies, such as GPOs and DFS, are build on FRS; both use it to replicate their file system–based information among domain controllers. GPOs use SYSVOL and FRS to store and replicate the GPO configuration stored in the GPT. DFS uses FRS to replicate information between multiple replicas in the same replica set. Of course FRS can also replicate other information—for example, the Netlogon folder, or any other folder you set up in the SYSVOL.

3.9   Replication registry settings

3.9.1   Replication priority

Replication can be tuned using registry settings. By default the registry settings are set for an optimum replication:

```
HKEY_LOCAL_MACHINE\SYSTEM\CurrentControlSet\Services\
NTDS\Parameters
```

The following keys can be used to modify the default behavior of Active Directory replication: Control the priority used by the replication thread. This is more interesting in a multi-CPU environment where a CPU could be dedicated to processing replication data, as follows:

- Replication thread priority high set to 1. If not set or set to 0, this gives the replication thread a low priority.

- Replication thread priority low set to 0. By default this value is set to −1, which simply means that the key should be ignored.

3.9.2 Replication packet size

Tune packet sizes and number of objects per packet for each type of replication: intrasite RPC, intersite RPC, and intersite SMTP. The values are as follows:

- Replicator intrasite packet size (objects)

- Replicator intrasite packet size (bytes)

- Replicator intersite packet size (objects)

- Replicator intersite packet size (bytes)

- Replicator async intersite packet size (objects)

- Replicator async intersite packet size (bytes)

Synchronous replication computes packet size dynamically, to best use of available system memory. Objects/packets start at 100 for a 100 MB or smaller server and increase to 1,000 for servers of 1 GB or more.

In term of bytes sent, 100 MB or smaller servers send 1 MB; 1 GB or larger servers send 10 MB. Asynchronous packets are fixed at 100 objects and 1 MB.

3.9.3 Replication latency

Notification

Replication latency can be adjusted by setting the following values:

- Replicator notify pause after modify (secs) to control the number of seconds to wait after a modification occurs on a DC before notifying the first replication partner.

- Replicator notify pause between DSAs (secs) to control how much time the replication partner will wait to notify the next replication partner in the replication topology.

Replication TCP/IP port number

Directory replication uses dynamically mapped ports. However, the port number can be statically assigned by editing the following registry key:

```
HKLM\System\CurrentControlSet\Services\NTDS\Parameters\
TCP/IP Port
```

3.9.4 Knowledge consistency checking

Triggering the KCC

The following registry setting can be used to set a different check interval
for triggering the KCC:

```
HKLM\System\CurrentControlSet\Services\NTDS\Parameters\
Repl topology update period (secs)
```

Logging when KCC is running

It is possible to log in the event log when the KCC is started and when it
has completed the generation or evaluation of the replication topology. The
registry key is:

```
HKEY_LOCAL_MACHINE\System\CurrentControlSet\Services\
NTDS\Diagnostics
```

The key value to set is 1 Knowledge Consistency Checker with a value
of 3. If this value is set, then the KCC will log two events, as follows:

1.   Event 1,009, which will be logged when the KCC is started.

2.   Event 1,013, which is logged when the KCC is terminating.

3.10 Replication tools

3.10.1 Age of directories

One of the problems with Active Directory replication topologies or any
large directory topology is that it's very hard to see the big picture. As sites
are added and linked to other sites, the DCs at those sites start creating connection objects with DCs at other sites.

Most of the tools available today provide information for single servers
and their immediate replication partners, but none is really showing the
entire topology in a single view.

Because of this, during the past months I have been working on a mid-
night project: a tool that allows viewing the site topology in a graphical fashion and viewing it entirely—that is, both intrasite and intersite topologies.

The tool is nicknamed "Age of Directories" (AoD). The idea of the tool
came from watching my ten-year-old son, Alexandre, play the Microsoft
game Age of Empires, a strategy game where different civilizations make
war with each other while building their infrastructures and advancing

technologically. Alexandre was using the map editor provided in the game to build his own world. I thought that a similar approach would be very appropriate for viewing Windows 2000 infrastructures, so I built a map engine performing very similar functions. Well, I omitted the soldiers and war engines—even though sometimes they would be very appropriate.

AoD provides a world in perspective and is capable of retrieving configuration information from a DC via ADSI. Using that information, it creates the graphical representation of sites, site links, DCs, GCs, and the connection objects linking them.

The tool also allows filtering out distinct naming contexts, has zoom-in/zoom-out functions, and allows saving a snapshot (view of a topology) to a file. The snapshot can later be refreshed with the latest information. To do this AoD reconnects to the Active Directory via ADSI and downloads the latest information

AoD also allows you to manipulate the objects: Sites and DCs can be dragged and dropped in other locations in the map. Connection objects are Bezier curves, which can be resized/reshaped. This is particularly useful

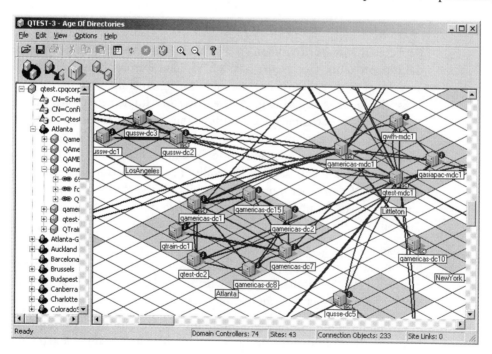

Figure 3.34   *Age of Directories*

when there is a DC crossing a connection object between two other DCs. Using curves to display connection objects allows shaping the replication topology so that everything can be viewed simultaneously. Double-clicking on DCs will connect to the systems to retrieve further information, such as the version of Windows 2000 they are running, status information, and more. (See Figure 3.34.)

At the time of this writing, Compaq Computer Corp. has not decided what to do with the tool. I maintain AoD as a spare-time hobby and have plans for the next version of Windows 2000.

3.10.2   Replmon, RepAdmin, DSASTAT, and DCDIAG

Troubleshooting Active Directory replication may not be an easy task without the help of some tools. The most important tools are the following:

- Replmon and RepAdmin
- DSASTAT
- DCDIAG

Replication Monitor and RepAdmin

Replication Monitor (replmon) is a powerful monitoring tool provided in the support tools. (See Figure 3.35.) The main features of replmon are to provide up-to-date information and monitoring capabilities for one or more DCs. Replmon is key in large Active Directory implementations, since it can provide important data concerning the status of specific replication topologies, trust relationships, and groups policy objects. While replmon is capable of detecting replication errors, it can also be used to synchronize entire naming contexts and has the ability to collect performance data of a particular DC. Another interesting capability is the ability to display replication metadata for objects. This is useful when troubleshooting conflicts or checking whether or not specific values are up-to-date.

Replmon is capable of providing group policy objects replication status by comparing the version of the local GPOs to the versions provided by SYSVOL. Finally, another interesting feature is the ability to check the servers that host the operation master roles.

While replmon uses a graphical user interface, RepAdmin is a command line tool. RepAdmin provides a subset of the functionality of replmon. Repadmin is more suited to scripts automating monitoring tasks. Similar to replmon, RepAdmin can be used to synchronize naming contexts and retrieve the replication status of DCs.

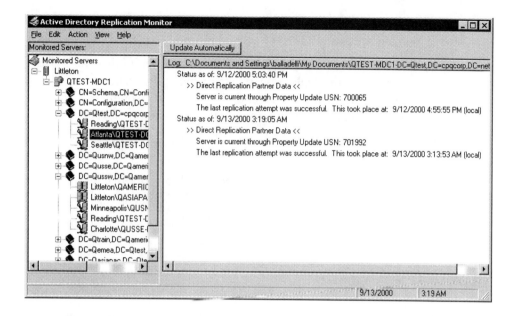

Figure 3.35   *Replication Monitor*

DSASTAT

DSASTAT performs tests and returns naming context differences between DCs. DSASTAT is a command line tool that determines differences between servers by comapring the following information:

- Size of database

- Number of objects

- Size of objects

- Attributes per object

If DSASTAT is used to check the validity of GCs, it will verify each domain partition hosted on the server against the original domains. This is an interesting tool that can be used when a corrupted DC is suspected.

DCDIAG

DCDIAG performs several tests on DCs to verify that they perform functions correctly and will report any error. DCDIAG focuses on DC functions such as the following:

- Explicit trust validation and replication. This test verifies the validity of explicitly created trust relationships and their replication status within the domain. DCDIAG will not verify Kerberos trusts; it's recommended that NETDOM be used instead.

- Topology integrity and replication. These tests verify that the DC is connected to the replication topology and verify that replication is performed normally. If replication is late or disabled an error will be displayed. DCDIAG will also check the BHSs and the ISTG.

- File replication services. This test verifies that the FRS service is available.

- DNS record generation. This is performed to verify that all resource records have been correctly generated on the DNS server.

- LDAP connectivity. This test checks that the server can be connected via LDAP.

3.11   Summary

The design of a fine-tuned replication topology is key when architecting a Windows 2000–based infrastructure aimed at large enterprises. The Active Directory is already used by a number of applications, including the version of DNS provided with Windows 2000 to store its data. This uses the replication mechanism to ensure that other DNS servers receive updates.

The Platinum version of Microsoft Exchange Server uses the Active Directory to store information about mailboxes and servers.

All other Microsoft BackOffice applications are likely to use the Active Directory after they have been upgraded for Windows 2000.

Customer solutions can also integrate their data with the Active Directory. Active Directory–enabled applications can modify the schema to add their own object classes. Instances of these classes will replicate using the same replication topology already in place.

Because Windows 2000 and many applications depend on the Active Directory, the replication topology must be carefully planned to provide the foundations for disseminating potentially large amounts of information. Planning for the deployment of the Active Directory is a critical part of any Windows 2000 implementation project.

4

Database Sizing and Design

4.1   Introduction

One of the major benefits of migrating to Windows 2000 is the ability to consolidate servers. Consolidation is about reducing the number of domains and reducing the number of servers and DCs. The trend in Windows 2000 designs is fewer but larger servers. The rationale behind consolidating servers is to reduce the hardware costs as well as management and troubleshooting costs. In other words, the goal is to reduce the total cost of ownership.

Understanding the Active Directory database is an essential part of the Windows 2000 design and particularly its consolidation efforts. The whole process of consolidation involves sizing DCs and GCs for large organizations with the goal of centralizing servers as much as possible. During this process, particular attention is paid to the choice of hardware and storage for these servers. The trend in scalable designs is to separate the server sizing and the storage design. This greatly simplifies the approach. In the server design, the CPU and memory considerations are addressed. In the storage design, the I/O subsystem and I/O performance are addressed.

This chapter reviews the Active Directory database architecture, explains the I/O patterns of the Active Directory, and discusses how the database works. We will then put into practice lessons learned in terms of optimization and storage design and go through the steps of creating, populating, and searching a very large Active Directory domain. We will review the tests and steps we perform when we create an Active Directory domain containing more than 100 million objects.

4.2 Active Directory storage architecture

4.2.1 Extensible storage engine

To create and maintain a large implementation of the Active Directory, it is important to understand how the Active Directory database works and what happens when an object is created. Understanding how the database works is key to tune it for optimum performance.

The AD store is based on the Extensible Storage Engine (ESE). This is based on the same database engine that is shipped with Microsoft Exchange. The ESE is not the Microsoft Jet database, but a variant called Jet Blue.

There are a number of reasons for Microsoft to choose the ESE as the database engine for the Active Directory. These include the following:

- Scalability—Microsoft Exchange already uses this database and it is not uncommon to see 100-GB databases deployed at customer sites.

- Performance—If well tuned, the database is quite fast and can handle enterprise requests very well.

- Recovery—This is the most important reason. In case something goes wrong—a disk crashes, the system crashes, or the software crashes—the ESE allows the recovery of the database into a usable state.

The AD storage architecture is composed of multiple layers, as shown in Figure 4.1. The top layer is formed by a number of APIs to allow integra-

Figure 4.1
AD database architecture

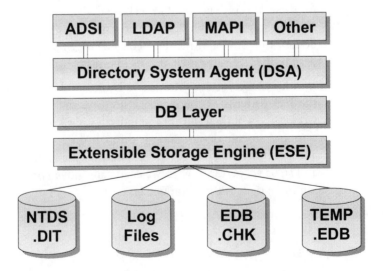

tion or applications with the Directory System Agent (DSA). This is the directory layer, which handles all access to the ESE engine through a database (DB) layer.

The DSA handles the hierarchical namespace of the OU and other containers in the AD. The ESE layer handles a flat representation of the namespace via a set of tables and stores these tables in the ESE files. The role of the DB layer is to manipulate the hierarchical representation of the objects into a flat format, which can then be stored as tables in the ESE.

The ESE is composed of multiple files. These are as follows:

- NTDS.DIT is the directory store. This is the actual database where the Active Directory objects reside.

- EDB log files contain objects from transactions. These objects may not yet have been saved in NTDS.DIT. The ESE uses these files, called *transaction logs*, to secure information on disk.

- EDB.CHK, or the checkpoint file, contains the current transaction state and is used when restoring log files. Information stored in this file indicates the latest transaction that has been saved in NTDS.DIT and can be used in a restore to reconstruct the database to its original state by indicating the latest transaction from the log files that were saved.

- TEMP.EDB contains the transactions in progress while a new log file is being created. Transaction logs in the Active Directory have a fixed size of 10 MB. Once this size is reached, a new transaction file is created. While the new file is being created, if there are incoming operations, they are saved in this file.

- RES1.EDB, RES2.EDB. These files have a total size of 20 MB. They are used only in case the disk is filled up. This allows an administrator to be informed that the disk holding the transaction logs is almost full while the services remain available. An administrator can then perform a backup of the transaction logs on the drive, causing their deletion by the system.

4.2.2   I/O patterns for the ESE

The files used by the ESE are fundamentally different. To understand their differences we need to look at their I/O patterns. The I/O pattern is a combination of multiple factors, including the I/O size and how the database is accessed. To adapt a storage solution for the Active Directory and tune it to increase performance, it's important to understand the I/O pattern of these files. This is because, depending on the I/O pattern, a particular tuning option will be used for the storage solution. Using the wrong tuning setting can result in a loss in performance. When building Active Directory storage, this is the key knowledge that allows choosing the settings for the various AD storage files in order to optimize access, and therefore performance, appropriately.

The I/O pattern for NTDS.DIT is the following:

- NTDS.DIT is a database that is normally used for read-mostly operations. Active Directory normal operations are 70 percent to 90 percent of reads.

- Each record stored in the database is exactly 8 KB.

- Access to the database is done asynchronously. This means that a write operation will return immediately; however, the caller does not know immediately if the operation was successful or not.

- Access is performed in a multithreaded way. This means that multiple threads can access the database to read and to write data. When putting in perspective the multithreaded and asynchronous access to the Active Directory, it's clearly a very scalable design that was adopted. Threads must perform tasks very quickly to scale to allow several hundred concurrent accesses. They are created to perform a specific task very quickly and once done they can perform another task and respond to the queries of another client.

- Data are saved randomly in the database. This means that if an object composed of multiple large (bigger than 8 KB) attributes must be retrieved, then the values of these attributes are spread in the database and are not sequential.

The I/O pattern for the log files is the following:

- The log files are intended for write operations only

- Each record stored in the database is exactly 8 KB, similar to NTDS.DIT.

- Writes are synchronous. This means that the caller will wait until the operation is completed and will then know the result of the operation.

- Access is performed by a single thread, which means only one write operation is in progress at any time. If the LSASS needs to perform multiple write operations, it must queue them and wait for the current one to complete.

■ Access to the data is sequential, which means that the data are stored contiguously in the log file.

4.2.3 Active Directory transaction logs

Logging is the action of saving data in a log file before it is saved in NTDS.DIT. Data are written to the log file and to a cache in memory simultaneously. This is done as an atomic operation or transaction to ensure commitment from both sides that the data are safe before saving these data in NTDS.DIT.

Figure 4.2 shows a write operation that is sent to LSASS.EXE via one of the APIs supported by the Active Directory. When, for example, an administrator creates an object in the Active Directory, such as a user or a contact, the request is sent via one of the APIs to the LSASS process. This process maintains the Active Directory.

Once LSASS has received the request it passes the write operation to the DB layer, which in turn transforms the data to a format understandable by the ESE. The write request is executed in the following steps to ensure that the data remain secure while these data are saved to NTDS.DIT:

1. LSASS receives an operation that involves a write operation to execute.

2. The ESE generates a transaction and saves the data in a memory block. This is the cache of the log files.

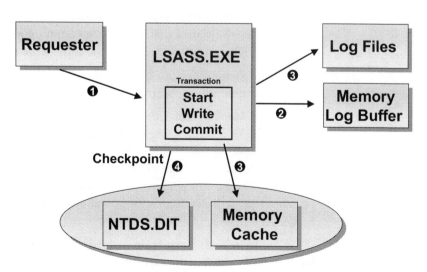

Figure 4.2
Write operations in the Active Directory

3. Two operations are then performed atomically. This means that if one of the operations aborts, then the entire transaction is aborted and an error is returned to the caller of the operation.

The first operation consists of saving the data in the memory cache of NTDS.DIT. The second operation consists of saving the data in the transaction logon files. As soon as both operations acknowledge that they have successfully achieved their tasks, the operation as a whole is committed.

LSASS is a multithreaded program, and operations are not instantly saved in NTDS.DIT. Every once in a while, LSASS checks the pages that haven't been saved but are stored in its memory cache and will save them. In case the system crashes and LSASS wasn't able to save the pages in memory, once rebooted it can automatically recover the pages because the same information was securely placed in the log files. Windows 2000 disables the cache on drives where the Active Directory is installed. This allows LSASS to know when the data are actually safely stored on disk.

Logging is the fundamental technology underneath the ESE. The goal of logging is to be able to recover the database in case of the following:

- Power failure
- Disk crash
- Software crash
- Any other corruption

The goal of logging is to recover the data in a consistent state. To do so, the ESE uses the transactions to ensure commitment that the data have been correctly saved before discarding the copy in the log buffer in memory.

ESE transaction logs can be set into two modes of operations: circular logging and noncircular logging.

Circular logging limits the number of log files that are created. By default, when circular logging is enabled, 20 log files are created. When the twenty-first log file must be created, the first one is deleted. This number can be modified in the registry. One of the advantages of circular logging is that storage size is under control. For 20 log files, a maximum of 200 MB are allocated on disk. Circular logging is the default and the recommended mode.

When noncircular logging is enabled, files are created on an as-needed basis; as long as there is storage available, new files are created. Noncircular log files are removed when they are successfully backed up. Windows 2000 is configured to use circular logging by default. While for Exchange a backup operation cleans the transaction logs, Active Directory cleans the log files every 12 hours. This is known as the garbage collection interval. This means that backup procedures must take into consideration that rolling transactions forward to restore a failed database may not be a viable solution. For this reason, it's important to keep the Active Directory available by adding multiple DCs per domain. As long as a DC remains available, the Active Directory is up and running. A restored DC from tapes will finish to synchronize by replicating the missing data from one of the DCs in the domain. Therefore, a best practice in a production environment is to have at least two DCs per domain. The DCs can be configured in the following way:

- One DC for the infrastructure master. This DC can also be configured as the RID master.

- One replica DC configured as the PDC emulator.

The two DCs are the minimum per domain; however, in a large environment, it is often recommended partitioning the physical layout of the Active Directory into multiple sites. In that case, it is good practice to place at least two DCs per site. If the sites have an Exchange 2000 server or if the network connection to a remote site is unpredictable, then it is also advised to place a GC there. The reasoning behind placing a GC next to Exchange 2000 is due to the great dependency of Exchange to access information stored in the GC—namely, the address book. If the connectivity to a remote site containing a GC is uncertain, then having a local GC at the site is also a good practice. GCs are required during the authentication process.

4.3   I/O fundamentals

4.3.1   Data rate

Another important aspect required for tuning the storage is to understand the data rate requirements for the Active Directory. The data rate is the speed at which the data are transmitted and is the ratio between the number of I/Os per second versus the size of these I/Os.

Figure 4.3 compares different data rates and shows the amount of megabytes per second that are required by the Active Directory during operations. The figure puts data rates and request rates in perspective. On the right side, the lowest curves are 1 KB and 2 KB for SQL, 8 KB for ESE I/Os, 16 KB (or even 32 KB) for data warehousing, and 64 KB for video on demand.

Figure 4.3
Data rates

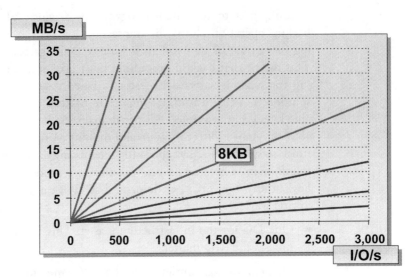

Figure 4.3 shows that for 2,000 8-KB I/Os, there is an actual data rate of less than 12 Mb/s. Note that an old SCSI-2 narrow bus could service this type of data rate. This means that the Active Directory does not use a large bandwidth for I/O operations. This implies that a storage solution providing large I/O bandwidth is not appropriate for Active Directory storage. In order to understand this in more detail, we need to look at some I/O performance principles.

4.3.2   I/O performance

How is it possible to use the I/O pattern information gathered above to improve the performance of a server? To address this question, we need to step back and look at some I/O fundamentals.

Figure 4.4 shows a curve that represents the response time generally observed on a single disk, but it could be a controller or a volume; only the scale changes.

Unlike CPUs, drive speeds haven't been progressing as fast. It's true that if we compare the first drive that shipped in 1956 and the latest drives that shipped in 1999 we see that we went from a mere 5-MB storage to 50 GBs—that's 10,000 better. However, in terms of speed, while progression was significant, it wasn't accelerating as fast as CPU speeds. In other words Moore's Law does not apply to storage.

When a request is sent to a single disk I/O, it returns in 12 ms for the old 7,200 RPM drives and 8 ms for the latest 10,000 RPM drives. This is a

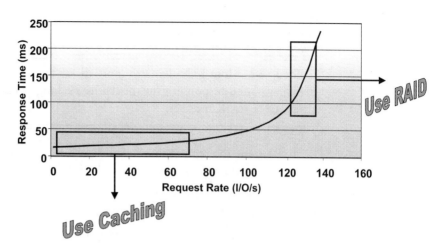

Figure 4.4
I/O performance cache and RAID

number that improves every year—but not dramatically. This number covers the rotation of the platters, the head seeking, the data transfer rate, and assumes that there is no I/O queue (queue lengths are discussed in the following text).

As the demand of I/O increases, each of these I/Os takes longer to execute and they grow in an exponential curve. This is primarily due to queuing. A spindle (or drive) can only accommodate a certain number of I/Os. When there are more I/Os than the drive can sustain, the I/Os are put in a queue. This queue is called the *queue length*. High queue lengths cause long response times.

This helps you tailor your solution to your problem. If you need to satisfy a greater number of I/Os in a reasonable response time, your solution is to use RAID's striping technology. That increases the number of spindles and, globally, improves the capacity of the volume to service more I/Os per second.

If the response time is your concern, caching is the solution. By adding memory to the controller, response time is decreased. That can help turn a 12-ms I/O into a 2-ns I/O. The paroxysm of caching is the solid-state disk, which has as much memory as storage. It has fast response time and is expensive.

As mentioned, Windows 2000 turns caching off on drives where Active Directory is installed. Some RAID controllers support caching in a way that is transparent to Windows 2000, and the best controllers protect the cache with batteries in case there is a power failure. Turning caching on greatly increases the risk of corrupting the Active Directory storage unless the battery system is properly set and maintained. We will return to caching and batteries later in this chapter.

Golden rule: More I/Os demand more disks sharing the load by working together; faster response time demands caching, because memory will always be faster than drives.

To illustrate the request rate versus capacity approach, review this simple example: to store and use 360 GB worth of data. What are the alternatives?

At the top of Table 4.1, you have the 47-GB disk drives that come in a form similar to the 23 GB, at approximately the same performance.

We need 16 23-GB disk drives to hold a 360-GB database and deliver 1,120 I/Os (at a 70 ms response time).

At the other extreme, if we use 2.1-GB disk drives we need 172 spindles, and combined they deliver 17,200 I/Os. Perhaps this is extreme, but a solution is going to occur between these two extremes, depending on the application.

Given the I/O pattern of the Active Directory, to increase the I/O requests it's important to have as many spindles working together as possible. In other words, the size of the drives does not matter; the number of drives is the key for Active Directory performance.

Table 4.1   *Number of Spindles to Improve I/Os per Second*

Drive (GB)	Form Factor	Number of Spindles	I/Os per Drive	Total I/O per Second
47	5 1/4	8	70	560
23	5 1/4	16	70	1,120
18	3 1/2	20	100	2,000
9	3 1/2	40	100	4,000
4.3	3 1/2	84	100	8,400
2.1	3 1/2	172	100	17,200

Redundant Arrays of Independent Disks

Redundant Arrays of Independent Disks (or Drives) (RAID) is a technology that spreads data across multiple drives to increase throughput; it uses error correction schemes to achieve data reliability. There are height levels of RAID from RAID0 to RAID7. Some RAID levels can be the bases for hybrid levels, such as RAID0+1, which we will discuss later.

RAID0

The RAID0 level is a nonredundant array of drives linked together via striping.

Striping is the fundamental technology behind RAID arrays; the technology allows creation of a logical volume composed of a number of connected, striped, physical volumes.

RAID0 is a scheme that achieves maximum parallel disk accesses with no redundancy. There is no extra overhead associated with striping. Sequential blocks of data are written across multiple disks in stripes.

The size of a data block, which is known as the *stripe width*, varies with the implementation, but is always at least as large as a disk's sector size. When it comes time to read back this sequential data, all disks can be read in parallel.

Advantages include the following:

- Disk striping without parity provides very high performance.
- It is the least-expensive level, since extra disks are not required for redundant information.

Disadvantages include the following:

- There is no data redundancy.
- One failed drive renders the whole array unavailable and is therefore not a recommended solution in a production environment.

RAID1

RAID1 is usually called *mirroring*. It provides complete redundancy by writing identical copies of all data on a pair of disks. Multiple pairs of disks can be installed in a system. Note that a mirror can consist of three disks.

The overhead of performing duplicate writes is relatively low, because they can be done in parallel. However, since write operations are performed in synch, write operations are as fast as the slowest of the drives.

In addition to fault tolerance, mirroring also gives improved read performance. Since the drives are duplicates, data can be read from both drives in parallel.

Advantages include the following:

- It offers higher write performance than levels 3 or 5.

- It can be combined with the disk striping of level 0 to provide the highest performance. This is often referred to as "RAID10" or "RAID0+1."

- In the event of a single disk failure, the controller uses either the mirror drive or the data drive for data recovery and continues operation.

Disadvantages include the following:

- It is relatively expensive, due to additional disk requirements.

- The overhead costs equal 100 percent.

- The usable storage capacity is 50 percent.

RAID3 and RAID4

RAID3 and RAID4 are a stripe with a parity disk. This parity disk is written in the same way as the parity bit in normal RAM, where it is the exclusive or (XOR) of the data bits.

In RAM, parity is used to detect single-bit data errors, but it cannot correct them because there is no information available to determine which bit is incorrect. With disk drives, however, we rely on the disk controller to report a data read error. Knowing which disk's data are missing, we can reconstruct it as the XOR of all remaining data disks, plus the parity disk.

As a simple example, suppose we have four data disks and one parity disk. The sample bits are as follows:

Disk 0	Disk 1	Disk 2	Disk 3	Parity
0	1	1	1	1

The parity bit is the XOR of these four data bits, which can be calculated by adding them up and writing a "0" if the sum is even and a "1" if it is odd. The sum of Disk 0 through Disk 3 is "3," so the parity is 1.

If we attempt to read back these data, and find that Disk 2 gives a read error, we can reconstruct Disk 2 as the XOR of all the other disks, including the parity. In the example, the sum of Disks 0, 1, 3, and parity is "3," so the data on Disk 2 must be 1.

Advantages include the following:

- It offers high read/write performance in large file applications, such as CAD/CAM and imaging.

- It has good availability because an array can continue to operate in the event of a disk failure. This is an advantage of all redundant RAID levels.

- It offers more reasonable disk costs than RAID1.

Disadvantages include the following:

- It shows poor performance in high I/O request rate applications (transaction reads/writes), such as transaction processing and relational databases.

- It has poor write performance due to parity generation.

- There is high regeneration impact when operating with a failed disk.

- It withstands only one disk failure. This is also a disadvantage of other redundant RAID levels.

RAID3 is difficult to implement due to block-size requirements and the need for all disks to be synchronized. Typically, a modified form of level 3 is used like RAID 4, which is not a common level, and will not be discussed here.

RAID5

RAID5 is a stripe of drives with a parity information spread among the drives in the set. The overhead of a RAID5 set is equal to a drive in the set. For example, if we have six drives of 18 GB forming a RAID5 set, the total amount of space will be: $(18 * 6) - 18 = 90$ GB.

RAID5 gives superior performance on all multitasking read operations (sequential or random) and on sequential reads in a single-tasking environment. In all these cases, all disks can be read in parallel.

Writes incur a performance penalty on RAID5. Updating the parity block requires two extra reads (one of the old data block and one of the old parity block) and one extra write (of the parity block). This penalty is reduced to one extra read for sequential writes, because the parity block will already be in the cache. However, this write performance penalty may not be significant on most systems. It is typically stated that only about 10 percent of all disk activity on client/server systems is write operations. If that figure is true for your system, the RAID5 write penalty may have no great effect on performance.

You can avoid the RAID5 write performance penalty at some additional cost in extra disks by using RAID0+1. RAID0+1 (also known as RAID10) was not mentioned in the original 1988 article that defined RAID1 through RAID5. The term is now used to mean the combination of RAID0 (striping) and RAID1 (mirroring). Disks are mirrored in pairs for redundancy and improved performance, and then data are striped across multiple disks for maximum performance.

Advantages include the following:

- It offers high read performance in high I/O request applications.
- There is good availability, since an array can continue to operate in the event of a single disk failure.

Disadvantages include the following:

- It shows poor performance in high data transfer rate applications.
- It has poor write performance due to parity generation.
- There is high regeneration impact when operating with a failed disk.

RAID10

RAID10 is a stripe of mirrors. Basically it's a stripe (RAID0) of a number of RAID1 sets.

RAID10 combines RAID0 and RAID1 advantages in terms of performance; however, it has all the RAID1 disadvantages, which are related to percentage of storage availability and costs.

Obviously, RAID10 uses more disk space to provide redundant data than RAID5. However, it also provides a performance advantage by reading from all disks in parallel while eliminating the write penalty of RAID5.

In addition, RAID10 gives better performance than RAID5 when a failed drive is not replaced. Under RAID5, each attempted read of the failed drive can be performed only by reading all the other disks. On RAID10, a failed disk can be recovered by a single read of its mirrored pair. Figure 4.5 illustrates RAID10.

Comparing RAID performance levels

Figure 4.6 shows that the least-expensive disk configuration is a single drive. Among the storage technologists this is known as Just a Bunch of Disks (JBOD). This means that single drives aren't expensive; however, they are poor in performance and induce point of failures. If a single drive fails, the data may be lost.

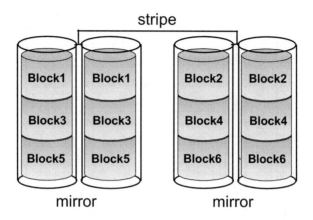

Figure 4.5
RAID10

The best performing and available solution is RAID0+1, but it is also the most expensive.

RAID5 and RAID1 provide reasonable performance at reasonable prices and availability.

Comparing the performance of RAID levels relative to the percentage of read operations is also a way to determine which RAID level best fits the Active Directory requirements. Figure 4.7 illustrates the cost of different RAID levels depending on the percentage of write operations performed. By looking first at the extremes, RAID5 is 25 percent efficient in a 100 percent write-operation environment, compared with 100 percent efficiency for RAID0. As already mentioned, this is because RAID5 requires four disk

Figure 4.6
Comparison of RAID levels

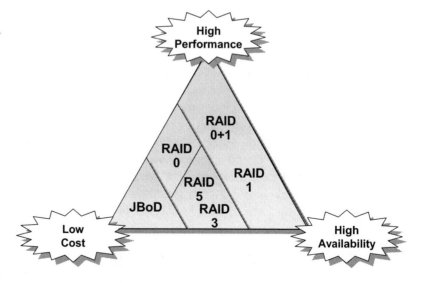

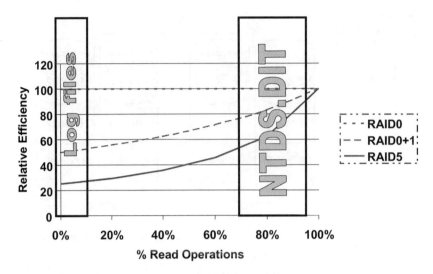

Figure 4.7
Comparing RAID levels for Active Directory

I/Os for each single write operation to the volume. For example, you should not try to put the Active Directory transaction logs on a RAID5 volume. RAID0+1 has half the efficiency of RAID0. This is the case if we assume the same number of spindles.

When looking at performance for read operations, for 100 percent of read operations the efficiency is similar for all kinds of volumes, and this is normal. Multiple spindles will work concurrently to read the data, and there is no overhead involved. This explains why RAID5 is appropriate for archiving where you read more than you write.

4.3.3 Cache

There are four forms of cache: writeback, write gathering, read, and reada-head. As mentioned, Windows 2000 disables the cache on drives where the Active Directory is installed. However, Windows 2000 turns off software cache. The cache I'm about to mention resides on storage controllers and is not seen by the operating system. It's very important to understand the limitations of the storage controller if caching is turned on. The risk is that if LSASS performs a write operation to the database, once the I/O successfully completes, the DC assumes that the data reside safely on disk. This may not be the case if the server is connected to a storage controller that uses caching, since the data may still reside in the controller's memory. Caching must be protected by a good battery system and not all storage controllers support it. Due to this reason Windows 2000 turns off caching by default where the Active Directory is installed, but cannot reach the cache available on the high-end storage controllers. Enabling caching on the controller must be done only if the storage controller provides the necessary features (dual batteries, battery status checks, and more) to prevent a corruption in the database in case of power failure.

Writeback cache is generally implemented at the RAID controller level. The goal of writeback cache is to reduce the amount of time required to perform a write operation. I/Os can be achieved in nanoseconds instead of milliseconds. This is because control is returned once the I/O is written to the memory cache. The controller then writes the I/O to the physical drive.

The size of the cache is not very important as long as data can be flushed faster than they arrives and it is large enough for the largest I/O burst.

Another important feature of writeback cache is write gathering, which allows the gathering of multiple writes to the same location; when it receives the last write, it will then copy all the data to disk. In other words, multiple small sequential writes are combined into one large one. This improves writes to the log files, since it avoids several writes of 8 KB.

Controller cache can also be used for read operations. There are two types of read cache: read cache and reach-ahead cache.

Read cache stores in the controller's memory the last blocks read. This is useful when the same blocks are read over and over again. In the case of the Active Directory, this is not useful because the Active Directory has its own cache implemented in the LSASS process. The amount of cache depends on the version of Windows 2000 and the amount of physical memory on the system. Server will use 512 MB of cache max. Advanced Server will use up to 1 GB. I've seen LSASS growing up to 750 MB in a stressed environment. For that reason, read controller cache will not be used even if available, since the LSASS process will be able to perform cached operations by itself.

Another type of cache is readahead cache. This type of cache involves caching the next block of data during read operations. This could be useful when data are stored sequentially; however, LSASS stores data randomly in the NTDS.DIT database—therefore the next block may not belong to the current operation. This is also not useful for the transaction logs, because they work in a 100 percent write mode only.

4.3.4 Summary for I/O fundamentals

RAID is key for proper performance and protection of the AD database. In a large Active Directory implementation a 18-GB disk drive will do no good for the performance of the database even if it is half the size. This is because I/Os are the main driving factor for good AD performance. CPUs are always faster, and memory is becoming cheaper; however, storage is slower to improve. Special care must be taken when designing the storage subsystem.

RAID brings load balancing across multiple spindles. For multi-threaded, concurrent I/Os, it helps in eliminating "hot" spindles and can improve performance by factors of two, three, or even more depending on usage.

RAID also helps build large logical volumes that do not fill up as easily. Do not fill up storage to more than 70 percent; leave room for expansion.

RAID, and in this case *parity* RAID, protects you against hardware failures. Parity RAID (RAID5) prevents loss of information even if you lose an entire disk.

RAID allows for more disks and more spindles to provide more capacity to handle peak I/Os, and it brings better performance overall.

4.4　Building a very large Active Directory

Let's put into practice some of the design principles and fundamental concepts learned in the previous section. Let's create an Active Directory database large enough to contain the white pages of the United States: 100 million subscribers. The goals are as follows:

- Load the database from real data and look at loading techniques.

- Tune the AD database and storage so that queries take two seconds or less.

- Replicate the data to a second DC to provide redundancy and availability.

To load the database from real data we will look at various loading techniques, including scripting and programming as well as tools.

Tuning the Active Directory is an important step to increase performance; we will concentrate on the indexing technique as well as tuning the Active Directory by separating the location of files depending on their I/O pattern.

Replication of the Active Directory is a mandatory step in any production environment to increase the availability of the directory data. As long as a DC is available, the Active Directory remains available. We will then look at best practices and recommendations for storage settings and RAID levels.

This project is based on tests performed on real data shortly after Windows 2000 was shipped. The Active Directory domain is available via the Internet for anyone to test. The URL of the Web server accessing the domain is available below.

Very honestly, when we started this project, we initially looked at ways to put the Active Directory on its knees. We wanted to know how many objects could be loaded comfortably in the Active Directory and what the performance issues were in extreme situations. We then looked at the kind of corporations that could benefit from a very large directory service, and we talked to a few of them. It's becoming clear that more and more corporations are moving into the e-business era. Many of the mobile telecom operators require a way to store the names of the subscribers as well as the services provided to them. In the telephony market we are talking about millions of people.

Another interesting aspect of the telecom and particularly the set-top box market: Several companies are providing services to people's homes; these services include TV as well as internet and telephony services.

Another interesting market is the automotive one. Many automobile manufacturers are looking at providing Internet access in cars. All the data related to these services must be stored in a scalable and available directory service.

These are only a few examples of how large directories are required in real business problems. Because of this, we took the challenge very seriously—after all, if you can tune comfortably a 100-million database, you will have no problem with 10 or even 1 million.

4.4.1   Preparing the Active Directory storage

The Active Directory is a true transactional database. Transactions are captured in log files before they are committed to the database (NTDS.DIT). The load program can only generate objects quickly if it is facilitated by fast hardware that has storage configured in an optimal fashion. In particular, it's critical to separate the I/O path to the transaction logs (which are serviced by one thread) away from the path to the database. To protect the database, the Active Directory must reside on a RAID5 or RAID0+1 volume. The controller is configured with well-protected writeback cache, which reduces the queue length for I/Os. Splitting the I/O traffic and enabling writeback caching allowed the eight-way Compaq Proliant processor used for the load to work at a consistent rate and use the power of its CPUs. During the initial tests, the CPUs were working at about 20 percent of capacity; however, once the writeback cache was enabled, they used 100 percent of CPU time, or close to it.

We started by looking at the database sizing requirements. In other words, we need to plan for enough storage for all the objects. Furthermore, given that the Active Directory storage is partitioned into multiple files, we need to understand the requirements for each file. For this, we looked at the work performed by Andreas Luther from Microsoft in terms of capacity planning. We wanted to create either user or contact objects. Each user object will use approximately 4.3 KB and unless we need to provide authentication services to the millions of people in the phone book, to use user objects is a bit of overkill. We decided to use contacts instead. While contacts provide most of the attributes available to user objects, they are much cheaper and faster to generate. An empty contact uses approximately 1.5 KB of storage space. Every additional attribute costs about 100 bytes. We planned for ten new attributes: common name, first name, surname, initials, display name, street address, city, state, zip, and telephone number. According to the calculations provided in Andreas's work, we needed enough storage for approximately 280 GB. However, since we don't recommend filling drives more than 70 percent, we really needed 360 gigabytes of storage, or close to it. In a RAID5 configuration, 360 GB requires 36-GB drives. A RAID5 set cannot be configured with more than 12 drives and 12 18-GB drives only provides 216 GB of disk space from which we must remove the overhead due to the parity information.

Another possibility is to use RAID0+1, since half of the drives are used to mirror the other half. That solution requires 48 18-GB drives, which is the maximum number of drives allowed in a Compaq StorageWorks ESA12000. The ESA12000 has two HSG80 redundant controllers, each managing 24 drives. We used 10,000 RPM 18-GB drives, which provides a total of 864 GB of usable disk space. Furthermore, we really wanted to use only half of the ESA12000 to allow a second DC to use the remaining storage. In previous tests we used RAID5 and a single DC. Given that we had a single ESA12000 to perform this test, we decided to compromise availability for performance and used several RAID0 stripes. In a production environment we would never recommend using RAID0, so don't try this with your production storage—this is a demo configuration. The ESA12000 can be configured in a Storage Area Network (SAN) fashion. We used switches to allow the two DCs to connect to the HSG80s in the ESA12000.

Connectivity is done using fiber-optic cables, which provide high-speed bandwidth. Switches allow us to separate storage from servers and are a fundamental component in SANs. We also configured the ESA12000 to limit the visibility of the storage sets to specific DCs. Servers and storage are connected to the same storage network. We wanted to avoid the typical mistake of two DCs accessing the same storage space.

Finally we configured the ESA12000 in the following way:

- We created six RAID0 sets, each containing six drives. Two DCs can then be configured to access three RAID0 sets each. This provides 324 GB for each DC when the three sets are striped. We used the striping features provided by the disk management snap-in. This allows creating a volume set containing multiple storage volumes provided by the RAID controller.

- We then created additional RAID0 configuration sets for the transaction logs. The disk space for transaction log does not need to be important in normal operations. The Active Directory is configured by default to use circular logging and removes the transaction log files every 12 hours as part of the garbage collection process. However, we needed more space than normal since we were going to perform some specific indexing tasks. This is discussed in more detail in the following text.

Once the volumes have been created, it is possible to configure the Active Directory while executing the Active Directory Installation wizard (also known as DCPROMO). DCPROMO is a wizard composed of forms with fields for specifying domain information and other settings for creating or joining an existing forest. One of the forms allows defining the location of the NTDS.DIT file and the transaction logs. We placed the NTDS.DIT file in the large volume composed of several stripes and the transaction logs in their own separate volume. Once the domain was created and the two DCs running and available, we started the loading phase of the project.

4.4.2   Active Directory loading techniques

The first approach we will look into for loading objects into the Active Directory involves Active Directory Service Interface (ADSI). ADSI is an API in the form of COM interfaces. The name is misleading, since ADSI can connect to different types of directories and not just the Active Directory. The directory services supported by ADSI are as follows:

- Active Directory

- Any LDAP-compliant directory, such as Novell NDS or Microsoft Exchange Server

- Windows NT 4.0. Even though the SAM database is not really considered a directory, it contains directory information accessible via ADSI.

ADSI can be used with any COM-aware language, such as Visual BASIC, Java, various scripting languages, and Visual C++. We opted for Visual C++ because it provides the ability to run multiple threads of execution and is, in our opinion, the fastest approach. We would not like to start another religious debate about the merits of one language versus another. So let's simply say that given that we know C++ better than BASIC or Java, the decision was simple. We wrote a multithreaded program loading the objects structured in organizational units. We will review the important portions of the program in the next section.

An early version of the program generated object names randomly. The program used a configurable number of concurrent threads to access the Active Directory. When we ran the program for the first time, it generated 16-million objects in two weeks. While this is a nice start, we looked at ways to improve it and load a lot more data in an equivalent amount of time. We also modified the program to load real data from the U.S. phone book. We will look also at an alternative, which involves a combination of LDIF and LDAP. LDIF (LDAP Interchange Format) allows directory information to be stored in flat text files and is designed for use as the basis to exchange data between directories.

In order to use real data, we first needed to find it. We partnered with Microsoft and got input data for the U.S. phone book from Info USA Inc., which provided it in the form of seven CDs containing highly compressed data (zipped text files). Each state was provided in a separate file. The semantic of those data was provided to us, so we wrote a data parser to extract the data and generate LDIF files, which were then loaded into the Active Directory using LDIFDE, a standard Windows 2000 utility program. The data parsing program takes care of data validation, such as managing phone book entries that have unlisted telephone numbers (those with 000-000-0000).

We could have generated a single LDIF file, but we believe it is faster to create multiple smaller files instead. This is because LDIFDE creates a temporary file used to store parsed data. The temporary LDIF file becomes as big as the original. This means that a single, large LDIF file may mean creating and accessing a several hundred–gigabyte temporary file, which isn't very fast. Therefore, when using LDIFDE, it's easier and faster to use several small files rather than one big one. We created multiple files, each containing approximately 250,000 records.

Translating the phone book data into LDIF format offered us a number of advantages. The LDIF files could be transferred around Compaq to allow a number of different teams to develop their own tests by loading a massive directory. The format of LDIF is easy to understand and debug. And, most important, the load program is able to generate new Active Directory objects at the rate of over 130 objects per second.

To speed things up further, data are loaded using a lazy commit process. This means that the data are loaded into memory and the system can proceed without receiving confirmation that these data have also been saved to disk. The database engine manages buffers in memory and arranges for them to be fully committed when system load allows. This process is well understood in the database world and is acceptable if data are protected with an appropriate RAID level and by separating the transaction logs and database files on different physical volumes.

Using LDIF files is also a recommended approach when adding schema records in the Active Directory. The schema can only be extended; this means that if a class or attribute with a mistyped name is created, it is not possible to undo the changes, unless performing an authoritative restore from tapes. A recommended approach for modifying the Active Directory schema is to create an LDIF file and test it using a separate forest. If the tests are successful, then the LDIF file can be applied to the production forest without the fear of mistyping an attribute or class name if the whole process is done manually.

4.4.3 Multithreading access to the Active Directory

The first approach to accessing, creating, and managing data stored in the Active Directory is via ADSI. On a multiprocessor system, and given the nature of LSASS, a multithreaded access approach brings better performance than a similar one based on single-threaded languages such as Visual BASIC.

We have written a Microsoft Foundation Classes (MFC)–based application. MFC provide a convenient object-oriented encapsulation over the WIN32 basic API. The MFC classes hide the complexity and overhead of WIN32 and provide a very easy mechanism to create threads.

In MFC you can create two types of threads: UI threads and working threads. UI threads can create user interface objects and can receive WIN32 messages related to the window objects they created. Working threads, on the other hand, are not intended to create UI objects; they are intended to execute background tasks and then exit. We have used working threads.

Visual C++ developers may want to read on. However, if you are as inspired by pointers and C++ classes as crocodiles are by yogurt, you may want to skip the following and jump to Section 4.4.4, which discusses transforming data into LDIF.

To create a thread in the MFC environment is a matter of calling a single function, AfxBeginThread, and passing the following three arguments:

1. A pointer to a structure passed as an opaque long value. Opaque means that the pointer is not typed and will need to be cast to the correct structure type. This pointer can also be pointing to a class.

2. The address of the function executing the thread.

3. The priority of the thread. Windows 2000 supports several thread priorities. Priorities can be as low as taking time when CPU is idle or as high as real time, which won't give the user interface a chance to continue until the thread executes all its tasks and exits.

You can create as many threads as you want. In our program we decided to create as many threads as the number of requested horizontal OUs we needed to create. If, for example, we wanted to create 100 horizontal OUs, each containing 10 child Ous, and in each OU we created 1,000 objects, we would have 100 threads creating 10,000 objects each for a total of 1,000,000 objects. The following code snippet shows the creation of the threads:

```
// Create as many threads as there are horizontal OUs to
// generate
for ( UINT i = 0; i < m_numOU; i++ )
{
    // Save this context so that the thread can
    // retrieve the data
    // This object will be destroyed by the thread
    CAddUsersData *pA = new CAddUsersData();

    // The ID will be used to compute unique
    // OU names and user names
    pA->SetId( i );

    // Save the UI information to allow the thread to
    // update the status
```

```
    pA->SetAddUsersDlg( this );

    // Rock & Roll!
    AfxBeginThread( ThreadProc, pA, THREAD_PRIORITY_IDLE
);
}
```

CAddUsersData is a class containing information gathered in the user interface. It contains the following:

- The LDAP-distinguished name of the DC to connect to for creating the users
- The prefix for the generation of the OU and object names
- The number of horizontal OUs (also used to generate the concurrent number of threads)
- The number of levels that we want to create
- The number of objects that we want to create in each OU

The THREAD_PRIORITY_IDLE value simply means that each thread will run at the lowest possible priority, basically taking CPU time when the processors are doing nothing. The MFC manual references the other priorities.

Once each thread is created, the ThreadProc function is invoked. This function executes the thread and creates the objects in the Active Directory. The first thing this function does is to initialize COM in order to use ADSI. Initialization of COM is done by calling CoInitialize().

Then the function binds to the DC for creating the objects; it uses ADSI for this as follows:

```
// Bind to the given server
hRes = ADsGetObject( server,
                     IID_IADsContainer,
                     (void**)&pContainer );
```

ADsGetObject does not require credentials to be passed because it uses the current credentials. To specify different credentials you must use AdsOpenObject, as follows:

```
// Connect to the sites container to retrieve the sites
hRes = ADSOpenObject( server,
                      username,
                      password,
                      ADS_SECURE_AUTHENTICATION,
                      IID_IADsContainer,
                      (void**) &pContainer );
```

The creation of the object is then performed using the following calls:

```
// Create the OU
if ( SUCCEEDED( hRes ) )
{
   hRes = pContainer->Create( TEXT("organizationalUnit"),
                             name,
                             (IDispatch **) &pNewObject );

   // Get the OU interface from the object
   if ( SUCCEEDED( hRes ) )
   {
     hRes = pNewObject->QueryInterface( IID_IADsOU,
                                       (void **)&pOU );
   }
}
```

The TEXT macro transforms a character string from ASCII format into Unicode. Unicode stores character information in 16 bits—unlike ASCII, which uses 7 bits for the U.S. character set and an 8th bit for international codes, such as characters with accents. When using ADSI you must use Unicode, which involves having specific constant definitions for the project and different project entries. The constant definitions are _UNICODE and UNICODE, and the entry point symbol for the program is: wWinMainCRT-Startup.

Now that we have an OU created, let's populate it by creating the objects in it, as follows:

```
// Create the user.
hRes = pOU->Create( TEXT("user"),
                    name,
                    (IDispatch **) &pNewObject );
```

With the user created, the returned pNewObject pointer allows us to query an ADSI user object interface with which we can populate the object with attributes. Note that return values checking was removed for the sake of brevity.

```
IADsUser *pUser = NULL;
hRes = pNewObject->QueryInterface( IID_IADsUser,
                                   (void **)&pUser );
```

Now we can add values to the user object, as follows:

```
hRes = pUser->put_FirstName( firstName );
hRes = pUser->put_LastName( lastName );
hRes = pUser->Put( TEXT("sAMAccountName"), name );
```

```
hRes = pUser->SetPassword( password );
hRes = pUser->put_EmailAddress( mail );
hRes = pUser->put_Description( description );

// Flush the data
hRes = pUser->SetInfo();
```

Finally, don't forget to clean up the COM interfaces by calling the `Release()` method and deallocating any memory used, as follows:

```
if ( pContainer!= NULL )
    pContainer->Release();
if ( pNewObject != NULL )
    pNewObject->Release();
if ( pUser != NULL )
    pUser->Release();
```

4.4.4   Transforming data into LDIF

Another method for loading objects in the Active Directory is via Light-weight Directory Interchange Format (LDIF). LDIF is a file representation of LDAP queries and commands. Data stored in LDAP compliant directory services can be exported/imported to or from an LDIF file.

When we received the data from Info USA Inc., they were provided in the form of zipped files, which, when unzipped, became very large (several gigabytes) text files containing the records of the white pages.

We wrote a Visual C++ tool, which reads records from those huge files and transforms them into several smaller LDIF files ready to be imported.

The output LDIF files container records appear as follows:

```
# Create the OU
dn: OU=NH,DC=usa,DC=compaq,DC=com
changetype: add
objectClass: organizationalUnit

# Create the contact
dn: CN=r0000010045,OU=NH,DC=usa,DC=compaq,DC=com
Changetype: add
objectCategory:CN=Person,CN=Schema,CN=Configuration,DC=u
sa,DC=compaq,DC=com
objectClass: contact
cn: r0000010045
displayName: JOE SMITH
sn: SMITH
givenName: JOE
```

```
streetAddress: 8 MAIN ST AMHERST NH
l: AMHERST
postalCode: 03031
st: NH
telephoneNumber: 603 9738129
```

Loading data using LDIFDE

LDIFDE is a tool that ships with Windows 2000's resource kit. It allows exporting data from the Active Directory into files and allows loading saved information stored in LDIF files into the Active Directory.

To import the generated files into the Active Directory, we use the following LDIF command:

```
C:\> LDIFDE -k -y -i -f nh001.LDF
```

-k means to ignore errors if the object as already been created. This is important, because we may have to restart loading files when problems occur. -y instructs LDIFDE to use lazy commit. Lazy commit provides faster writes to the Active Directory, because data are not immediately committed to the Active Directory storage, but are committed later as soon as there are idle cycles. However, control is returned faster to the tool, which can process the following object. -i indicates the records are to be imported. -f allows us to specify the input LDIF file containing the objects to process.

In our case, we have a number of files to load and have therefore automated the load process with the following Visual BASIC procedure, which will look for LDIF files and as it finds them, will load them in the Active Directory:

```
Dim fso
Set fso = CreateObject("Scripting.FileSystemObject")

Dim filespec

Dim i
i = 0

Set objArgs = Wscript.Arguments


filespec = objArgs(0) & i & ".ldf"
Set ws = CreateObject("Wscript.Shell")
do while fso.FileExists(filespec)
```

```
Wscript.Echo filespec
ws.run "LDIFDE -y -k -i -f " & filespec, 6, TRUE

i = i + 1
filespec = objArgs(0) & i & ".ldf"
```

Loop

The script can be executed in multiple command prompt windows. Since each script is loading a different state, this allows a parallel load to be performed.

4.4.5 Tuning for performance

Indexing the content of the Active Directory

The Active Directory has indexing capabilities to optimize queries to objects and attributes stored in the database. Indexing improves perfor mance drastically. With a 100-million-objects database, it could take several minutes for a query to return without indexing; with indexing, however, we can have results in a matter of seconds. Indexing, however, requires additional space in the transaction logs. This space will be cleaned up during the garbage collection phase of DCs.

Indexing can be performed on specific attributes. This provides great flexibility, since not all the attributes are likely to be searched, and, more importantly, not all attributes require the same level of indexing. Every attribute defined in the schema is an object of type attributeSchema. One of the attributes of that object is searchFlags, which is stored as an integer. The searchFlag is a combination of bit values. These are as follows:

- 1 = Index over attribute only

- 2 = Index over container and attribute

- 3 = Add this attribute to the Ambiguous Name Resolution (ANR) set (should be used in conjunction with 1)

- 8 = Preserve this attribute on logical deletion—that is, make this attribute available when the object is transformed into a tombstone

If bit 1 is set on the searchFlags of an attribute, that attribute will be searched for on all containers. This may not be optimum when looking for common names such as "Smith." Searching all containers may be slow. We experienced various performance results, sometimes peaking at 30 seconds or more for queries to return.

Bit 2 will allow container-specific searches and dramatically increase the overall speed for queries. Setting this bit was the determining factor for the speed of searches in the Active Directory. Searches for common names took a second to return with results. This is a value that cannot be entered using the MMC schema snap-in. To set this bit you must use ADSI Edit or LDP (shipping with the support tools).

Bit 4 is usually combined with bit 1; this allows Ambiguous Name Resolution (ANR) to find results when the value entered for the query wasn't accurate or complete.

Bit 8 allows us to keep the attribute when the object is deleted and transformed into a tombstone. The transformation of an object into a tombstone will by default remove the value of most attributes, and, therefore, the object cannot be recovered unless a restore from backups is performed.

Replicating to a second DC

A single system containing a large number of objects is a single point of failure. To remove this single point of failure we have to let a second DC join the domain containing the U.S. white pages. We have tested two scenarios, as follows:

1. Have two systems loading the objects in the active directory in parallel. This implys that the systems are replicating to each other while the objects are loaded.

2. Let a new DC join a system while the load is in progress and is well advanced.

The two systems loading objects in parallel allow us to speed up the load considerably. However, the default replication settings will allow about 30 objects per second in packets containing about 900 objects. This is not very fast, and we have looked at improving performance by increasing the number of objects per packet or increasing the byte size of the objects and reducing the latency for replication notification.

It's quite important to control the amount of objects in the replication packets. If a lot of objects are packed, then this operation will increase the time and memory used to create these packets. We increased the number of objects per packet but not drastically.

We believe replication is well optimized for normal Active Directory loads; however, it is not well adapted to extremely large loads. I don't think this is a very big problem for 99 percent of the current implementations of Windows 2000, but given that the number of Active Directory–enabled applications will increase, and as directory consolidation takes place, future versions of Windows 2000 will need to take replication for large directory services into consideration.

It took quite some time to get all the data replicated to the second DC. The initial test of spreading the load of generating objects provided a faster approach to get all the objects in both servers. Replication is not very fast for large amounts of objects; therefore, we strongly recommend performing backups on every DC once the load is performed. The data backed up on a DC cannot be restored on another one; therefore, it's important to choose which DCs will be protected by backups. Backups are not normally necessary on every DC if the replication speed and the number of objects can be replicated from a working DC within an acceptable time. In our case, where a second DC joins a domain containing 100 million objects, a month and a half of replication effort was required, which is not acceptable in the case of recovering a production environment from a disaster. From an operational perspective, full online backups of the Active Directory database, which is over 260 GB in size, take approximately 12 hours. (See Figure 4.8.)

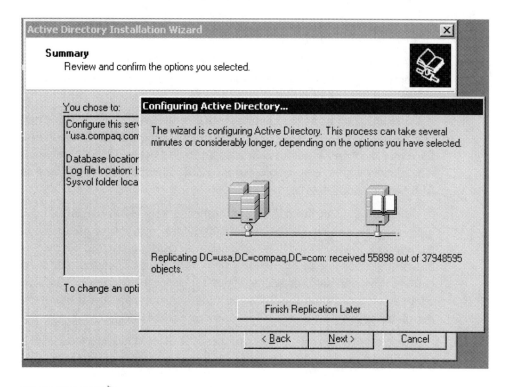

Figure 4.8 *Joining a large domain*

4.5   Searching the Active Directory database

There are several ways to perform a query in the Active Directory. Some of these are as follows:

- Find People. This is a dialog box provided in the Start menu under the Search submenu. A number of directories can be searched, including the Address Book, Yahoo!, Bigfoot, VeriSign, the Active Directory, and more. Find People uses GCs (port 3268) when searching the Active Directory—not DCs.

- Active Directory Users and Computers snap-in. The primary purpose of the Users and Computers snap-in is to manage the security principals stored in the Active Directory. This snap-in is limited in the number of simultaneous objects it can display. By default only 2,000 objects can be displayed. This number can be increased; however, there will be a penalty in speed since the snap-in can display only about 30 objects per second. Administrators can use the search feature of the snap-in to retrieve specific objects.

- Scripts can also be written to perform queries using ADSI via the interface IDirectorySearch.

- Web interface combined with scripting technology. This is the approach that we used. This is discussed in more detail in the following text.

Michael Craig from the Compaq office in Bellevue wrote a Web interface based on Active Server Pages (ASP) performing queries in the Active Directory database. His approach was to provide an easy-to-use user interface coupled with a remote access to the Active Directory database using an ADO connection.

Michael wrote an input ASP page, called `pbSearch.asp`, controlling a TreeView component. This component allows creating a hierarchy of names, and Michael used it to organize the cities and states, so that by browsing it's possible to define the scope of the query. Users can select the entire country, a state, or a city. Once the scope of the query has been selected, users can enter the last name and, optionally, the first name of the person being searched for; hitting return triggers the query.

Triggering the query invokes another ASP page. Data are passed to it from the `pbSearch.asp` page as hidden form variables—for example:

```
http://demo.esc.compaq.com/phonebook/
pbResults.asp?sn=smith&givenname=michael&Submit=Search&l
=BELLEVUE&st=WA
```

The ASP page starts by building the LDAP query using the passed parameters:

```
strSearchBase="LDAP://" & searchserver & "." &
searchdomain & "/"
if st<> "" then
    strSearchBase=strSearchbase & "ou=" & st & ","
end if
strSearchBase=strSearchBase & ldapDomain
```

The variable `strSearchBase` is built using predefined variables containing the name of the domain and the name of the DC. It uses the passed arguments to further refine the search string, as follows:

```
LDAP://escdemo1.compaq.com/ou=WA,ou=usa,dc=compaq,
dc=com
```

Then, the a search filter is created. This allows limiting the query for a specific object class and for objects containing specific values in their attributes, as follows:

```
strFilter="(&(objectClass=contact)"& stSearchText &
                lSearchText & snSearchText &
                givennameSearchText & ")"
```

which results in:

```
((objectClass=contact)(st=WA)(l=BELLEVUE)(sn=smith)
(givenname=michael))
```

Once the search string and search filter are defined, we have to tell AD which attributes we want returned:

```
strAttribs =
"givenname,sn,l,st,postalcode,name,telephonenumber,
streetAddress"
```

Depending on the input parameters, we can decide whether the query involves a subtree or if it will be executed in a single level. Subtree queries are more resource intensive.

```
if st="" then
    strScope="subtree"
else
    strScope = "onelevel"
end if
```

Finally, once all the parameters have been processed and the scope and filters created, we can build the query string that will be used with ADO:

```
sql = "<" & strSearchBase & ">;" & strFilter & ";" &
      strAttribs & ";" & strScope
```

This gives us:

```
<LDAP://escdemo1.usa.compaq.com/
ou=WA,ou=usa,dc=compaq,dc=com>;(&(objectClass=contact)
(st=WA)(l=BELLEVUE)(sn=smith)(givenname=michael));
givenname,sn,l,st,postalcode,name,telephonenumber,
streetAddress;onelevel
```

The ASP page then instantiates an ADO object to perform the query, as follows:

```
set oLDAPCon = server.createobject("adodb.connection")
oLDAPCon.cursorlocation=adUseServer
oLDAPCon.provider = "ADsDSOObject"
oLDAPCon.Properties("User ID") = logonname
oLDAPCon.Properties("Password") = logonpassword
oLDAPCon.Properties("Encrypt Password") = true
oLDAPCon.Properties("ADSI Flag") = ADS_FAST_BIND
oLDAPCon.open "Active Directory Provider"

set oLDAPCmd=server.CreateObject("ADODB.Command")
set oLDAPCmd.ActiveConnection=oLDAPCon

oLDAPCmd.CommandText=sql
oLDAPCmd.Properties("Size Limit") = maxrecords
oLDAPCmd.Properties("Time Limit") = 60

on error resume next

set oLDAPrs=oLDAPCmd.Execute

if oLDAPCon.Errors.Count>0 then
   dim objError
   for each objError in oLDAPCon.Errors
      dbg objError,"ADO/ADSI Error"
      dbg sql,"SQL"
   next
   Response.Write "There was an error in processing your
request."

else

on error goto 0
```

```
if not oLDAPrs.EOF then
   iRecordCount=oLDAPrs.recordcount
   if iRecordCount >= maxRecords then
      ' response.write "(Results limited to first " &
maxrecords & ")<p>"
      iRecordCountOut=">" & maxrecords
   else
      iRecordCountOut=iRecordCount
   end if
dim fldGivenname,fldSn,fldL,fldSt,fldPostalCode,fldName,
fldHomePhone,fldStreet

set fldGivenName=oLDAPrs(0)
set fldSn=oLDAPrs(1)
set fldL=oLDAPrs(2)
set fldSt=oLDAPrs(3)
set fldPostalCode=oLDAPrs(4)
set fldName=oLDAPrs(5)
set fldHomePhone=oLDAPrs(6)
set fldStreet=oLDAPrs(7)

do until oLDAPrs.eof
   ...display recordset
```

Figure 4.9 displays the Web interface in action. It took less than a second to find nine records containing Karen Forster in the entire U.S. database. It took two seconds to build the HTML page with the results. This shows that the Active Directory can be extremely fast if proper tuning and design are applied.

4.5.1 Recommendations

Designing the AD database is a fundamental part of Windows 2000 planning and design. Depending on the load of the DCs, a particular configuration can be applied to considerably increase performance figures.

We recommend separating the log file disk and the disk hosting NTDS.DIT. For the log file disk, we recommend using a RAID1 (mirror).

For NTDS.DIT, we recommend a RAID5, given the amount of read operations. In large implementations of the Active Directory we recommend using RAID0+1.

We recommend using circular logging for the Active Directory storage and planning a backup strategy. Strategy for backups should be based on the number of objects stored in the Active Directory and the amount of time

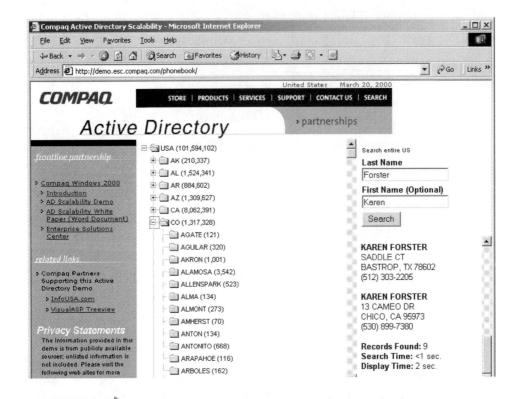

Figure 4.9   *Searching the Active Directory via a Web interface*

required to replicate them from other DCs. If the amount of time is unacceptable, then the DC should be backed up.

We also recommend protecting the operating system and page file with a RAID1 configuration. For optimum performance the operating system and page file should not be stored with the NTDS.DIT and transaction log files.

4.6   Summary of test data

The following chart shows the states and their population sizes:

USA1		USA2	
State	**Population**	**State**	**Population**
AK	210,337	MT	339,503
AL	1,524,341	NC	2,687,613

USA1		USA2	
State	**Population**	**State**	**Population**
AR	884,602	ND	255,369
AZ	1,309,627	NE	615,795
CA	8,062,391	NH	483,166
CO	1,317,328	NJ	2,293,942
CT	1,156,308	NM	507,717
DC	186,562	NV	454,734
DE	239,026	NY	5,791,130
FL	5,613,077	OH	3,327,036
GA	2,719,589	OK	1,186,356
HI	289,932	OR	1,120,201
IA	1,103,188	PA	4,284,375
ID	425,705	RI	333,074
IL	3,282,268	SC	1,270,942
IN	1,951,665	SD	272,034
KS	949,048	TN	1,995,570
KY	1,288,343	TX	5,965,164
LA	1,447,457	UT	561,392
MA	2,151,237	VA	2,214,633
MD	1,446,611	VT	280,060
ME	576,292	WA	1,866,219
MI	2,987,176	WI	2,002,762
MN	1,755,127	WV	677,222
MO	1,887,040	WY	173,316
MS	870,500	CA2	8,062,391
		TX2	5,965,164
Total	45,634,777	**Total**	54,986,880
Total population: 100,621,657			

Note: CA and TX were loaded twice to reach the magic 100-million objects mark. The load was performed on two concurrent DCs, which were also replicating information to each other.

5

Fundamentals of Windows 2000 Security

This chapter provides an introduction to Windows 2000 security. It covers general security concepts, such as the goals of security and the fundamentals of cryptography. The bulk of the chapter discusses two fundamental operating system security services and the way they are implemented in Windows 2000: access control and auditing. Since authentication is such a big topic, it will be covered in detail in Chapter 6. The reason why we will spend so much time on security is not just because we like it so much, but mainly because we think that a solid understanding of the Windows 2000 security features is a key requirement for the creation of a secure and reliable enterprise Active Directory infrastructure.

5.1 Introduction to Windows 2000 security headlines

The next five chapters of this book will focus on Windows 2000 security. We will cover operating system security, security management, and public key infrastructures. As an introduction, here are the Windows 2000 security headlines.

5.1.1 Integrated with the directory services

Windows 2000 security is tightly integrated with the Windows 2000 directory system: the Active Directory. This integration is implemented as follows:

- The Active Directory is used to store security-related account information.

- Access to the Active Directory is secured via the operating system: The operating system enforces the Windows 2000 access control model on all directory objects. Also, the operating system authenticates every directory access.

5.1.2   Based on open standards

Windows 2000 security is based upon numerous open standards. Open standards facilitate security interoperability between Windows 2000 and other operating system environments. Some well-known open security standards supported in Windows 2000 are Kerberos, an authentication protocol for distributed systems (Kerberos V5 is defined in RFC 1510); IPsec (the security architecture for the Internet Protocol, which is defined in RFCs 1825 through 1827); and L2TP (Layer 2 Tunneling Protocol, which is defined in the Internet draft: *draft-ietf-l2tpext-l2tpbis-00.txt*). IPsec and L2TP are two well-known tunneling standards.

5.1.3   Support for strong security

Windows 2000 includes support for several strong security protocols and technologies. Strong means that it is very hard, if not impossible, to compromise the security of the protocol or technology. Windows 2000 provides the following:

- Incorporates Kerberos V5 as the default authentication protocol (the NT4 default was NTLM). Kerberos V5 is widely regarded as a strong authentication protocol.

- Support for multifactor authentication using a smart card and PIN code.

- Support for public key infrastructures (PKI) and public key–enabled applications.

5.1.4   Support for single sign-on

Windows NT has always provided a single sign-on. The purpose of single sign-on is to minimize the number of times the user must enter his or her credentials (user ID and password). The user authenticates once at the beginning of a logon session; from that moment on, he or she should be able to access any resource in the domain or the domain tree (without an additional credential prompt). Windows 2000 extends the single sign-on process as follows:

- Windows 2000 now supports Kerberos as an authentication protocol. Kerberos is an open standard implemented on different platforms.

- Windows 2000 supports the SSL and TLS protocols. The X509v3 certificates used in these protocols can be used as credentials for Windows authentication. For more information about SSL version 3 go to *http://home.netscape.com/eng/ssl3/ssl-toc.html*; TLS version 1 is defined in RFC 2246 (available from *http://www.ietf.org*).

5.2   Security basics

In this section we will try to answer two fundamental security questions: What services should a security solution provide, and what are the basic concepts of cryptography? A good understanding of these basic concepts will facilitate the reading of the other security chapters of the book.

5.2.1   Security goals and services

The implementation of a security solution obviously serves some goals. The main goal of a security solution is to protect information assets stored on and transmitted between computer systems. These information assets may be attacked by internal or external hackers, or even employees, intentionally or unintentionally. Security is built on some typical security services, which we will explain in the following text.

Throughout this section you should remember the following three important facts:

1.   The implementation of a security solution is always a trade-off between security and ease of use. Ease of use usually means less or even no security. Good security usually means no ease of use. It's a big challenge for every security architect to find the right balance between the two.

2.   Security is everybody's responsibility. The creation of a secure IT environment is not just the responsibility of your organization's IT staff. Everyone in the organization has a responsibility to respect and implement the corporate security policies.

3.   Different levels of security needs may coexist in a single organization. Your CIO and the executive staff will obviously have higher security needs then the office maintenance personnel.

Operating system security goals and services

Operating system security is based upon three core services: authentication, authorization (or access control), and auditing. Although these three services serve three different goals, they are interdependent: A good auditing system depends on a good authorization system, which, in turn, depends on a good authentication system (as illustrated in Figure 5.1).

Authentication

Before an entity is given access to a resource or a service on a Windows 2000 system, the operating system must be sure of who it is dealing with. The primary purpose of the authentication process is to answer the question: Who or what is the system talking to? Chapter 6 will cover Windows 2000 authentication in depth.

Access control

Once an entity has been authenticated we need some way to restrict its access to the resources available on a computer: not everyone can access every computer resource. This defines the role of authorization or access control: It provides an answer to the question: What can the entity do and how can it do it? Windows 2000 access control will be covered later in this chapter.

Auditing

The auditing system of an operating system is the system that keeps track of all security activities that occur on a computer system; its primary purpose is the detection of any security-related event. Windows 2000 auditing will be covered later in this chapter.

Communications security goals and services

Windows 2000 is not just an operating system, it is also a network operating system providing services to run client/server applications in a distributed environment. This has an important impact on the security perimeter that needs to be protected; also, the communication medium used by clients and servers needs to be taken into account. This medium can run over your corporate LAN or WAN, via a PSTN (Public Switched Telephone Network), or via the Internet. Since the rise of the Internet, communications security has become a must-have feature for every OS. In this section we will explain the five core communications security services.

Figure 5.1
OS security pyramid

Communications security goals

Most communications security solutions offer the following security services: confidentiality, authentication, nonrepudiation, integrity, and anti-replay protection.

Confidentiality Confidentiality protects against unauthorized disclosure of information. The two following examples illustrate the need for confidentiality:

1. You decide to buy a book on the Web site of your favorite bookshop; at the end of your order you fill in your credit card number. What you certainly don't want is that your credit card number is sent in clear view over the Internet.

2. To log on to a Windows 2000 domain, you fill in your user ID and password. Your client software will send your credentials to the DC so it can validate them and give you access to the domain. We cannot send the user ID and password in the clear over the wire; for a hacker it is not that difficult to read them off the wire and to perform a spoofing (impersonation) attack using your identity afterwards.

Integrity A security service that provides integrity protection protects against undetected modification of a message. When we send a message and a malicious person intercepts it, modifies it, and sends it on to the recipient, we want to provide a way for the recipient to detect that the original content of the message has been changed.

Integrity protection is very important in financial and medical environments where sensitive data are sent over a public communication medium. When dealing with money or with medical data, it is a key requirement to have the exact data and that the data remain unchanged while they are transmitted over a public communication carrier.

Authentication   Network authentication can be subdivided into two categories: message authentication and authentication of persons (also known as identification). Message authentication provides a way to ensure that the alleged sender of a message is the one from whom it originates. Identification gives another person a way to check a person's identity.

When authentication happens in two directions, we can call it mutual authentication. Most Web transactions only require the client to authenticate to the server. Mutual authentication assures the client he or she is talking to the right Web server and not to a fake one.

Antireplay protection   Antireplay protection makes it impossible for one of the entities involved in a communication to repeat an already completed request—in other words, to resend a previous message.

Antireplay protection is very important when dealing with financial transactions: If you initiate a transaction from your account to the account of a supplier, you do not want a malicious supplier to record your transaction and replay it later in order to reinitiate the same transaction to his or her account.

Nonrepudiation   Nonrepudiation protects against denial by one of the entities involved in a communication of having participated in all or part of the communication. In a paper and pencil world, a manual signature provides nonrepudiation.

As with authentication, nonrepudiation can occur in two directions, as follows:

1.   Nonrepudiation of sending protects against denial by the sender.

2.   Nonrepudiation of receiving protects against denial by the receiver.

Nonrepudiation is very important for e-commerce applications. For a mail-order company, for instance, that decided to let its customers order through electronic mail, nonrepudiation is a basic requirement. It is very important to have proof of the customer's order; this gives the company a way to protect against the customer denying the purchase of the goods.

Table 5.1 *All-Time Favorite Security Goals*

All-Time Favorite Security Goal	Meaning
Defense in depth	The defense in depth rule states that not just one security solution should be implemented but that different solutions should be combined into one solution framework. In other words, information security is not a question of this OR this but rather of this AND this. This approach has the additional advantage that the different solutions can supplement each other.
Ease of use	Ease of use assures that a security system is used when appropriate and that its use doesn't depend on the complexity of its implementation: If a user encounters too many difficulties while working with a security system, he or she could prefer to do the same job without the security system. A way to provide ease of use is to centralize all security administration tasks and to make the application of security measures transparent to the user. This principle is used by Windows 2000 Group Policy Objects.
Performance	As with ease of use, performance also assures that a security system is used when appropriate. It guarantees that a security system's use doesn't depend on its execution speed. If it takes you several minutes to send one secured e-mail, you might consider sending the mail without security (or upgrading your machine).
Availability	Availability protects against interruption. It guarantees that the security system and the information protected by the security system are available all the time. Excellent examples of security solutions providing availability are backup software and fault-tolerant solutions, such as hardware or software clustering or RAID.
Cost	This is a key factor that is often forgotten. In many organizations it's the decisive parameter when choosing the final security solution.

All-time favorites

Table 5.1 explains some all-time favorite security goals: defense in depth, ease of use, performance, availability, and cost.

5.2.2 An introduction to cryptography

On the basic level, most security solutions, including PKI, rely on cryptography. Literally translated from Greek, "cryptography" is the science of "hidden writing." As will be illustrated in this chapter, cryptographic solutions can offer much more than just confidentiality protection. They can also offer integrity, data authentication, identification, and nonrepudiation services.

This chapter will not provide all the details behind cryptography; it will give enough information to understand the references to cryptography in the rest of the book. If you want to know all the details read one of the

Figure 5.2
Cryptographic terminology

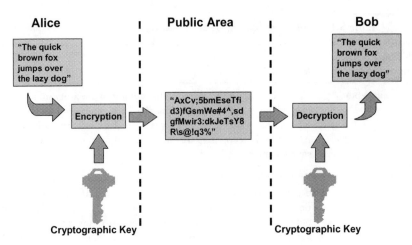

following excellent books: *Handbook of Applied Cryptography* by Van Oorschot and Menezes or *Applied Cryptography* by Bruce Schneier. If you want to read a good high-level overview of cryptography, read Chapter 6 of Bruce Schneier's most recent book, *Secrets and Lies*.

Cryptography is based upon two processes: encryption and decryption (as illustrated in Figure 5.2). Encryption transforms the cleartext (or plaintext) into ciphertext. To get back to the plaintext, given the ciphertext, the inverse transformation is applied to the ciphertext; this process is called *decryption*.

In modern cryptography both processes (encryption and decryption) are based on mathematics. The three basic cryptographic primitives, all derived from mathematical functions, are symmetric ciphers, asymmetric ciphers, and hash functions.

1. Symmetric ciphers use mathematical transposition and substitution functions. Transposition means that characters are moved to a different position in the ciphertext; for example if "jan" is the cleartext, a possible ciphertext resulting out of a transposition of the cleartext would be "anj." Substitution means that characters are replaced by other characters: for example, the "j" by the "z," the "a" by the "r," and the "n" by the "j." In this example the ciphertext would be "zrj."

2. Asymmetric ciphers are built on difficult or hard mathematical problems, such as the factorization problem, the discrete logarithm problem, or elliptic curve theory. The factorization problem is explained later when we discuss the RSA asymmetric cipher.

3. Hash functions use mathematical one-way functions. We come back to one-way functions later in this chapter.

These three primitives all have different characteristics and, thus, all serve different security goals. Most security solutions combine them in what is known as hybrid cryptographic solutions.

In most cryptographic solutions the algorithms behind the primitives are public. This makes it possible to analyze them and to develop more efficient implementations. Because the algorithms are public, we need something else to provide secrecy: that's the goal of a cryptographic key. It is a secret input parameter for a cryptographic algorithm (as illustrated in Figure 5.2). The use of keys promotes the reuse of the same algorithm for different secure communications. Private algorithms provide secrecy because only the users of the algorithm know them. Although public algorithms are available to everyone, they can be reused for secret communications because of the secret key concept.

When evaluating different cryptographic solutions, you should always consider the following:

- The cost of breaking the cipher should exceed the value of the encrypted information.
- The time required to break the cipher should exceed the useful lifetime of the information.

The following examples illustrate the second consideration: It doesn't make sense to protect highly confidential data using a cryptographic algorithm that could be hacked in less then a day. It could, however, make sense to use the same algorithm to protect data that are obsolete after one day.

Symmetric and asymmetric ciphers

In this section we will differentiate between two basic ciphers based on the key material that is used: symmetric ciphers and asymmetric ciphers.

Symmetric ciphers

Symmetric ciphers are the oldest and most used cryptographic ciphers. In a symmetric cipher the key used to decipher the ciphertext is the same as (or can be easily derived from) the key used to encipher the cleartext (as illustrated in Figure 5.3). This key is called the *secret key*. The way this cipher provides secrecy is by sharing the secret key only between the participants to the secure communication process. In practice this requires the key generated at one side of the communication channel to be sent to the other side of the channel using a secret channel. "Secret channel" in this context

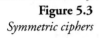

Figure 5.3
Symmetric ciphers

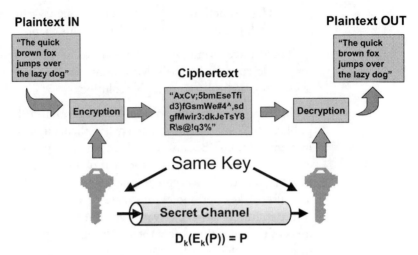

means protecting the confidentiality of the key, or keeping the key secret. The most widely used symmetric cipher is the Data Encryption Standard (DES).

The strength of a symmetric cipher depends on three variables, as follows:

1. The block length or the number of bits the symmetric cipher operates on during one round; DES operates on 64-bit blocks.

2. The key length: The longer the key, the bigger the keyspace, and the more difficult it becomes for a hacker to guess the right key. A typical DES key is 56 bits long.

3. The random number generator used to generate the symmetric key. If the same key is generated several times, it becomes easier to guess the key used for the encryption. This is an often overlooked critical parameter.

The constantly increasing processing power of computer systems and the above parameters explain why the original implementation of the DES is not safe anymore and why it is currently being replaced by stronger algorithms derived from DES, such as DESX and 3DES. There's also a new U.S. federal standard in the making that will shortly replace DES: the Advanced Encryption Standard (AES). AES should (at a minimum) support block sizes of 128 bits and key sizes of 128, 192, and 256 bits. It operates on 128-bit blocks and can use variable key sizes (128, 192, or 256 bits). In October 2000, the NIST decided to select Rijndael as the cipher for the AES. Rijndael has been developed by a group of Belgian cryptographic experts. More information on Rijndael can be found at *http://*

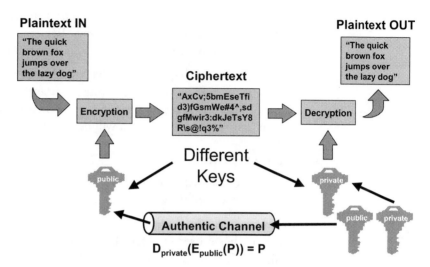

Figure 5.4
Asymmetric ciphers

$$D_{private}(E_{public}(P)) = P$$

www.esat.kuleuven.ac.be/cosic. To get the latest news on the AES development, surf to *http://csrc.nist.gov/encryption/aes.*

Asymmetric ciphers

Asymmetric ciphers are the most recent cryptographic ciphers. Contrary to a symmetric cipher, an asymmetric cipher uses two keys: one key that is kept secret and known to only one person (the private key) and another one that is public and available to everyone (the public key). The two keys are mathematically interrelated, but it is impossible to derive one key from the other. An important advantage of an asymmetric cipher is that its secrecy does not depend on the secrecy of the key that is exchanged between the communicating entities (the public key), but rather on the secrecy of the key that is never exchanged (the private key), as illustrated in Figure 5.4. As a consequence, an asymmetric cipher does not require a secret channel for public key exchange—only an authentic channel. "Authentic channel" in this context means assuring the recipient of the public key of the origin of the key. Well-known asymmetric ciphers are the Diffie-Hellman algorithm, RSA, and DSA.

The strength of an asymmetric cipher depends on the difficulty of resolving the mathematical problem behind it and on the key length. Let's illustrate this using the best-known asymmetric cipher, RSA:

- RSA is based on the mathematical problem of factorization. This problem tells us that it is easy to generate two large primes and to multiply them, but, given a large number, it requires a huge amount of computation to find the two prime factors. Because of their difficult mathematical background, asymmetric ciphers are regarded as offering stronger security than symmetric ciphers. Remember that symmetric ciphers are based on simple substitution and transposition methods.

- The length of the biggest factorable number is, due to the ever-increasing processing power, growing constantly: currently a key length of 768 bits is recommended for personal use of RSA. If you want military-grade security, you will need 2,048-bit keys.

Comparing the two

So what are the advantages of using an asymmetric cipher over using a symmetric cipher? Some of the advantages are as follows:

- An important advantage of asymmetric ciphers over symmetric ciphers is that no secret channel is needed for the exchange of the public key: The receiver only needs to be assured of the authenticity of the public key. Symmetric ciphers require a secret channel to send the secret key, generated at one side of the communication channel, to the other side.

- Asymmetric ciphers also create lesser key management problems than symmetric ciphers: Only 2n keys are needed for n entities to communicate securely with one another. In a system based on symmetric ciphers we would need $n(n - 1)/2$ secret keys. In a 5,000-employee organization, for example, the deployment companywide of a symmetric crypto-based security solution would require more than 12 million keys. The deployment of an asymmetric solution would require only 10,000 keys.

- A disadvantage of asymmetric ciphers over symmetric ciphers is that they tend to be about 1,000 times slower. Slower means that it takes about 1,000 times more CPU time to process an asymmetric encryption or decryption than a symmetric encryption or decryption.

- Symmetric ciphers can be cracked by doing a "brute-force attack," in which all possible keys are tried out until the right key is found.

Because of these characteristics asymmetric ciphers are typically used for data authentication (through digital signatures), for the distribution of a symmetric bulk encryption key (this technique is also known as a *digital envelope*), for nonrepudiation services, and for key agreement. Symmetric ciphers are used for bulk encryption.

Asymmetric ciphers are the only ciphers that can provide nonrepudiation services. This is due to their unique mathematical background; in short, if the signature on a digital document can be validated using a valid public key, the user cannot deny having signed the message using his or her private key. True nonrepudiation services not only require the use of asymmetric ciphers but also the presence of a trusted time stamping service and a legal or policy framework that fixes the liabilities and responsibilities of all parties involved.

Hash functions, message authentication codes, and digital signatures

A hash function is a cryptographic primitive used for integrity, confidentiality, and authentication services. It takes an input of an arbitrary length and reduces it to a fixed-size string (as illustrated in Figure 5.5). The output of a hash function is also known as a digital fingerprint or a "hash." Hash functions are one-way functions, which means that it is impossible to obtain the original text given the unique fingerprint. Well known examples of hash functions are MD5 (MD stands for Message Digest) and the Secure Hash Algorithm (SHA). MD5 generates a 128-bit hash; SHA generates a 160-bit hash.

The primary function of hash functions is to offer a detection mechanism against message tampering: The sender first calculates the hash of the message and attaches it to the message. If the original message is changed during transmission, reapplying the same hash function will result in another hash. This offers the receiver a way to check whether the integrity of the original message is still valid after being transmitted over a public medium.

Hash functions are often used to protect the confidentiality of passwords; storing the hash of a password in a centralized database guarantees

Figure 5.5
Hash function

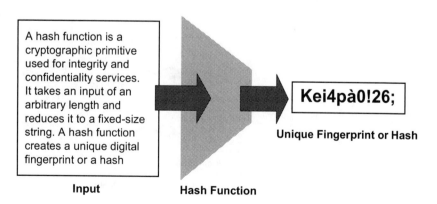

A hash function is a cryptographic primitive used for integrity and confidentiality services. It takes an input of an arbitrary length and reduces it to a fixed-size string. A hash function creates a unique digital fingerprint or a hash

Kei4pà0!26;

Unique Fingerprint or Hash

Input　　　　**Hash Function**

that nobody can get to the password—at the same time it provides a way to check whether a given password is valid.

Hash functions are also a building block for cryptographic authentication solutions. Two basic types of cryptographic authentication solutions exist, as follows:

1. Message Authentication Codes (MACs). MACs can provide data origin authentication. They are the result of a hash function and a symmetric cipher. Before a message is signed with a secret key (known only by the two communicating parties), it is compressed using a hash function.

2. Digital signatures. Digital signatures can provide data origin authentication and identification. Identification is also known as the authentication of persons. A digital signature combines an asymmetric cipher with a hash function. The process of digital signature generation (sender side) and verification (receiver side) is illustrated in Figure 5.6. Using a hash function, a unique hash value is computed from the original (unencrypted) message, which is then encrypted using the sender's private key and is added to the end of the message (the message digest). Along with the message, the recipient opens the digital signature and uses the

Figure 5.6
Digital Signature generation and verification

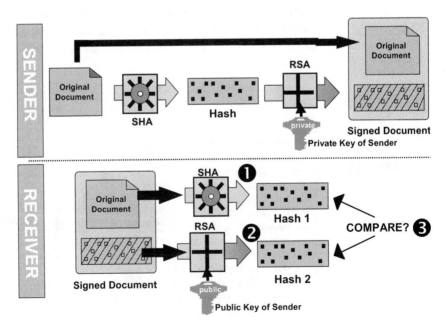

sender's public key to decrypt the hash value (step 2 in Figure 5.6). The same hash function is used to recompute the hash on the message (step 1). This hash will differ from the original (the one coming with the message) if the message contents are off by even 1 bit (step 3). If they are different, the recipient is notified that the contents of the message may have changed.

Hybrid cryptographic solutions

Most real-world security problems requiring a high-quality security solution are solved by combining basic cryptographic primitives (symmetric, asymmetric ciphers, and hashing algorithms) into a hybrid cryptographic system.

A hybrid system uses a symmetric key and algorithm to encrypt the plaintext, then uses the recipient's public key to encrypt the symmetric key (into what is called a lockbox) and attaches it to the message along with the encrypted information being sent to the recipient. This technique is also known as the creation of a digital envelope. The recipient uses the private key to decode the lockbox and retrieve the symmetric key with which the message can be decrypted. This method uses fast symmetric key encryption on the bulk of the message and retains the benefits of more secure public key encryption. By using the recipient's public key to encrypt the lockbox it also ensures that only the intended recipient (who has a private key) can get to the symmetric key.

Two examples of hybrid cryptographic solutions are the Encrypting File System (EFS) and S/MIME. Both will be discussed later in this book. Figure 5.7 illustrates S/MIME, a protocol for secure messaging and an excellent example of a hybrid cryptographic solution. In a typical S/MIME scenario, Alice wants to send a secure message to Bob. Secure means guaranteeing confidentiality, integrity, authentication, and nonrepudiation. The S/MIME exchange illustrated in Figure 5.7 can be split into six steps, as follows:

- Step 1: Alice creates a digital signature for the message using her private key.

- Step 2: Alice encrypts the message using a bulk encryption key.

- Step 3: To create a secure channel protecting the confidentiality of the encryption key, Alice encrypts the encryption key with the public key of Bob. This results in the lockbox.

- Step 4: Bob decrypts the lockbox using his private key. This results in the bulk encryption key.

Figure 5.7
Hybrid cryptographic solution

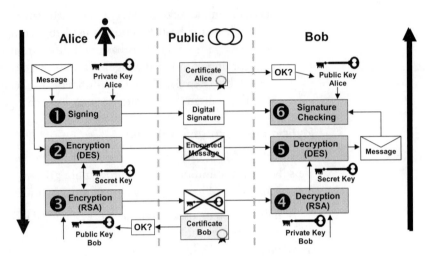

- Step 5: Using the bulk encryption key Bob decrypts the message. This gives Bob the readable message.

- Step 6: Bob verifies the authenticity and integrity of the message by verifying the digital signature using Alice's public key.

Note the use of certificates in this example. Certificates contain public keys and offer a way to verify the authenticity of public keys. We will come back to certificates in Chapters 8 and 9 of this book.

Cryptographic protocols

Cryptographic protocols are protocols whose implementation is based on cryptographic primitives or protocols that are related to the use of cryptographic primitives. In what follows we'll discuss two cryptographic protocols: identification and key management protocols. As will be explained in this chapter and the following security chapters, both protocols play a crucial role in Windows 2000.

Identification protocols

Identification protocols are used to authenticate a user. At the basic level identification protocols use cryptographic methods. Most protocols use a challenge-response mechanism, which brings together several cryptographic primitives. NTLM, for instance, the default identification protocol of NT4, combines hashing (MD4) and symmetric cipher (DES) primitives.

Looked at from a higher level most of them are based on knowledge, possession, or a combination of both.

The simplest identification protocols are based on knowledge: Users are authenticated based on their knowledge of a password or a pin code. As you might know, the use of just a password for identification is not a very safe identification method: End users just happen to choose very straightforward passwords and write or stick them down almost everywhere. Not all identification methods based on passwords are unsafe: The S/KEY standard, for instance, uses a system of one-time passwords and is a very safe identification system.

Smart cards or tokens are a much better alternative, especially if they're combined with the knowledge method. Windows 2000 supports smart cards and tokens (e.g., SecurID) out of the box, as a method to log on to a Windows 2000 domain.

Much more advanced identification systems are biometric- or reaction-based. Although some of them are not yet perfected (it happens that legitimate users fail the identification and that intruders are accepted as genuine), there are also reliable systems available on the market today. Compaq's Fingerprint Identification Technology (FIT) is considered one of the reliable biometric-based identification systems.

Key management protocols

Key management protocols are a key issue when implementing cryptographic solutions in a larger environment. Every cryptographic primitive that has been discussed so far (except for hash functions) makes use of cryptographic keying material, whose confidentiality, integrity, and authenticity must be protected when distributed over a public channel. Remember that the distribution of symmetric keys requires a secret channel, whereas the distribution of public keys only requires an authentic channel. To distribute the keying material in a secure way in a large environment, distributed systems such as Windows 2000 use key management protocols that are based on other basic cryptographic primitives. (See Table 5.2.)

Key management protocols can be classified based on their key management topologies, as follows:

- The Web of Trust Topology: in this topology all entities exchange keys with one another and decide upon which keys they trust. There is no concept of a centralized trusted entity used for key management. A big drawback of this topology is that it is very difficult to scale it on a large organization. A well-known example of a system using this approach is PGP (Pretty Good Privacy), a standard for secure messaging. As we will see later on, the basic idea behind the

Table 5.2   *Classification of Key Management Protocols*

Key Management Topology	Key Material	Trusted Third Party?	Example
KDC Topology	Symmetric keys (secret keys)	Yes: Key Distribution Center (KDC)	Kerberos
Web of Trust Topology	Asymmetric keys (public and private keys)	No	Pretty Good Privacy (PGP)
CA Topology	Asymmetric keys (public and private keys)	Yes: Certification Authority (CA)	S/MIME-based secure mail solution

web of trust is also present in Windows 2000: A user can make his or her own trust decisions regarding public keys.

- Topologies using a Trusted Third Party (TTP): In large environments it is not a very good idea to let every user exchange a secret with every other user. In a company with 5,000 employees 2.5 million keys would be needed to let everyone communicate with everyone else in a secure way. What's needed in these environments is a central trusted entity. Trusted third party topologies can be further subdivided based on the keying material the third party is dealing with.

- Key Distribution Center (KDC) topologies deal with secret keys: In this topology all entities exchange a secret key with a trusted third party, called the KDC, who they trust to generate other secret keys. KDC topologies facilitate the exchange of secret keys used for symmetric cipher operations. A good example of such a system is the Kerberos protocol, the default authentication protocol of Windows 2000: In Windows 2000 every DC is automatically defined as a Kerberos KDC. We will discuss Kerberos extensively in Chapter 6.

- Certification Authority (CA) topologies are dealing with public (and private) keys: In this topology a trusted authority, called the CA, certifies the user's public keys. If a user trusts a CA to certify his or her public key, the user will also trust all other public keys that have been certified by the same CA. CAs facilitate the definition of trust and the exchange of trustworthy public keys. A CA has a big advantage over a KDC in that it doesn't have to be online all the time. A good example of this topology is the advanced security system of Exchange (which uses S/MIME). Windows 2000 comes with CA software out of the box. We discuss Windows 2000 CAs extensively in Chapters 8 and 9.

Table 5.3 *Windows 2000 Security Technologies and Cryptography*

Technology	Symmetric Ciphers	Asymmetric Ciphers	Hash Functions
Kerberos	DES	RSA	
EFS	DESX	RSA	MD5
IPsec	DES, 3DES	Diffie-Hellman	MD5, SHA

Note that trusted third party topologies not only reduce the number of keys needed, but they also take away the need for a key database containing an entry for every user on every machine on the network. TTPs allow for a single centralized key database. We will discuss TTPs in Chapter 6.

Cryptography in Windows 2000

Table 5.3 shows some of the key technologies of Windows 2000 and the cryptographic primitives upon which they are based.

5.3 Windows 2000 communications security

This book does not contain a detailed discussion of the communications security features of Windows 2000. In this section we will explore the communications security protocols available in Windows 2000 and how they fit into the TCP/IP networking model. After this we will focus on two communications security areas for which Windows 2000 provides a lot of new features: virtual private networking and remote access security.

5.3.1 Windows 2000 communications security protocols in the TCP/IP networking model

Communications security solutions can be applied at the different layers of the TCP/IP networking model. By applying several security solutions at different levels in the TCP/IP stack, a tighter and more solid security framework can be obtained. (This is an excellent example of the defense in depth principle, which was explained earlier in this chapter.) Figure 5.8 illustrates which layer is affected by the communications security protocols included in Windows 2000, as discussed in the following list:

- End-to-end security is provided at the application layer. Secure RPC and S/MIME can provide communications security on the application layer.

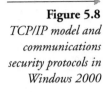

Figure 5.8
TCP/IP model and communications security protocols in Windows 2000

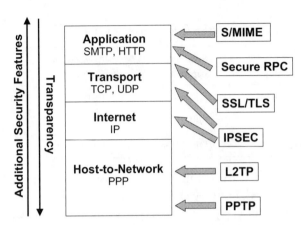

- Session security is provided at the level sitting between the application layer and the transport layer. SSL (Secure Sockets Layer) and TLS (Transport Layer Security) both provide session layer communications security.

- TCP, UDP, and IP protocol-level security is provided at the Internet and transport layers: IPsec is a well known Internet and transport layer communications security protocol.

- Windows 2000 communications security protocols operating on the host-to-network layer are PPTP and L2TP.

Figure 5.8 illustrates some interesting details related to communications security and the TCP/IP networking model, as follows:

- Since a direct link to a user is needed, nonrepudiation, identification, and authorization regarding a specific user can only be provided at the application layer.

- Security solutions applied below the application layer occur completely transparent to the user.

- The higher the TCP/IP stack level, the more security features can be provided. The lower the TCP/IP stack level, the more general solutions are; generality has the additional advantage of transparency for the user.

5.3.2 Virtual private networking

Windows 2000 comes with extended support for tunneling protocols and Virtual Private Networking (VPN). Using a VPN an organization can ensure secure networking over an untrusted communication channel (such as the Internet). For a detailed overview of VPNs in Windows 2000, we refer to Thaddeus Fortenberry's book, *Windows 2000 Virtual Private Networking*.

Tunneling is based upon the encapsulation mechanism, which is the building block of the OSI and TCP/IP networking models. The TCP/IP model mentioned previously is a simplified version of the OSI networking model; the concept of encapsulation originally comes from the OSI model but can be used as well for the TCP/IP model. In these models a packet consists of a header and a body part; the body part contains the packet's "payload," or the information that must be transmitted between the sender and the receiver. Among the information contained in a header are generic packet information and packet routing information.

Encapsulation can be explained as follows: As a message flows through the TCP/IP stack from the application down to the physical layer, a layer-specific header is added to the packet at each layer. At the receiver side it happens the other way around: The lower-level header is stripped off as the packet goes up higher in the TCP/IP stack. Tunneling provides some kind of secure encapsulation; it adds extra headers to a packet that can be used to provide confidentiality, integrity, and authentication services.

A typical tunneling solution consists of three protocol types, as follows:

1. The carrier protocol provides the network connectivity between the end points of the tunnel.

2. The passenger protocol is the protocol that is being encapsulated.

3. The encapsulation protocol is the protocol that is used to create, maintain, and tear down the tunnel and to encapsulate the data.

Table 5.4 *Windows 2000 Tunneling Protocols*

TCP/IP Layer	Tunneling Protocol	Carrier Protocol	Passenger Protocol	Encapsulation Protocol
Layers 3 + 4	IPsec	IP	Tunnel Mode: IP	Encryption: ESP[*]
	IPsec	IP	Transport Mode: Any protocol above IP	Authentication: AH[†]
Layer 1	PPTP	IP	PPP	GRE[‡]
	L2TP	IP	PPP	/

[*] ESP = Encapsulating Security Payload
[†] AH = Authentication Header
[‡] GRE = Generic Routing Encapsulation

Table 5.4 lists the tunneling protocols that are supported in Windows 2000 and their main characteristics.

The support for the L2TP (Layer 2 Tunneling Protocol) and IPsec protocols is new for Windows 2000; PPTP (Point-to-Point Tunneling Protocol)) was already supported in NT4. Windows 2000 comes with a new PPTP version: Among its new features is support for MSCHAPv2 (MSCHAPv2 provides mutual authentication and improved encryption) and support to create server-to-server tunnels.

5.3.3   Remote access security

Windows 2000 comes with the following new RAS security features:

- Windows 2000 RAS client and server software both include support for the Extensible Authentication Protocol (EAP). EAP is an authentication negotiation protocol for RAS: Using EAP an RAS client and server can negotiate the authentication protocol that will be used during an RAS connection. Windows 2000 EAP supports MD5, CHAP (EAP-MD5 CHAP), TLS (EAP-TLS), and SecurID tokens (SDI EAP), as well as the PPP authentication mechanisms supported in NT4: PAP, CHAP, MSCHAP (versions 1 and 2), and SPAP (Shiva PAP). EAP-TLS is the strongest RAS authentication mechanism that has ever been available in a Microsoft RAS environment: It uses public key cryptography (and thus requires the use of certificates) and can provide mutual authentication (if both the client and the server have a certificate).

- Windows 2000 comes with SecurID ACE/Agent software. This software enables strong two-factor RAS user authentication using SecurID token technology from RSA security (formerly known as Security Dynamics).

- Windows 2000 comes with RADIUS Server software. RADIUS (Remote Address Dial-in User Service) is an IETF standard (defined in RFCs 2138 and 2139) that provides authentication, authorization, and accounting services for dial-up networking. A RADIUS environment consists of RAS clients, one or more RAS servers, and a RADIUS Server. The Windows 2000 RADIUS Server is called Internet Authentication Services (IAS). A Windows 2000 RAS Server can use the IAS server (or a third-party RADIUS Server) as its authentication and accounting provider.

- Windows 2000 supports RAS policies, allowing network administrators to grant remote access connection permission based on attributes such as account group membership, time of day, connection media type, or the phone number the user is calling from.

5.4 Windows 2000 operating system security

In the following text we will focus on operating system security. Because many of the technologies explained in this section already existed in previous versions of the Windows NT operating system, we will focus on the differences in the way these technologies are implemented in the Windows 2000 operating system. Remember that operating system security is based upon three core services: authentication, authorization (or access control), and auditing. In this chapter we will focus on authorization and auditing; chapter 6 is dedicated to authentication.

5.4.1 Core concepts

Windows 2000 operating system security is (just like NT4) based upon the following core concepts: security principal, domain, SID, domain controller (DC), logon names, trust relationships, LSA, LSA policy, and secure channels.

Security Principals

In a Windows environment any entity that can be uniquely identified is a security principal. Users and machines are examples of security principals. Because security principals can be identified, they are unique within a certain environment and can be distinguished from one another. A new feature of Windows 2000 is that machines are now real security principals; they can identify themselves to any other principal; this was not the case in NT4.

As we explained previously, identification can use different identification methods (knowledge, biometric data, etc.). All of these methods use different credentials or things that uniquely identify an entity. Knowledge-based identification, for example, uses a user name and a password; biometric identification can use a fingerprint.

Besides credentials every security principal also has a set of unique identifiers. Examples of identifiers are the logon name, the Security Identity (SID), and the Global Unique Identifier (GUID) (SID and GUID are explained below).

So what's the use, besides identification, of being a security principal? Every security principal can be used in Windows 2000 security-related processes, such as access control and delegation. A security principal can be granted access to other objects (this process is known as access control). It can also be granted administrative permissions (this process is known as delegation). Both access control and delegation use the security principal's SID to uniquely identify the security principal.

Password credentials

Let's look a little bit more at password credentials. Although they are not the best way to identify security principals they are certainly the most widely used security principal credentials. A better alternative is smart card–based credentials; we will discuss this in Chapters 6 and 9. What's different between the way passwords were implemented in NT4 and in Windows 2000? A first, very noticeable difference you may come upon is in the way an administrator resets passwords in Windows 2000: Right-click the account and select Reset Password…. Another key difference is the maximum password length. In NT4 passwords were limited to 14 characters; in Windows 2000 the limit is 127 characters (if AD is installed). From a security point of view it's a good idea to use longer passwords for important administrator accounts.

An interesting password detail is related to the password of machine security principals: The OS changes the machine password automatically every 30 days. Unlike user passwords a machine's password cannot be reset from the Windows 2000 GUI; you can, however, use the command prompt tool Netdom with the /resetpwd switch (this tool comes with the support tools) to force a machine password change. Doing so will write a copy of the new password to the local LSA database and to the Active Directory.

Windows 2000 supports some interesting registry hacks to change the machine password update behavior. They are all located in the HKLM\system\currentcontrolset\services\netlogon\parameters container and are listed in the Table 5.5. From a security point of view it may be a bad idea to disable password changes because it makes machines more vulnerable to hacker attacks.

Logon names

A Windows 2000 user can log on to Windows 2000 in two ways: using his or her down-level NT4 account name or using his or her Windows 2000 Universal Principal Name (UPN). A UPN is of the format *username@company.com,* a down-level account name has the format *domainname\username.* The nice thing about using a UPN to log on is that it takes away the requirement of entering a domain name in the logon dialog box. When you

---

Table 5.5 *Machine Password Update Registry Hacks*

Can Be Applied To...	Parameter	Values	Meaning
Workstations	DisablePasswordChange (REG_DWORD)	0	Workstation automatically changes machine account password.
		1	Workstation never changes machine account password (this does not prevent manual change).
	MaximumPasswordAge (REG_DWORD)	1–1,000,000 days	Interval for automatic machine password change (only used of DisablePasswordChange is disabled).
DCs	RefusePasswordChange (REG_DWORD)	0	DC accepts machine password changes.
		1	DC rejects machine password changes.

type your UPN, the domain entry box will be automatically disabled. UPNs will be discussed in detail in Chapter 6.

Security identifiers

Every security principal created in the domain (the AD) or the local security database (the SAM) gets a unique Security Identifier (SID). SIDs are used to identify a security principal in access control and administrative delegation settings.

The SID for a domain account is created by the domain's trusted authority (the DC); the SID for a local account is created by the local trusted authority (the Local Security Authority or LSA). The SID of a domain account is stored in the objectSid attribute of the account's AD object; the SID of a local account is stored in a secured registry portion (the SAM).

An important property of a SID is its uniqueness in time and space: a SID is unique within the scope of the environment where it was created (domain or local computer). It is also unique in time: If you create an object "Paul," delete it, and recreate it with the same name, the new object will never have the same SID as the original object. There are some exceptions to this uniqueness rule: the well-known SIDs—for example, the SID of the Everyone or Administrators groups. The well-known SIDs are fully documented in the Windows 2000 resource kit and the Microsoft Platform SDK.

Table 5.6   *SID Structure*

Field	Example: S-1-5-32-544
Character S identifying the object as a SID	S
The revision level of the SID structure	1
An identifier for the authority that issued the SID (5, for example, stands for a Windows NT/Windows 2000 system). Possible values for this field are: 0, 1, 2, 3, or 5.	5 (SECURITY_NT_AUTHORITY)
A variable number of identifiers for subauthorities, also known as relative identifiers (RIDs): They uniquely identify the security object relative to the authority issuing the SID.	32 (SECURITY_BUILTIN_DOMAIN_RID)
	544 (DOMAIN_ALIAS_RID_ADMINS)

Let's have a look at what a SID looks like. The different parts of a SID are shown in Table 5.6.

A SID is not the same as a GUID. Both are created when a security principal is created. The SID is an object's unique identifier within a domain; it can be used for security-related processes. The GUID is an object's unique identifier within the Active Directory, it cannot be used in any security-related process. The GUID of an object never changes, whereas the SID does: for example when a user object is moved between two domains. A GUID is stored in an object's objectGUID AD attribute.

Some interesting utilities to translate user IDs to SIDs and the other way around are available on the Internet. Look at the sysinternals Web site for the getsid utility (*http://www.sysinternals.com*); on the ntbugtraq Web site you can find a copy of user2sid and sid2user (*http://www.ntbugtraq.com*). To translate an object's GUID to its AD Distinguished Name, have a look at the resource kit utility guid2obj.

Domain

As in NT4 a domain defines a security and management boundary. It is an administrative grouping of users, machines, and resources (e.g., file and printing services). Every domain has a central trusted authority (earlier in this chapter we called this a trusted third party). In NT4 and Windows 2000, this authority is known as a domain controller. The domain controller maintains the centralized domain security database containing the identifiers and authentication credentials of the different domain security principals. The centralized database obviously simplifies centralized security administration. Because a domain defines a security boundary, it can be linked to a specific security policy, which is only valid within that particular domain.

As mentioned previously, Windows 2000 allows you to build domain trees and forests. In Chapter 2 we also explained how closely the concept of a Windows 2000 domain is intertwined with the DNS namespace design. In this and in the next chapter we will explain how trust relationships can be set up between different domains to enable cross-domain resource access.

DC

A domain controller (DC) is a computer that holds the domain security database, and that authenticates security principals for domain resource access. It is the domain's trusted authority. A domain can contain multiple DCs and, thus, multiple trusted authorities. All DCs hold the same domain security database.

The default domain security database of Windows 2000 is the Active Directory, which replaces the SAM used in Windows NT 4.0. In Windows 2000 every DC contains a read/write copy of the domain directory database. This is different from Windows NT4 where the Primary DC (PDC) was the only one to host a read/write copy. All other Windows NT4 DCs held a read-only copy of the domain database and served as Backup DCs (BDCs).

Windows 2000 supports mixed mode domains. This means that a domain can contain both NT4 DCs and Windows 2000 DCs at the same time. To support down-level DCs within a Windows 2000 domain a single DC is nominated to act as the PDC emulator. PDC emulator is one of the FSMO (flexible, single-master operation) roles. There can only be one PDC in a domain (remember NT4) so hence the name "single master." The Windows 2000 FSMO roles are explained in Chapter 1.

Another security-related FSMO role hosted on a DC is the RID master. Most operations on directory objects can be performed as multimaster operations. Others can only be done at one DC. An excellent example of such an operation is the management of the RIDs. The concept of a RID was explained in the previous section. RIDs need to be unique relative to the subauthority that issues them (in this case a domain). The RID master allocates a pool of RIDs for each of the other DCs and keeps track of the sets of allocated RIDs.

Trust relationships

Trust relationships define an administrative and communication link between two domains. A trust relationship enables users to access resources that are located in a domain different from their proper definition domain. Remember that the creation of a trust between domains will not automatically grant users access to resources in the trusting domains; the domain administrator still has to assign access rights for the users on the appropriate resources.

Windows 2000 supports transitive trusts. In Chapter 6 we will explain why transitive trust is just a logical concept and how it relies on Kerberos and the GC.

Windows 2000 includes some important changes in the way trust relationships are created and managed. A feature that greatly simplifies trust management is the automatic creation of default trusts relationships as part of the DCPROMO process. Obviously trust relationships can still be created manually. To create a trust, use the Active Directory domains and trusts MMC snap-in. As in NT4, the creation of unidirectional trust relationship requires configuration changes in both domains on both sides of the trust. During manual trust setup you will be prompted to enter a trust password (at both sides). When trusts are created automatically, this trust password is generated and exchanged without any administrator intervention.

Let's look at what's behind a trust relationship and what happens when you manually set up a one-way trust relationship in Windows 2000 (everything is illustrated in Figure 5.9).

In a trust relationship there's always a trusting and a trusted domain. When a domain administrator of domain "south" decides to trust another domain, "north," "south" is the trusting domain and "north" is the trusted domain. When the domain administrator sets up the trust, the operating system will create a trusted domain object (account) for the "north" domain in the AD domain NC of domain "south." Linked to this object there's a password (just as for any other account) that is stored in the trusted domain object's unicodepwd attribute. As with any other account, this password should be changed at regular intervals—in Windows 2000 this happens automatically every 30 days; in NT4 every 7 days. When you set up a trust relationship manually in Windows 2000 you will be prompted to enter this password.

You can look at the trusted domain account objects using the MMC users and computers MMC snap-in or using ADSIEDIT; they are located

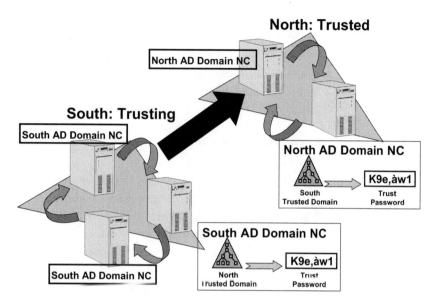

Figure 5.9
Trust relationships:
behind the scenes

in the domain NC, underneath the System container. In this example the "south" domain will contain a trusted domain object named "north."

What will this trusted domain account north be used for? One of the things it is used for is the setup of a secure channel between the domains "north" and "south." A secure channel is set up when the first DC of domain "north" boots up and on the condition that a DC of domain "south" is available. The concept of a secure channel will be explained in greater detail later on in this chapter. Anyway, before a secure channel can be set up domain "north" should authenticate to domain "south": to authenticate, "north" will use its trusted domain account and the associated trust password.

In order for "north" to authenticate to "south," it also needs a copy of the trust password of the "north" trusted domain object. That's why when the trust relationship is set up, Windows 2000 will also create a trusted domain object in the north domain; this object will be named "south" and will hold the same password as the other object in the other domain. This object is created when the administrator of the trusted domain "north" adds the name of the trusting domain "south" in the list of trusting domains (in the Trusts tab of a domain object's properties, in the MMC Active Directory domains and trusts snap-in).

Because any DC can be the first one to boot up and to set up the secure channel with the other domain, the trusted domain object and the trust password should be available on every DC. In Windows 2000 the trusted domain object is stored as a trusteddomain object in the LSA database. It is also contained in the AD domain NC using the schema class "secret."

In NT4 trusted domain global LSA secrets were stored in the LSA database, which is a part of the system registry. They were replicated using SAM replication. The LSA, its database, and its policy objects are discussed in the following text.

Local Security Authority and LSA policy

The Local Security Authority (LSA) is a protected Windows 2000 OS kernel subsystem (visible in the task manager as the lsass process). It plays a crucial role in the authentication and authorization of security principals. The role of the LSA for authentication is discussed in more detail in Chapter 6. Among its tasks are user credential validation and access token generation. The LSA also enforces the local security policy, including the auditing policy, memory quotas, user logon rights, and privileges.

To make the link between the LSA and two other key Windows security concepts, "trusted authority" and "DC," just remember that the LSA is a machine's local trusted authority and that a DC is a domain's trusted authority. All this shows once more the importance of "trust" in the Windows security model.

The LSA maintains its proper database containing all security information local to a system. The information stored in the LSA database is also known as the LSA policy; the objects stored in the LSA policy are known as policy objects. Physically the LSA database is a secured part of the registry, stored underneath the security key.

Different kinds of policy objects are stored in the LSA database: policy, account, and private data objects, as follows:

- A policy object determines who can access the LSA database. It also contains global system information such as system memory quota and auditing settings. Every system has a single policy object.

- An account object contains information that's specific to a user or group—for example, user logon rights, privileges, and quotas.

- A trusted domain object stores information about a trusted domain. The name and SID of the domain and the account name and password needed to send authentication requests to that domain.

- A private data object is used to store confidential information such as system or service account passwords. LSA private data objects are also known as LSA secrets. There's a limit on the number of LSA secrets that can be stored in the LSA database; in Windows 2000 this limit is 4,096. An LSA secret is encrypted using a system-specific key and stored in the LSA database (with the exception of Windows 2000 global LSA secrets [see below]). LSA secrets can be one of the following types: local, global, or machine LSA secrets. Local and machine LSA secrets can only be read locally from the machine that stores them; global LSA secrets are replicated between DCs. MS uses special naming conventions to store these special LSA secret types in the security key of the registry: "L$" for local, "G$" for global, and "M$" or "NL$" for machine LSA secrets.

A good example of a global LSA secret is the trusted domain object, explained in the previous section. A good example of a machine LSA secret is the machine password linked to a machine's domain account. To look at how the machine password is stored as an LSA secret, open up the registry editor and choose the HKEY_LOCAL_MACHINE hive; change the permissions on the security key to give the administrators Full Control access and open up the policy\secrets key: It contains a special key named "$machine.acc" used to store the machine password.

As mentioned earlier there is an important difference in the way the Windows 2000 OS deals with trusted domain objects on domain controllers: a copy of the trusted domain object is also stored in the AD domain NC and replicated between all DCs. Also, a Windows 2000 client's (workstation or member server) LSA database will contain more instances of the trusted domain object than its NT4 predecessor. This is due to Windows 2000 support for transitive trust. We will come back to this in Chapter 6.

Secure channels

In a Windows domain environment a secure channel provides a secure communication path between security principals. Secure means providing authentication of the requester, as well as confidentiality, integrity, and data authentication services for the data sent across the channel. A secure channel always involves a DC. A secure channel is set up between the following:

- A workstation or member server and a DC located in the same domain.

- DCs located in the same domain.

- DCs located in different domains.

You can look at a secure channel as the enabler of secure communication between machines and their trusted authority in the same domain and between the trusted authorities of different domains. The security services offered by a secure channel are based on the machine account's password.

Some examples illustrating the role of a secure channel: a secure channel enables secure replication of Active Directory data between multiple DCs in the same and different domains. Also the exchange of the challenge-response messages and pass-through authentication in an NTLM authentication sequence takes place across a secure channel.

Secure channels are set up at system startup time. To authenticate the requestor of the secure channel, different accounts are used depending on where the secure channel is set up:

- Between a workstation or member server and a DC located in the same domain, the workstation or member server's machine account is used.

- Between DCs located in the same domain, the DC's machine account is used.

- Between DCs located in different domains, the "trusteddomain" account is used.

The service responsible for the set up of the secure channel is the NetLogon service. An important difference in the way a secure channel is set up between Windows 2000 and NT4, is the way the requester locates a DC. In NT4, the localization method was dependent on the way the machine's NetBIOS name resolution was configured; in Windows 2000, a DC is

Table 5.7   *Secure Channel Security Registry Hacks*

Registry Parameter	Meaning
Requiresignorseal	If set to 1, secure channel traffic must be either signed or sealed; if this cannot be done, the system refuses to set up a secure channel. If set to 0, the use of signing and sealing will depend on the outcome of the negotiation between the two entities.
Sealsecurechannel	Encrypt secure channel traffic (if set to 1).
Signsecurechannel	Sign secure channel traffic (if set to 1). If Sealsecurechannel is set, the channel will be sealed and not signed.
RequireStrongKey	If set to 1, this enforces the use of a strong 128-bit key for securing the channel. 128 bit key encryption will only be used if both sides of the channel support 128-bit encryption (this setting requires the high-encryption pack for Windows 2000 or Windows 2000 Service Pack 1).

Table 5.8 *Secure Channel Troubleshooting Tools*

Tool (Available From)	Function
Netdom.exe (Support Tools)	Command prompt tool enabling an administrator to check the status of secure channel (/query switch) and to reset it (/reset switch).
Dommon.exe (Resource Kit)	GUI tool enabling an administrator to check the status of secure channels between DCs in its own and in other domains.
Nltest.exe (Support Tools)	Command prompt tool enabling an administrator to check the status of a secure channel (/query and /sc_query switch) and to reset it (/sc_reset switch).
Dcdiag (Support Tools) dcdiag.exe and netdiag.exe	Command prompt tool to test DCs. Running the tool with the /Outbound-securechannels switch will test secure channels. (Important note: Dcdiag only works for "explicit" trust relationships.)
Netdiag (Resource Kit)	The "Trust" test queries for secure channels and validates them.
Setprfdc.exe (NT 4 SP4)	Enables the specification of a preferred list of DCs for secure channel setup.

located using DNS. (Remember from the good old NT4 days: B, P, M, or H node types.)

Besides authentication of the requester a secure channel also provides confidentiality, integrity, and data authentication services for the data sent across the channel. These security services can be fine-tuned using the registry hacks shown in Table 5.7 (located in the HKLM\System\CurrentControlSet\Services\Netlogon\Parameters registry folder). These parameters (explained in Knowledge Base article Q183859) should not be confused with "SMB signing and sealing" (explained in Knowledge Base article Q161372). Obviously these hacks can also be controlled using Windows 2000 group policy object settings. By default every Windows 2000 workstation and server has the Sealsecurechannel and Signsecurechannel parameters set.

In a Windows NT 2000 environment, many logon problems are caused by secure channel problems. This means you should have some adequate troubleshooting tools at your disposal. Table 5.8 lists the tools you can use to monitor, test, and troubleshoot your Windows 2000 secure channels and where you can find them.

5.4.2 **Authentication**

Before an entity is given access to a resource or a service on a Windows 2000 system, the operating system must be sure of whom it is dealing with.

The primary purpose of the authentication process is to answer the question: Who or what is the system talking to? Chapter 6 is dedicated to Windows 2000 authentication.

5.4.3   Access control

Once an entity has been authenticated, we need some way to restrict its access to the resources available on a computer or in a domain: Not anyone can access every computer or domain resource. This is the goal of authorization or access control: It protects against unauthorized use and provides an answer to the question: What can the entity do and how can it do it?

Authorization typically deals with three entities (as illustrated in Figure 5.10): a subject that wants to access an object; the access control itself is enforced using a third entity, a "reference monitor." This third entity is known in a Windows environment as the Security Reference Monitor (SRM); it is part of the operating system kernel.

Access control not only deals with access to visible objects, such as files, printers, registry keys, and AD objects, but also with access to less-visible ones such as processes and threads. It also controls the ability to perform system-related tasks, such as change the system time and shut down the system. Microsoft calls these system-related tasks "user rights."

Access control model

Although Windows 2000 includes quite a few new access control features, the access control model is basically the same as the one that was used in NT4. It is based upon the following key concepts: access token, access mask, security descriptor, and impersonation. Figure 5.11 brings these different concepts together.

Figure 5.11 shows how, upon every object access, an object's security descriptor is checked against the access token and the access mask by an operating system component called the Security Reference Monitor (SRM).

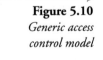

Figure 5.10
*Generic access
control model*

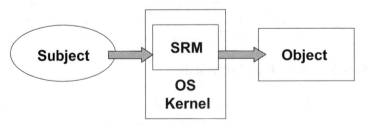

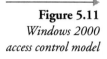

Figure 5.11
*Windows 2000
access control model*

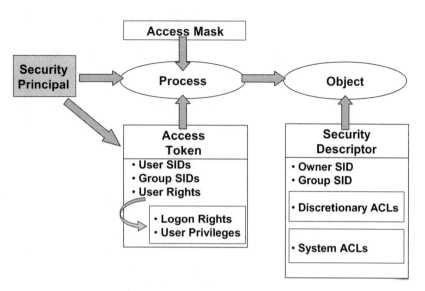

The access token and access mask are both linked to a process that impersonates a user. The following list defines these terms:

- Impersonation means that a process acts on behalf of a user.

- The access token contains a user's access control data (for example, group memberships).

- The access mask tells the SRM what the process wants to do with the resource (read? write?).

- The security descriptor tells the SRM who can do what with an object.

Based on the outcome of the comparison process, the SRM will decide if the process can access the resource. To inform the process of what it can do, the SRM will return another access mask, the granted access mask. In the following paragraphs we will examine these key concepts in detail and link them to the subject and object we introduced in the previous section.

To allow the operating system to associate a user's authorization data (the user's rights and group memberships) with every process that is started by the user, Windows 2000 uses an object called the access token. Access tokens are bound to a user's logon session. They are generated on every machine the user logs on to, independently of the logon type (interactive, network, etc.). (The difference between interactive and network logon is explained in Chapter 6.) An access token is always local and never travels across the network. The operating system component that generates access tokens is the Local Security Authority (LSA). Besides the user's domain authorization data an access token also contains the user's local authorization data. This is the access control information stored in the local security database (the SAM, which is a portion of the system registry). It includes local group memberships and local user rights. We will discuss access tokens and their content in Chapter 6. A complete overview of all the fields in the access token can be found in the Windows 2000 resource kit or the Microsoft platform SDK.

The main access control structure on the object side is called a *security descriptor*. A security descriptor tells the access control system who can do what with the object. The security descriptor of an AD object is stored in the object's ntsecuritydescriptor property. The security descriptor of a file system object is stored in the NTFS file system. Every object that has a security descriptor linked to it is called a *securable object*. Securable objects can be shared between different users: examples are a file, a folder, a file system share, a printer, a registry key, an AD object, a service, and so on.

An object's security descriptor contains a set of Access Control Lists (ACLs). An ACL is composed of multiple Access Control Entries (ACEs). An ACE is also referred to as a *permission*. So what's in an Access Control Entry? An ACE links a SID (a security identity) to an access right (read, write, delete, execute). Typical examples of permissions are "user A can read file B," or "user C can print on printer D." A complete overview of all the access rights supported in Windows 2000 can be found in the Windows 2000 resource kit or the Microsoft platform SDK.

Table 5.9 *Windows 2000 Impersonation Levels*

Impersonation Level	Meaning
Anonymous	The process impersonates an anonymous user (this means unidentified user); the access token will not contain any access control information.
Identify	The process can use the identity of the user for its own security processes; it cannot impersonate the user.
Impersonate	The process can act on behalf of a user to access resources on the local machine; the access token will contain the user's access control information.
Delegate	A service can act on behalf of a user to access resources on the local machine and also on remote machines; the access token will contain the user's access control information.

Every security descriptor contains two types of ACLs: discretionary and system ACLs, as follows:

- Discretionary ACLs contain ACEs that are set by the owner of an object; they are called "discretionary" because their content is set at the owner's discretion. Ownership is another very important concept in the Windows security model. By default, the owner of an object is the entity that created the object. Ownership can be transferred to other entities by the default owner or by an administrator. To take a look at the discretionary ACLs of a file system object you can use the command prompt tools cacls, xcacls, or showacls; for an AD object you can use dsacls; and for a service you can use svcacls. We will discuss these tools later in the chapter.

- System ACLs contain object-auditing settings and are set by an administrator. They are nondiscretionary: They are not related in any way to the owner of an object. SACLs are not the only thing that's needed in order to enable auditing on the object level; you also need to enable *Audit object access* in a machine's audit policy. We will discuss auditing in general later in this chapter.

In the NT4 and Windows 2000 access control model a user never accesses a resource alone; there's always a server process that acts on behalf of a user. This is known in Windows terminology as *impersonation*. When a process impersonates a user it means that it runs in the security context of the user and that it uses the user's access control attributes.

The degree to which a process can act on behalf of a user can be controlled using impersonation levels. Impersonation levels are set in an access token. Windows 2000 understands the following impersonation levels: anonymous, identify, impersonate, and delegate. They are explained in Table 5.9. The anonymous and delegate impersonation levels are brand new to Windows 2000. The delegate level is the only impersonation level that can be controlled from the administration interface. In Chapter 6 we will discuss the delegate impersonation level and the way it differs from the impersonate impersonation level.

Access control changes

Windows 2000 includes some important changes to Access Control Lists (ACLs), the associated Access Control Entries (ACEs), the way that access control is administered, and the ACL evaluation rules. Microsoft included the following major access control changes:

- Inclusion of a new ACL editor

- Fine-grain control over inheritance
- Support for object-type ACEs
- Support for property- and property set–based ACEs
- Support for extended rights
- New ACL evaluation rules

In the following text, Windows 2000 objects can refer to any securable object. These can be file system, share, printer, registry, Active Directory (AD), or service objects. A securable object can also be a less-tangible object, such as a process or a Windows station.

Some securable objects can contain other securable objects; they are called *container objects*. A container object can be a file system container (a folder), a registry container (a key), a printer container (a printer contains documents), or an Active Directory container (an OU).

Table 5.10 shows a subset of the securable objects available in Windows 2000 and which new access control feature is or can be applied to the ACL. This table does not list all Windows 2000 objects on which access control can be set; for example, service and windows station objects are missing.

Table 5.10   *New Windows 2000 ACE Features*

Access Control Feature	Securable Object				
	AD Object Permissions	NTFS Object Permissions*	Registry Object Permissions	Share Object Permissions†	Printer Object Permissions
New ACL editor	Yes	Yes	Yes	Yes	Yes
Fine-grain inheritance control	Yes	Yes	Yes	No	No
Object-type ACEs (v4)	Yes	No	No	No	No
Property-based ACEs (v4)	Yes	No	No	No	No
Extended rights and property sets (v4)	Yes	No	No	No	No
New ACL evaluation rules	Yes	Yes	Yes	Yes	Yes
ACL version	4	2	2	2	2

*NTFS object permissions require the NTFS file system.

†Share object permissions can be set on objects on the NTFS or the FAT file system.

Some of the new features (the ones marked with "v4" in Table 5.10) are part of a new ACL version (version 4). In Windows 2000 this new ACL version has been implemented only for AD objects. The main change in version 4 ACLs is the support for object-type ACEs. Object-type ACEs enable property based ACEs, extended rights, and property sets. The principal reason why Microsoft incorporated these new ACL version changes was to enable the definition of access control on AD objects in a more granular way. These changes also enable fine-grain administrative delegation on AD objects—another key feature of Windows 2000.

The new ACL editor

To enable a proper display of the ACE changes mentioned above Microsoft provided a new ACL editor. This new editor was shipped for the first time with NT4 SP4; it was installed together with the Security Configuration Editor (SCE).

The most important characteristics of this ACL editor are its object independency (the same editor is used to set access control on different types of securable objects) and its support for "deny" ACEs and the new ACL evaluation rules. The new ACL evaluation rules and how they affect what's displayed in the ACL editor will be discussed later on.

A fundamental difference with its NT4 predecessor is its capability to display negative ACEs (also known as "deny" ACEs). Although NT4 supported negative ACEs, the ACL editor couldn't deal with them. If in NT4

Figure 5.12
Windows 2000
ACL editor GUI

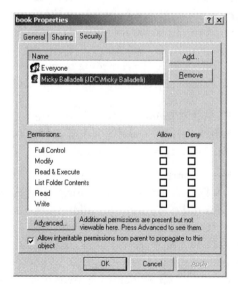

you set deny ACEs programmatically, an error message was displayed when using the NT4 ACL editor.

The new ACL editor also has a brand-new Graphical User Interface (GUI), consisting of a basic and an advanced view. Figure 5.12 shows the basic view of the new ACL editor; pushing the Advanced... button brings you to the advanced view. The advanced view is used to set more granular access permissions, control inheritance, change ownership, and set auditing settings.

The permissions displayed in the basic view of the ACL editor are in fact groups of permissions. To see what permissions are contained in a group of permissions, go to the advanced view of the ACL editor. The use of groups of permissions in the basic view can lead to situations such as the one illustrated in Figure 5.12. In this example, the administrator denied access to user Micky Balladelli to read the attributes of the book file system folder. Since read attributes is an individual permission rather than a group of permissions, it will not be displayed in the basic view of the ACL editor.

Fine-grain control over inheritance

ACL inheritance is a mechanism that lets container objects pass access control information to their child objects. A container's child objects can be noncontainer objects but also other container objects. From an administrator point of view ACL inheritance simplifies access control management. The administrator can set the ACL on a parent object and, if inheritance is enabled, shouldn't bother about setting ACLs on child objects. From a software logic point of view ACL inheritance makes access control evaluation much more complex. The software needs to consider multiple ACLs: not just an object's proper ACLs (also known as explicit ACLs) but also all the inherited ACLs. Inherited ACLs can come from an object's immediate parent but also from parent objects higher up in a hierarchy.

Comparing NT4 and Windows 2000 inheritance   Table 5.11 compares ACL inheritance between NT4 and Windows 2000. NT4 clearly offered no or very limited means to control ACL inheritance.

A major difference with NT4 is the Windows 2000 support for dynamic inheritance. In NT4 inheritance was static. This meant that the parent object's permissions did not affect the child object unless the administrator selected *Replace Permissions on Subdirectories and Replace Permissions on Existing Files* in NT4's Folder Permissions dialog box. The Windows 2000 support for dynamic inheritance means that Windows 2000 will automatically update the child's ACLs when the parent object's ACLs change. Note

Table 5.11   *Comparing Inheritance between NT4 and Windows 2000*

NT4	Windows 2000
Static inheritance	Dynamic inheritance.
ACL inheritance can be configured on file system objects.	ACL inheritance can be configured on file system, registry, and AD objects.
ACL inheritance can be enforced.	ACL inheritance can be blocked and enforced.
Inherited ACLs overwrite existing ACLs.	Inherited ACLs do not overwrite existing ACLs.
No way to remove inherited ACLs.	Inherited ACLs can be removed from child objects.
Inherited ACLs are not recognizable.	Inherited ACLs are recognizable: they are displayed differently in the ACL editor.

that in Windows 2000, for noncontainer objects, dynamic inheritance will take place only if the child object has explicit ACLs linked to it; if it hasn't inheritance remains static.

Another important difference is that Windows 2000 does not overwrite the child's proper explicit ACEs with the inherited parent ACEs. Windows 2000 simply adds inherited ACEs to the child's ACLs and tags them with a special inherited flag. You can observe the presence of this flag in the advanced view of the ACL editor (as illustrated in Figure 5.13). (Inherited permissions cannot be viewed frm the ACL editor's basic view.) To stress the

Figure 5.13
Inheritance in the advanced view of the ACL editor

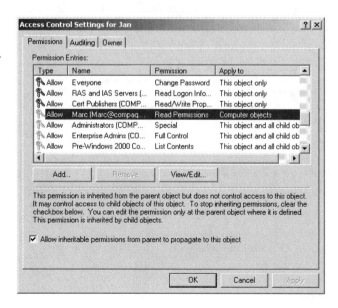

fact that inherited ACLs cannot be edited in the ACL editor of a child object Microsoft grays out the keys in the type column for inherited permissions; also, Microsoft added an explanatory text in the dialog box telling the user "this permission is inherited" and "you can edit the permission only at the parent object." In NT4 inherited permissions could be edited on the child object, because both the child object's proper ACLs and the inherited ACLs were merged, making the inherited ACLs unrecognizable.

An interesting detail from both an ACL inheritance and an AD replication point of view is the way ACL changes on AD container objects are replicated in the Active Directory. Since AD is a multimaster database, ACL changes made on one instance of AD also need to be replicated to every other instance of the AD database. To limit bandwidth use Microsoft only replicates the top-level ACL change "Between" AD instances. This feature, combined with the Windows 2000 dynamic inheritance, means that when access control is evaluated on a child AD object, it should always have the latest ACL information—unless some change on another AD instance hasn't replicated to the child object's AD instance.

Controlling inheritance   By default, Windows 2000 ACL inheritance automatically flows from container objects to all child objects. This default behavior can be modified by blocking ACL inheritance on a child object or by limiting the inheritance scope on a container object. Thanks to these features both entire subtrees and leaf objects can be excluded from ACL inheritance in an object hierarchy (as illustrated in Figure 5.14). What these features really mean is that ACEs marked as inheritable are not written to the ACLs of child containers or objects. On the file system level you may

Figure 5.14
Controlling inheritance using blocking

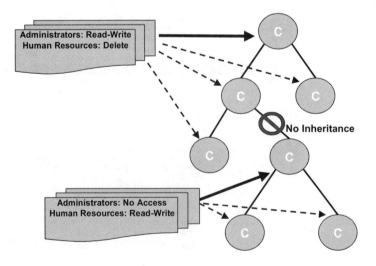

Figure 5.15

Setting inheritance in the ACL editor (part 1)

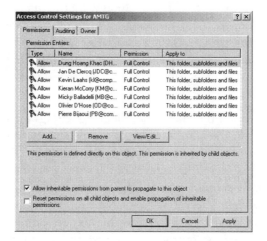

want to do this to apply special access control rules to the departmental folder of one of your organizations very special departments.

In the following text we will focus on NT file system and version 2 ACL inheritance. We discuss AD object and version 4 ACL inheritance later in the chapter. Just remember that, contrary to version 4 ACLs, version 2 ACLs can only differentiate between container and noncontainer object types.

To block inheritance on the child object level uncheck the Allow inheritable permissions from parent to propagate to this object (available in both the basic and the advanced view of the ACL editor) (as illustrated in Figure 5.12 for the basic view and Figures 5.15 and 5.16 for the advanced view). If

Figure 5.16

Setting inheritance in the ACL editor (part 2)

you uncheck this box, Windows 2000 will bring up a dialog box that gives you the option to *Copy previously inherited permissions to the object* or to *Remove the inherited permissions and keep only the permissions explicitly specified on this object.* The first choice removes the inherited flag from inherited ACEs and makes them explicit ACEs; the second choice effectively removes inherited ACEs.

To get around the inheritance blocking settings mentioned in the previous paragraph, the administrator of a child's parent container can enforce the writing of the inheritable ACEs to the child object's ACEs or take ownership of the object. Enforcement of the writing of inheritable ACEs is done using the *Reset permissions on all child objects and enable propagation of inheritable permissions* check box (available from the advanced view only) (as illustrated in Figure 5.15). For now this may appear to be against the rule of discretionary access control. In a subsequent section, we will explain why this is not against the rule. We will come back to taking ownership in a later paragraph on inheritance blocking and object ownership.

Another way to control inheritance on the parent container level is by using ACL inheritance scoping. File system ACL inheritance scoping is based on some special inheritance flags (listed in Table 5.12) that are added to a parent object's ACEs. The flags can be set from the advanced view of the ACL editor, using the View/Edit... pushbutton (as illustrated in Figure 5.16). In the *Apply onto* list box, different scopes can be selected: "This folder only," "Files only," and so on. Table 5.12 shows the inheritance flags corresponding to the setting chosen from the *Apply onto* list box. A leaf file

Table 5.12   *Inheritance Flags Corresponding to the File System ACL Apply onto Setting*

	Inheritance Flag		
Apply onto... Setting	**Inherit Only (IO)**	**Container Inherit (CI)**	**Object Inherit (OI)**
This folder only			
This folder, subfolders, and files		X	X
This folder and subfolders		X	
This folder and files			X
Subfolders and files only	X	X	X
Subfolders only	X	X	
Files only	X		X

system object obviously doesn't have these settings; in this case the *Apply onto* box just shows "This object only."

A flag that is not listed in Table 5.12 is the nonpropagate flag. This one is not set by using the *Apply onto* list box but by using the *Apply these permissions to objects and/or containers within this container only* check box (this checkbox is available from the advanced view only [View/Edit... pushbutton]) (as illustrated in Figure 5.16). The nonpropagate flag and the corresponding check box control the recursion depth of the inheritance. If you select the check box, the parent's ACL settings will only be propagated one level down the hierarchy (only to child objects, not to grandchild objects); if you clear it, inheritance will be applied recursively all the way down the folder tree.

Inheritance blocking and object ownership   It's very interesting to look at the combination "inheritance blocking" and "object ownership"; not just because this has had a lot of press attention over the last year (see Netware's claim in "The NDS Advantage: AD Security" at *http://www.novell.com/competitive/nds/security.html* and Microsoft's reply in "Novell Wrong About Windows 2000 Security Hole" at *http://www.microsoft.com/windows2000/news/bulletins/novellresponse3.asp*), but also because understanding both concepts are key to understanding Microsoft's AD security model.

In the AD security model an administrator or object owner can always take control over any AD object. This means that a domain administrator can at any point change the access control permissions of an AD object, even if he is not listed as the owner and even when the owner of the object has blocked inheritance of parent object ACE settings. An important consequence of this is that if you want to fully exclude an administrator from access to a particular set of AD objects, there's only one viable solution: put the objects in a separate domain. A domain is the only security container for which access can be completely blocked to administrators of other domains and that can have a completely autonomous administration model.

This unlimited power of an administrator is not a security flaw but rather a fundamental design decision Microsoft made during the AD security design. Although it's true that this "feature" conflicts with the concept of "discretionary access control," it may in some scenarios also be a very helpful concept—for example, when the administrator of a particular OU leaves the company and blocks access to the OU, an administrator can at least reclaim ownership of the OU and access the objects in it. Note also that ownership changes always generate an event log entry; an administrator could never take ownership unnoticed.

Object type–based ACEs

Object type–based ACEs are a new feature of version 4 ACLs. Microsoft implemented them in Windows 2000 for AD objects. Object type–based ACEs include two new ACE fields: an object type field and an inherited object type field. Using these fields an administrator can create fine-grain access control settings for AD objects, as follows:

- He or she can define which object types an ACE applies to. The object type field of an ACE refers to an object GUID. The GUID can be linked to an object type, an object property, a set of object properties, or an extended right.

- He or she can define which object types will inherit the access control information defined in an ACE. The ACE field used for this feature is the inherited object type field. As with the object type field, it contains a GUID.

The following sections explain how you can set access control based on the object type, a property, a property set ,or an extended right. We will also come back to the effect of object type–based ACEs on AD object ACL inheritance.

Setting access control based on the object type   Object type–based ACEs can be used to set access control based on the object type. Let's illustrate this with an example. As mentioned earlier, AD objects can be grouped in containers, which are called Organizational Units (OUs). Figure 15.7 shows

Figure 5.17
Object type–based
ACEs

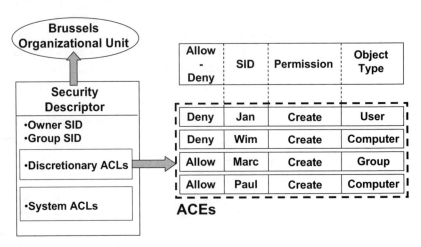

Allow - Deny	SID	Permission	Object Type
Deny	Jan	Create	User
Deny	Wim	Create	Computer
Allow	Marc	Create	Group
Allow	Paul	Create	Computer

how access control could be set on the Brussels OU using object type–based ACEs. We can determine the following from Figure 5.17:

- Jan cannot create user child objects in the Brussels OU.

- Wim cannot create computer child objects in the Brussels OU.

- Marc can create group child objects in the Brussels OU.

- Paul can create computer child objects in the Brussels OU.

Figure 5.18 shows how these object type–based ACEs are displayed in the ACL editor. You get this view from the advanced view of the ACL editor. Figure 5.19 shows how one of the ACEs (the one that allows Marc to create group objects) is set in the advanced view.

Here's an interesting note about the use of the ACL editor for AD object access control management. Since the number of object types stored in an AD object is relatively big, the ACL editor only displays a subset of the object types. To modify the object types displayed in the ACL editor, you can edit the dssec.dat file, which is located in the %systemroot%\System32 directory of every DC. This file contains a bracketed entry for every object type. If an object type's "@" value is set to "7," the type is not displayed, if it's set to "0," it is displayed. To reflect the changes made to dssec.dat, close and restart the MMC AD User and Computers snap-in.

Figure 5.18
Object type–based ACEs in the ACL editor (part 1)

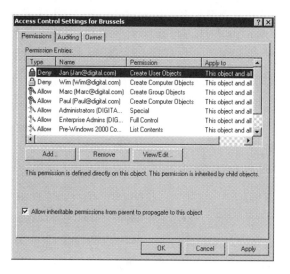

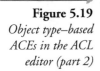

Figure 5.19
Object type–based ACEs in the ACL editor (part 2)

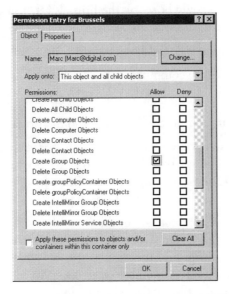

Setting access control based on a property or a property-set Object type–based ACEs can be used to set access control based on an object property or a set of object properties. Examples of user object properties are a user's First Name, Home Directory, City, and Manager's Name. Sample user object property sets are Phone and Mail Options, Account Restrictions or Personal Information, Public Information, and Home Address. The Public Information property set covers the following properties: a user's e-mail addresses, Manager, and Common Name attributes.

Figure 5.20
Property and property set–based ACEs

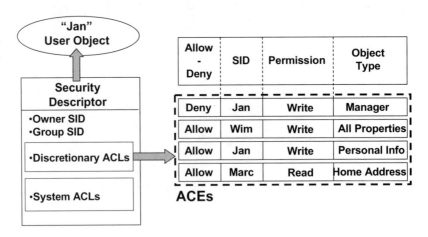

How to create custom property sets for your organization is explained in the Windows 2000 platform SDK.

Figure 5.20 shows how access control can be set on an AD user object, "Jan," based on its properties and the available property sets. We can determine the following from Figure 5.20:

- Jan cannot change the name of his manager.

- Wim can change all properties of Jan's user object.

- Jan can change his own personal information.

- Marc can read all information contained in Jan's Home Address property set.

Figure 5.21 shows how these property-based ACEs are displayed in the ACL editor. Figure 5.22 shows how one of the ACEs (the one that allows Jan to change his personal information) is set in the advanced view.

As with object types, the number of properties linked to an AD object is relatively large, and, again, the ACL editor only displays a subset of the object properties. To modify the properties displayed in the ACL editor, you can edit the same dssec.dat file. Beneath every object type there's a list of its properties. If a property is set to "7," it is not displayed; if it's set to "0," it is displayed.

Figure 5.21
Property-based ACEs in the ACL editor (part 1)

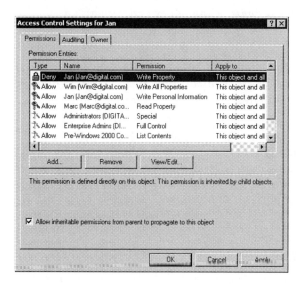

Figure 5.22
Property-based
ACEs in the ACL
editor (part 2)

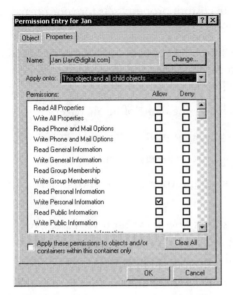

Setting access control using an extended right   Extended rights are special AD object–related actions or operations that are not covered by any of the standard Windows 2000 access rights (read, write, execute, delete). What makes them so special is that they cannot be linked to object properties. Good examples are the mailbox-specific "send as" and "receive as" extended rights. Although extended rights are not linked to object properties, they are displayed together with the standard object permissions in the ACL editor. To get an overview of the extended rights, open the Extended Rights container of the Windows 2000 AD configuration NC (you can look at the AD content using the ADSIEDIT tool). As with property sets, an organization can create additional extended rights; the way to set this up is explained in the Windows 2000 platform SDK.

Object type–based ACEs and inheritance   An object type–based ACE contains a special field, which can be used to define which child objects will inherit the ACE. This is why version 4 ACE inheritance can be limited to more object types than just container and non container objects. If you look into the *Apply onto* list box of an AD box, you'll notice many different object types.

Figure 5.13 showed the effect of this feature regarding the way inherited ACEs are displayed in the advanced view of an AD child object's ACL editor. In the example we're dealing with a user object "Jan." The ACL editor's advanced view displays all inherited ACEs: the ones that apply to user objects and the ones that don't. Notice that Microsoft added an explanatory text that says ". . . does not control access to this object" for inherited object type–based ACEs that do not apply to user objects.

In the first release of Windows 2000 some of the new inheritance features described in the section about comparing NT4 and Windows 2000 inheritance are not fully implemented on the level of AD object ACL inheritance (e.g., inheritance blocking). This probably has to do with the use of the new ACL version for AD objects and the complexity of implementing object-specific ACEs.

The ACL evaluation process

Previously, we introduced the entities involved in the access control evaluation: the subject (using an access token and an access mask), the object (having a security descriptor), and, of course, the Security Reference Monitor (SRM). In this section, we will look at how the SRM decides upon letting a process access a resource or keeping a process from accessing a resource. We will explain how the SRM generates the granted access mask, based on the access token, the access mask, the security descriptor, and the ACL evaluation rules.

The basic process   The basic process can be summarized as follows:

- The SRM receives an access token and an access mask from some server process.

- For every access right contained in the access mask the SRM will check the DACL of the object's security descriptor. It will check every ACE for an allow or deny permission that matches that particular access right and the user SID or one of its group SIDs. Remember, users and groups are identified in ACEs using their SIDs; a user and its group SIDS are listed in the access token.

- This process will end when one of the following occurs:

  - The SRM reaches the end of the object's security descriptor and didn't find a match for every requested access right. The granted access mask will be cleared and access will be denied. This is very important: If not every requested access right matches, access is denied.

  - The SRM found matching allow permissions for all the access rights that were requested in the access mask. The granted access mask will be complete and access will be allowed.

■ The SRM finds a deny permission for one of the access rights that was requested in the access mask. The granted access mask will be empty and access will be denied.

The evaluation rules and order   All the access control changes listed in the previous sections forced Microsoft to review the discretionary ACL evaluation rules and order. The new DACL evaluation order is illustrated in Figure 5.23. Microsoft calls this evaluation order the *canonical order*. An interesting property of the new ACL editor is that it displays the ACEs in canonical order in the advanced view (as illustrated in Figures 5.13, 5.15, 5.18, and 5.21).

This evaluation order contains three fundamental rules:

1.   Explicitly defined access control settings always have precedence over inherited access control settings. This a direct consequence of the discretionary access control model used in Windows NT and Windows 2000.

2.   Tier 1 parent access control settings have precedence over tier 2 parent access control settings.

3.   "Deny" permissions have precedence over allow permissions. If this were not the case, a user with a "deny" access right could still be allowed to access a resource based on an "allow" ACE for one of his or her groups. In this case the evaluation order would be: "allowed for the group"/"deny for the user"; since processing stops when all access rights in the access mask are granted, the evluation process wouldn't even get to the "deny" ACE.

Figure 5.23
Canonical evaluation order

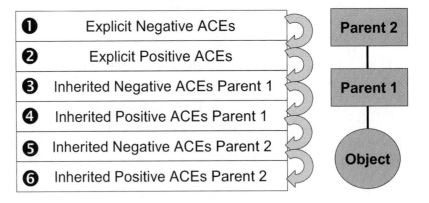

In the ACL evaluation process special care must be taken of empty DACLs and the absence of a DACL (also known as the NULL DACL). An empty DACL doesn't grant access to anyone. A missing DACL gives access to everyone. In this case the SRM simply copies the requested access mask to the granted access mask.

Figures 5.24 and 5.25 give some ACL evaluation examples. In both examples a process impersonating a user, "Jan," is requesting read and delete access to a resource. The user, "Jan," is a member of two groups "Consultants" and "AMTG."

In the first example (Figure 5.24), access is denied based on a deny delete permission for the "Consultants" group (this an inherited ACE). Note that even though "Jan" was granted read access the granted access mask is empty.

In the second example (Figure 5.25) access is allowed based on an "allow" read permission for "Jan" (explicit permission) and an "allow" delete permission for "AMTG" (inherited permission). The granted access mask has both the read and delete access rights set.

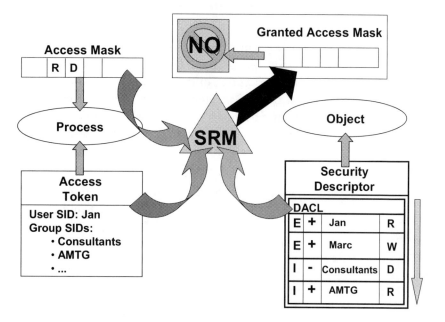

Figure 5.24
ACL evaluation example 1

Figure 5.25
ACL evaluation
example 2

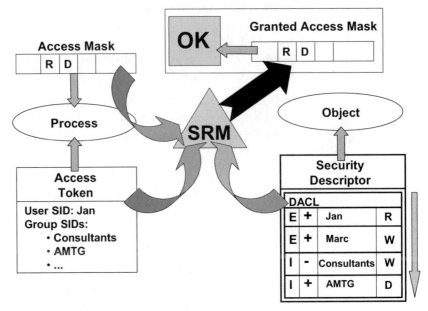

Authorization intermediaries

In large distributed environments such as a Windows 2000 domain, consisting of many subjects and even many more objects, the management of authorization data may become a very tedious and time-consuming task. With the exception of the inherent permission to deny or grant access to an object that's given automatically to the owner of the object, all other permissions must be set manually by an administrator or by the object owners. To ease access control management Windows 2000 includes the following intermediaries sitting between subjects and objects: groups and user rights:

- Groups provide a way to group entities with similar capabilities. They facilitate the access control management of object permissions. Typically all authenticated Windows 2000 entities (users, machines) with similar resource permissions (or user rights: See next paragraph) are added to the same group.

- User rights define the capabilities of subjects to manage system resources and to perform system-related tasks. For instance: Who can log on locally to a DC? Who can change the system time? Who can load device drivers? They facilitate access control management for system resources and system-related tasks. User rights should not be confused with access rights; user rights apply to a computer system, access rights apply to an object. The Windows 2000 access rights were explained earlier in this chapter.

Even though they both serve different access control goals, group intermediaries can be used to ease the administration of user rights intermediaries. For example, you can give all the members of the help desk department the right to reset the system time on your DCs.

Windows 2000 groups

The following list gives an overview of the major differences between the way groups are implemented in NT4 and Windows 2000:

- Windows 2000 provides two types of groups: security groups and distribution groups; the latter category is typically mail-oriented. This demonstrates the tight integration of the new version of the Exchange Mail Server (Exchange 2000) with the Windows 2000 operating system. Contrary to a security group, a distribution group does not have a SID and thus cannot be used in any security-related process (access control or delegation).

- Windows 2000 includes four types of security groups. They are listed in Table 5.13 giving their usage scope (Where can I use the group?), their content scope (What can be contained in the group?), and the

Table 5.13 *Windows 2000 Groups*

Type of Group	Usage Scope	Content Scope	Group definition Storage	Group membership Storage
Universal groups	Global	• Principals from any domain • Universal groups from any domain • Global groups from any domain	AD Domain NC Global Catalog	AD Domain NC Global Catalog
Global groups	Global	• Principals from the same domain • Global groups from the same domain	AD Domain NC Global Catalog	AD Domain NC
Domain local groups	Local domain	• Principals from any domain • Universal groups from any domain • Global groups from any domain • Domain local groups from the same domain	AD Domain NC	AD Domain NC
Local groups	Local computer	• Principals from any domain • Universal groups from any domain • Global groups from any domain	SAM	SAM

database or file that holds the group definition and membership. Note that the four types are only available if the domain is running in native mode.

The usage scope column deserves some more explanation. A global usage scope means that the group can be used in the ACL of any object, anywhere in the forest. A local usage scope means that the group can be used only in the ACL of an object in the local domain (for a domain local group) or in the ACL of an object on the local computer (for a local group).

■ The group scope and group type of domain local and global groups can be changed, if the domain is running in native mode.

■ Windows 2000 groups (with the exception of local groups) can be nested. An administrator can, for instance, create a global group, Employees, and within it two other global groups: Consultants and Managers. This feature is only available if the domain is running in native mode. Note that local groups cannot contain any other group with the exception of the groups controlled by the operating system, discussed later in the chapter. Nesting can be used to get around the 5,000-member Windows 2000 group limit.

■ The membership of any group type can be controlled using the Security Configuration and Analysis tool (SCA) (for local groups) and using Group Policy Object (GPO) settings (for universal, global, and domain local groups). We will discuss the SCA later in this chapter; GPOs will be covered extensively in Chapter 7.

A special note should be made about local groups. As Table 5.13 shows, local groups are very different from the three other group categories: they are only meaningful on the local computer, cannot be nested, and are stored in the SAM (the system registry). Local groups are sometimes referred to as *aliases*. An alias identifies an object in a different way. A local group can be an alias for any other security principal; in this case the link between the alias and the object is established by adding the security principal to the local group. On a server running your company's ERP application—for example, you can create a local group alias named "ERP users"; in ERP users you could embed any other user or group defined in your forest.

Groups in mixed and native mode   The availability of some of the group features listed in the previous section depends on whether the Windows 2000 domain is running in mixed or native mode. Remember that a

Table 5.14   *Effect of the Windows Domain Modes on Windows 2000 Groups*

Mixed Mode	Native Mode
Two group scopes: global and local	Four group scopes: global, domain local, local, and universal
Two group types: security and distribution	Two group types: security and distribution
DCs share local groups.	All domain computers share domain local groups.
Custom local groups can be defined on any machine.	Custom local groups can be defined on any machine with the exception of DCs.
Groups cannot be nested.	Groups can be nested (with the exception of local groups).
Group scope and type cannot be changed.	Group scope and type can be changed.

Windows 2000 domain must run in mixed mode as long as it contains down-level DCs. Table 5.14 lists the group feature differences between mixed and native modes.

Default security groups   The goal of this section is not to provide a complete overview of all the default Windows 2000 security groups. We will focus on the differences with NT4. Table 5.15 lists the new default security groups.

The pre-Windows 2000 compatible access group deserves some more explanation. It enables applications that cannot run with the strict permissions enforced by a Windows 2000 DC, to run in a Windows 2000 environment. It enables them to read the AD user and group objects. If the *Pre-Windows 2000 compatible access* option is selected during the Windows 2000 AD installation process, the "Everyone" group is added to this group.

A very powerful type of group is the security group whose membership is controlled automatically by the operating system. Although their membership cannot be controlled, they can be used for delegation and for access control settings. To illustrate the power of these groups, let's take the example of the dial-up and interactive groups: These groups allow you to separate users who are working from their homes from normal users, and set access control settings on corporate resources accordingly. An interesting characteristic of these groups is also the way they are replicated between AD instances: Even though they may contain thousands of objects, their membership is not replicated.

Table 5.15 *New Windows 2000 Groups*

Default Group Name	Group Scope	Meaning
Pre-Windows 2000 Compatible Access	Built-in Local	Members of this group have read access to all attributes on user and group AD objects.
Enterprise Admins	Universal (native mode) Global (mixed mode)	The Enterprise Admins group exists only in the root domain of an AD forest. The members of this group can make forest-wide changes and change the AD configuration NC.
Schema Admins	Universal (native mode) Global (mixed mode)	The Schema Admins group exists only in the root domain of an AD forest. The members of this group can change the AD schema NC.
Group Policy Creator Owners	Global	Members of this group are authorized to create new Group Policy Objects in the AD.
Enterprise DCs	Global	Includes all DCs of the domain.
Domain Computers	Global	Includes all computers that joined the domain, including DCs.
DnsAdmins	Domain Local	Members of this group can administer the Windows 2000 DNS service.

These groups can be classified in two categories: the built-in groups and the well-known security principals groups. The first ones are stored in the builtin container of every AD domain. The well-known security principals are stored in the AD configuration NC in a container with an identical name. All these special security groups are listed in Table 5.16. Note that not every built-in group is automatically populated by the operating system—for example, server operators, backup operatiors, and so on.

Windows 2000 administrator groups The pyramid shown in Figure 5.26 shows the level of administrative privileges Windows 2000 gives to its default security groups. Table 5.17 shows the default memberships of these groups on a Windows 2000 workstation, member server, and DC. Notice that some of the groups are not available on all computer types (NA) and that others are by default created empty (—).

Let's look in more detail at the power of the Windows 2000 Enterprise Admins, Domain Admins, and Administrators groups. It is also worth comparing these groups to the administrator groups available in NT4.

Table 5.16   *Groups Controlled by the Operating System*

Groups	Membership—Meaning
Everyone	Includes all users, as well as guests and anonymous users
Anonymous Logon	Includes all users who logged on anonymously
Authenticated Users	Includes all users who authenticated to the operating system
Network	Includes all users logged on through a network connection
Dial-up	Includes all users logged on through a dial-up connection
Batch	Includes all users logged on through a batch scheduler connection
Interactive	Includes all users logged on interactively
Service	Includes all principals logged on as a service
Enterprise DCs	Includes all DCs in a Windows 2000 forest
Terminal Server User	Includes all users who have logged on to a Terminal Services Server
System	Represents the local system
Creator Owner	Placeholder used for inheritance: It is replaced by the creator owner of the object that inherits the permission
Creator Group	Placeholder used for inheritance: It is replaced by the primary group of the creator owner of the object that inherits the permission.
Self	Placeholder—represents the object to whose ACLs "Self "is added

Figure 5.26
*Windows 2000
administrator
pyramid*

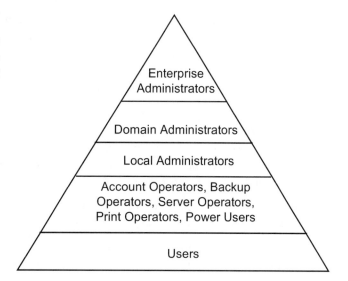

Table 5.17   *Windows 2000 Administrator Groups*

Group	Default Members on Workstations, Member Servers	Default Members on DCs
Enterprise Admins	NA	Administrator of forest root domain
Domain Admins	NA	Administrator of the domain
Administrators	Administrator, Domain Admins*	Administrator, Domain Admins, Enterprise Admins
Users	Authenticated Users, Domain Users*	Authenticated Users, Domain Users, Interactive
Power Users	Interactive Users	NA
Account Operators	NA	—
Server Operators	NA	—
Backup Operators	NA	—
Print Operators	NA	—

*The Domain Admins is added to the local Administrators group when the machine joins a domain; same thing for the Domain Users and the local Users group.

NT4 had two administrator groups: Domain Admins and Administrators, as follows:

1. The Administrators group on DCs was one and the same group, shared between all DCs of a domain. A member of this group had the right to manage all domain resources, including users, groups, rights, account policy, audit policy, trusts, shares, and the services on all DCs. The Administrators group on a member server or a workstation had the right to manage all resources on the local workstation or member server system.

2. The Domain Admins group itself didn't have proper rights. Members of the Domain Admins group received administrative rights over every system in a domain, because, by default, when a system joined the domain, the Domain Admins group was added to the local Administrators group.

Windows 2000 has three administrator groups: Enterprise Admins, Domain Admins, and Administrator, as follows:

■ The Enterprise Admins group is created in the first domain that's created in the forest, when this domain is switched to native mode. The

Enterprise Admins group also exists when the root domain of a forest is in mixed mode; however, in mixed mode it is a global security group. When you switch the domain to native mode, it will be automatically converted to a universal security group. The Enterprise Admins group is added automatically to every Administrators group of the DCs in every domain that joins the forest. This means that by default a member of the Enterprise Admins group can manage the configuration of a forest and also every DC in the forest. Table 5.18 lists some Windows 2000 administrative tasks that require enterprise administrator rights and permissions. The Enterprise Admins group is not added to the Domain Admins group and the Administrators group on member servers and workstations. However, since a member of the Enterprise Admins group can manage the group membership of every group in a domain, he or she can manage the group

Table 5.18 *Administrator Tasks that Require Enterprise Administrator Permissions*

Task	Reason
Create new domain in forest	▪ Creates crossRef objects in CN=Partitions, CN=Configuration
Manage Sites and Subnets	▪ Creates and modifies objects in CN=Sites, CN=Configuration subtree
Install Enterprise Certification Authority	▪ Creates CA object in CN=Public Key Services, CN=Services, CN=Configuration
Install Certification Authority for a child domain	▪ Creates objects in CN=Public Key Services, CN=Services, CN=Configuration subtree
Create Admission Control Service (ACS) policies	▪ Creates subnet objects in CN=Subnets, CN=Sites, CN=Configuration ▪ Creates CN=ACS, CN=Subnets, CN=Sites, CN=Configuration, and objects in this subtree
Install first Exchange 2000 server in forest	▪ Extends schema configuration NC ▪ Creates objects in CN=DisplaySpecifiers, CN=Configuration subtree ▪ Creates CN=MS Exchange, CN=Services, CN=Configuration, and objects in this subtree
Authorize a DHCP server	▪ Creates CN=DHCPRoot, CN=NetServices, CN=Services, CN=Configuration and objects in this subtree
Set up printer location tracking	▪ Set location attribute on subnet or site objects in CN=Sites, CN=Configuration subtree ▪ Set location attribute on computer object in any domain
Set up Simple Certificate Enrollment Protocol (SCEP)*	▪ Changes ACL on objects in CN=Public Key Services, CN=Services CN=Configuration subtree

*SCEP support comes as an add-on with the Windows 2000 resource kit; more information on SCEP can be found in Chapter 8.

membership of every group in a domain, and can add him- or herself to the Domain Admins group. This will give him or her access to every DC, member server, and workstation in that domain.

- The same rules as in NT4 apply to the Domain Admins and the Administrators groups on member servers and workstations.

A key problem of NT4 is its inflexible character on the level of granular administration. If you wanted to give an administrator permission to manage a subset of your domain accounts, you added him or her to the Domain Admins group. This gave him or her administrative control not just over the subset but over every account in your domain.

Windows 2000 includes major enhancements on the level of granular administration. In Windows 2000 it is possible to grant an administrator the permission to manage only a subset of the domain accounts.

Default group permissions and rights   A very important difference with NT4 is that Windows 2000 does not assign any default permissions or rights to the groups whose membership is automatically populated by the operating system. Some exceptions to this rule exist. For example, the Everyone group is granted read access to some file system and registry objects for backward compatibility with applications requiring anonymous read access. Also, the interactive group is used on Service ACLs where access depends on how you are logged on to the system rather than who you are logged in as. Instead, Windows 2000 only uses the groups whose membership can be controlled by an administrator to set default permissions and rights; these groups are the Users, Power Users, and Administrators groups. We will discuss these groups in the following text.

For workstation and member server computers, Windows 2000 provides the following permissions and rights for the Users, Power Users, and Administrators groups:

- Members of the Users group do not have broad read/write as in NT4. These users have read-only to most parts of the system and read/write only in their own profile folders. Users cannot install applications that require modification to system directories nor can they perform administrative tasks.

- Members of the Power Users group have all the access that Users and Power Users had in Windows NT4. Power Users have read/write to other parts of the system in addition to their own profile folders. They can perform per-machine installs and uninstalls of applications that do not install system services. They also can customize system-wide resources, such as the system time, display settings, shares, power configuration, printers. In Windows 2000, Microsoft tried to cut back the use of Power Users as much as possible. Applications satisfying the Windows 2000 Application Specification can run successfully as normal Users. Thus, in case all your applications are Windows 2000 compliant, you can increase security on your workstations by removing the Interactive Users from the Power Users group. You can find more information at *http://msdn.microsoft.com/winlogo/win2000.asp.*

- Members of the Administrators group have the same level of rights and permissions as they did for Windows NT4. Administrators can perform all operating system functions. An administrator can grant to himself or herself any right that an administrator does not have by default.

For servers configured as DCs, Windows 2000 provides the following permissions and rights for the Users, Operators, and Administrators groups:

- Members of the Users group do not have broad read/write permissions as in NT4. For example, unlike in NT4, users can only access DCs over the network; interactive logon to DCs is not granted.

- Members of the Account Operators, Server Operators, Backup Operators, and Printer Operators groups have the same access as in NT4.

- As in NT4, members of the Administrators group have full control of the system.

Group usage guidelines   A Windows 2000 administrator faces the same access control administration problem as was encountered in NT4: The administrator needs to give a universe of users access to a universe of resources. It's clear that groups can make the life of an administrator easier; which guidelines should the administrator follow? Here are some starting points:

- Use global groups to group users, use local groups (SAM local or domain local) to set the ACLs on resources, put global groups into local groups.

- Use universal groups to give users access to resources that are located in more than one domain. This means putting global groups into universal groups; put the universal groups into local groups and use these local groups to set ACLs.

- Use universal groups when their membership is static. Universal groups can cause excessive network traffic when their membership changes frequently. The reason for this was shown in Table 5.18. The membership of a universal group is stored in the Global Catalog (GC), which is replicated forest-wide. This is another reason to put users into global groups and the global groups into universal groups: Global groups should normally be more static than user membership.

Windows 2000 user rights

User rights can be split into two categories: logon rights and user privileges. Logon rights control who can log on to a computer system and how he or she can do the logon. User privileges are used to control access to system resources and system-related operations.

User rights are machine-specific; they are enforced by the LSA. As in NT4, user rights can be set on the machine level. To set them on a Windows 2000 machine you can use the Local GPO editor (LGPO) or the command prompt utility ntrights.exe (part of the resource kit). In Windows 2000 user rights can also be set and enforced globally using GPO settings. Table 5.19 lists user rights that are new to Windows 2000.

User rights versus user permissions   User rights are very different from user permissions (defined in an ACE). User rights ease the access control management for system resources and system-related tasks. Permissions are not intermediaries; they control the access to any securable object. Also, permissions affect only a particular object or a group of objects on a computer system; user rights affect the entire computer. Finally, user rights are set by a GPO administrator; permissions are set by the owner of an object or by the administrator of a computer system.

If user rights conflict with permissions, user rights will always have precedence. For example, if an administrator has the right to back up files and directories on a system, and the owner of some files stored on the system has explicitly denied the administrator access to these files, the administrator will still be able to back up the files.

Administrative delegation

Administrative delegation is the ability to delegate part of the administrative tasks to another administrator. Delegation is made possible thanks to changes to the Windows 2000 access control model and the inclusion of a special container, called an organizational unit (OU) in the Active Direc-

Table 5.19   *New Windows 2000 User Rights*

User Right	Meaning
Deny access to this computer from network, deny logon as a batch job, deny local logon, deny logon as a service	Prohibits an entity from connecting to the computer from the network, to log on as a batch job, to log on locally, or to log on as a service. These four rights all have a corresponding grant right. If both the grant and deny rights are set, the deny right will overrule the grant right.
Enable computer and user accounts to be trusted for delegation	Allows the user to change the Trusted for Delegation property on a user or computer object. Besides this right the user must also have write access to the object's account control flags.
Remove computer from docking station	Allows the user of a portable computer to undock the computer by clicking Eject PC on the Start menu. This feature protects against theft on docking stations that have special security options to anchor the portable.
Synchronize directory service data	Allows a process to synchronize AD data. Obviously, this right is relevant only on DCs.

tory. Besides delegation OUs can also help to provide a hierarchical view of objects within a domain. You should remember the following OU facts:

- OUs are not security principals (they don't have a SID). Because of this they cannot be used in ACLs; also, you cannot delegate administrative tasks to an OU. This makes them very different from groups. This does not mean that you cannot use ACLs to provide access control on OU objects.

- An object can only be contained in a single OU, although, from a hierarchical point of view, an object can have multiple parent OUs.

- OUs are bound to a single domain; an OU cannot span multiple domains.

The following example illustrates the use of organizational units: Jan De Clercq is defined as a user account in the *compaq.com* domain. He is a member of the Applied Microsoft Technology Group (AMTG). AMTG is a subgroup of the Technology Leadership Group (TLG). TLG is part of Compaq Professional Services (Compaq PS). This organizational structure can be reflected in the OU structure of the *compaq.com* domain, illustrated in Figure 5.27. The nesting of OUs is reflected in Jan De Clercq's distinguished name (every Active Directory object has a distinguished name): CN=Jan De Clercq, OU=AMTG, OU=TLG, OU=Compaq PS, DC= compaq, DC=com.

Figure 5.27
Organizational
unit hierachy
example

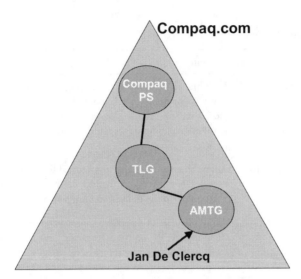

Suppose we want to do the following: Everyone in the AMTG department needs to access a folder on File Server 1. Everyone from TLG must have access to a database on File Server 2. In Windows 2000 we cannot resolve this by just adding the OUs to the ACLs of the resources (remember: OUs aren't security principals); we will need to create different security groups to set the resources' ACLs.

To facilitate the creation of a group containing all member objects of an OU, Microsoft created the Add Members to a Group menu option. You'll find this option when you right-click an OU object. MS does not provide a tool to dynamically synchronize OU content and group membership.

Setting up administrative delegation

To set up administrative delegation Microsoft has provided a delegation wizard on the level of sites, domains, and OUs. The delegation wizard allows an administrator to choose among a set of predefined delegation tasks (listed in Table 5.20). An administrator can also create customized tasks to fit to its organizational needs; these can be based on object-types and general or property-based permissions.

Administrators who are familiar with the new ACL editor and the changes on the level of the ACL model in Windows 2000 can do without the delegation wizard, and set delegation through a site, OUs, domains, or any other object's ACL editor.

To reflect the administrative delegation on the level of the administrator interface Windows 2000 allows you to develop customized administration

Table 5.20 *Predefined Windows 2000 Delegation Tasks*

Domain	Join a computer to the domain
	Manage group policy links
Site	Manage group policy links
OU	Create, delete, and manage user accounts
	Reset passwords on user accounts
	Read all user information
	Create, delete, and manage groups
	Modify the membership of a group
	Manage group policy links

interfaces; Microsoft calls them Taskpads. To create a taskpad you use the Taskpad View wizard. To get to this wizard open a new MMC console and add a snap-in; right-click the snap-in container and select New Taskpad View... in the menu. Customized MMC consoles and Taskpads can be saved as regular files; if you want, you can send them by mail to the administrator who needs them. To limit who can modify the MMC console or Taskpad you can change the Console Mode. Four console modes can be defined: Author Mode (full access), User Mode – full access (prevents a user from modifying console properties and adding or removing snap-ins), User Mode – limited access, multiple window (user can create new windows but not close existing ones), User Mode – limited access, single window (user cannot create new windows). You can find the console mode in the options dialog box, available from the MMC's Console menu.

An interesting third-party tool that can be used to set delegation using specific "roles" is DM/ActiveRoles from Fastlane Technologies. DM/ActiveRoles allows you to consolidate the access control settings used in AD's delegation model into logical roles.

Administrative delegation sample

The following example illustrates how you could use OUs and delegation in a Windows 2000 domain. Built into this domain are three administrative levels: the domain level (the users container), the location level (the location OUs, Brussels and Valbonne), and the business unit level (the Research and Consulting OUs). (See Figure 5.28.)

Figure 5.28
Administrative delegation sample

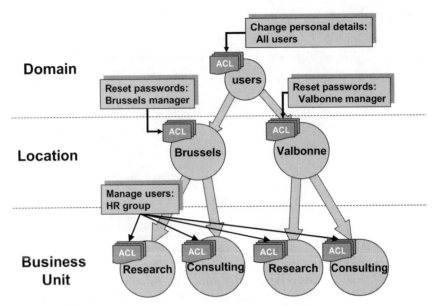

The three administrative levels are described in detail in the following list:

1. On the users container level, the administrator decided to give all users permission to manage their own personal details. To do this the administrator gave *Read Personal Information and Write Personal Information* permission to the Self group. This enables a user to read and write his own and only his or her own personal information.

2. On the location level, the administrator decided to give the location managers for the Valbonne and Brussels locations the permission to reset the passwords on all objects in that location. To do this the administrator delegated the *Reset passwords on user accounts* task to the location managers' accounts.

3. On the business unit level, the administrator decided to give members of the Human Resources (HR) group the permission to manage user accounts in the Research and Consulting business units of all locations. To do this the administrator delegated the *Create, delete, and manage user accounts* task to the HR group for both the research and consulting BUs. Notice that the same HR group has user managament permission over OUs in different locations.

Access control troubleshooting and administration tools

Table 5.21 lists the access control troubleshooting and administration tools that are shipped with Windows 2000 or as part of the Windows 2000 resource kit or the Windows 2000 support tools.

Table 5.21   *Access Control Tools*

Tool	Explanation
Windows 2000 Tools	
cacls	A command-line tool to view and update file system ACLs.
Resource Kit Tools	
Appsec	A GUI-based tool that allows administrators to restrict users' access to a predefined set of applications on the network.
Showpriv	A command-line tool that displays the privileges granted to users and groups.
Svcacls	A command-line tool to set ACLs on service objects (enables administrative delegation on the service level).
Enumprop	A command-line tool that can be used to look at the security descriptor of an AD object.
Global	A command-line tool that displays the members of global groups.
Grpcpy	A GUI-based tool that enables users to copy the user names in an existing group to another group in the same or another domain.
Local	A command-line tool that displays the members of local groups.
ntrights	A command-line tool that can be used to grant or revoke Windows 2000 rights for a user or group.
permcopy	A command-line tool that copies share permissions and file ACLs from one share to another.
perms	A command-line tool that displays a user's access permissions for a specified file or set of files.
showacls	A command-line tool that enumerates access rights for files, folders, and trees.
showgrps	A command-line tool that shows the groups to which a user belongs.
subinacl	A command-line tool to transfer security information from user to user, from local or global group to group, and from domain to domain.
showmbrs	A command-line tool that shows the user names of members of a given group.
Usrtogrp	A command-line tool that adds users to a local or global group according to information contained in a user-specified input text file.
xcacls	A command-line tool that can be used to set all file system security options accessible in Windows Explorer from the command line.

Table 5.21   *Access Control Tools (continued)*

Tool	Explanation
Support Tools	
Acldiag	A command-line tool that helps diagnose and troubleshoot problems with permissions on Active Directory objects.
Dsacls	A command-line tool that facilitates the management of ACLs for AD objects.
Sidwalker	Sidwalker consists of three separate programs. Two of these, Showaccs and Sidwalk, are command-line tools for examining and changing ACEs. The third, Security Migration Editor, is an MMC snap-in for editing mapping between old and new SIDs.
Sdcheck	A command-line tool that displays the security descriptor for any AD object.

5.4.4   Auditing

The auditing system of an operating system keeps track of all activities that occur on a computer system. It is another critical operating system security service, which can help you detect dangerous attacks occuring on your Windows 2000 computer system. It is important to stress that auditing keeps track of *all* activities: It not only gathers security-related information but also application- and system service–related information. In the following text, we will first discuss some general Windows 2000 auditing topics and tools; later we will look in more detail at security-related auditing in Windows 2000.

General Auditing: The Event Viewer and the Event Logs

When discussing general auditing in Windows 2000, we must address two topics: Event Logs and the Event Viewer. The Windows 2000 operating system gathers all events in Event Log files. By default these files (*.evt) are located in the <%systemdirectory%>\config\ subdirectory.

The Event Viewer is the Windows 2000 primary and only Event Log viewer. For every Event Log entry, the Event Viewer shows an event description, the account that caused the event, the event type (warning, error, information), the event ID, the source (originating service), and the date and time of the event. If the event description is missing, possibly the service's event DLL is not loaded on the system; the MS Knowledge Base article Q165959 explains how to load this DLL.

From a troubleshooting point of view, the event description and the event ID are the most important fields; the event ID allows you to look up up the event in the Microsoft Knowledge Base. The Event Viewer also allows the Event Logs to be displayed in a filtered manner.

You may have some difficulty locating the Event Viewer in the Windows 2000 interface; it is now integrated within the computer management MMC snap-in; of course, it can also be viewed as a standalone MMC snap-in. As in NT4 you can launch the Event Viewer from the command prompt by typing eventvwr.

Compared with its NT4 predecessor, the Event Viewer has been extended: It includes a set of new folders to gather auditing information related to certain OS core services (such as the Directory Service, the DNS Server and the File Replication Service). The services or applications that are logging their events to a particular folder can be found in the HKLM\SYSTEM\CurrentControlSet\Services\EventLog\<Log-name>\sources registry entry. Also, the description portion of the events has been extended, facilitating troubleshooting. Some events even include an HTTP pointer to the Microsoft online support site. Last but not least the event logs can now also be accessed using the WMI management interface.

As with NT4, the Event Viewer includes an application (to log program-specific information), security (to log security events), and system log (to log system-related events). The application log entries are fixed and set by the application developer. The system log entries are fixed as well and set by the OS. By default no security entries are logged; the security entries that are logged are configured by an administrator, as will be explained in the next section. If you need to, you can log your own events to the event log of a local or a remote computer using the resource kit utility logevent. This can be used to log, for example, the outcome of a batch script to the event logs. Typing logevent –m \\compaqdc1 –s E "Script Failed" at the command prompt will log an error saying "Script Failed" to the event log of the computer named compaqdc1.

The Windows 2000 Event Log files have, like their NT4 predecessors, a limited size. The size of a log file can be set per individual event viewer container. The default log files are named Appevent.evt, Secevent.evt, Sysevent.evt, ntds.evt, dnsevent.evt, and ntfrs.evt. The maximum log size is 999 MB (default is 512 KB). To cope with this limited size different retention policies can be set per individual container, as follows:

- Overwrite events as needed: When this option is set, the oldest events will automatically be overwritten with newer events when the log file fills up.

- Overwrite events older than X days: When this option is set, only events older than X days will be overwritten. If all events older than X days are overwritten, no more events are logged. Logging will start again from the moment some older events expire (or reach the X days limit).

- Do not overwrite events: When this option is set, no events are overwritten. When the log is full, logging stops. Logging can only be started again by manually clearing the logs.

Two features that are still missing from the Windows 2000 Event Viewer and its Event Log system is the ability to set up centralized logging and to archive Event Log settings in a professional manner. Centralized logging in this context means real-time gathering in a single, centralized database of all log events of all your computer systems. Organizations that want to keep track of the content of their Event Logs over time need to put in place some special archival procedures. Also, to enable centralized logging, special scripts or specific third-party software products are required.

To archive the log file content you can simply rely on your standard backup utility, or you can set up some special system using, for example, the resource kit command prompt utility dumpel.exe. In both cases you will have to align the log settings described above with your archival procedure to make sure that no log entries are lost. Dumpel dumps the Event Log content for a local or remote system in a tab-separated text file. Using the tool you can, for example, dump the Event Logs of all your DCs to a text file at regular intervals (using a scheduled batch script). Besides dumpel other third-party tools are available to dump the Event Log content: eventsave (*http:/// www.heysoft.de*) and ntolog (*http:///www.ntobjectives.com*).

The Security Configuration and Analysis (SCA) tool, as well as the security portion of the Windows 2000 GPOs, includes some interesting Event Viewer configuration settings. The GPO settings can be used to centrally control and manage the event viewer settings. The settings are in Table 5.22, together with their corresponding registry entry. The first four settings can be set for the application, security, and system log. The last one is only for the security log.

RestrictGuestAccess and CrashOnAuditFail are two critical parameters from a security point of view. CrashOnAuditFail prevents unauthorized actions from occurring when they cannot be logged in the security log. RestrictGuestAccess prohibits members of the Domain Guests group from viewing the information in one of the Event Log containers.

Table 5.22 *Event Viewer Registry Hacks*

Setting	Registry Entry
	HKLM\System\CurrentControlSet\Services\Eventlog\<log name>\
Maximum log file size	MaxSize (REG_DWORD)
Restrict guest access to log	RestrictGuestAccess (REG_DWORD)
Retention policy and retention method	Retention (REG_DWORD)
	HKLM\System\CurrentControlSet\Control\LSA\
Shut down the computer when the security audit log is full	CrashOnAuditFail (REG_DWORD):

Security-related auditing

The security auditing system in Windows 2000 is very closely related to the access control system. As with the access control settings, auditing settings can be set on individual objects and are stored in an object's security descriptor. Each time an object is accessed its auditing settings are checked to see whether this type of access needs to be audited. In the following text, we will focus on how to set up security-related auditing in Windows 2000. We will shortly introduce the Security Configuration and Analysis tool (SCA), a tool you can use to analyze security-related settings.

Setting up security-related auditing

As in NT4, Windows 2000 security logging is disabled by default. To set up security event logging you must define a security audit policy and set auditing properties for a number of event categories on the object level. Once set up, Windows 2000 will log the security-related events to the security container of the Event Viewer. Remember that to look at the content of this container you need to be a local administrator on the system. The content of the other containers can be looked at by any user.

A Windows 2000 audit policy defines which categories of audit events will be recorded in a computer's local security log. It is defined through Group Policy Object settings on the domain, site, or OU level. You can find the audit policy in the GPO computer configuration, underneath Windows Settings\Security Settings\Local Policies\Audit Policies. You can also set the audit policy locally using the Local Security Settings configuration tool or the command prompt resource kit tool auditpol.exe. Auditpol can also be used to set the audit settings on a remote machine. To run it remotely you need administrator rights on the target computer.

Table 5.23   *Audit Policy Categories*

Audit Policy Category	Meaning
Audit Account Logon Events	Monitors network logon.
Audit Account Management	Monitors creation, deletion, and modification of security principals.
Audit Directory Access	Monitors administrative access to AD.
Audit Logon Events	Monitors interactive logon.
Audit Object Access	Monitors access to all securable objects (objects with an ACL).
Audit Policy Change	Monitors policy changes.
Audit Privilege Use	Monitors priviliged access to resources by the system or accounts that have system priviliges.
Audit Process Tracking	Monitors access to executable files (DLL, EXE).
Audit System Events	Monitors system events.

Table 5.23 shows the event categories that can be logged. For all categories you can set auditing for both successful and failed attempts.

To set up auditing on the object level, right-click the object, select properties; open up the Security tab, click advanced, and select the Auditing tab. You'll see that you can set up auditing based on the account or group performing an action and the type of action being performed (as illustrated in Figures 5.29 and 5.30). As with access control Microsoft included some important changes on the level of object auditing, as follows:

- Windows 2000 permits a much finer granularity for object and property auditing than NT4. As with access control, auditing settings can be defined based on object types and object properties.

- Windows 2000 includes the capability to define auditing "inheritance" between parent and child objects.

- The object auditing administration interface has been extended to reflect the changes we just mentioned and is integrated with the new Windows 2000 ACL editor.

The security configuration and analysis tool

The Security Configuration and Analysis (SCA) tool can be used to analyze and configure the security settings (including the auditing settings) on a Windows 2000 or NT4 computer. SCA was introduced in SP4 for NT4; an updated version is provided with Windows 2000. In NT4, the tool was

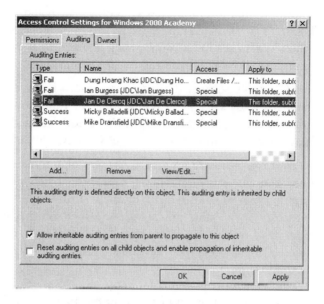

called Security Configuration Editor (SCE). The Windows 2000 SCA version includes support for the new security features of Windows 2000.

To analyze and configure security settings SCA uses the values that are defined in the SCA security template. Windows 2000 ships with a set of predefined security templates (we will come back to them in Chapter 7). The templates can be edited manually using Notepad or using the "security templates" MMC snap-in. They contain all kinds of Windows 2000 security-related parameters: ACLs on file system and registry objects, Event Log settings, restricted groups (to set group membership), registry keys and values, system service, account policy, and audit policy settings. So far SCA cannot handle NTFS share and printer permissions.

SCA uses a security database (secedit.sdb) in which one of the security templates is loaded. The SCA engine can be run from the MMC snap-in or from the command prompt (using the secedit executable). The same engine is used for the security portion of the Windows 2000 GPO settings.

SCA is a great step forward in the area of automated security configuration. You can easily extend the tool using batch scripting or any other scripting tool to control centrally the security of all the machines in your network—at the same time, you can gather security information. A good example of this has been developed by Pauli Hopea of Tieturi Knowledge-pool, Finland. You can download Pauli's sample scripts from *http://www.tieture.fi/scts*.

Third-party security auditing and monitoring tools

To provide an adequate level of Windows 2000 operating system auditing and monitoring in accordance with your company's security policy, you might need more tools than the ones MS gives you for free with the OS, the support tools, and the resource kit. The third-party tools we will discuss here can be classified as follows:

- Windows 2000–specific auditing and monitoring tools: Event Log, Registry and Access Control Analyzers.

- General auditing and monitoring tools: Port Scanners (vulnerability scanners), Packet Sniffers, and Intrusion Detection Systems (IDS).

Table 5.24 provides a rough overview of the products available on the market. Although most of them will work on Windows 2000, we do not guarantee that they will. Table 5.24 is mainly based on the products that were available for NT4; most of the vendors will provide a version for Windows 2000. If you want more details, contact the vendor, or check out their Web site.

Windows 2000–specific security auditing and monitoring tools

This section lists products that can provide additional auditing and monitoring functionality for typical Windows 2000 components such as the event logs, the registry and the file system.

A copy of CyberSafe's Log Analyst and Seagate's Crystal Reports comes for free with the Windows 2000 resource kit.

Table 5.24 *Third-Party Auditing and Monitoring Tools*

Company	Product	Web Site
Event Log Analyzers		
CyberSafe	Log Analyst	http://www.cybersafe.com
Seagate	Crystal Reports	http://www.seagatesoftware.com
NT Objectives	NTLast – VisualLast	http://www.ntobjectives.com/
SomarSoft	DumpEvt	http://somarsoft.com
Systemtools	Event Log Monitor	http://www.systemtools.com
Registry Analyzers		
SomarSoft	Dumpreg	http://somarsoft.com
Pedestal Software	Intact	http://www.pedestalsoftware.com/
System Internals	Regmon	http://www.sysinternals.com
Tripwire	Tripwire	http://www.tripwiresecurity.com
Access Control Analyzers		
SomarSoft	Dumpsec	http://somarsoft.com
System Tools	Security Explorer	http://www.systemtools.com

General auditing and monitoring tools

In this section we'll discuss some general auditing and monitoring tools that can be used for and from other platforms than just Windows 2000. Some of the tools (e.g., some port scanner and packet sniffer tools, such as Nmap, Saint, Nessus, QueSO) cannot run on Windows 2000, although they can be used to scan Windows 2000 related network traffic.

Port scanners and packet sniffers   Table 5.25 lists some of the port scanner and packet sniffer tools currently on the market.

The Windows 2000 Network Monitor (Netmon) comes with the Windows 2000 OS code.

Intrusion detection systems   The goal of Intrusion Detection Systems (IDSs) is to detect a hacker breaking into your corporate IT infrastructure or a legitimate user misusing your IT resources. Many organizations neglect the enemy inside: the legitimate user who is misusing, by accident or intentionally, your IT infrastructure. Recent studies (the FBI computer crime survey) show that about 60 percent of the attacks are carried out by legitimate users.

Table 5.25   *Port Scanner and Packet Sniffer Tools*

Company	Product	Web Site
Point One	UltraScan	http://www.point1.com\ultrascan\
The Nessus Project	Nessus	http://www.nessus.com
NT Objectives	NTO Scanner	http://www.ntobjectives.com
Winternals	TCPview Pro	http://www.winternals.com
Insecure.org	Nmap	http://insecure.org
World Wide Digital Security	Saint	http://www.wwdsi.com
The Apostols UNIX Cult	Queso	http://www.apostols.org
Network Associates	Sniffer (formerly netxray)	http://www.nai.com
Microsoft	Netmon	http://www.microsoft.com

Table 5.26   *IDS Products*

Company	Product	Web Site
AXENT Technologies	NetProwler—Intruder Alert	http://www.axent.com
Cisco Systems	Cisco Secure IDS—NetRanger	http://www.cisco.com
Internet Security Systems	RealSecure—System Scanner	http://www.iss.net
Norton–Symantec	Norton Internet Security 2000	http://www.symantec.com/sabu/nis
RSA security	Kane Security Analyst	http://www.rsa.com
Network Associates	Cybercop	http://www.nai.com
Bindview	NOSadmin	http://www.bindview.com
Cybersafe	Centrax	http://www.cybersafe.com
Agilent Technologies	SFProtect	http://www.agilent.com
NetworkIce	Black Ice	http://www.networkice.com
Webtrends	Webtrends Security Analyzer	http://www.webtrends.com

Table 5.27 *OS Security Summary*

OS Security	Windows 2000 Highlights
Authentication	▪ Default authentication protocol: Kerberos ▪ Credential store: Active Directory or SAM ▪ Negotiate support for NTLM and Kerberos
Authorization	▪ Fine-Grain Access Control ▪ Support for Administrative Delegation
Auditing	▪ Extended Event Viewer ▪ Security Configuration and Analysis tool (SCA) ▪ Fine-Grain Auditing (property level)

An intrusion can be defined as any attempt to compromise the confidentiality, integrity, availability, or authenticity of one of your corporate IT resources.

Intrusion detection tools can be categorized in two classes: audit tools and analysis tools. Audit tools should detect misuse of any corporate IT resource; analysis tools try to detect deviations from normal system usage patterns. One of the tasks of an analysis tool is to analyze the audit trails. Table 5.26 lists some well-known IDS products and their vendors.

The ISS System Scanner is a Windows 2000–specific IDS system; a copy of it comes with the Windows 2000 resource kit.

5.5 Summary

Table 5.27 shows the highlights of the three main OS security building blocks in Windows 2000. We will cover Windows 2000 authentication in great detail in the next chapter.

6

Windows 2000 Authentication

In this chapter we will look at the most important operating system security service and how it is implemented in Windows 2000: authentication. We will look at the Windows 2000 authentication architecture and at the nuts and bolts of the Kerberos authentication protocol: how it compares to NTLM, how it can be used as a single sign-on solution between different operating systems, and so on.

6.1   Introduction

Before an entity is given access to a resource on a Windows 2000 system, the operating system must validate the entity's identity and check whether it can access that particular resource. The latter process is known as access control; it was discussed in the previous chapter. The first process is known as authentication, and it will be discussed extensively in this chapter. The primary purpose of authentication is to prove and validate an entity's identity. It answers the question of who or what is the system talking to?

In a Windows environment, you bootstrap the authentication process by pressing CTRL+ALT+DEL (known as the Secure Attention Sequence [SAS]) to log on to a machine or a domain (this is called an interactive logon). A valid interactive logon results in a local logon session. If you want to access a resource located on another machine during your logon session, another authentication process will be started (this is called a noninteractive logon). A valid noninteractive logon results in a network logon session.

Every entity that authenticates to a Windows 2000 system is called a principal. A principal is identified by its Security Identifier (SID); to prove its identity during an authentication process, a principal uses credentials. Credentials allow principals to be distinguished from one another and to identify them. Examples of credentials are a principal's account name and its password. Don't confuse principal and account. An account is a record in an authentication authority's database; a principal is an entity that can be identified by a Windows 2000 system. If the operating system accepts this type of credential for authentication, the fact that the principal knows its account name and password is regarded by the operating system as a proof of its identity. Remember from the previous chapter that the OS may well accept other credentials. In Windows 2000, for example, you may use a smart card and a PIN code or a fingerprint.

The component that handles authentication on the operating system side is known as the authentication authority. The authentication authority differs depending on what you're logging on to. If you log on locally to a machine, it is the Local Security Authority (LSA) on the machine itself; but if you log on to a domain, authentication is performed against the LSA of a DC. To be able to validate a principal's identity the authentication authority needs a copy of a principal's credentials; they are stored in the authentication database.

A Windows 2000 authentication process can use different authentication protocols: NTLM (NT LAN Manager), Kerberos, SSL (TLS), Distributed Password Authentication (DPA), and so on. The manner in which these protocols are embedded in the Windows 2000 authentication architecture is explained in the next section.

6.2   Windows 2000 Authentication Architecture

Since its early days, one of the most important design principles of NT has been modularity. NT's authentication architecture is an excellent example of a modular architecture built upon different abstraction layers. In Windows 2000 this architecture is basically the same as the one used in NT4. Ninety percent of the changes that Microsoft incorporated can be described as the plugging in of supplementary security modules.

Windows 2000 is built upon four basic logon types: local (or interactive) logon, network (or noninteractive) logon, batch, and service logon. Batch logon is used by task schedulers (e.g., the "at" or "WINat" service); service logon is used by services. All of them have slightly different architectures. In the following text, we will focus on local and network logon.

6.2.1   Architecture for interactive authentication

The architecture for interactive authentication is illustrated in Figure 6.1. An interactive authentication starts whenever a user initiates an SAS

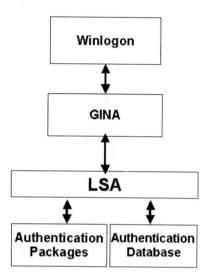

Figure 6.1
Interactive
authentication
architecture

sequence. This makes the Winlogon service call the GINA module. (GINA stands for Graphical Identification and Authentication.) Winlogon is the OS component that provides interactive authentication. GINA is the component responsible for displaying the logon interface, extracting the user's credentials, and passing them to the Local Security Authority (LSA).

The Local Security Authority is the OS kernel component that acts as authentication authority: It interacts with the local security database and the authentication packages and handles user authentication. To decide if a user is permitted to log on the LSA relies on both authentication packages and security databases.

Authentication packages are software packages that implement different authentication protocols. In NT4 the only available authentication package was MSV1_0. MSV1_0 was the package that performed a passthrough authentication if there wasn't a credential store (a SAM database) available locally to validate the user's credentials. Software vendors can implement their own authentication package to provide other authentication protocols.

Windows 2000 comes with two authentication packages: MSV1_0 and Kerberos. You can find out which authentication package DLLs are available at your machine by looking into the HKEY_LOCAL_MACHINES\System\CurrentControlSet\Control\Lsa\AuthenticationPackages registry location. The Kerberos authentication package cannot handle local logon requests on workstations or member servers. Kerberos requires the presence of a Key Distribution Center (KDC) service, which is only available on a Windows 2000 DC.

The authentication database stores the credentials needed during the authentication process. In this context "authentication database" refers to the same concept as security database. NT4 machines, Windows 2000 workstations, and member servers store credentials in the SAM database (which is part of the system registry). A Windows 2000 DC stores credentials in the Active Directory. In the first case, the credentials contain local accounts; in the second, domain accounts.

6.2.2 Architecture for noninteractive authentication

Figure 6.2 provides a simplified overview of the noninteractive authentication architecture used in a distributed application consisting of a client and a server component. A good example of a distributed application is an Outlook client accessing an Exchange mailbox. This architecture introduces two new important concepts: the Security Support Provider Interface (SSPI) and Security Support Providers (SSPs).

Communication between the client and the server component happens via communication protocols. These protocols can be typical LAN communication protocols such as SMB and RPC, or typical Internet-oriented communication protocols such as HTTP, POP3, NNTP, and LDAP.

The SSPI is an Application Programming Interface (API), sitting between the communication protocols and the security protocols; it has two important functions, as follows:

1. Its primary function is to abstract the commonalities of different authentication protocols and to hide their specific implementation details. For example, Kerberos and NTLM both use the concept of a master key; NTLM, however, uses a challenge-response mechanism, while Kerberos relies on a ticketing system.

2. Abstract communication protocols from security protocols. Any security protocol should be available to any communication protocol; or, in other words, the implementation of a security protocol should not contain any communication protocol–specific code.

A Security Support Provider (SSP) is a software module that implements a security protocol. SSPs can be plugged into the SSPI. Out-of-the box Windows 2000 supports the following SSPs: NTLM, Kerberos, SChannel (SSL and TLS), and Distributed Password Authentication (DPA). The NTLM SSP supports LAN Manager authentication, NTLM version 1, and NTLM version 2. NTLM is the default authentication protocol of NT4.

Figure 6.2
Noninteractive
authentication
architecture

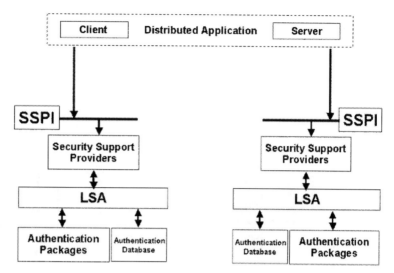

DPA is a challenge response–based authentication protocol introduced in the Microsoft Commercial Internet System (MCIS). Software vendors can also implement their own SSP to provide other security models. In the next release of Windows 2000 (*Windows.net*, codenamed "Whistler"), Microsoft will provide a "Digest authentication" SSP.

Notice in Figure 6.2 that SSPs access authentication packages via the LSA. It also shows the LSA communicating with the authentication database: remember from the previous section that the LSA validates credentials by comparing them with the entries in its authentication database. One concept not shown in Figure 6.2 is that most SSPs rely on Cryptographic Service Providers (CSPs). CSPs are modules that provide basic cryptographic functions. For example, encryption using the Data Encryption Standard (DES), signing using RSA, or hashing using Message Digest 4 (MD4). SSPs can call on different CSPs thanks to another abstraction layer introduced in NT4: the CryptoAPI (or CAPI). The Crypto API will explained in Chapter 8.

Because the model shown in Figure 6.2 contains multiple authentication protocols (SSPs), there has to be some kind of negotiation between the client and the server before the actual authentication can take place. To enable the negotiation Microsoft included a special SSP called Negotiate; it is illustrated in Figure 6.3. This package is based on the Simple and Protected GSS-API Negotiation Mechanism (SPNEGO), as defined in Internet draft RFC 2478: The Simple and Protected GSS-API Negotiation Mechanism. In order to negotiate an authentication protocol the Negotiate package has

Figure 6.3
*Role of the
Negotiate SSPI*

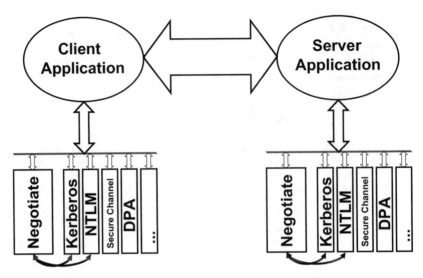

to know how to communicate with the corresponding authentication package. So far the Negotiate SSP can only deal with the Kerberos and NTLM package.

So how does this negotiation work? The first SSP that is called by the SSPI when a call for authentication comes in is the Negotiate SSP. The client Negotiate package then sends a list of available SSPs to the server. Finally, the server Negotiate package picks an SSP based on its locally available SSPs and communicates it to the client. Although this negotiation clearly adds some communication overhead, it offers much more flexibility.

In Windows 2000 the Negotiate SSP's first choice for authentication is Kerberos. It will fall back to NTLM if the following conditions are present:

- No KDC service (read Windows 2000 domain controller) is available in the domain.

- A service's Service Principal name (SPN) is not registered (SPNs will be explained in Section 6.6.1). For example, when a user tries to access a file share on a server of which the host SPN is not registered, the user will be authenticated using NTLM.

Also, if the use of Kerberos is not feasible, the Negotiate SSP will first try NTLM version 2, then NTLM version 1, and then LAN Manager authentication. The supported NTLM SSP protocols can be configured using the LMCompatibilityLevel registry key; for more information, take a look at Microsoft Knowledge Base article Q147706, "How to Disable LM Authentication on Windows NT."

An excellent tool to get a deeper understanding of how the SSPI really works is the SSPI workbench. It is written by Keith Brown from Develop-Mentor and can be downloaded from the Microsoft MSDN Web site *http://www.microsoft.com/msdn.*

6.2.3 Authentication architecture overview

The most important updates to the Windows 2000 authentication architecture are as follows:

- Kerberos, the new default authentication protocol, has been implemented as both an authentication package and a Security Support Provider (SSP). The rest of this chapter will focus on the Kerberos authentication protocol.

- Windows 2000 includes another new SSP: the Negotiate package.

- On a DC the authentication credentials are stored in the Active Directory.

Table 6.1 gives an overview of the different authentication types, the authentication packages, and SSPs available in NT4 and Windows 2000.

Table 6.1 *Overview of Windows 2000 Authentication Types, Packages, and SSPs*

Authentication Type	Machine–Domain Logon	Logon From	Authentication Package		Security Support Provider (SSP)	
Interactive authentication	Machine logon	Non-DC	NT4	MSV1_0	NT4	NA
			Win2K	MSV1_0	Win2K	NA
		DC	NT4	MSV1_0	NT4	NA
			Win2K	Kerberos	Win2K	NA
	Domain logon	Any Machine	NT4	MSV1_0	NT4	NA
			Win2K	Kerberos	Win2K	NA
Noninteractive authentication	NA	Any Machine	NT4	MSV1_0	NT4	NTLM
			Win2K	Kerberos	Win2K	Negotiate Kerberos NTLM Secure Channel

6.3   Introducing Kerberos

In Greek mythology Kerberos is a three-headed dog who guards the entrance to the underworld. In the context of this book Kerberos refers to the authentication protocol developed as part of the MIT Athena project.

Kerberos is embedded in Windows 2000 as the new default authentication protocol. Every Windows 2000 workstation and server includes a client Kerberos authentication provider. Windows 2000 does not include Kerberos support for other Microsoft platforms. If you want your NT4, Windows 95, or 98 clients to authenticate using Kerberos, you'll need to upgrade your workstation to Windows 2000 Professional. In the early days of Windows 2000 Microsoft promised to include Kerberos support for Windows 95 and 98 in the Directory Service Client, an add-on for Windows 95 and 98, which can be found on the Windows 2000 Server CD. The same is true for the NT4 Directory Service Client, which Microsoft released in September 2000. You can download it from the Microsoft Web site.

A little more about the dog's three heads: they stand for authentication, access control, and auditing. The basic Kerberos protocol (version 5, as defined in RFC 1510) only deals with authentication. Microsoft's implementation of the protocol also includes extensions for access control. So far no Kerberos implementation covers auditing. But there's more than the three As: Later in this chapter we'll explain how one of the secret keys exchanged during the Kerberos authentication sequence can be used for packet authentication, integrity, and confidentiality services.

Another way to look at the dog's three heads is as the basic entities the protocol is dealing with. There are always three: two entities that want to authenticate to one another (e.g., a user and a resource server) and an entity that mediates between the two—a trusted third party, or in Kerberos terminology, the Key Distribution Center (KDC).

6.3.1   Kerberos positioning

Figure 6.4 positions NTLM, Kerberos, and SSL-TLS together with the main cryptographic technology they rely upon. (SSL stands for Secure Sockets Layer; TLS for Transport Layer Security; TLS is SSL version 3.1.) NTLM relies on symmetric key cryptography. SSL-TLS uses asymmetric key cryptography. Windows 2000 Kerberos comes in two flavors: standard Kerberos (as defined in RFC 1510) is based on symmetric key cryptography; Kerberos PKINIT uses asymmetric key cryptography.

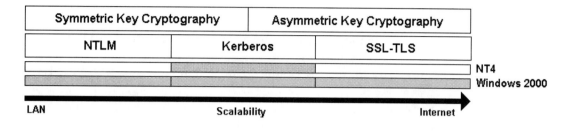

Figure 6.4 *Kerberos positioning*

Authentication protocols purely based on asymmetric cryptography scale better than protocols based on symmetric cryptography. In asymmetric solutions, the trusted third party doesn't need to be online all the time. Of the two symmetric solutions, Kerberos and NTLM, Kerberos scales better than NTLM. This is mainly due to the Kerberos ticketing system. Still, Kerberos cannot scale to environments such as the Internet. For Internet authentication the best available solution remains SSL-TLS.

Compared with their symmetric-key counterparts asymmetric crypto–based authentication protocols are more complex to administer. Asymmetric cryptography is also a relatively new technology. This is one of the main reasons why Microsoft didn't choose a full asymmetric crypto–based solution and instead incorporated Kerberos as the new default authentication protocol of Windows 2000.

6.3.2 Kerberos Advantages

In this section, we will explain the key differences between NTLM and Kerberos and the advantages Kerberos brings to the Windows 2000 operating system and its users. This section is just an introduction; in later sections, we will look at the technical details.

Faster authentication

The core of the Kerberos protocol uses a unique ticketing system, providing faster authentication, as follows:

- Every authenticated domain entity can request tickets from its KDC to access other domain resources.

- The tickets are considered access permits by the resource servers.

- The ticket can be used more than once and can be cached on the client side.

When a resource server or the KDC gets a Kerberos ticket and a Kerberos authenticator from the client, the server has enough information to authenticate the client. If the resource server is not a DC, NTLM requires the server to contact a DC to validate a user's authentication request (this process is known as pass-through authentication). Thanks to its ticketing system, Kerberos does not need pass-through authentication. This is why Kerberos accelerates the authentication process. A downside to the ticketing system is that it puts a greater workload on the client.

Mutual authentication

Kerberos supports mutual authentication. This means that the client authenticates to the service that's responsible for the resource and that the service authenticates to the client. This is a big difference from NTLM. The NTLM challenge/response provides only client authentication: The server challenges the client, the client calculates a response, and the server validates that response. Using NTLM users might provide their credentials to a bogus server.

Transitive trust

As in NT 4.0, a trust between two Windows 2000 domains facilitates cross-domain resource access and creates cross-domain account visibility. In Windows 2000 Microsoft simplified trust creation and management by letting you create trusts automatically as part of the domain hierarchy building process (DCPROMO) and by allowing transitive trust. Although they are created automatically, so far there's no simple way to turn trust relationships off.

Transitive trust means that if both *europe.compaq.com* and *us.compaq.com* trust *compaq.com*, then *europe.compaq.com* implicitly trusts *us.compaq.com*. In the current version of Windows 2000, however, this is only true if both the *europe* and the *us* domain are in the same Windows 2000 forest. So far, trust relationships between forests are always nontransitive. Transitive trust reduces the number of trusts needed for authentication. In Figure 6.5, only four trusts are needed (between each parent and child domain) to obtain authentication interoperability between all three domains. NT4 would have needed six trust relationships to do the same thing.

Transitive trust is only a logical concept—no shared secret exists between the DCs of the domains that share a transitive trust. This means that for authentication to occur between entities on opposite ends of a transitive trust, the authentication process will not flow across the transitive trust but through the trust path. This is illustrated in Figure 6.5. It shows the mes-

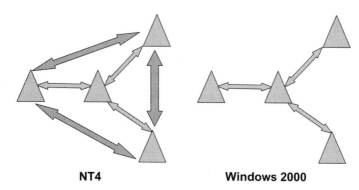

Figure 6.5
*Number of trust
relationships
required in
Windows 2000
and NT4*

NT4   **Windows 2000**

sage flow needed to authenticate a user defined in *europe* and logging on to a machine in the *us* domain. The flow follows the trust path, not the transitive trust.

Kerberos is an open standard

Microsoft based its Kerberos implementation on the standard defined in RFC 1510 (this is Kerberos V5). This is why Kerberos can provide single sign-on between Windows 2000 and other OSs supporting an RFC1510 based Kerberos implementation. Over the past years, Microsoft has been actively involved in the Kerberos standardization process. Microsoft software engineers participated in the creation of the standards and standard drafts listed in Table 6.2.

Support for delegation

Delegation can be looked at as a next step after impersonation. Thanks to impersonation a service can access local resources on behalf of a user; thanks to delegation a service can even access remote resources on behalf of a user. What delegation really means is that user A can give rights to intermediary machine B to authenticate to an application server C as if machine B were user A. This means that application server C will base access control decisions on user A's identity rather than on machine B's account. Delegation is also known as authentication forwarding. In Kerberos terminology this means that user A forwards a ticket to intermediary machine B, and machine B then uses user A's ticket to authenticate to application server C.

You can use delegation for authentication in multitier applications; an example of such an application is database access using a web front end, where the browser, the web server, and the database server are all running on a different machine. In a multitier application authentication happens on different tiers; preferably every authentication process can use the same

Table 6.2   *Kerberos IETF Standards and Drafts*

Standard or Draft Name	Available From
The Kerberos Network Authentication Service (V5)	*http://www.ietf.org/internet-drafts/draft-ietf-cat-kerberos-revisions-04.txt*
Public Key Cryptography for Initial Authentication in Kerberos (PKINIT)	*http://www.ietf.org/internet-drafts/draft-ietf-cat-kerberos-pk-init-10.txt*
The Simple and Protected GSS-API Negotiation Mechanism (RFC 2478)	*http://www.ietf.org/rfc/rfc2478.txt*
Generating KDC Referrals to Locate Kerberos Realms	*http://www.ietf.org/internet-drafts/draft-swift-win2k-krb-referrals-00.txt*
The Windows 2000 RC4-HMAC Kerberos Encryption Type	*http://www.ietf.org/internet-drafts/draft-brezak-win2k-krb-rc4-hmac-01.txt*
User to User Kerberos Authentication Using GSS-API	*http://www.ietf.org/internet-drafts/draft-swift-win2k-krb-user2user-00.txt*
Extension to Kerberos V5 for Additional Initial Encryption	*http://www.ietf.org/internet-drafts/draft-ietf-cat-kerberos-extra-tgt-02.txt*
Extending Change Password for Setting Kerberos Passwords	*http://www.ietf.org/internet-drafts/draft-trostle-win2k-cat-kerberos-set-passwd-00.txt*

credentials. In such an application setup it is impossible to use NTLM for authentication on every link, simply because NTLM does not support delegation.

Support for smart-card logon

Through the Kerberos PKINIT extension Windows 2000 includes support for smart-card logon. Smart-card logon provides much stronger authentication than password logon does, because it relies on two-factor authentication: To log on, a user needs a smart card and its PIN code. Smart-card logon also offers stronger security in general: it blocks Trojan Horse attacks that attempt to grab a user's password from the system memory.

6.3.3   **Comparing Kerberos with NTLM**

Table 6.3 compares Kerberos, the default authentication protocol of Windows 2000, to NTLM, the default authentication protocol of NT4. It also lists the main features of both protocols introduced in the previous sections.

Table 6.3   *Kerberos–NTLM Comparison*

	NTLM	Kerberos
Cryptographic Technology	Symmetric Cryptography	Basic Kerberos: Symmetric Cryptography Kerberos PKINIT: Symmetric and Asymmetric Cryptography
Trusted Third Party	DC	Basic Kerberos: DC with KDC service Kerberos PKINIT: DC with KDC service and Enterprise CA
Microsoft-Supported Platforms	Windows 95, Windows 98, NT4, Windows 2000	Windows 2000
Features	Slower authentication because of passthrough authentication	Faster authentication because of unique ticketing system
	No mutual authentication	Mutual authentication
	No support for delegation of authentication	Support for delegation of authentication
	No support for transitive trust if the authenticating DC is an NT4 DC. Support for transitive trust if the authenticating DC is a Windows 2000 DC.	Support for transitive trust
	No support for smart-card logon	Support for smart-card logon
	Proprietary Microsoft standard, poorly documented	Open standard, fully documented
	No protection for access control data carried in NTLM messages[*]	Cryptographic protection for access control data carried in Kerberos tickets

[*]This was the case for NTLM version 1; this problem has been resolved in NTLM version 2.

6.4   Kerberos: the basic protocol

The following text explains the basic Kerberos protocol as it is defined in RFC 1510. Those not familiar with Kerberos may be bewildered by the need for numerous diverse keys to be transmitted around the network. In order to break down the complexity of the protocol we will approach it in five steps, as follows:

- Step 1: Kerberos authentication is based on symmetric key cryptography.

- Step 2: The Kerberos KDC provides scalability.

- Step 3: A Kerberos ticket provides secure transport of a session key.

- Step 4: The Kerberos KDC distributes the ticket by sending it via the client.

- Step 5: The Kerberos ticket-granting ticket limits the use of the entities' master keys.

Before starting to explore how Kerberos works, we must explain the notations that will be used in the illustrations, as follows:

- u stands for user, s stands for resource server, k stands for KDC.

- S stands for session key; Sus means the session key shared between the user and the resource server.

- M stands for master key; Mu is the master key of the user.

- Illustration (1) in Figure 6.6 represents the session key shared between the user and resource server.

- Illustration (2) in Figure 6.6 represents the same session key, but this time encrypted.

- Illustration (3) in Figure 6.6 represents the same session key, encrypted using the master key of the user.

To ease reading we will talk about a client, Alice, and a resource server that authenticate using Kerberos. The identities used in this Kerberos

Figure 6.6
Session keys and encrypted session keys

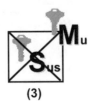

(1)   (2)   (3)

authentication exchange are Alice's SID and the SID of the service account that is used by the application or the service responsible for the resource. To be fully correct we should discuss the service account of the service, but this would not facilitate ease of reading. Also, when we discuss Alice, we really mean the LSA on Alice's machine impersonating Alice and acting on her behalf. From now on the following words are synonyms: principal, security principal, and entity; domain and realm.

6.4.1   Step 1: Kerberos authentication is based on symmetric key cryptography

To authenticate entities Kerberos uses symmetric key cryptography. In symmetric key cryptography the communicating entities use the same key for both encryption and decryption. The basic mathematical formula behind this process is the following:

$$D_K(E_K(M)) = M$$

If the encryption (E) and decryption (D) processes are both using the same key (K), the decryption of the encrypted text (M) results in the readable text (M).

This is what happens when Alice wants to authenticate to a resource server using a symmetric key cipher (illustrated in Figure 6.7):

- Alice encrypts her name and the current time stamp using a symmetric key.

- The encrypted message and Alice's name are sent to the resource server.

- The resource server decrypts the message.

- The resource server checks Alice's name and the time stamp (this is the result of the decryption process). If they're OK, Alice is authenticated to the server.

Why does this process authenticate Alice to the resource server? If the resource server can successfully decrypt the message, meaning if it results in Alice's name and an acceptable time stamp, the resource server knows that only Alice could have encrypted this information, since she's the only one, besides the resource server, who knows the symmetric key. An "acceptable time stamp" means that resource server compares the time stamp received in Alice's encrypted packet against the local time. If the time skew between these two time stamps is too big, the resource service will reject the authentication attempt, since a hacker could have replayed Alice's original authen-

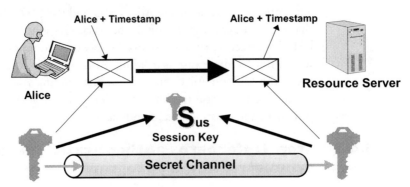

tication packet. Notice the differences and similiarities with NTLM. Both Kerberos and NTLM use symmetric cryptography for authentication: "If you can prove you know your secret key, I believe you are who you say you are." In NTLM the knowledge of the secret key is proven using a challenge-response mechanism. Kerberos uses symmetric encryption of the time stamp and the user's name to do the same thing. The encrypted packet containing Alice's name and the time stamp is known in Kerberos as the authenticator, the symmetric key is called a session key. A session key exists between all Kerberos principals that want to authenticate to each other.

A critical element in the above exchange is the time stamp: it provides authenticator uniqueness and protects against replay attacks. Without the authenticator, a hacker could grab a ticket off the network and use it to impersonate Alice to a resource server. The time stamp explains the time sensitivity of Kerberos and of Windows 2000 in general. We will discuss extensively the importance of time for Windows 2000 authenticity in Section 6.7.5.

Remember from the introduction that Kerberos can provide mutual authentication. To provide this the Kerberos protocol includes an additional exchange that authenticates the server to the client. In the previous example, it means that, in turn, the server will encrypt its name and the current time stamp and send it to Alice.

A big problem when using a symmetric protocol is the distribution of the secret key: in practice the key is generated at one side of the communication channel and should be sent to the other side of the communication channel in a secure manner; secure means that the confidentiality of the key should be protected. If anybody could read the secret key when it's sent across the network, the whole authentication system becomes worthless: the secrecy of the secret key is a vital part of a symmetric cipher.

Steps 2, 3, and 4 explain how the Kerberos developers have resolved the problem of secure session key distribution.

6.4.2 Step 2: The Kerberos KDC provides scalability

The Kerberos protocol always deals with three entities: two entities that want to authenticate to one another and one entity that mediates between these two entities for authentication: the Key Distribution Center (KDC). Why do we need a KDC? (See Figure 6.8.)

Suppose that Alice is part of a workgroup consisting of five entities, which all want to authenticate to one another using symmetric key cryptography. Since every entity needs to share a secret key with every other entity, we'll need ten keys. The mathematical formula behind this is $n(n-1)/2$. In a 50,000-employee company we would need about 1,500,000,000 keys. Not only would we have to deal with an enormous amount of keys, there would also be an enormous amount of small authentication databases: There would be one on every client, containing all the secret keys of the entities the client wants to authenticate. This solution is clearly not scalable at the level of a large company.

To make Kerberos more scalable the Kerberos developers included the concept of a Key Distribution Center (KDC). The Key Distribution Center (KDC) is a trusted third party with whom every entity shares a secret key. This key is called the entity's master key. All entities trust the KDC to mediate in their mutual authentication. The KDC also maintains a centralized authentication database containing a copy of every user's master key.

Figure 6.8
A KDC provides scalability

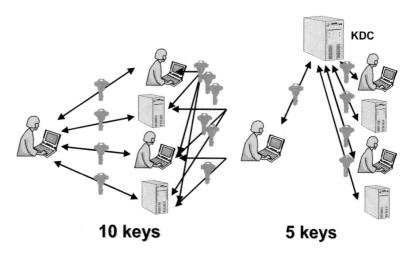

10 keys   **5 keys**

In Windows 2000 the KDC is a service that is installed on every DC as part of the DCPROMO Active Directory installation process. Every Windows 2000 DC runs a KDC service and hosts a portion of the Active Directory (AD), the centralized authentication database. The KDC itself is made up of two subservices: the Authentication Service (AS) and the Ticket-Granting Service (TGS); in other Kerberos implementations these two subservices can run on different machines—this is not possible in Windows 2000.

An interesting note: A standard Kerberos domain is made up of a master KDC and one or more slave KDCs. The master KDC is collocated with a read/write copy of the authentication database (single-master model). In Windows 2000 every KDC server hosts a read/write copy of the domain portion of the Active Directory (multimaster model). Note that if a domain has multiple DCs, this feature can provide fault tolerance for the authentication process and the authentication database. If one DC is down, another one can automatically take over; also, the AD is replicated between DCs.

The concept of a master key is not new to Windows 2000 and Kerberos: It already existed in NT4. In both NT4 and Windows 2000, the master key is derived from an entity's password. The password is a secret key shared between all the security principals and the KDC. (Note that we're talking about symmetric key cryptography.) Both the entity and the KDC must know the master key before the actual Kerberos authentication process can take place. For obvious security reasons the AD never stores the plain password but a hashed version. The hash algorithm used for password hashing is MD4.

An entity's master key is generated as part of the domain enrollment process—for example, when the administrator enrolls the user and enters a password. A machine's master key is derived from the machine password that is automatically created when an administrator joins the machine into a domain.

6.4.3   Step 3: A Kerberos ticket provides secure transport of the session key

Figure 6.9 shows the three basic entities the Kerberos protocol deals with: a client (Alice), a resource server, and a Key Distribution Center (KDC). Figure 6.9 also shows the master keys shared between the entities participating in the authentication process and the KDC. Also note that the KDC consists of two subservices: an Authentication Service (AS) and a Ticket-Granting Service (TGS). We'll discuss this difference later in this chapter.

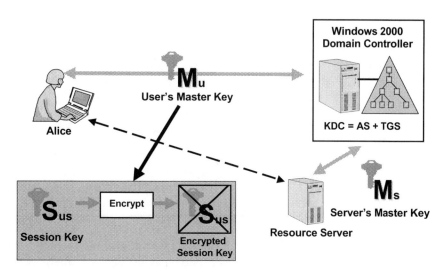

Figure 6.9
Kerberos entities and master key concept

Remember that in the first step we talked about the problem of distributing the secret key (the session key) when dealing with symmetric key ciphers. The following text explains how Kerberos resolves this problem.

Previously, we explained that every entity shares a master key with the KDC. We also said that all entities trust the KDC to mediate in their mutual authentication: trust in this context also means that every entity trusts the KDC to generate session keys. In the scenario shown in Figure 6.9, the resource server would never trust Alice to generate session keys, because Alice hasn't yet authenticated to the resource server (the other way around wouldn't work either).

So far so good: Alice needs to authenticate to the resource server and requests a session key from the KDC. The KDC will generate the session key and distribute it to both entities. The quality or the randomness of the session key is dependent on the quality of the random number generator of Windows 2000. Remember that the session key is the key introduced in step 1; it is the one used for authentication. The master key was introduced in step 2. The following text makes the link between the session key and the master key and explains why we need a master key.

After the KDC has generated the session key, it must communicate it to both Alice and the resource server. To secure the transport of the session key to a particular entity Kerberos encrypts it with the master key of that entity. As there are two entities, Alice and the resource server, two encrypted versions of the session key must be generated: one encrypted with Alice's master key; one encrypted with the master key of the resource server.

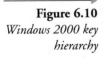

Figure 6.10
*Windows 2000 key
hierarchy*

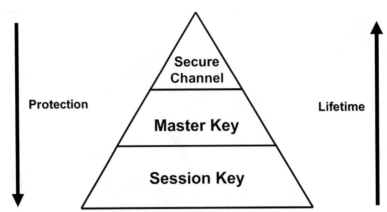

In Kerberos terminology, the session key encrypted with the resource server's master key is known as a ticket. A Kerberos ticket provides a way to transport a Kerberos session key securely across the network. Only the destination resource server and a Windows 2000 DC can decrypt it.

By securing the transport of the session key using the master key, Kerberos creates what is known as a key hierarchy. Figure 6.10 shows the Windows 2000 key hierarchy; it consists of the following entities:

- The session key (or short-term key). A session key is a secret key shared between two entities for authentication purposes. The session key is generated by the KDC. Since it is a critical part of the Kerberos authentication protocol, it is never sent in the clear over a communication channel: It is encrypted using the master key.

- The master key (or long-term key). The master key is a secret key shared between each entity and the KDC. It must be known to both the entity and the KDC before the actual Kerberos protocol communication can take place. The master key is generated as part of the domain enrollment process and is derived from a user's, a machine's, or a service's password. The transport of the master key over a communication channel is secured using a secure channel.

- The secure channel. When Windows 2000 is using a secure channel, it is using a master key to secure the transport of another master key. The following example illustrates the secure channel concept. When you create a new user, the user's password will be sent to the DC using a secure channel. The secure channel in this case is made up of the master key shared between the workstation you're working on and the DC. In this case the master key is derived from the workstation's machine account password. The concept of a secure channel was also explained in the previous chapter.

In the key hierarchy shown in Figure 6.10 the following are also true:

- Higher-level keys protect lower-level keys.

- Higher-level keying material has a longer lifetime than lower-level keying material.

- Lower-level keying material is used more frequently for sending encrypted packets across the network. As a consequence, there's a higher risk for brute-force attacks on these packets; this means that the associated keys should be changed more often.

6.4.4 Step 4: The Kerberos KDC distributes the ticket by sending it via the client

The KDC can distribute the encrypted session keys to Alice and the resource server in the following two ways (remember that the session key is encrypted once with Alice's master key and once with the resource server's master key):

- Method 1: The KDC could send it directly to both Alice and the resource server (as shown in Figure 6.11).

- Method 2: The KDC could send the two encrypted session keys to Alice. Alice could send out the resource server's encrypted session key later on in the Kerberos authentication sequence (as shown in Figure 6.12).

Method 1 has the following disadvantages:

- The resource server has to cache all the session keys: one session key for each client that wants to access a resource on the server. This would also impose a huge security risk on the server side.

- Synchronization problems could occur: The client could already be using the session key while the resource server hasn't even received its copy yet.

Because of the disadvantages associated with Method 1, Kerberos uses the alternative shown in Method 2 (see Figure 6.12):

- Both the encrypted session keys (the one for Alice, encrypted with Alice's master key, and the one for the resource server, encrypted with the resource server's master key) are sent to Alice.

Figure 6.11
Kerberos ticket
distribution—
Method 1

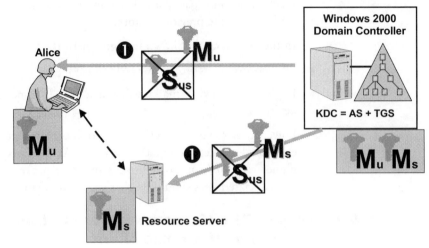

- Alice can decrypt the packet encrypted with her master key and get out the session key. Alice's system can now cache both Alice's copy of the session key and the server's copy of the session key (contained in the ticket).

- When Alice needs to authenticate to the resource server, the client will send out the server's copy of the session key.

The key advantage of Method 2 lies in its unique caching architecture. Alice's machine can cache tickets and reuse them. Also, it takes away the need for the server to cache the tickets. It receives them from the client as needed. This architecture makes the Kerberos protocol stateless on the

Figure 6.12
Kerberos ticket
distribution—
Method 2

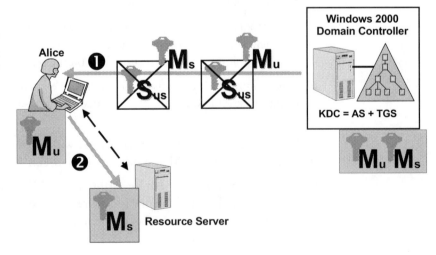

server side. This has obvious advantages if you want to implement some load balancing or redundancy solution on the server side: You will not need to bother about keeping the session keys synchronized between the different DCs.

On the client side tickets are kept in a special system memory area, which is never paged to disk. The reuse of the cached tickets is limited, because of a ticket's limited lifetime and renewal time. Windows 2000 maintains a ticket cache for every logon session. The ticket cache is purged when the logon session ends; it is preserved when a system is in hibernation mode. The cache can be purged manually using the klist.exe or kerbtray.exe tools, explained later in this chapter.

6.4.5 Step 5: The Kerberos ticket-granting ticket limits the use of the entities' master keys

There's yet another important weakness in the protocol that we haven't addressed so far. The session key that is sent back from the KDC to Alice is encrypted using Alice's master key (as shown in Figure 6.13). This encrypted packet is sent over the network every time Alice needs a session key to authenticate to a resource server. This means that there are many opportunities for hackers to intercept the encrypted packet and to perform (offline) a brute-force attack to derive the user's master key.

In a brute-force attack, a hacker tries to guess the key that was used to encrypt a packet by trying out all the possible keys and looking at the result. Such attacks are not unrealistic. Remember the tools that were available in NT4 to do brute-force attacks on the SAM database or on authentication packets sent across the network, such as the L0phtcrack tool from the

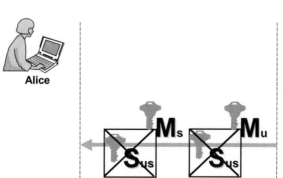

Figure 6.13
The use of the master key

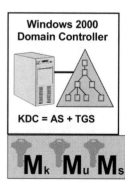

L0pht Heavy Industries (previously called Cult of the Dead Cow) hacker group.

There's clearly a need here for a strong secret to replace Alice's master key. This will be the role of the session key shared between each entity and the KDC. "Strong secret" in this context means less susceptible to brute-force attacks. To resist these attacks there are two possibilities. Use longer keys (longer keys create bigger key spaces and make it more difficult to guess the right key) or change the keys more often, which limits the chance for brute-force attacks (in other words, limit the lifetime of the keys; this principle is often referred to as Perfect Forward Secrecy [PFS]). The Kerberos developers have chosen the latter.

This new session key will replace Alice's password to authenticate Alice to the KDC after the initial authentication. Although it has an identical function (authentication), the session key introduced in this step is not the same as the one used previously. This session key is shared between Alice and the KDC; the other session key is shared between Alice and the resource server. Just as with Alice's master key, both Alice and the KDC must know this session key. To securely transport this session key we will use the same principles as the ones described in steps 3 and 4, as follows:

- Step 3: Kerberos uses a ticket to provide secure transport of the session key: the special ticket used here is known as the Ticket-Granting Ticket (TGT).

- Step 4: Kerberos distributes the tickets by sending them out via Alice. The KDC sends the TGT to Alice; Alice caches the TGT and can send it to the KDC as needed. There's no need for the KDC to cache the TGTs of every client.

Figure 6.14 shows how this new session key (S_{ku}) and the associated TGT are used in the basic Kerberos protocol exchange, as follows:

- Alice sends a logon message to the DC. This message is secured using Alice's master key, derived from Alice's password. The encryption of this request is not part of the basic Kerberos protocol as defined in RFC 1510; it's based on the extension known as preauthentication data. Preauthentication data will be explained later on in the text.

- The KDC will then send out a secured copy of the session key to be used for authentication between Alice and the KDC for the rest of the logon session (this session key will replace the user's master key). The copy of the session key encrypted with KDC's master key is called the TGT.

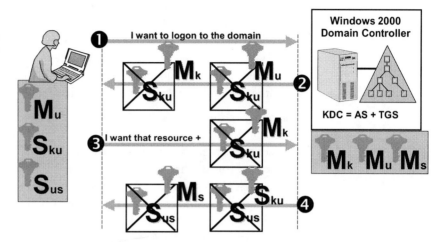

Figure 6.14
The role of the Kerberos TGT

- The session key and the TGT will be cached in Alice's local Kerberos ticket cache.

- Later on, when Alice wants to access a resource on the resource server, the security process acting on Alice's behalf will send out a request for a ticket to the KDC using the locally cached TGT. The request for the resource will be secured using the session key S_{ku}.

- Finally, the KDC will send back a ticket and a new session key to Alice, which she can use later on to authenticate to the resource server. Notice that in Figure 6.14 the new session key is not encrypted using Alice's master key, but using the newly created session key S_{ku}.

The following are more thoughts on this basic Kerberos protocol Exchange:

- The TGT is reused to request tickets for other application or resource servers. The reuse of the TGT is limited by its lifetime. The lifetime of the TGT not only limits the use of the TGT itself but of all the tickets obtained using a particular TGT as well. For example, if I have a TGT that's about to expire in a half hour, every new ticket I get will also expire at the same point in time (even though the default lifetime of a ticket may be one hour).

- Ticket requests don't require further use of the client's master key. This means that once you have a session key, there's no more need to cache the master key on the client, which is very good from a security point of view. Microsoft Windows 2000 still caches the master key, because it needs it for NTLM authentication to down-level clients.

- During the logon session a weak secret (the master key derived from a client's password) is exchanged for a strong secret (the session key contained within the TGT). In other words, at logon time and at each TGT renewal the user will authenticate to the KDC with his or her master key in subsequent ticket requests the user will authenticate using the session key, which is contained in the TGT.

- The newly created session key (S_{ku}) doesn't need to be cached on the KDC: the KDC gets it from the client each time the client requests a new service ticket. S_{ku} is encrypted using the KDC's master key (remember: this is what they call the TGT). This feature makes Kerberos stateless on the KDC side, which has, as for resource servers, obvious advantages if some load balancing or redundancy technology has to be implemented on the KDC side. This is the case in Windows 2000; every DC has a KDC service.

6.4.6 Bringing it all together

In this section, we'll bring together all the elements of the previous five steps to explain the complete Kerberos protocol. Figure 6.15 shows the complete Kerberos protocol, as it occurs when a user logs onto a domain and when he accesses a resource during his logon session. Kerberos protocol consists of three subprotocols (or phases), each one made up of two steps. In the following listing, the cryptic names in parentheses are the names of the Kerberos protocol messages, as they are called in the Kerberos standard documents.

- Phase 1: Authentication Service Exchange (happens once per logon session).

  - Step 1: Authentication Server Request (KRB_AS_REQ). Alice logs onto the domain from her local machine. A TGT request is sent to a Windows 2000 KDC.
  - Step 2: Authentication Server Reply (KRB_AS_REP). The Windows 2000 KDC returns a TGT and a session key to Alice.

- Phase 2: Ticket-Granting Service Exchange (happens once for each resource server)

  - Step 1: TGS Request (KRB_TGS_REQ). Alice wants to access a resource on a server. A ticket request for the Resource Server is sent to the Windows 2000 KDC. This request consists of Alice's TGT and an authenticator. Remember from step 1 that the authenticator is the basic entity used for Kerberos authentication:

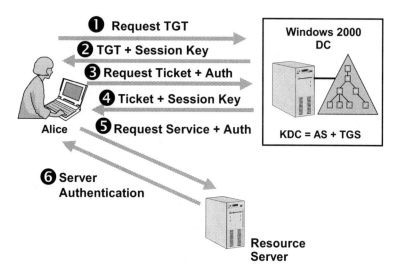

Figure 6.15
*The complete
Kerberos protocol*

It contains the user's ID and the current time stamp and is encrypted using the session key shared between the two entities that need to authenticate to one another.

  ▪ Step 2: TGS Reply (KRB_TGS_REP). The Windows 2000 DC returns a ticket and a session key to Alice.

• Phase 3: Client Server Authentication Exchange (happens once per server session)

  ▪ Step 1: Resource Server Request (KRB_AP_REQ). The ticket is sent to the resource server. Upon receiving the ticket and the authenticator, the server can authenticate Alice.

  ▪ Step 2: Resource Server Reply (KRB_AP_REP). The server replies to Alice with another authenticator. On receiving this authenticator, Alice can authenticate the server.

In this exchange the following keys and tickets are cached on Alice's computer: the TGT, the ticket used to authenticate to the resource server, and two session keys, one to authenticate to the KDC and one to authenticate to the resource server.

6.4.7 Kerberos data confidentiality, authentication, and integrity services

Windows 2000 includes the Kerberos extensions, which can be used to provide data confidentiality, authentication, and integrity for messages that are sent after the initial Kerberos subprotocol steps. These extensions are known as KRB_PRIV (data confidentiality) and KRB_SAFE (data authentication and integrity). They are based on the existence of a session key between two entities at the end of each Kerberos authentication protocol exchange, as follows:

- The session key can be used to sign a message (data authentication and integrity). A hash, the result of the application of a hash function on a message, can be encrypted using the session key. A hash encrypted with a session key is called a Message Authentication Code (MAC).

- The session key can be used to seal a message (data confidentiality) by encrypting a message using the session key.

A protocol that uses this session key to add signing functionality to its messages is the Server Message Block (SMB) protocol (currently known as the the Common Internet File Sharing [CIFS] protocol). The use of digital signatures on SMB messages can be controlled using the EnableSecuritySignature and the RequireSecuritySignature registry values. On the server side these two values are located in HKLM\System\CurrentControlSet\Services\LanManServer\Parameters; on the client side in HKLM\System\CurrentControlSet\Services\Rdr\Parameters (as documented in Knowledge Base Article Q161372). Note that enabling SMB signing will have a significant impact on performance.

6.5   Logging on to Windows 2000 using Kerberos

Now that we've explained the basic Kerberos protocol we can discuss some real-world Windows 2000 Kerberos logon examples. In this section we will look in detail at both local and network logon in a single- and a multiple-domain environment.

In the following text, we will also discuss the Authentication Service (AS) and Ticket-Granting Service (TGS) concepts. These are the two sub-services that make up the KDC service.

6.5.1   Single-domain logon

A single-domain logon occurs when the following takes place:

- Alice is logging on from a machine that is a member of the domain where Alice's account has been defined (this is a local logon).

- Alice accesses a resource located on a machine that is a member of Alice's logon domain (this is network logon).

Local logon

Figure 6.16 and the following list show what happens during a local logon in a single-domain environment:

1.   Alice presses <CTRL><ALT><DEL> and chooses to log on to the domain.

2.   The client software acting on behalf of Alice tries to locate a KDC service for the domain; this is done by querying DNS. The Kerberos package will retry up to three times to contact a KDC. It initially waits ten seconds for a reply and will wait an additional ten seconds on each retry. In most cases a KDC is already known; the discovery of a DC is also part of the secure channel setup that occurs before any local logon.

3.   Once the DC is found, Alice sends a Kerberos authentication request to the DC. This request authenticates Alice to the DC and contains a TGT request (KRB_AS_REQ).

4.   The Authentication Service authenticates Alice, generates a TGT, and sends it back to the client (KRB_AS_REP).

5.   The local machine where Alice logged on is, as with any other domain resource, a resource for which Alice needs a ticket. Alice sends a ticket request to the DC using her TGT (together with an authenticator) (KRB_TGS_REQ).

6.   The TGS of the DC checks the TGT and the authenticator, generates a ticket for the local machine, and sends it back to Alice (KRB_TGS_REP).

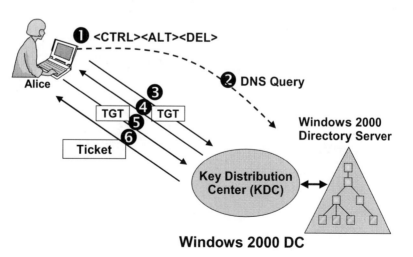

Figure 6.16
Local logon in a single-domain environment

7. On Alice's machine, the ticket is presented to the Local Security Authority, which will create an access token for Alice. From then on, any process acting on behalf of Alice can access the local machine's resources.

This first example showed how Kerberos uses DNS to locate a KDC service. Windows 2000 publishes two special Kerberos SRV records to DNS: _kerberos and _kpasswd.

Network logon

When Alice, who is already logged on to a domain, wants to access a resource located on a server within the same domain, a network logon happens. In this case, the logon sequence is the following (as illustrated in Figure 6.17):

1. Alice sends a service ticket request to the DC using her TGT (together with an authenticator) (KRB_TGS_REQ).

2. The TGS of the DC checks the authenticator, generates a service ticket, and sends it back to Alice (KRB_TGS_REP).

3. Alice sends the ticket (together with an authenticator) to the resource server (KRB_AP_REQ).

4. The resource server verifies the ticket and the authenticator. After the verification, it sends another authenticator to Alice for resource service authentication (KRB_AP_REP).

Figure 6.17
Network logon in a single-domain environment

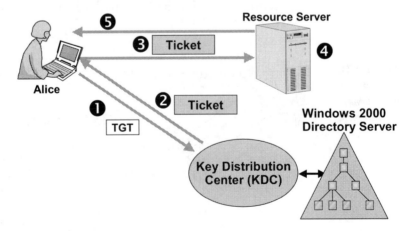

6.5.2 Multiple-domain logon

A multiple-domain logon occurs when the following takes place:

- Alice is logging on from a machine member of a domain different from the one where Alice's account has been defined (this is a logon logon).

- Alice is accessing a resource located on a machine that is a member of a domain different from the one where Alice logged on (this is network logon).

In the following examples we will use the concepts referral ticket and interrealm key; they will be explained in a subsequent section.

Local logon

Figure 6.18 shows a typical multiple-domain environment, consisting of a parent domain, *compaq.com*, and two child domains, *NA* (North America), and *Europe*. In the local logon example, Alice's account is defined in the *Europe* domain. Alice logs on from a workstation whose account is defined in the *NA* domain.

The local logon process can be subdivided into the four following steps:

- Step 1: AS exchange (KRB_AS_REQ and KRB_AS_REP):

  - To log on, Alice sends a TGT request to a KDC in *Europe.compaq.com*. The AS request and reply are sent to the KDC of

Figure 6.18
Local logon in a multiple-domain environment

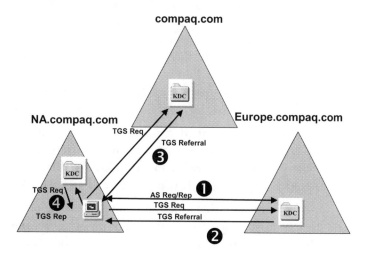

Europe.compaq.com. Only a KDC of Alice's account domain can authenticate Alice (credentials are never replicated between DCs of different domains).

- Steps 2, 3, and 4: TGS exchanges (KRB_TGS_REQ and KRB_TGS_REP):

  - To request a ticket for Alice to authenticate to the *NA* workstation, a TGS request is sent to the KDC of *Europe.compaq.com.*
  - The KDC of *Europe.compaq.com* cannot issue a ticket that allows Alice to authenticate to the workstation in *NA.* Only a KDC of *NA* can return such a ticket. Therefore, the TGS reply contains a referral ticket to the domain closest to *NA.compaq.com* (from a DNS point of view) and with which *NA.compaq.com* has a real Kerberos trust. In this example, it is *compaq.com.* The concept of a "real trust relationship" will be explained in a later section, "Multiple domain logon: behind the scenes."

    To create trust relationships in a forest Windows 2000 calls on DNS; at run time, however, it calls on AD. If Windows 2000 would also use DNS at run time, it would be impossible to discover short-cut trust relationships.
  - On receiving the referral ticket, Alice locates a KDC of the intermediary domain *compaq.com* and sends a TGS request, including the referral ticket to that KDC.
  - The KDC in *compaq.com* decrypts the ticket using the interrealm key (shared between *Europe.compaq.com* and *compaq.com*) and detects it contains a ticket request for a workstation in *NA.* The KDC checks on the domain closest to *NA.compaq.com* from the *compaq.com* point of view, with which it has a real trust relationship, and sends Alice a referral ticket to this domain.
  - Alice asks a KDC of *NA.compaq.com* for a ticket for the local workstation. Finally, a KDC of *NA.compaq.com* will send Alice a TGS reply with a valid ticket for the workstation.

The amount of interdomain authentication traffic occurring in this scenario should not be overestimated for two reasons: The size of Kerberos tickets is relatively small and the referral traffic does not occur at every resource access (tickets have a lifetime and are cached).

An interesting side note is to look at what happens if, at some point in the above exchange, the administrator of the *Europe* domain decides to disable Alice's account. The answer to this question is pretty straightforward. The KDC of *Europe* will continue to issue tickets as long as the original

TGT is valid; the same thing is true for the *NA* domain. The disabled account will only be detected when Alice gets a new TGT.

Network logon

Let's look at what happens with a local logon in a multiple-domain environment. Again, we're using the example of a parent domain and two child domains. In the network logon example, Alice is logged on to the *NA* domain (Alice and computer account are defined in the *NA* domain). Alice wants to access a resource hosted on a server in the *Europe* domain.

The network logon process can be subdivided into the following four steps (as illustrated in Figure 6.19):

Steps 1, 2, and 3: TGS exchanges:

- Before Alice can contact the KDC in realm *Europe.compaq.com*, she must have a valid referral ticket to talk to the KDC of that domain. Since there is no direct trust between *Europe.compaq.com* and *NA.compaq.com*, Alice must request the referral ticket via an intermediary domain.

- Alice first requests a referral ticket for the KDC of the domain closest to the *Europe.compaq.com* domain; this is *compaq.com*. Since there is a direct trust between *NA.compaq.com* and *compaq.com*, Alice can request this ticket from her own KDC. The KDC will return a referral ticket encrypted with the interrealm key shared with between *NA.compaq.com* and *compaq.com*.

Figure 6.19
Network logon in a multiple-domain environment

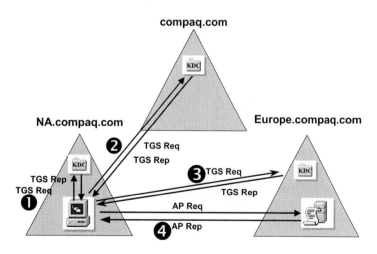

- Armed with this referral ticket, Alice can send a TGS request to the KDC of realm *compaq.com*, requesting a referral ticket for the KDC of the *Europe.compaq.com* realm. Since there is a direct trust between *compaq.com* and *Europe.compaq.com*, the KDC of *Europe.compaq.com* can answer this request. The returned referral ticket will be encrypted with the interrealm key shared between *compaq.com* and *Europe.compaq.com*.

- With the above referral ticket, Alice finally can send a TGS request to a KDC of realm *Europe.compaq.com* to request a service ticket for the target file server.

    Step 4: Application Server Exchange:

- With the service ticket received from the target server's KDC, Alice sends an access request (consisting of the ticket and an authenticator) to the target server.

- During the last step, the target server will authenticate back to Alice.

The effect of short-cut trusts on multiple-domain logon traffic

A typical scenario when you would create a short-cut trust is a Windows 2000 domain tree, where a massive amount of authentication traffic occurs between two domains logically linked together using a transitive trust. The short-cut trust example illustrated in Figure 6.20 shows how the number of referrals is reduced and how the trust path used during authentication is shortened; note that the KDC in *NA.compaq.com* can detect the existence of the short-cut trust when querying AD. It has enough intelligence to refer Alice directly to the KDC in *Europe.compaq.com*.

Figure 6.20
Effect of a short-cut trust on muliple-domain logon traffic

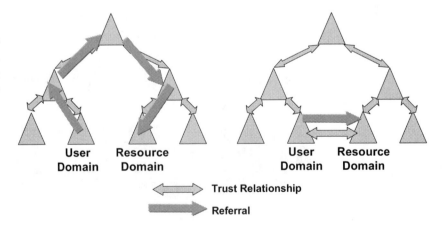

In the example in Figure 6.19 the creation of a short-cut trust between *NA* and *Europe* would affect the authentication steps as follows:

- Step 1: Alice uses her TGT to obtain a ticket from a KDC in the *NA* domain for the resource server in the *Europe* domain. The KDC in the *NA* domain isn't the authoritative KDC for the resource server's *Europe* domain, so the KDC in the *NA* domain refers Alice to the domain closest to the target domain the *NA* domain has a real trust relationship with. This domain is *Europe*.

- Step 2: A KDC in the resource server's *Europe* domain, authoritative for that domain, generates a ticket for Alice.

- Step 3: Alice uses the ticket to access the resource server.

Multiple-domain logon: behind the scenes

In this section, we'll explain some of the concepts behind multiple-domain logon: referral tickets, interrealm keys, Authentication service, and Ticket-Granting Service. To fully understand multiple-domain logon, we will also introduce two special Kerberos principals: the domain trust account and the krbtgt principal. We will also explain what we mean by a "real" trust relationship.

Domain trust accounts   To enable interdomain authentication every domain trusted by domain A is registered in domain A's AD domain NC as a special Kerberos principal, also known as a domain trust account. Interdomain authentication traffic (the referral tickets mentioned previously) are secured using the master key and the session key of these domain trust account principals (see also LSA trusteddomain object discussion in the previous chapter). The domain trust account's keys are also referred to as interrealm keys. As for any other account, the domain trust account's master key is the account's password. Also, as for any other account, the password of a domain trust account is changed on a regular schedule.

The master key of the domain trust account also explains the "real" trust relationship concept we referred to in the previous sections. A real trust relationship is nothing else than a shared secret (a key) between the DCs of two different domains, as follows:

- If only domain A is registered as a domain trust account in domain B, we have a one-way trust going from B to A (domain B trusts domain A). In this scenario the master key of the domain trust account of domain A is the shared secret behind the one-way trust.

- If only domain B is registered as a domain trust account in domain A, we have a one-way trust going from A to B (domain A trusts domain B). In this scenario the master key of the domain trust account of domain B is the shared secret behind the one-way trust.

- If both are registered as domain trust accounts, we have a two-way trust. In this scenario the master key of the domain trust account of both domains is the shared secret used for the two-way trust relationship.

The creation of the domain trust accounts and their master keys (the interrealm keys) happens automatically during the DCPROMO process when a domain joins an existing domain tree. More details on the types of trust relationships are provided later on in this chapter.

Now it should also be clear why the Kerberos authentication traffic follows real trust relationships—also known as the trust path (based on domain trust accounts)—and not transitive trust links. A transitive link is not secured; there's no shared secret between two domains linked using a transitive trust. The reason for this is pretty obvious: there are no domain trust accounts defined between two domains linked using a transitive trust. If you don't have a secret you cannot use the trust link to send authentication traffic. This is also why a transitive trust is just a logical concept.

The krbtgt account   To explain the use of the KRBTGT account we must first explain why the Kerberos KDC is made up of two subservices: the Authentication Service (AS) and the Ticket-Granting Service (TGS). The services offered by a KDC can be split into two service categories; each subservice has a set of different tasks, as follows:

- The Authentication Service authenticates accounts defined in the domain where the AS is running and issues TGTs for these accounts.

- The Ticket-Granting Service issues tickets for resources defined in the domain where the TGS is running.

Splitting up the KDC into two subservices offers the flexibility to run the two subservices on two different servers; unfortunately, this is not supported in Windows 2000.

The AS and TGS services share a secret that is derived from the password of the krbtgt principal. The krbtgt principal is the security principal used by the KDC; its master key will be used to encrypt the TGTs that are issued by the KDC. The krbtgt account is created automatically when a Windows 2000 domain is created. It cannot be deleted and renamed. As with any other account, its password is changed regularly. In the Windows 2000 users and computers snap-in this account is always shown as disabled.

Multiple-domain logon revisited   Now that we've explained interrealm key, krbtgt, domain trust account, and what's behind a real trust relationship, let's look once more at how multiple-domain logon works. A basic rule in Kerberos is that to access a resource a user needs a ticket. How can Alice get a ticket for a resource contained in a domain different from Alice's definition domain? Remember that a ticket for a resource can only be issued by an authoritative DC. Let's once again use the example of Alice defined and logged on in domain *NA.compaq.com*, who decides to access a resource in *Europe.compaq.com* (as illustrated in Figure 6.21).

To resolve this issue Kerberos uses referral tickets, domain trust accounts and interrealm keys. In this scenario, the KDC of *NA.compaq.com* would issue a referral ticket to Alice to access *compaq.com*. What is a referral ticket? A referral ticket is a TGT, which Alice can use in domain *compaq.com* to get a ticket for a resource in that domain. The KDC of *NA.compaq.com* can issue such a TGT because *compaq.com* is a principal (remember the domain trust account) in its domain. How can the KDC of *compaq.com* trust a TGT that was issued not by itself, but by the KDC of *NA.compaq.com*? The KDC of *compaq.com* will decrypt the TGT with the interrealm key of its domain trust account in *NA.compaq.com*. If the decryption comes out valid, the KDC will consider the TGT trustworthy. The same things will happen

Figure 6.21
Multiple-domain logon revisited

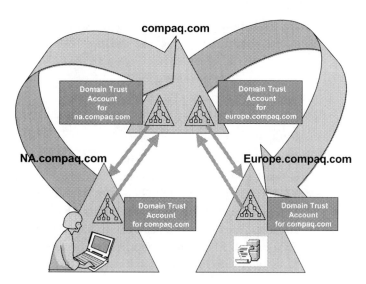

when *compaq.com* issues a referral ticket for Alice to request a service ticket to a KDC in the *Europe.compaq.com* domain.

The referral process we just explained relies heavily on AD and the Global Catalog (GC). First, it uses the GC to find out, given the Service Principal name (SPN) in which domain the resource is located and thus which DC can issue a ticket to access the resource. The service that's responsible for a resource is always registered in the GC. SPNs (and UPNs) are unique identifiers for users and services that want to authenticate using Kerberos. SPNs (and UPNs) are explained in detail in Section 6.6.1. Then it uses AD to find out the domain closest to the target domain to which Alice should be referred. Since GCs are not shared between forests, referrals and Kerberos authentication will not work between forests.

6.5.3   Kerberos in the Windows 2000 startup and logon sequence

So far, we've explained the Kerberos authentication sequence in all its possible flavors. In the following text, we will look at where the Kerberos authentication sequence fits into the Windows 2000 machine startup and user logon sequence. We will see that the Kerberos authentication sequence is executed more than once during machine startup and that machine startup and user logon includes much more than just user and machine authentication.

Machine startup

Figure 6.22 shows the different processes that take place during a regular Windows 2000 client machine startup. The different processes are as follows:

- The client starts up. The network interface is initialized. If the machine is not configured with static IP configuration information, it will run through the DHCP configuration process to obtain its IP configuration.

- Once the client's network interface has been configured and the network protocol stack has been initialized, the machine will launch a DNS query for an LDAP service (Windows 2000 DC) to one of its configured DNS servers. The DNS query will look for an _ldap._tcp.default-first-site-name._sites.dc._msdcs.<domain name> SRV record. (The site name depends on the one registered on the machine, by default it is default-first-site-name).

- When an LDAP service (Windows 2000 DC) has been located, the client will launch an LDAP query for a DC of the machine's defini-

Figure 6.22
Machine startup

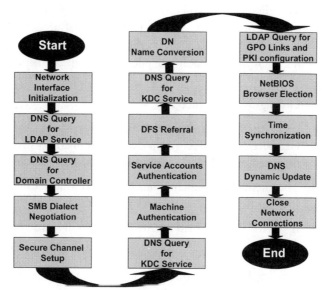

tion domain to the LDAP server ("definition domain" means the domain containing the machine account).

- The client will then negotiate an SMB dialect with the DC. The Server Message Block protocol (SMB) is an important file sharing protocol in both NT4 and Windows 2000. It is used to provide remote file services in a distributed client/server environment. Later on in the startup, it will be used by the client to download configuration information (including GPO settings) from the DC.

- Next, the client will set up a secure channel with the DC. To do this it will connect to the DC's netlogon service. The secure channel is needed to send confidential information, such as authentication data, from the client to the DC in a secure way. Secure channels were explained in detail in Chapter 5.

- Once the secure channel has been set up, the client will launch another DNS query to its DNS server to find an authentication server (in Windows 2000, a DC running a KDC service). The DNS query will look for a _kerberos._tcp.default-first-site-name._sites.dc._msdcs.<domain name> SRV record. The site name depends on the one registered on the machine; by default it is default-first-site-name.

- The machine Kerberos authentication phase takes place.

- The Kerberos authentication takes place for every service that is not running using the local system account.

- The client will then connect to the IPC$ share on the DC and start the Distributed File System (DFS) referral process. The DFS referral process downloads DFS configuration information from the DC to the client (downloading happens using the SMB protocol).

- The client launches an RPC call to the DC to convert its name into a Distinguished name (DN).

- Using the DN the client can then perform an LDAP query against its DC to find out the group policies applied to it. The group policy information is downloaded using the SMB protocol.

- The client then launches another LDAP query to the DC to find out PKI configuration information (e.g., What are the Enterprise CAs?).

- If NetBIOS is enabled on the client, it will start a browser election.

- The client performs time synchronization with its DC.

- Finally, the client launches a DNS query for the start of authority of its DNS domain; the client then performs a dynamic update of its DNS records on the DNS server returned from the previous query.

- The client startup will be completed by closing down the connections with the DC.

User logon

Once a machine has been started up, a user can log on to it interactively. Figure 6.23 shows the different processes that take place during a regular Windows 2000 user logon. As we will see, the user logon process is much shorter than the machine startup process. The different processes are as follows:

- After the machine has started up successfully, a CTRL-ALT-DEL screen will be displayed on the screen, permitting the user to start an interactive logon session by pushing CTRL-ALT-DEL.

- The user presses CTRL-ALT-DEL, fills in a set of credentials, and presses OK or Enter.

- The user Kerberos authentication sequence takes place.

- The machine launches an RPC call to the DC to convert the user name to a Distinguished name (DN).

- Using the DN the client can then perform an LDAP query against its DC to find out the group policies applied to the user. The user group policy information is downloaded using the SMB protocol. At the

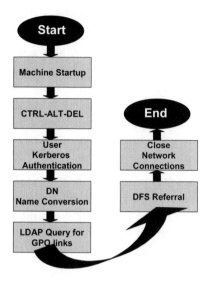

Figure 6.23
User logon

same time DFS referral information linked to the user will be downloaded.

- The user logon will be completed by closing down the connections with the DC.

6.6 Advanced Kerberos topics

In this section we'll focus on some advanced Kerberos topics: Kerberos principal identifiers, the link between authentication and authorization, the content of Kerberos tickets and authenticators, the details behind smartcard logon, Kerberos transport protocol and port usage.

6.6.1 Principal identifiers

One of the great features of Kerberos is its support for mutual authentication. The enabling technologies for mutual authentication are Kerberos itself, User Principal names (UPNs), and Service Principal names (SPNs). In this section, we'll explore UPNs and SPNs.

User principal names

Windows 2000 users can log on to a Windows 2000 domain using an NT4-like account name or using a User Principal Name (UPN). A Windows 2000 account also has other identifiers associated with it: the X.500

DN (Distinguished Name), the GUID, and the SID. In this section we focus on names that can be used to log on to Windows 2000.

The concept of a UPN is an extension to the standard Kerberos protocol. A UPN must be unique in the forest. Every user also keeps his or her down-level NT4-like logon name: <domain Name>\<SAM Name>. Contrary to the UPN, the NT4-like logon Name must only be unique in the domain. The UPN is stored in the userprincipalname property of a Windows 2000 account. It is validated at logon time first by searching the local Active Directory domain NC, and then the GC.

A UPN consists of a principal's name, an @ symbol, and a DNS domain name. (UPNs are defined in RFC 822.) There's no need for the DNS domain Name to correspond to the domain containing the user account. It needs to correspond to a domain that has a trust relationship with the principal's domain or to an alternate domain name listed in the UPNsuffixes property of the Partitions container (part of the configuration naming context). UPNsuffixes can be set from the Windows 2000 GUI: Use the properties of the active directory domains and trusts container in the Active Directory Domains and Trusts MMC snap-in (as illustrated in Figure 6.24).

The UPN stays the same independently of what happens with the user principal after its creation. The following administrative actions do not affect the UPN: moving a user principal to another domain and renaming a user principal's NT4-like name.

Figure 6.24
Setting the
UPNsuffixes
property from the
Windows 2000
GUI

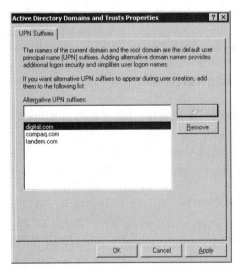

From a user's point of view, Windows 2000 UPNs enable the user to log on with his or her e-mail address. This can be risky from a security point of view: A hacker sniffing SMTP traffic can immediately catch half of the user's credentials.

Service Principal Names

A Service Principal Name (SPN) is a service identifier. Once you can identify a service, you can also authenticate it and that's what we want in Kerberos mutual authentication. As with UPN, an SPN must be unique in the Windows 2000 forest. It is associated with a service's logon account; associated means that the SPN is stored in the service logon account's AD object ServicePrincipalName attribute. An SPN can only be associated with one account. To look at the SPNs associated with a machine account use the support tools tool, adsiedit, or use the resource kit tool, setspn. Typing **setspn –l <machinename>** at the command prompt will list all the SPNs linked to <machinename> (as illustrated in Figure 6.25).

To enable a user to construct the SPN without knowing the service's logon account, SPNs have a fixed format and do not contain any reference to the service account. This format is ServiceClass/Host:[Port]/[Servicename], where:

- ServiceClass is a string identifying the service. Examples are www for a Web service, and ldap for a directory service.

- Host is the name of the computer on which the service is running. This can be NetBIOS or a DNS Name. Since a NetBIOS name is not necessarily unique in the forest, it's advisable to use DNS Names.

- Port is an optional parameter for the service port number. It enables the user to differentiate between multiple instances of the same service running on the same machine.

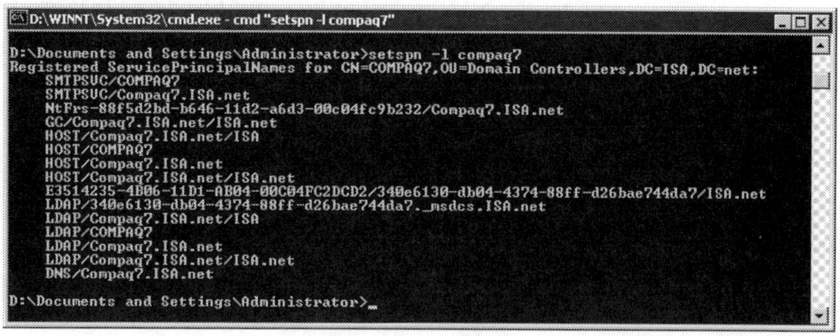

Figure 6.25
Using setspn to display the SPNs linked to a machine

- ServiceName is an optional parameter used to identify the data or services provided by a replicable service or to identify the domain served by a replicable service. A replicable service is a service running on different machines and whose data are replicated among different machines.

Let's look at how SPNs fit into the Kerberos authentication. We will take the example of a user who decides to access a file on another server during his or her logon session. The steps are as follows:

1. The Kerberos software on the client side constructs a Kerberos KRB_TGS_REQ message, containing the user's TGT and the SPN of the service responsible for the file the user wants to access. Notice that the client can construct the SPN even though he or she doesn't know the service account. The Kerberos software sends this message to the user's authentication DC.

2. The KDC will query the AD (in the first place the local domain NC, afterwards the GC) to find an account that has a matching SPN (this process is also known as resolving the SPN). If more than one account is found, the authentication will fail.

3. Given the service account and its master key (which is also stored in AD), the KDC will construct a service ticket, and send it back to the client. (This is the KRB_TGS_REP message.)

4. Next step is the client sending a KRB_AP_REQ message to the file server (including the service ticket and a Kerberos authenticator).

5. In the last step, the service will authenticate back to the client (KRB_AP_REP message). This is where the real mutual authentication happens.

One more remark on step 1. In most cases the Kerberos software may not get the SPN from the user, but just an LDAP or HTPP URL. Windows 2000 includes a special OS function called DsCrackNames, which can make conversions between different naming formats. This function can, for example, transform an LDAP URL to an SPN.

To end our discussion about SPNs let's take a look at the conditions that should be met in order for mutual authentication to work. They are as follows:

- Both the user's and the service's account must be defined in a mixed- or native-mode Windows 2000 domain.

- Both accounts must be defined in domains that are part of the same Windows 2000 forest. Remember that the KDC queries the GC to locate the service account associated with an SPN. In Windows 2000, GCs do not span forests.

- The user must be authenticating from a Windows 2000 machine and the service must be running on a Windows 2000 machine. The reason for this is that an SSP is needed that supports mutual authentication; so far only the Kerberos and the Negotiate SSP support mutual authentication.

- The SPN must include the full DNS name of the server on which the service is running.

6.6.2 Delegation of authentication

Windows 2000 Kerberos supports delegation of authentication (introduced in version 5 of the Kerberos protocol), an important authentication feature for multitiered applications. In a multitier application a client needs to be authenticated on multiple machines, preferably all using the same credentials. Delegation was not supported by NTLM. NTLM requires a copy of an account's hashed password (its master key) to be available on the machine that initiates the authentication. For obvious reasons an account's master key is never sent across during an NTLM-based network logon; hence, NTLM can only work for single-tier authentication.

Because the Kerberos credentials (the authenticator and the ticket) are less critical than the master key used in NTLM, Kerberos can support the forwarding of these credentials to other machines. Why are they less critical? Remember the key pyramid: The use of a session key is much more limited in space and time than a master key. This doesn't mean forwarding should be completely unlimited; you don't want machines to forward the user ticket of any user to any other machine on the network. In Section 6.7.2, we'll explain how Kerberos delegation can be limited in space.

In Kerberos terminology delegation means that the KDC can issue a ticket with a network address that is different from the address of the principal that requested the ticket. The KDC will do so after having validated the forwarded ticket it got from the requester.

Kerberos delegation uses some specific flags, which can be set in a ticket. The Kerberos standard (RFC 1510) defines four types of flags, listed in Table 6.4. Windows 2000 currently only supports the "forwardable" and "forwarded" flags. Notice in Table 6.4 that "forwardable" is a much more

Table 6.4   *Kerberos Ticket Delegation Flags*

Flag	Meaning
Proxiable	Tells the TGS that a new service ticket with a different network address may be issued based on this ticket
Proxy	Indicates that the ticket is a proxy ticket
Forwardable	Tells the TGS that a new TGT with a different network address may be issued based on this TGT
Forwarded	Indicates that this ticket has been forwarded or was issued based on an authentication using a forwarded TGT

powerful concept than "proxiable." A forwardable ticket is a TGT, a proxiable ticket is a plain ticket; a ticket can be used for one single application, a TGT for multiple applications.

Figure 6.26 gives a practical example of the Kerberos delegation process. Imagine that we are dealing with Alice using a browser, and she wants to access a SQL server database using a Web front-end hosted on an Internet Information Server. Another example is a user checking his or her mail in an Exchange Server mailbox using a Web front end (IIS–IE, also known as Outlook Web Access). Here's what's happening during this particular delegation process:

- During the authentication sequence (KRB_AS_REQ and KRB_AS_REP) Alice requests and receives a forwardable TGT and the associated session key from the KDC. Windows 2000 TGTs are forwardable by default.

- Later on in her logon session Alice accesses a resource on the IIS server and obtains a ticket and a session key for the IIS server (KRB_TGS_REQ and KRB_TGS_REP). (Step 1)

- Alice then decides she wants to launch a query against the SQL server database using a Web front end located on the same IIS Server. To do so Alice will forward her TGT and the associated session key to the IIS Server. To assure the confidentiality of the session key, it is encrypted using the session key, which Alice and the IIS Server share. (Step 2)

- Using Alice's forwardable TGT the IIS Server can request a new ticket to access the SQL server database server. The KDC will notice the request is coming from an IP address different from the one mentioned in the TGT. (Step 3)

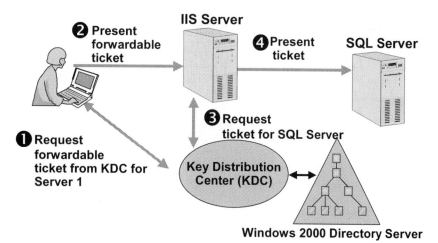

Figure 6.26
Kerberos delegation in a Windows 2000 environment

- Because the TGT is forwardable, the KDC agrees to issue a new ticket. This new ticket will contain Alice's identity and authorization data. Coming with the ticket is a new encrypted session key. (Step 4)

- The IIS Server authenticates to the SQL server database server using the new ticket and the new session key. The SQL server database thinks it is dealing with Alice, although, the messages are originating at the IIS Server. (Step 4)

To make this Kerberos delegation example work the following conditions should be met:

- The account impersonating the user on the IIS Server must be trusted for delegation.

- Alice's account should be trusted for delegation; it cannot have the *Account is sensitive and cannot be delegated* property set.

- All machines involved should have the Kerberos SSP installed.

- All services involved should be Kerberized; This is the case for IE5, IIS5, SQL Server 2000, and Exchange 2000.

6.6.3 Windows 2000 and transitive trust relationships

Windows 2000 includes support for transitive trust relationships. A transitive trust allows a trust to go through other trusts in order to reach an intended destination domain. For example, suppose you want to go from A to D, but do not have a direct trust to D. You do, however, have a trust with B, and C trusts B, and D trusts C; as a consequence, A can trust D. Transitive trusts allow indirect trust relationships.

Table 6.5   *Windows 2000 Trust Types and Characteristics*

Type	Creation	Default Characteristics
Tree-Root trust Between two tree root domains in same forest	Implicitly, DCPROMO	Transitive, two-way
Parent-Child trust Between parent-child domain in same tree	Implicitly, DCPROMO	Transitive, two way
Short cut (cross-link) trust Between any domain in same forest	Explicitly	Transitive, one- or two-way
External trust Between domains in different forests	Explicitly	Nontransitive, one- or two-way
Non-Windows trust Between two Kerberos KDCs (e.g., between a Windows 2000 domain and an MIT Kerberos-based domain)	Explicitly	Nontransitive, one- or two-way

Transitive trust is possible thanks to two important Windows 2000 features: the Kerberos authentication protocol and the ability to share configuration information among all domains in the same forest. The latter enables a parent domain to share its direct trust relationships not only with its child domains, but also with any domain in the same forest.

Windows 2000 Kerberos trust relationships created implicitly or explicitly within the same forest are transitive by default. Explicit trusts between forests (external trusts) or trusts to non-Win2K domains, such as a UNIX Kerberos domain (non-Windows trust), are nontransitive by default. While a non-Windows trust can be made transitive using the netdom utility, an external trust cannot. It is always nontransitive. This means that if you want authentication interoperability between two domains that are part of different forests, you have to establish a trust relationship between the two domains manually. Table 6.5 outlines the different Windows 2000 trust types and their default characteristics.

Be careful when relying on transitive trust in mixed-mode domains. Since NT4 DCs do not support Kerberos and cannot access the forest configuration information, transitive trust will only work if a user is authenticated by a Windows 2000 DC. Consider the network logon example illustrated in Figure 6.27. A user defined in *NA* logged on from a Windows 2000 workstation in *NA* is accessing a resource in the Belgium domain (*Be.EMEA.compaq.com*). There's a transitive trust between *NA* and *Europe*,

Figure 6.27
Transitive trusts in
mixed-mode
domains

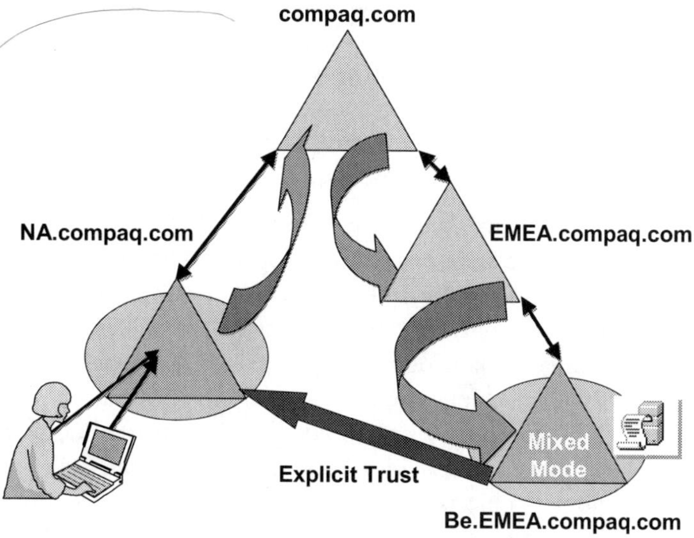

and between the *NA* and *Be* domains. In this scenario authentication will fail if the DC authenticating the user in the *Be* domain is an NT4 DC. Because of the NT4 DC, authentication will fall back to NTLM. NTLM does not understand transitive trust and requires a real trust. What does this mean? When the NT4 DC receives the authentication request from the user in *NA*, it cannot create a trust path back to the *Be* domain because NT4 and NTLM can only deal with single hop trusts. NTLM would work in this scenario if an explicit trust relationship was defined between the *NA* and *Be* domains. In short, resources in a Windows 2000 forest are accessible via transitive trust if one of the following conditions is met:

- The resource server is part of a native-mode domain.

- The resource server is part of a mixed-mode domain, where all domain controllers have been upgraded to Windows 2000.

- The resource server is part of a mixed-mode domain and the domain controller answering the authentication request is a Windows 2000 domain controller (if this is not the case you end up with the example explained above).

Also tricky are trust relationships set up between Windows 2000 forests (external trusts). These relationships are always nontransitive. Kerberos authentication will never work across these trust relationships—even though the machines on both ends are Kerberos-enabled, they do not share a common configuration. Another reason why transitivity will not work in this scenario is because of the way mutual authentication works. Kerberos requires a valid UPN and SPN. SPNs are resolved through the GC. Since a GC does not span forests, authentication will fail if the SPN or UPN cannot be resolved. In other words, transitive trust also requires the availability of a common GC accessible to both entities that want to authenticate. This interforest transitive trust issue should be resolved in the next release of Windows 2000, Windows.Net, codenamed Whistler.

Users working from Windows 2000 workstations can see the effect of transitive trusts when they log on. They can choose every domain with which their domain has a direct trust or an indirect trust. An NT 4.0 end user sees only the direct trusts of his or her domain. The LSA database trusteddomain object (explained in the previous chapter) of a Windows 2000 machine contains both direct and indirect trusted domains; on an NT4 machine it only holds the direct trusted domains. A Windows 2000 administrator can view trust relationships and their properties through each domain objects' properties in the AD domains and trusts MMC snap-in, or by using the netdom.exe or nltest.exe command prompt utility. Typing nltest /server:<servername> /trusted-domains will list all the trusted domains, including the ones connected via a transitive trust (they are tagged "Direct Outbound")

6.6.4 From authentication to authorization

This chapter is all about authentication. In this section we want to link Windows 2000 authentication to authorization. Figure 6.28 illustrates the link between these two core operating system security services.

In the following text, we will explain how we get from the Kerberos ticket (the basic entity used for authentication) to the access token (the basic entity used for authorization). An important component in this process is the Privilege Attribute Certificate (PAC). Microsoft uses the PAC to include authorization data (e.g., global group memberships, etc.) in every Kerberos TGT and ticket.

Let's get back to a normal Kerberos authentication sequence. Again, we're dealing with three entities: a user, Alice; a resource server; and a Kerberos KDC. Once Alice's workstation has located a DC, it will request a Ticket-Granting Ticket. The KDC will generate the PAC, embed the authorization data, put the PAC into a TGT, and send the TGT to Alice. These authorization data are as follows:

- Alice's global group memberships and domain local group memberships: These are available from the KDC's local Active Directory (domain NC).

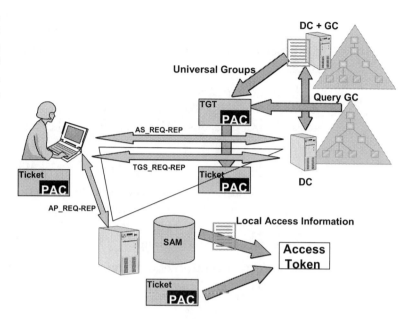

Figure 6.28
From Windows 2000 authentication to authorization

- Alice's universal group memberships: these are available in the GC. For more information on the GC, read Chapter 3. The GC is a subset of the AD domain naming context, which is replicated to every other domain. If the KDC server doesn't host a GC, the KDC service will need to query a GC on another DC. Table 6.6 gives an overview of where group and group membership definitions are stored depending on the group type.

- The user rights assigned to Alice or any of her groups (universal, global, and domain local). These are available from the DC's LSA database.

Table 6.6   *Windows 2000 Groups: Group Membership and Definition Storage Locations*

Group Type	Group Definition Storage	Group Membership Definition Storage
Universal group	AD: GC	AD: GC
Global group	AD: GC	AD: Domain NC
Domain local group	AD: Domain NC	AD: Domain NC
Local group	SAM	SAM

Alice then decides she wants to access a resource hosted on a member server. Alice sends a request for a ticket to the KDC. This ticket will contain the same PAC as the one contained in the TGT. The ticket is sent back to Alice.

Alice authenticates to the resource server using the ticket. The LSA on the resource server will generate Alice's access token (for use in subsequent access control decisions). Within the access token the LSA will embed the following:

- Alice's authorization data found in the ticket's PAC.

- Alice's authorization data found in the local security database (SAM): These are the local group memberships for Alice and any of Alice's groups (universal, global, or domain local) and the user rights for Alice and any of Alice's groups.

To look at the contents of your access token use the Windows 2000 SDK tool, mytoken, or the whoami tool accompanying the Windows 2000 resource kit.

Key things to remember from this section are the following:

- The PAC data are added to a ticket on the KDC level and are inherited between subsequent TGT and ticket requests and renewals. The PAC data are not refreshed at ticket-request time; this means that if a user's group memberships change during its logon session, the user will have to logoff/logon (just as in NT4) or purge the Kerberos ticket cache (using the klist utility).

- The presence of at least one DC hosting a GC per domain tree is mandatory to log on a normal user. An exception to this rule is an account that is a member of the administrators or domain administrators groups: he or she can log on even when a GC server is not available.

- To avoid the need for a GC and to get around possible logon failures when a GC is not available, the following registry key can be set: HKLM\System\CurrentControlSet\Control\Lsa\IgnoreGCFailures (as documented in Knowledge Base article Q241789).

6.6.5 Analyzing the Kerberos ticket and authenticator

This section provides some inside information on the Kerberos ticket and authenticator. The concepts of a ticket and an authenticator and the relationship between the two are illustrated in Figure 6.29. Remember that the

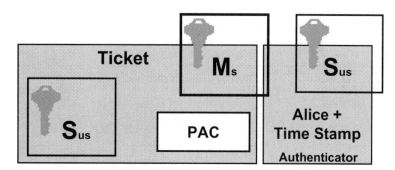

Figure 6.29
*Relationship
between Kerberos
ticket and
authenticator*

primary purpose of a ticket is to securely transport the session key to be used for authentication between two entities. A ticket can only be decrypted by a KDC and the Destination Resource Server. This way the client can never decrypt and change its own authorization data (the information contained in the PAC). An authenticator is the Kerberos object providing the actual authentication. An authenticator can be checked by anyone possessing the corresponding session key.

Ticket content

Table 6.7 shows the ticket fields, their meaning, and whether they are sent in encrypted format across the network.

The privilege attribute certificate

Shortly after the release of Windows 2000, Microsoft got some negative press attention because of the way they used the authorization data field in a Kerberos ticket. Microsoft calls this field the Privilege Attribute Certificate (PAC). Shortly after the press incident, Microsoft published the PAC specification on their Web site. You can download it from *http:// www.microsoft.com/technet/security/kerberos/default.asp.*

An important PAC security detail is that its content is digitally signed. By signing the access control data, a hacker cannot make modifications to the data without being detected. This was possible in NTLM version 1. Access control data that were part of NTLM messages were not protected. Microsoft corrected this error in NTLM version 2 (included in Windows 2000 and all the NT4 service packs from NT4 SP4 on). The Windows 2000 Kerberos ticket PAC's content is signed twice, as follows:

- Once with the master key of the KDC (this is the master key linked to the krbtgt account). This signature prevents malicious server-side services from changing authorization data. The LSA on the server

Table 6.7   *Kerberos Ticket Content*

Encrypted?	Name	Meaning
No	Tkt-vno	Version number of the ticket format
No	Realm	Name of the realm (domain) that issued the ticket.
No	Sname	Name of the server (principal name)
Yes	Flags	Ticket options
Yes	Key	Session key
Yes	Crealm	Name of the client's realm (domain)
Yes	Cname	Client's name (principal name)
Yes	Transited	Lists the Kerberos realms that took part in authenticating the client to whom the ticket was issued
Yes	Authtime	Time of initial authentication by the client. The KDC places a time stamp in this field when it issues a TGT. When it issues tickets, the KDC copies the authtime of the TGT to the authtime of the ticket
Yes	Starttime	(Optional) Time after which the ticket is valid
Yes	Endtime	Ticket's expiration time
Yes	Renew-till	(Optional) Time period during which the ticket is automatically renewed without the client having to provide his or her master key
Yes	Caddr	(Optional) One or more addresses from which the ticket can be used. If omitted, the ticket can be used from any address.
Yes	Authorization data	(Optional) Privilege attributes for the client. Microsoft calls this part the Privilege Attribute Certificate (PAC).

side will require a validation of the signature for every ticket coming from a service that is not running using the local system account. To validate the signature the server needs to set up a secure channel with the KDC that signed the authorization data. This extra validation step might remind you of NTLM and its passthrough authentication; this time the passthrough is not used for the validation of a response but for the validation of a digital signature.

- Once with the master key of the destination service's service account (the destination service is the one responsible for the resource the user wants to access). This is the same key as the one used to encrypt the ticket content. This signature prevents a user from modifying the

PAC content and adding his or her own access control data. This signature can be considered overload, since the ticket content (and with it the PAC) is also encrypted with the same master key.

Kerberos preauthentication data

Preauthentication is a feature introduced in Kerberos version 5. With preauthentication data, a client can prove the knowledge of its password to the KDC before the TGT is issued. In Kerberos version 4 anyone, including a hacker, can send an authentication request to the KDC; the KDC doesn't care. It doesn't even care about authenticating the client: Authentication is completely based on the client's ability to decrypt the packet returned from the KDC using its master key.

Preauthentication also lowers the probability for an offline password-guessing attack. Without preauthentication data, it is easy for a hacker to do an offline password-guessing attack on the encrypted packets returned from the KDC. During an offline password-guessing attack a hacker intercepts an encrypted packet, takes it offline, and tries to break it using different passwords. (This is also known as a brute-force attack, where a hacker tries out different keys [in this case passwords] to decrypt a packet until he or she finds the right key that decrypts the packet in cleartext.) To augment his chances, a hacker can even send out a dummy request for authentication; each time he or she will get back another encrypted packet, which means the hacker gets another chance to do a brute-force attack on the encrypted packet and to guess the user's master key.

In a regular logon session the preauthentication data consist of an encrypted time stamp. When logging on using a smart card, the preauthentication data consist of a signature and the user's public key certificate. In Windows 2000 preauthentication is the default. An administrator can turn it off using the *Don't require Kerberos preauthentication* check box in the account options. This might be required for compatibility with other implementations of the Kerberos protocol. Preauthentication affects the content of a ticket: every ticket contains a special flag to indicate the use or non-use of preauthentication.

Kerberos encryption types

Windows 2000 Kerberos supports the following cryptographic algorithms: RC4-HMAC (see *http://www.ietf.org/internet-drafts/draft-brezak-win2k-krb-rc4-hmac-01.txt*) DES-CBC-CRC, and DES-CBC-MD5. The default

Table 6.8   *Kerberos Encryption Types Key Lengths*

Algorithm	Authentication	Confidentiality Protection
RC4-HMAC	128	56[*]
DES-CBC-CRC	56	56
DES-CBC-MD5	56	56

*Upgradeable to 128-bit keys with the Strong encryption fix installed.

encryption algorithm is RC4-HMAC. There are two reasons why Microsoft did not use DES as the default algorithm:

- Ease of upgrading from NT4 to Windows 2000. The key used for RC4-HMAC can also be used with the Windows NT 4 password hash.

- Export law restrictions. In the early stages of the Windows 2000 development, 56-bit DES could not be exported outside the U.S. Because Microsoft wanted to use the same Kerberos encryption technology in both the domestic and export versions of the product, they chose the 128-bit RC4-HMAC alternative. RC4-HMAC was already exportable at that point in time.

Kerberos can be forced to use DES by setting the *Use DES encryption for this account* property on the Windows 2000 account. This may be needed for authentication interoperability with other non–Windows 2000 systems. The algorithm used for a Kerberos ticket can be checked using the klist or kerbtray resource kit utilities.

Table 6.8 shows the algorithms and their supported key lengths. When the Windows 2000 Strong encryption fix has been installed, RC4-HMAC can use 128-bit keys for bulk encryption. A Windows 2000 domain can contain a mix of clients with and without the fix installed. Windows 2000 Kerberos will automatically choose the strongest available encryption algorithm.

Authenticator content

Table 6.9 shows the authenticator fields, their meaning, and whether they are sent in encrypted format across the network.

TGT and ticket flags

In this section, we will focus on the TGT and ticket flags. The ticket flags and their meaning are explained in Table 6.10.

Table 6.9 *Kerberos Authenticator Content*

Encrypted?	Name	Meaning
Yes	Authenticator-vno	Version number of the authenticator format. In Kerberos v5 it is 5.
Yes	Crealm	Name of the realm (domain) that issued the corresponding ticket.
Yes	Cname	Name of the server that issued the corresponding ticket (principal name)
Yes	Cksum	(Optional) Checksum of the application data in the KRB_AP_REQ
Yes	Cusec	Microsecond part of the client's time stamp
Yes	Ctime	Current time on client
Yes	Subkey	(Optional) Client's choice for an encryption key to be used to protect an application session. If left out, the session key from the ticket is used.
Yes	Seq-number	(Optional) Initial sequence number to be used by the KRB_PRIV or KRB_SAFE messages (protection against replay attacks)

Table 6.10 *Kerberos Ticket Flags*

Flags	Meaning
Forwardable	Indicates to the Ticket-Granting Server that it can issue a new ticket-granting ticket with a different network address based on the presented ticket.
Forwarded	The ticket has either been forwarded or was issued based on authentication involving a forwarded ticket-granting ticket.
Proxiable	Indicates to the Ticket-Granting Server that only non-ticket-granting tickets may be issued with different network addresses.
Proxy	The ticket is a proxy.
May be postdated	Indicates to the Ticket-Granting Server that a postdated ticket may be issued based on this ticket-granting ticket.
Postdated	End service can check the ticket's authtime field to see when the original authentication occurred.
Invalid	The ticket is invalid.
Renewable	The ticket is renewable. If this flag is set, the time limit for renewing the ticket is set in RenewTime. A renewable ticket can be used to obtain a replacement ticket that expires later.
Initial	The ticket was issued using the AS protocol instead of being based on a ticket-granting ticket.

Table 6.10	*Kerberos Ticket Flags (continued)*
Flags	**Meaning**
Preauthenticated	Indicates that, during initial authentication, the client was authenticated by the KDC before a ticket was issued. The strength of the preauthentication method is not indicated but is acceptable to the KDC.
Hardware preauthentication	Indicates that the protocol employed for initial authentication required the use of hardware expected to be possessed solely by the named client. The hardware authentication method is selected by the KDC, and the strength of the method is not indicated.
Target trusted for delegation	This flag means that the target of the ticket is trusted by the directory service for delegation.

Some important notes on the use of the ticket flags in Windows 2000 Kerberos:

- By default, every Windows 2000 ticket has the forwardable flag set. This default behavior can be reversed by setting the *Account is sensitive and cannot be delegated* property on an account object. Windows 2000 Kerberos does not support proxy tickets.

- By default, every Windows 2000 ticket has the renewable flag set. "Renewable" means that a ticket can be renewed, it does not always mean that an existing ticket is automatically renewed. In Windows 2000, for example, the operating system will not automatically request a new ticket (a TGT or a service ticket) when it expires. It will, however, get a new ticket when it needs one. As long as a user's credentials are cached locally this will happen without an additional password prompt.

- By default, every Windows 2000 ticket has the preauthenticated flag set.

- Every Windows 2000 TGT has the initial flag set.

- A Windows 2000 ticket has the *Target trusted for delegation* flag set if the service or user account to which the ticket belongs has the *Account is trusted for delegation* property set. Or, in the case of a computer or a service using the local system account, if the computer object has *Trust computer for delegation* set.

A single ticket can contain multiple flags. The flags are added to a Windows 2000 ticket's properties as a hexadecimal 8-bit number, of which only the first four bits are significant. One bit can refer to different flags. If flags

Table 6.11   *Kerberos Ticket Flags and Bit Values*

Bit 1		Bit 2		Bit 3		Bit 4	
8	N/A	8	Proxy (4)	8	Renewable (8)	8	N/A
4	Forwardable (1)	4	May be postdated (5)	4	Initial (9)	4	Target trusted for delegation (12)
2	Forwarded (2)	2	Postdated (6)	2	Preauthenticated (10)	2	N/A
1	Proxiable (3)	1	Invalid (7)	1	Hardware preauthentication (11)	1	N/A

refer to the same bit position, they are added hexadecimally. This hexadecimal number is displayed when looking at the ticket cache using the resource kit tool klist; the other resource kit tool, kerbtray, automatically converts the number to its appropriate meaning. Table 6.11 shows the bit values and the associated ticket flags.

To facilitate the analysis, Table 6.12 lists the results of adding hexadecimal numbers. Hexadecimal A equals 8 + 2 (decimal 10); hexadecimal D equals 8 + 4 + 1 (decimal 13).

Some examples of typical ticket flags are as follows:

- 0x40e00000

  4 (Forwardable)
  e = 14 = 8 (Renewable) + 4 (AS:Initial ticket) + 2 (PreAuth)

Table 6.12   *Decimal and Hexadecimal Flag Values*

	8	4	2	1
A	*		*	
B	*		*	*
C	*	*		
D	*	*		*
E	*	*	*	
F	*	*	*	*

Figure 6.30
Domain layout

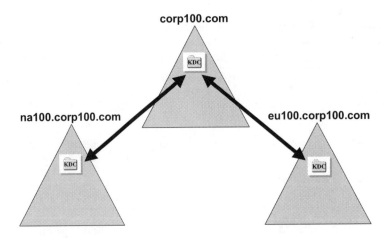

- 0x40840000

    4 (Forwardable)
    8 (Renewable)
    4 (Target trusted for delegation)

To illustrate the way the flags are used let's examine a local logon and a network logon. The domain layout used in these logon sequences consists of one parent domain, *corp100.com*, and two child domains, *eu100.corp100.com* and *na100.corp100.com* (as illustrated in Figure 6.30). The klist command prompt tool used to look at the content of the ticket cache comes with the Windows 2000 platform SDK; the GUI tool, kerbtray, comes with the Windows 2000 resource kit.

Local logon example   A user defined in the *na100* domain logs on to the *na100* domain from machine dc2-na100, which is also part of the *na100*

Figure 6.31
*klist results for
local logon*

```
C:\WINNT\System32\cmd.exe                                        _ □ x
Microsoft Windows 2000 [Version 5.00.2072]
(C) Copyright 1985-1999 Microsoft Corp.

C:\>klist tickets

Cached Tickets: (2)

    Server: krbtgt/NA100.CORP100.COM@NA100.CORP100.COM
       KerbTicket Encryption Type: RSADSI RC4-HMAC(NT)
       TicketFlags: 0x40e00000
       Start Time: 8/18/1999 10:35:25
       End Time: 9/17/1999 10:35:25
       Renew Time: 10/17/1999 10:35:25

    Server: DC2-NA100$@NA100.CORP100.COM
       KerbTicket Encryption Type: RSADSI RC4-HMAC(NT)
       TicketFlags: 0x40a40000
       Start Time: 8/18/1999 10:35:26
       End Time: 9/16/1999 10:35:26
       Renew Time: 10/17/1999 10:35:25
```

domain. Kerbtray or *klist tickets* reveal the following local ticket cache content (see Figure 6.31):

- 1 TGT for the *na100* domain

- 1 ticket for the local machine: dc2-na100

Network logon example   The same user accesses a resource located on machine dc1-eu100 in the *eu100* domain. Kerbtray or *klist tickets* reveal the the local ticket cache content (see also Figure 6.32).

This time the cache contains six tickets, of which four are TGTs. The 4 TGTs reflect the Kerberos referral process: There's one TGT for *corp100*, one for *eu100*, and two for *na100*. The tickets are for the user's local machine (dc2-na100) and for the resource machine in the *eu100* domain (dc1-eu100).

Figure 6.32
klist results for
network logon

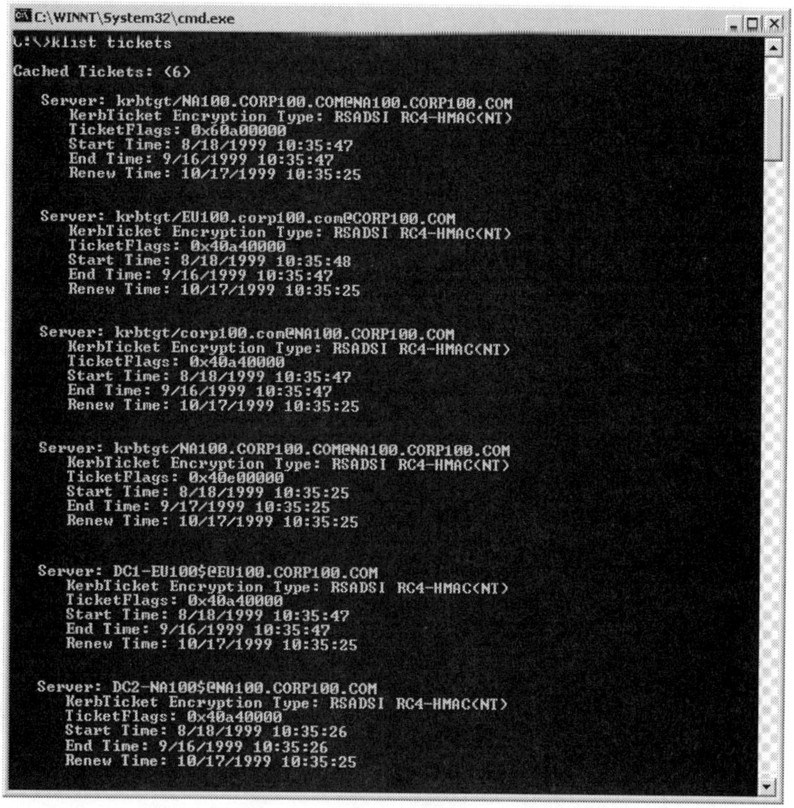

Let's take a closer look at the four TGTs.

- TGT 1 for *na100*

  Flags: 40e
  4 (Forwardable)
  e = 14 = 8 (Renewable) + 4 (AS:Initial ticket) + 2 (PreAuth)

- TGT 2 for *na100*

  Flags: 60a
  6 = 4 (Forwardable) + 2 (Forwarded)
  a = 8 (Renewable) + 2 (PreAuth)

- TGT 3 for *corp100*

  Flags: 40a
  4 (Forwardable)
  a = 8 (Renewable) + 2 (PreAuth)

- TGT 4 for *eu100*

  Flags: 40a: see TGT3

6.6.6 Kerberized applications

Kerberized applications are applications that use the Kerberos authentication protocol to provide authentication, and maybe, in a later phase, to provide encryption and signing for subsequent messages. Authentication can be related to a user, a machine, or a service (any principal). In its current release, Windows 2000 includes the following Kerberized applications:

- LDAP to AD
- CIFS/SMB remote file access (CIFS stands for Common Internet File System—more info at *http://www.cifs.com*)
- Secure dynamic DNS update (explained in Chapter 2)
- Distributed file system management
- Host to host IPsec using ISAKMP
- Secure intranet Web services using IIS
- Certificate request authentication to Certification Authority (CA)
- DCOM RPC security provider

6.6.7 Smart-card logon

Windows 2000 includes extensions to Kerberos version 5 to support public key–based authentication. These extensions are called PKINIT, as defined in *draft-ietf-cat-kerberos-pk-init-09.txt*. Although Microsoft claims to adhere to this draft, they didn't implement one of the required algorithms: Diffie-Hellman. PKINIT enables smart-card logon to a Windows 2000 domain. PKINIT allows a client's master key to be replaced with its public key credentials in the Kerberos authentication request (KRB_AS_REQ) and reply (KRB_AS_REP) messages. This is shown in Table 6.13.

PKINIT introduces a new trust model in which the KDC isn't the first entity to identify the users (as was the case with the master key concept). Prior to KDC authentication, users are identified by the Certification Authority (CA) in order to obtain a certificate. In this new model the users and the KDC obviously all need to trust the same CA.

Figure 6.33 and the following list show the way Kerberos smart-card logon works (notice that the cryptic names of the Kerberos messages have changed):

- Alice starts the logon process by introducing her smart card and by authenticating to the card using her PIN code. The smart card contains Alice's public key credentials: her private-public key pair and certificate.

- A TGT request is sent to the KDC (AS); this request contains the following (PA-PK-AS-REQ):

  - Alice's principal name and a time stamp
  - The above signed with Alice's private key
  - A copy of Alice's certificate

Table 6.13 *Mapping the Standard Kerberos Master Key to the PKINIT Public-Private Key*

Standard Kerberos Use of Master Key	PKINIT Replacement
Client-side encryption of the preauthentication data	Private key
KDC-side decryption of the preauthentication data	Public key
KDC-side encryption of session key	Public key
Client-side decryption of session key	Private key

Figure 6.33
Smart-card logon

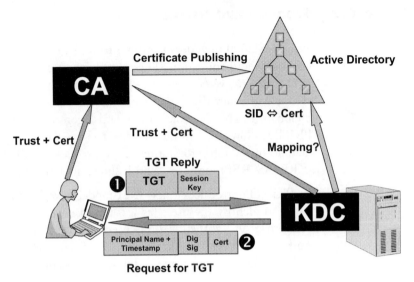

- To validate the request and the digital signature on it, the KDC will first validate Alice's certificate. The KDC will query the Active Directory for a mapping between the certificate and a Windows 2000 SID; if it finds a mapping, it will issue a TGT for the corresponding SID.

- The KDC sends back the TGT to Alice. Alice's copy of the session is encrypted with her public key (PA-PK-AS-REP).

- To retrieve her copy of the session key Alice uses her private key.

6.7   Kerberos configuration

6.7.1   Kerberos GPO settings

The Windows 2000 account policies (part of the GPO computer configuration) include a special subfolder for Kerberos-related policy settings. It contains the following GPO entries:

- Maximum lifetime for service ticket: in Microsoft terminology, a service ticket is a plain Kerberos ticket; its default lifetime is ten hours.

- Maximum lifetime for user ticket: in Microsoft terminology, a user ticket is a Kerberos TGT; its default lifetime is ten hours.

- Maximum lifetime for user ticket renewal: by default, the same ticket (service or user ticket [TGT]) can be renewed up until seven days after its issuance. After seven days, a new ticket has to be issued.

- Maximum tolerance for computer clock synchronization: this is the maximum time skew that can be tolerated between a Kerberos authenticator's time stamp and the current time at the KDC or the resource server. Kerberos is using a time stamp to protect against replay attacks. Setting this setting too high creates a bigger risk for replay attacks. The default setting is five minutes.

- Enforce user logon restrictions: This setting enforces the KDC to check the validity of a user account every time a ticket request is submitted. If a user doesn't have the right to log on locally or if the user's account has been disabled, he or she will not get a ticket. By default, the setting is on.

Another Kerberos-related GPO entry is located in local policies/user rights assignment subcontainer: checking *Enable computer and user accounts to be trusted for delegation* sets the trusted for delegation property of user and computer objects in a domain, site, or organizational unit.

An important detail is that the Kerberos GPO settings can be defined only once for each AD domain. You cannot define custom Kerberos settings for a particular OU or site.

6.7.2 Kerberos-related account properties

Every Windows 2000 user account has a set of Kerberos-related properties. Most of them are related to Kerberos delegation, one is related to the use of preauthentication, and one is related to the choice of the Kerberos encryption algorithm.

Every user account has the properties *Account is trusted for delegation* and *Account is sensitive and cannot be delegated*. Every machine account has the *Trust computer for delegation* property. These settings can be used to limit Kerberos delegation in space (for a limited set of users or service accounts on a predefined set of machines). The technical details behind delegation were explained earlier in this chapter. By default *Account is trusted for delegation* and *Trust computer for delegation* are disabled. An exception are DCs: they are always trusted for delegation. If the check box in a user or machine object's properties is checked, it means that the user or machine account can forward the credentials of any Kerberos principal. In Kerberos terminology this means that the acount can act as a delegate. Setting this property adds the *Target trusted for delegation* (also called OK_AS_DELEGATE) flag to the account's tickets. If a user account has the *Account is sensitive and cannot be delegated* property set, the administrator instructs the KDC not to issue any forwardable tickets to that particular user account.

Do not require Kerberos preauthentication must be set when the account is using a Kerberos implementation that does not support preauthentication. As discussed earlier, Windows 2000 Kerberos supports preauthentication. *Use DES encryption for this account* must be set for an account using a Kerberos implementation that only supports DES encryption. Windows 2000 Kerberos uses RC4-HMAC for encryption; DES is the encryption algorithm defined in the first version of Kerberos.

6.7.3 Kerberos authentication database security

The credentials (a user's ID and hashed password) used during the Kerberos authentication sequence are stored in the Active Directory. Anyone with sufficient cryptographic knowledge who can access the authentication database and obtain the user credentials could impersonate any user. Since we're dealing with a multimaster directory model, the risk for unauthorized access is even bigger.

Accessing the credentials is, however, not that simple, as shown in the following list:

■ Access to every Active Directory object is validated by the Directory Service Agent (DSA), which is linked to the Local Security Authority (LSA). The LSA and DSA are both part of the Windows 2000 kernel.

■ To protect against offline attacks (e.g., on a copy of the Active Directory database located on a backup tape) the Active Directory can be encrypted with a special key called the syskey. This feature was also available in NT4 to protect the SAM. If you're implementing this solution, look for a very safe place to store the symmetric key (the syskey) used for encryption. Also, remember that you cannot use syskey on just one DC. If you use it on one DC, you have to use it on every DC. Futhermore, syskey makes it impossible to do a remote reboot of the DC.

■ Replication of AD information among Windows 2000 DCs occurs across a secure channel. The secure channel guarantees the confidentiality of the replicated data.

In high-security environments, it can be appropriate to install the KDC service on a DC that is located in a room with sufficient physical security provisions.

6.7.4 Kerberos transport protocols and ports

RFC 1510 defines that a Kerberos client should connect to a KDC using the connectionless UDP protocol as a transport protocol (port 88). Microsoft Kerberos uses TCP to take advantage of TCP's bigger Maximum Transmission Unit (MTU) capacity. Microsoft uses TCP if the ticket size is bigger than 2 KB. Any ticket fitting in a 2-KB packet is sent using UDP. UDP has a 1,500-octet MTU limit. Windows 2000 Kerberos tickets can easily grow beyond this limit if they are carrying a large PAC field. The use of TCP is in accordance with the revised RFC 1510 (see *draft-ietf-cat-kerberos-revisions-04.txt*, June 25, 1999, at *http://www.ietf.org*).

The default limit of 2 Kb can be changed using the following registry hack:

HKEY_LOCAL_MACHINE\SYSTEM\CurrentControlSet\
    Control\Lsa\Kerberos\Parameters
Value Name: MaxPacketSize
Data Type: REG_DWORD
Value: 1–2,000 (in bytes)

Setting this value to 1 will force Kerberos to use TCP all the time.

Kerberos uses port 88 on the KDC side and a variable port on the client side. If your Kerberos clients communicate only with Kerberos V5 KDCs

Table 6.14   *Kerberos-Related Ports*

Port	Protocol	Function Description
88	UDP TCP	Kerberos V5
750	UDP TCP	Kerberos V4 authentication
751	UDP TCP	Kerberos V4 authentication
752	UDP	Kerberos Password Server
753	UDP	Kerberos User Registration Server
754	TCP	Kerberos slave propagation
1109	TCP	POP with Kerberos
2053	TCP	Kerberos demultiplexor
2105	TCP	Kerberos encrypted rlogin

(Windows 2000), it's enough to keep port 88 open on your firewall. If they communicate with Kerberos V4 KDCs, remember to open up port 750. Table 6.14 gives an overview of all Kerberos-related ports. If you're interested in monitoring and parsing Kerberos network traffic using network monitor: a special parser DLL is available from Microsoft.

6.7.5 Kerberos time sensitivity

Time is a critical service in Windows 2000. Time stamps are needed for directory replication conflict resolution (see Chapter 3) and also for Kerberos authentication: Kerberos uses time stamps to protect against replay attacks. Out-of-sync clocks between clients and servers can cause authentication to fail or extra authentication traffic to be added during the Kerberos authentication exchange.

To illustrate the importance of time for Kerberos authentication let's look at what really happens during a KRB_AS_REQ and KRB_AS_REP Kerberos exchange:

1.   A client uses the session key it got from the KDC to encrypt its authenticator; the authenticator is sent out to a Resource Server together with the ticket.

2.   The Resource Server compares the time stamp in the authenticator with its local time; if the difference is within the allowed time skew, it goes to step 5. By default the maximum allowed time skew is five minutes; remember that this setting can be configured through domain-level GPOs.

3.   If step 2 failed, the Resource Server sends its local current time to the client.

4.   The client sends a new authenticator using the new time stamp it got from the Resource Server.

5.   The Resource Server compares the new time stamp it got from the client with the entries in its replay cache (this is a list of recently received time stamps). If it finds a match, the client's authentication request will fail.

6.   The Resource Server adds the time stamp to its replay cache; client authentication has succeeded.

Note in the exchange above the extra authentication traffic generated by steps 3 and 4.

The service responsible for time synchronization between Windows 2000 computers is the Windows Time Synchronization Service (W32time.exe). The time service is compliant with the Simple Network Time Protocol (SNTP) as defined in RFC 1769. RFC 1769 is available at *http://www.ietf.org/rfcs/rfc1769.txt.*

Basic SNTP operation

All Windows 2000 machines have W32time installed by default. Only machines that are joined in a domain will start the W32time service automatically. A Windows 2000 machine will perform time synchronization at machine startup and at regular intervals.

At machine startup, a Windows 2000 client contacts an authenticating DC and exchanges packets to determine their time difference. The W32time service on the DC side will determine what time the client's local time should be converged to (this is called the target time). The client will adjust its local time accordingly using the following rules. If the target time is ahead of local time, local time is immediately set to the target time. If the target time is behind local time, the local clock is slowed over the next 20 minutes to align the two times, unless local time is more than two minutes out of synchronization, in which case the time is set immediately.

At regular intervals, the client machine will perform time checks. This means that the client connects to its authenticating DC once each "period." The initial period is eight hours. If the local time is off from the target time by more than two seconds, the period is divided by two. This process is repeated until either the local and target time are within two seconds of each other, or until the period is reduced to 45 minutes.

If local and target time are within two seconds of each other, the period is doubled, up to a maximum period of eight hours.

The default time convergence hierarchy constructed in a Windows 2000 forest adheres to the following rules:

- All client desktops and member servers nominate as their inbound time partner the authenticating DC (the DC returned by DSGetDC-Name()). If this DC becomes unavailable, the client reissues its request for a DC.

- All DCs in a domain nominate the Primary Domain Controller (PDC) flexible, single-master operation (FSMO) to be the inbound time partner.

Figure 6.34
Sample SNTP hierarchy

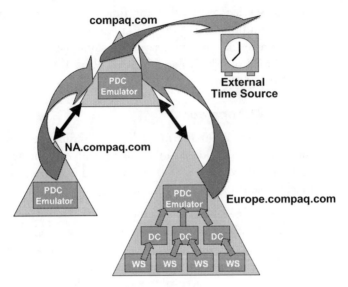

- All PDC FSMOs in the enterprise follow the hierarchy of domains in their selection of an inbound time partner.

- The PDC FSMO at the root of the forest is authoritative and can be manually set to synchronize with an outside time source.

This default hierarchy can be modified by using the utilities explained in the next section. If you want, you can link up any machine in your Windows 2000 forest with an external time source. A sample SNTP hierarchy is shown in Figure 6.34.

Configuring SNTP

The following registry parameters related to W32time can be set (registry path: HKLM\System\CurrentControlSet\Services\w32Time\Parameters):

- NTPServer (REG_SZ): NTP serverName or IP address

- Type (REG_SZ): NT5DS or NTP

The first registry entry can be set using the NET TIME /SETSNTP: <ntp server> command. To query the same registry entry use NET TIME /QUERYSNTP.

A more advanced tool, which can be used to view and to change the SNTP configuration, is w32tm.exe. It can be used to test and configure the time service or to manually synchronize time.

6.8   Kerberos and authentication troubleshooting

In the next two sections, we'll explore some basic Kerberos and Windows 2000 authentication troubleshooting tools. An indispensable tool for every administrator is the Event Viewer; Section 6.8.1 describes some common Kerberos error messages as they appear in the Event Viewer.

6.8.1   Kerberos error messages

The error messages listed in Table 6.15 appear in the Event Viewer. They can give you some interesting hints for troubleshooting Kerberos authentication problems.

Table 6.15   *Kerberos Error Messages and Meaning*

Code	Short Meaning	Error Explanation
0x6	Client principal unknown	The KDC could not translate the client principal Name from the KDC request into an account in the Active Directory. To trouble-shoot this error check whether the client account exists in AD, whether it hasn't expired, and whether AD replication is functioning correctly.
0x7	Server principal unknown	The KDC could not translate the server principal name from the KDC request into an account in the Active Directory. To trouble-shoot this error check whether the client account exists in AD, whether it hasn't expired, and whether AD replication is functioning correctly.
0x9	Null key error	Keys should never be null (blank). Even null passwords generate keys, because the password is concatenated with other elements to form the key.
0xE	Encryption type not supported	The client tried to use an encryption type that the KDC does not support, for any of the following reasons: The client's account does not have a key of the appropriate encryption type; the KDC account does not have a key of the appropriate encryption type; the requested server account does not have a key of the appropriate encryption type. The type may not be recognized at all, for example, if a new type is introduced.
0x17	Password has expired	This error can be caused by conflicting credentials. Let the user log off and then log on again to resolve the issue.
0x18	Preauthentication failed	This indicates failure to obtain ticket, possibly due to the client providing the wrong password.

Table 6.15   *Kerberos Error Messages and Meaning (continued)*

Code	Short Meaning	Error Explanation
0x1A	Requested server and ticket do not match	This error will occur when a server receives a ticket destined for another server. This problem can be caused by DNS problems.
0x1F	Integrity check on decrypted field failed	This error indicates that there's a problem with the hash included in a Kerberos message. This could be caused by a hacker attack
0x20	Ticket has expired	This is not a real error; it just indicates that a ticket's lifetime has ended and that the Kerberos client should obtain a new ticket.
0x22	Session request is a replay	This error indicates that the same authenticator is used twice. This can be caused by a hacker attack.
0x19	Preauthentication error	The client did not send preauthentication, or did not send the appropriate type of preauthentication, to receive a ticket. The client will retry with the appropriate kind of preauthentication (the KDC returns the preauthentication type in the error).
0x25	Clock skew too great	There is a time discrepancy between client and server or client and KDC. To resolve this issue synchronize time between the client and the server.
0x26	Bad address in Kerberos session tickets	Session tickets include the addresses from which they are valid. This error can occur if the address sending the ticket is different from the valid address in the ticket. A possible cause could be an Internet Protocol (IP) address change invalidating any existing cached tickets.
0x3C	Generic error	A generic error; for example, a memory allocation failure.
0x29	Kerberos AP exchange error	This indicates that the server was unable to decrypt the ticket sent by a client—meaning that the server doesn't know its own secret key, or the client got the ticket from a KDC that didn't know the server's key.

6.8.2   Troubleshooting tools

Microsoft delivers several tools to troubleshoot Kerberos. They are spread across the resource kit, the support tools, and the platform SDK. Most of them are command prompt tools. (See Table 6.16.)

Table 6.16 *Kerberos Troubleshooting Tools*

Tool	Comments
mytoken.exe (Platform SDK)	Command prompt tool to display the content of a user's access token: This includes the user's rights and group memberships.
klist.exe (Resource Kit)	Command prompt tool to look at the local Kerberos ticket cache. Klist can also be used to purge tickets.
Kerbtray (Resource Kit)	GUI tool that displays the content of the local Kerberos ticket cache. (See Figure 6.35.)
Netdiag (Support tools)	Netdiag helps isolate networking and connectivity problems by providing a series of tests to determine the state of your network client. One of the netdiag tests is the Kerberos test (netdiag was named nettest before Windows 2000 Beta 3). To run the Kerberos test, type **netdiag /test:Kerberos** at the command prompt.
Replication monitor (Support tools)	Using replication monitor an administrator can check not just the replication traffic but also the number of AS and TGS requests and the FSMO roles.
Network monitor (Server CD)	Network monitor doesn't come out of the box with a parser for the Kerberos protocol. A special Kerberos parser DLL is, however, available from Microsoft.

Figure 6.35
Kerbtray tool showing the Kerberos ticket cache

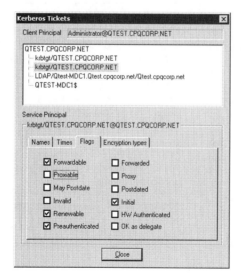

Table 6.17   *nltest Switches and Meaning*

Nltest	Windows 2000 Support Tools
Nltest /trusted_domains	Find out all the trusted domains
Nltest /dclist:<domainname>	Find out all the DCs of domain <domainname>
Nltest /whowill:<domainname> <useraccount>	Find out whether the domain <domainname> has a DC available that can authenticate user <useraccount>
Nltest /finduser:<username>	Find the trusted domain that has a user named <username>

Nltest can be used to test and to find out information about trust relationships. (See Table 6.17.)

Netdom can be used to manage domains and trust relationships from the command prompt. (See Table 6.18.)

Table 6.18   *Netdom Switches and Meaning*

Netdom	Windows 2000 Support Tools
Netdom TRUST /d:<trusteddomain> <trustingdomain> /ADD /Ud:<accounttrusted> /Pd:<passwordaccounttrusted> /Uo:<accounttrusting> /Po:<passwordaccounttrusting>	Creates a trust relationship from the <trustingdomain> to the <trusteddomain> using the given accounts and passwords. Adding the switch /TWOWAY after the /ADD switch will create a bidirectional trust relationship.
Netdom TRUST /d:<trustedrealm> <trustingdomain> /ADD /PT:<trustpassword> /REALM	Creates a trust relationship from the <trustingdomain> to the non-Windows 2000 Kerberos realm <trustedrealm>; sets the trust password to <trustpassword>. To make it a bidirectional trust add /TWOWAY; to make it a transitive trust add /TRANS:yes.
Netdom TRUST <trustingdomain> /d:<trusteddomain> /TRANS:yes	Makes the trust relationship between <trustingdomain> and <trusteddomain> transitive.
Netdom TRUST /d:<trusteddomain> <trustingdomain> /REMOVE	Removes a trust relationship between the <trustingdomain> and the <trusteddomain>.
Netdom TRUST /d:<trusteddomain> <trustingdomain> /VERIFY	Verifies the trust relationship between the <trustingdomain> and the <trusteddomain>.
Netdom TRUST /d:<trusteddomain> <trustingdomain> /Ud:<accounttrusted> /RESET	Resets the secure channel between <trustingdomain> and the <trusteddomain>.
Netdom TRUST /d:<verifieddomain> /VERIFY /KERBEROS	Verifies Kerberos authentication (referrals) between the local workstation and a Kerberos service in <verifieddomain>.

Table 6.19 *Setspn Switches and Meaning*

Setspn	Windows 2000 Resource Kit
Setspn –l <servername>	Lists all the SPNs linked to <servername>.
Setspn –r <servername>	Resets the default SPNs for <servername>.
Setspn –a <SPN> <servername>	Adds <SPN> for <servername>; an SPN usually has the following format: <servicename>/<server DNS name>.
Setspn –d <SPN> <servername>	Deletes <SPN> for <servermame>.

Setspn allows you to manage (view, reset, delete, add) service principal names (SPNs). (See Table 6.19.)

6.9   Kerberos interoperability

As mentioned earlier in this chapter, Kerberos is an open standard, which has been implemented on different platforms. Because of this, Kerberos can be used as a single sign-on (SSO) solution among different OS platforms and applications.

6.9.1   Non-Windows 2000 Kerberos implementations

Table 6.20 lists other Kerberos implementations and the platform on which they are available. At the time of this writing, Microsoft had only conducted interoperability tests between Windows 2000 and MIT Kerberos and CyberSafe TrustBroker.

Table 6.20 *Kerberos Implementations for non–Windows 2000*

Kerberos Implementation	Platform
MIT Kerberos v1.1	NetBSD
CyberSafe TrustBroker	UNIX, MVS, Windows 95, NT4
Sun SEAM	Solaris
DCE Kerberos (IBM)	AIX, OS/390
Computer Associates Kerberos (Platinum [OpenVision])	Windows 95, 3.1, 3.11
Heimdal	UNIX

6.9.2   Comparing Windows 2000 Kerberos to other implementations

Before going into the details of the interoperability scenarios, it's interesting to look at what makes Windows 2000 Kerberos different from the other implementations. The MS implementation of Kerberos differs in the following ways:

- It is tightly integrated with the Windows 2000 OS: Every Windows 2000 system runs the Kerberos SSP, every DC has a KDC service.

- Kerberos principals locate the KDC using DNS. Windows 2000 DNS includes special SRV records that point to the location of a Kerberos KDC.

- Microsoft implemented the RC4-HMAC encryption algorithm (56/128-bit keys) as the preferred Kerberos encryption type; Microsoft still supports DES-CBC-CRC and DES-CBC-MD5 (56-bit keys) for interoperability reasons.

- The Microsoft implementation does not support the MD4 checksum type.

- Windows 2000 does not include support for DCE-style cross-realm trust relationships.

- Microsoft uses its proprietary SSPI to access Kerberos services; there's no support for the raw krb5 API.

- Microsoft uses the authdata field in the ticket to embed access control data.

6.9.3   Interoperability scenarios

In this section we will focus on setting up Kerberos interoperability between Windows 2000 Kerberos and a Kerberos implementation that runs on top of UNIX platforms. Kerberos authentication interoperability can be set up in three different ways.

- The Windows 2000 Kerberos KDC is the KDC for both Windows 2000 and UNIX principals (the principals are administered from the Windows KDC). (Scenario 1)

- The UNIX KDC is the KDC for both Windows 2000 and UNIX principals (the principals are administered from the Unix KDC). This scenario includes no Windows 2000 DCs. (Scenario 2)

- A cross-realm trust relationship is defined between a Windows 2000 domain and a UNIX Kerberos realm. (A part of the principals is administered from the Windows KDC; another part is administered from the UNIX KDC.) In this case, there are two KDCs—one KDC on each side of the trust relationship. (Scenario 3)

In the following text, we'll explain these scenarios.

Lots of valuable information on how to set up interoperability can be found in the following white papers: "Windows 2000 Kerberos Interoperability" available from *http://www.microsoft.com/windows2000/library/howitworks/security/kerbint.asp* and "Kerberos Interoperability: Microsoft Windows 2000 and CyberSafe ActiveTrust" available from *http://www.cybersafe.com/news/whitepapers.html*.

Principals defined in Windows 2000 KDC

This scenario allows Kerberos principals on both Windows 2000 and non-Windows 2000 platforms to log on using Windows 2000 credentials and a Windows 2000 KDC. To enable a user to log on to Windows 2000 from a UNIX workstation, the UNIX krb5.conf Kerberos configuration file must be edited to point to the Windows 2000 KDC. Afterwards the user can log on using his or hers Windows 2000 account and the kinit command (kinit is the equivalent of log on in Unix Kerberos implementations).

The setup gets a little bit more complicated when enabling a service, running on a UNIX platform, to log on using Windows 2000 credentials and a Windows 2000 KDC. In this scenario the Windows 2000 administrator has to run through the following configuration steps:

- Edit the krb5.conf file on the UNIX machine to point to the Windows 2000 KDC.

- Create a service account for the UNIX service in the Active Directory

- Use ktpass.exe to export the newly created service account's credentials from AD and to create a keytab file. The keytab file contains the password that will be used by the UNIX service to logon to the Windows 2000 domain. Ktpass.exe is shipped with the Windows 2000 resource kit.

- Copy the keytab file to the UNIX host and merge it with the existing keytab file.

The following example illustrates this last scenario. A company has a UNIX database server whose content should be accessible through a Web interface for every Windows 2000 user. To set this up, configure the database service as a principal in the Windows 2000 domain, and install an IIS Server as a Web front end for the Database Server. To allow for credential forwarding between a Windows 2000 user and the IIS server, the IIS Server must be trusted for delegation.

Principals defined in non-Windows 2000 KDC

This scenario allows Kerberos principals on both Windows 2000 and non-Windows 2000 platforms to log on using UNIX credentials and a UNIX KDC. For a standalone Windows 2000 workstation or member server to use a UNIX KDC, the following steps must be taken:

- Create a host for the workstation in the UNIX realm.

- Configure the Windows 2000 workstation or member server using ksetup.exe to let it point to the UNIX KDC and realm and to set the machine password (this will automatically switch the workstation or member server to workgroup mode). Ksetup.exe is shipped with the Windows 2000 resource kit.

- Restart the workstation or member server and run ksetup.exe again to map local machine accounts to UNIX principals.

Cross-realm trust

This is probably the most flexible interoperability scenario available. This scenario will enable non–Windows 2000 Kerberos principals to log on to their UNIX KDC and to access resources in a Windows 2000 domain and vice versa: for Windows 2000 principals to log on to their Windows 2000 KDC and to access resources in a UNIX realm.

The setup of a cross-realm trust between Windows 2000 and a UNIX realm is relatively straightforward. On the Windows 2000 side two things must be done: a trust relationship must be created using the AD domains and trusts snap-in and a realm mapping for the UNIX realm should be added to the system registry. To add a realm mapping use the ksetup tool. A realm mapping should not only be added on the Windows 2000 DC, but on every machine from which resources will be accessed in the UNIX realm. On the UNIX side, a trust relationship can be created using the kadmin tool.

If all user accounts are defined in the UNIX realm or in the Windows 2000 domain, a domain layout very similar to the NT4 master domain model of account domains and resource domains is created. In that case, the UNIX realm acts as a master account domain containing all the accounts. The Windows 2000 domain acts as a resource domain, containing resources and mappings from the UNIX accounts to Windows 2000 SIDs (or the other way around).

Besides the creation of a cross-realm trust, the scenario where the UNIX realm functions as a master domain requires more configuration on the Windows 2000 side. The reason for this is the difference in the accounting and access control systems used in Windows 2000 and UNIX. Whereas UNIX relies on principal Names for both accounting and access control, Windows 2000 relies entirely on Security Identities (SIDs). Even though there's a trust relationship between the UNIX realm and the Windows 2000 domain, users authenticated through the KDC in the UNIX account domain can by default not access any resource in the Windows 2000, because they do not have a SID.

To resolve this problem shadow or proxy accounts must be created on the Windows 2000 side. A proxy account is an attribute (the altSecurityID attribute) of a Windows 2000 account that contains a UNIX principal name. In other words, proxy accounts provide a way to map a UNIX account to a Windows 2000 account or SID.

Let's look at what will happen in this scenario when a UNIX principal wants to access a resource hosted on a machine that is a member of a Windows 2000 domain (illustrated in Figure 6.36):

- The UNIX principal is logged on to the UNIX domain; its credential cache will contain a TGT for the UNIX domain. (Step 1)

- The UNIX principal wants to access a resource in the Windows 2000 domain. Its local KDC refers it to the Windows 2000 KDC. (Step 2)

Figure 6.36
UNIX–
Windows 2000
single sign-on using
a cross-realm trust

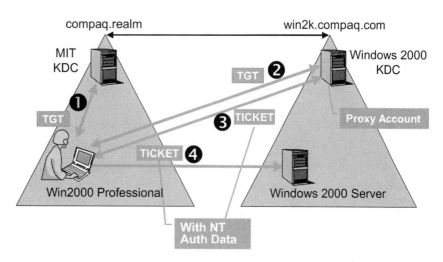

- The Windows 2000 KDC creates a new service ticket for the UNIX principal to access the resource. Since the TGT used by the UNIX principal contains an empty PAC, the Windows 2000 KDC will query the Active Directory for an account mapping between the UNIX principal and a Windows 2000 SID. The newly issued service ticket will contain the PAC data corresponding to the Windows 2000 SID. (Step 3)

- Using the service ticket the UNIX principal authenticates to the machine hosting the resource. (Step 4)

In case the Windows 2000 domain also contains NT4 servers that can serve only NTLM authentication requests, this scenario also requires some password synchronization tool between the UNIX realm (where the accounts and their passwords are defined) and the Windows 2000 domain. Such a tool is available in CyberSafe's TrustBroker product.

6.10 Summary

By implementing Kerberos in Windows 2000 Microsoft has clearly ameliorated and extended the authentication process. This chapter certainly showed that Kerberos is a very powerful, but at the same time very complex protocol. Mainly because of its symmetric cryptography roots, Kerberos is a typical LAN intranet–oriented authentication protocol. The inclusion of PKINIT is a first step towards the inclusion of public key-based authentication mechanisms for Kerberos and toward the widening of the Kerberos application area.

7

Group Policy and OU Design

This chapter introduces AD user and computer configuration management and one of its key features: group policy. We will look in detail at the technology behind group policy, what you can do with it, and how you can troubleshoot group policy objects (GPOs). At the end of the chapter we will also examine Windows 2000 group policy and OU design, and how group policy can impact your OU design.

7.1   Group policy

7.1.1   An introduction to Windows 2000 group policy

In Windows 2000, group policy refers to a group of software technologies that allows centralized configuration and change management of user and computer environments. It covers five major areas: local registry management, software deployment, folder redirection, scripts, and security settings management. Through its tight integration with Active Directory, group policy is highly scalable and extensible.

Group policy should not be confused with system policy or user profiles. As will be explained later on in this chapter, Windows 2000 group policies are very different from NT4 system policies. In Windows 2000 Microsoft has extended and optimized the capabilities of system policies. Also, policies are not the same as profiles, as defined in the following:

■ Policies define a set of user environment settings that are enforced by a domain or system administrator; a profile contains a set of user settings that can be changed by the user.

■ Policies are enforced independently of the machine from which a user logs on to a Windows 2000 domain; if profiles are not roaming, they do not follow the user and are different on every machine.

Group policy objects

The basic unit of Windows 2000 Group Policy is a Group Policy Object (GPO). A GPO is a collection of policy configuration settings that can be linked to an Active Directory container (a domain, site, or OU). The administration interface for GPOs is the MMC group policy snap-in, also known as the group policy editor (GPE). To help you understand this chapter, we recommend that you play around with the GPE.

Using the GPE an administrator gets a clear overview of everything that can be configured through GPO (as illustrated in Figure 7.1). When loading the group policy snap-in you can choose among the local computer GPO (LGPO) or any of the other GPOs available from the DCs in your logon domain or one of its trusted domains (use the Browse button). Each group policy object has two subcontainers: one containing the computer configuration settings and another one containing the user configuration settings. Each of these subcontainers contains more containers, one for each category of settings that can be configured through group policy, as follows:

- The Software Settings subcontainer lists the software packages deployed using GPO.

- The Windows Settings subcontainer has different subcontainers for the configuration of scripts, security settings, Internet Explorer maintenance, folder redirection and remote installation services. Notice that most of the settings in the Security Settings container are also displayed in the Security Configuration and Analysis tool (SCA) MMC management interface (see Chapter 5).

- The Administrative Templates subcontainer lists the registry settings that can be configured through GPO.

The settings defined in a GPO apply to all computer and user objects contained in the AD container to which the GPO is linked. By default a GPO applies as a whole to an AD container: the computer portion applies to every computer object, and the user portion applies to every user object in the container. GPOs do not apply to any other nonuser or nonmachine object member of an AD container (e.g., printers, shares, etc.). GPOs can be applied partially to an AD container. This means that the user or the machine portion of the GPO can be disabled. To do this, select the properties of the GPO object and check *Disable User Configuration settings*, *Disable Computer Configuration Settings*, or both (as illustrated in Figure 7.2).

When a GPO object is created, it is by default linked to an AD container. This behavior can be reversed by enabling the GPO entry *Create new Group Policy Object links disabled by default*. Because the GPO itself and the

Figure 7.1
GPE and different containers and settings

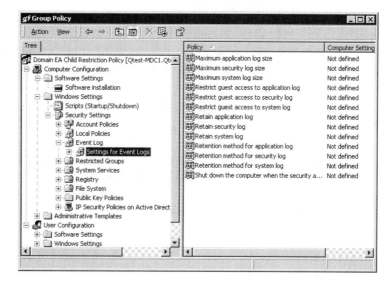

link between the GPO and the AD container are two different AD entities, a GPO can exist in AD without being linked to an AD container. A GPO AD object contains all the policy settings. A GPO link is an attribute of the AD container it is linked to. The same GPO object can be linked to multiple AD containers. As will be explained in detail later in the chapter, a GPO object is partially stored in AD and partially in the system volume (SYS-VOL), and a GPO link is stored in AD.

Figure 7.2
Disabling the user or the machine portion of a GPO

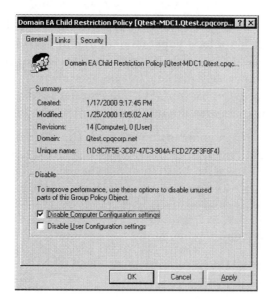

Local versus nonlocal GPOs

Windows 2000 supports two basic types of GPOs: local GPOs (LGPOs) and nonlocal GPOs. A key difference between these two GPO types is their application scope, or the group of objects to which the GPO settings can be applied.

A nonlocal GPO is a GPO that can be linked to multiple AD container objects, such as sites, domains, and OUs. The application scope of a nonlocal GPO is set by an administrator when he or she links the GPO to an AD container. A nonlocal GPO has a unique AD identifier (GUID) and is defined and stored on the DCs of a specific domain. A nonlocal GPO can be used to configure all the settings explained at the beginning of this chapter. Sometimes they are referred to as AD GPOs.

Regarding the application scope of a nonlocal GPO, always remember the following:

- They apply to all computer and user objects that are contained in the AD container to which they are linked. They do not apply to groups or any other objects (printers, shares, etc.) contained in the AD object.

- A nonlocal GPO can be linked to more than one AD object. This means that, for example, a GPO object can be linked to both an OU and a site. Since GPO links are stored in the GC, a GPO object can be linked to objects in a domain different from the GPO's definition domain (although we don't advise you to do this).

A local GPO is a GPO that is stored on and linked to exactly one machine. It has a local application scope. An LGPO applies only to the machine where it was defined and to the users logging on to that machine. Every Windows 2000 machine (member servers and workstations, with the exception of DCs) has a LGPO. DCs do not have a local GPO; instead, they can be configured through the default DCs nonlocal GPO.

LGPOs have nothing to do with the Active Directory. They do not have a GUID and cannot be centrally administered and distributed throughout your organization. An LGPO can only be used to configure local security settings, local account, and password policies and scripts; application deployment or folder redirection cannot be set on the LGPO level.

Predefined GPOs

Windows 2000 comes with two predefined GPOs: the default DCs and the default domain policy GPO:

1. The default domain policy GPO is the GPO that is automatically applied to every user and computer object in a Windows 2000 domain. It is linked to an AD domain object. To explore or edit the settings of the default domain GPO, right-click the domain container in the AD user and computers snap-in, select Properties, and then the Group Policy tab. The default domain policy is the only policy that can be used to control the security settings (password quality, account lockout, etc.) of AD account objects (also known as global accounts)

2. The default DCs GPO is the GPO that is automatically applied to every Windows 2000 DC. It is linked to the DCs organizational unit (OU). To explore or edit the settings of the default DCs GPO, right-click the DCs OU in the AD user and computers snap-in, select Properties, and then the Group Policy tab. Interesting detail: if you move a DC to another OU, it may end up with different security policies (account policy, user rights, etc.). This was impossible in NT4. In NT4 all DCs always had the same security policy.

The power of group policy

A Windows 2000 administrator can use group policy to control and enforce the following user-, machine-, and desktop-related configuration settings:

- Desktop management settings covering registry, security, Internet Explorer, and folder redirection configuration.

- Software installation settings covering automatic software installation, publishing, updating, and removal.

- Machine and user scripts configuration settings covering the definition of user logon and logoff scripts and machine startup and shutdown scripts.

- Remote installation services (RIS) configuration settings, enabling a complete remote unattended installation of the Windows 2000 operating system.

In the following sections we will explore some of the powerful configuration options of group policy in more detail. We will focus on the features related to user data and settings management and software installation and maintenance. Microsoft usually calls this group of features IntelliMirror. Later on in the chapter we will explain the software technology behind these configuration options.

We will not cover the remote operating system installation and Internet Explorer maintenance GPO configuration features. Internet Explorer maintenance allows centralized configuration of most of the IE configuration settings. Both remote OS installation and IE maintenance settings are configurable in the user portion of a GPO.

Registry management

GPO registry management settings allow an administrator to centrally control the content of any setting in the user (HKEY_CURRENT_USER) or machine (HKEY_LOCAL_MACHINE) portion of the system registry. We will explain later in the chapter how a Windows 2000 administrator can customize the list of registry settings enforced through GPO.

GPO registry management allows an administrator to set the following settings (as illustrated in Figure 7.3):

- Settings to configure Windows components, such as Internet Explorer, Windows Explorer, MMC, NetMeeting, Task Scheduler, and Windows Installer.

- Start menu and Taskbar settings.

- Desktop settings to configure the Active Desktop and the Active Directory folder in My Network Places.

- Control Panel settings to control the behavior of the Add/Remove Programs, Display, Printers, and Regional Options Control Panel folders.

- Network settings to control the properties of offline folders and the configuration of network and dial-up connections.

- System settings to control logon/logoff, disk quotas, the DNS client, group policy, and Windows file protection.

- Printer settings.

All of these settings are grouped in the GPE Administrative Templates container.

The Windows 2000 registry management portion of a GPO covers the functionality offered in NT4 system policies. The technology used for it is very similar to the one used for NT4 system policies. Key differences with system policy are GPO's support for nonpersistent registry changes and for true registry setting enforcement. A GPO will not tattoo the registry. Registry changes applied through group policy do not overwrite the registry settings on disk. They just update the registry settings that are loaded in

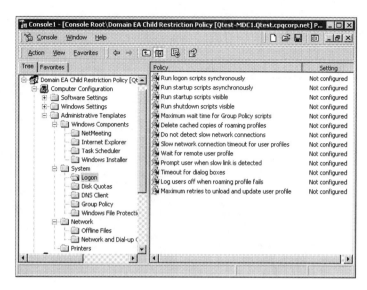

Figure 7.3
GPO registry management settings categories

system memory. Thanks to this feature a normal user cannot change the settings enforced through GPO, as a user could do in NT4 with system policies.

Security management

The security management portion of a Windows 2000 GPO enables centralized management of security settings. All these settings, except for one that's user-bound, are machine-bound (we will come back to this later in this chapter). GPO security management includes configuration options for the following (as illustrated in Figure 7.4):

- Account policies: to set password, account, and Kerberos settings

- Local policies: to set auditing, user rights, and security options

- Event log settings: to set properties of the application, system, and security logs

- Restricted group settings: to configure the membership of security-sensitive groups

- System services settings: to configure security and startup settings for services

- Registry settings: to configure security (ACLs) on registry keys

- File system settings: to configure security (ACLs) on files and folders

Figure 7.4
*GPO security
management
settings categories*

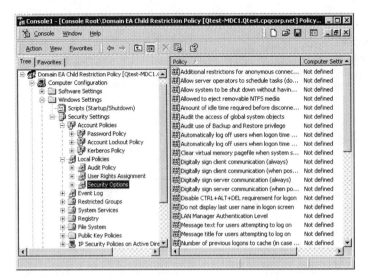

- Public key policies: to configure the Enterprise Data Recovery Policy (EDRP), root CAs, and so on

- IP security policies: to configure IPsec-related settings

The account policies and local policies deserve a bit more explanation. Local policies always refer to local machine settings, not domain-wide settings. (They are stored in the LSA database.) Account policies can refer to local accounts or domain accounts. Account policies for domain accounts can only be set in the default domain policy. This means that password, account lockout, and Kerberos policies for domain accounts can be defined only once: on the domain level using the default domain policy. Account policies set in other GPOs, will not affect domain account policies, but will affect local account policies.

Local account policies means policies linked to accounts stored in the SAM (the local security database). Since AD DCs have a dormant SAM, it is of no use to set account policies in the default DCs policy. It will, however, affect the accounts of machines with an active SAM, that is, member servers and workstations.

GPO security management is closely related to the Security Configuration and Analysis (SCA) tool, discussed in Chapter 5. It complements the SCA by enabling the enforcement of security settings on the domain, OU, and site level. Both the SCA and GPO security management are using the same client-side extensions and database. We will discuss this later in the chapter.

In the GPO security management portion, Microsoft brought together the configurations of several security settings that previously, in NT4, were spread across different administration tools. GPO security management also complements other Windows 2000 security administration tools, such as the local users and groups MMC snap-in. Compared with its NT4 predecessor the local users and groups MMC snap-in lacks functionality. The audit policy, password policy, and account policy have now been integrated into the GPO security management portion. Table 7.1 gives an overview of the different security setting categories configurable through the GPO security settings and their NT4 administration tool counterpart.

Table 7.1   *GPO Security Settings Containers and Equivalent NT4 Administration Tool*

Security Settings Subcontainer (Windows 2000)	Equivalent NT4 Administration Tool (NT4)
Account policies	
Password policy	User manager => policy/account policy
Account lockout	User manager => policy/account policy
Kerberos policy*	NA
Local policies	
Audit policy	User manager => policy/audit policy
User rights assignment	User manager => policy/user rights
Security options	NA
Event log*	Event Viewer => log/event log settings
Restricted groups*	NA
System services*	Control Panel => services
Registry*	NA
File system*	NA
Public key policies†	NA
IP security policies	NA

*Not configurable on Windows 2000 Professional

†This is an exception to the machine-bound rule; public key–related security settings can also be configured on the user level.

Software installation

Using the GPO software installation tools an administrator can set up automatic application deployment for machines in the Windows 2000 organization. Deploy in this context means three things: install applications, update applications, and remove applications. Application deployment can be set up on the site, the domain, and the OU level, but not on the local GPO (LGPO) level. Software installation using GPOs uses Windows installer service technology.

Applications can be installed in two different modes. They can be assigned to users and computers, or they can be published to users, as follows:

- Use assignment mode when the application you want to deploy is a required application that should be available to every user or on every computer in your organization. When an application is assigned, a shortcut to the application's executable will be advertised in the Start menu. When the machine reboots, the first time the user starts the program from the Start menu, or the first time the user opens an object whose file type is linked to the application, the application will be installed.

- Use publishing mode when the application you want to deploy is not a required application. Publishing works as follows: when a user opens the Control Panel and selects the Add/Remove Programs applet, the operating system queries the Active Directory to determine the applications that have been published to that particular user. When publishing applications the decision to install the application is up to the user. A published application is advertised in the Active Directory, not on the user's desktop.

When deleting the installation package from the GPO, GPO-based software installation allows an administrator to specify whether to uninstall an application immediately or to allow users to continue to use the application. Also, previous installations of a product can be removed when these installations were not done using GPO.

Although GPO-based software installation offers lots of interesting configuration options, it does not reach the feature level offered by a dedicated software distribution package, such as Microsoft's SMS.

Scripts

Windows 2000 includes important enhancements to support automatic script execution. The execution of scripts can be set and enforced through

Table 7.2   *Windows 2000 GPO Script Options*

Script Type	Executed When?	Where Configured?
Startup script	Machine startup	GPOt
Logon script	User logon	GPO
Legacy logon script	User logon	Properties of an Active Directory User object
Logoff script	User logoff	GPO
Shutdown script	Machine shutdown	GPO

GPOs. Windows 2000 comes out of the box with the Windows Scripting Host (WSH). WSH is a scripting engine supporting VBScript, JScript, and extensions for other script languages such as Perl and Rexx.

GPO script configuration is done through the scripts subcontainer in the Windows Settings container (available in both the user and the machine portion). GPO allows the definition of multiple user and machine scripts, multiple parameters per script, and the order of script processing (in the case of multiple scripts). Also, in Windows 2000 scripts can be executed at different moments in time (at logon, logoff, startup, or shutdown). NT4 supported only user logon scripts. Table 7.2 gives an overview of when scripts can be executed and where they are configured.

The legacy logon script in Table 7.2 is the classic NT4 logon script, configured in the properties of a user object. To make the life of an administrator easier Microsoft recommends not using legacy logon scripts: Troubleshooting becomes a nightmare when both a GPO logon script and a legacy logon script have been defined. Anything that could be done with a legacy script can now be done with GPO-defined scripts.

The order in which the scripts are listed in Table 7.2 is the order in which they would be executed when all of them were applicable. By default, an NT4 logon script is executed after the GPO scripts have finished running. This behavior can be changed by setting the GPO entry *Run Logon Scripts Synchronously.* If this setting is disabled, the Explorer shell (and thus the NT4 logon script) will start running before the GPO scripts have finished running. This could possibly lead to inconsistent results. On the other hand, you might need to set the logon scripts to run asynchronously. For example, if you want to make use of some environment variables in your scripts. Environment variables are not available if the user shell has not been loaded.

Table 7.3   *Script-Related GPO Settings*

GPO Portion	GPO Path	GPO Entry
Computer Configuration	Windows Settings\Script\Startup	
	Windows Settings\Script\Shutdown	
	Administrative Templates\System\Logon	Run Logon Scripts Synchronously
		Run Startup Scripts Asynchronously
		Run Shutdown Scripts Visible
		Run Startup Scripts Visible
		Maximum wait time for Group Policy scripts
User Configuration	Windows Settings\Script\Logon	
	Windows Settings\Script\Logoff	
	Administrative Templates\System\Logon/ Logoff	Run Logon Scripts Synchronously
		Run Legacy Logon Scripts Hidden
		Run Logon Scripts Visible
		Run Logoff Scripts Visible

Run Logon Scripts Synchronously can be set on both the computer- and the user-configuration level. The computer setting has precedence over the user setting. An identical setting can be set for startup scripts—this time only on the machine level. If startup scripts are enforced to run synchronously, it will be impossible for a user to log on before all startup scripts have completed. Table 7.3 shows all script-related settings that can be set through GPO.

An interesting parameter is the *Maximum wait time for group policy scripts*. This parameter is used to set the total time for all scripts configured through GPO to finish running. The default limit is ten minutes. If the scripts have not finished running after ten minutes, they will be interrupted and an error event will be logged. GPOs also include a setting to make scripts run visible. By default, Windows 2000 GPO configured scripts run in the background. This is not true for legacy logon scripts, which by default run visible.

The scripts that are referred to in the GPO settings should be located in the Scripts subcontainer of the system volume. This makes them available throughout your enterprise, thanks to FRS replication. Also it gives you the option to refer to the scripts independently of the server on which they are stored. Just type \\<domain name>\sysvol\<domain name>\ scripts or \\<domain.name>\netlogon. By default the scripts directory of the SYSVOL is shared as netlogon to make the logon scripts accessible to down-level clients.

Folder redirection

Folder redirection is the ability to store the content of specific user profile folders on a server instead of the user's workstation. Folder redirection can be looked at as a next step after home directories. One of the goals of folder redirection is to reduce a user's system management tasks. Many help-desk calls originate from users stuffing their hard disks to a level where the system halts. Using folder redirection, user files can automatically and transparently be stored on a central server.

Windows 2000 folder redirection can be configured through site, domain, or OU GPOs. It can be set for the following user profile folders: Application Data, Desktop, My Documents, My Pictures, and the Start menu. The use of folder redirection has some important advantages, as follows:

- Because it reduces the size of the user profile, it can reduce logon time. This will have a big impact when using roaming profiles, in which case profiles are downloaded from a central location at logon time.

- Redirecting a subset of the profile folders to a central server means that these folders can be made available to the user anywhere he or she logs on.

- You can combine folder redirection with fault-tolerant DFS shares to enhance user profile folder availability.

- By storing some of the key user profile folders on a central server, the maintenance (backup-restore) of these folders can be taken care of by your organization's IT department.

Folder redirection can be configured in different ways: everyone's folder can be redirected to the same location (basic configuration), or many different locations can be configured, and users can be redirected to these locations based on their group membership (advanced configuration). Also, an administrator can configure what happens when the folder redirection GPO setting is removed: Are the data left in the remote location or is the

Table 7.4   *Comparing the Features of NT4 System Policy and Windows 2000 Group Policy*

NT4, Windows 95, Windows 98 System Policies	Windows 2000 Group Policy Objects (Administrative Templates)
Are linked to domains	Can be linked to domains, sites, and organizational units
System policy application can be filtered using user security groups.	GPO application can be filtered using user or computer security groups.
Persistent registry and user profile changes: Settings can only be removed by reversing the policy or by manual user edits.	Nonpersistent registry changes
Not secure: A user who has access to a registry editor can change system policy settings.	Secure: Only an administrator with sufficient permissions can change GPO settings.
Can be used for registry-based desktop control	Can be used for registry-based desktop control and to control a user's complete computing environment
All settings are stored in a single file.	Settings are stored in different files and in the Active Directory.
Both machine and user system policy settings are evaluated and applied at user logon.	Machine group policy settings are evaluated and applied at machine startup, user policy settings at user logon. Both categories are automatically refreshed after startup and after logon.
Are edited using the system policy editor (poledit.exe)	Are edited using the group policy MMC snap-in (group policy editor [GPE])

folder automatically redirected back to the corresponding folder in the user's profile?

Comparing Windows 2000 group policy to NT4 system policies

Table 7.4 compares the features of NT4 system policy to those of Windows 2000 group policy.

7.1.2   The software technology behind group policy

This section contains detailed information on the way GPOs work. First we will discuss GPO storage, afterward we will explore GPO application.

GPO storage

In this section, we will look in detail at how GPOs are stored. Which GPO portions are stored in the AD? Which ones are stored on the file system (the system volume)? A discussion of GPO storage can be split into three sub-topics: nonlocal GPO storage, GPO link storage, and local GPO (LGPO) storage.

If needed, GPO information can be stored outside the default Windows 2000 GPO storage areas. This, however, requires custom development.

Nonlocal GPO storage

A nonlocal GPO consists of two parts: a group policy container (GPC), stored in the Active Directory, and a group policy template (GPT), stored on the file system (on the system volume [SYSVOL]). Both the GPC and the GPT are available on Windows 2000 DCs. They are replicated among DCs using different mechanisms: The GPC is replicated using AD replication; the GPT is replicated using the File Replication Service (FRS). For more information on AD replication and FRS, see Chapter 3.

The group policy container A GPC is stored in the AD domain NC. The Distinguished Name (DN) of a GPC has the following format: CN=<Pol-icy-GUID>,CN=Policies,CN=System,DC=<domain name> (as illustrated in Figure 7.5). Notice that the GPC is identified with a GUID, not with a friendly display name. The GPC has two subcontainers: a Machine container and a User container. Table 7.5 shows the most important attributes of an AD GPC object and their meaning.

Figure 7.5
*Checking GPC
AD storage
using adsiedit*

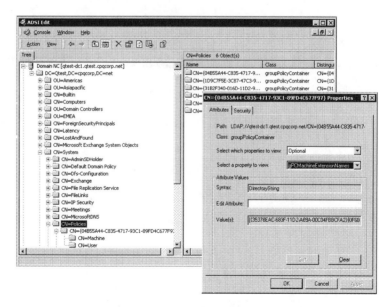

Table 7.5   *Active Directory GPC Object Attributes and Their Meaning*

Attribute Name	Meaning
Displayname	The friendly display name used in the GPE.
Flags	Indicates which GPO portions are disabled: 1 = user portion disabled, 2 = computer portion disabled, 3 = both disabled.
GPCFileSysPath	Points to the file system location of the corresponding GPT. The path has the following format (also known as a fault-tolerant path): \\<Domain DNS Name>\SysVol\<Domain DNS Name>\Policies\{Policy GUID}.
GPCFunctionalityVersion	The version number of the group policy snap-in extension (GPE) that created the GPO
GPCMachineExtensionNames	The client-side extensions needed to execute the machine portion of the GPO format: [<GUID of client-side extension> <GUID of MMC extension> <GUID of second MMC extension if appropriate>]
GPCUserExtensionNames	The client-side extensions needed to execute the user portion of the GPO format. Same as for GPCMachineExtensionNames
VersionNumber	The GPO version (as in gpt.ini)

Figure 7.6
Checking GPT file system storage using Explorer

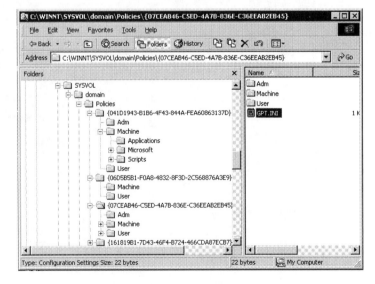

The group policy template   A GPT is stored in the system volume (SYSVOL) on the file system. The system volume is available on every Windows 2000 DC. The default file system path to a GPT is the following: %systemdrive%\winnt\sysvol\sysvol\<Domain DNS Name>\Policies\<Policy GUID> (as illustrated in Figure 7.6). Table 7.6 shows the default folder structure for a GPT.

We will discuss the meaning of most of the files mentioned in Table 7.6 later on in this chapter. An important file is the gpt.ini file. It contains the GPO version number, which is also contained in the Versionnumber attribute of the GPC. The version number is used to check whether the

Table 7.6   *Nonlocal GPO GPT Default Folder Structure*

Directory Name	Comments
<Policy GUID>	Contains the gpt.ini file
Adm	Contains the administrative templates (*.adm files)
Machine	Contains the Registry.pol file for the machine-bound registry settings
Applications	Contains machine-bound application installation packages
Microsoft	
Windows NT	
SecEdit	Contains the GptTmpl.inf for security settings
Scripts	
Shutdown	Contains machine shutdown scripts
Startup	Contains machine startup scripts
User	Contains the Registry.pol file for the user-bound registry settings
Applications	Contains user-bound application installation packages
Documents and Settings	Contains the Fdeploy.ini for folder redirection
Microsoft	
RemoteInstall	Contains the Remote OS installation preferences (Oscfilter.ini)
IEAK	Contains the IE configuration settings (Install.ins file)
Scripts	
Logoff	Contains user logoff scripts
Logon	Contains user logon scripts

GPO file system (GPT) and AD (GPC) contents are synchronized. Both could get out of sync because both are using different replication mechanisms to replicate their contents between DCs. If this is the case, the GPO will not be applied.

Nonlocal GPO storage overview   Table 7.7 shows where the GPO settings of the different GPO-enabled technologies are stored—in AD, in the SYSVOL, or in both. The table shows that the bulk of the GPO content is stored in the SYSVOL with a few exceptions, such as software installation packages and IPsec policy definitions. A special case is the storage of public key policies; they are not stored in AD or the SYSVOL. Public key policies are stored in the system registry.

Table 7.7   *Storage Locations of GPO Settings of Different GPO-Enabled Technologies*

	Stored in SYSVOL	Stored in AD
Administrative Templates	Adm subdirectory	No
Registry.pol	Machine and user subdirectory	No
Security Settings	Machine\Microsoft\Windows NT\ secedit subdirectory	No
Public Key Policies	No	No
IP security Policies	No	Ipsec policy definition: CN=IP Security,CN=system, DC=<Domain DNS Name> Ipsec link: CN=ipsec,CN=windows, CN=Microsoft,CN=machine
Software Installation	Package: User\Applications or Machine\ Applications Subdirectories	PackageRegistration: CN=Packages,CN=Class Store,CN=Machine
Scripts	User\scripts and Machine\Scripts subdirectories	No
Microsoft Internet Explorer Maintenance	User\Microsoft\IEAK subdirectory	No
Remote Installation Services	User\Microsoft\RemoteInstall	No
Folder Redirection (fdeploy.ini)	User\documents and settings subdirectory	No

GPO link storage

GPO links are stored as attributes of the AD objects to which they are linked. To find out all the AD objects a particular GPO is linked to, right-click the GPO object, select properties, and go to the Links tab. Pushing *Find Now* will bring up all the AD objects to which the GPO is linked. Behind the scenes Windows 2000 will query AD for all occurrences of the GPO's GUID. This GUID is contained in the GpLink attribute of the AD objects to which the GPO is linked.

AD objects have two attributes, which refer to GPO links, as follows:

1.   The GpLink attribute stores the LDAP path to the GPC of the GPOs linked to the object, and the GPO link options *No Override* and *Disabled*. Because this attribute is replicated to the AD GC, a GPO can be referenced to or from a domain other than its definition domain. Table 7.8 gives some sample values for the GpLink attribute.

2.   GpOptions stores the block policy inheritance GPO property; 1 means that this property is set; 0 means it isn't.

The meaning of no override and block policy inheritance will be explained later in the chapter. Setting the GPO link to disabled unlinks the GPO from the AD object; this can be useful to allow safe editing of the GPO definition. In a production environment, this is a necessity. If a GPO is enabled while it is being edited, the changes to the GPO are applied immediately to all the objects to which it is linked. To set the disabled property, open up the properties of an object the GPO is linked to, go to the Group Policy tab, select options, and check the *Disabled* check box. GPOs

Table 7.8 *AD Object GpLink Attribute Entries*

GpLink Entry	Meaning
[LDAP://CN={007BECC6-08ED-4DEE-8D94-F5B4966A90CA},CN=Policies,CN=System,DC=compaq,DC=com;0]	Default setting
[LDAP://CN={007BECC6-08ED-4DEE-8D94-F5B4966A90CA},CN=Policies,CN=System,DC=compaq,DC=com;1]	GPO disabled
[LDAP://CN={007BECC6-08ED-4DEE-8D94-F5B4966A90CA},CN=Policies,CN=System,DC=compaq,DC=com;2]	No override set
[LDAP://CN={007BECC6-08ED-4DEE-8D94-F5B4966A90CA},CN=Policies,CN=System,DC=compaq,DC=com;3]	GPO disabled and no override set

can be set disabled by default by setting the GPO entry *Create new Group Policy Object links disabled by default* (located in the user configuration\ administrative templates\system\group policy). An alternative is to disable both the user and the machine portion of the GPO in the properties of the GPO object.

Local GPO storage

Local GPOs only have a group policy template (GPT) portion. Since a specific LGPO exists for every Windows 2000 machine (server, DC, and workstation), they cannot be stored in the SYSVOL. The definition of local GPOs is stored in the %systemroot%\System32\GroupPolicy directory. Table 7.9 shows the default folder structure for the GPT of an LGPO.

Since LGPOs include less configuration options than nonlocal GPOs, their folder structure is simpler. As Table 7.9 shows, the subfolders for

Table 7.9   *Local GPO GPT Default Folder Structure*

Directory Name	Comments
GroupPolicy	Contains the Gpt.ini file
Adm	Contains the administrative templates (*.adm files)
Machine	Contains the Registry.pol file for the machine-bound registry settings
Scripts	
Shutdown	Contains machine shutdown scripts
Startup	Contains machine startup scripts
User	Contains the Registry.pol file for the user-bound registry settings
Microsoft	
IEAK	Contains the IE configuration settings (Install.ins file)
LOCK	
RemoteInstall	Remote OS installation preferences (Oscfilter.ini)
Scripts	
Logoff	Contains user logoff scripts
Logon	Contains user logon scripts

application deployment (Applications) and folder redirection (Documents and Settings) are missing. Also, the machine security configuration (secedit) folder is missing, because the security configuration files are not stored in the LGPO folder but in the %systemdrive%\winnt\security folder.

Since an LGPO doesn't have a GPC counterpart, there's more information contained in its gpt.ini. Besides the GPCUserExtensionNames, GPC-MachineExtensionNames, and GPCFunctionalityVersion fields, it also has an Options field. This field indicates whether the user or the machine portion of the LGPO has been disabled, or whether both are disabled (values: 0 = both enabled, 1 = disable user, 2 = disable computer, 3 = both disabled).

GPO application

In this section, we will explore how GPOs are applied on the Windows 2000 client side. We will take a closer look at the client-side GPO engine, the application sequence, the default application mechanisms, and the ways these default mechanisms can be modified.

GPO application process

GPOs are automatically applied at machine startup, user logon, and at regular intervals, as follows:

- At machine startup the machine portion of the GPOs is applied.

- At user logon the user portion of the GPOs is applied.

- Periodic GPO updates happen every 90 minutes for the user portion and for the machine portion of workstations and member servers. The machine portion of DCs is updated every five minutes. Periodic GPO processing deals with every GPO setting with the exception of the following GPO categories:

  - Software installation and folder redirection
  - Every category that has the *Do not apply during periodic background updating* GPO option or the NoBackgroundPolicy registry key set.

GPO application can be activated manually by running the secedit command prompt tool, as follows:

- Run secedit /REFRESHPOLICY MACHINE_POLICY to refresh the machine portion.

- Run secedit /REFRESHPOLICY USER_POLICY to refresh the user portion.

- Adding the /ENFORCE switch applies the GPO even if no changes have occurred to the GPO definition since the last update.

The periodic GPO update interval can be configured using the following GPO entries:

- In Computer Configuration\Administrative Templates\System\ Group Policy: *Group policy refresh interval for computers* and *Group policy refresh interval for DCs*.

- In User Configuration\Administrative Templates\System\Group Policy: *Group policy refresh interval for users*.

The update interval can be set anywhere between 0 and 64,800 minutes. Setting it to 0 minutes will enforce a GPO update every seven seconds. You can also set a random offset, which is used to spread the load of automatic GPO updating on the DC side. The offset can be set anywhere between 0 and 1,440 minutes. Putting this setting to 30, will add a time period between 0 and 30 minutes to the default update interval.

Client-side GPO engines   GPO application is done by a set of client-side extensions (CSEs). Each extension (they are all listed in Table 7.10) is responsible for the client-side configuration of a particular GPO area. Later in the chapter, we will look at the detailed operation of the registry management (userenv.dll), the security management (scecli.dll and scesrv.dll), and the software installation (appmgmts.dll) CSE.

All CSEs are configurable through the registry and through GPO administrative templates settings. The registry settings are located in the registry folder HKEY_LOCAL_MACHINE\software\Microsoft\windows-NT\currentversion\winlogon\gpextensions. Table 7.10 shows the different CSE configuration registry settings and their meaning. An important side note: only administrators have write access to these parameters.

The GPO CSE configuration settings are located in the computer configuration\administrative templates\system\group policy GPO folder. The following CSE parameters can be set:

- *Allow processing across a slow network connection* determines whether the GPO CSE will run when a slow network connection is detected. (registry setting: NoSlowlink)

- *Do not apply during periodic background updating* determines whether the GPO CSE will run during a user's logon session, based on the periodic GPO updates. Background GPO updates can corrupt some of the user processes. (registry setting: NoBackgroundPolicy)

Table 7.10   *CSE Registry Entries*

Registry Entry	Meaning
Dllname	Name of CSE DLL
ProcessGroupPolicy	Enables CSE GPO processing
NoMachinePolicy	Disables CSE GPO machine portion processing
NoUserPolicy	Disables CSE GPO user portion processing
NoSlowlink	Disables CSE GPO processing across slow link
NoBackgroundPolicy	Disables CSE GPO periodic background processing
NoGPOListChanges	Disables CSE GPO processing without changes
EnableAsynchronousProcessing	Enables asynchronous CSE GPO processing

- *Process even if the group policy objects have not changed* determines whether the GPO CSE will reapply the GPO even if none of its settings has changed since the previous execution. By default, a GPO is only applied if changes have occurred. (registry setting: No-GPOListChanges)

A setting that cannot be set is the time slot the system reserves for CSE GPO application. If a CSE has not finished applying its GPO settings after 60 minutes, the CSE will be stopped and part of the settings will not be applied.

The registry management client-side engine   The CSE that applies GPO registry settings is userenv.dll. Remember that GPO registry management is using an engine that's very similar to the one used for NT4 system policy. Just as with NT4 registry settings and system policy, Windows 2000 registry settings are enforced using administrative templates and registry policy files.

Administrative templates   Administrative templates are files containing metadata: They list the registry entries that can be managed through GPO and their possible values. As in NT4, administrative templates have an *.adm extension, are customizable, and can contain settings that apply to the user (HKEY_CURRENT_USER) or the machine (HKEY_LO-CAL_MACHINE) portion of the registry.

Despite many similarities there are some major differences between NT4 and Windows 2000 administrative templates. Windows 2000 administrative templates have the following features:

- Support for unicode encoding, NT4 administrative templates only support ASCII encoding.

- Support for the Windows 2000 policy clean-up registry locations

- They can contain the following tag values:

    - The explain tag provides inline help. Explain tags are used to clarify the effect of changing a particular policy setting.
    - The version tag enables the specification of the policy-editing tool: The NT4 system policy editor is version 2; the Windows 2000 group policy editor is version 3. NT4 administrative templates cannot be opened from the Windows 2000 MMC group policy snap-in; the same is true for Windows 2000 templates in the NT4 system policy editor.

The administrative templates shipping with Windows 2000 are located in the winnt\inf directory. To load these templates into the GPE, right-click the Administrative Templates container and select Add/Remove Templates (as illustrated in Figure 7.7). If a template is loaded into a GPO, it is copied from the winnt\inf directory to the adm subdirectory of the GPT. The template of an LGPO is saved in the %systemdrive%\winnt\system32\group-policy\adm directory. The templates can be categorized based on the

Figure 7.7
Loading administrative templates into the GPE

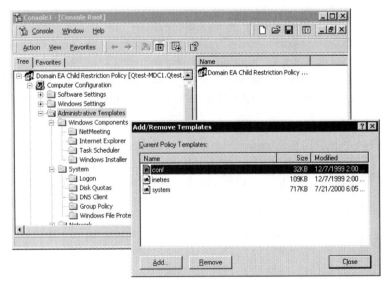

Table 7.11 *Administrative Templates*

Type	Editing Tool	Administrative Templates
GPO-only templates	MMC group policy snap-in (GPE)	system.adm, wmp.adm, conf.adm, and inetres.adm
System policy–only templates	NT4 system policy editor	common.adm, windows.adm, and winnt.adm
IEAK-only templates	IEAK administration tool	inetcorp.adm and inetset.adm

administration interface, which can be used to display their settings (see Table 7.11).

This categorization explains why the System policy only and IEAK only administrative templates are loaded in a special container when they are loaded in the GPO MMC snap-in. System policy–only templates are loaded in the Unsupported Administrative Templates container; IEAK-only templates are loaded in the IE Maintenance Only container.

Registry policy files Registry policy files contain the actual registry entry values enforced using GPO registry management. Unlike NT4, Windows 2000 uses separate files to hold the user and the machine portions of the policy; both are named registry.pol. Also, separate registry.pol files are created per GPO. Windows 2000 saves the two registry policy files in the file system portion (GPT) of the GPOs: The user registry.pol file is saved in the user subdirectory of the GPT; the machine registry.pol file is saved in the machine subdirectory of the GPT.

In NT4 all policy settings were contained in a single file named ntconfig.pol (for NT4 clients) or config.pol (for Windows 95, 98 clients). This single file contained all the registry changes that were enforced within the scope of a particular domain. In an NT4 environment, all changes were distributed to everyone, even if some of them were only targeted at specific users or groups.

A Windows 2000 registry.pol is a unicode-formatted text file, containing a header and a body. The header contains a registry file signature and the version number of the GPE that created the file. The body contains a list of semicolon-separated registry entry definitions.

Before the GPO registry settings are applied, the userenv.dll CSE process will merge the registry.pol files of the different GPOs into a single registry policy file for both the user and the machine portions. The user settings are merged into the ntuser.pol file. It is located in the user's profile subfolder, underneath Documents and Settings. The machine settings are merged into another registry.pol file. This one is located in the winnt\system32\group-policy\machine folder.

The security settings client-side engine   The GPO security settings are applied by the scecli.dll (for clients) or the scesrv.dll (for servers). Most of the settings (with the exception of the Kerberos, public key, and IPsec policy settings) set using GPO security management can also be enforced using the Security Configuration and Analysis (SCA) tool.

Both GPO security management and the SCA tool are using the same client-side engines (scecli.dll or scesrv.dll) and database (secedit.sdb) to enforce the security settings.

When group policy is applied the client-side engine downloads all gpttmpl.inf files that are part of a GPO applied to the machine or user. The gpttmpl.inf is located in the GPT portion of a GPO (machine\Microsoft\windows NT\secedit). The client-side engine brings all security settings, nonlocal and local, together in the \winnt\security\templates\policy directory. When you open up this folder, you'll see it contains a set of *.inf files and a file with a *.dom extension. The last one is the security policy enforced on the domain level.

The *.inf files are called security configuration templates. They list predefined security settings and are stored in the %systemdrive%\winnt\security\templates directory. As with the administrative templates used for registry management, the security configuration templates are customizable.

Microsoft provides two basic categories of security configuration templates: default and incremental security templates, as follows:

Default security templates contain the default Windows 2000 security settings, as they are applied to a Windows 2000 system during a normal installation. Default templates can be used to configure a machine upgraded from NT4 to Windows 2000 to the level of the default Windows 2000 security settings.

Incremental security templates define higher or lower security levels; they can be used to bring a machine from the default security level to a higher or lower security level. The compatws.inf template, for example, loosens security on a Windows 2000 Professional machine to allow applications to write to more registry keys. The hisecdc.inf template, on the other hand, tightens the security of a Windows 2000 DC. An incremental tem-

Table 7.12   *Security Templates*

Security Template Category	Template Name	Meaning
Default Templates	Basicdc.inf	The default template for a Windows 2000 DC
	Basicsv.inf	The default template for a Windows 2000 server
	Basicwk.inf	The default template for a Windows 2000 workstation
Incremental Templates	Compatws.inf	Compatible incremental template for a Windows 2000 workstation
	Securedc.inf	Secure incremental template for a Windows 2000 DC
	Securews.inf	Secure incremental template for a Windows 2000 workstation
	Hisecdc.inf	High-security incremental template for a Windows 2000 DC
	Hisecws.inf	High-security incremental template for a Windows 2000 workstation

plate should never be applied without first applying a default template. Microsoft defines three levels: compatible, secure, and high secure.

Each of these categories contains specific templates for a Windows 2000 workstation, server, and DC. The security configuration templates available in Windows 2000 are listed in Table 7.12.

According to your security needs you can load the appropriate templates into the SCA or GPO interfaces. To load a template in the GPO interface, right-click the Security Settings container, and select Import Policy (as illustrated in Figure 7.8)

The security settings are the only GPO settings that can be copy-pasted or imported/exported between different GPOs. Export can be done on the LGPO level: Right-click the Security Settings container and select Export Policy. *Local policy* will export the LGPO inf file; *Effective policy* will export the resulting policy.

The software installation client-side engine   GPO-based software installation is done by the appmgmts.dll CSE. The software technology behind GPO-based software installation is known as Windows Installer. The Windows Installer software engine is installed with every Windows 2000, Windows NT4 SP3 or post-SP3, and Windows 98 installation. Add-ons are available for Windows 95 and NT4 pre-SP3 installations. Plenty of techni-

Figure 7.8
*Importing security
templates for a
GPO's security
settings*

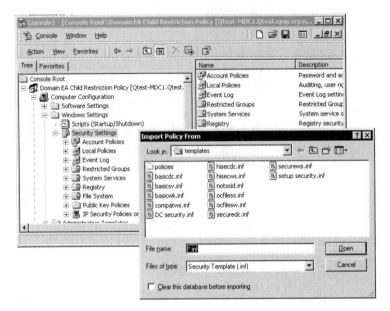

cal details on Windows Installer are available from the Microsoft platform
SDK.

To be able to use Windows Installer and GPOs to deploy applications a
special application installation package must be available. This package is
also known as the *.msi file. Every Windows 2000 certified application
must have such a package. Besides automated installation using GPOs,
Windows Installer also allows for manual enforcement of an installation. To
do this, use the msiexec.exe command prompt tool. For example,
Msiexec.exe /I c:\myapplication.msi forces the installation of the application
myapplication, whose *.msi file is located on the C: drive.

When a GPO software installation package is created, it affects both the
GPC and the GPT portion of the GPO. In the GPC portion, the CN=
packages,cn=class store,cn=machine,cn=<policyguid>,cn=policies,cn=system,
dc=<domain name> container holds a packageregistration object for every
package. This object has some important attributes, shown in Table 7.13.

On the GPT level, the applications\script subdirectory contains an
ade.cfg file and an *.aas file. The ade.cdg file contains important Windows
Installer configuration information; the *.aas file contains the installation
script.

Table 7.13   *Important packageregistration Object Attributes*

Packageregistration Attribute	Meaning
Msifilelist	points to *.msi location
Msiscriptname	A(Assigned) / P(Published)
Msiscriptpath	points to *.aas location

GPO application sequence

The application scope of a GPO (explained earlier in this chapter) determines on which objects the settings defined in the GPO are applied. Windows 2000 GPOs can have four different application scopes: local (L), site (S), domain (D), and organizational unit (OU). In a pure Windows 2000 environment the default GPO application sequence is: local GPO, site GPOs, domain GPOs, OU GPOs (as illustrated in Figure 7.9). This sequence is easy to remember using the mnemonic LSDOU. By pure I mean that all machines involved are Windows 2000 machines and that no NT4 system policy is in place.

Things get a little bit more complicated when we add NT4 system policy to the application sequence. You can look at system policy as another application scope: an NT4 system policy in a Windows 2000 domain will apply to every user logging on to the domain from any NT4, Windows 2000, Windows 95, or Windows 98 domain member. In this case, the sequence becomes: NT4 system policy, local GPO, site GPOs, domain GPOs, OU GPOs (as illustrated in Figure 7.9). This sequence is easy to remember using the mnemonic 4LSDOU.

Application sequence example   Explaining the rules described previously is easier when using an example. In this example (illustrated in Figure 7.10), we will examine how GPOs are applied to user A, defined in root domain *compaq.com*, who is logging on to computer B, defined in child domain *NAmericas.compaq.com*. User A is a salesperson working in the NYC office; function and location are reflected in domain *compaq.com*'s OU structure. Computer B is located in site Midwest. The computer is a desktop computer administered by the IT department of the Chicago office. Both computer type and IT department are reflected in *NAmericas.compaq.com*'s OU structure (as illustrated in Figure 7.10).

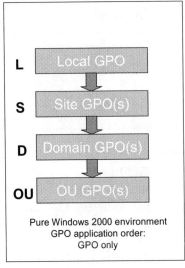
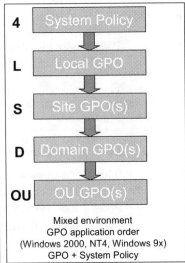

Figure 7.9
*GPO application
sequence*

Pure Windows 2000 environment
GPO application order:
GPO only

Mixed environment
GPO application order
(Windows 2000, NT4, Windows 9x)
GPO + System Policy

The following GPOs are set (shown as buckets in Figure 7.10):

- One GPO (1) is linked to *compaq.com*, two GPOs ([2] and [3]) are linked to *NAmericas.compaq.com*.

- One GPO is linked to the sales (4), NYC (5), and Chicago (6) OUs; two GPOs are linked to the desktop OU ([7] and [8]).

- One GPO is linked to the Midwest site (9).

Figure 7.10
*GPO application
example*

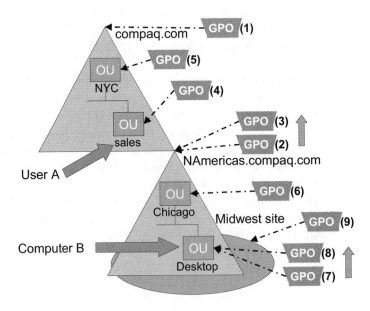

What is the order in which the GPOs listed above will be applied to computer B when starting up and to user A when logging on to domain *compaq.com* from computer B? The GPOs will be applied in the following order:

Computer B starts up:

1.   Machine portion of the LGPO

2.   Machine portion of the Midwest site GPO (9)

3.   Machine portion of the *Namericas.compaq.com* domain GPOs: in order of preference—(2) and (3)

4.   Machine portion of the Chicago OU GPO (6)

5.   Machine portions of the GPOs (7) and (8) for the desktop OU: in order of preference—(7) and (8)

User A logs on:

6.   User portion of the LGPO

7.   User portion of the *compaq.com* domain GPO (1)

8.   User portion of the GPO (5) for OU NYC and GPO (4) for OU sales

Notice in the application order above that GPO inheritance occurs on the OU level but not on the domain level. Only the GPOs (2) and (3), linked to domain *NAmericas.compaq.com*, are applied to computer B, not GPO (1), which is linked to domain *compaq.com*. Also, when multiple GPOs are linked to an object, they are processed in an order of preference. The order of preference is the order in which the GPOs were linked to the object. It's the reverse of the order shown in an object's GPO tab. Note as well that OUs are processed hierarchically from top to bottom.

Sequence of events during machine startup and user logon   The following list of events shows where the GPO application sequence fits in a normal machine startup and user logon sequence:

1.   From the moment the network has been started and the machine account has logged on to the domain, the GPO engine will request a list of applicable GPO settings to a Windows 2000 DC.

2.   The DC will query the Active Directory for the applicable GPO settings and send the list back to the machine.

3.   Based on the list it got back from the DC, the GPO engine will retrieve the GPO settings from the system volume (or for some

settings from the Active Directory). At this moment in time the GPO engine knows which GPO settings need to be applied and which CSEs it needs to call upon. Remember that the CSE GUIDs are stored in the properties of the Active Directory GPCs.

4. The GPO engine applies the machine GPO settings. The order in which machine GPOs are processed is based on the mnemonic 4LSDOU.

5. The GPO startup scripts are executed (execution is hidden). By default the Windows logon window will not appear before all machine GPO settings have been applied. This behavior can be changed by setting the *Apply group policy for computers asynchronously during startup* in the GPO administrative settings.

6. The user logs on using CTRL-ALT-DEL; after successful authentication the user profile will be loaded.

7. The GPO engine applies the user GPO settings. The order in which user GPOs are processed is based on the mnemonic 4LSDOU.

8. The GPO logon scripts are executed (execution is hidden). By default, the user's desktop will not appear before all user GPO settings have been applied. This behavior can be changed by setting the *Apply group policy for users asynchronously during logon* in the GPO administrative settings.

9. The logon scripts defined on the user object level are executed (by default the execution is visible).

10. The user shell is started with the desktop set in the user profile and the GPO settings.

For a very detailed overview of the sequence of events during machine startup and user logon, including the way GPOs are applied, enable advanced logging. You can do this by creating the UserEnvDebugLevel value at the following registry location and setting it to 30002 for verbose logging or 30001 for errors and warnings only. The registry location is HKEY_LOCAL_MACHINE\Software\Microsoft\Windows NT\CurrentVersion\Winlogon. The log file userenv.log is saved in %SystemRoot%\Debug\UserMode.

GPO application particularities   The normal GPO application sequence explained previously can be somewhat different in certain circumstances. Some of these behaviors happen automatically, others can be enforced.

Next, we'll look at GPO loopback, asynchronous application of GPOs, the application of GPOs across slow links, and GPO application enforcement.

Loopback application   The default GPO application process explained before can be modified by running GPOs in loopback mode. GPO loopback processing is a property that can be set in the machine portion of a group policy: Computer Configuration\Administrative Templates\System\ Group Policy*User group policy loopback processing mode*. This is very important: loopback applies to a machine, not a user.

Loopback application enables a Windows 2000 administrator to enforce the application of the user GPO settings defined in GPOs linked to the machine object, and to override the user GPO settings defined in GPOs linked to the user object. Loopback processing can be a viable option to enforce the user settings linked to the computer-specific GPOs of kiosk computers. On a typical kiosk computer, user GPO settings should never be applied; on the other hand, kiosk computer GPO settings should always be enforced. Loopback application may also be an interesting setting to deal with roaming users: You may not want the GPO settings defined in the user's definition domain to prevail over settings defined in the computer domain.

During normal GPO processing, the computer GPO settings applied are based on the location of the computer account in the Active Directory; the user GPO settings applied are based on the location of the user account in the Active Directory. When loopback has been enabled on the machine level, the GPO engine will launch, at user logon, a query to AD to determine the machine GPOs. This will enable the GPO engine to reapply the GPOs linked to the machine object. This time it will not apply the machine portion but the user portion of the GPO.

GPO loopback can be set in two different modes: replace and merge, as follows:

1.   When loopback is set to replace mode, both the computer and user settings are applied based on the location of the computer account in the Active Directory. In other words, the location of the user account in the Active Directory is ignored.

2.   When loopback is set to merge mode, the computer settings are applied based on the location of the computer account in the Active Directory. The user settings will be applied twice: first in the normal way and then based on the location of the computer account in the Active Directory.

Table 7.14 and Figure 7.11 illustrate the differences between the two modes. Loopback processing works only if both accounts involved (the user and the computer account) are members of a Windows 2000 domain. Loopback processing will not work when one of the accounts involved is a member of an NT4 domain.

The left column of the table shows which GPOs are linked to which AD objects (see also arrows in Figure 7.11). The other columns show the GPO processing order for normal processing, loopback processing in replace mode, and loopback processing in merge mode. Note that in loopback replace mode the GPOs that should be applied to the user object are simply ignored and replaced by the GPOs applicable to the machine object (1-2-3-4). In loopback merge mode the user GPOs are evaluated first (2-5-6), followed by the machine GPOs (1-2-3-4).

Asynchronous application   GPO execution is by default synchronous. This means that a user cannot log on before machine policies have been applied. Also, the user shell and desktop are not launched before all user policies have been applied. This behavior can be changed by setting the two settings

Table 7.14   *Normal GPO Processing versus Loopback Replace and Merge Mode GPO Processing*

GPOs		GPO Scope	Normal Processing	Loopback Replace Mode	Loopback Merge Mode
Site => GPO1	Machine startup	Site	GPO1 (machine)	GPO1 (machine)	GPO1 (machine)
Domain => GPO2		Domain	GPO2 (machine)	GPO2 (machine)	GPO2 (machine)
OU1 => GPO3		OU1	GPO3 (machine)	GPO3 (machine)	GPO3 (machine)
OU2 => GPO4		OU2	GPO4 (machine)	GPO4 (machine)	GPO4 (machine)
OU3 => GPO5	User Logon	Site	NA	**GPO1 (user)**	NA
OU4 => GPO6		Domain	GPO2 (user)	**GPO2 (user)**	GPO2 (user)
		OU1–OU3	GPO5 (user)	**GPO3 (user)**	GPO5 (user)
		OU2–OU4	GPO6 (user)	**GPO4 (user)**	GPO6 (user)
		Site	NA	NA	**GPO1 (user)**
		Domain	NA	NA	**GPO2 (user)**
		OU5	NA	NA	**GPO3 (user)**
		OU6	NA	NA	**GPO4 (user)**

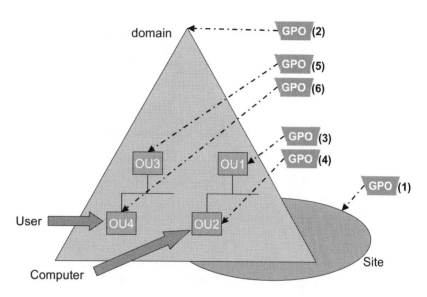

Figure 7.11
Normal and loopback processing evaluation example

listed in Table 7.15, which are located in the GPO computer portion. Asynchronous application will speed up the startup and the logon process, but might also lead to unpredictable results.

Application across slow links By default, Windows 2000 will apply only administrative templates and security settings to GPO entries when a user logs on across a slow link. By default, software installation, folder redirection, and scripts are not applied. This default behavior can be changed by setting the connection speed limit, determining what is considered slow (the default is 500 Kb/s), and by setting the slow link application behavior for the different GPO subportions. The speed limit can be set separately for the GPO user settings and the GPO computer settings. To detect the actual connection speed, Windows 2000 uses a special algorithm, which pings DCs, and calculates the actual speed by comparing the start of the ping to the return of the response. (See Table 7.16.)

Table 7.15 *GPO Asynchronous Application Settings*

Computer	Computer configuration\administrative templates\group policy
	Apply group policy for computers asynchronously during startup
	Apply group policy for users asynchronously during logon

Table 7.16   *GPO Settings for GPO Application Across Slow Slinks*

Computer	Computer configuration\administrative templates\group policy
	Group policy slow link detection
	Registry policy processing
	Internet Explorer maintenance policy processing
	Software installation policy processing
	Folder redirection policy processing
	Script policy processing
	Security policy processing
	IP security policy processing
	EFS recovery policy processing
	Disk quota policy processing
User	User configuration\administrative templates\group policy
	Group policy slow link detection

Application enforcement   Windows 2000 GPOs normally just apply the changes that happened to the GPO since the last application. To enforce application, even if no change occurred, an administrator can set *Process even if Group Policy Objects have not changed* in the GPO properties of every GPO subportion (machine and user; see Table 7.17).

GPO application mechanisms

GPO application is based on three mechanisms: inheritance, accumulation, and filtering. Next, we'll explain these three mechanisms and the default GPO application rules in which they result. We'll also look at how you can modify these default rules by using mechanisms such as enforcing and blocking.

GPO Inheritance and accumulation   Inheritance and accumulation are the two most important GPO application mechanisms:

- Inheritance means that settings defined on the level of a parent object are inherited by its child objects. A Windows 2000 GPO setting is configured when it is set in the enabled or disabled state or when it is

Table 7.17 *GPO Application Enforcement GPO Settings*

Computer	Computer configuration\admin templates\system\group policies
	Registry policy processing
	Internet Explorer maintenance policy processing
	Software installation policy processing
	Folder redirection policy processing
	Script policy processing
	Security policy processing
	IP security policy processing
	EFS recovery policy processing
	Disk quota policy processing

set to a specific value. The standard GPO inheritance rules between parent and child objects are the following:

- If a parent has configured a setting and a child has not, the parent's setting is inherited by the child.
- If a parent has configured a setting that does not conflict with the child's setting (e.g., if the parent has a logon script set and the child does too), the child will inherit the parent's setting and will also apply its own setting.
- If a parent has configured a setting that is conflicting with the child's setting (e.g., if the parent has a setting set to enabled and the child has the same setting set to disabled, the child's setting will have precedence (in this case the setting will be disabled). An exception to this rule happens when the parent has set disabled and the child enabled; in this case, the disabled setting will be inherited by the child.

- Accumulation is a direct consequence of inheritance: Because unconfigured settings do not override configured settings, the settings applied to an object will be the sum (or accumulation) of all settings previously applied to it by the different GPOs.

Accumulation and inheritance are illustrated in Table 7.18. The leftmost column of the table shows the GPO application order (from top to bottom). The table shows the inheritance and accumulation process for six

Table 7.18   *GPO Inheritance and Accumulation Example*

GPO Scope	Settings					
	S1	S2	S3	S4	S5	S6
Local (LGPO A)	I	O	NC	3	NC	NC
Site (GPO B)	NC	NC	NC	5	NC	Script1.bat
Domain (GPO C)	I	NC	NC	4	NC	NC
OU1 (GPO D)	NC	I	O	NC	4	Script2.bat
OU1 (GPO E)	NC	O	I	NC	3	Script3.bat
OU2 (GPO F)	NC	NC	NC	2	NC	NC
Object (result)	**I**	**O**	**I**	**2**	**3**	**Script1.bat** **Script2.bat** **Script3.bat**

NC = Not Configured; I = Enabled; O = Disabled; 2–8 = Value Settings

different settings (S1 to S6). Setting number 6 defines a script. The resulting setting is shown in the bottom row (in bold).

If multiple GPOs are set on the same level, the GPO with the highest priority will be the last one to be processed. The GPO with the highest priority is the one that's highest in the list available from an object's Group Pol-

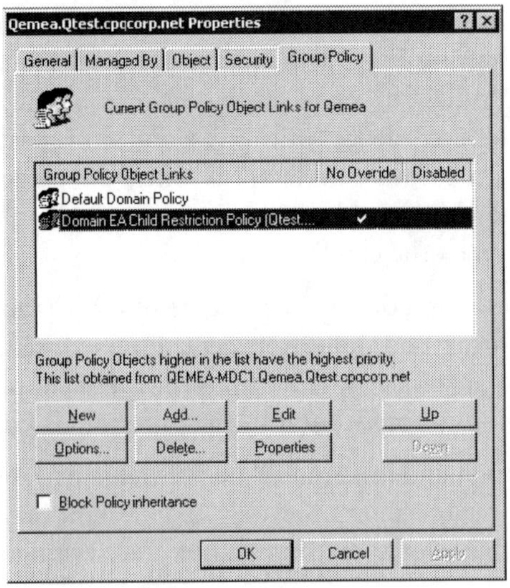

Figure 7.12
*Setting inheritance
blocking on an OU
object*

icy tab. This is illustrated in Figure 7.12. In this case the domain EA child restriction policy will be applied first, followed by the default domain policy. Here, the default domain policy has the highest priority.

Enforcing and blocking GPO inheritance   Windows 2000 inheritance can be enforced and blocked. Enforcement always takes precedence over blocking.

Inheritance blocking is a property that can be set on domain and OU Active Directory objects (as illustrated in Figure 7.12). It cannot be set on a site and an LGPO object. Blocking applies to every GPO that's applied to the domain or OU object. Since it's a property of an AD object, blocking is not related in any way to an LGPO. Blocking means that GPO settings defined on a particular level cannot be overridden by GPO settings defined on a higher level. The effect of blocking is illustrated in Table 7.19. In this example, GPO enforcement is blocked on the OU1 object level.

Enforcement, or No Override, in Microsoft terminology, is a property that is set on a GPO link object (as illustrated in Figure 7.13). Contrary to blocking, enforcement applies to one, and only one, GPO, and only for the AD object it is linked to. Enforcement means that a GPO setting linked to an object higher up in the hierarchy will be enforced, independently of the GPO settings applied to an object lower in the hierarchy. A No Override GPO setting also overrides the GPO settings of AD objects marked with

Table 7.19   *GPO Blocking Example*

GPO Scope	Settings					
	S1	S2	S3	S4	S5	S6
Local (LGPO A)	I	O	NC	3	NC	NC
Site (GPO B)	NC	NC	NC	5	NC	Script1.bat
Domain (GPO C)	I	NC	NC	4	NC	NC
OU1 (GPO D)	NC	I	O	NC	4	Script2.bat
OU1 (GPO E)	NC	O	I	NC	3	Script3.bat
OU2 (GPO F)	NC	NC	NC	2	NC	NC
Object (result)	I	O	I	2	3	Script2.bat Script3.bat

NC = Not Configured; I = Enabled; O = Disabled; 2–8 = Value Settings

Figure 7.13

Setting No Override in the properties of a GPO link object

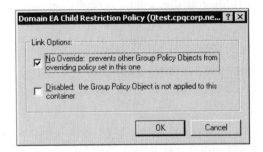

block policy inheritance. The effect of enforcement is illustrated in Table 7.20: GPO B on the site level is enforced, while blocking is set for OU1.

If No Override is set on different levels in the GPO hierarchy, the No Override linked to the GPO that's highest in the hierarchy will have precedence. As shown in Table 7.20, if both the GPO B site and GPO C domain links have the No Override property set, the settings defined in GPO B will be enforced and override the settings in GPO C.

A GPO link that has No Override set will also override other GPOs on the same level (linked to the same object) that do not have this property set. If it is set on different GPO links linked to the same object, the No Override that will be enforced is the one that's linked to the GPO with the high-

Table 7.20   *Enforcement and Blocking Example*

GPO scope	Settings					
	S1	S2	S3	S4	S5	S6
Local (LGPO A)	I	O	NC	3	NC	NC
Site (GPO B)	NC	NC	NC	5	NC	Script1.bat
Domain (GPO C)	I	NC	NC	4	NC	NC
OU1 (GPO D)	NC	I	O	NC	4	Script2.bat
OU1 (GPO E)	NC	O	I	NC	3	Script3.bat
OU2 (GPO F)	NC	NC	NC	2	NC	NC
Object (result)	I	O	I	5	3	Script2.bat Script3.bat Script1.bat

NC = Not Configured; I = Enabled; O = Disabled; 2–8 = Value Settings

est priority. GPO priority can be set using the Up and Down pushbuttons in the Group Policy tab of the properties of an AD object (as illustrated in Figure 7.12).

GPO filtering   GPO filtering is the ability to limit GPO application to a subset of the machine or user accounts contained in the AD container (OU, site, or domain) to which the GPO is linked. This is done by setting specific ACLs on the Active Directory GPOs (as illustrated in Figure 7.14). GPO objects have a special ACL entry, Apply Group Policy, which can be set to allow or deny. GPO filtering can be looked at as a special type of delegation.

For a GPO to apply to a user or a machine account, the machine or user account needs to have both Apply Group Policy and Read permission set in the GPO's ACL. (*Permission set* means: set to allow.) By default every GPO object's ACL has this property set for the authenticated users group. The easiest way to filter GPO application is by using groups (by the way, this is the main reason why GPOs are called group policy objects).

GPO filtering applies to the GPO object as a whole. What cannot be done is enforcing only a portion of the GPO for a particular security group, although you can use security groups to fine-tune the application of certain GPO portions, such as folder redirection and software installation.

Figure 7.14
Setting up GPO filtering

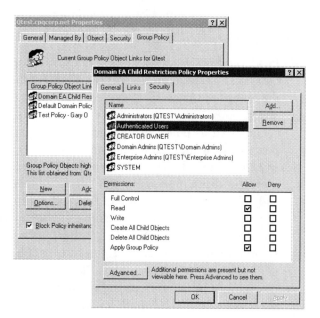

Filtering can also be set for the LGPO. This time we're not dealing with Active Directory–based filtering, but with a kind of file system–based filtering. To filter the application of an LGPO you will set file system ACLs on the %systemdrive%/winnt/grouppolicy subdirectory.

The default security settings on a GPO object are as follows:

- *Authenticated Users: Read, Apply Group Policy.* This means that all accounts that have successfully logged on to a Windows 2000 system get by default the GPOs applied.

- *Local System, Domain Admins, and Enterprise Admins: All permissions, except for Apply Group Policy.* Since all administrators are also part of authenticated users, the GPOs are, by default, also applied to them.

7.1.3 Implementing Windows 2000 GPOs

Planning and designing Windows 2000 GPOs

In the previous section, we looked at what you can do with Windows 2000 GPOs and what's behind them. In what follows, we will look at how you can implement Windows 2000 GPOs in your organization.

GPO design models

GPOs can be linked to AD objects in a number of different ways:

- Layered versus monolithic GPO design:
  - In a layered design the same GPO setting can be defined in multiple GPO objects, located on different levels of the AD hierarchy. In the example in Figure 7.15 both the users and servers policy contain script policy settings, both the Europe and servers policy contain security policy settings, and both the Europe and machines policy contain application policy settings.
  - In a monolithic design a setting is defined in exactly one GPO. It is evident that a monolithic GPO design will be easier to manage and will make the delegation of GPO administration much more straightforward. An extreme example of a monolithic design is the one where GPOs are only linked to the leaf objects of the AD tree. A monolithic design can be enforced by setting No Override on GPO objects that are on a higher level in the GPO hierarchy. In the example in Figure 7.16 the account policy is defined only in the domain-level GPO; both leaf OUs Paris and Valbonne have a GPO linked to them with specific scripts and application policy settings.

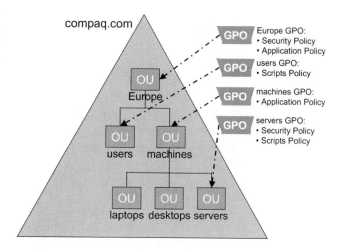

Figure 7.15
Layered GPO design

- Single GPO type versus multiple GPO type design:
  - In a single GPO type design a GPO covers only one area of the GPO settings. For example, a GPO called machine scripts, covering just machine startup and shutdown scripts, another one called user security settings, covering just the GPO security settings related to a user. A single GPO type design will result in more GPOs per object, but will, on the other hand, give more flexibility when setting up GPO administration delegation. In the example in Figure 7.17 the servers OU has three GPOs linked to it. They all contain a very specific set of GPO settings: one contains script settings, another one application settings, and another one security settings.

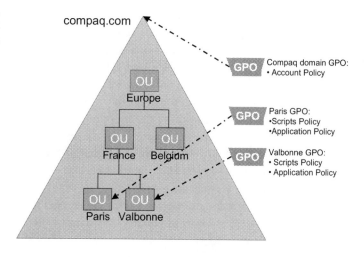

Figure 7.16
Monolithic GPO design

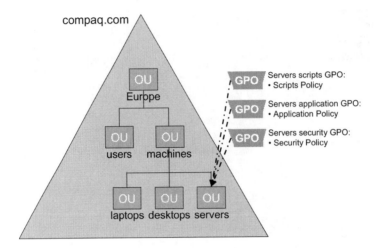

Figure 7.17
Single GPO type design

- In a multiple GPO type design one GPO covers different GPO areas. For example, a GPO called Marketing Division might as well cover the logon scripts as the security settings for the marketing users. A multiple GPO type design will result in fewer GPOs, but will be less flexible for delegation. In the example in Figure 7.18 the servers GPO contains different types of GPO settings, for script, application, and security.

- Functional roles versus team design. The choice between these two GPO design types is strongly dependent on the way your organization is organized and managed.

  - In a functional role design, specific GPOs are created for each of the functional or business groups within your organization. For example, a GPO for sales, another one for marketing, and yet another one for research. If your organization's OU structure is aligned with your functional structure, a one-on-one mapping can be done between GPOs and OUs. If this is not the case, you can link the functional GPOs to a parent object or to every object containing entities to which the GPO should be applied, and then filter the application of the functional GPO using a security group for the appropriate function. In the example in Figure 7.19 specific GPOs are defined for the different functions within the *compaq.com* organization: marketing, sales, and research. Each function also has its proper OU.

  - In a team design, specific GPOs are created for the different teams in your organization. Teams have a more changing character and

Figure 7.18
Multiple GPO type design

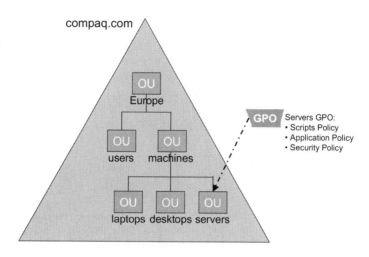

are less persistent over time than functions. In most organizations there's very little chance that your OU design will reflect the teams within your organization. Hence, the application of the team GPOs should be filtered using team-specific groups. Groups allow for fast modification of GPO applications in fast-changing organizations. Although in the example in Figure 7.20 the Wireless team GPO is linked to the research OU, the GPO settings defined in the Wireless team GPO do not apply to all the members of the research OU. The application of the Wireless team GPO is filtered using a specific Wireless team group. The same is true for the IPaq sales team and the IT marketing team GPO.

Figure 7.19
Functional roles in GPO design

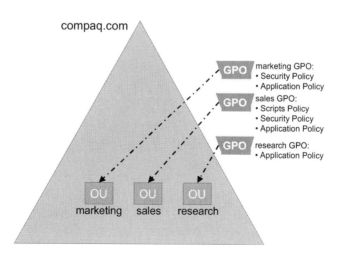

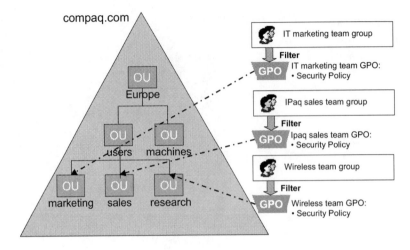

Figure 7.20
Team GPO design

- User- and machine-specific versus public computing environment design:

  - In a user- and machine-specific design specific GPOs are created only for machine settings and others only for user settings. In this design the user portion or the machine portion of the GPOs should be disabled, depending on the GPO type you're dealing with. In the example in Figure 7.21 a specific GPO exists for the user objects in the *compaq.com* domain and for the machine objects in the domain. In the *compaq.com* user domain GPO the machine portion is disabled. In the *compaq.com* machine domain

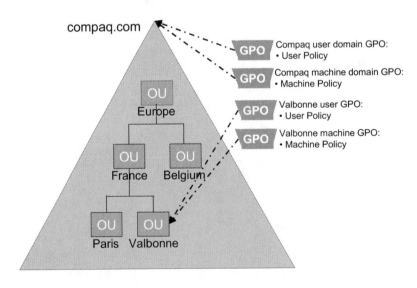

Figure 7.21
User- and machine-specific GPO design

GPO the user portion is disabled. The same principle is applied on the level of the GPOs for the Valbonne OU.

* In a public computing environment design specific GPOs supporting GPO loopback mode will be created. In this case the machine settings will always override the user settings, independent of the other GPOs that might enforce certain user settings. This is an interesting design option for kiosks, roaming users, or public PC environments.

Microsoft group policy scenarios   Microsoft has provided a set of group policy scenarios, describing several possible GPO configurations for different environments. They can be downloaded from the Microsoft Windows 2000 Web site.

The scenarios are a Kiosk PC, a Task Station, an Application Station, a Public Computing Environment (PCE), a Low TCO Desktop, and a Laptop. The Kiosk PC scenario gives little freedom to its user. It is a computer in a public environment that is dedicated to running one application. A Task Station–based computer is the same as the Kiosk-based computer except that a user has the ability to save data and some user settings. The Application Station configuration is identical to the Task Station scenario except that more applications are available to users. In the Public Computing

Table 7.21   *Microsoft Group Policy Scenarios Characteristics*

Scenario	(A)	(B)	(C)	(D)	(E)	(F)	(G)
Kiosk PC	1	No	No	No	No	1	No
Task Station	Multiple	Yes	Yes	My Documents and Application Data	No	1	No
Application Station	Multiple	Yes	Yes	My Documents and Application Data	No	Up to 5	No
PCE	Multiple	Yes	Yes	My Documents and Application Data	Some desktop settings	> 3	Yes
Low TCO Desktop	Multiple	Yes	Yes	My Documents and Application Data	Almost all settings	> 3	Yes
Laptop	1	Yes	Yes	My Documents and Application Data	Some desktop and configuration settings	> 3	Yes

(A) number of users, (B) roaming user profile support, (C) user data saved, (D) folder redirection, (E) user can customize settings, (F) assigned applications, (G) published applications.

Environment scenario, a user is allowed even more freedom to customize his or her computer. The Low TCO Desktop and the Laptop scenario speak for themselves. Table 7.21 gives an overview of the main features of each scenario.

Interoperability with NT4 system policies

Earlier in this chapter, we explained the differences between NT4 system policies and Windows 2000 GPOs. In this section, we will look at coexistence. GPO migration will be covered in Chapter 10. Many organizations running NT4 have implemented system policies and will face a period of coexistence during the Windows 2000 implementation. This period ends when all systems are migrated to Windows 2000.

Coexistence

In a mixed environment consisting of Windows 2000, Windows NT4, and Windows 95 and 98 machines, the following rules apply for the application of system policies and GPOs:

- Only system policy (config.pol file) can be applied to Windows 95 and 98 machines.

- Only system policy (ntconfig.pol file) can be applied on Windows NT4.0 machines.

- Both GPO and system policy can be applied on Windows 2000 machines. Table 7.22 gives an overview of the applied policies, depending on the domain where the user and the machine account are defined (NT4 or Windows 2000).

Remember that NT4 system policy tattoos the registry. A good practice is to disable the processing of the NT4 system policy on a Windows 2000 machine. To do so, create the registry value HKEY_LOCAL_MA-CHINESoftware\Microsoft\Windows\CurrentVersion\Policies\SystemDisableNT4Policy (value: REG_DWORD) and set it to 1 (hex). You can also set the *Disable system policy (use group policy only)* in the GPOs.

GPO administration and maintenance

In this section, we will look in more detail at GPO administration and maintenance: the definition of GPOs, GPO administrative delegation, and GPO troubleshooting and modeling tools.

Table 7.22   *Policies Applied Depending on the Domain where the User and the Machine Account are Defined (NT4 or Windows 2000)*

Scenario	When?	What Affects the Client
1 – Pure Windows NT 4.0		
Machine—NT 4.0	Machine startup	Machine LGPO (only if changed)
	User logon	Machine system policy
	Machine refresh (MF)	
	MF before user logon	Machine LGPO only (only if changed)
	MF after user logon	Machine LGPO + machine system policy
User—NT 4.0	User logon	User system policy
	If LGPO changes	User LGPO + user system policy
	User refresh	User LGPO + user system policy
2 – Mixed (Migration): Machine NT4.0/User Windows 2000		
Machine—NT 4.0	Machine startup	Machine LGPO (only if changed)
	User logon	Machine system policy
	Machine refresh (MF)	
	MF before user logon	Machine LGPO only
	MF after user logon	Machine LGPO + machine system policy
User—Windows 2000	User logon	Group policy
	User refresh	User group policy
3 – Mixed (Migration): Machine Windows 2000/User NT4.0		
Machine—Windows 2000	Machine startup	Group policy
	Machine refresh	Machine group policy
User—NT 4.0	User logon	User system policy
	If LGPO changes	User LGPO + user system policy
	User refresh	User LGPO + user system policy

Table 7.22   *Policies Applied Depending on the Domain where the User and the Machine Account are Defined (NT4 or Windows 2000) (continued)*

Scenario	When?	What Affects the Client
4 – Pure Windows 2000		
Machine—Windows 2000	Machine startup	Group Policy
	Machine refresh	Group Policy
User—Windows 2000	User logon	Group Policy
	User refresh	Group Policy
5 – Non-Active Directory		Local group policy only

GPO definition

Group policy is defined through the MMC group policy editor snap-in. This snap-in is also accessible through the Active Directory sites and services snap-in (dssite.msc) to set site GPOs, and the Active Directory users and computers snap-in (dsa.msc) to set domain and OU GPOs. (See Table 7.23.) The group policy editor is made up of several snap-in extensions, which can be added or removed to fit your administration needs. To add or remove an extension, select the Extensions tab in the Add/Remove Snap-In dialog box. A fully customized GPO editor can be created by defining a Taskpad; to do this select the GPO object and choose Action, New Taskpad View.

The GPE can also be started from the command prompt. Type **gpedit.msc** to edit the LGPO, gpedit.msc /gpcomputer:"<computer FQDN>" to access the LGPO of another computer, or **gpedit.msc /gpobject:"<GPO AD LDAP path>"** to access a nonlocal GPO.

Earlier in this chapter, we explained how GPO information is replicated between DCs (using AD and FRS replication). A multimaster model is nice, but can be dangerous when simultaneous updates happen on the same object from different DCs. In this case, there will always be a winner and a loser; the GPO updates made by the losing administrator will be lost. In the ideal case, an administrator should always update GPOs on the same DC. This will eliminate the possibility of replication conflicts.

To minimize the number of times GPO update loss can occur, Windows 2000 allows you to influence DC selection. These DC selection options can be set from the GPE's View menu (as illustrated in Figure 7.22) or using the GPO entry *Group Policy domain controller selection* in user configuration\

Table 7.23 *GPO administration interfaces*

GPO Scope	MMC Snap-In
Local	Group Policy
Site	Active Directory Sites and Services
	Group Policy
Domain	Active Directory Users and Computers
	Group Policy
OU	Active Directory Users and Computers
	Group Policy

administrative templates\system\group policy. Three options can be set, as follows:

1. *The one with the operations master token for the PDC emulator.* Using this choice all GPO updates will be performed on the FSMO PDC emulator. This is the default.

2. *The one used by the Active Directory Snap-ins.* Using this choice all GPO updates will be performed on the DC you're currently connected to from the MMC.

3. *Use any available domain controller.* In this case any available DC can be chosen to perform the updates.

If the GPE cannot get to the DC that has been set in the DC selection, it will bring up an error message and give you the option to cancel the operation or to select another DC.

The best choice is PDC emulator. In some cases, *Use any available domain controller* may be chosen for update performance reasons, but this choice can have a very inconsistent outcome. You may want to do this to

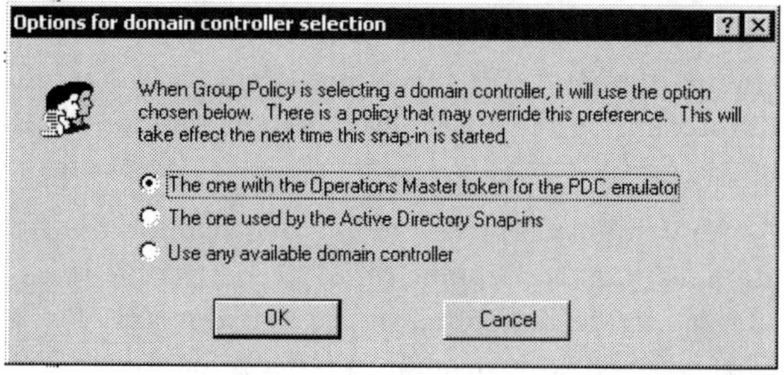

Figure 7.22
Setting GPO DC selection options

give an administrator in a remote site, connected to the FSMO PDC emulator using a bad link, the ability to update particular GPOs.

GPO administrative delegation

As with any other Active Directory object, the administration of GPOs can be delegated. Three common GPO administration tasks can be delegated: the creation of GPOs, the creation of GPO links, and the editing of GPOs. (See Table 7.24.) If you're an experienced administrator, you can change the ACLs on the object to set delegation. If you're not, Microsoft embedded some tools to facilitate the setup of administrative delegation.

Since the creation of a nonlocal GPO object affects Active Directory, a Windows 2000 account that wants to create a nonlocal GPO object will need logon access to a DC. There's even more than that: The account needs read/write access to the system volume and modify rights on the appropriate domain, site, or OU object. In addition, the Windows 2000 account should be logged on to the domain where the GPO will be stored or to a trusted domain of this domain.

The permission to create GPO child objects in a domain is by default given to members of the Group Policy Creator Owners group, and the Administrators, Domain Admins, and Enterprise Admins groups. Obviously every account that has the permission to create a GPO object also has the permission to edit it. However, it will not allow the account to link the GPO to an AD object.

The permission to edit a newly created GPO is by default given to the creator of the GPO object, the Operating System (system group) and the Domain Admins and Enterprise Admins groups. As with the create permission, the edit permission will not allow an account to link the GPO to an AD object.

Giving an account the *Manage Group Policy Links* task will allow the account to prioritize the GPOs linked to an object, to disable the GPO link, and to enforce the application of the GPO (No Override setting). It will not allow the account to block inheritance on the object level. This requires the *Read GPOptions* and *Write GPOptions* ACLs to be enabled for the account on the object level. Also, it will not allow the account to create or edit GPOs.

An administrative delegation that requires special attention is the creation, editing, and linking of GPOs on the site level. The GPOs linked to sites are by default stored in the root domain of a Windows 2000 forest. This means that by default, in order to be able to create a site GPO, you'll

Table 7.24 *GPO Administrative Delegation*

Delegated Task	Microsoft Method	AD Object ACL Equivalent
Create GPOs	Add account in Group Policy Creator Owners global security group.	Use security settings of CN=Policies,CN=System,CN=<domain name> AD container object (use adsiedit) and give account *Create All Child Objects* permission.
Create GPO links	Use Delegation wizard on the object level: delegate *Manage Group Policy Links* task to account.	Use security settings of object and give account *Read GPLink* and *Write GPLink* permissions on the object.
Edit GPOs	Use security settings of GPO object and give account *Full Control* permission.	Use security settings of GPO object and give account *Full Control without Apply Group Policy* permission.

need to be an administrator of the root domain or an enterprise administrator. This default behavior can be changed by pointing the AD sites and services snap-in to another DC when the site GPO is created. To do this, right-click the AD Sites and Services container object in the snap-in and choose Connect to DC.

The application of the GPO settings to a Windows 2000 machine or user object can be looked at as a special kind of delegation. In order for a GPO to be applicable when a machine starts up or when a user logs on, the user or machine account needs read and apply group policy permission on the GPO object. By default, the Authenticated Users group has these permissions. Knowing this you'll notice that all the groups, which have by default GPO create and edit rights, do not have the apply group policy permissions. In other words: By default, accounts that can edit a GPO are not subjected to it. This is true even if the accounts are a member of the container object.

To make the administrative delegation complete you can, besides setting the ACLs, also customize the administrator interface. You can create a custom MMC GPE or a Taskpad. You can also limit access to the GPE and its extensions by setting the GPO entries in User Configuration/Administrative Templates/Windows Components/Microsoft Management Console.

GPO troubleshooting

To troubleshoot GPOs an administrator needs auditing tools, log analysis tools, GPO search tools, and reporting tools. In some situations even more powerful tools, such as diagnosis and analysis tools, are required.

Figure 7.23
*Machine GPO
history in the
registry*

Above all an administrator needs adequate help files that explain the GPO settings. Some GPO settings are very tricky and hard to understand. Microsoft embedded adequate help files in the GPO editor. Every GPO setting has an Explain tab that explains the effect of enabling or disabling the setting.

Microsoft offers some GPO troubleshooting tools in the Windows 2000 resource kit, which will be explained later in this chapter. For logging Microsoft relies on its classical tools (e.g., Event Viewer).

So far, Microsoft has not delivered a modeling tool. At the time of this writing Microsoft is developing such a tool, which is called RSOP (Resultant Set Of Policies). A very good third-party troubleshooting, modelling, and reporting tool is FAZAM (Full Armor Zero Administration for Windows 2000).

GPO logging   The primary source of GPO logging information is the GPO application history, which is written to the registry. (See Figure 7.23.) History logging is enabled by default. GPO applications can also be logged to the Event Viewer's application log or to the userenv.log file. Both are disabled by default.

Logging defaults   The GPO application history gives a chronological overview of the application of the different GPOs, ordered by GPO client-side extension. The history is located in the following registry locations:

- HKEY_LOCAL_MACHINE\Software\Microsoft\Windows\Current-Version\Group Policy\History; for the GPOs applied to the local computer

- HKEY_CURRENT_USER\Software\Microsoft\Windows\Current-Version\Group Policy\History; for the GPOs applied to the user

Beneath these registry keys is a set of keys named after the GUIDs of the CSEs that have run on the client. Each CSE key has another set of subkeys, each one representing a GPO object. The GPO objects are listed in chronological order. Each GPO subkey contains a set of values; their meaning is explained in Table 7.25.

Logging options   To log GPO application information to the Event Viewer set the following registry setting:

> Key: HKEY_LOCAL_MACHINE\Software\Microsoft\
>   Windows NT\CurrentVersion\Diagnostics
> Value: RunDiagnosticLoggingGroupPolicy
> Value Type: REG_DWORD
> Value Data: 1

Table 7.25   *GPO History Registry Entries*

Registry Value	Meaning
DisplayName	Friendly name of the GPO
DSPath	DN of the GPC path in AD (not for LGPOs)
Extensions	List of all CSEs linked to GPO, together with the GUID of their MMC snap-in. Format: [{CSE GUID}{MMC snap-in GUID}]
FileSysPath	File system path to the GPT (in SYSVOL)
GPOLink	GPO application scope ※ 0 = unlinked ※ 1 = local ※ 2 = site ※ 3 = domain ※ 4 = OU
GPOName	GUID for nonlocal GPOs; local group policy for LGPOs
Options	Disabled and No Override GPO link options
Version	GPO version, used to detect GPO changes

The source of the entries will be userenv or application management. The diagnostics key does not exist by default. The RunDiagnosticLogging-GroupPolicy setting is not needed when you already set the value RunDiag-nosticLoggingGlobal. The diagnostics key can also contain a specific entry to enable logging for remote boot (RunDiagnosticLoggingIntelliMirror) and application deployment (RunDiagnosticLoggingAppDeploy).

The Windows 2000 GPO client-side GPO engine will write GPO application logging information to the %SystemRoot%\Debug\UserMode\ Userenv.log file when you set the following registry entry (restart the computer after setting this value):

Key: HKEY_LOCAL_MACHINE\Software\Microsoft\
    Windows NT\CurrentVersion\Winlogon
Value: UserEnvDebugLevel
Value Type: REG_DWORD
Value Data: 0x30002 (hex) for verbose logging
             0x30001 (hex) for errors and warnings only
             0x30000 (hex) disables logging

This is very similar to the way system policy logging was set up in NT4. However, in NT4 a special debug version of the userenv.dll needed to be copied to the winnt\system32 directory (this DLL was available from the NT4 DDK and SDK). Also, in NT4 the UserEnvDebugLevel variable had to be set to 0x10002 and the userenv.log file was located in the root directory of the system drive.

Basic GPO Troubleshooting tools   Microsoft provides two basic GPO troubleshooting tools in the Windows 2000 resource kit: gpresult.exe and gpotool.exe. Gpresult can be used on any Windows 2000 machine, but gpotool can only be used from Windows 2000 DCs.

Table 7.26   *gpresult Switches*

gpresult.exe	Meaning
/v	Verbose mode
/s	Super verbose mode (includes registry settings)
/c	Computer settings only
/u	User settings only
/?	help

Gpresult, the group policy results tool shows which GPOs were applied and when they were applied. It also lists GPO properties (such as the GPC and the GPT version) and the currently logged-on user, as well as the settings applied to a machine: registry settings, redirected folders, published and assigned applications, scripts, and IPsec settings. It does not list the details related to security policies, IE maintenance, and EFS recovery. When registry settings have been applied outside the GPO registry folders (the ones that tattoo the registry), gpresult will display a warning message. The tool can also be used to list general machine and user properties, such as machine and user group memberships. See Table 7.26.

Gpotool, the group policy verification tool, can be used to check the consistency of GPOs and their components (GPC and GPT) on a DC. Gpotool can also check the ACLs on the system volume and list GPO properties, such as the creation date, the friendly name, the user, and machine client-side extensions (CSEs). (See Table 7.27.)

Since gpotool can show the GPO status on different machines, it can also be used to troubleshoot GPO replication between DCs. Another tool that can do this is the Active Directory replication monitor (replmon.exe), shipping with the Windows 2000 support tools. A nice feature of replmon is that it can be used to force replication. To look at the GPO properties with replmon, right-click the DC object and select Show Group Policy Object Replication Status. This will bring up a dialog box showing the names of the different GPO objects, their GUID, and the GPT (SYSVOL) and GPC version number.

Advanced GPO troubleshooting tools The tools explained previously are not sufficient to troubleshoot GPOs in a large corporate Windows 2000 environment. A good third-party, advanced GPO troubleshooting tool is

Table 7.27 *gpotool Switches*

gpotool.exe	Meaning
/gpo:GPO	Preferred GPOs (GUID or friendly name)
/domain: name	DNS domain name for hosting domain
/dc:DC	Preferred DCs
/checkacl	Verify SYSVOL ACL
/verbose	details

FullArmor's FAZAM. FAZAM is more than just a troubleshooting tool. It can also be used for GPO modeling, analysis, and diagnosis. At the time of this writing, Microsoft was developing a similar tool, called RSOP (Resultant Set Of Policies). RSOP will not be available until the next release of Windows 2000, code named "Whistler."

FullArmor FAZAM   FullArmor Zero Administration for Windows 2000 is an indispensable administration tool for GPO administrators in a corporate environment. (See Figure 7.24.) It provides advanced troubleshooting, modeling, and reporting capabilities. Detailed feature and pricing information can be found at *http://www.fullarmor.com*. The major strengths of FAZAM are as follows:

- The FAZAM administrator MMC snap-in gives a complete overview of the GPOs that are linked to a Windows 2000 domain and its OU subcontainers. From a single interface the administrator can create new GPOs; link and unlink GPOs; modify GPO settings; and set filtering, GPO link properties (disable, No Override), and object properties (blocking). The GPO settings are summarized in a well-organized report shown in the snap-in's right pane.

- FAZAM comes with an advanced GPO search function, which allows searches based on GPO name, GPO GUID, or registry entry.

Figure 7.24
FAZAM administration interface

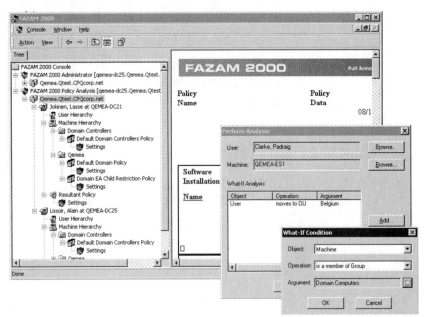

- FAZAM supports backup and restore of GPOs. The administrator can choose to back up just the settings, the links, or the security settings (filtering), or any combination of them. FAZAM also supports backup and restore scripting. Scripting uses the FAZAM2000.Policy-Manager object, WSH, and VBscript.

- FAZAM can diagnose current GPO settings and analyze future GPO settings. Both functions are available from the tool's policy analyis MMC snap-in. The analysis function calculates the GPO settings that will be applied when a particular user logs on to a particular machine. The interface shows the user portion, the machine portion, and the resultant policy. Analysis can also take into account certain conditions: What happens if a user or a machine moves to another OU? What if a user or a machine becomes a member of another group?

- FAZAM supports copy and paste, and import, export, and merge of GPO settings between GPOs. Copying and pasting will overwrite all GPO settings with the exception of software installation and IPsec settings. Importing GPO settings will overwrite all the settings. A special function is Merge, which will apply the rules of one GPO to another one. To do this it will follow the rules of GPO inheritance.

Two limitations of FAZAM in its current release are that its RSOP function does not handle site-level group policy objects and group policy objects that use loopback processing mode.

GPO design considerations and best practices

The following list explains some general GPO design recommendations and best practices; they are based on real-life experiences that occurred during some of the Windows 2000 designs led by Compaq Global Services.

- Limit the number of GPOs that need to be processed at startup and logon time. There are two reasons for doing so: Troubleshooting the resultant set of policies is difficult with many GPOs; also, the logon time may become very slow when too many GPOs are applied to an object.

- Disable the GPO portions (computer or user) that are not used.

- Limit the use of inheritance enforcement and blocking. Both settings make GPO troubleshooting much more complex.

- Do not use cross-domain GPO references. The GPT portion of a GPO is only replicated within a domain. The downloading of cross-domain GPOs will be slower and will have a negative impact on bandwidth use.

- Limit the linking of a single GPO to multiple AD objects. Too many GPO links make GPO administration much more complex.

- Limit the use of loopback processing and GPO filtering—mainly for performance reasons.

- Clearly define who can administrator GPOs. Also, limit the number of GPO administrators. The effect of a wrong GPO setting can impact your entire Windows 2000 domain.

- Set the GPO setting *Create new group policy object links disabled by default*. GPO settings are applied immediately, even when editing the GPO.

- Document your GPO design and the individual GPO settings. A simple spreadsheet will do.

- Perform detailed testing before applying any GPO in your production environment.

- Before activating a GPO setting make sure that you fully understand its effect. The Windows 2000 resource kit contains a special help file (gp.chm), which explains all the possible GPO settings in detail.

- Use GPO logging and the resource kit utilities, gpresult and gpotool. Consider the use of FAZAM if you have a big and complex Windows 2000 environment.

7.2   Organizational unit design

In this section, we will look at organizational units (OUs). What are they? What can you do with them? And, what do you need to think about when planning and designing an Active Directory OU hierarchy?

7.2.1   Defining organizational units

Active Directory OUs are custom administrator-defined AD containers. An OU can contain different types of AD objects: users, computers, printers, and also other OUs. Objects contained in the same OU have something in common; that's why you group them into a container. If they don't have a common characteristic, there's no need to create an OU. This also means it's a bad idea to create just placeholder OUs.

So what's behind this common characteristic? To explain this you first need to know what you can do with OUs. Organizational units enable an administrator to set up two very important Windows 2000 features: administrative delegation and GPO application. Administrative delegation allows you to delegate part of your AD administrative tasks to another administrator. Objects in the same OU may have common administration needs. GPO application allows you to set the configuration of user and computer environments. Objects in the same OU may have common application, configuration, and security needs.

Note that OUs are not a solution for all common configuration or security needs. For example, Kerberos and password policy settings can only be set on the domain level. If you want to have different password policies for two different groups of users, it won't help you to put these users in two separate OUs. The only solution would be to put them in two separate domains and apply a different password policy to every domain.

In Windows 2000 OUs do not have a security identity (SID). This means that you cannot refer to them in any security-related operation such as delegation or access control. You cannot delegate administrative control to the members of an OU using an OU, neither can you set access control on an object using the OU. This is what makes groups so different from OUs.

Because of the above feature, you may end up with a need for two entities: a group to give access control to a set of users and an OU to apply GPOs to the same set of users. To facilitate the creation of a group that has the same membership as an OU, Microsoft has provided the following feature: if you right-click an OU in the MMC user and computers snap-in, you can select *Add members to a group…*, which allows you to copy the members of an OU easily to a security group.

7.2.2   Organizational unit design considerations

Given the fact that OUs can be used for both delegation and GPO application there are two key motivators driving an OU design:

- To delegate administration over a part of the AD objects to another administrator. Delegation can be set up in such a way that a set of objects of the same type contained in the same OU is administered by the same administrator. You may, for example, want to delegate the permission to reset passwords of the user objects in OU Brussels to the Brussels administrator. In many organizations administrative delegation may be driven by pure business requirements or by pure political requirements.

- To apply the same GPOs to a set of AD objects or to give them a set of common security settings. The reason we put these two together is because security settings are defined as part of the GPO definition. A GPO linked to an OU might, for example, install a common set of applications on all machine objects contained in that OU, or it might enforce a common set of NTFS access control settings.

A very important and very difficult decision that has to be made during OU design is how objects will be grouped together. When doing so you'll try to answer the following questions: What are the common characteristics of the objects in my AD? And, if they have something in common, is there a need to create a separate OU for them? For example, it doesn't make sense to create an OU called Printers in Paris if you're not planning to do something with that particular OU (i.e., to delegate administration on it or to apply GPOs to it).

The following list gives some examples regarding how you could group your AD objects together using OUs:

- Object-type based. Create separate OUs for user, computer, and printer objects:
  - Create OUs for administrators and regular users (both user objects), create OUs for workstations, laptops, member servers, and DCs (all of them are computer objects).
  - For servers you could create an OU structure based on the server function—for example, file and print servers, database servers, Web servers, DHCP servers, DNS servers, system management servers, and so on.
  - For users you could create an OU structure that is function-based—for example managers, consultants, researchers, and so on.

- Geography-based. Create separate OUs per geographical location (e.g., America, Europe, AsiaPac). Within Europe you could create more sub-OUs that are country-based (e.g., United Kingdom, Belgium, France).

- Business unit–based. Create separate OUs per business unit (e.g., engineering, research, sales, marketing, etc.).

- Project-based. Create separate OUs for the different projects running in your organization at a particular moment in time.

Another key decision you'll have to make during OU design is the OU hierarchy depth. We strongly recommend limiting the levels in an OU hierarchy to five or six. Why? Too many OU levels will negatively impact performance in the following ways:

- GPO application processing at machine startup time and user logon time

- The application of access control inheritance from parent OU objects down to all their child objects. Remember that Windows 2000 supports dynamic ACL inheritance. ACL inheritance is applied on the moment a change is made on the parent object—not when a child object is accessed.

Microsoft differentiates between three OU models based on the OU hierarchy depth. Their characteristics are shown in Table 7.28.

Figure 7.25 shows a sample organizational unit hierarchy for a company called Pandora. The hierarchy is made up of three levels of OUs. The rationale behind this OU hierarchy is as follows:

- Level 1 is based on geography. Pandora has three major geographic locations (UK, France, and Italy). IT management is decentralized. Each location has an IT staff, which manages the IT resources in its geography.

- Level 2 is based on object types. Per geography there's an OU for administrators, users, desktops, laptops, and servers. The reason for this level is due to GPO application. The user environment of an administrator is different from the user environment of a user. A desktop has security settings applied to it that are different from the ones applied to servers.

- Level 3 is another level based on object type. It contains sub-OUs for users and servers, both based on their function: sales, consultants, and

Table 7.28 *Microsoft OU Models*

MS OU Model	OU Levels	Used for...
Flat	2	Small- or medium-sized companies
Narrow	3 to 5	Medium-sized companies
Deep	5+	Large companies

Figure 7.25
*Sample OU
hierarchy for*
Pandora.com

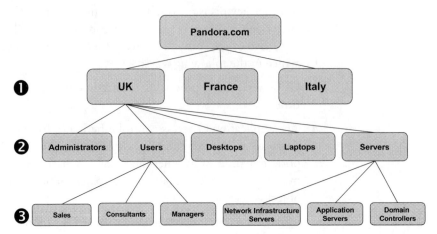

managers for users, and network infrastructure servers, application servers, and DCs for servers. This level is driven by both delegation and GPO application. The applications installed on DCs are different from the ones installed on application servers. Both server types are managed by different people. Members of the marketing OU have access to other applications and get a desktop different from the one used for members of the managers OU.

7.3 Summary

Active Directory comes with great new configuration and administration features, of which the ones discussed in this chapter (group policy objects and OUs) are certainly the most important. The primary goal of this chapter was to give you some insight as to how GPOs and OUs really work and what you need to think about when implementing them in your organization. By showing you the complexity of the technology behind GPOs and OUs we've certainly frightened some of you. But don't be afraid—just be aware that planning, designing, and implementing GPOs, OUs, and delegation are among the most complex tasks in building a corporate AD infrastructure.

Windows 2000 Public Key Infrastructure

This chapter focuses on public key infrastructure (PKI)—a crucial technology for distributed and heterogeneous computer environments that require a security system to provide authentication, confidentiality, and nonrepudiation services. This chapter provides background information on PKI, what you can use it for, how you can implement it on top of a Windows 2000 Active Directory infrastructure, and what components make up the Windows 2000 PKI. In Chapter 9, we will look at the steps you need to consider when planning and designing a Windows 2000 PKI.

8.1   An introduction to public key infrastructure

What is a public key infrastructure? A public key infrastructure (PKI) provides a set of security building blocks, which can be used by distributed applications to provide strong security services to their users. Among the building blocks that can be offered by a PKI are identification, data authentication, confidentiality, integrity, and nonrepudiation.

It's important to stress the last letter of the acronym PKI. A PKI is an *infrastructure.* Many applications can build on it to provide strong security (as illustrated in Figure 8.1). In the next chapter we will discuss some PKI-enabled applications that can be built on top of a Windows 2000 PKI. Market analysts project Web, VPN, and e-mail as the top three applications that

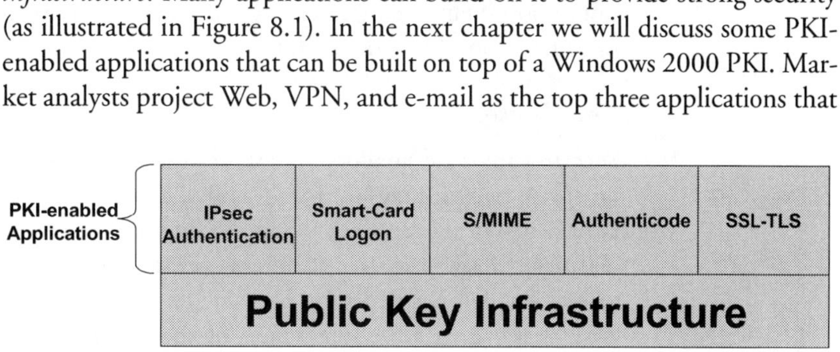

Figure 8.1
PKI is an infrastructure

PKI-enabled Applications	IPsec Authentication	Smart-Card Logon	S/MIME	Authenticode	SSL-TLS
Public Key Infrastructure					

will very likely be PKI enabled on a widespread scale during the years to come.

At the heart of a PKI is cryptography and, more specifically, asymmetric cryptographic ciphers. Asymmetric ciphers deal with public keys and private keys. A PKI provides services to manage these keys and their entire life cycle. Among these services are certification, user registration, key generation, key update, certificate publishing, certificate renewal, and certificate revocation. Cryptography is discussed in Chapter 5.

In this section, we will look at the components upon which a PKI is built, PKI standards, and the requirements for a PKI. All these topics will be examined from a Windows 2000 Active Directory infrastructure point of view.

8.1.1   PKI components

PKI is built upon the following key concepts: certificates, certification authorities (CA), registration authorities (RA), directories, and the concept of trust, as indicated in the following list:

- A PKI is made up of one or more certification authorities.
- Certification authorities issue certificates.
- Registration authorities are the administrative interfaces to a PKI.
- Certificates are published in a directory.
- The fundamental question that is resolved in a PKI is which public keys are trustworthy?

PKI also deals with other topics, such as policies, liability statements, and so on, which are not at all technology oriented. Throughout this section we will also pay attention to the standards PKI and its components are built upon. Standards are key when discussing interoperability between PKI products from different vendors.

Certificates

A certificate is a digital document attesting to the binding of a public key to an entity (which may be an individual, a computer, or a service). It creates confidence in the legitimacy of an individual's public key. In other words, a certificate allows the user of the certificate to verify the claim that a specific public key belongs to a specific individual. This is why a digital signature is part of the certificate. The issuer of the certificate, a trusted certification authority, applies the digital signature.

Certificates (which contain a digital signature) are the enablers of other digital signatures used for the authentication of entities communicating across a public communication channel. The nice thing with digital signatures is that physical identification, dependent on place and time, can be replaced by logical identification, which is independent of place and time. The logical identification can take place between any entities, anywhere on the network. Digital signatures were explained in detail in Chapter 5.

Besides a public key and the user's identity, a certificate also contains other data: the certificate serial number, the issuing CA's identity, and so on. A certificate may even contain other user attributes, such as a user's shoe size, home address, and so forth. A standard format for the content of certificates is defined in the ITU-T X.509 standard. So far, three versions of the X.509 standard have been published. Most software products, including Windows 2000 PKI and CA software, support X.509 V3. Table 8.1 gives a detailed overview of the X.509 certificate format.

Table 8.1   *X.509 Standard for Certificates and CRL Formats*

X.509 Field Name	Field Meaning	X.509 Version/Optional–Required/ Criticality for Extensions
Version	X.509 certificate version	V1 Required
SerialNumber	Unique serial number of the certificate	V1 Required
Signature	Digital signature	V1 Required
Issuer	Distinguished name of the issuing CA	V1 Required
Validity	Start and end date of the certificate	V1 Required
Subject	Distinguished name of the certificate subject	V1 Required
SubjectPublicKeyInfo	Information on the subject's public key	V1 Required
IssuerUniqueIdentifer	Unique identifier of the certificate issuer	V2 Optional
SubjectUniqueIdentifier	Unique identifier of the certificate subject	V2 Optional
Extensions		V3 Optional
AuthorityKeyIdentifier	Identifies public key to be used for certificate verification	V3 Optional—always Noncritical
SubjectKeyIdentifier	Identifies public key being certified	V3 Optional—always Noncritical
KeyUsage	Identifies purpose for which the certified public key is used	V3 Optional—Critical or Noncritical

Table 8.1   *X.509 Standard for Certificates and CRL Formats (continued)*

X.509 Field Name	Field Meaning	X.509 Version/Optional–Required/ Criticality for Extensions
PrivateKeyUsagePeriod	Indicates period of use of private key corresponding to certified public key	V3 Optional—always Noncritical
Certificate Policies	Identifies certificate policies, recognized by issuing CA, that apply to this certificate	V3 Optional—Critical or Noncritical
PolicyMappings	For CA certificates only—maps policy defined in one domain to policy in another domain	V3 Optional—always Noncritical
SubjectAltName	Alternative names for the certificate subject	V3 Optional—Critical or Noncritical
IssuerAltName	Alternative names for the certificate issuer	V3 Optional—Critical or Noncritical
SubjectDirectoryAttributes	Lists directory attributes for the certificate subject	V3 Optional—always Noncritical
BasicConstraints	CA: Can public key listed in this certificate be used to verify other certificates? PathLengthConstraint: Maximum number of certificates that can follow this certificate in certificate path	V3 Optional—Critical or Noncritical
NameConstraints	Lists name constraints for subject names in certificates part of certificate path	V3 Optional—Critical or Noncritical
PolicyConstraints	Lists policy requirements for certificates part of certificate path	V3 Optional—Critical or Noncritical
CRLDistributionPoints	Identifies CRL distribution point	V3 Optional—Critical or Noncritical
Signature	Digital signature on certificate content	V1 Required

The most important characteristic of X.509 version 3 (as opposed to the previous versions) is its support for certificate extensions. Using extensions, extra fields can be added to the certificate. Some extensions have been predefined in the X.509 standard, but an organization might as well decide to add its own custom extensions. Extensions can be marked as critical; this means that they must always be considered during certificate validation.

A term that has been used a lot in PKI-literature over the past months is qualified certificate. A certificate is called qualified if it has been issued by a CA that is adhering to a predefined set of quality requirements, such as the availability of a secure directory for certificate publishing, immediate revocation, or personnel with expert PKI knowledge. More information on this concept is available in the corresponding IETF draft, downloadable from *http://www.ietf.org/internet-drafts/draft-ietf-pkix-qc-03.txt.*

Certificate characteristics

Certificates have a limited lifetime, can be revoked, and can be used in different PKI-enabled applications.

An X.509 certificate's validity field contains a start and an end date delimiting the lifetime of the certificate. This validity limitation helps cope with advances in cryptography and computer science. Cryptographic ciphers using 1,024-bit keys that are secure now may be cracked in a couple of days a few years from now.

Certificates can be revoked; revocation may be needed due to private key compromise or loss. One of your PKI users might, for example, lose his or her laptop, containing all the private keys. When this occurs, the administrator of the CA should add the certificate (corresponding to the compromised private key) to a blacklist. This blacklist is called the certificate revocation list (CRL). The reason why a certificate, having the corresponding private key compromised, should be added to a CRL is directly related to security. If a hacker has access to the compromised private key, he or she can decrypt any information encrypted with the corresponding public key; he or she can also impersonate the user by forging the user's digital signature. Therefore, use of the public key should be prohibited from the moment private key compromise is detected. In order for the revocation to be efficient, the CRL must be checked every time the certificate is used. The X.509 standard defines a format for Certificate Revocation Lists (CRLs). Table 8.2 gives a detailed overview of the X.509 CRL format.

Certificates can be used in different PKI-enabled applications: for smart-card logon, to encrypt files, to digitally sign e-mail, to encrypt e-mail, and so on. Some certificates can be used for just one application (or purpose in Microsoft terminology); others can be used in multiple applications. The applications a certificate can be used for are defined in some predefined X.509 fields. Before a PKI-enabled application accepts a certificate it should check whether the certificate contains the appropriate application use extensions. We will discuss the single- and multipurpose certificates supported in Windows 2000 in Section 8.2.3.

Certificates in Windows 2000

In Windows 2000 the certificate format and content can be looked at in great detail by double-clicking a certificate. Certificates are accessible from the file system, the MMC certificates snap-in, or the Internet Explorer

Table 8.2   *X.509 CRL Fields*

X.509 Field Name	X.509 Version/Optional–Required/ Criticality for Extensions
Version	Optional
Signature	Required
Issuer	Required
ThisUpdate	Required
NextUpdate	Optional
RevokedCertificates	Optional
UserCertificate	Required
Revocationdate	Required
CRLentryExtensions	Optional
ReasonCode	Optional—always Noncritical
HoldInstructionCode	Optional—always Noncritical
Invaliditydate	Optional—always Noncritical
CertificateIssuer	Optional—always Critical
CRLExtensions	Optional
AuthorityKeyIdentifier	Optional
IssuerAltName	Optional
IssuingDistributionPoint	Optional—always Critical
DeltaCRLIndicator	Optional—always Critical

certificates viewer. Using the Details tab of the certificate GUI you can look at all the X.509 fields and their content (as illustrated in Figure 8.2). You can select to view the X.509 v1 properties only, extensions only, critical extensions only, properties only, or all X.509 fields. On the bottom of the first tab of the certificate properties you can see whether a private key corresponding to the certified public key is available on your local computer system.

If you select Edit Properties in the Details tab, you will notice that a Windows 2000 certificate comes with additional non-X.509 properties. The friendly name, the description, and the certificate purposes. The

Figure 8.2
*Windows 2000
certificate viewer*

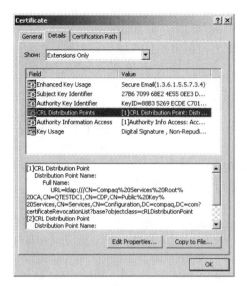

friendly name and description fields are used to customize the display of the certificate in the certificate console. The certificate purposes field lets the certificate user make his or her own trust decisions; in other words, a user may decide that he or she trusts a particular certificate only for a limited set of applications or purposes.

Windows 2000 certificates and private keys are stored encrypted in a user's profile. Access to the profile's PKI data is unlocked after a valid Windows 2000 authentication. As with for private keys the secure storage of certain certificate-types is very important (e.g., for trust anchor certificates). We will discuss certificates and private key storage extensively later on in this chapter.

If user profiles are stored on a central server, Windows 2000 can provide roaming support for certificates: In this case a user's certificates are made available to him or her on any machine in the Windows 2000 forest. If no roaming profile support is available, certificates can be manually ported between machines. To do this use the export and import wizards, available from the MMC certificates snap-in or from the IE certificates viewer. Windows 2000 certificates can be exported and imported in four different formats, as follows:

- DER encoded (*.cer): certificate-only format, DER encoding (no certificate chain). DER is a binary encoding format for certificates. A good document about DER can be downloaded from *ftp://ftp.rsa.com/pub/pkcs/doc/layman.doc*.

- Base64 encoded (*.cer): certificate-only format, Base64 encoding (no certificate chain). Base64 is a text-based encoding format for certificates. Base64 is defined as part of the MIME specifications (Part 1) in RFC 1521 (downloadable from *http://www.ietf.org*).

- PKCS7 encoded (*.p7b): can be used to encode the certificate together with its certificate chain (optional).

- PKCS12 encoded (*.pfx): the personal information exchange format. This format can encode and encrypt the certificate together with the corresponding private key. Since this format exports the private key, the resulting *.pfx file is password protected.

Export and import are wizard based; the wizard can be started from the MMC certificates snap-in or from the IE certificates viewer. An easy way to export a certificate from the IE certificates viewer is by simply dragging it from the viewer to the desktop. Using the Advanced button in the IE certificates viewer the user can set the default export format (DER, Base64, or PKCS7) and whether the complete certificate chain should be exported as well (PKCS7 only). At the time of this writing IE (version 5) did not support the export of certificates in PKCS12 format. It is supported in IE 5.5.

Certification and registration authorities

A certification authority is a trusted third party that issues public key certificates. When a CA issues a certificate, it establishes and vouches for the authenticity of a user's public key. To do so the CA applies a digital signature on the certificate's content (including the user's public key) and adds the signature to the certificate (as illustrated in Figure 8.3). To verify a certificate issued by a CA, one needs the CA's public key. By using the CA's public key the digital signature can be verified.

In most PKI-enabled applications a key pair, consisting of a private and a public key, is generated on the client machine. The private key is stored locally; the public key is presented to a certification authority for certification. Certification means that CA will sign the content of the certificate using its own private key. An often-overlooked detail is identification. Before the CA actually generates the certificate it must be sure that the public key (and with it the private key) really belong to the user who's requesting the certificate.

Since a CA has a public key and a private key, it also has its own certificate that certifies the CA's public key. A CA certificate is signed by the CA itself (in the case of a root CA) or by another CA.

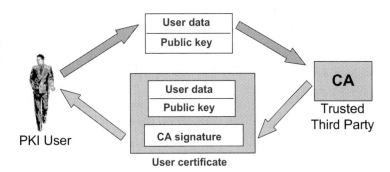

Figure 8.3
The role of a
certification
authority (CA)

A critical component of a PKI is the private key of the CA. If this key is compromised, the complete PKI, and with it the trust infrastructure, falls down. When installing CA software most system administrators forget that the CA's private key is stored on disk just like the rest of the installed CA software. Recent hacker attacks have shown that it is not that difficult to get to the private keys. Different strategies can be used to protect against possible CA private key compromise or at least to minimize the risks, as follows:

- Keep the CA offline, disconnected from the network, when off duty; in other words, when it is not needed for certificate generation and issuance.

- Store the CA private key on a special hardware device, such as a smart card or a Hardware Security Module (HSM). By far the best, but also the most expensive, solution is to store the private key on an HSM.

- Provide adequate logical, physical, organizational, and communication security measures on the level of the CA server or hardware.

Directories

A PKI can use a directory to store certificates and CRLs. Most PKI products (including Windows 2000 PKI) require the directory to be LDAP and X.500 compliant. We will not elaborate on these standards; they've been addressed repeatedly throughout the book. The presence of a directory is not always a requirement. In Windows 2000, for example, you can build a PKI that is based on standalone certification authorities. In this scenario a much simpler certificate and CRL sharing mechanism (e.g., a shared folder) can be sufficient.

If you plan to use a directory in a Windows 2000 environment, it's wise to use the Active Directory. AD is tightly integrated with the Windows 2000 OS. AD is also a good choice from a TCO point of view: You can leverage the investment for your corporate Windows 2000 Active Directory. Integration of Windows 2000 PKI with another directory system (e.g., the Isocor or Netscape directories) will demand more resources.

When using a directory in a PKI, a critical requirement is availability. PKI users should have access to other users' certificates and revocation lists on a permanent basis. In most environments availability of the directory is even more critical than the availability of the certification authorities.

Policies

The majority of the guidelines in this chapter focus on the technical aspects of the PKI infrastructure design and planning. An important nontechnical aspect often forgotten by technically oriented planners is the definition of the certificate policies (CPs) and certificate practice statements (CPSs), both derived from your company's security policy (SP). The CPs and the CPSs help the user of a public key infrastructure to determine the level of trust he or she can put in the certificates that are issued by a CA.

The availability of policies is critical when dealing with a PKI used to secure highly confidential or very valuable information. When using PKI to secure some low-end applications within your internal network, the creation of a CPS and PS might not be an absolute necessity. In this case, some extra clauses regarding the use of PKI and certificates in your company added to the agreement your employees sign at the start of their employment would do.

The security policy (SP) is a high-level document created by the corporate IT group. It defines a set of rules regarding the use and provision of security services within the organization and should reflect your organization's business and IT strategy. As a sort of context definition for corporate security services, it should answer high-level PKI questions such as what applications should be secured with certificates, and what kind of security services should be offered using certificates?

A certificate policy (CP) focuses on certificates and the CA's responsibilities regarding these certificates. It defines certificate characteristics such as use, enrollment procedure, liability issues, and so on. The X.509 standard and the European Electronic Signature Standardization Initiative (EESSI) define a CP as "a named set of rules that indicates the applicability of a certificate to a particular community and/or class of application with common security requirements." (The X.509 standard can be downloaded from *http://www.itu.int/itudoc/itu-t/rec/x/x500up/x509.html*. More information on

EESSI is available from *http://www.ict.etsi.fr/eessi/EESSI-homepage.htm.*) A CP typically answers the following questions:

- What type of applications can the certificate be used for?

- How can a user enroll for the certificate?

- How are users identified when they request a certificate?

- What is a certificate's lifetime?

- How is renewal defined? Is a new key pair generated at every certificate renewal?

- What key lengths and ciphers are used to generate the certificate?

- Where is the private key stored? How should it be protected? Can it be exported?

- What about the CA's liability when its private key is compromised?

- How should users react when they lose their private keys?

The CP is defined by a group of people within your organization known as the policy authority; this group should consist of representatives of the different core departments of your organization: management, legal, audit, human resources, and so forth. Overall the policy authority members will also be members of the group that defined the SP; this assures that the CP is in line with the SP.

The certificate practice statement (CPS) translates certificate policies (CPs) into operational procedures on the CA level. The CP focuses on a certificate; the CPS focuses on a certification authority (CA). Both the EESSI and the American Bar Association (ABA) define a CPS as "a statement of the practices that a certification authority employs in issuing certificates." A CPS answers the following questions:

- What certificate policy or policies does the CA implement?

- What are the policies for certificate issuing? How are certificates issued? Are they issued directly to users, or into a directory? What types of certificates will the CA issue and to which users?

- Who can administer the CA? What subtasks are delegated to the different administrators?

- What are the revocation policies? How is certificate revocation handled? When is a certificate revoked (conditions)? Where are CRLs published? How often are the CRLs updated?

- How is the access to the CA physically and logically secured?

- Who is responsible for backing up the CA?

- What about the quality of the CA certificate and private key? What's the lifetime of the keys and the certificate? What's the CA key length? Where and how is the private key securely stored?

- What's the policy for CA rollover? When is a new certificate generated? When are both a new certificate and a new key pair generated?

The CPS should be defined by members of your IT department, people who are operating and administering the IT infrastructure, in cooperation with the people who defined the CP. Good examples of a CPS can be found on the Web sites of the following commercial CAs:

- Globalsign: *http://www.globalsign.net/repository*

- Verisign: *http://www.verisign.com/repository/CPS*

- Entrust.net: *http://www.entrust.net/about/cps.htm*

A reference to the CP and CPS to which the CA adheres can be made available in the CA certificate. To do this the CA has to embed a unique CP Object Identifier (OID) in its certificate's CertificatePolicies extension. This will allow the user of the certificate to reject certificates issued under a policy the user doesn't adhere to. More detailed information can be added by including a pointer to the appropriate CPS or a short text notice. The way to do this in Windows 2000 will be explained in Chapter 9.

An OID is an object identifier. It is a string of numbers based on a hierarchical dot notation. The OID format has been defined in the ITU X.209 standard. OIDs are maintained by the ISO standardization organization. To get an OID for your certificate policy you should go to your local ISO naming authority. A list of these authorities can be found at *http://www.iso.ch/infoe/agency/agenlist.html*. An easy way to look up an OID assignment is available from the following Web site: *http://www.alvestrand.no/harald/object-id/top.html*. The Web site *http://www.alvestrand.no/harald/objectid/index.html* contains general OID information.

More information on CPs and CPSs is available in documents downloadable from the following Web sites:

- The EESSI report "Electronic Signature Standardization" available from *http://www.ict.etsi.org/eessi/EESSI-homepage.htm*

- RFC 2527 (also known as PKIX part 4), "Internet X.509 Public Key Infrastructure Certificate Policy and Certification Practices Framework" *available from http://www.ietf.org*

- Entrust white paper, "Certificate Policies and Certification Practice Statements" available from *http://www.entrust.com*

It's all about trust

The fundamental question that must be answered in a corporate PKI is which public keys are trustworthy? Public keys are used in asymmetric ciphers offering strong security services to distributed applications. This is only possible if the public component of an asymmetric cipher, the public key, is trustworthy.

Trust in a PKI starts off with trust in the CA issuing certificates. Anyone trusting the CA, trusts every certificate it issues. Trust of the CA in this context means that you believe that a particular CA can create legitimate certificates that uniquely bind information about an individual to a public key. You'll trust a public key when you're convinced that it corresponds to the private key belonging to the one entity mentioned in the public key certificate. The reason you believe that is because you trust the CA that issued the certificate. The word believe in the previous sentence shows that trust in a PKI, in a certificate, or in a public key is not a scientific fact; in many cases it is based on some assumption.

The ITU-T X.509 standard (paragraph 3.3.23) also uses the term *assumption* in its trust definition: "An entity can be said to trust a second entity when it (the first entity) makes the assumption that the second entity will behave exactly as the first entity expects. This trust may apply only for some specific function. The key role of trust in the authentication framework is to describe the relationship between an authenticating entity and a certification authority; an authenticating entity should be certain that it can trust the certification authority to create only valid and reliable certificates."

Trust relationships in the certificate world are very similar to trust relationships in the real world. Three types of trust relationships can be defined (as illustrated in Figure 8.4), as follows:

- Direct trust relationships. In a direct trust relationship user A trusts user B's certificate, because user A knows user B personally; anything (including B's certificate) user A gets from user B is considered trustworthy by user A. If the same is true the other way around, there's a mutual or bidirectional direct trust relationship between A and B. If everybody has a direct trust relationship with the same entity, this entity becomes a trusted third party.

- Third-party trust relationships. In this trust relationship a direct trust relationship exists between user A and a third-party C and also

Figure 8.4
PKI trust
relationships

Direct Trust

Third-Party Trust

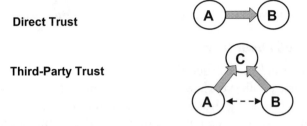

Extended Third-Party Trust

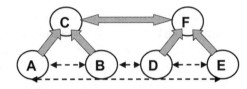

between the same third-party C and user B. As a consequence there's an implicit trust between A and B. A third-party trust relationship is based on the transitivity of other direct trust relationships. Transitivity of trust relationships greatly simplifies trust management; it also reduces the number of trusts needed between entities that want to interoperate. As a consequence third-party trust is a scalable solution for large organizations.

- Extended third-party trust relationships. If A and B have a trust relationship with C, D, and E with F, and a trust relationship is set up between C and F, we can have extended third-party trusts. The trust relationship between A and F, for example, is an extended third-party trust based on the transitivity of third-party trust relationships.

The trust question is easy to resolve in environments consisting of a single CA. It becomes more difficult if an organization decides to have multiple CAs or if certificate-based security interoperability is needed between the users of your corporate CA and the users of the CAs of your partner organizations. How will the users decide which CAs are trustworthy in that case? Will they need to trust every individual CA? Or should they trust only one CA? All these questions will be answered in Section 8.1.2.

8.1.2   PKI trust models

From the moment you decide to implement multiple CAs you'll need to consider the trust model. In a PKI the trust model defines how the trust relationships between the different CAs are defined and managed. Obviously, the trust models also have an important impact on the CAs and certificates that are "trusted" by the users of a PKI. Three major trust models can be used to define the trust relationships between the certification authorities in a corporate Windows 2000 PKI, as follows:

1.   The hierarchical trust model

2.   The distributed trust model

3.   The browser trust model

A fourth and a fifth model could be added to the list: the hybrid model and the user-centric trust model, as follows:

4.   A hybrid trust model combines different trust models into one.

5.   In a user-centric trust model every user makes his or her own trust decisions. This is the model used in Pretty Good Privacy, the well-known secure mail application. Given its decentralized character and its lack of scalability, we won't consider this trust model as an acceptable model for the creation of a PKI in a large company.

Of course, Windows 2000 supports the hybrid model. It even supports a sort of user-centric trust model.

As will be explained, the most important differentiators between these models are the number of trust anchors available in the model and the way that they are made available to the users of the PKI system. A trust anchor can be looked at as the starting point of the trust. The trust in a trust anchor is not based on technology but on a regular human trust: you or the enterprise you work for trusts a CA, because you or your enterprise believe it will issue trustworthy certificates. The trust in any certificate issued by a trust anchor can be verified using cryptographic technology.

In the following paragraphs we will look at why your organization might need multiple CAs and the different trust models that are supported in Windows 2000. We will also discuss an important technique to provide interoperability between different trust models: cross-certification. This technique is not available in the current release of Windows 2000. However Windows 2000 has a tool to get around this limitation.

Why multiple CAs?

Within your organization you may require multiple CAs for the following sizing, fault tolerance, or load-balancing reasons:

- Possibly your organization needs too many certificates to be maintained by one CA.

- To spread the request load you may want to set up multiple CAs.

- Multiple CAs also provide fault tolerance. If one CA is down, another one can handle the certificate requests.

There can be other environmental- or organizational-related reasons to set up multiple CAs, as follows:

- Sites connected using low bandwidth links may all need their own CAs.

- Your organization may require different CAs for partners and employees (internal, external PKI).

Setting up multiple CAs also provides more flexibility, as follows:

- You can support applications that require different security policies. Suppose, for example, you have one certificate-based application dealing with large financial transactions and another dealing with the distribution of nonconfidential corporate information. Both use certificates for client authentication, but the first obviously needs a much higher level of user identification than the second. CA servers in such cases also require different degrees of physical and logical security. The first CA's private key could be stored on a Hardware Security Module (HSM).

- You can set up different maintenance and administration rules for the different CAs. For example, you can define different backup schemes and different CA key and certificate change intervals. You can also shut down part of your CAs for maintenance without affecting the other CAs.

- You can map the PKI structure to the organizational structure more effectively. Organizations often have units that require different security policies. Members of the human resources department should have to satisfy higher security requirements to get a certificate than should members of the logistics department, which usually do not deal with confidential information.

- You can map the PKI structure to the organization's geographical structure more effectively. Some locations may require different security policies.

- You can cope with political requirements. A part of your organization might require its own CA, because it cannot tolerate any external involvement in security-related topics such as PKI.

- Multiple CAs can limit the negative consequences of CA private key compromise. If your organization has one CA whose private key is compromised, everyone will be affected. If there's more than one CA, only the entities trusting that CA will be affected.

Remember that availability of the CA is not a key requirement and is not a real reason to create multiple CAs. One of the key features of a CA is that it doesn't need to be online all the time. Only at certificate request time and for certificate revocation.

Hierarchical trust model

A hierarchical trust model consists of a tree of CAs. The top of the hierarchy is a root CA—it is also known as the trust anchor of the hierarchy and, as such, is the only entity authorized to sign its own certificate. The self-signed root certificate makes it impossible for just anyone to pretend to be the root CA: only the root CA knows and possesses its private key.

In a hierarchy the root CA certifies the tier 1 CAs (one tier below), which, in turn, certify the tier 2 CAs, and so on. The nonroot CAs are called subordinate CAs. The hierarchical trust model provides delegation, so a CA can delegate part of its certificate-issuing responsibilities to a lower-level CA. Organizations with a clear hierarchical structure can easily be mapped to the hierarchical CA trust model.

A hierarchy can contain two types of subordinate CAs: intermediate CAs and issuing CAs. Issuing CAs issue certificates to users. In theory, intermediate CAs should issue only subordinate CA certificates. This allows you to take intermediate CAs offline, which can provide another level of security. To take an intermediate CA offline you can shut down the entire machine or just stop the CA service when it is not performing any certificate-related task. You can also install it on a machine that is not part of your Windows 2000 domain—one that is not connected to any network and that is shut down most of the time.

When implementing a Windows 2000 CA hierarchy it's advisable to use standalone CAs for the root and intermediate (every nonissuing CA). This will facilitate taking these CAs offline. Doing so will also give you more CA configuration options. The issuing CAs can be Windows 2000 Enterprise CAs. The difference between Windows 2000 Enterprise and standalone CAs is explained later in this chapter.

Figure 8.5 illustrates a hierarchical trust model in a Windows 2000 environment. It shows how a Windows 2000 PKI hierarchy can span multiple forests: domain trust relationships and CA trust don't necessarily need to collide. The advantages and disadvantages of using a hierarchical trust model are summarized in Table 8.3.

Figure 8.5
*Hierarchical trust
model in Win2K*

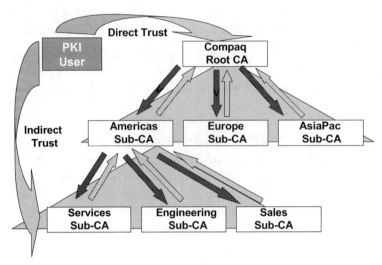

Table 8.3   *Advantages and Disadvantages of the Hierarchical Trust Model*

Hierarchical Trust Model

Advantages:

- Scalability. As your organization or its certificate use grows, you can create new subordinate CAs without affecting the existing trust infrastructure.
- Efficient certificate validation system for a large organization having multiple CAs. Any entity trusting the root CA implicitly trusts any certificate issued below it in the hierarchy.
- Additive policies. A policy exists between every parent CA and its child CAs that is additive at each lower level: the lower the level, the more precise the policies.
- Containment if an intermediate CA is compromised; only the certificates within the hierarchy below the compromised CA must be reissued.
- Integration with third-party product CA hierarchies. A Windows 2000 CA can be integrated within another hierarchy consisting of third-party CA software.
- CRL generation can be partitioned: Each CA has one CRL.
- Trust validation during certificate registration can be brought closer to the PKI user. The trust infrastructure can be mapped to existing human trust relationships.

Disadvantages:

- The basic policy is determined and enforced by the root CA: Everyone in the hierarchy has to agree with the general policy governing the PKI.
- If the root CA is compromised, all users of every CA below it are affected.
- It's not possible to add and integrate another hierarchy without reissuing all the certificates from the existing hierarchy. The same is true for splitting. The hierarchy that is split off will have to regenerate all the certificates it issued.

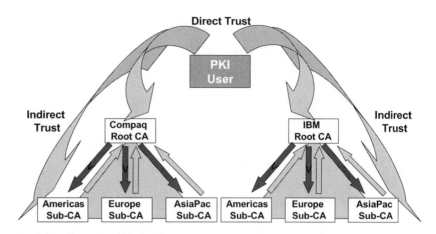

Figure 8.6
*Distributed trust
model in Win2K*

Distributed trust model

In a distributed trust model there's more than one trust anchor. For example: a subset of the user community trusts CA1; another subset trusts CA2. CA1 and CA2 can be the root CAs of two distinct hierarchies. To a certain extent the distributed trust model can be compared with a Windows 2000 forest; as with a Windows 2000 forest consisting of multiple domain trees, a distributed trust model can consist of multiple hierarchical CA trees.

The distributed trust model allows the creation of distinct PKI trust units. To enable interoperability between these units of trust most PKI products support the concept of cross-certification. Windows 2000 does not allow cross-certification, but is using the concept of Certificate Trust Lists (CTLs). CTLs are similar to the browser trust model, explained in the following text.

Figure 8.6 illustrates a distributed trust model in a Windows 2000 environment. It shows once more how a Windows 2000 PKI hierarchy can span multiple forests. (See also Table 8.4.)

The browser trust model

The browser trust model is the trust model used in a Web browser. Every Web browser comes preinstalled with a set of trusted CA certificates. At first glance this model may appear very similar to the distributed trust model. This model is illustrated in Figure 8.7. However, there are differences, as follows:

- In the browser trust model every user has more than one trust anchor. Every CA whose certificate is embedded in the user's browser.

Table 8.4   *Advantages and Disadvantages of the Distributed Trust Model*

Distributed Trust Model

Advantages:

- If one CA's key is compromised, damage can be limited to that CA and its trust unit.
- Trust agreements (CTLs) can be fine-tuned on the level of time and supported applications.
- Within a trust unit: all advantages of the hierarchical trust model.
- Ability to integrate or split an existing PKI.

Disadvantages:

- To enable interoperability among the trust units in Windows 2000, CTLs must be created. CTLs are very different and much more limited than true cross-certification.
- Within a trust unit: all disadvantages of the hierarchical trust model.

- The model has more similarity to the hierarchical model than to the distributed trust model. By embedding CA certificates in the browser software, the software vendor acts as a type of root CA. Instead of signing the CA certificates using its private key, the software vendor embeds the certificates in its software. Because they are embedded, browser users think that the CA certificates are trustworthy.

- This brings up another key difference: in the browser model it's not really the user who makes trust decisions, but the software vendor. Because of this some organizations may not accept this trust model at all. A user may well modify the trust decisions made by the software vendor: he or she can mark CA certificates as untrustworthy.

In Windows 2000 the Web browser certificate store and a PKI entity's certificate store collide. The list of CA certificates embedded in the

Figure 8.7
*Browser trust
model*

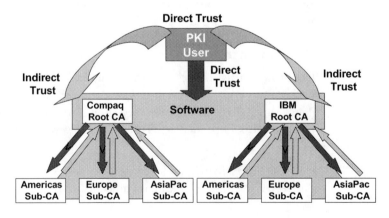

Table 8.5   *Advantages and Disadvantages of the Browser Trust Model*

Browser Trust Model

Advantages:

▓ Trusted CA certificates can be distributed easily to all PKI entities in an organization.

Disadvantages:

▓ Not suitable for high-security environments.

Windows 2000 certificate store can be modified using a customized IE software package or using Windows 2000 GPO settings. To create a customized IE package the administrator should use the Internet Explorer Administration Kit (IEAK).

The concept of Certificate Trust Lists (CTLs), used in Windows 2000 to get around the lack of cross-certification features, is also based on the browser trust model. To provide interoperability among distinct PKI trust units a Windows 2000 administrator can define CTLs containing other CAs' certificates signed with a special private key (bound to a special certificate used for CTL signing). The CTLs are distributed using the Windows 2000 GPOs and are, as with the browser, embedded in the PKI entity's certificate store. (See also Table 8.5.)

Linking trust models together

We previously discussed the fact that distinct trust units can be linked together and provide public key–based security interoperability using the concept of cross-certification. What is cross-certification? Cross-certification between two CAs means that a CA issues a certificate to the other CA. If this happens in only one direction, the cross-certification is unidirectional; if it also happens in the other direction, the cross-certification is bidirectional. When looking at this from a hierarchical point of view you can say that in a cross-certification model every CA is a root and subordinate CA at the same time.

Cross-certification also includes more than just technology: In a real cross-certification a policy agreement is set up between the two cross-certifying CAs. Cross-certification can also limit the trust based on different constraints: naming, timing, policy, or path-length constraints, as follows:

■ A naming constraint can be linked to a trust unit; for example, certificates issued by the CA of Compaq are trusted; the ones issued by the IBM CA are not.

- Timing limits the validity of cross-certificates in time.

- Policy constraints limit the validity of a cross-certificate to certain certificate types (e.g., only e-mail certificates).

- Path-length constraints limit cross-certification transitivity or the number of allowed hops.

One of the major strengths of cross-certification is that it does not affect previously issued certificates or subsequently issued ones. An alternative to cross-certification to link two distinct hierarchies together would be the creation of a super root CA certifying both root CAs; however, this would require all certificates in both hierarchies to be reissued.

Cross-certification is a feature that is missing in the current release of Windows 2000. Microsoft promised to include it in one of the upcoming Windows 2000 releases. Currently Windows 2000 PKI is using the browser trust model to link different PKI domains together. To do this it uses the CTLs concept. You can put an expiration date on a CTL and limit it to a subset of certificate types. As with regular cross-certification, CTLs can provide uni- or bidirectional trust.

Although the Windows 2000 CTL model serves the same goal as cross-certification, it is fundamentally different from it in the following three ways:

- Policy enforcement in the CTL model is very limited: only expiration date and certificate type specifications.

- CAs don't issue certificates to one another. There is just an exchange of CA certificates between two organizations.

- CTLs are defined on the Active Directory level (using GPOs). As a result, people other than the ones administering your CAs may administer CTLs. Real cross-certification happens on the CA level.

User trust decisions

Although Windows 2000 PKI trust can be highly structured and driven by corporate administrator decisions, a Windows 2000 PKI user still has some freedom on the level of trust decisions. In your organization a CA certificate may automatically be trusted following some corporate-level administrator decision. A user can override this temporarily, and deny the trust. We use the term "temporarily" because organizational trust decisions are enforced using GPOs. Every time the GPO gets applied the certificate will be trusted again. In a hierarchical trust model this could mean that from a user's point of view the root CA shouldn't necessarily be its trust anchor in any case. A user can define his or her trust anchor at any level of the hierarchy: at the root CA level or at the level of any subordinate CA.

Windows 2000 even supports fine-grained individual trust decisions: A user may decide to trust a CA certificate only for a particular set of applications, or "purposes" in Windows 2000 terminology. This can be done from the advanced view in the Internet Explorer certificates dialog box or from the properties in the MMC certificates snap-in. In the MMC snap-in a user can choose to enable all purposes, disable all purposes or enable only a subset of the purposes. Using the IE interface trust decisions can be set per purpose.

8.1.3   PKI standards

We've already mentioned the use of the X.509, LDAP, and X.500 standards in PKI environments. Standards are, also for a PKI, very important for interoperability reasons. Two other PKI-related standards not discussed so far are PKCS and PKIX:

- The Public Key Cryptography Standards (PKCS) are a set of standards (15 so far) related to the use of PKI: They define message formats for certificate requests, certificate transport, Diffie-Hellman key agreement, RSA encryption and signing, and so on. A complete list of the PKCS standards is given in Table 8.6. More information on the

Table 8.6   *PKCS Standards*

PKCS #1	RSA Encryption Standard
PKCS #2	Integrated in #1
PKCS #3	Diffie-Hellman Key Agreement Standard
PKCS #4	Integrated in #1
PKCS #5	Password-Based Cryptography Standard
PKCS #6	Extended-Certificate Syntax Standard
PKCS #7	Cryptographic Message Syntax Standard
PKCS #8	Private Key Information Syntax Standard
PKCS #9	Selected Attribute Types
PKCS #10	Certification Request Syntax Standard

Table 8.6   *PKCS Standards (continued)*

PKCS #11	Cryptographic Token Interface Standard
PKCS #12	Personal Information Exchange Syntax Standard
PKCS #13	Elliptic Curve Cryptography Standard
PKCS #15	Cryptographic Token Information Format Standard

PKCS standards is available from the Web site of RSA security at *http://www.rsasecurity.com/rsalabs/pkcs/*.

- PKIX stands for Public Key Infrastructures based on X.509 certificates; it's a PKI standardization effort driven by the IETF. The PKIX working group has already produced several important RFCs, of which an extensive list can be found at *http://www.ietf.org/html.charters/pkix-charter.html*. Throughout this chapter we will discuss several of these standards.

8.1.4   PKI requirements

The following text lists some high-level PKI requirements. At the end of the chapter, after discussing the Windows 2000 PKI capabilities, we will look at how Windows 2000 PKI can correspond to these requirements.

A Public Key Infrastructure should contain the following components:

- A certification authority to issue certificates
- Registration authorities to perform PKI user–related administrative tasks.
- A directory to store certificates and CRLs.
- Client-side software to provide transparent and easy-to-use access to the PKI functionalities listed below.

It should provide the following functionalities:

- A revocation system to prevent improper use of a certificate.
- An automatic key update facility to transparently renew certificates and key pairs.
- A key history facility to archive the keys used to encrypt persistent data.
- A key backup and recovery facility for fault tolerance and recovery of private encryption keys in case of loss.

- Support for nonrepudiation, including secure storage of the signing private key.

- Support for secure certificate storage. Certificates that are trust anchors are of great importance in certificate chain validation and hence have to be stored in a secure manner.

- Support for cross-certification; this enables certificate-based inter-operability between two distinct PKI administrative domains.

Another interesting view regarding the requirements for a PKI can be found in Bruce Schneier's article "Ten Risks of PKI: What You're Not Being Told about Public Key Infrastructure" available from his Web site: *http://www.counterpane.com/pki-risks.html.*

8.2   Windows 2000 PKI basics

In this section we'll look at the added value of using Microsoft PKI as the building block for advanced security in your organization. Before discussing possible deployment scenarios of Windows 2000 PKI, we also need to take a closer look at all of its core components: the certificate server, the CryptoAPI, the protected store, and the Active Directory.

8.2.1   Why use the Microsoft PKI?

At the core of the Microsoft PKI shipping with Windows 2000 is version 2 of Microsoft's certificate server. Version 2 is more scalable, flexible, standards-based, and extensible than its NT4 Option Pack predecessor, as follows:

- Scalability. The Windows 2000 CA can scale up to 1 million certificates per CA. At the time of this writing Microsoft had tested up to 5 million certificates per CA. This is mainly due to the adaptation of JET technology for the CA database. Another important scalability factor is the full support for multiple-level CA hierarchies, consisting of a root CA and multiple levels (up to 40) of subordinate CAs. The initial NT4 product only supported two-level hierarchies.

- Flexibility. Windows 2000 PKI is also flexible. The CA service can be installed in two modes: enterprise or standalone; each mode is built to fit particular enterprise security needs. Compared with version 1 the CA service also offers many more configuration options.

- Interoperability. To provide interoperability, Microsoft PKI supports the major open standards for PKI: ITU-T X.509, IETF PKIX, and

PKCS. A Windows 2000 CA can easily be integrated into a PKI consisting of other vendors' CA products. It also supports a range of cryptographic algorithms: RSA, DSA, and so on.

- Extensibility. The Windows 2000 CA is extensible. The CA policy and exit modules can be customized to meet different security needs. Windows PKI also provides a true extensible security infrastructure: multiple applications coming out of the box with Windows 2000 can build on it to provide strong security services.

- Pricing. Windows 2000 has an important price advantage over some of the advanced PKI products, such as Entrust, Baltimore, and ID2. It is true, however, that these products offer some interesting features not available in Windows 2000 PKI. The fact that Windows 2000 PKI comes out of the box with the Windows 2000 server software also allows you to leverage the investment in a Windows 2000 infrastructure.

8.2.2   Windows 2000 PKI core components

Certificate server

Microsoft first shipped their Certificate Server as part of the Option Pack for NT4. Windows 2000 comes with version 2 of the product. In the following text, we will focus on the architecture of Microsoft's Certificate Server and its specific configuration options. Certificate Server can be installed as a root or a subordinate CA, as an enterprise (AD integrated), or standalone CA (non-AD integrated).

The Windows 2000 Certificate Server provides the following core services: It receives and processes certificate requests, issues certificates according to a security policy, renews and revokes certificates, publishes and delivers certificates, creates and publishes CRLs, and logs all certificate and CRL transactions in a log database.

The administrative interface of Microsoft Certificate Server version 1 was mainly Web based. Some settings could also be administered using the certutil.exe tool. In Windows 2000 CA management can be done from an MMC snap-in. Windows 2000 still supports the command prompt tool certutil.exe and Web interfaces.

Certificate Server architecture

The architecture of the Microsoft Certificate Server is illustrated in Figure 8.8. At the heart of Certificate Server sits an engine (certsrv.exe), which

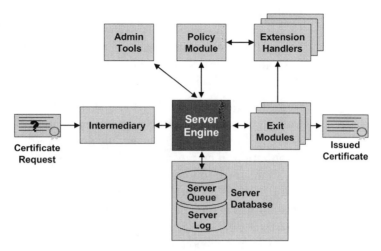

Figure 8.8
Certificate Server architecture

generates the certificates and directs the message flow between the other components. The engine communicates with three important modules: the entry, policy, and exit modules, as follows:

- The entry module accepts PKCS 10- or keygen (Netscape)-formatted certificate requests coming in over HTTP, RPC, or another custom transport, or even in file format. It's only job is to place the certificate requests in a queue for treatment by the policy module. It isolates the CA from communicating with any specific transport.

- The policy module is the CA's most important module. It's the module that implements and enforces the CA policy rules set by the CA administrator. It deals with user identification, certificate issuance, renewal, and revocation. It tells the CA engine if the certificate needs any additional settings (X.509 extensions). If any settings must be modified; and if a certificate request should be issued, denied, or left pending. Windows 2000 comes with one module supporting two policy types. The enterprise and standalone policy. Details on the two policy types will follow. To check out the policy module that has been installed on a CA, look at its properties on the level of the MMC snap-in GUI or use certsvr.exe with the –z switch from the command prompt.

- The exit module distributes and publishes certificates, certificate chains, and CRLs in PKCS7 format. The PKCS7 file can be written to a file or transported across HTTP, RPC, or any other custom transport. The Windows 2000 CA can support multiple exit modules, by which certificates, certificate chains, and CRLs can be published and distributed to different locations at the same time—LDAP directories, file shares, Web directories, or an ODBC-compliant database. You could also create an exit module that automatically sends the certificates via e-mail to the user or that publishes them to a third-party directory.

Both the exit and the policy module are customizable and replaceable; for both some configuration settings can be changed through the Windows 2000 GUI. If the policy or exit module doesn't correspond to the needs of an organization, they can develop their own modules in Visual BASIC or C++ and plug them into the CA architecture. All this is documented in the platform SDK. The entry module is noncustomizable. The default Windows 2000 policy module is called certpdef.dll; the default exit module is called certxds.dll (both are located in the system32 directory). If you plan to use a custom policy module it's advisable to install your CA first in standalone mode and then install the custom policy module.

Both the policy and the exit module can be configured using the certification authority management snap-in or using the certutil command prompt utility; using the properties of the CA object you can plug in a newly created policy module (DLL), configure the X.509 extensions (CRL distribution points, authority information access), and configure CRL publication (as illustrated in Figure 8.9). We will discuss the certutil utility later on in the book.

Certificate Server also has its own database and communicates with intermediaries and extension handlers, as follows:

- Certificate Server uses its database to store all certificate transactions and status information. It is located in the certlog folder of the system32 directory. Certificate Server communicates with the database through the certdb.dll. In the Windows 2000 release of Certificate Server, Microsoft changed its database technology to JET. The same technology is used for Active Directory and the Exchange databases. This switch gave the Windows 2000 CA a scalability injection. As with any other major Windows 2000 service, Certificate Server has its own MMC snap-in. This is a major difference from the NT4 version, where administration was completely Web based.

- Applications that help the client in generating PKCS10-formatted certificate request files and getting PKCS7-formatted certificates back from the CA to the client are known as intermediaries. They are not part of the CA architecture. Intermediaries are bound to a specific transport protocol. Besides the generation of PKCS-formatted messages, an intermediary also gathers the user-specific data required for

Figure 8.9
*Configuring exit
and policy module
properties using the
CA object
properties*

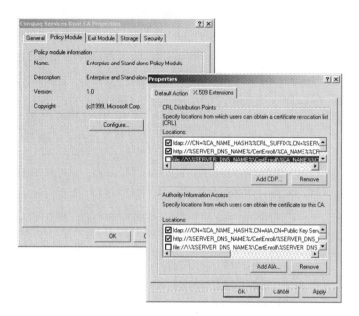

Figure 8.9
*Configuring exit
and policy module
properties using the
CA object
properties*

a certificate request and adds required request attributes; for example, a request that is sent to a Windows 2000 Enterprise CA should mention a certificate template. Examples of Windows 2000 intermediaries are the Web enrollment pages—an HTTP intermediary—and the MMC certificates snap-in, containing the certificate request wizard—a DCOM-RPC intermediary. As with the entry module, an intermediary isolates the CA from communicating with any specific transport.

- As previously mentioned, one of the policy module's responsibilities is to add X.509 extensions to the certificates issued by the Windows 2000 CA. If a company wants to add custom extensions requiring a special encoding (other than date, long, and binary string), a special extension handler can be written and plugged into the CA architecture. An extension handler is an encoder for special extension formats.

The architecture we just described is very similar to the architecture of CS version 1. Later on in the chapter you'll see that Microsoft added lots of configuration options related to the policy and exit modules.

Enterprise versus standalone CA

The Windows 2000 Certificate Server can be installed in one of two modes: standalone mode or enterprise mode (as illustrated in Figure 8.10). In both modes root and subordinate CAs can be installed. To install a CA in enterprise mode, two requirements must be met, as follows:

1.   The account installing the CA should be an enterprise administrator or a domain administrator of the root domain of the forest.

2.   The server on which the enterprise CA is installed should be a member of a domain with a functioning AD.

Installing the Certificate Server in enterprise mode provides full integration with the Active Directory. It activates the enterprise mode of the Windows 2000 policy module. A Windows 2000 enterprise CA offers the following advantages:

■   An Enterprise Certificate Server can use the Active Directory to store and publish certificates and CRLs. Each certificate published in the AD is automatically mapped to the Windows 2000 account of its requester. The certificate is added to the multivalued user certificate attribute of the user object. Note that not every certificate generated by an enterprise CA is published in AD (e.g., an enrollment agent or CTL signing certificate). An enterprise CA will also publish every certificate to the user's profile.

■   The Active Directory contains the location of enterprise certificate servers. When a system requests a certificate, it can query the GC to find a CA.

■   Thanks to the publication of certificates in AD any internal PKI client can launch LDAP queries on the Active Directory (in fact, the GC) to look up and retrieve certificates.

Figure 8.10
Choosing the Certificate Server mode during installation

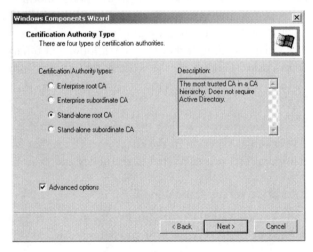

- The ability to provide smart-card logon to your Windows 2000 domain. Smart-card certificates are automatically mapped to Windows 2000 accounts during the smart-card enrollment process. During the logon process the Kerberos KDC queries the Active Directory for a mapping between the user's certificate and a Windows 2000 account.

- Support for certificate templates. The certificate types that can be issued are dependent on the available certificate templates. Certificate templates are explained in detail in Section 8.2.3. You can set the types of certificates issued by a CA by loading the appropriate templates in your CA's policy module. A certificate issued by an enterprise CA contains a reference to the template that was used to generate it.

- The integration with AD also means that an enterprise CA can use the Windows 2000 default authentication protocol Kerberos to authenticate user certificate requests. User data needed for some of the certificate fields can also be retrieved automatically from the AD using RPC-DCOM calls or using HTTP requests. These two features enable automated certificate approval and automated certificate enrollment (for computer certificates). Also, a certificate issued by an enterprise CA contains a reference to the Windows 2000 User Principal Name (UPN) of the object the certificate belongs to (part of the certificate's SubjectAltName field)

- Integration with Windows 2000 authentication also means that you can take advantage of the integration of certificate templates with the Active Directory. You can set ACLs on certificate templates just as you can on any other Active Directory object. This enables you to control who can get which type of certificates, based on, for instance, group membership. ACLs set on the templates are stored in the AD configuration NC and are available forest-wide. During a certificate request the CA service will impersonate the user, and the user's access token will be compared with the ACLs set on the templates.

In standalone mode the CA can issue Web authentication (SSL, TLS), e-mail protection (S/MIME), server authentication, code signing, time stamp signing, IPsec certificates, or any other certificate that has a customized OID (these types of certificates are known as *extended key usage* certificates, named after the certificate field where the OID is stored). The user certificate request interface is Web based and communicates with the CA using HTTP. Since a standalone CA has no access to AD, user identification information required for the certificate needs to be filled in manually by the user on the CA's Web site. To verify a user's identity a standalone CA requires an administrative action: by default, every request is set to pending and the CA administrator has to approve it manually. This setting can be reversed by checking the *Always issue certificates* check box in the properties of the CA object. Certificates that are not downloaded from the CA's Web site within ten days are purged. Contrary to an enterprise CA a standalone CA does not support certificate templates.

Pending certificate requests are saved on the client side in the certificate store's Request container. Physically this container is located at the following registry location: HKEY_CURRENT_USER\software\Microsoft\systemcertificates\Request\Certificates. On the Certificate Server side they are saved in the edb.log file (located in the CA's certlog subdirectory). The same database will also store the issued certificates that have not been downloaded by their requesters.

The default behavior of a standalone CA can be modified somewhat by editing the certdat.inc file and by using the certutil utility. By modifying the nPendingTimeoutDays setting in the certdat.inc file (located in the c:\winnt\system32\certsrv directory) you can set the amount of days before a certificate is purged from the CA's Web site. In the same file you can set some of the default certificate entries: sDefaultCompany, sDefaultOrgUnit, sDefaultLocality, sDefaultState, and sDefaultCountry.

By default a standalone CA does not publish the issued certificates to AD. To let a standalone publish certificates to the AD the Certificate Server administrator can do the following:

- Run the following command on the Certificate Server to tell the exit module to publish certificates to the Active Directory: **certutil –setreg exit\PublishCertFlags EXITPUB_ACTIVEDIRECTORY**. After doing this you'll notice in the CA's exit module configuration that the *Allow certificates to be published to Active Directory* is checked (although it is still grayed out).

- Set the Certificate Server virtual Web directory certsrv to require identification: clear the *Anonymous access* check box and select the *basic authentication*, *digest authentication*, or *integrated windows authentication* check boxes.

Afterwards, if a user wants his or her certificate published into Active Directory, he or she can do the following:

- Select Advanced Request on the Certificate Server's Choose Request Type Web page.

- Select *Submit a certificate request to this CA using a form* option on the Advanced Certificate Requests Web page.

- Type **CertificateTemplate:User** in the *Attributes* section of Additional Options.

Independent of this method and the CA installation mode the user can always manually publish certificates to AD by dragging them from the Personal to the Active Directory User Object container in the certificates MMC snap-in. An administrator can use the MMC domain users and computers snap-in to publish a user certificate to the AD; he or she can add it from the certificate store or from a file. The same interfaces can be used to remove a user certificate from AD.

It's clear that the standalone mode involves much more administrative overhead. Standalone mode is clearly targeted toward the issuance of certificates to external users (extranet users) who do not have an internal Windows 2000 account. Standalone mode can also be an interesting solution to take advantage of the new features of the Windows 2000 CA in an existing Windows NT4 environment without having to install the Active Directory and other Windows 2000 features, such as dynamic DNS. For your information, the basic design principle behind the Windows 2000 standalone CA is very similar to the one used in Netscape's Certificate Management System.

Table 8.7 compares the default characteristics of a Windows 2000 standalone and enterprise CA.

Registration authorities

Previously we introduced another critical PKI component: RAs. The current version of Windows 2000 PKI does not support real RAs, in the sense of a separate entity or service dealing with user registration. Windows 2000, however, supports some RA functionalities through the use of special enrollment agent certificates (OID 1.3.6.1.4.1.311.20.2.1—certificate request agent). Enrollment agent certificates can be used for the following:

- Smart-card bulk enrollment. An administrator with a special certificate request agent certificate can bulk enroll users' certificates on smart cards and act as a registration authority for smart-card certificates.

- Integration with Exchange KMS. If your organization has implemented Exchange advanced mail security (S/MIME) in combination with Microsoft Certificate Server, the Exchange Key Management

Table 8.7   *Windows 2000 Standalone versus Enterprise CA*

Windows 2000 Standalone CA	Windows 2000 Enterprise CA
Extranet-Internet certificate user oriented	Windows 2000 intranet certificate user oriented
Non-AD integrated	AD integrated
CA location not published to AD	CA location published to AD
User interface is Web forms based	User interface is GUI based (MMC) or Web forms based
User communication with CA is based on HTTP	User communication with CA is HTTP or RPC/DCOM based
Can issue limited set of certificate types and any certificate defined using a custom OID; does not support certificate templates	Can issue all Windows 2000 certificates defined in the Windows 2000 certificate templates
User has to enter identification information manually at certificate request time	User identification information automatically retrieved from Active Directory
By default, certificate requests are set to pending	Certificate requests automatically validated using integrated Windows 2000 authentication
Manual certificate approval	Can take advantage of Windows 2000 authentication and access control model for certificate request approval
Certificate downloaded to user profile when certificate is retrieved from CA Web site; by default no certificate publishing	Certificate automatically downloaded to user profile and in some cases published to AD
CRL and CA certificate can be published to AD; this is not the default	CRL and CA certificate published to AD
Does not support AD-based certificate lookup and retrieval	Supports AD-based certificate lookup and retrieval
Does not support smart-card logon	Supports smart-card logon
Can be installed on Windows 2000 DC, member server, or standalone server (not member of any domain)	Can be installed on Windows 2000 DC or member server

Server acts as an RA. It identifies users and passes the certificate requests to the Windows 2000 CA.

RAs will be discussed in more detail in Chapter 9.

Active Directory

As discussed in the beginning of this chapter, a directory is one of the core components of a PKI. In Windows 2000 the Active Directory is an obvious choice. As will be explained, AD is the only possible choice if you want to take advantage of some typical Windows 2000 AD–based PKI features (enterprise CA) or PKI-enabled applications (smart-card logon).

Windows 2000 PKI is very tightly integrated with AD services. Examples of this integration are the user group policy objects used to distribute trusted CA information to Windows 2000 Professional workstations. Windows 2000 PKI becomes even more tightly integrated with AD when deploying Windows 2000 enterprise Certificate Servers, as follows:

- CRLs, CA, and some user certificates issued by the Certificate Server are automatically published in the Active Directory (as part of the domain and configuration NC; for details see Table 8.8), generally in Distinguished Encoding Rules (DER) encoded binary X.509 format. This enables users to query the GC and retrieve certificates or CRLs. AD's replication model also ensures that certificate information is distributed throughout the Windows 2000 forest.

- AD offers certificate server location information. To find an enterprise CA a user simply can query the Active Directory.

- The CA can take full advantage of the Windows 2000 authentication and access control model to identify user certificate requests and of the user information stored in AD to fill in user certificate fields.

- Users can log on to Windows 2000 using PKI-based credentials: a private key and a certificate, both stored on a smart card.

Table 8.8 shows the Windows 2000 PKI information that is published in the Active Directory, as well as where it is published in the AD. (To look at the PKI information contained in AD you can use the support tools tool adsiedit.exe.)

The following list clarifies several of the entries in Table 8.8:

- The AIA container contains the CA certificates of all CAs (root and subordinate CAs) located on servers that are a member of your Windows 2000 forest. The CaCertificate attribute not only stores the current CA certificate but also the CA certificate history.

- The CDP is the Active Directory CRL Distribution Point (CDP), which allows PKI users to download the latest CRL from the AD. The CDP container contains one subcontainer per CA. Within every container multiple CRLs can be stored. Every time the CA key pair and certificate are renewed, a new CRL is generated. (Windows 2000 PKI uses a unique CRL per CA. In the current release delta or partitioned CRLs are not yet supported.)

Table 8.8   *Windows 2000 PKI Information Stored in AD*

Naming Context	Object Distinguished Name (DN)	Key Attributes
Configuration	CN = AIA, CN = Public Key Services (container)	CaCertificate
	CN = CDP, CN = Public Key Services (container)	CertificateRevocation
	CN = Certificate Templates, CN = Public Key Services (container)	Pkicriticalextensions Pkidefaultcsps Pkidefaultkeyspec Pkienrollmentaccess Pkiexpireationperiod Pkiextendedkeyusage Pkikeyusage Pkimaximumissuingdepth Pkioverlapperiod
	CN = Certification Authority, CN = Public Key Services (container)	Cacertificate Authorityrevocationlist Certificaterevocationlist
	CN = Enrollment Services, CN = Public Key Services (container)	Certificate Templates
	CN = NTAuthTemplates, CN = Public Key Services	CaCertificate
Domain and GC	User Object	UserCert (single-valued attribute; OID: 1.2.840.113556.1.4.645) UserCertificate (multi-valued attribute; OID: 2.5.4.36) UserSMIMECertificate (multivalued attribute; OID: 2.16.840.1.113730.3.140)

- The Certificate Templates container contains the different certificate template definitions (as illustrated in Figure 8.11). The ACL set on these templates allows or disallows a user to enroll for a certain certificate type. Since their definition and ACL settings are part of the configuration NC, they can be defined only once, for the entire forest.

- The CA contains all the enterprise root CAs.

- The Enrollment Services container contains an entry for every CA that is a member of your Windows 2000 forest. Every CA's certificate templates attribute lists the templates that are loaded and made avail-

Figure 8.11
*Looking at the
content of the
Certificate
Templates
container using
adsiedit*

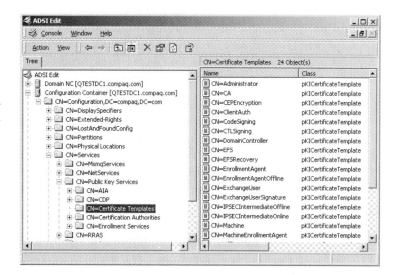

Figure 8.11
*Looking at the
content of the
Certificate
Templates
container using
adsiedit*

able to the end users. This attribute will be empty for standalone CAs, since they do not support certificate templates.

- The NTAuthTemplates object's CaCertificate attribute determines which CAs can issue smart-card logon and enrollment agent certificates.

To look at all CA-related AD entries in the configuration NC of your Windows 2000 forest, you can also use the certutil tool with the –v –ds switch; this will bring up the contents of the CAs, enrollment services, AIA, and CDP containers. All configuration NC PKI entries are also visible from the Public Key Services container in the sites and services MMC snap-in. This is the preferred location to set ACLs on certificate templates.

If a CA is removed from your Windows 2000 forest, the CA object in the Enrollment Services container will be removed; the other entries remain. This will make it impossible for PKI clients to request new certificates from the CA, while still giving them the ability to retrieve the CA's certificate and CRLs.

All standard Windows 2000 user certificates are stored in the AD in a user object's multivalued UserCertificate. Certificates are also published in the Global Catalog. When user certificates are stored in the Active Directory, keep in mind the impact this has on the size of the AD database. The average size of one certificate is about 1,200 bytes.

Another interesting sidenote: AD supports third-party CAs to publish their certificates using LDAP. This will only work if the appropriate user objects are already in place. Also, at the time of this writing, AD did not support LDAP referrals when writing attributes to AD. This means that to write a certificate to a user object that's not contained in the domain to which you're connected, you'll have to manually connect to a GC server in that particular user's domain. Remember that a domain's GC portion is read-only on the GC servers of any other AD domain.

To query the AD for user certificates you can use the Search…For People function available from the Windows 2000 start menu. The last tab of the user object properties is named digital IDs and contains all the user's AD-published certificates. The same interface can be used to export certificates to a file; afterwards you can import the certificate-file into your personal certificate store.

CryptoAPI and cryptographic service providers

The CryptoAPI is an Application Programming Interface (API), which enables programmers to add cryptography-based security services, such as authentication, confidentiality, and integrity, to their applications. It hides the implementation details of cryptographic algorithms to the programmer. The CryptoAPI is subdivided into two main levels, as follows:

- Level 1 provides the "real" cryptographic services to applications: it generates cryptographic keys, performs hashing, digital signing, and data encryption and decryption. It also interacts with the Cryptographic Service Providers (CSPs). CSPs are software libraries containing implementations of cryptographic algorithms and ciphers. The use of libraries creates a pluggable provider model. Third-party vendors can plug their proper CSP in the OS and provide their specific security services to applications. To embed a CSP into Windows it should be cryptographically signed by Microsoft. How to do this is described in the CSP Development Kit available from Microsoft. In Windows 2000 level 1 has been extended with new CSPs, implementing the DSA/DSS digital signature algorithm and the Diffie-Hellman key exchange protocol.

- Level 2 contains the CryptoAPI interface and as such processes the application messages passed through the CryptoAPI. Level 2 performs message encoding and decoding to and from the PKCS7, PKCS10, and ASN.1 message formats. In Windows 2000 level 2 has been extended with certificate management services to generate, manage, and validate certificates and to interact with the certificate stores.

The CryptoAPI is fully documented in the Windows 2000 platform SDK. Programmers can use CryptoAPI to develop customized CryptoAPI-based applications such as the following:

- Tools that set and retrieve private key properties (e.g., a tool to make the private key exportable).

- Tools to query user, machine, or service certificate stores and to retrieve the certificate properties.

CSPs can be implemented in both software and hardware. So far, two smart-card vendors' CSPs are included in the Windows 2000 product: the Gemplus and Schlumberger smart card CSPs. A hardware implementation of a CSP provides better security; it offers better tampering protection and detection mechanisms.

A CSP does more than just provide the implementation of a cryptographic cipher. CryptoAPI stores sensitive keys (session keys and private keys) into key databases embedded in the CSPs. The CSP key database contains a key container for each user, named after the user's logon name. The key containers are stored in the registry, on the file system or on a smart card. These containers can only be accessed through the CryptoAPI, by using the appropriate CryptoAPI functions.

CSPs located on different machines cannot communicate directly. It happens though that keys need to be exchanged between different CSPs. CryptoAPI allows sensitive keys to be exported from a CSP's key container and transported in a secure manner to another CSP (e.g., using the PKCS12 certificate and private key transport format). To do this, keys are encrypted with a symmetric key or with the public key of the destination user. These encrypted keys are known in Microsoft literature as key BLOBs.

Table 8.9 gives an overview of the CSPs that come preinstalled with Windows 2000.

Windows 2000 users who have the high encryption pack installed get another CSP: the Microsoft Enhanced Cryptographic Service Provider. The Enhanced CSP includes support for 56-bit DES, 3 DES (112-bit two-key and 168-bit three-key), 1,024-bit RSA, and 128-bit RC2 and RC4. The base CSP only supports 512-bit RSA and 40-bit RC2 and RC4. The high encryption pack for Windows 2000 can be downloaded from *http://windowsupdate.microsoft.com*. It also comes pre-embedded with Windows 2000 Service Pack 1.

Table 8.9   *Windows 2000 Cryptographic Service Providers (CSPs)*

CSP Name	Description
MS Base Cryptographic Provider v1.0	Base CSP
MS Base DSS Cryptographic Provider	Includes support for DSA and SHA
MS Base DSS and Diffie-Hellman Cryptographic Provider	Superset of previous row, includes support for the Diffie-Hellman key agreement protocol
MS Diffie-Hellman SChannel Cryptographic Provider	SChannel CSP
MS RSA SChannel Cryptographic Provider	SChannel CSP
MS Exchange Cryptographic Provider v1.0	Exchange-specific CSP
Gemplus GemSAFE Card CSP v1.0	Gemplus hardware CSP for smart-card support
Schlumberger Cryptographic Service Provider	Schlumberger hardware CSP for smart-card support

Key and certificate storage

As discussed previously, PKI and PKI-enabled applications rely on private keys and certificates containing public keys. In the PKI requirements listed previously in this chapter we mentioned the importance of secure private key and certificate storage, as follows:

- Private keys are personal keys, which should only be accessed and used by their owner. The secure storage of a user's private key is critical: It has an important impact on the amount of trust you have in the user's public key.

- Certificates are stored in an entity's personal certificate store. Some of the certificates in this store are implicitly considered trustworthy and can function as a trust anchor for cryptographic certificate validation. It is very important that access to the certificate store is controlled and authenticated. If anyone (including hackers) can put certificates in the store, a user could end up using fake certificates or certificates that are not trustworthy.

In the following text, we'll discuss in detail the Windows 2000 certificate store and protected store (used for secure private key storage).

Certificate stores

As mentioned previously, one of the CryptoAPI's tasks is certificate management. The Windows 2000 CryptoAPI provides tools (programmatic functions and procedures) to store, retrieve, delete, list, and verify certificates.

Certificates, together with CTLs and CRLs are stored in the Windows 2000 certificate store. Each Windows 2000 user, machine, and service has his or her certificate store.

The Windows 2000 certificate store is divided into two abstraction layers (as illustrated in Figure 8.12): the logical certificate store and the physical certificate store. The purpose of this architecture is to abstract physical certificate storage from logical certificate categories. A Windows 2000 PKI user shouldn't bother about where a certificate is stored physically but rather about what he or she can do with it. The Windows 2000 certificate store also provides ways to combine multiple physical stores into one logical store or, vice versa, to provide automatic content inheritance from one physical store to multiple logical stores.

Table 8.10 and Figure 8.12 show the different logical and physical stores available in Windows 2000. Table 8.10 also shows in which entity's certificate stores they are available: user, machine, or service entities. The names in parentheses in the first column are the registry names of the logical stores.

A user can look at the content of its certificate stores using the MMC certificates snap-in or the lightweight certificate viewer, which is accessible via the Internet Options/Content/Certificates menu in Internet Explorer. In the MMC snap-in the user can also see the physical stores: to do this select Options in the MMC View menu, and select the *Physical Certificate Stores* check box. To look at the user or machine certificate store from the command prompt you can use certutil (available only from the Windows

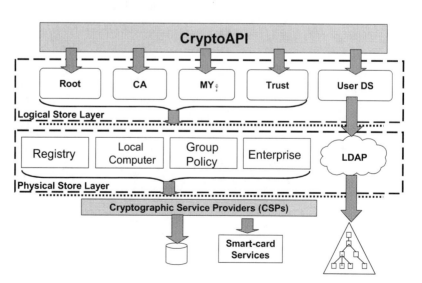

Figure 8.12
Physical and logical certificate stores

Table 8.10   *Logical and Physical Certificate Stores for User, Machine, and Service Principals*

Logical Store	Physical Store	User, Machine, Service
Personal (MY)	Registry	U, M, S
Trusted Root Certification Authorities (ROOT) (also known as the Root Store)	Registry	U, M, S
	Local Computer	U, S
	Enterprise	M
Enterprise Trust (TRUST)	Registry	U, M, S
	Group Policy	U, M
	Local Computer	U, S
	Enterprise	M
Intermediate Certification Authorities (CAs)	Registry	U, M, S
	Group Policy	U, M
	Local Computer	U, S
	Enterprise	M
Active Directory User Object (USERDS)	User Certificate	U
Other People	Registry	U, M
	Group Policy	U, M
	Local Computer	U
	Enterprise	M
Request (REQUEST)	Registry	U, M
	Group Policy	U, M
	Local Computer	U
	Enterprise	M
SPC	Registry	M
	Group Policy	M
	Enterprise	M

2000 Server CDs): use it with the –store switch to display the machine certificate store, with the –user –store switches to display the user certificate store, and replace –store with –verifystore if you want not only to list but also to verify the certificates in a store.

Windows 2000 archives expired or renewed certificates and their private keys. This enables a user to check the signature on an old document, even if the original certificate has expired or been renewed. To look at the archived certificates that are part of an entity's certificate store, select archived certificates in the view options of the MMC certificates snap-in. The same menu contains a check box to look at the certificates in an entity's certificate store, based on the purpose or application for which they can be used.

In the following text, we will look in more detail at the content of the physical and the logical certificate stores.

Logical certificate stores   Figure 8.13 shows the logical certificate stores as you view them from the certificates MMC snap-in. Let's run through all of them and look at their content:

- The Personal store contains the certificates, CRLs, and CTLs that are stored in a user's profile. Certificates in this folder also have their corresponding private key stored in the user portion of the system registry. The user portion of the registry is also a part of the user's profile. You can look at the personal certificate files in the Documents and Settings\<*username*>\ApplicationData\Microsoft\SystemCertificates\My file system folder.

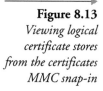

Figure 8.13
Viewing logical certificate stores from the certificates MMC snap-in

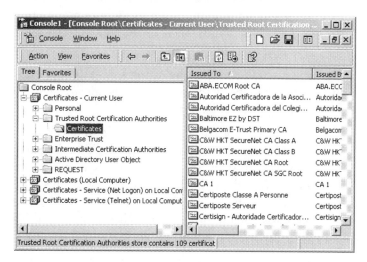

- Trusted Root Certification Authorities contains by definition only self-signed root CA certificates; in practice, also nonroot CA certificates can be added to this store. They can be internal as well as external CA certificates. The main characteristic of the CA certificates in this store is that they are regarded as trust anchors.

- Enterprise Trust contains CTLs; CTLs are signed lists containing CA certificates, which are downloaded to a Windows 2000 client using GPOs. The CA certificates part of a CTL are considered trust anchors if the CTL signing certificate is valid.

- Intermediate Certification Authorities contains root or intermediate CA certificates and CRLs. The CAs can be internal Windows 2000 CAs as well as CAs external to the company. The certificates in the Trusted Root Certification Authorities store are not trust anchors. If they are marked as trustworthy, this is because their certificate chain contains the certificate of a trustworthy CA certificate that's part of one of the two previous containers.

- The Active Directory User Object container holds user certificates that are published in the Active Directory as part of a user's user certificate property. This store only exists for user accounts; it does not exist for machine or service accounts.

- The Other People folder contains other people's certificates; certificates that don't have their corresponding private key stored in the profile of the user who is logged on.

- The Request folder contains certificate request files. These files are created when a user is requesting a certificate to a standalone Windows 2000 CA or when an enterprise CA goes offline during certificate enrollment.

- The SPC container holds software publisher certificates, certificates that can be used to verify authenticode signed code downloaded using Internet Explorer.

A very important logical certificate store is the Trusted Root Certification Authorities container. Certificates that are part of this container are considered trust anchors, a critical element in the certificate validation process. During the validation process every certificate's certificate chain must validate to a trust anchor in order for the certificate to be accepted by the Windows 2000 security system. The content of the Trusted Root Certification Authorities container results from the following different actions:

- Distributed via the Trusted Root CAs GPO setting.

- Installed out of the box with the Windows 2000 software; Windows 2000 comes with a list of more than 100 preloaded CA certificates. Remember that this is a negative point. By embedding root CA certificates in the software Microsoft creates an implicit trust.

- Added to the machine store by the local machine administrator.

- Added via the AD as the result of an enterprise or root domain administrator installing a CA in the Windows 2000 forest or as the result of an enterprise or root domain administrator adding a CA to AD manually using the dsstore resource kit tool (using the –addroot switch).

Knowing all this you can perform the following operations on the level of the MMC certificates snap-in to move certificates around between logical certificate stores, as follows:

- Publish user certificates to the Active Directory. The MMC certificates snap-in has built-in drag-and-drop functionalities. To publish one of your certificates to AD, simply pull it to the Active Directory User Object container. Doing this will strip off the friendly name attribute of your certificates. This attribute is only available on the file system level.

- Trust or untrust CA certificates. To untrust a CA certificate, simply cut it out of the Trusted Root Certification Authorities container and paste it into the Intermediate Certification Authorities container. From a security point of view it's best to move all CA entries, which Microsoft puts by default in this container, from the Trusted Root CAs to the Intermediate CAs container, unless you implicitly trust Microsoft-embedded trustworthy trust anchors in your software.

Physical certificate stores   Figure 8.14 shows the physical certificate stores as you view them from the certificates MMC snap-in. Let's run through all of them and look at their content:

- The Registry (.default) store is an entity's personal certificate, CRL, and CTL store. For a user it is part of the user portion of the system registry, which is part of the user's profile. The Registry store contains both certificates that have their corresponding private key stored in the user profile and others that haven't. The Trusted Root Certification Authorities subpart of this store on the user level is also known as the user's root store. All certificates in this store are trust anchors. Because certificates (and private keys) are stored in the profile, they can be made accessible from any computer the user logs on to—on

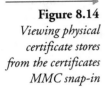

Figure 8.14
*Viewing physical
certificate stores
from the certificates
MMC snap-in*

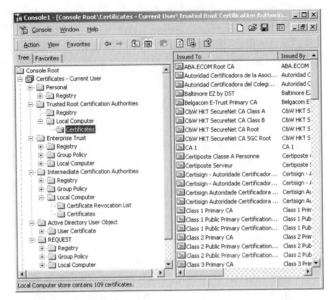

the condition that your environment supports roaming profiles stored on a central server. Looking in a user's profile you'll notice that certificates are stored in the My\Certificates container (Documents and Settings\<usename>\ApplicationData\Microsoft\SystemCertificates\My\Certificates).

■ The Local Computer (.localmachine) store is the local machine's certificate, CRL, and CTL store; it is part of the all users user profile. You might have noticed in Table 8.10 that user and service accounts have a physical local computer store for most of the logical stores. This is a very nice feature, since it removes unnecessary duplication of certificates, CRLs, and CTLs. For example, external root CA certificates shouldn't be stored in every store. Windows 2000 stores them once in the machine certificate store, and puts a pointer to this store in every other user and service certificate store that's logging on to that machine. The content of the local computer certificate store is stored twice: in the all users user profile and in the HKEY_LOCAL_MACHINE registry hive. You can find it at the following locations:

  ▪ For the file system: \Documents And Settings\All Users\Application Data\Microsoft\RSA\MachineKeys.

  ▪ For the registry: HKLM\software\Microsoft\systemcertificates\my. Notice in this folder that the subfolder root contains the certificates of all trusted root CAs (HKLM\software\ms\system-certificates\root) and that the subfolder ca contains the certificates of all intermediate CAs (HKLM\software\ms\systemcertificates\ca).

- The Group Policy (.grouppolicy) store contains the certificates (Trusted Root Certification Authorities) and CTLs that are distributed via GPO settings (more information on these settings can be found in Chapter 9). GPO certificate and CTL content are not automatically merged with the user and computer certificate stores; they are stored in a separate registry area, as follows:

  - HKLM\software\policies\Microsoft\systemcertificates (for machine certificates)
  - HKCU\software\policies\Microsoft\usercertificates (for user certificates)

- The User Certificate (.usercertificate) contains the user certificates that are published in a user's user certificate Active Directory attribute.

- The Enterprise container contains the certificates of root CAs that are stored in the Active Directory configuration NC. These certificates are set when an enterprise administrator installs a root CA in the Windows 2000 forest. They are physically stored in the Active Directory and in the registry, as follows:

  - For the Active Directory: CN = Certification Authority, CN = Public Key Services and CN = NTAuthTemplates
  - For the registry: HKLM\software\Microsoft\enterprisecertificates\ntauth and HKLM\software\Microsoft\enterprisecertificates\root

Table 8.11 shows where the physical stores' content is originally located, where it is stored on the client side, and when it is copied from its original location to the client certificate store.

Knowing all this you can perform the following operation on the level of the MMC certificates snap-in. You can make a CA certificate available to every user logging on to the machine. To do this, drag the certificate from the registry to the local computer Trusted Root Certification Authorities store. Doing this on the user level (remember, the Trusted Root Certification Authorities container is the user's root store) will bring up a dialog box requesting whether you want to add or delete a certificate from the root store.

Table 8.11   *Physical Store Details*

Physical Store	Original Location	Physical Location on PKI Client Side	Copied When?
Registry	NA	User: File system (profile): Documents and Settings\<user-name>\ApplicationData\Microsoft\SystemCertificates\My\Certificates	NA
		Machine, Service: see (1) (Local Computer, below)	
Local Computer (1)	Machine Registry	Machine Registry: HKLM\software\Microsoft\systemcertificates\my	Log on from computer
		File System (profile): \Documents And Settings\All Users\Application Data\Microsoft\RSA\MachineKeys	
Group Policy	SYSVOL and AD	Machine Registry: HKLM\software\policies\Microsoft\systemcertificates	GPO application event
		User Registry: HKCU\software\policies\Microsoft\usercertificates	
User Certificate	NA*	NA	Certificate enrollment event
Enterprise	AD configuration NC: CN = Certification Authority, CN = Public Key Services and CN = NTAuthTemplates, CN = Public Key Services	Machine Regisrty: HKLM\software\Microsoft\enterprisecertificates	Auto enrollment event

*The client certificate store contains an LDAP pointer to certificates stored in AD.

Protected store

User private keys are, similar to certificates, stored in the user's profile. This is not true if smart cards are used and the smart-card vendor provided a smart card–specific CSP. In this case private keys are not stored in the profile but on the card, which is, of course, much more secure. The private keys are stored in the subdirectory Application Data\Microsoft\Crypto\RSA. Unlike certificates, which are public, private keys should remain confidential.

In Windows 2000, private keys are protected by a user's master key. The master key is a random symmetric key, which is generated automatically and renewed periodically. The master key is generated using the RC4 algorithm. RC4 will generate a 128-bit master key if the Enhanced CSP is available and a 56-bit master key if only the Base CSP is available. The master key is stored encrypted in the protect folder of a user's profile (Path: Application Data\Microsoft\Protect\<UserSID>). The user's profile protect folder is created the first time a user generates a private–public key pair. The system service that encrypts and decrypts a user's master key is the protected storage service. Windows 98 and Windows 2000 install the protected store service as a part of the operating system (in earlier versions it was installed with Internet Explorer 4). The information about the protected store that Microsoft has released to the public has always been, for security reasons, very scarce. In the next version of Windows, Windows.NET, Microsoft will embed a brand-new protected store service.

To store the master key securely, the protected storage service performs the following cryptographic operations on the master key:

- It encrypts the master key, the user's SID, and the user's logon password using RC4. The result of this operation is then hashed using HMAC-SHA1 and stored in the protect folder.

- To enable the protected storage service to access the user's master key in case the user's password has changed, the service encrypts and hashes the master key a second time using the following steps. It encrypts the user's master key using RC4. The result of this operation is then hashed together with the DC's master key using HMAC-SHA1 and stored in the protect folder. You can look at this as a type of backup for the master key. To generate the second encryption the user's symmetric master key is sent across secure RPC to the DC. A DC's master key is stored in the registry HKEY_LOCAL_MACHINE/ SAM folder.

An extra level of protection for the master key (remember the principle of defense in depth) can be added by configuring a Windows 2000 system key. The system key provides another level of master key encryption; the system key can be stored on a floppy disk, hard disk, or simply derived from a password. The configuration of the system key was explained in Chapter 6.

Two private key properties that impact the key's security level are whether the key is exportable and whether it has strong private key protection enabled.

To enable all-time data recovery and to protect against cracking attacks, private keys used for recovery of encrypted data should be backed up or exported from the Windows 2000 system and stored on some other secure medium. To make the private key exportable the user should check *Mark keys as exportable* in the Advanced Certificate Request options on the Web enrollment pages. This option is only available if the certificate will be used for key exchange only. A key can also be made exportable programmatically, by setting the CRYPT_EXPORTABLE property. How to do this is explained in detail in the platform SDK. If you want more than just backup and you really want to delete the local private key (to protect against cracking attacks), don't forget to check the option to delete the private key if the export succeeds.

Private key exportability is a predefined property, which is set in the certificate templates used when requesting certificates to an enterprise CA. The private keys of certificates for user signature, user, CTL signing, smart-card user, smart-card logon, enrollment agent, code signing, client authentication, and administrator are by default marked as nonexportable. Windows 2000 private signing keys are always marked as nonexportable. Signing keys should never be copied or stored on a medium different from the one that was used to store the private key when it was generated. This could be a serious security risk: a malicious person could export another person's private key and impersonate him or her. The private keys of EFS and EFS recovery certificates are by default exportable, for obvious data recovery reasons.

In both the Web enrollment pages and the certificate request wizard a user can choose to enable strong private key protection. This feature has been available from NT4 Service Pack 4 and Internet Explorer version 5 onward. This means that the user will be prompted every time the private key is used by an application. Two levels of strong private key protection can be set: high and medium (this is the default). High means that the user will, besides being prompted, also be asked to enter a password. The password is used by the protected storage service to add another security level for private key storage.

Private keys for which this property should be set are the ones that are linked to EFS recovery, smart-card enrollment agent, code signing, and

CTL signing certificates. Compromise and misuse of these private keys would damage your complete corporate PKI environment.

8.2.3 Windows 2000 certificates and their life cycle

In this section we will focus on the certificates that are generated by the Windows 2000 CAs and their life cycle. What types of certificates can be generated by a Windows 2000 CA? How is a Windows 2000 certificate validated? How does Windows 2000 handle certificate revocation and revocation checking?

Windows 2000 certificate types

To deal with different certificate types Microsoft has chosen to implement a flexible and modular architecture. The uses of a certificate are defined, together with many other characteristics, in certificate templates. A certificate template defines the certificate characteristics shown in Table 8.12.

The definition of the templates is stored in the registry of servers hosting a Windows 2000 CA (HKLM\Software\Microsoft\Cryptography\template-cache) and in the Active Directory configuration NC (cn = certificate templates, cn = public key services, cn = services, cn = configuration). A subset

Table 8.12 *Certificate Template Attributes*

Registry Value	AD Object Attribute	Meaning
CriticalExtensions	pKICriticalExtensions	X.509 extensions that are marked as critical
SupportedCSPs	pKIDefaultCSPs	The CSPs that can be used to generate and manage the certificate
Security	pKIEnrollmentAccess	ACL on the certificate template determining who can enroll for this certificate type
ValidityPeriod	pKIExpirationPeriod	Default certificate lifetime
ExtKeyUsageSyntax	pKIExtendedKeyUsage	Definition of extended key usage field (based on OIDs)
KeyUsage	pKIKeyUsage	Definition of key usage: signature, exchange, or both
Pathlen	pKIMaxIssuingDepth	For subordinate CAs only: length of certificate chain
RenewalOverlap	pKIOverlapPeriod	Determines when to start renewal procedure (before expiration) for autoenrollment machine certificates

of a certificate template's definition is displayed in the MMC certification authority snap-in: right-click a template and select properties.

Certificate templates can be used for two things: to set which users can request which type of certificate and to define the CA issuing policy, as follows:

- Certificate templates can be used to define the issuing policy of an enterprise CA; in other words, to define what certificate types a CA can issue. You can load and unload them to and from a CA's supported certificates container to enable/disable the CA to issue certain certificate types. Templates cannot be used when dealing with a standalone CA.

- On the Windows 2000 forest level certificate templates can be used to define which users can request which certificate types. Certificate templates are normal AD objects: You can set a certificate template's ACLs to define which users can enroll for them. To set the ACLs you can use the AD sites and services snap-in: All templates are available from the certificate templates container in the Public Key Services container.

Table 8.13 lists the certificate templates supported in Windows 2000. For every template it lists the supported applications (or purposes). It shows also the corresponding OID for every purpose. An OID, or object identifier, is a unique identifier for an object in the X.500 namespace.

Table 8.13   *Windows 2000 Certificate Templates*

Template Name	Meaning	Supported OIDs
Administrator	Code Signing	1.3.6.1.5.5.7.3.3
	MS Trust List Signing	1.3.6.1.4.1.311.10.3.1
	Encrypting File System	1.3.6.1.4.1.311.10.3.4
	Secure e-mail	1.3.6.1.5.5.7.3.4
	Client Authentication	1.3.6.1.5.5.7.3.2
CA	Certification Authority	
CEPEncryption	Certificate Request Agent	1.3.6.1.4.1.311.20.2.1
ClientAuth (Authenticated Session)	Client Authentication	1.3.6.1.5.5.7.3.2
CodeSigning	Code Signing	1.3.6.1.5.5.7.3.3

Table 8.13 *Windows 2000 Certificate Templates (continued)*

Template Name	Meaning	Supported OIDs
CTLSigning	MS Trust List Signing	1.3.6.1.4.1.311.10.3.1
DomainController	Client Authentication	1.3.6.1.5.5.7.3.2
	Server Authentication	1.3.6.1.5.5.7.3.1
EFS	Encrypting File System	1.3.6.1.4.1.311.10.3.4
EFSRecovery	File Recovery	1.3.6.1.4.1.311.10.3.4.1
EnrollmentAgent	Certificate Request Agent	1.3.6.1.4.1.311.20.2.1
EnrollmentAgentOffline	Certificate Request Agent	1.3.6.1.4.1.311.20.2.1
ExchangeUser	Secure e-mail	1.3.6.1.5.5.7.3.4
	Client Authentication	1.3.6.1.5.5.7.3.2
ExchangeUserSignature	Secure e-mail	1.3.6.1.5.5.7.3.4
	Client Authentication	1.3.6.1.5.5.7.3.2
IPSECIntermediateOnline	IPsec tunnel endpoint authentication	1.3.6.1.5.5.8.2.2
IPSECIntermediateOffline	IPsec tunnel endpoint authentication	1.3.6.1.5.5.8.2.2
Machine	Client Authentication	1.3.6.1.5.5.7.3.2
	Server Authentication	1.3.6.1.5.5.7.3.1
MachineEnrollmentAgent	Certificate Request Agent	1.3.6.1.4.1.311.20.2.1
OfflineRouter	Client Authentication	1.3.6.1.5.5.7.3.2
SmartCardLogon	Client Authentication	1.3.6.1.5.5.7.3.2
	Smart-Card Logon	1.3.6.1.4.1.311.20.2.2
SmartCardUser	Secure e-mail	1.3.6.1.5.5.7.3.4
	Client Authentication	1.3.6.1.5.5.7.3.2
	Smart Card Logon	1.3.6.1.4.1.311.20.2.2
SubCA	Subordinate Certification Authority	
Time Stamping	Time Stamping	
User	Encrypting File System	1.3.6.1.4.1.311.10.3.4
	Secure e-mail	1.3.6.1.5.5.7.3.4
	Client Authentication	1.3.6.1.5.5.7.3.2
UserSignature	Secure e-mail	1.3.6.1.5.5.7.3.4
	Client Authentication	1.3.6.1.5.5.7.3.2
WebServer	Server Authentication	1.3.6.1.5.5.7.3.1

The certificate templates that are designated as offline (see Table 8.13) are certificates for which the CA will not retrieve any user information from the Active Directory at certificate request time. This means that the requester has to provide the necessary information. Offline templates are mainly used for non–Windows 2000 PKI clients, such as non-Microsoft IPsec clients or nonAD integrated Web servers, that don't have an object entry in the AD. The template for a subordinate CA is also an offline template, because the administrator has to enter specific sub-CA information at installation time.

Table 8.13 shows the Windows 2000 support for both single-use and multiple-use certificates (or single- and multiple-purpose certificates, as Microsoft calls them). Windows 2000 PKI users can choose for which applications they will trust a multiple-use certificate; to do this a user should edit the properties of the certificate.

The Windows 2000 certificate life cycle

The life of a certificate can be subdivided into three phases, in which different processes can occur. The phases are: start, issued, and end. Table 8.14 lists the processes that are linked to every phase and the way the processes can be initiated: automatically or manually. The complete certificate life cycle is illustrated in Figure 8.15.

Table 8.14 also shows the characteristics of the Windows 2000 PKI product and of more advanced non-Microsoft PKI products supporting "managed PKI." Good examples of managed PKIs are the PKI software from Entrust and Baltimore.

Figure 8.15
*The Windows
2000 certificate
life cycle*

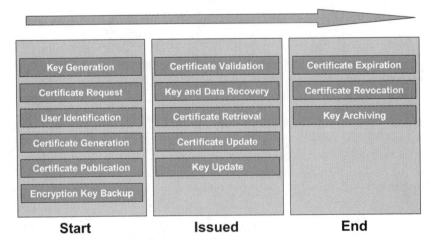

Start	Issued	End
Key Generation	Certificate Validation	Certificate Expiration
Certificate Request	Key and Data Recovery	Certificate Revocation
User Identification	Certificate Retrieval	Key Archiving
Certificate Generation	Certificate Update	
Certificate Publication	Key Update	
Encryption Key Backup		

Table 8.14   *Certificate Life Cycle in a Windows 2000 and a Managed PKI*

		Windows 2000 PKI	Managed PKI
Start	Key generation	Automatic	Automatic
	Certificate request	Automatic/Manual	Automatic/Manual
	User identification	Automatic/Manual	Automatic/Manual
	Certificate generation	Automatic	Automatic
	Certificate publishing	Automatic	Automatic
	Encryption key backup	Manual	Automatic
Issued	Certificate validation	Automatic	Automatic
	Key and data recovery	Manual	Manual
	Certificate retrieval	Automatic/Manual	Automatic/Manual
	Key update	Manual	Automatic
	Certificate update	Automatic/Manual	Automatic
End	Certificate revocation	Manual	Manual
	Certificate expiry	Automatic	Automatic
	Key archiving	Manual	Automatic

The automation of the certificate life cycle is very important from an end-user and management ease of use point of view. This is the main advantage of a managed PKI solution: Most processes are automated. The Windows 2000 PKI comes with a lot more automation than its predecessor, NT4 PKI. We will run through all the processes in the following text.

Certificate enrollment

Certificate enrollment enables a user, machine, or service to participate in PKI-enabled applications or processes. Certificate enrollment consists of a cycle of events: key generation, certificate request, identification, certificate generation, publishing, and encryption key backup.

Certificate enrollment can be started manually by a user account or an administrator account. In some applications it requires an initiative of both the user and the administrator account. A good example of this is Exchange's secure mail enrollment model. In Exchange 5.5 and Exchange 2000 the administrator enables a user to enroll for certificates by creating a kind of authorization code and sending it to the user; the user then can use the code to enroll for certificates.

Normally the user (be it a user, machine, or service account) of the certificate initiates enrollment. In Windows 2000 there's one exception to this rule: smart-card enrollment. In this enrollment model an administrator with a special certificate is allowed to enroll for a certificate on a user's behalf and load it on the user's smart card. We will discuss smart-card enrollment in Chapter 9.

Before a user can enroll for a certificate from a Windows 2000 Enterprise CA, the following conditions must be met: the user must have enroll permission on the Enterprise CA level; the appropriate permissions on the certificate template (enroll and read), and the right certificate template should be loaded on the CA. For a Windows 2000 standalone CA only enroll permission is required.

Enrollment can also be initiated automatically, but only for machine accounts (this is known as autoenrollment). Some examples of automated machine enrollment, are as follows:

- Every Windows 2000 DC automatically gets a DC certificate when the machine joins a domain in which an enterprise certification authority is defined.

- An administrator can set a GPO setting that automatically enrolls a number of machines for an IPsec or SSL certificate. The actual enrollment is initiated when the autoenrollment event occurs on the machine.

In the following text, we will look at the key elements of certificate enrollment, as follows:

- Enrollment interfaces

- Key and certificate request generation

- Requester identification

- Certificate generation, distribution, and publication

Enrollment interfaces   Windows 2000 comes with three certificate enrollment interfaces, as follows:

- Web interface. To enroll for certificates from an enterprise or a standalone CA using a Web browser, the user has to go to the URL: *http://<CAservername>/certsrv/*.

- GUI interface. A user can enroll for certificates from an enterprise CA using the certificate request wizard, available from the MMC certificates snap-in.

- Command prompt interface. A user can enroll for certificates from an enterprise CA using the command prompt utility certreq; the syntax is CertReq [-rpc] [-binary] [-config ConfigString] [-attrib AttributeString][RequestFile [Certfile[CertChainFile]]].

Both the Web interface and the MMC snap-in are intermediaries. Intermediaries were discussed earlier in the chapter.

Table 8.15 lists the key differences between the two main enrollment interfaces: the Web interface and the GUI interface. The identification protocols mentioned in the table are addressed in more detail in the following text.

The Web interface is made available through the certificate services Web enrollment support, an option that's selected by default when installing a CA. Its only installation requirement is a functioning IIS Web server. The Web server will host the Certsrv virtual directory and application, as well as the Certcontrol and CertEnroll virtual directories; these are all created during the Web interface installation process. The CA web interface is accessible via *http://<servername>/certsrv.*

Table 8.15 *Certificate Enrollment Interfaces Characteristics*

	Web Interface	GUI Interface (Certificate Request Wizard)
Communication protocols	Between client and CA Web site: HTTP Between CA Web site and CA: DCOM RPC	Between client and CA: DCOM RPC
Authentication protocols	※ Anonymous Access (default for standalone CA) ※ Basic Authentication (default for enterprise CA) ※ Digest Authentication ※ Integrated Windows Authentication* (default for enterprise CA)	NTLM Kerberos
Available for which CA types	Standalone and Enterprise CA	Enterprise CA only

*Integrated Windows authentication includes support for three Authentication Security Support Providers (SSPs): Negotiate, Kerberos, and NTLM.

The CA that the Web interface is communicating with shouldn't necessarily be on the same machine as the interface itself: when installing the Web interface on a server that doesn't have a CA installed, the installation program will prompt you for a CA server, which the interface has to point to. This also means you can deploy multiple CA Web interfaces on the same or on a different machine pointing to the same Certificate Server. This can give you an elegant way to deal with, for example, the different language requirements of your PKI clients. Just deploy one Web interface per language you need to support.

The CA Web interface is built on ASP pages, which detect the client's browser type. If these pages detect Internet Explorer, they will use the Certificate Enrollment Control (CEC) and its ActiveX controls. If it detects a Netscape browser, it will generate Netscape-specific pages. Netscape uses a special HTML tag, the keygen tag, for the generation of key material and the submission of the public key as part of an HTML form. More information on this tag can be found at *http://developer.netscape.com/docs/manuals/ htmlguid/tags10.htm#1615503*.

Table 8.16 shows the certificate enrollment choices that are available from the Web interface. Some slight differences exist between the Web interface for a standalone and an enterprise CA. The Web certificate enrollment interface gives far more choices to the user than the certificate enrollment wizard. Using the wizard you can choose the certificate template, the CSP, and whether you want strong private key protection. It also allows you to select the CA and give a friendly name and a description to your certificate (things that cannot be done using the Web interface).

In case your organization has special requirements, Windows 2000 makes it relatively easy for a developer to modify existing or develop custom certificate request interfaces. Windows 2000 comes with two reusable software modules, which can be called from any customized certificate enrollment application. These modules are ActiveX controls and are called the Certificate Enrollment Control (CEC) and the Smart-card Enrollment Control (SEC).

Both controls are located in the %windir%\system32\certsrv\certcontrol\x86 directory on the server side and in the %windir%\system32 directory on the client side. A client-side copy of the controls is needed to enable the control to write to the local certificate stores. In case they are not available locally, the Web enrollment interface will download them. If this doesn't work, they can be downloaded manually (given that the user has sufficient permissions) and registered using regsvr32.exe. The CEC and SEC are extensively documented in the Windows 2000 security platform SDK.

Table 8.16   *Windows 2000 CA Web Interface Options*

Windows Windows 2000 CA Web Interface Options	Remarks
1. Retrieve the CA certificate or certificate revocation list	
1.1. Install this CA certification path	
1.2. Choose file to download (DER or Base64 encoded)	
1.2.1. CA certificate	
1.2.2. CA certification path	*.cer format
1.2.3. Latest CRL	*.p7b format
	*.crl format
2. Request a certificate	
2.1. User certificate request	Standalone CA:
2.1.1. Standalone CA: Web browser or e-mail protection; enterprise CA: User certificate	Fill in name, e-mail, company, dep, city, stat, country (all filled in except for name and e-mail)
	Enterprise CA:
	Data retrieved automatically from AD
2.1.2. More options	
2.1.2.1. CSP + enable strong private key protection	
2.2. Advanced request	
2.2.1. Submit a cert request to this CA using a form	Standalone CA:
	Fill in name, e-mail, company, dep, city, stat, country (all filled in except for name and e-mail)
	Enterprise CA:
	Data retrieved automatically from AD
2.2.1.1. Certificate template (enterprise CA only)	
2.2.1.2. Intended purpose (standalone CA only)	client authentication . . . other (given OID)
2.2.1.3. Key options	
2.2.1.3.1. CSP	
2.2.1.3.2. Key usage (Exchange, signature, both)	Exchange: symmetric key exchange only
2.2.1.3.3. Key size	Signature: signing only
2.2.1.3.4. Create new key set and set container name	
2.2.1.3.5. Use existing key set and container name	
2.2.1.3.6. Enable strong private key protection	
2.2.1.3.7. Mark keys as exportable	Impossible for digital signature private keys
2.2.1.3.8. Use local machine store	Store certificate in local machine certificate store (needs local administrator rights)

Table 8.16   *Windows 2000 CA Web Interface Options (continued)*

Windows Windows 2000 CA Web Interface Options	Remarks
2.2.1.4. Additional options	
2.2.1.4.1. Hash algorithm	
2.2.1.4.2. Save request to PKCS10 file	
2.2.2. Submit a cert request using Base64 PKCS10 or renewal request using Base64 PKCS7	
2.2.2.1. Base64 encoded request (PKCS10 or PKCS7)	
2.2.2.2. Additional attributes	
2.2.3. Request a certificate for a smart card on behalf of another user using the smart-card enrollment station	Enterprise CA only
2.2.3.1. Certificate template	Enterprise CA only
2.2.3.2. CA	
2.2.3.3. CSP	
2.2.3.4. Admin signing certificate	
2.2.3.5. User to enroll	
3. Check on a pending certificate	Standalone CA only

The SEC ActiveX control (scrdenrl.dll) enables an administrator who has an enrollment agent certificate to request certificates on behalf of other users and to store them on a smart card.

The CEC ActiveX control (xenroll.dll) can be looked at as a kind of PKCS10-PKCS7 gateway sitting between an application and the CA. The first version of the CEC shipped with the NT4 option pack; Windows 2000 comes with a newer version. The CEC does the following:

- It accepts certificate requests in binary string format, coming from an application.

- It generates a key pair.

- It puts the public key and other user data in a standardized PKCS10 message (this message is signed with the newly generated private key).

- It links the newly generated key pair to a dummy certificate, which is stored in the request folder of the requester's certificate store;

- It sends the PKCS10 certificate request message to the CA.

When the application gets back a PKCS7 message from the CA, it will send it to the CEC. The CEC will then pull the certificate or certificate chain from the PKCS7 message and store the certificate or certificate chain in the appropriate certificate store.

Both the Web enrollment interface and the certificate request wizard, discussed previously, reuse the CEC.

Key and certificate request generation   Certificate enrollment starts with key generation. Key generation generates a private and public key. Once generated the private key is stored in a secure place (a secure file system location or, in the best case, a smart card). The public key is prepared for certification. In Windows 2000 the tasks of key generation, secure private key storage, and preparation of the public key for a certificate request are all performed by the CEC (xenroll.dll).

Most PKI-enabled applications use a single key pair; some use a dual key pair or even a triple key pair. Most secure mail applications providing key recovery use a dual key pair. The reason for doing this is to enable support for both encryption key recovery and nonrepudiation services. Both services have different requirements. Nonrepudiation and digital signatures require that access and use of the signing private key are strictly limited to one user. Key recovery requires the private decryption key to be archived in some centralized database. In most cases the key pair is generated on the client side; in secure mail applications the encryption key pair is generated on the server side. In a triple key pair model, one pair is used to identify a user, one pair is used for digital signatures, and another is used for data encryption. This model is used in the digital signature and smart-card standards created by the Swedish government.

Recall that the public key is prepared for certification. This typically means that the public key is embedded in a certificate request. Such a request contains not only the public key but also the identity of the requester, the publication location (certificate store), and some typical request attributes dependent on the CA to which the request is sent. A commonly used certificate request format is defined in PKCS10.

Windows 2000 supports PKCS10 and also the Simple Certificate Enrollment Protocol (SCEP). SCEP is a protocol developed by Verisign and Cisco. So far, only Cisco network devices are SCEP-enabled. A Cisco router for example can enroll for an IPsec certificate with a Windows 2000 CA using SCEP. To enable a Windows 2000 CA to support SCEP install the mscep.dll shipping with the Windows 2000 resource kit. A detailed procedure on how to set this up is also available from the resource kit.

To view the content of a Windows 2000 certificate request look at the contents of the request certificate container in a user's certificate store

Figure 8.16
*Content of a
certificate request*

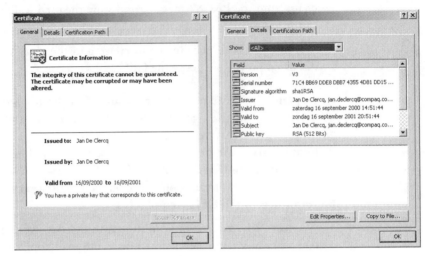

(accessible via the MMC certificates snap-in; see Figure 8.16). Note that the General tab of the certificate request properties shows an integrity error. Requests sent to a standalone CA are by default saved in this container, as well as any failed requests to an Enterprise CA.

Requestor identification   Before the certificate is actually generated by the CA, the CA will validate the certificate request (this includes the validation of the request format) and identify the requesting user. Identification is an often-forgotten, critical step of certificate enrollment. Identification means that the CA will check whether the entity requesting the certificate is really the one that's mentioned in the request message and whether the same entity possesses the private key corresponding to the public key.

In Windows 2000 the identification method depends on the enrollment interface and on the type of CA used. When enrolling using the certificate enrollment wizard, an enterprise CA authenticates users using the Kerberos protocol or NTLM if a Kerberos KDC is not available. The authentication protocol used when enrolling through the Web interface depends on the CA type: a standalone CA is by default using anonymous access, while an enterprise CA is by default using basic and integrated Windows authentication.

In the case of the Web interface, authentication settings can, of course, be changed on the level of the certsrv Web page in the Internet services manager MMC snap-in. If both basic and integrated Windows together with digest authentication are selected, the order of priority is the following: integrated Windows authentication, basic authentication, and digest authentication. If also anonymous access is selected, the previous authentication methods are only selected if the NTFS access control settings are set on the level of the Certificate Server Web site's resources. Although it's not a good idea to use anonymous access to identify a certificate request, this is a case where you might need to change the ACL settings on the CA object (who has enroll permission?) and on the certificate templates (in the case of enterpise CA: who can get which certificate types?). Anonymous access uses the IUSR_<servername> ID to request a certificate.

When the Web enrollment pages are located on a computer other than the CA computer, we're dealing with a multitier application, where authentication happens on two levels: between the browser and the Web server and between the Web server and the CA server. In this case you also need to keep in mind the following:

- Using Kerberos on both authentication levels works only if the computer (hosting the Web enrollment pages) is trusted for delegation and if all computers involved are Windows 2000 computers.

- Using NTLM on both authentication levels will never work, since NTLM doesn't support delegation of authentication.

Certificate generation, distribution, and publication During certificate generation the CA will sign the certificate content using its private key. The data contained in the certificate are those the CA received with the client's certificate request. In the case of an enterprise CA some of the requester's data are found in the Active Directory. Some certificate parameters, such as some Windows 2000–specific certificate extensions and the certificate lifetime, are not received from the client but enforced by the CA itself.

A nice feature related to the certificate lifetime is the following: to prevent orphaned certificates, a Windows 2000 CA will never issue certificates whose lifetimes extend beyond the CA's certificate lifetime. If this weren't the case, the certificates would automatically be invalidated, since they could never be related to a valid CA certificate. An example of this feature. If a request is sent to create a certificate with a two-year lifetime, and CA's certificate is about to expire in one year, the CA generates a certificate with a lifetime slightly shorter than one year.

Once generated the certificate can be distributed and published. Most PKI systems publish the certificate in a directory. In Windows 2000, enterprise CAs publish some certificate types into the Active Directory. To publish certificates to additional locations (e.g., other LDAP directories or web sites) you should develop custom exit modules, which can be plugged into the Windows 2000 CA architecture. If you want to do this, remember that no matter which exit modules are installed, certificates will not be published unless the publication location is specified in the certificate request.

To distribute the certificate back to the user a Windows 2000 enterprise CA sends a copy to the user using the PKCS7 message format. Certificates that are returned from the CA are by default installed in the user's certificate store. When requesting a certificate from the Web enrollment pages, the user can set an option to store the returned certificate in the local machine's certificate store. This way the certificate becomes available to any user logging on to the system. A standalone CA stores the newly generated certificate on the CA's Web site, from where it can be retrieved by the user.

Another interesting detail regarding certificate publication is the following: the machine account of the server hosting the CA should be a member of the cert publishers global group. Members of this group are the only ones that can write certificates to the user certificate attribute of user objects, defined in a particular domain NC. This is good to know when troubleshooting certificate publication problems between parent and child domains, where an enterprise CA, located on a server in the parent domain, needs to publish certificates belonging to user objects defined in the child domain. The problem is that by default the machine account of the CA server will not be a member of the cert publishers group in the child domain. You can do three things to resolve this problem: add the server's account to the cert publishers group, switch to native mode and make cert publishers a universal group, or add the machine account of the CA server to the ACL of every user object in the child domain.

Key backup, recovery, and archiving   So far, Windows 2000 doesn't come with a general key backup utility integrated with certificate enrollment. The secure mail enrollment model used by Exchange 5.5 and Exchange 2000 does provide encryption key backup at enrollment. In Exchange, the Key Management Server (KMS) copies the newly-generated private encryption key and certificate into a centralized database. This enables two things: decryption of encrypted mail after a user has left the company and recovery of the user's keys and certificates in case he or she loses the primary copy (stored on a local hard disk or on a smart card) of the keys and certificates.

Encryption key backup is a requirement in most PKI-enabled applications dealing with persistent data. Examples are secure mail, file encryption, and so on. In Chapter 9 we will look at both the key backup model used by Exchange and the one used by the Windows 2000 Encryption File System (EFS).

Windows 2000 doesn't come with a built-in facility to support key archiving. Key archiving serves other goals than key backup. It is the long-time storage version of key backup. It is mainly done for auditing or legal purposes.

Certificate validation

Certificate validation is the process by which a Windows 2000 PKI-enabled application finds out whether a certificate and the public key contained in it are trustworthy for use in security-related processes. During certificate validation a Windows 2000 PKI application will check the following: time, digital signature, formatting, and revocation. The flow used during the validation is illustrated in Figure 8.17. The different checks are explained in the following text.

- Digital signature check. This means that the digital signature applied by the issuer of the certificate will be validated. To be able to do this the validation software needs a trustworthy public key. This can be the public key of the issuing CA or the public key of another CA that's part of the certificate's certificate chain. In other words: Availability of the public key is not enough—the public key must be trusted by the verifying entity. From a technological point of view, certificate trust in the Microsoft world means that the certificate is added to the Trusted Root Certification Authorities container in the client's certificate store or that the same container contains the certificate of a CA that is part of the certificate's certificate chain. In Windows 2000 domain administrators can set the content of this list through the use of group policy objects. Certificate chain validation (trust check in Figure 8.17) can be viewed as a subprocess of the digi-

Figure 8.17
Windows 2000
certificate
validation steps

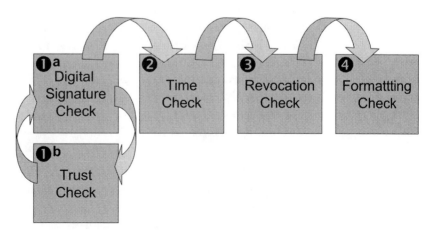

tal signature check. We will come back to certificate chain validation
in the sections below, "Regular certificate chain processing" and
"CTL certificate chain processing."

- Time check. This means that the start and end date of the certificate
  are compared with the current time. The reason a certificate's lifetime
  is limited is mainly to cope with the advances in computer technology: every year it becomes easier to break a 512-bit key asymmetric
  cipher.

- Revocation check. This means that the certificate is checked for revocation. Windows 2000 supports certificate revocation list distribution
  points (CDPs). CDPs can provide automated certificate revocation
  checking. From an interoperability point of view it's important to
  know that CDPs are also an ITU-T standard, defined in one of the
  subparagraphs of the X.509 standard.

- Formatting check. This means that the format of the certificate is
  checked and validated, according to the standard certificate format
  defined in the ITU-T X.509 standard and some specific rules defined
  on the level of the PKI-enabled application. This also includes the
  validation of the certificate's extensions. Among a certificate's extensions is a set of critical extensions, which must be validated by every
  application. The validation or evaluation of other extensions depends
  on the PKI application that is using the certificate. Most S/MIME
  applications, for instance, will evaluate the certificate subject's RFC
  822 name. It will be compared with the sender entry in the header of
  the SMTP message. This check protects against impersonation or
  man-in-the-middle attacks. In such attacks a malicious entity reuses
  the identity of another entity. The same thing is done by most SSL
  implementations. SSL compares the subject's RFC 822 name with
  the name contained in the URL. The RFC 822 name is a regular
  SMTP mail address, such as *jan.declercq@compaq.com*.

Regular certificate chain processing   So what is a certificate chain, and
why do we need to process it during certificate validation? The concept of a
certificate chain originates from the world of the hierarchical trust model.
In this model every end-entity's certificate chain consists of all the CA certificates on the path between the end entity and root CA of the hierarchy.
Also, every certificate always contains a pointer to its parent or issuing CA.

During certificate validation the certificate validation software processes
a certificate's chain. This process can be split into two subprocesses: chain
construction and chain validation, as follows:

- During chain construction the certificate validation software runs through the certificate's chain until it finds a trusted CA certificate, also known as a trust anchor. In Windows 2000 every certificate that is part of the Trusted Root Certification Authorities container in an entity's certificate store is considered a trust anchor.

- During chain validation the certificate validation software walks the chain in the opposite direction (top-down) and validates every CA certificate that's part of the chain. To validate a certificate, that's a part of the certificate chain, it should be available locally in the Trusted Root Certification Authorities, Enterprise Trust, or Intermediate Certification Authorities certificate containers of an entity's certificate store. Identification of a CA certificate is based on the Authority Key Identifier field in the certificate under Verification. This field contains the serial number of the CA certificate. When it is not available locally, the Windows 2000 PKI software will do the following to obtain a local copy of the certificate:

  - It will try to download the certificate from an online location: to do this it will use a certificate's Authority Info Access (AIA) field, which contains an LDAP, FTP, HTTP, or file system pointer to a location where the certificate is stored. If the AIA field has multiple entries, the entries will be tried out in the order in which they're listed in the field. The certificates that can be downloaded this way will be stored in the appropriate container in the entity's certificate container for future reference. These containers are the Trusted Root Certification Authorities for self-signed certificates and the Intermediate Certification Authorities for all the others.
  - If the issuer's certificate hasn't been found after doing all of the above, the PKI software will try to locate the certificate in the local certificate store using the Issuer Unique Identifier certificate field.
  - If the certificate is not available, verification will fail. If it is, the validation process will run (for every certificate in the chain) through all the steps that were explained above: time, digital signature, formatting, and revocation checking. An interesting side note regarding the time check: CA certificates that are part of a certificate's chain and that are expired on the moment of certificate validation are accepted as long as they were valid on the moment of the issuance of the certificate that is under validation. This could never happen with certificates issued by a Windows 2000 CA anyway. A Windows 2000 CA will never issue a certificate that exceeds its proper CA certificate's lifetime.

Certificates can get to an entity's certificate store in different ways: preinstalled with the Windows 2000 or IE software, applied by a GPO setting, downloaded via the AD DS enterprise root store or using a manual user download (from the Web, the file system, an FTP share, or the AD).

When a user downloads a certificate using the Windows 2000 CA Web interface he or she has the choice to download just the certificate or the certificate together with all the certificates that are part of its certificate chain. This can be very advantageous during certificate validation: All CA certificates are directly available on the client and there's no need for the client software to download the certificate using the AIA pointers. Another example of an application supporting such features is the Microsoft implementation of the S/MIME protocol for secure messaging: A signed message not only comes with the certificate of the signer but also with the complete certificate chain.

Figure 8.18 shows the certificate chain of a certificate that ends in a trusted CA certificate, and Figure 8.19 illustrates the certificate chain of a certificate that ends in an untrusted CA certificate as they are displayed in the Windows 2000 certificate properties.

Note the confusion caused by the interface in Figure 8.20: Even though one of the CA certificates QTest Root CA is not trusted, the end-user certificate, Jan De Clercq, is still displayed as valid. The General tab of the certificate viewer will display the correct information (as illustrated in

Figure 8.18
Certificate chain viewed from the certificate properties: trusted CA certificate

Figure 8.19
Certificate chain viewed from the certificate properties: untrusted CA certificate

Figure 8.20): It will tell you that "the certificate cannot be verified up to a trusted certification authority" and will show an invalid certificate icon.

This section has explained how certificates can be invalid for different reasons: expiration or other time problems, invalid signatures, unavailability of a trusted CA certificate, improper use, improper formatting, revocation, and so on. Finding out the exact reason why a certificate is not valid can be a very hard job.

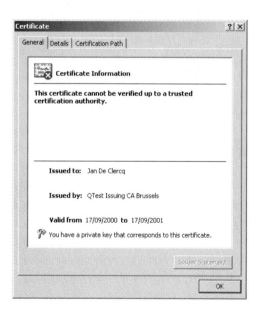

Figure 8.20
General tab of invalid certificate shown in Figure 8.19

CTL certificate chain processing   A special case of certificate chain processing is Certificate Trust List (CTL) certificate chain processing. CTLs are signed lists of trusted root CA certificates (a CTL can only contain self-signed root CA certificates), defined on the level of Windows 2000 GPOs, that are automatically downloaded to the Enterprise Trust container in an entity's certificate store. The Enterprise Trust container is not a Trust Anchor container; in other words, its content is not considered trusted by default. In order for a CTL and its content to be trusted, the CTL signing certificate should be valid. This means that the CTL signing certificate should pass the time, digital signature, formatting, and revocation checks.

In order for the digital signature check to succeed, the CTL signing certificate's certificate chain should contain a certificate that's part of the Trusted Root Certification Authorities container. In other words, the CTL signing certificate should be issued by a CA that is part of the Trusted Root Certification Authorities container, or at least one of the CA certificates in the CTL signing certificate's certificate chain should be issued by a CA that is part of that container.

Figures 8.21 and 8.22 show the certificate chain of a certificate that's part of a valid CTL and one that's part of an invalid CTL, as they are displayed in the Windows 2000 certificate properties.

Figure 8.21
Certificate part of a certificate chain of a valid CTL

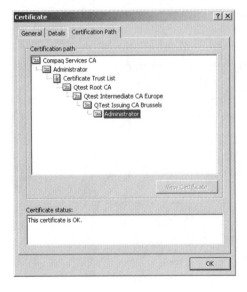

Key and data recovery

Key and data recovery are administrator-initiated processes, which are needed when dealing with persistent data secured using encryption technology. The inability to decrypt data when the encryption key is lost would result in data loss. The following paragraphs explain the difference between key and data recovery:

- Key recovery is used to recover a user's encryption keys when he or she has lost them. Key loss can occur because of deletion by purpose or by accident, or because of theft. An example of a system that deals solely with key recovery is the key recovery system shipping with the Entrust PKI software.

- Data recovery is used to decrypt user data. Data recovery can happen with the user's consent or without the user's consent. It can happen while the user is still a member of your organization or after he or she has left your organization. Encrypted data recovery is always preceded by key recovery.

The Windows 2000 recovery techniques mentioned in the following text support both key and data recovery. In all of them key refers to a bulk encryption key; the secure storage of the bulk encryption is guaranteed using asymmetric cryptography.

Figure 8.22
Certificate part of a certificate chain of an invalid CTL

Windows 2000 currently has two PKI-enabled applications supporting key and data recovery, as follows:

1.   The Encryption File System (EFS) uses a decentralized key and data recovery system, which enables an administrator to recover the EFS bulk encryption key and to decrypt a user's data. The recovery is decentralized, because the key recovery information is stored together with every encrypted file or folder.

2.   Exchange 2000 Advanced Security for secure (i.e., S/MIME-based) messaging uses a centralized key and data recovery system, which enables both the recovery of a user's encryption keys and the decryption of user data. This system uses a centralized database for the storage of key recovery information.

Both applications, EFS and S/MIME, will be discussed in great detail in Chapter 9.

Certificate retrieval

Certificate retrieval deals with the way certificates get to a user who needs them for certain PKI-based security operations. In Windows 2000 certificates can be retrieved manually from anywhere the CA publishes them. In the Active Directory, on a Web site, on an FTP share, or on a file share. Windows 2000 also allows automatic retrieval of certificates during certificate validation for certificate chain validation or revocation checking. The locations from which certificates and CRLs can be automatically retrieved are specified in the CRL distribution point (CDP) (for CRLs) and the Authority Information Access (AIA) (for CA certificates) extensions of a Windows 2000 certificate.

Exchange 2000 S/MIME sends the signing certificate with every signed message. This method of certificate retrieval is not specific to Windows 2000, but is part of the S/MIME specification for secure messaging.

Key and certificate update

To provide better security cryptographic keys and certificates should be updated regularly. Windows supports both manual and automatic key and certificate updating. The latter feature is only available to machine accounts. Machine certificates that are set for automatic enrollment will also be automatically updated when the autoenrollment event occurs. Updating the keys and certificates of a Windows 2000 CA requires a special procedure. This procedure will be discussed in Chapter 9.

To update your user keys and certificates you should use the MMC certificates snap-in: you can choose to renew an existing certificate using the same keys or by generating a new key pair. Renewing a certificate will archive the old certificate. Using the same interface you can also request a new certificate using the same keys and, of course, request a new certificate with a brand new key pair.

Certificate revocation

One of the key problems in the creation of PKIs over the past years has been the problem of certificate revocation and, more particularly, the problem of automated revocation checking. Remember that revocation checking is a subpart of the certificate validation process. Automated revocation checking is critical for PKI systems that deal with important and valuable information or transactions. In such systems using a certificate without revocation checking can be very dangerous. Imagine that confidential information is encrypted with a public key, of which the corresponding private key has been compromised. If a hacker stole the private key, he or she has potential access to confidential data.

Different, mostly theoretical, models for automated revocation checking are available in the PKI world. Most of them, with the exception of Certificate Revocation Trees (CRTs) and the Online Certificate Status Protocol (OCSP), are based on Certificate Revocation Lists (CRLs): Complete CRLs, Authority Revocation Lists (ARLs), CRL Distribution Points (CDPs), Enhanced CRLs, Delta CRLs, and Indirect CRLs. We will not discuss all these methods, since they are beyond the scope of this book. For a good overview read *Understanding Public Key Infrastructure* by Carlisle Adams and Steve Lloyd. Windows 2000 supports CRL Distribution Points (CDPs). In its next release Microsoft is planning support for Delta CRLs. CDPs are a certificate extension defined in the X.509 v3 standard. In its current release Windows 2000 also supports the Netscape revocation extensions.

So how do CDPs work? How can they provide an adequate and automated certificate revocation checking mechanism? The manner in which CDPs work is illustrated in Figure 8.23 and discussed in the following list:

- Each certificate generated by a Windows 2000 Certificate Server includes one or more pointers to a CDP. A CDP can be a URL (HTTP, LDAP, FTP) or a file share.

- A Windows 2000 PKI client application that is CDP-enabled will, each time it uses a certificate, check the local system cache for a valid

Figure 8.23
Windows 2000
CRL distribution
points (CDPs)

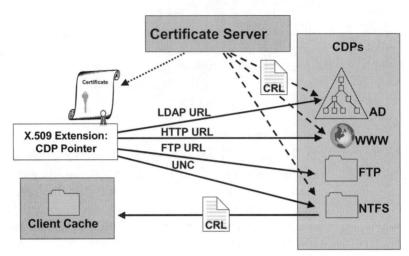

CRL. If it doesn't find one, it will check the certificate's CDPs for an up-to-date CRL. If a new CRL is available, it will download it from the CDP and cache it locally for the lifetime of the CRL. If a certificate does not contain any CDPs, the PKI client application will query the certificate's issuing CA for a CRL. At the time of this writing, only four Microsoft software products were CDP-enabled: Windows 2000, Internet Explorer 5.0 and 5.5, and Internet Information Server 5.0.

- In order for CDPs to work not only certificate and PKI client application support is required, but also the CA should support them. For every CDP the CA should have a corresponding exit module, which can publish the CRLs to the appropriate file system, FTP, Web, or Active Directory CDP. Windows 2000 comes with an exit module that can support AD, Web, and file system CDP publishing.

Besides automated revocation checking CDPs can also increase CRL availability. Each certificate can contain different CDPs. If one CDP is unavailable, the CRL can be found at another one. This feature is not supported in the current release of Windows 2000.

CDPs are not a remedy to reduce the size of CRLs; a Windows 2000 CA generates by default a single CRL. A single, large CRL downloaded to all your PKI clients at regular intervals can seriously impact bandwidth usage. To limit the size of the CRLs you can do one of the following three things:

1.   Define multiple CAs. If you define multiple CAs, with each CA having its own CRL, the size of those individual CRLs will be

much smaller than the size of the CRL generated when you would have created just one CA.

2.   Generate certificates with a short lifetime. Windows 2000 CRLs are self-cleaning, which means that expired certificates are automatically removed from the CRL.

3.   Generate a new CA key pair. Every time the CA key pair is renewed, a new CRL will be generated. The new CRL will be signed using the newly generated private key.

Netscape is using a proprietary online certificate revocation checking method. They embed a custom extension, the netscape-revocation-url, in all their certificates; it points to a Web page where the certificate revocation can be checked. To send the revocation checking request to the Web page Netscape is using the HTTP GET method with a URL, which is the concatenation of the netscape-revocation-url and the serial number of the certificate that needs to be checked. The response that comes back from the Web server is a document with content-type application/x-Netscape-revocation; it contains a single digit, which is 1 if the certificate is not valid or 0 if the certificate is valid. To enable a Windows 2000 CA to issue certificates containing this extension use the certutil tool: certutil –setreg Policy\revocationtype +AspEnable. You will also have to restart the CA service to make this change effective.

Certificate expiration and certificate lifetimes

A certificate expires at the moment in time set in the certificate's validity field. The issuing CA sets this field automatically, without any user choice or intervention. An exception to this rule is the lifetime of a root CA certificate that can be set manually at installation time. The certificate lifetime preferences are set differently on enterprise and standalone CAs, as follows:

■   On a standalone CA the certificate lifetime is set in the system registry. Both the ValidityPeriod and ValidityPeriodUnits keys refer to certificate lifetime. They are located in HKEY_LOCAL_MACHINE\SYSTEM\CurrentControlSet\Services\CertSvc\Configuration\<CAName>. The default lifetime of certificates issued by a standalone CA is one year.

■   On an enterprise CA the certificate lifetime can be set in the registry or on the certificate template level. All certificate templates have two-year lifetimes, with the exceptions of a DC and a subordinate CA certificate, which have five-year lifetimes. Certificate lifetimes that are defined on the template level cannot be modified. The setting in the registry is used when no lifetime is defined on the certificate template level. The default lifetime of certificates issued by an enterprise CA is two years.

Standalone CAs offer the highest level of flexibility regarding certificate lifetime definition: they do not use certificate templates and hence can control the lifetime of every certificate they issue.

Windows 2000 certificate lifetimes support nested validity dates; this means that a certificate can never have a lifetime that is longer than the certificate lifetime of its issuing CA. For example, if your CA's certificate is about to expire in 16 months and the default certificate lifetime is two years, the CA will issue certificates with a one-year lifetime. As a consequence, you should renew your CA certificates in time in order to have the ability to issue user certificates with a particular lifetime.

Within a PKI hierarchy the lifetime of entities' certificates will differ depending on the level where the entity is located in the hierarchy. This is because the higher the entity is in the hierarchy, the more security measures will be implemented to safeguard its private key. Remember that CA private key compromise at a higher level in a hierarchy has much more impact than at a lower level in the hierarchy. Also, consider the nesting validity dates feature of Windows 2000 PKI: since an issuing CA's certificate is part of the certificate chain of any certificate it issues, its own CA certificate should be valid in order for any of the issued certificates to be valid. Thus, the CA's certificate should have, under all circumstances, a lifetime that is longer than the lifetime of the certificates it issues.

8.3   Summary

In this chapter we introduced the concepts of PKI and the features of Windows 2000 PKI. It should now be clear that Microsoft has made as a priority the extension of its PKI capabilities in Windows 2000. In the next chapter, we will explain what to consider when planning and designing a Windows 2000–based PKI.

Building a Windows 2000 PKI

9

In Chapter 8, we introduced the basic building blocks of PKI and, more specifically, the building blocks of Windows 2000 PKI. In this chapter, we will look at the different steps you need to consider when planning, designing, and building a Windows 2000 PKI. We will also look at three applications, which can leverage your PKI investment: smart-card logon, the Encryption File System, and S/MIME for secure SMTP messaging. To end our discussion on PKI in Windows 2000 we will present a case study.

9.1 Introduction to running a Windows 2000 PKI project

As with any other IT project, a Windows 2000 PKI project can be subdivided into four key phases: assessment, design, implementation, and management.

During the assessment phase the current and future security requirements of an organization are analyzed. This can be done by running a security audit, performing a penetration test, or just by analyzing existing processes. Of course, the assessment phase also includes a business requirement analysis. The design phase deals with the technological design of the PKI solution and with some nontechnological design topics, such as the creation of Certificate Practice Statements (CPSs). The implementation phase takes care of the rollout of the PKI solution, its integration with the existing IT environment, and, prior to the rollout, the development of customized PKI applications or modules. Once PKI is installed and deployed across your enterprise you'll need to manage and maintain it: in the management phase you'll have to deal with the support model for the PKI (help desk, etc.), administrator and end-user training, and the management of the PKI components. The four major phases are illustrated in Figure 9.1. Notice that a PKI project can be iterative: during the implementation,

Figure 9.1
*The four major
phases of a PKI
project*

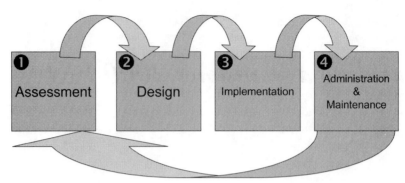

issues might come up that require a new assessment and changes to the original design.

9.1.1 Assessing the organizational needs for a PKI

During an assessment for a PKI project, you need to analyze your company's current and future security needs. Prior to assessment, you may need to gather some extra information. To do this you can organize a security audit or a penetration test.

In the following text, we focus on four key areas you should focus on during the assessment phase: the business requirement analysis, the decision on whether to insource or to outsource, the analysis of the applications that need PKI-based security, and the product choice.

Analyzing business requirements

The rollout of a Public Key Infrastructure (PKI) in a corporate environment is driven by core business needs, such as advanced security requirements for information storage and network communication. The business reason behind a corporate PKI rollout will have an impact on every step of your PKI planning and design. For example, the size of the investment a company makes in a PKI will depend upon the criticality of the business problem it wishes to resolve or the importance of the business processes whose security level it wants to improve by installing a PKI.

Some business security requirements don't need a certificate-based security solution and can be resolved with simpler arrangements. Also, because not every certificate-based solution requires rolling out an enterprise PKI, companies often decide to outsource the job or simply buy a limited set of certificates from a commercial certification authority.

Because of the business your organization is in you might have some extra PKI requirements, as follows:

- Availability. What sort of availability does the PKI need within the organization? This affects the CAs, the CA databases, and the directories used in the PKI solution.

- Scalability. Does the PKI have to be scalable? Will it have to cope with rapid growth of the number of required certificates? Does planning have to take into account possible future mergers? Will a lot more PKI-based applications be deployed in the near future?

- Performance. Public key cryptography operations place load and performance demands on client/server systems. Is it acceptable? Should hardware be upgraded? Should you buy and install special hardware that will speed up PKI functions?

- Cost. PKI products come in different flavors, with different features and in different price classes.

Which applications will be built on top of the PKI?

A PKI is an infrastructure and many Windows 2000 applications (built-in and otherwise) can take advantage of it to provide strong security: networking systems, VPN systems, ERP software, document signing, and smart card–based applications. The types of certificates that will be needed and the entities to which certificates will be issued (machines or users) depend on the applications you want to support in your corporate environment.

You can build the following types of Windows 2000 applications on top of a Windows 2000 PKI:

- Secure Web. In a corporate intranet or extranet environment, you can use certificates for strong authentication, using the Secure Sockets Layer (SSL) or Transport Layer Security (TLS) protocols. Both TLS and SSL can provide client authentication, server authentication, and data confidentiality. Each authenticated entity requires a certificate. If you host Web sites and directories on Microsoft Internet Information Server (IIS), you can map a certificate-based account to a Windows 2000 account. This way users authenticating using certificates are treated just like any other user in postauthentication processes, such as access control. On the IIS level, you can define one-to-one mapping or a many-to-one mapping, which maps certificates of the same type (e.g., issued by the same CA) to the same Windows NT account. Mapping definitions are contained in the IIS metabase or in the

Active Directory. A new feature of IIS5.0 running on top of Windows 2000 is the possibility to point a Web server to the Active Directory database to check for certificate mappings.

- Secure mail. Signing and sealing electronic mail messages using S/MIME (Secure Multipurpose Internet Mail Extensions) is also based on public key cryptography and certificates. Signing uses the sender's private key, sealing uses the receiver's public key. Microsoft Exchange, Outlook, and Outlook Express all can provide secure mail. Most secure mail applications use a dual key pair system to provide non-repudiation of signed mail messages and recovery of encrypted mail messages.

- File system encryption. Windows 2000 comes with the Encryption File System (EFS) extension to the NTFS version 5 file system. It provides file system–level encryption. A built-in EFS feature provides recovery of encrypted data by a person other than the one who originally encrypted the data. Because it performs encryption and decryption transparently, it is also easy to use. Windows 2000 allows you to encrypt files or folders through a GUI or a command-prompt interface.

- Code signing. This helps protect against downloads of altered (hacker) code from Web sites. Using a private key, the original code developer signs the code, and the user downloading a piece of it can use the developer's public key to verify the code's origin. The Microsoft code-signing technology is known as Authenticode.

- Smart-card logon. This provides strong two-factor authentication (based on knowledge of a PIN code and possession of a smart card) in a Windows 2000 domain environment. Classic Windows NT4 logon using a user ID/password provides one-factor authentication (based on knowledge only). Smart-card logon in Windows 2000 is implemented as an extension to the Kerberos protocol; it is called PKINIT because it uses public key cryptography only for initial authentication. The smart-card logon process replaces all occurrences of the user's password with the user's public key credentials. The Active Directory contains a mapping between a user's certificate and a Windows 2000 account.

- Secure Web and secure mail using Fortezza crypto cards (United States only). The Fortezza crypto card standard is a smart-card standard developed by the U.S. National Security Agency (NSA). Like any other smart card these cards can be used for secure storage of public key credentials. Fortezza also enables secure Web and secure mail applications that use public key technology.

- Virtual private networking. Windows 2000 supports the IPsec tunneling protocol, which can use certificates to authenticate between two IPsec tunnel end points. This is an ideal solution for strong authentication between two tunnel end points that are part of different domains not having a trust relationship set up. Untrusted domains cannot rely on the standard Windows 2000 authentication protocols such as Kerberos and NTLM.

- Remote access authentication. The Windows 2000 Remote Access Service (RAS) supports the Extensible Authentication Protocol (EAP), which uses (among other methods) TLS authentication. The IETF successor to SSL, TLS uses certificates for client and server authentication.

- Securing SMTP site connections. You can connect Windows 2000 sites with asynchronous SMTP connections, in which case the bridgehead DCs at both ends authenticate one another using certificates. Setting this up will also protect the confidentiality and integrity of the replication traffic.

- Any custom PKI-enabled application that uses CryptoAPI version 2. The Windows 2000 CryptoAPI dealing with PKI-related operations is fully documented in the Windows 2000 SDK and can be used to build many other PKI-enabled applications on top of Windows 2000.

Not all of the applications listed above require the presence of a corporate PKI or CA infrastructure. You can use EFS, for example, on laptops even if no CA is present.

Insource or outsource?

You have three choices when implementing and managing an enterprise PKI: insource, outsource, or a hybrid approach.

Insourced solutions are solutions you install, implement, administer, and maintain. Your IT department must take the lead in implementing all related PKI technologies: CA hardware, CA database, PKI directories, and the communication links between all participating entities. Naturally, this path offers you complete independence. You can create your own liability rules and security policies and can decide how to implement, administer, and maintain the PKI. You also have complete control over who gets a certificate.

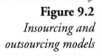

Figure 9.2
*Insourcing and
outsourcing models*

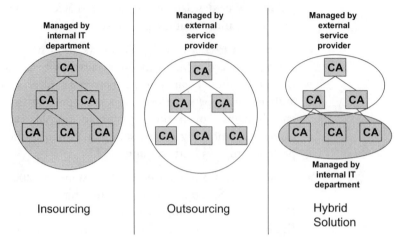

Outsourced solutions turn most of this over to another company. The degree of outsourcing can range from a little (generating some server certificates) to a lot (outsourcing multiple CA services that are dedicated to your company). Although you have to put a high level of trust in the company you hire, this is often the best solution for smaller companies or for those without the funds and resources required to install and maintain a proper PKI.

In today's PKI market there are plenty of outsourcing partners. An important factor to consider is whether you can trust the partner. Don't forget that you're dealing with security!

Hybrid solutions combine insourcing and outsourcing: Your company maintains part of the CAs in the hierarchy, another company maintains others. This model is probably the best choice for most companies. A company might have different security needs for different applications. Applications with high security needs could have their CAs managed and implemented by the company itself; the implementation and management of CAs used for applications with lower security needs could be outsourced. (See Figure 9.2.)

The topics outlined in Table 9.1 can help you to choose between an insourced, outsourced, or a hybrid approach.

PKI product choice

After the information gathering and assessment are done, after you've decided which applications you want to be PKI enabled, and after you've decided on insourcing or outsourcing, you'll need to decide on the PKI

Table 9.1 *Advantages and Disadvantages of Insourcing versus Outsourcing*

Insourcing	Outsourcing
Advantages	*Advantages*
▪ More and tighter control over certificate policy definition and management, certificate and key management, issuance, archiving, and recovery ▪ Tighter integration options: integration with enterprise directory and in-house applications ▪ Potentially stronger trust relationships with partners because of certificate policy control	▪ Leverage on expertise of PKI leaders ▪ Less effort for planning, design, administration, and maintenance ▪ Can be more cost effective for a small enterprise; the business with the external partner can be extended as need for PKI-enabled applications grows. ▪ Can be operational in a short period of time ▪ Requires less in-house expertise
Disadvantages	*Disadvantages*
▪ More costly (certainly for a small enterprise): cost of planning, design, administration, maintenance ▪ Requires more in-house expertise ▪ Possible complex integration and deployment ▪ Requires more time to plan, design, and deploy	▪ Less policy control and enforcement capabilities ▪ Less integration options ▪ Can be more costly for a large enterprise

product or PKI products you will implement. Key factors you need to consider here are as follows:

- Cost. How much will the PKI solution cost? What resources will be required to administer and maintain it?

- Ease of use. How difficult is it to enroll for a certificate? How long does it take? How long does it take to renew a certificate? How complex is PKI administration?

- Time to market. How long will it take to get the PKI into operation? How soon can you get an application running on top of it?

- Support for open standards. Is the PKI solution based on open standards? They are key to interoperability. The major ones are: X.509, PKCS, PKIX, and RFC 2459. The ITU-T X.509 standard defines a format for certificates. PKCS defines the format of public key-related messages. PKIX defines PKIs that use X.509 certificates. RFC 2459 defines the Internet X.509 PKI certificate and CRL profile.

- PKI management. What are the management features of a given solution? What features does your organization want?

As Table 9.2 shows, your product choice will definitely be impacted by whether you want to insource or outsource. When choosing to outsource,

Table 9.2   *Commercial CAs and PKI Software Vendors*

Outsourcing: Commercial CAs	Insourcing: PKI Software Vendors
▓ Globalsign	▓ ID2
▓ Verisign	▓ Entrust
▓ Entrust.net	▓ Baltimore Technologies
	▓ Xcert
	▓ Microsoft
	▓ Netscape
	▓ Siemens SSE
	▓ Utimaco

you'll have to choose among one of the commercial CAs. Insourcing lets you choose between different PKI software vendors.

Note that the list in Table 9.2 is not complete and that it's beyond the scope of this book to make a comparison between the different PKI products.

9.1.2   Designing, planning, and implementing a Windows 2000 PKI

In this section, we will focus on the different steps you need to consider when designing, planning, and implementing a Windows 2000 PKI.

Defining your topology

When designing your Windows 2000 PKI topology you need to think about the four topics outlined in the following text. For all of them you need to keep possible future extensions of your organization in mind:

- Decide on the number of CAs you want. Your organization may require multiple CAs for scalability, business, geographical, CA policy, or political reasons.

- Choose a trust model. The primary trust model of Windows 2000 is the hierarchical trust model. Windows also supports the distributed and browser trust model. When designing a hierarchical trust model, you will need to decide upon the number of hierarchical levels you'll need and on what those levels will be based (e.g., geography, business organization, etc.). In a distributed model, you'll need to decide upon the number of hierarchies necessary for your organization. In PKI projects of limited scope, you might choose a single CA solution. Given the growing interest in PKI, however, this is a bad idea. You should always consider the possibility of linking your CA trust model with others and provide ways to scale your CA trust model.

- Map the trust model to the Windows 2000 domain and site model. Because the trust model established between CAs is totally independent of the trust model existing among Windows 2000 domains, one CA can span multiple domains and a domain can contain multiple CAs. In Windows 2000 it's a good practice to increase availability by installing one Windows 2000 DC or GC server in each site. In a PKI environment, the availability of the CA services is less important than the availability of the directory that holds the certificates and the CRLs. If you integrate the Certificate Server with the Active Directory, the certificates and CRLs are automatically published to the directory and replicated throughout the forest as part of the GC. In some environments, such as the one illustrated in Figure 9.3, it might be a good idea to have one CA per group of sites. Figure 9.3 illustrates a multiple hub-and-spoke site model. In this case it's a good idea to deploy one CA per core site, simply for availability and performance reasons.

- Define relationships with external CAs or PKIs. When the PKI topology design is done, you should have a clear view on the trust relationships between your organization's CAs. To provide PKI interoperability between different CA domains Windows is using the

Figure 9.3
Example of CA trust model in a hub-and-spoke site model

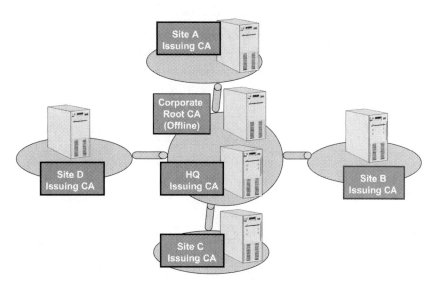

concept of Certificate Trust Lists (CTLs). You also need to decide on how you will link your PKI domain with other external PKI domains and whether there's a need to do this. If you're planning to use CTLs, think about the following. Which CA certificates will be contained in the CTLs? Will the trust be uni-or bidirectional? What will be the limitations on the CTLs? Which certificate types will it support? What will be its lifetime? Remember that setting up a link between different PKIs requires more than just a technology solution, you will also need to think about policy agreements.

Specifications of the individual CAs

CAs are your key PKI components, so you need to spend enough time and effort to create detailed designs of the individual CAs. Part of the parameters are set during the installation of your CA. Another part is set postinstallation, in the configuration phase. You need to consider the installation and configuration options outlined in Table 9.3.

Parameters set before or during CA installation

Before or during CA installation, you need to think about the following CA-related parameters: the CA architecture, its role, the specification of its keys and certificates, whether it will be offline or not, the CA naming conventions, the inclusion of a pointer to the CPS or to a short notice text in the certificates, and the CA's database specifications. In what follows we will not review topics that were discussed extensively in the previous chapter:

- The CA architecture design. Does your organization need CAs with a customized exit or policy module?

Table 9.3   *CA Configuration Options Before and During Installation and During Configuration*

Before or During Installation	During Configuration
CA architecture	CRL generation and distribution
CA role	Supported certificate types (certificate templates)
CA keys and certificates	Certificate characteristics
CA naming conventions	User identification
CA data storage locations	Certificate request interfaces
Definition of CPS	Hardening the CA server

- The CA role. Will the CA be a standalone or an enterprise CA? Will it be a root CA or a subordinate CA? If it is a subordinate CA, will it be an intermediate or an issuing CA? If it is a root or an intermediate CA, will it be configured as an offline CA? Note that a Windows 2000 PKI hierarchy can contain different types of CAs: an enterprise CA can be subordinate to a standalone CA or the other way around.

Offline CAs   To minimize the risk of CA private key compromise you may want to set up offline CAs. Within a certificate hierarchy, for example, it's advisable to take the nonissuing CAs (root CAs and intermediate CAs) offline. Taking a CA offline can mean different things, as follows:

- Take it off the network.

- Shut down the CA service.

- Shut down the CA machine.

- Install it on a standalone Windows 2000 server and thus set it up as a standalone CA. Since a CA is a trusted third party, which, in most scenarios, is administered by people other than domain administrators, it's advisable to install it on a standalone instead of a member server. Also, a nonissuing CA does not need AD.

- Remove a CA server's hard disk and store it in a vault to which only a very limited number of employees have access.

In case an offline CA needs to issue new certificates or CRLs, you'll need to bring it online again. If it is not connected to the network, you can use the following procedure to obtain a certificate for the new subordinate CA:

- During the subordinate CA installation, select *Save the request to a file*. The Microsoft certificate services will inform you that the installation is incomplete; put the request file (*.req) on a floppy disk and transport the floppy to the offline CA.

- Bring the offline CA online. Open the subordinate CA's request file from the offline CA, and copy the text between the BEGIN NEW CERTIFICATE REQUEST and END NEW CERTIFICATE REQUEST lines. Paste this text into the *Submit a saved request* page (advanced certificate request) of the offline CA's Web enrollment interface. Submit the request and save the newly generated certificate to the floppy disk.

- Transport the floppy to the subordinate CA; from the CA MMC snap-in, right-click the CA object and select *Install CA certificate*. The CA certificate will be installed and the subordinate CA service will be started up.

Also, you'll need to bring an offline CA online every time its proper certificate must be renewed. For this reason it's advisable to set the lifetime of an offline CA's certificate relatively high (10 or even 20 years).

Even though a CA is offline, the users of the certificates it issued need to be able to access its CRLs and CA certificate. This means it should be brought online at regular intervals to generate a new CRL (it doesn't matter if the CRL is empty, as long as it is available). The number of times the CA is brought online for CRL generation is obviously a tradeoff between better security and administrative overhead.

Also, when a CA is offline it doesn't mean you cannot publish its certificate and CRL in the Active Directory. Export them from the offline CA to a floppy disk; bring the disk to a machine that has access to AD, and publish them in AD using the Dsstore resource kit tool. Don't forget that you also have to change the CRL Distribution Point (CDP) and Authority Information Access (AIA) parameters in the CA's certificate (by using the capolicy.inf file), and in the CA's policy module. This change should be made before any certificate is issued.

CA keys and certificate   When you set up a CA, you have to choose the key length, the cryptographic service provider and the hash functions the CA will use for cryptographic operations (as illustrated in Figure 9.4). When installing a root CA, you can also set the lifetime of its certificate. For subordinate CAs the default lifetime is five years if the certificate is issued by an enterprise CA, it can be changed to anything else if it is issued by a standalone CA. From a security point of view it's advisable to renew a CA's

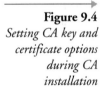

Figure 9.4
Setting CA key and certificate options during CA installation

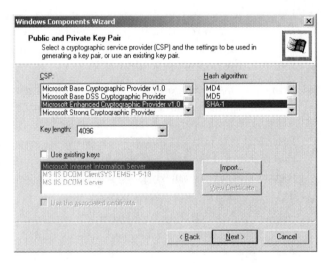

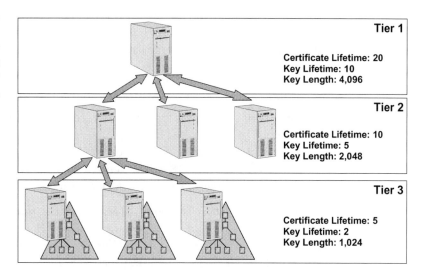

Figure 9.5
*Certificate lifetime
and key length in a
typical PKI
hierarchy*

keys at regular intervals. CA key renewal can be done independently of certificate renewal. It cannot be automated and is initiated by the CA administrator.

Figure 9.5 brings together certificate lifetime, key renewal, and key length; it gives an example of how these three key parameters could be defined for different CAs in a PKI hierarchy. Notice that the deeper you go in the certification hierarchy, the shorter the certificate lifetime, key lifetime, and key length become.

A key topic to remember is that the CA is the heart of your security system, and if its private key is compromised, so is the entire PKI. Protect against attacks by choosing the longest key possible—at least 1,024 bits—and by storing the CA private key in a secure place.

The place where the private key is stored depends on the CSP selected during the installation of the CA. A CSP can be software-based; for CA private key storage it should be, preferably, hardware-based. By far the safest way to store the CA's private key is on a specialized hardware device, a Hardware Security Module (HSM), available from vendors such as Atalla (more info at *http://www.atalla.com*) or nCipher (nForce, nShield: more info at *http://www.ncipher.com*). HSMs are very expensive. A cheaper alternative is a smart card. Windows 2000 supports different types of smart-card readers and smart cards.

Independent of the choice you make, you'll have to make sure that the device (disk, smart card, HSM, etc.) on which you store the CA's private key is physically secured. Put it in a highly secured area of your company's computer room, or lock it in a safe. If you're not planning to use any special hardware protection on your root CAs and intermediate CAs, remember that it is regarded as a best practice to keep these servers offline.

CA naming conventions   During CA installation, you will be prompted to enter the CA's identification information: the CA name, organization, organizational unit, city, state or province, country, e-mail, and CA description. Be sure to agree on the naming conventions before you start the installation. The naming choices made during installation not only affect the CA, they will also be the CA's common name in the Active Directory and will be reflected in every certificate the CA issues.

Behind the scenes, Windows 2000 generates a sanitized CA name; it's the truncated CA name without any non-ASCII characters and ASCII punctuation characters. It is needed for file names, key container names, and AD object names that cannot handle a CA name, including special characters. AD object names are limited to 64 characters: If a CA's name is longer than 64, it is truncated and appended with a hash calculated over the truncated part.

To look at all CA-related Active Directory names (including the CA sanitized names) run certutil with the –v –ds switches. (See Figure 9.6.)

Once you install the CA, you cannot change the server's name. To change the server name after installation you have to uninstall the CA, change the server's name, and then reinstall the CA.

CA database   The location of the database and its log files can be specified during CA installation. During installation, you'll also be asked whether you want to store the CA's configuration information on the file system. Doing this copies the CA's naming information and the CA's certificate to the file system (the configuration directory will automatically be shared as certconfig).

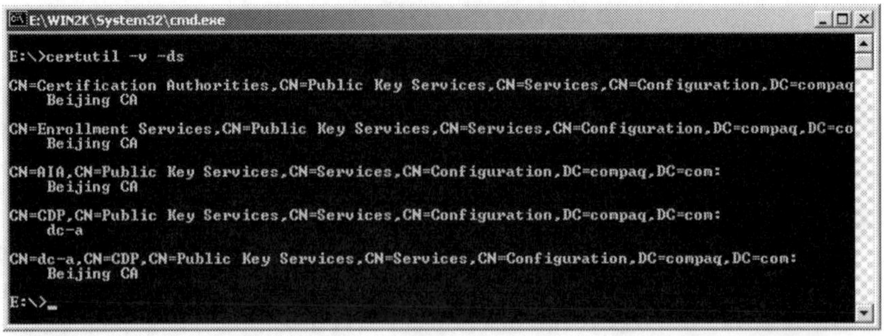

Figure 9.6
Using certutil to check the CA's sanitized names

```
E:\WIN2K\System32\cmd.exe                                          _ □ ×

E:\>certutil -v -ds
CN=Certification Authorities,CN=Public Key Services,CN=Services,CN=Configuration,DC=compaq
    Beijing CA

CN=Enrollment Services,CN=Public Key Services,CN=Services,CN=Configuration,DC=compaq,DC=co
    Beijing CA

CN=AIA,CN=Public Key Services,CN=Services,CN=Configuration,DC=compaq,DC=com:
    Beijing CA

CN=CDP,CN=Public Key Services,CN=Services,CN=Configuration,DC=compaq,DC=com:
    dc-a

CN=dc-a,CN=CDP,CN=Public Key Services,CN=Services,CN=Configuration,DC=compaq,DC=com:
    Beijing CA

E:\>_
```

The Windows 2000 CA database is a JET database. It is using the same database engine, the extensible storage engine (esent.dll), that is used in Exchange and the Active Directory. The CA database files are listed in Table 9.4. Just as with any other JET database a good practice is to split the database and its log files across different physical disk drives. By default all its files are located in the certlog subdirectory of the system directory. To find out the location of your CA database files type certutil –databaselocations at the command prompt. To change the location of the CAs database files you must change the registry values DBDirectory and DBLogDirectory located in the HKLM\System\CurrentControlSet\Services\Certsvc\Configuration registry folder.

The goal of the different files that make up a JET database was explained extensively in Chapter 4. We will discuss backup and restore of the CA database in a later section.

The Windows 2000 CA database is designed to support up to 1 million certificates; if every user has on average four certificates, this means that it can support approximately 250,000 users (these are Microsoft numbers). Since there's no limit on the number of CAs that can be supported in a single domain, Windows 2000 PKI is practically unlimited as far as the number of supported users and certificates are concerned.

The CA database format used in v2 of Certificate Server (the one shipping with Windows 2000) is different from the format used in v1 (the one shipping with the NT4 option pack). When upgrading from NT4 to Windows 2000, the database is converted automatically. To upgrade your CA database from v1 to v2, stop the CA service, use certutil –convertMDB to do the conversion, restart the CA service, and force the publication of a new

Table 9.4   *Windows Certificate Server Database Files*

Database File	Goal
<CA name>.edb	The CA store
edb.log	The transaction log file for the CA store
res1.log	Reservation log file to store transactions if disk space is exhausted
res2.log	Reservation log file to store transactions if disk space is exhausted
edb.chk	Database checkpoint file
tmp.edb	Temporary CA store

CRL. To look at the new schema layout of the Windows 2000 CA database type **certutil –schema** at the command prompt.

Other installation-time CA configurations   During enterprise or stand-alone CA installation or certificate renewal, you can add several custom extensions to the CA certificate, as follows:

- A custom issuer statement
- A custom Certificate Policies (CPs) field, pointing to all CPs to which the CA is adhering
- Custom CRL Distribution Points (CDPs)
- Custom Authority Information Access (AIA) points
- Custom enhanced key usage settings
- Custom certificate renewal settings

The last four extensions are only used when installing or renewing a root CA certificate. For subordinate CA CDPs, AIA settings are set by configuring the parent CA's policy settings.

To customize the CA certificate you need to create a policy statement file, capolicy.inf, and store it in the system directory (C:\winnt) prior to CA installation. The following is a sample capolicy.inf file:

```
[Version]
Signature="$Windows NT$"

[CAPolicy]
Policies=CompaqPolicy

[CompaqPolicy]
OID=1.1.1.1.1.2.3.4.5
URL = "http://www.compaq.com/certsvc/cp.asp"
URL = "ftp://ftp.compaq.com/certsvc/cp.asp"
URL = "ldap://ldap.compaq.com/certsvc/cp.asp"
Notice = "Compaq Certificate Policy"

[CRLDistributionPoint]
URL="http://www.compaq.com/Public/CompaqCA.crl"

[AuthorityInformationAccess]
URL="http:// www.compaq.com/Public/CompaqCA.crt"

[EnhancedKeyUsage]
OID=1.2.3.2.110
OID=1.2.3.2.111
```

```
[certsrv_server]
RenewalKeyLength=4096
RenewalValidityPeriod=4
RenewalValidityPeriodUnits=Years
```

The settings in the [CompaqPolicy] section will embed the following in the CA's certificate policies extension:

```
[1] CertificatePolicy:
    PolicyIdentifier=1.1.1.1.1.2.3.4.5
    [1,1]Policy Qualifier info:
        Policy Qualifier ID= CPS
        Qualifier: http://www.compaq.com/certsvc/cp.asp
    [1,2]Policy Qualifier info:
        Policy Qualifier ID= CPS
        Qualifier: ftp://ftp.compaq.com/certsvc/cp.asp
    [1,3]Policy Qualifier info:
        Policy Qualifier ID= CPS
        Qualifier: ldap://ldap.compaq.com/ certsvc/cp.asp
    [1,4]Policy Qualifier Info:
        Policy Qualifier ID= User Notice
        Qualifier: Notice Text= Compaq Certificate Policy
```

Parameters set during CA configuration

Once installed you have to configure your CA and all the settings related to the operation of your PKI environment. This includes configuration of CRL preferences, policy and exit module settings, loading of the appropriate certificate templates, delegation of administrative control, setting of identification options, setting up additional certificate request interfaces, and hardening the CA server. Again, in what follows we will not review topics that were discussed extensively in the previous chapter:

1.   CA identification options

2.   Certificate request interfaces

3.   Certificate templates and their ACLs set on forest level

CRL settings   In the planning for a PKI you should consider how CRLs will be generated, distributed, and checked. You need to think about the following CRL-related parameters: the period allowed between key compromise and certificate revocation, the CRL lifetime and publication interval, and the number and type of CRL Distribution Points (CDPs).

The period allowed between key compromise and certificate revocation is a parameter that should be agreed upon in the CP and mentioned in the CPS.

When setting the CRL lifetime and publication interval parameters, keep the following in mind:

- In Windows 2000 the CRL lifetime and publication interval are, although closely related, not the same. The CRL lifetime is deducted from the publication interval and is by default 10 percent longer than its publication schedule. This enables Windows 2000 to deal with the replication delay of CRLs that are published in AD. The CRL overlap can be set in the registry using the CRLOverlapPeriod, CRLOverlapUnits, and the Clockskewminutes parameters, that are located in the HKEY_LOCAL_MACHINE\SYSTEM\CurrentControlSet\Services\CertSvc\Configuration\<CA Name>\ registry hive. Here's an example: Imagine you have to deal with a replication delay of four hours. In this case, it would be wise to set the overlap period to five hours. The CRL lifetime resulting from the registry settings below would be: one week, five hours, and ten minutes, which is the sum of the CRLPeriod, CRLOverlapPeriod, and Clockskewminutes:

CRLPeriod	REG_SZ = Weeks
CRLPeriodUnits	REG_DWORD = 1
CRLOverlapPeriod	REG_SZ = Hours
CRLOverlapUnits	REG_DWORD = 5
ClockSkewMinutes	REG_DWORD = a

  Setting the CRLOverlapUnits parameter in the registry to 0 activates the default algorithm for the calculation of the CRL overlap.

- The shorter the CRL lifetime the faster the user is apprised of a revoked certificate. Setting CRL publication and thus CRL lifetimes too short can burden the network with numerous CRL downloads.

- Windows 2000 supports both automated and manual CRL publishing. To disable automatic CRL publishing, check the *Disable publication schedule* box or set the CRLPeriodUnits parameter in the registry to 0. Automatic CRL publication cannot be set to less than one hour. It is set on the CA level, in the properties of the Revoked Certificates container, available from the MMC CA snap-in.

- If some of your PKI-enabled applications have different CRL publication requirements, you'll have to install multiple CAs (e.g., one with a short publication schedule, which is used for an application with high security requirements, and another one with a longer schedule for an application with lower security requirements).

Figure 9.7
Publishing CRLs
manually

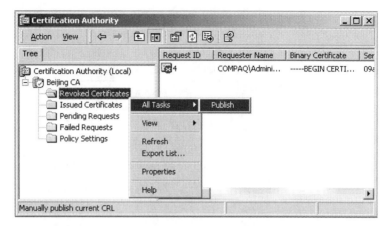

The previous text focused on automatic CRL publication. CRLs also can be published manually by right-clicking the Revoked Certificates container and selecting Publish (as illustrated in Figure 9.7).

Windows 2000 supports four types of CDPs: LDAP, file system, HTTP, and FTP-based CDPs. For CRL downloads within your Windows 2000 organization, the Active Directory is an obvious storage location; in this case, you will be using LDAP CDPs. If you also share PKI-enabled applications with entities outside your organization, you'll need to consider alternative CDP locations, such as FTP sites or Web pages.

CDPs are configured in the X.509 Extensions tab of the Policy Module Configuration dialog box, available from the properties of the CA object container (in the MMC CA snap-in). To define CDPs you should use the text string variables, also known as the replaceable parameter syntax, defined in Table 9.5. In the registry the text string variables are translated into numbered variables.

The renewal extension is the extension that is added to the CRL name when the CA's key pair has been changed, and thus when a CRL is generated. The %5 and %6 variables both point to the PKI entries in the Active Directory.

Remember that the CDP settings for the certificate of a root CA are configured during CA installation using the Capolicy.inf file, as explained earlier in this chapter. To use the replaceable parameter syntax for CDP and AIA specifications in the capolicy.inf file, you need to add an extra % before every parameter; for example, instead of %8, you should specify %%8. To

Table 9.5   *CDP Replaceable Parameter Syntax*

Text String Variable	Numbered Variable	Value
%SERVER_DNS_NAME%	%1	DNS name of CA
%SERVER_SHORT_NAME%	%2	NetBIOS name of CA
%CA_NAME%	%3	Name of CA
%CERT_SUFFIX%	%4	Renewal extension of CA
	%5	Location of domain root in AD
%CONFIG_NAME%	%6	Location of Configuration container in AD
%CA_NAME_HASH%	%7	Sanitized name of CA
%CRL_SUFFIX%	%8	CRL base file name and renewal extension for the CA

specify a space in the CDP or AIA, you need to add three extra % to the %20, so it becomes %%%%20.

Table 9.6 lists some sample file, AD, and Web CDPs.

Certificate characteristics   The administrator of a Windows 2000 CA can set the following certificate properties: the certificate lifetime, the CRL Distribution Points (CDPs), and the Authority Information Access (AIA) points. The CA administrator cannot influence a user's key pair lifetime; this is a user decision taken when the user renews certificates. Remember that machine certificates, resulting from an autoenrollment, will renew their key pair automatically at each automatic certificate renewal.

Table 9.6   *CDP Examples*

CDP	Sample CDPs
File CDP	File://\\%SERVER_DNS_NAME%\CertEnroll\%CA_NAME%%CRL_SUFFIX%.crl
AD CDP	ldap:///CN=%CA_NAME_HASH%%CRL_SUFFIX%, CN=%SERVER_SHORT_NAME%,CN=CDP,CN=Public Key Services, CN=Services,%CONFIG_NAME%?certificateRevocationList?base?objectclass= cRLDistributionPoint
Web CDP	Http://%SERVER_DNS_NAME%/CertEnroll/%CA_NAME%%CRL_SUFFIX%.crl

The way CDPs can be changed was explained previously. To set AIAs you can use the same procedure and variables as the ones outlined for CDPs.

The default certificate lifetimes and the way you can change the defaults were explained in Chapter 8. When planning for certificate lifetimes, you have to consider the lifetime and key length of the associated public-private key pair, the certificate and private key storage, the risk for attacks, the trust your organization has in the certificate subjects, the impact on network traffic, and the amount of administrative effort your organization can invest in certificate administration. These are as follows:

- The longer the lifetime of the public and private key pair, the more packets will be secured with the same key pair, and thus the more opportunities a hacker will get to break the mathematical problem behind an asymmetric cipher. Hence, it's a good practice to renew the key pair at each certificate renewal.

- Certificate lifetime is also related to key length. Because it takes less time to resolve the mathematical problem behind an asymmetric cipher using short keys, certificates certifying short public keys should have a shorter lifetime than the ones certifying long public keys.

- The storage of public key credentials on a dedicated hardware device, such as a smart card, and, consequently, the use of a hardware CSP, lower the risk for private key compromise. If there's less risk for compromise, you may as well lengthen the key pair and certificate lifetimes. The risk for attacks is also influenced by other IT environmental factors, such as the cryptographic knowledge of your employees.

- Certificate lifetime impacts the number of certificate renewal requests sent across your network. In environments with scarce bandwidth (e.g., users in remote sites connecting to a CA across a slow WAN) this can be a reason to lengthen certificates' lifetimes.

- If you're issuing certificates to users of your corporate extranet, the certificate lifetime might be shorter than when you're issuing certificates to users of your corporate intranet. Generally the level of trust an organization has in its internal users is higher than the level of trust it has in the external users of the corporate IT infrastructure.

CA administration delegation   Administration of the Windows 2000 CA can be delegated to different administrators by setting the appropriate ACLs on the CA object. Table 9.7 shows the permissions that can be set. CA administration delegation can be subdivided into three categories, as follows:

1.   CA manage permission: for administrators managing the CA configuration. This permission allows for fine-grained delegation—for example, CA management can be delegated for certificate revocation or certificate request approval.

Table 9.7   *CA Administrative Delegation: Basic Permissions and Default Membership*

	Meaning	Default Membership
Basic View		
Manage (1)	Accounts and groups that can manage CA using MMC snap-in or from command line	Administrators (local) Domain Admins Enterprise Admins
Enroll	Accounts and groups that can request certificates	Administrators (local) Domain Admins Enterprise Admins Authenticated Users
Read (2)	Accounts and groups that can read CA configuration information	Administrators (local) Domain Admins Enterprise Admins Authenticated Users
Advanced View		
Write Configuration	Accounts and groups that can change CA configuration information	Manage members (1)
Read Control	Accounts and groups that can view the CA configuration information	Read members (2)
Modify Permissions	Accounts and groups that can change CA security permissions	Manage members (1)
Modify Owner	Accounts and groups that can change ownership of a CA object	Manage members (1)
Revoke Certificates	Accounts and groups that can revoke certificates	Manage members (1)
Approve Certificates	Accounts and groups that can approve certificate requests	Manage members (1)
Read Database	Accounts and groups that can access and read the CA database	Manage members (1)

2.   CA read permission: for administrators needing just read permission to the CA configuration.

3.   CA enroll permission: for PKI clients that need to request certificates to the CA.

To view the CA permissions, right-click on the CA object in the MMC certification authority snap-in and select properties.

Although Windows 2000 offers plenty of flexibility for the definition of CA-related administrative tasks, it offers no or very little flexibility for the delegation of CA-related installations in a Windows 2000 forest. For example, in a forest only a root domain or an enterprise administrator can install an enterprise CA; the reason being that installation of an enterprise CA requires read/write access to the AD configuration NC. Consequently, an enterprise administrator cannot delegate the installation of an enterprise subordinate CA to an administrator of a child domain.

Hardening the CA server   A CA's private key is the most critical element of PKI security. If a root or intermediate CA's private key is compromised, part or even all of the certificates issued in your PKI become untrustworthy. The level of security provided by a CA on the level of the private key storage will also have an important impact on the amount of trust people have in the CA. This is why it is so important to store the CA's private key securely, to keep root and intermediate CAs offline, and to harden your CA server by boosting its physical, logical, communications, and organizational security. Some points to consider are as follows:

- Physical security. Install Certificate Servers on computers in secure areas, where physical access is controlled and there is protection against fire, power loss, and other disasters.

- Logical security. Implement software access control systems on the computer to prevent unauthorized access to computer systems. In a Windows 2000 environment, logical security depends on the quality of the operating system's authentication and access control system, as follows:

  - You can provide high-quality authentication by equipping all servers with smart-card readers, which provide two-factor authentication.
  - You can provide high-quality access control by checking the ACLs on all the server's resources at regular intervals using the Security Configuration and Analysis (SCA) tool.

- You can also use the SCA to audit the security settings on Windows 2000 servers. You can automate the SCA and run it at regular intervals in batch mode (using secedit.exe).

- Communications security. To provide communications security for the CAs (issuing CAs or other online CAs) that are connected to your production network, you can install them on a separate subnet, behind a dedicated firewall or router filtering out all non-PKI-related traffic.

- Organizational security. Make the administrators of the CA and the operators of the computer room where the CA server is located aware of the importance of the CA. Convince them that this is not an ordinary file and print server but a server used to secure your corporate IT environment.

Defining public key policy settings (GPO)

Windows 2000 GPO objects include some PKI-related entries: automated certificate request settings, trusted root certification authorities, enterprise trust, and encrypted data recovery agents. Table 9.8 shows the mapping between the PKI-related GPO settings, the GPO levels (domain, site, OU, or local), and the GPO portions (user or machine). Notice that the same settings occur on the site, domain, and OU level. Settings that are defined on the machine level are shared with all users logging on to the machine and all services that are running on the machine. Settings defined on the user level are only valid on the user level. Figure 9.8 shows the GPO containers holding the PKI-related settings.

Automated certificate requests

The automated certificate request GPO setting refers to automated certificate enrollment and renewal. Windows 2000 administrators can set machine accounts to enroll automatically for a certificate when they boot up or the next time their GPO settings are enforced. This feature enables you, for example, to autoenroll all machines located in one of your Windows 2000 sites. Automatic renewal starts automatically at some predefined moment, defined in the renewal overlap parameter of a certificate template, before the expiration of the certificate.

The following machine-related certificate types can be automatically requested: computer, DC, Ipsec, and enrollment agent. Automated enrolment can be very useful for IPsec or SSL certificate-based machine authentication. In the Automatic Certificate Request Setup wizard you can select

Table 9.8 *PKI-Related GPO Settings*

	GPO Level	User	Machine
Automated Certificate Request	Domain		X
	Site		X
	OU		X
	Local		
Trusted Root CAs	Domain		X
	Site		X
	OU		X
	Local		
Enterprise Trust	Domain	X	X
	Site	X	X
	OU	X	X
	Local		
Encrypted Data Recovery Agents	Domain		X
	Site		X
	OU		X
	Local		X

multiple enterprise CAs to service the request. This feature can provide some level of fault tolerance: If the first CA in the list is unavailable, the next one can be tried.

Let's look at the technical details of autoenrollment. Every time the GPO settings are applied to the machine, an autoenrollment event occurs. This event triggers more than just autoenrollment, as follows:

- The status of the current available machine certificates is checked against the autoenrollment object. This not only means that the machine will automatically enroll for a certificate, but also that it will reenroll in case of certificate revocation, certificate expiration, or even in the case where the CAs issuing the autoenroll certificate have been changed in the GPO setting.

Figure 9.8
PKI-related GPO
settings

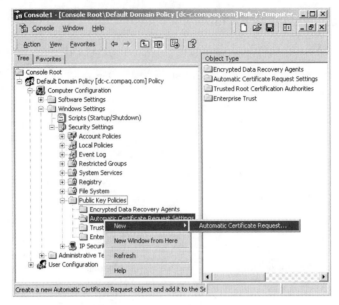

- Certificates of enterprise root CAs are downloaded from the DS-based enterprise root store to the machine's local trusted root certification authorities certificate store.

- Enterprise CA certificates are downloaded from the Active Directory–based NTAuth store to the local machine NTAuth store.

The autoenrollment event occurs when the GPO is pulsed: this happens automatically at machine startup or every eight hours; it can happen manually by using the resource kit tool Dsstore with the –pulse switch.

Independently of this setting every Windows 2000 DC that is part of a Windows 2000 forest containing an enterprise CA automatically enrolls for a DC certificate.

Trusted root CAs

The trusted root CAs GPO setting contains a list of trusted CA certificates. The name of the container is rather misleading: it can contain certificates of both root and subordinate CAs, as well as certificates of CAs internal or external to your Windows 2000 organization. Contrary to the enterprise trust setting, you cannot limit the trust of CA certificates in this container based on time or application (certificate template). The certificates that are part of this GPO setting will be downloaded to the Trusted Root Certification Authorities container of your Windows 2000 clients.

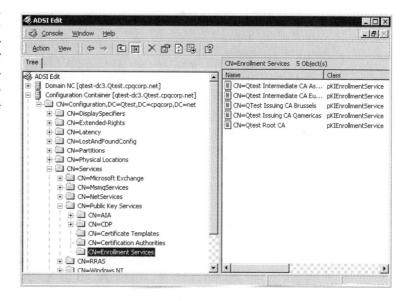

Figure 9.9
*Checking out the
content of the DS
enterprise root store
and the NTAuth
store using adsiedit*

Besides the use of this GPO setting, there are two other ways to auto-matically download CA certificates to users' Trusted Root Certification Authorities certificate store containers. Both the certificate entries in the DS enterprise root store and NTAuth store are downloaded to the trusted root certification authorities certificate store when the autoenrollment event occurs. Both containers are defined forest-wide in the AD configuration NC (as illustrated in Figure 9.9 and outlined in the following list).

- The DS enterprise root store:

  If a root domain administrator or an enterprise administrator installs an enterprise or standalone root CA in a Windows 2000 domain, a CA object is automatically added to the Active Directory–based enterprise root store. The multivalued Cacertificate attribute of the CA object contains the CA's certificate(s). This store is located in CN=< CA NAME >, CN=Certification Authorities,CN=Public Key Services,CN=Services,CN=Configuration,DC=<root domain in enter-prise>,DC=com. To display or modify (add/delete) the content of the DS enterprise root store you can use: **dsstore <DN of root domain (required) > [–display | –del | –addroot]**.

- The NTAuth store:

  If a root domain administrator or an enterprise administrator installs an enterprise CA in a Windows 2000 domain, a CA object is auto-matically added to the Active Directory–based NTAuth store. This

AD store contains the certificates of Enterprise CAs that are capable of issuing smart-card logon and enrollment agent certificates. The multivalued Cacertificate attribute of the CA object contains the CA's certificate(s). This store is located in CN=< CA NAME >, CN=Enrollment Services,CN=Public Key Services,CN=Services,CN=Configuration,DC=<root domain in enterprise>,DC=com.

Enterprise trust

The enterprise trust GPO setting contains a signed list of CA certificates of CAs that are internal or external to your organization and that need to be trusted by your internal Windows 2000 entities. The setting is referred to as a certificate trust list. The concept of CTLs was also used in Exchange 5.5 Advanced Security to enable S/MIME-based security interoperability between two organizations. To create a CTL an administrator needs a CTL signing or administrator certificate. By default members of the Enterprise Admins and Domain Admins groups can enroll for these certificates.

Using the enterprise trust GPO setting the trust definition can be fine-tuned based on *Certificate type* and *Validity period.* This is very different from the trusted root certification authorities GPO setting: a CA that is trusted using this setting is by default trusted for all purposes and for its entire lifetime.

- *Certificate type* allows you to specify that certificates coming from a particular CA are trusted only for some uses or purposes (such as secure e-mail). Besides the certificate purposes available by default, you can also add your own purposes. To do this, add the appropriate OID in the User-Defined Purposes dialog box. These purposes are listed in the *subject usage* extension of the CTL.

- *Validity period* allows you to specify that certificates coming from a particular CA are trusted only if they are used within a certain time period. If the administrator doesn't specify a time limit, the CTL expires when the CTL signing certificate expires. The CTL validity period can be specified in months and days; it is listed in the *effective date* and *next update* extensions of the CTL.

- Besides the *subject usage, effective date*, and *next update* fields, the CTL format used by Microsoft also contains a version number, a list identifier, the subject algorithm, the thumbprint algorithm, a thumbprint, and a friendly name. A CTL's properties are displayed in the CTL dialog box, which opens up when double-clicking a CTL. The same dialog box can be used to view the CTL signature.

Encrypted data recovery agents

The encrypted data recovery agents GPO setting is used to define accounts that have the ability to recover Encrypting File System (EFS) data. A Windows 2000 domain administrator can grant this privilege to a limited number of Windows 2000 accounts. Only accounts that have an EFS recovery certificate can be added to this setting. You can add accounts by pointing to their recovery certificates stored in the Active Directory or on the file system.

9.1.3 Windows 2000 PKI management

In this section we will focus on the key administrative and maintenance tasks related to a Windows 2000 PKI: CA and directory backup and restore, CA certificate rollover, and last but not least, troubleshooting tools.

The primary Certificate Server administration interface is a Microsoft Management Console (MMC) snap in (as illustrated in Figure 9.10). You can use it to stop and start the CA service, revoke certificates, issue CRLs, add certificate templates, back up and restore the CA, and look at the CA database contents. You can set permissions on the level of the CA container, which allows you to delegate CA-related administrative tasks.

CA-directory backup/restore

As with any other critical component of your Windows 2000 infrastructure, it's very important to have solid backup-restore procedures for your CA and its database. Windows 2000 comes with two built-in tools for backup and restore of a Windows 2000 CA: the regular ntbackup utility and the CA-specific backup utility.

Figure 9.10
The Windows 2000 CA MMC snap-in

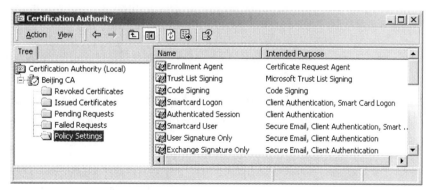

Table 9.9   *CA File System Level Data*

Name	Notes
CA Configuration directory	Only available if created during CA installation (shared as certconfig)
CA Database directory	Default: <system root>\system32\certlog
CA Web directory	Default: <system root>\system32\certsrv

The regular Windows 2000 backup and restore utility (ntbackup) can be used to back up all the CA file system–level data listed in Table 9.9.

An interesting side note: The ntbackup utility is the one that causes a checkpoint to be written to the Certificate Server log files. If you do not use ntbackup, the Certificate Server log files will accumulate.

The CA-specific backup/restore utility is available from the CA MMC snap-in (in the form of a wizard) and from the command prompt (using the certutil utility). The CA-specific backup/restore utility can back up and restore the CA database, the CA private key and certificate, or all of them together. During the backup the CA certificate and private key are exported to a PKCS12 file. Obviously, you'll need to provide a password to secure the PKCS12 file containing the private key. The certutil backup-restore switches and their meaning are explained in Table 9.10.

Both the MMC wizard and certutil allow you to specify which parts of the CA database you want to back up: only the CA configuration information, only the logs and request queues, or both. The configuration information should only be backed up when needed—or in other words, when the CA's configuration has changed. Note that the configuration information the wizard backs up is very limited: it does not include CA policy or exit module settings, ACLs set for delegation, or the CA registry settings; it just backs up the CA naming information and certificate. To back up these other settings it's better to use the regular ntbackup, which makes a backup of the complete system state.

Before starting the backup be sure you have prepared a separate backup medium or at least a separate folder, different from the CA configuration folder on the CA server. Also, the backup will fail if the folder you are using is not empty. The CA's certificate log and pending certificate request queue can be backed up in an incremental manner. An incremental backup can be saved at the same location as a full backup. When doing a restore from a full backup and a set of incremental backups, never restart the CA service if not

Table 9.10   *certutil Backup/Restore Switches*

Certutil Backup/Restore Command	Meaning
certutil [options] –config ConfigString] –backup|restore BackupDirectory [password [incremental] [KeepLog]]	Backs up or restores the CA database, certificate, and private key[*]
certutil [options] [–config ConfigString] –backupDB|restoreDB BackupDirectory [[incremental] [KeepLog]]	Backs up or restores the CA database[*]
certutil [options] [–config ConfigString] –backupKey|restoreKey BackupDirectory [password]	Backs up or restores the CA certificate and private key[*]

*–config: backs up CA configuration; keeplog: backs up certificate log and pending certificate request queue.

all incremental backups have been restored; if you do, you'll lose all the changes since the last full or incremental backup that was ran before restarting the CA service.

CA rollover

In PKI terminology, CA certificate rollover is the generation of a new CA certificate. Rollover is needed in the following scenarios:

- (A) Extending the CA certificate lifetime:

  As with any other certificate, the CA certificate has a validity period. Timely renewal of the CA certificate is critical for two reasons: First, the lifetime of the certificates issued by a CA is automatically reduced as the CA's certificate is approaching its expiration date. Second, A CA cannot issue any new certificates or CRLs if it doesn't have a valid certificate. A new CA certificate can be based on the same key pair as its predecessor—this means that the lifetime of the old certificate is simply extended—or it can use a newly generated key pair. Generating a new key pair has these advantages:

  - Better security. A CA is the most critical PKI component; reusing keys gives hackers more opportunities (and more time) to derive and compromise your CA's private key. Since we're talking about asymmetric ciphers, the risk that a hacker will succeed in breaking the asymmetric cipher and deriving the CA private key is obviously very low.
  - The generation of a new CRL. We previously explained how the generation of a new CA key pair and certificate also generates a new CRL.

When the CA administrator chooses to generate a new certificate and at the same time generate a new key pair, the old certificates that were issued by the CA before the renewal and that were signed with its old private key will not be invalidated. The old CA certificates remain trustworthy.

- (B) CA private key compromise:

An extreme scenario, which can require CA certificate rollover, is CA private key compromise. A new private key means a new public key and thus a new certificate. The important question here is whether your certificate clients will still trust your CA if its private key has been compromised. Remember that CA private key protection is extremely important! This scenario requires that your CA certificate be put on a CRL. To revoke a root CA's certificate use the certutil utility with the certificate's serial number as a parameter. Revoking a subordinate CA's certificate can be done from the parent CA's CA MMC snap-in. Contrary to the previous scenario, CA private key compromise will make the old CA certificate untrustworthy: Validation of certificates issued by the CA using the CA's old certificate will fail.

- (C) CRL partitioning:

Indirectly this can be another reason for CA rollover: when the CRL is getting too big and you want to partition your CRLs or start all over with a new CRL.

To support the previous scenarios, Windows 2000 supports the following rollover methods:

- Renewing the CA certificate: This means issuing a new CA certificate with the same public and private key material as the old CA certificate, but with an extended validity period. This is a rollover solution for scenario (A).

- Reissuing the CA certificate: This means issuing a new CA certificate with a new public and private key and validity period. This is a rollover solution for scenario (A), (B) and (C). Reissuing is a solution to get around CRL sizing problems and results in the generation of a new CRL. Reissuing means new CA keys, which means that another private key will be used to sign the revoked certificate information.

To renew or reissue a CA certificate, you simply run the renewal wizard from the CA snap-in. You are asked if you want to reuse the same key pair (renew) or generate a new one (reissue). The wizard will bring up different dialog boxes depending on whether you're dealing with a root CA or a subordinate CA. Remember that a root CA has a self-signed certificate, a subordinate CA's certificate is signed by its parent CA; this means that in the case of a subordinate CA certificate renewal or reissue, you'll have to go back to the parent CA.

Certificate renewal or reissue affects the version number of the CAs certificate; the CA version is an extension that is part of all MS CA certificates. Renewal will add 1 to the CA certificate's version number; reissue will add 1,2. Another way to distinguish between renewal and reissue on the level of the CA certificate properties is the following: reissue will generate a new subject key identifier field. This is pretty obvious since the CA's key pair has been changed. Of course reissue will also change the version number of the CRL.

Troubleshooting and administration tools

The primary administration interface to the Windows 2000 PKI services is the CA MMC snap-in. Windows 2000 and the Windows 2000 resource kit also come with command prompt PKI administration and troubleshooting tools: certutil, certreq, certsrv, and dsstore.

Certsrv with the –z switch can be used to run the CA service in diagnostic mode. You cannot use this switch if your CA is up and running as a service.

Table 9.11 lists what you can use the certutil tool for.

Table 9.11   *certutil Switches*

Goal	Tool
Display CA configuration information	certutil [options] –dump
Display CA configuration string	certutil [options] –getconfig
Retrieve the CA signing certificate (and chain)	certutil [options] –v [–config ConfigString] –ca.cert CACertFile certutil [options] –v [–config ConfigString] –ca.chain OutCACertChain-File
Revoke certificates	certutil [options] [–config ConfigString] –revoke SerialNumber
Publish the CRL	certutil [options] [–config ConfigString] –CRL [OutFileResult|–]
Check certificate validity	certutil [options] –verify CertFile [CACertFile]
Approve or deny pending certificate requests	certutil [options] [–config ConfigString] –deny RequestId

Table 9.11   *certutil Switches (continued)*

Goal	Tool
Set extensions on pending certificate requests	certutil [options] [–config ConfigString] –setattributes RequestId AttributeString
Verify a key set	certutil [options] –verifykeys KeyContainerName CACertFile
Decode or encode Base64	certutil [options] –decode InFile OutFileResult certutil [options] –encode InFile OutFileResult
Shut down the CA server	certutil [options] [–config ConfigString] –shutdown
Display the CA database schema	certutil [options] [–config ConfigString] –schema
Convert CS 1.0 database to CS 2.0 database	certutil [options] [–config ConfigString] –ConvertMDB
Back up and restore CA keys and database	certutil [options] [–config ConfigString] –backup|restore Backup-Directory [password [incremental] [KeepLog]] certutil [options] [–config ConfigString] –backupDB|restoreDB Backup-Directory [[incremental] [KeepLog]] certutil [options] [–config ConfigString] –backupKey|restoreKey Backup-Directory [password]
Display CA database locations	certutil [options] [–config ConfigString] –databaselocations
Display certificates in the machine certificate store	certutil [options] –store [CertificateStoreName [CertIndex [OutputFile]]]
Display certificates in the machine certificate store and verify certificates and private keys	certutil [options] –verifystore CertificateStoreName [CertIndex]
Display certificates in the user certificate store	certutil [options] –user –store [CertificateStoreName [CertIndex [OutputFile]]]
Display error code message text	certutil [options] –error ErrorCode
Import certificates into the database	certutil [options] [–config ConfigString] –importcert Certfile [Flags]
Set and display CA registry settings	certutil [options] [–config ConfigString] –getreg [{ca|restore|policy|exit} [\ProgId] \RegistryValueName certutil [options] [–config ConfigString] –setreg [{ca|restore|policy|exit}\[ProgId]\RegistryValueName
Create or remove CA Web virtual roots and file shares	certutil [options] –vroot [delete]
Add the Netscape certificate revocation extension to every issued certificate	certutil [options] –SetReg Policy\RevocationType [+|–]AspEnable

Table 9.12   *certreq Switches*

Goal	Tool
Request certificates	CertReq [–rpc] [–binary] [–config ConfigString] [–attrib AttributeString] [RequestFile [Certfile[CertChainFile]]]
Retrieve certificates, that were set to pending	CertReq –retrieve [–rpc] [–binary] [–config ConfigString] [RequestId [Certfile [CertChainFile]]]

Using the certreq tool you can request and retrieve certificates from the command prompt, as shown in Table 9.12.

Using dsstore, the directory services store tool, you can accomplish the goals outlined in Table 9.13.

Table 9.13   *dsstore Switches*

Goal	Tool
Trigger the autoenrollment object	dsstore –pulse
Check and manipulate DC certificates	dsstore [–domain <target domain>] –dcmon
Manage certificates in the DS enterprise root store	dsstore <DN of root domain (required) > [–display | –del | –addroot]
Check on validity of a smart-card certificate	dsstore –checksc
List information about enterprise CAs	dsstore –tcainfo
List information about a machine's certificates	dsstore – entmon <machine name>
List information about machine objects	dsstore –macobj <machine name, SAM style>
Add non-Windows 2000 CAs or offline CAs	dsstore <DN of root domain (required)> –addroot <.crt file> <ca name>
	dsstore <DN of root domain (required)> –addcrl <.crl file> <ca name> <machine name>
	dsstore <DN of root domain (required)> –addaia <.crt file> <ca name>

9.2   Building and using applications on top of Windows 2000 PKI

One of the key messages you should remember from Chapter 8 is that a PKI is an infrastructure, of which multiple applications can take advantage to provide strong public key cryptography–based security. In this section, we will look at two of Windows 2000's most important PKI-enabled applications: the Encrypting File System (EFS) and S/MIME, a standard for secure messaging. We will also explore the support for smart cards in Windows 2000 and how PKI-enabled applications can leverage the advanced security features offered by smart cards.

9.2.1   Encrypting file system

The disclosure of confidential information to unauthorized parties is a serious threat from which any organization should be protected. On a Windows platform an obvious solution is to implement an efficient authentication and access control system. Both NT4 and Windows 2000 implement such systems as part of the operating system. This way, the only way a hacker can get to the files is by getting around the operating system. Some hackers have succeeded in doing this; remember the NT4 war stories regarding the ntfsdos, ntfs driver for Linux, and getadmin tools. A more efficient protection mechanism against both accidental disclosure and theft of information by either internal or external entities is encryption. If somebody circumvents the OS kernel–level protection, there's another encryption-based level of protection.

The Encrypting File System (EFS), a feature of the Windows 2000 NTFS version 5 file system, provides file system–level encryption of files and folders stored on Windows 2000 NTFS volumes. Before Windows 2000, NT users had to look at the products of other vendors to implement an encryption solution. At the end of this section we will list some encryption solutions from other vendors.

NTFS files and folders can be encrypted manually by checking the *Encrypt contents to secure data* box in the advanced properties or by choosing the Encrypt command on a file or folder's short-cut menu. If you set the encryption attribute on the folder level, newly created files in the folder will be automatically encrypted. Unless you check the *Apply changes to this folder, subfolders, and files* box, files that already existed in the folder before the encryption attribute was set will not be encrypted. The same is true for decryption.

Table 9.14 *Cipher Switches*

Command	Effect
Cipher /E /A /I <path>	Encrypts all files and subfolders in the specified file system path and ignores possible errors
Cipher /D /A /I <path>	Decrypts all files and subfolders in the specified file system path and ignores possible errors
Cipher /E /A <path>/*.txt <path>/*.bat	Encrypts all txt and bat files in the specified file system paths
Cipher /E /A /F <path>/*.*	Forces the encryption of all files in the specified file system path; files encrypted previously are reencrypted
Cipher <path>	Shows the EFS status (U or E) of all files in the specified file system path

The Encrypt/Decrypt short-cut menu option is disabled by default. To enable it, add EncryptionContextMenu with REG_DWORD value 1 to the HKEY_LOCAL_MACHINE\Software\Microsoft\Windows\Current-Version\Explorer\Advanced registry key.

The cipher.exe tool can be used to automate and enforce encryption from the command prompt. You can include it in a user's logon or logoff script. In Windows 2000 you could automatically distribute these scripts throughout the enterprise using GPOs. Table 9.14 lists some sample cipher commands and their effect.

EFS internals

The software technology behind EFS is a good example of a hybrid cryptographic solution (explained in Chapter 5) combining the power of both asymmetric and symmetric ciphers. EFS uses a symmetric cipher (DESX) to perform the bulk encryption and an asymmetric cipher (RSA) to provide secure storage of the bulk encryption key (as illustrated in Figures 9.11 and 9.12). The bulk encryption key is known as the File Encryption Key (FEK).

The encrypted FEK is stored along with every encrypted file or folder, in the NTFS $EFS attribute. The $EFS attribute is stored in a file's logged tool stream attribute ($Logged_Utility_Stream). Changes to this attribute are logged in the NTFS change log. EFS encrypts an NTFS file's content, contained in the unnamed $data stream, as well as every additional NTFS file stream.

Multiple encrypted versions of the FEK are stored: one for the account that encrypted the information and one for every recovery agent. The first is

Figure 9.11
*How EFS
encryption works*

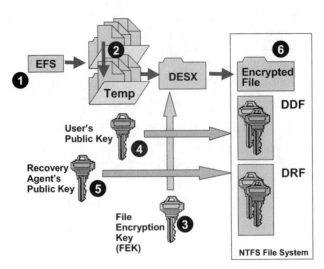

stored in the Data Decryption Field (DDF), the latter in the Data Recovery Field (DRF). DDF and DRF are also known as key rings; the DDF contains one, the DRF can contain several key entries (one for every recovery agent). When using EFS don't forget that the account that can encrypt data is not restricted to the owner of the data. In order to encrypt a file you don't need file or folder ownership but you need at least read/write permission to the file or folder.

DDFs and DRFs contain besides the encrypted bulk encryption key, information that facilitates the lookup of the account's private key, which is needed for the decryption of the FEK:

- The account's distinguished name
- The CSP (Cryptographic Service Provider) used for encryption/ decryption
- The location the CSP uses to store the certificates (certificate store container)
- The certificate thumbprint

To retrieve a private key the Local Security Authority (LSA) will pass the certificate's thumbprint and certificate store to the CSP. The $EFS file attribute (containing a file's DDFs and DRFs) also contains a checksum, which is used by the EFS system to detect integrity changes on the DDF and DRF level. This protects against tampering with the EFS data on the file system level.

Figure 9.12
How EFS
decryption works

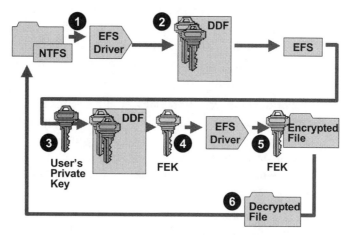

To look at the content of the DDF and DRF fields you can use the command prompt resource kit tool efsinfo or the tool efsdump available from the sysinternals Web site (*http://www.sysinternals.com*). Efsdump displays the contents of the DDF and DRF key rings. For each entry it shows the account name and the subject's distinguished name. With efsinfo you can do the same and even more. Two interesting efsinfo switches are /C and /Y. The /C switch displays the certificate thumbprints of the encryption and recovery certificates, referred to in the DDF and DRF rings. The /Y switch displays the thumbprint of a user's local EFS certificate. To look at both the DDF and DRF fields and the associated certificate thumbprints, use **efsinfo /u /r /c <filename>** (as illustrated in Figure 9.13).

All EFS operations (encryption, decryption, and recovery) are fault tolerant and are logged. During an EFS operation a hidden log file (named efs0.log) is created in the hidden system volume information folder. Besides a log file the EFS system also creates a temporary backup of the file being encrypted in the file's directory (named efs0.tmp). If your system crashes

Figure 9.13
Using efsinfo

```
C:\WINNT\System32\cmd.exe                                    _ □ ×

C:\Customers>efsinfo /u /r /c ITproject.txt

C:\Customers\

ITproject.txt: Encrypted
  Users who can decrypt:
    QTEST\Administrator (CN=Administrator)
    Certificate thumbprint: 6C8D F332 9A46 1B98 9E3F F511 1D77 4AA4 1FD7 86E3
  Recovery Agents:
    QTEST\gonzalez (OU=EFS File Encryption Certificate, L=EFS, CN=gonzalez)
    Certificate thumbprint: F919 BD8D FEB6 1EF9 E7E9 5F14 8476 A50D 88FF 8432

C:\Customers>_
```

during an EFS encryption operation, the EFS operation will be rolled back and the original, possibly corrupted, file will be replaced with the backup file. To look at what's happening behind the scenes on the file system level when using EFS you can use sysinternals' Filemon tool (available from their Web site).

For obvious security reasons the FEK is never paged to disk. However, some applications dealing with an encrypted file might copy some of the cleartext to the paging file. Since the paging file is a system file and thus cannot be encrypted, Microsoft advices to clear the paging file at system shutdown. This can be automated by selecting the GPO setting *Clear virtual memory page file when system shuts down.*

The generation of a private-public key pair and a special EFS certificate happens transparently. When the user checks the encrypted property, chooses the encrypt option in the context menu, or encrypts a file or folder using the cipher command prompt tool, the system will automatically generate a private-public key pair and send a public key certification request to a Windows 2000 enterprise CA. If no CA is available, a certificate will be generated by a CSP on the local machine. This enables EFS to function even in the absence of a CA.

Once the EFS certificate is created or downloaded to the local certificate store, a reference to it (the certificate hash) is put in HKEY_CURRENT_USER\Software\Microsoft\Windows NT\CurrentVersion\EFS\CurrentKeys\CertificateHash. This value can be retrieved from the registry using the efsinfo tool with the /Y switch.

The following certificate templates can be used for EFS operations: user, administrator, and basic EFS. EFS certificates can be issued by a Windows 2000 standalone or enterprise CA. Possibly some third-party PKI software vendors will support the issuance of EFS certificates in the near future.

As with any other personal certificate, EFS certificates (and with them the EFS public keys) and EFS private keys are stored in the user's profile. More information on the storage of certificates and private keys can be found in Chapter 8. EFS certificates can be stored on a smart card; however, in the first release of Windows 2000 EFS could not access certificates stored on smart cards.

One of the key features of EFS is privacy. Encrypted data are only accessible by the account that performed the encryption. So what about encrypted file sharing? This means guaranteeing confidentiality (privacy) while at the same time letting multiple accounts access the file. This is a feature that could be useful on a departmental file server, for example.

Microsoft lets you add more accounts programmatically through the EFS AddUsersToEncryptedFile API function. For obvious reasons, this function can only be executed by the owner of the data or a recovery agent.

The enabling of real encrypted file sharing requires more than just programmatical changes. On a departmental file server an account other than an administrator or a recovery agent might need to decide which encrypted files are accessible to which users. Typically, this would be a job for the manager of a department. Microsoft promised to add EFS encrypted file sharing in the next major Windows 2000 release (also known as Whistler or Windows.Net). This illustrates that the current version of Windows 2000 EFS is targeted at laptop or single-user privacy. This does not mean that EFS could not be used to encrypt a user's home directory located on a central server. Later in this chapter we will list some other third-party products that can provide sharing of encrypting files on the server side.

EFS recovery

A key feature of EFS is its ability to recover encrypted files or folders when a user's private key is lost. Loss of private keys can occur because of hardware or software problems on a user's computer. Recovery can also be useful when an employee has left the company, when his or her account and profile are deleted, and when access is needed to files previously encrypted by that employee.

Recovery means that a Windows 2000 account (the recovery agent), other than the original account that encrypted the data, can decrypt the FEK and recover the user's data. The recovery agent can recover a file if his or her public key was used to encrypt the FEK and the resulting encrypted FEK is part of the encrypted file's NTFS $EFS attribute. In other words, when the account was defined as a recovery agent at the moment the file was encrypted. A recovery agent also needs to have a special key pair and a special certificate (an EFS recovery certificate) before the EFS encryption process takes place.

Recovery agents can be defined on the domain, site, organizational unit, or local machine level. You use the Windows 2000 Group Policy Object (GPO) Encrypted Data Recovery Policy (EDRP) entry to define them (as illustrated in Figure 9.14). The EDRP entry contains the EFS recovery certificates of Windows 2000 accounts designated as recovery agents by the GPO administrator. To facilitate the life of administrators Microsoft provides a wizard to set the recovery agents on the GPO level. The recovery certificates can be downloaded from the Active Directory or can be imported in *.cer format. EFS recovery certificates have file recovery (OID

Figure 9.14
Setting up the EDRP using GPOs

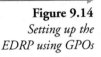

1.3.6.1.4.1.311.10.3.4.1) in the enhanced key usage field. They can be generated by an enterprise or a standalone CA; or even without the intervention of any CA. The recovery certificates that are in place after Windows 2000 installation are generated by the local machine.

To enable EFS recovery no CA is required. However, within a Windows 2000 environment the use of an enterprise CA for the generation of EFS certificates will offer more flexibility and centralized control over EFS recovery, as follows:

- An organization can provide EFS recovery privileges (in the form of an EFS recovery certificate) to specific administrator accounts; the organization can give them the privilege for a specific OU, site, domain, or machine.

- An organization can control the validity of the EFS recovery privilege because it has control over the lifetime and revocation of the associated EFS recovery certificate.

The default recovery agent is the administrator account. On a standalone machine, this is the local administrator account. On a machine member of a domain, it's the domain administrator. In many environments, this is fine; in others, it should be changed. It's a good practice to change the default domain recovery account administrator anyway.

The EDRP policy settings are downloaded to the machine at startup, at the predefined GPO update interval, or when GPO application is enforced. Changes in the EDRP content are not applied immediately to every encrypted file or folder in the EDRP scope. EFS will enforce and apply the change at the first decryption after the EDRP change. Remember that to define a new DRF, EFS needs the FEK; the FEK is only available at decryption time. In some Windows 2000 books, this is referred to as the EDRP lazy update.

Because of this feature, you should always archive the private keys and certificates of old recovery agents (in other words, keep the recovery agent private key and certificate history). By doing this you'll always be able to access every encrypted file, even those that haven't been opened since an EDRP change occurred (those where the FEK is still encrypted with a recovery agent's old public key). To archive a recovery agent's private key and certificate export them using the certificate export wizard. To find out which archived keying material you should use for a recovery, use the efs-info tool with the /C switch to retrieve the recovery agent's certificate thumbprint from the encrypted file.

Special care should be taken regarding the place where the archived recovery agent private keys are stored. They should be protected from unauthorized access. Remember that anyone possessing the recovery private key can read any encrypted file or folder within the EDRP scope. A good practice is to put the private key on a floppy disk or on a smart card and lock it in a safe. Also, when requesting a recovery certificate using the CA web interface, be sure to check *Enable strong private key protection* in the advanced request settings to provide another level of software protection.

Besides archiving the recovery agent's private key, you should also delete it from the local system. *Delete the private key if export is successful* is an option that can be set in the certificate export wizard. The reason for doing this is related to a fundamental security principle: encryption keys should never be stored near the files they secure. This is a must do for standalone machines; it is less critical for machines in a domain, where the recovery agent's private key is almost certainly located on another machine. In the summer of 1999 a hacker found this weakness and got lots of press attention. A less-secure alternative is to use a dedicated highly secure workstation, preferably off the network, which has a local copy of the recovery private key and is only used for EFS recovery.

The preferred procedure to recover an encrypted file is the following: let the user back up the file using NTbackup (NTbackup is the only way that an encrypted file can be exported from a Windows 2000 system without decrypting it). Let the user send it to a recovery agent using a secure channel. Let the recovery agent do the recovery, and let the recovery agent send the decrypted file back to the user, once more using a secure channel. A secure channel can be created by delivering the file out of band using a floppy, by copying it to a share across a VPN tunnel, or by sending it using a secured S/MIME mail message. Another, less secure and thus less preferred, way is to use a dedicated machine to perform the recovery of encrypted files.

EFS can be disabled based on the simple fact that EFS will not work if no EDRP is defined; using this workaround, you can disable EFS on the domain, site, OU, or machine level, as follows:

- To disable EFS on the domain, site, or OU level delete the EDRP policy or define an empty EDRP policy. In these cases you have to be careful about the special EDRP inheritance rules:
  - A deleted EDRP policy is not inherited from a higher level to a lower level.
  - An empty EDRP policy is inherited from a higher level to a lower level.

- To disable EFS on the machine level delete the EDRP policy or define an empty EDRP policy. Once more be careful about EDRP inheritance: if an EDRP policy has been defined on a higher level (domain, site, OU) it will be applied and override the empty or missing local EDRP policy.

If you want to enable EFS afterwards, be sure you have a copy of the recovery agent's certificate before deleting it from the EDRP (you can, for example, export it to a floppy disk or another medium).

To disable EFS on the file or folder level do the following:

- To disable EFS on the folder level set the system attribute and/or create a special entry in the folder's desktop.ini file (add *disable=1* underneath the [Encryption] section).

- To disable EFS on the file level set the system attribute.

EFS caveats and pitfalls

This section lists some special EFS features you need to consider when planning a corporate EFS deployment. Some of these features are very poorly documented; you can look at them as caveats and pitfalls.

To do EFS decryption operations you need access to the private key. As long as this can be done, any file encrypted with the corresponding public key can be decrypted. Microsoft has built in some features to facilitate access to the private key when a user is encrypting files on a file server from his or her workstation. Windows 2000 will automatically build a local user profile on the file server that contains a copy of the user's EFS certificate and private key. A copy of this EFS certificate and private key will also be available in the user's profile on the local workstation. A tricky detail in this scenario is that the file server machine account has to be trusted for delegation. Why? This is related to impersonation. To be able to decrypt the encrypted copy of the private key in the user profile the server process impersonating the user needs a valid Kerberos ticket. To obtain this ticket, the process must use Kerberos delegation.

Also, keep in mind that EFS encryption and decryption always happen locally. If you decrypt a file on a remote machine, the file will be decrypted remotely and will be send in the clear over the network. EFS does not provide communication security; if you need communication security, use a tunneling protocol. Some third-party products, discussed later in the chapter, can provide communication security for encrypted files.

EFS cannot be used to encrypt system files. Encrypting system files would block Windows 2000 system startup. The reason for this is that private keys are needed for system file decryption, and they cannot be accessed during system startup. Private keys are only available after a valid authentication, happening during a user's logon session. Also keep in mind that NTFS compression and encryption are mutually exclusive. Before an encrypted file or folder can be compressed, it should be decrypted.

As mentioned earlier, an encrypted copy of a user's private key is stored in his or her user profile. The profile that is chosen (from the local documents and settings folder or from the central roaming profile folder) is based on the user SID validated by the OS during the authentication phase. When using EFS, this has two important consequences, as follows:

- User accounts, SIDs, and profiles used when logging on locally are different from the ones that a user gets when he or she logs on to a domain. In other words, files that are encrypted while a user is logged on to a domain cannot be accessed while the user is logged on locally (and vice versa).

- With the exception of some system SIDs and standard group SIDs, SIDs linked to the same user account name in two different Windows 2000 installations will be different. In other words, if a user installs Windows 2000, encrypts some files, reinstalls Windows 2000, and then tries to access the files using the same account, this will not be possible, since the SIDs are different.

To get around this problem, the user should export his or her private key to a floppy before reinstalling and then import it from the floppy after reinstalling. Alternatively, the user could have decrypted the data with the old SID and then re-encrypted it with the new SID.

The tight integration of EFS with Windows 2000 offers numerous advantages—to name a few: encryption and decryption take place transparently as the file is read or written to disk, files are automatically encrypted when they are created or copied in a folder with the encryption attribute set, and so on. Be aware of the difference between copying and moving. Contrary to copying a file, moving a file keeps the encryption state of the file, independent from the encryption state of the destination folder. If an unencrypted file is moved to an encrypted folder, it remains unencrypted.

When setting the encryption attribute on a folder, you are asked whether you want to apply the change to the folder only or to all its subfolders and files as well. Applying encryption to all the subfolders and files will possibly make some of them inaccessible to their owners. Remember that encryption is not restricted to the owner of a file or folder. A similar dialog box appears when you're encrypting a single file in a folder; it asks whether you want to encrypt the file only or also the parent folder. Choosing the latter option will have the same negative effect on files owned by other accounts.

Table 9.15   *File Encryption Products*

Company or Product Name
Utimaco
Data Fellows Fsecure
Entrust ICE
PGP
WinMagic Securedoc
Norton For Your Eyes Only
RSA SecurPC
NovaStor-Authentex DataSafe
PC Guardian Encryption Plus
Safeboot (Fischer)
Compaq Drivelock

EFS alternatives

EFS is a good solution for desktop encryption; however, it lacks some features on the server side. If your company is looking for an advanced server-side encryption product, you might take a look at some of the products listed in Table 9.15, or you might decide to invest in a corporate deployment of the Exchange 2000 Web store. The Exchange 2000 web store content is accessible via the file system, and can contain S/MIME encrypted messages. The combination S/MIME-Web store has some server-side features that are missing in the current version of EFS (e.g., file sharing, etc.).

The products listed in Table 9.15 can be categorized in file system–level encryption solutions, file and folder–level encryption solutions, and disk encryption solutions. EFS is a good example of a file system–level encryption solution. The solutions differ in the way they protect the encryption keys, the level on which the encryption and decryption take place, the support for single or multiuser access, and the way they implement recovery of the encryption keys, as follows.

- An encryption key can be protected with another symmetric key or with a public key.

- The encryption key can be stored on the computer system or on some special device (smart card, token).

- Recovery keys can be stored with every file (decentralized) or in a central database.

- Encryption/decryption can happen on the disk level, on the file or folder level, or on the file system level.

- Some encryption systems are single-user oriented; others can give multiple users access to the encrypted files.

9.2.2   S/MIME

In the following text, we will look at how Microsoft has build S/MIME support into Exchange 2000 and Outlook and how it is integrated with the Windows 2000 PKI. Outlook 2000 and Outlook Express 5.0 (on the client side), combined with Exchange 2000 (on the server side), have the potential to become Microsoft's first mature S/MIME platforms. Both platforms benefit from the Windows 2000 PKI and provide enhanced S/MIME security options and S/MIME interoperability with non-Microsoft mail clients.

S/MIME basics

Secure MIME (S/MIME) is the Internet's de facto standard for secure messaging. An Internet mail message consists of a message header, which contains sender and recipient information, and an optional message body. Thanks to MIME, which the IETF defined in Requests for Comments (RFCs) 2045 through 2049, a message body can contain data types other than flat ASCII. You can use MIME to add nontextual objects, such as images, audio, formatted text, and Microsoft Word documents, to messages. MIME terminology refers to a data type as a content type. A multipart content type lets you embed different content types in one message body. In a multipart body, boundaries mark the beginning and end of each content type.

S/MIME provides security extensions that let MIME entities encapsulate security objects, such as digital signatures and encrypted messages. S/MIME adds new MIME content types that provide data confidentiality, integrity protection, nonrepudiation, and authentication services: application/pkcs7-MIME, multipart/signed, and application/pkcs7-signature. The MIME content type application signals that the message carries data as a MIME attachment and that an application (in this case, the mail client's S/MIME functionality) must process the data before the recipient can view those data. As the Table 9.16 shows, the attachment's extension differs depending on the S/MIME service that the content type provides. The MIME header specifies the name of the MIME attachment. Some mail clients, such as clients of non-S/MIME-enabled systems or early versions of S/MIME, need the attachment to recognize a message's S/MIME content. Other mail clients rely completely on the content-type information to identify MIME entities;

Table 9.16   *S/MIME Content Types and Services*

MIME Content Type	MIME Subtype	S/MIME Type	S/MIME Service	Attachment Extension
Application	pkcs7-MIME	Signed data	Guarantees data integrity, authentication, and nonrepudiation; uses opaque signing.	.p7m
		Enveloped data	Guarantees data confidentiality	.p7m
Multipart	signed	NA	Guarantees data integrity, authentication, and nonrepudiation; uses clear signing.	NA
Application	pkcs7-signature	NA		.p7s

these clients ignore the attachment names. S/MIME secures only the message body. Header information must remain unencrypted for messages to relay successfully across gateways on the path between sender and recipient.

As Table 9.16 shows, you can use the application/pkcs7-MIME content type or a combination of the multipart/signed and the application/pkcs7-signature content types to sign a message body. Each application implements a different signature type: clear or opaque. These two signature types let S/MIME-enabled and non-S/MIME-enabled mail clients exchange signed messages. A clear signed message separates the digital signature from the signed data; an opaque signed message binds the signature and the message in one binary file.

Exchange Server S/MIME support

Microsoft Exchange Server has always (since version 4) provided the Advanced Security subsystem to let users secure their mail messages. Advanced Security guarantees confidentiality and message content integrity and verifies the sender's authenticity. Advanced Security provides end-to-end message security from the moment the sender signs and encrypts the message until the receiver reads it. The message stays encrypted even while it is stored in the Exchange Server's Information Store (IS) or in a user's personal folder. Microsoft builds Advanced Security around the optional Key Management Service (KMS).

From the beginning, Advanced Security has included a unique key recovery feature that lets you recover copies of users' lost or deleted encryption keys. Don't confuse key recovery with key escrow: key escrow deals with government access to encrypted user data, whereas key recovery deals with users' access to their encrypted data. In Advanced Security, key recovery is server-oriented. The KMS database contains copies of each Advanced Security–enabled user's current and previous private encryption keys.

This method of key storage explains the use of a dual-key-pair system, in which users have one key pair for encryption and another pair for signing. Advanced Security couldn't guarantee trustworthy digital signature services if it used only one key pair and stored the pair's private key in the KMS database for key recovery purposes. Digital signatures require that only users can access their private signing keys (otherwise, anyone could impersonate a particular user). Therefore, Exchange Server stores the signing pair's private key only on the client side. You can observe the use of dual key pairs every time a user is enrolled in Advanced Security: Using the certsrv tool you can see how the CA issues two new certificates (as illustrated in Figure 9.15).

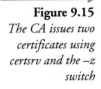

Figure 9.15

The CA issues two certificates using certsrv and the –z switch

The server-oriented approach results in more administrative overhead. Administrators must enroll users in Advanced Security, put a regular KMS database backup scheme in place, and recover users' encryption keys when necessary. Advanced Security's support for dual key pairs is an important interoperability topic: not all vendors' S/MIME products support the dual-key-pair system.

The Exchange Server KMS has evolved to deliver practical secure messaging. Originally, the KMS generated X.509 version 1 certificates. An important change occurred in Exchange Server 5.5 Service Pack 1 (SP1). Beginning with SP1, you can outsource certificate generation to Microsoft Certificate Server (which generates X.509 version 3 certificates). In this scenario, the KMS becomes a Registration Authority (RA). To enable the Exchange 2000 KMS to use X.509 version 3 certificates, you no longer need to install the special CA policy module (expolicy.dll) on Certificate Server. The policy module included with Windows 2000 Certificate Server already understands Exchange 2000.

A core change in Exchange 2000 is the integration of its directory and AD. Microsoft unifies Exchange 2000 directory objects and Windows 2000 directory objects: a mailbox is now a mailbox-enabled user object, a custom recipient is a mail-enabled contact object, and a distribution list (DL) is a mail-enabled distribution group. The administration benefits are clear: you can set users' security- and mail-related properties through one interface. Open the MMC users and computers snap-in, and double-click any user object to view its properties (including the Exchange features settings). The new interface lets you enroll a user in Advanced Security, revoke a user's certificate, and recover a user's private encryption key.

The directory integration between Exchange 2000 and Windows 2000 also impacts KMS Advanced Security: Active Directory (AD) stores certificates, CRLs, and encryption preferences. This means that any client that can browse AD can access the location information of your corporate AD-integrated enterprise CA servers. Also, for the Exchange 2000 KMS, pointing the KMS to one fixed-certificate server (the way you do in Exchange Server 5.5) is unnecessary. If the KMS CA goes down, the KMS automatically queries AD to find another CA—an important fault-tolerant, flexible feature, which also removes the need for complicated KMS CA rollover procedures.

Since Exchange Server 5.5 SP1, Advanced Security supports the definition of certificate trust lists. CTLs let you set up certificate-based security interoperability without the need for a hierarchical relationship between two CAs. As explained previously in this chapter, Windows 2000 implements CTLs through the enterprise trust group policy object entries. Exchange/Outlook do not yet fully support the GPO-based CTL settings: an Outlook 2000 client still gets its CTL from the AD. The KMS creates this CTL from the corresponding GPO CTL entries on the KM Server and publishes the CTL to the AD. Microsoft plans to fully support GPO CTL settings in a future version of Outlook.

What about CRLs? The new KMS still maintains its CRL in the KMS database (kmsdir.edb) and publishes the CRL to the AD. The KMS needs this CRL to publish revoked X.509 version 1 certificates and to let mail clients with Outlook 98 or earlier get a CRL. By default, the Windows 2000 KMS CA publishes its CRL to the AD and to the CA's Web directory. The Exchange Server Advanced Security X.509 version 3 certificates that the Enterprise Certificate Server issues also incorporate Windows 2000's changes to automated CRL checking. Each certificate now includes pointers to CRL distribution points. To take advantage of CDPs, you need a mail client such as Outlook Express 5.0 distributed with Internet Explorer (IE) 5.0 or Outlook 2000. To enable CDP support in Outlook 2000, you must create the HKEY_LOCAL_MACHINE\SOFTWARE\Microsoft\Cryptography\{7801ebd0-cf4b-11d0-851f-0060979387ea} registry key, add the PolicyFlags registry value, and set it to 0x00010000.

Microsoft client S/MIME support

Outlook 2000 is the latest version of Microsoft's full-blown mail client. Microsoft also offers Outlook Express 5.0, a lightweight Internet-oriented mail client, which Microsoft distributes with Internet Explorer (IE) 5.0. You can connect Outlook Express 5.0 to Exchange 2000 or Exchange Server 5.5 through SMTP and POP3 or IMAP4, and you can connect the mail client to a directory through LDAP. Table 9.17 shows an overview of these clients' main S/MIME features.

Table 9.17   *Outlook Client S/MIME Features*

	Outlook 2000 Corporate/Workgroup Mode[*]	Outlook 2000 Internet Mail Only Mode[*]	Outlook Express 5.0[†]
Encryption key recovery	Yes	No	No
CDP support	Yes[‡]	Yes[‡]	Yes
Private key storage	Protected store, optional Syskey protection	Protected store, optional Syskey protection	Protected store, optional Syskey protection
Support for clear and opaque signing	Yes	Yes	Yes
S/MIME enrollment	KMS, internal CA, commercial CA	Internal CA, commercial CA	Internal CA, commercial CA
S/MIME enrollment initiator	Administrator (KMS), user (other)	User	User
Certificate renewal	Automated (revocation, expiration)	Warning (revocation, expiration)	Warning (revocation, expiration)
LDAP support	Yes[**]	Yes	Yes
PKCS12 support	Yes	Yes	Yes

*Outlook 2000 version 9.0.0.2711

†Outlook Express version 5.00.2919.6700

‡To enable CDP support in Outlook 2000, you must create the HKEY_LOCAL_MACHINE\SOFTWARE\Microsoft\Cryptography\{7801ebd0-cf4b-11d0-851f-0060979387ea} registry key, add the PolicyFlags registry value, and set it to 0x00010000.

**If the LDAP directory service is added to the Outlook profile.

You can install Outlook 2000 in one of two e-mail modes: Corporate/Workgroup or Internet Mail Only. (You can also select the No E-mail mode.) The two e-mail modes support different protocols: Corporate/Workgroup is a complete MAPI mail client, which provides additional support for SMTP and POP and optional support for LDAP (through the LDAP directory service). Internet Mail Only is an ISP-oriented mail client, which provides SMTP, IMAP, POP, and LDAP protocol support. You can use the Reconfigure Mail Support button in Outlook 2000's Mail Services Options dialog box to switch between modes. Outlook 2000 reconfigures the mode at the machine level: the reconfiguration applies to every user who logs on to the machine.

From an S/MIME standpoint, a fundamental difference exists between the two modes. When you want to provide encryption key recovery for your enterprise mail clients, install your Outlook 2000 clients in Corporate/Workgroup mode. This mode lets you enroll clients in Exchange 2000 Advanced Security and lets mail clients take advantage of the S/MIME encryption preferences that Exchange 2000 stores in the Active Directory.

The administrator of the Exchange 2000 KMS initiates Advanced Security enrollment. The administrator generates and distributes enrollment tokens, which clients can use to enroll for S/MIME certificates and keys. Both Outlook 2000 and Outlook Express can use an inhouse or a commercial CA to enroll for a certificate, although only the KMS CA, which is loaded with Exchange 2000–specific certificate templates, can generate Advanced Security certificates.

Certificate renewal is as important as enrollment. Every Microsoft mail client mentioned previously warns users when their certificates expire or when the CA or KMS administrator has revoked the certificates. Outlook 2000's Corporate/Workgroup mode, combined with the Exchange KMS, offers the highest level of automation: A dialog box prompts users to enroll for new certificates, which the CA transparently generates when users accept the prompt. Users of Outlook 2000 Internet Only mode or Outlook Express 5.0 must rerun the enrollment process to replace expired or revoked certificates.

You don't need to install personal S/MIME certificates or enroll in Advanced Security to read signed messages in Outlook 2000 or Outlook Express 5.0. Outlook Express 5.0 users don't even need a personal S/MIME certificate to send encrypted mail. When a client receives a message with a valid signature, the software automatically adds the sender to the Outlook Express Contact List. A Contact list entry contains the sender's account certificate; after you have an account's certificate, you can send encrypted mail to that account. Outlook 2000 requires users to manually add senders to the users' Contact lists or Personal Address Books (PABs), and users must have personal S/MIME certificates to send encrypted messages.

Both Outlook 2000 Internet Only mode and Outlook Express 5.0 support LDAP. Mail clients can connect to any LDAP-compliant directory and download account information, including certificates, to the clients' PABs. LDAP support can also be provided in Corporate/Workgroup mode by adding the LDAP directory service to your Outlook profile. Contrary to the Outlook Express and Internet Only mode LDAP service, this LDAP service does not support the downloading of certificates. In Outlook 2000

Corporate/Workgroup mode only MAPI can be used to download certificates from the Exchange directory.

Windows 2000 automatically publishes in AD, as an attribute of the client's account, the certificate of a mail client that enrolls with a Windows 2000 enterprise CA. (Windows NT 4.0 publishes only the certificates of clients enrolled in Advanced Security in the Exchange directory.) To enable Outlook 2000 Internet Only mode to browse AD, create a new Directory Service (DS) account that connects to a Windows 2000 DC through port 3268 (the GC port). Standard Outlook 2000 in Corporate/Workgroup mode can connect only to AD. Outlook Express 5.0 can browse AD by default.

Windows 2000 automatically adds all certificates used in a user's logon session to the user's personal certificate store. Outlook 2000 and Outlook Express 5.0 can download certificates from a directory or receive certificates attached to signed mail messages.

Service release 1 for Office 2000 comes with a set of S/MIME-related add-ons for Outlook 2000. In SR1 Microsoft has implemented some of the S/MIME enhanced security services (ESS) as defined in RFC 2634: signed receipts and message labeling. It also comes with support for multiple levels of encryption and digital signatures, the Diffie-Hellman key agreement protocol, and so on. SR1 can be installed on a Windows 2000 machine only and it requires, after installation, a set of registry hacks to be activated. Figure 9.16 shows the S/MIME security options that can be set on a message after SR1a has been installed. More information on the Office 2000 SR1a S/MIME features is available in the following Windows 2000 Magazine article: *http://www.win2000mag.com/Articles/Index.cfm?ArticleID=8910*.

S/MIME and other SMTP security aspects

When your company is planning for a complete SMTP security solution, you should look for more than just an S/MIME implementation. S/MIME provides encryption and signing for MIME-formatted messages transported using the SMTP protocol. You should also think about content blocking, user blocking, virus protection, and mail archiving, as follows:

- Content blocking deals with policy enforcement on mail content (content being the information itself or just the file type). Exchange comes with some basic SPAM blocking functionality. Advanced content blocking support can be found in products such as Tumbleweed's MMS suite (formerly Worldtalk Worldsecure) or Content Technologies' MIMEsweeper.

Figure 9.16
*SR1a message
S/MIME security
options*

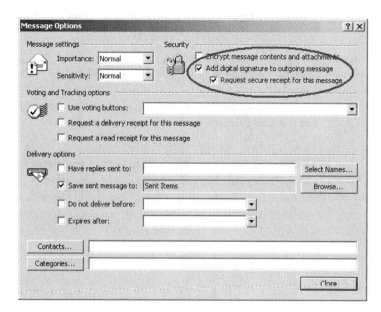

- User blocking enables you to define rules on the SMTP gateway level to determine to which internal or external recipients users can send mail messages and from which internal or external senders users can receive mail messages. The products offering content blocking can also provide advanced user-blocking functionalities.

- Virus protection (AV) software scans mail messages for viruses. A best practice is to provide virus scanning on different levels and to use different scanning engines (remember the principle of defense in depth). Numerous AV products are available that can integrate with Exchange 2000.

- Mail archiving copies every incoming and outgoing message into a special archival repository. Archiving is a legal requirement for some companies.

An important detail to keep in mind is that end-to-end encryption and AV/content scanning are mutually exclusive. You can combine the security requirements by implementing encryption on the gateway level; this means that a message will be scanned for viruses and content before it is encrypted (vice versa for incoming messages). Products that offer S/MIME functionality on the gateway level are available from companies such as Viasec, Tenfour, Tumbleweed, Content Technologies (SecretSweeper), and Hummingbird.

9.2.3   Leveraging smart cards for PKI-enabled applications in Windows 2000

Smart cards offer secure credential (private keys and certificates) storage for PKI-enabled applications. Remember from Chapter 8 that the use of smart cards may be a requirement for PKI-enabled applications where user identification and nonrepudiation are top priorities.

If you have the appropriate smart-card driver and CSP installed, you can write any certificate and its private key to a smart card. Unfortunately, not every PKI-enabled application supports smart-card credential storage. At the time of this writing, Windows 2000 came with built-in support enabling the following applications to store their PKI-based credentials on smart cards:

- S/MIME for secure mail

- Smart-card logon for two factor–based authentication to a Windows 2000 domain (based on Kerberos PKINIT)

- SSL authentication for secure Web authentication

- Remote access authentication for secure authentication of remote access clients (possible thanks to the Windows 2000 support for the Extensible Authentication Protocol [EAP])

We will now focus on the built-in Windows 2000 smart-card support, Windows 2000 smart-card logon, and a third-party software you can use to extend the Windows smart-card capabilities on the Windows 2000 platform itself and also on other Windows platforms.

Basic Windows 2000 smart-card support

Out-of-the-box Windows 2000 comes with support for the smart-card readers listed in Table 9.18. All readers in the table are Windows 2000 compliant, which means that they are listed on the Windows 2000 Hardware Compatibility List (HCL). The HCL is available from the Web at: *http://www.microsoft.com/hcl/default.asp*. All Windows 2000–compatible smart-card readers support the PC/SC smart-card interface. More information on the PC/SC smart-card interface standard is available from *http://www.pcsc-workgroup.com/*.

Installation of the smart-card readers is straightforward; Windows 2000's plug-and-play technology automatically recognizes the type of reader. Smart-card readers can be used to read smart cards, but they can also write to smart cards.

Table 9.18 *Windows 2000 Smart-Card Readers*

Smart-Card Reader	Interface
Compaq basic smart-card reader	RS-232
Bull CP8–Smart TLP3	RS-232
Gemplus–GCR410P *http://www.gemplus.com/*	RS-232
Gemplus–GPR400 *http://www.gemplus.com/*	PCMCIA
Hagiwara Flashgate SmartMedia R/W	USB
Hewlett-Packard Protect Tools Serial Smart-Card Reader	RS-232
Litronic–220P	RS-232
Rainbow Technologies–3531	RS-232
SCM Microsystems SwapSmart	RS-232
SCM Microsystems SwapSmart	PCMCIA
Towitoko Chipdrive micro	RS-232
Utimaco Cardman	RS-232
Utimaco Cardman	USB

Windows 2000 natively supports two types of smart cards: the Gemplus GemSafe and Schlumberger CryptoFlex cards. Smart cards from other vendors (e.g., ActivCard smart cards) are supported if you add the appropriate Cryptographic Service Providers (CSPs). The support for smart cards depends on the availability of a special smart card CSP, which enables the operating system to communicate with the card for cryptographic operations and smart-card initialization and configuration. This includes PIN code storage and change management. Both the Gemplus and Schlumberger CSP are shipping with Windows 2000 out of the box.

Associating a PIN code with a smart card and its content binds the card to the entities knowing the PIN code (this is also known as smart-card personalization). The PIN code can be changed when a user or an administrator enrolls for a smart-card certificate. Other advanced PIN code management tasks, such as setting the number of bad attempts after which the card is locked or unlocking the card, require special software. This software can be bought from some smart-card vendors. The default PIN code for the Gemplus card is 1234, for the Schlumberger card it's 00000000.

Windows 2000 comes with two smart card–related certificate templates: smart-card user and smart-card logon. The smart-card user template offers not only client authentication and smart-card logon but also support for secure e-mail; in other words, the certificates and private keys that are stored on the smart-card can be used for smart card logon, SSL-TLS client authentication, and S/MIME-based secure e-mail. Smart-card certificates are visible in the user's certificate store, part of the user profile.

In a Windows 2000 environment a user can enroll for smart-card credentials, a smart-card private key and certificate, provided the user has the appropriate permissions on the level of the smart-card certificate templates. An alternative is to let the smart cards be loaded centrally on a smart card enrollment station by an administrator having a special enrollment agent certificate. Given the importance of smart-card enrolment from a security point of view and given the difficulty of the procedure, the use of a smart-card enrollment station is the preferred way to enroll users in your corporate environment for smart-card logon. Smart-card enrollment automatically generates keys and certificates on the smart card and writes them to the card memory. It also publishes the certificates in the Active Directory, as an attribute of the user object.

The smart-card enrollment station interface is Web based. Only administrators who have an enrollment agent certificate in their personal certificate store can request smart-card certificates on behalf of another user. Behind the scenes the smart-card certificate requests are signed using the administrator's private key. The CA validates the requests by using the administrator's corresponding public key. If you check the ACLs on the enrollment agent certificate template, you'll notice that by default only domain administrators and enterprise administrators can enroll for an enrollment agent certificate.

From the previous paragraph, it should be clear that enrollment agent certificates and smart-card enrollment stations should be handled with extreme caution. An administrator with an enrollment agent certificate can impersonate anyone in the corporate network; the administrator is the one generating a user's smart-card credentials, so he or she can use them as well. If someone succeeds to log on to an enrollment station using the administrator's credentials, this person can do even more harm; he or she can request smart-card certificates on behalf of anyone in the organization and impersonate anyone on any smart-card-compliant machine. Therefore, it's advisable to install a smart-card enrollment station on a dedicated, highly secured machine; limit the number of enrollment agent administrators; use a special CA to issue smart-card certificates; implement strict ACLs on the enrollment agent certificate templates; and write special policies to regulate the use of enrollment agent certificates and smart-card enrollment stations.

Smart-card logon

Smart-card logon in Windows 2000 is based on an extension to the Kerberos protocol, called PKINIT: Public Key technology for Initial authentication. The details of PKINIT were explained in Chapter 6. Remember that in PKINIT all occurrences of the hashed password in the initial Kerberos authentication sequence are replaced by a user's public and private keys. The use of smart cards for identification has the following advantages:

- Smart cards offer a user identification alternative that's much better than plain password identification. Smart card logon is based on two-factor authentication. It combines knowledge (of an alphanumeric PIN code) and possession (of the smart card).

- Smart-card logon is more difficult to crack. The smart-card logon sequence relies on asymmetric keying material instead of symmetric-based hashed passwords. Symmetric-based methods can always be cracked using a brute-force attack.

- Smart cards offer secure and tamper-resistant credential storage: The user's credentials (private keys and certificates) never leave the card; all critical calculations using asymmetric cryptography occur on the card itself.

- Smart cards can provide roaming of credentials. A user can log on and have access to his or her credentials from every system that has a smart-card reader installed.

Smart-card logon obviously requires the presence of a Windows 2000–compatible smart-card reader on every machine from which a smart-card logon will be initiated. Installing a smart-card reader on a Windows 2000 machine will change the GINA (the screen that pops up when you press <CTRL> <ALT> <DEL>), as illustrated in Figure 9.17.

Since smart-card logon certificates are mapped automatically to the appropriate Windows 2000 account, smart-card enrollment requires the presence of an enterprise CA. In order for smart-card logon to work in a Windows 2000 environment, both the DC, validating the smart-card authentication request, and the user, logging on using a smart card, must have valid certificates issued by a Windows 2000 enterprise CA. Valid means that both certificates can chain up to a trusted CA and that none of

Figure 9.17
Smart-card logon
interface

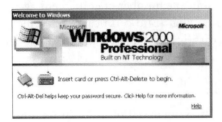

the certificates in the DC's or the user's certificate chain is revoked. In order
to check for revocation, the appropriate CRLs should be available and time-
valid and the CDPs should be reachable. Remember that in a Windows
2000 domain every DC automatically receives a certificate from the
moment an enterprise CA is online.

A nice feature of smart-card logon in Windows 2000 is that OS behavior
for smart-card removal can be set. The smart-card removal behavior can be
configured in the machine security options of the domain, site, OU, and
local computer GPO objects at the following location: Computer Configu-
ration\Windows Settings\Security Settings\Local Policies\Security Options.
The values that can be set are No Action, Lock Workstation, and Force
Logoff. Windows 2000 also allows an administrator to force the use of a
smart card for logon. By default a user who has a smart card can still log on
using his or her password. This privilege can be taken away by checking the
box *Smart card is required for interactive logon* on the level of the user object
account properties.

Extending smart-card capabilities and management features

An interesting third-party product you can use to extend smart-card capabilities and management features on Windows platforms is Gemplus Enterprise. Gemplus Enterprise is currently available in version 1.1; version 2 is
planned for early 2001—more info at *http://www.gemplus.com/products/soft-
ware/gemsafe/gse.html*. Gemplus Enterprise consists of two major components: the GemSafe Enterprise Suite, to be deployed on the server side, and
the GemSafe Enterprise Workstation software, to be deployed on the client
side. GemSafe Enterprise supports Windows 2000, but also Win9x and
NT4.

Gemplus Enterprise is tightly integrated with the Windows 2000 PKI
and security model. It links up with a Windows 2000 enterprise CA, relies
on Security Identities (SIDs) and certificates for authentication, and
respects the cryptographic architecture of Windows (CryptoAPI, CSPs).
The installation of the product requires an AD schema update and the
creation of a set of special AD objects (containers, groups, etc.). The schema

Table 9.19   *Gemplus Enterprise Administrative Delegation and Capabilities*

Capabilities	Administrator	Smart-Card Operator	Smart-Card User
Define different administrator levels for smart-card administrative tasks	Yes	No	No
Issue, revoke, reissue cards	Yes	No	No
View smart-card information and properties	All cards	All cards	Own card
Diagnose smart cards	All cards	No	No
Block and unblock smart cards	All cards	No	No
Reset and change PIN codes	No	All cards	Own card
Erase smart cards	No	All cards	No

update obviously happens forest-wide; the product-specific objects are needed in every domain where the GemSafe Enterprise smart-card management utilities will be used.

The most important feature of Gemplus Enterprise is the way it can extend the smart-card management capabilities of Windows 2000. It allows you to define different smart-card administrative levels. You can define an administrator, smart-card operators, and smart-card users. All of them are linked to a Windows 2000 SID. Table 9.19 gives an overview of the different capabilities that are linked to the three administration levels.

Figure 9.18
GemSafe Enterprise card management interface

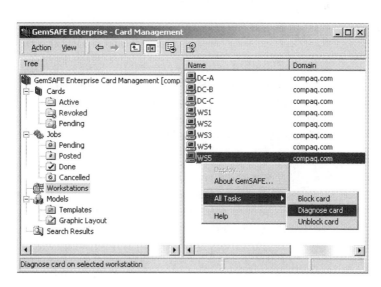

Table 9.20   *Gemplus Enterprise: Supported Platforms and PKI-Enabled Applications*

Operating System	Supported PKI-Enabled Applications
Windows 2000 Professional	Smart-card logon, secure e-mail, Web authentication, document signing
Windows NT4, SP4, or higher	Smart-card logon, secure e-mail, Web authentication, document signing
Windows NT4 and SP3	Secure e-mail, Web authentication, document signing
Windows 95/98	Secure e-mail, Web authentication, opening signed documents

Figure 9.18 shows the card management MMC snap-in, used by the administrator of a Gemplus Enterprise domain setup. The objects and containers displayed in this interface are AD objects (part of the domain NC).

Gemplus Enterprise also adds smart-card capabilities to other Windows platforms and other PKI-enabled applications (see Table 9.20).

9.3   PKI case study

To illustrate how to plan and design an enterprise PKI, this section uses a scenario based on the fictional DigiPaq Company. DigiPaq is a multinational company with customers in North America, Europe, and Asia. DigiPaq is a market leader in IT services and IT hardware ranging from desktops to mainframe systems. Last year's strong growth in e-commerce services has strengthened DigiPaq's market position by allowing it to buy one major competitor in Europe and one in Japan.

9.3.1   DigiPaq's business requirements analysis

One of DigiPaq's key business requirements is to get new technology implemented as soon as possible within the internal IT infrastructure. DigiPaq has deployed new workstations worldwide: Pentium III systems with 256 Mb RAM. They currently run Windows NT4 workstation, but DigiPaq is planning to deploy Windows 2000 and migrate all systems before mid-2001.

Recently, there was a serious security breach. An employee intercepted an e-mail message from one of the key technology managers and passed it through to a competitor. Not surprisingly, the CIO now wants to implement a system to encrypt and authenticate mail messages as soon as possible. DigiPaq also plans to deploy PKI worldwide, but to keep control completely under its own IT department. They plan to roll out the PKI first in three regional headquarters and to complete the deployment by the end of 2000. The head of IT created a PKI-based application priority list, as follows:

- Secure e-mail

- Encryption of laptop data

- Secure Web access to intra- and extranet Web sites with both client and server authentication

- Smart-card logon to servers

- Secure Internet connection of some smaller locations to the headquarter locations

The secure e-mail and Web access application should be interoperable with similar systems implemented by DigiPaq's partners. After weaker financial results this quarter, the CIO cut back a project to provide each employee with a home PC. Minimizing educational costs for technology deployed over the next year is also a priority.

9.3.2 DigiPaq's PKI topology

DigiPaq decided to create their own PKI topology, primarily to retain complete control over the issuance of certificates that are used in their corporate environment. They decided to implement two PKI hierarchies: one overall hierarchy for the whole company and one for the recently purchased Europe-based service company. The decision to go with two hierarchies was primarily political: the service company wants to administer its own CA hierarchy and wants to have complete control over its PKI trust decisions.

DigiPaq will set up a CTL-based trust relationship between the two hierarchies for secure e-mail and Web authentication. The service company has agreed to make the trust two-way. DigiPaq also wants to set up trust links with its main partners for secure e-mail (S/MIME) and extranet access (SSL). Partners who don't have their own CA can enroll for an SSL or S/MIME certificate from the DigiPaq standalone CA, which is accessible on a secured Web page on DigiPaq's Web site and will be subordinate to the DigiPaq corporate root CA.

The corporate PKI hierarchy (as illustrated in Figure 9.19) will consist of a root CA (in Europe); and a subordinate CA for the Americas; one for Europe, Middle East, and Africa (EMEA); and one for Asia-Pacific (Asia-Pac) (all these are issuing CAs). The Europe Services PKI hierarchy will consist of a root CA and a subordinate CA (the latter is an issuing CA). For

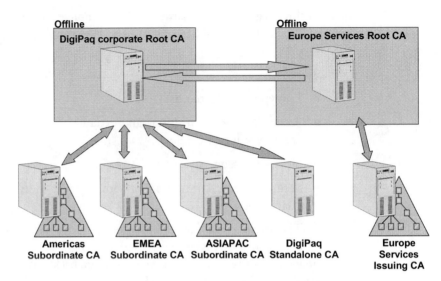

Figure 9.19
DigiPaq's PKI

security reasons both root CAs will be installed as offline CAs, disconnected from the network and not part of any Windows 2000 domain.

DigiPaq's Windows 2000 domain structure consists of two forests (as illustrated in Figure 9.20): a corporate Windows 2000 forest and a single-domain forest in the DigiPaq demilitarized zone (called DEF). The corporate forest consists of one parent domain (*DigiPaq.com*) and one child domain (*Europe.DigiPaq.com*). The DigiPaq corporate subordinate CAs are installed on Windows 2000 DCs belonging to the DigiPaq parent domain.

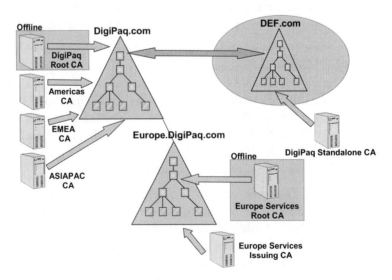

Figure 9.20
DigiPaq's domain infrastructure and PKI

The European services company's subordinate CA is installed on a Windows 2000 controller belonging to the *Europe.DigiPaq.com* child domain. Remember that the two root CAs are installed as offline CAs. The DEF domain contains DigiPaq's standalone CA (not integrated with the Active Directory). It also contains a Web server that hosts a secured Web site through which external partners can download DigiPaq's CA certificates and CRLs, access the standalone CA to request new certificates, and query the Active Directory of *DEF.com* to download certificates of DigiPaq users

The certificates of the users in the DigiPaq domain are replicated to the Active Directory in the DEF domain. Users' queries coming from the Web site are sent as LDAP calls to the Active Directory. To handle certificate replication between *DigiPaq.com* and *DEF.com*, DigiPaq runs Microsoft's Active Directory Connector (ADC) between the two Active Directories. (Another product such as Compaq's LDSU would also work.)

9.3.3 DigiPaq's CA specification

DigiPaq decided to integrate four of their CAs with the Active Directory and to keep the standard enterprise policy module on all of them. The four CAs will all have CRLDPs defined that point to the Active Directory and to a Web directory from which partners can get the latest CRLS. The CA located on the DMZ and the two root CAs will be installed in standalone mode.

To provide access to the CRLDPs and root certificates of the offline root CAs, the CRLDP and AIA pointers will be changed in the policy settings of both root CAs. The CRLDPs will be pointed to a location that is online all the time.

All CA servers will be installed on dedicated servers in a high-security room. Only CA administrators will be able to log on locally; users will need to use smart-card authentication to access the servers. The IT department will harden the CA servers by creating a checklist of Windows 2000–related security settings that will be applied and regularly checked using secedit.exe. All issuing CAs will have their private key stored on smart cards. The smart cards will be stored in a highly secured area.

The IT department will create a customized Web page where partners can enroll for a client authentication certificate. Access will be secured using digest authentication. The same Web page will contain a link to a page from which partners can download DigiPaq's CRLs, user certificates, and root certificates.

DigiPaq will set CRL lifetime to one month and will shorten it to one week when more certificates are issued. The root CA certificate has a lifetime of two years; subordinate CA certificates have a lifetime of one year. Only the certificate templates that are really used will be loaded on the CAs. To control which users can get which certificate types, special Windows 2000 groups will be created and set in the ACLs of the certificate templates.

9.4   Summary

The PKI software shipping with Windows 2000 offers a great level of flexibility and scalability to organizations that are planning to deploy public key–based security solutions within their enterprise. Microsoft has clearly chosen the open standards track to implement their PKI solution, which is very important from an interoperability point of view. A critical factor, which can drive the decision to set up a Windows 2000–based PKI, is cost: Windows 2000 PKI is substantially cheaper than products from other vendors.

If you're planning to implement a Windows 2000-based PKI, remember that, just as with any other PKI product, a large amount of the planning, design, and administration work related to a PKI is nontechnical. Also remember that a PKI is an infrastructure, which not only affects different applications but also all entities dealing with your corporate IT infrastructure, from simple users to your CIO.

If you're not convinced of the qualities of Windows 2000 PKI, wait until you see the next major Windows release, code named "Whistler." Whistler will include numerous extensions and enhancements over its predecessor including support for Delta CRLs, editable certificate templates, cross-certification, registration authorities, and key archival and recovery, to name a few.

10

Migrating to Windows 2000

10.1 Introduction

Migrating to Windows 2000 involves a number of preparation steps and a thorough understanding of the various migration techniques and their implications.

Before the actual migration is even attempted, a full design of the future Windows 2000 infrastructure must be achieved. In other words, the design phase in the Windows 2000 project will define what the future infrastructure will look like. The migration phase will define the steps involved in getting there.

The migration phase must provide a strategy for migrating the current infrastructure to Windows 2000 without interrupting daily business. This is a very challenging aspect of the migration. Global corporations may have a large existing infrastructure composed of many Windows NT 4.0 domains. Compaq, for example, had 13 account domains and more than 1,700 resource domains. It is often the case that corporations or conglomerates don't really know how many domains exist in their infrastructure. One of the design goals is to reduce the number of domains and store the resources they contain in organizational units. These containers may replace resource domains, since Windows 2000 provides the ability to delegate administrative rights at the level of organizational units. Collapsing domains into organizational units is not something that can be achieved overnight. The migration phase of a 100,000-seat company may take several months. It is not possible to stop all operations while the migration phase is in progress. Therefore, the migration of these domains requires accepting a coexistence phase, where some of the accounts or resources have already been migrated to Windows 2000, while some haven't. In this chapter, we will review the various migration techniques and their implications, as well as best practices to reduce the risks involved in the migration phase.

10.2   Windows NT 4.0 access validation

Migrating to Windows 2000 from Windows NT 4.0 requires understanding the security mechanisms behind authentication and access control. While we will review how Windows NT performs access control, security mechanisms are explained in more detail in Chapter 5.

Security Identifiers (SIDs) are unique identifiers for security principals, such as users, groups, and computers. Resources are protected using Access Control Lists (ACLs). ACLs contain SIDs and permissions. This allows administrators to define which operations can be performed by security principals.

When moving security principals between domains, the SID associated with these objects will change. One part of a SID always refers to the domain where the security principal was created. Whenever a security principal is moved to a different domain, a new primary SID has to be created. This has implications in terms of access control, since SIDs are used to control access rights to resources. If a security principal with access to a resource is moved to a different domain, then access to the resource is lost, since the new SID generated in the new domain is not the same as the one stored in the ACL. More importantly, if the security principal was explicitly denied access to the resource, the move, and therefore the generation of a new SID, will grant access to the security principal, since it will be identified by a different SID.

So, for example, if we assume that we have a user named Joe in the account domain *Accounts*, and Joe was denied access to a folder in the resource domain *Resources*, by moving Joe's account to a new domain, the SID will change. This SID is not known in the *Resources* domain and potentially Joe could access the forbidden folder.

In any case, as soon as disruption is introduced due to a loss of identity by the generation of a new SID in domain movements of security principals, the migration is no longer transparent, since users are affected. As a result of this, costs of migration are increasing due to calls to the help desk. A well-planned migration phase, as well as Windows 2000 migration techniques will avoid this situation.

Windows NT 4.0 supports two types of groups: local and global. Global groups contain users and are visible by trusting domains. Local groups can contain global groups and users from trusted domains as well as users from the same domain. Local groups are not available outside the domain in which they belong.

When users authenticate, they receive a token from the system hosting the resource to which access is desired. The token contains the list of SIDs that the user is allowed. These are, as follows:

- The user's own primary SID

- Some of the well-known SIDs, such as Everyone or Authenticated Users

- The SIDs of the groups of which the user is a member

The user can perform the operation defined by the permissions stored in the ACL of a resource provided that the token contains a matching SID. Access Control Lists are composed of Access Control Entries (ACEs). Each ACE contains a SID and a permission. Access is granted or denied by matching the SID in the ACE with the associated permission.

10.3   Preparing for a migration

Performing a migration involves choosing a strategy and defining contingency plans for each migration step. A preparation is necessary and it basically involves going through the various phases of a Windows 2000 project. These phases can be broken down as follows:

- Assessment

- Planning and design

- Pilot

- Implementation and migration

10.3.1   Assessment phase

The assessment phase of the project evaluates the infrastructure in place and provides critical information essential for learning about current administrative practices. This information will also be used for reducing the risks associated with the migration. The assessment phase is a discovery phase where the following information is gathered:

- Business drivers for migrating to Windows 2000. The goal is to understand the role and scope of the new infrastructure. Many companies will migrate to reduce costs, some will be interested in building a foundation for Exchange 2000, and others will want a stronger and flexible environment for an e-business strategy. Understanding the business drivers allows the project team to design the new Windows

2000 infrastructure accordingly. For example, the design principles for an infrastructure dedicated to an ASP will be different from the ones applied in a global deployment for Exchange 2000—that is, the ASP will probably be more centralized and consolidation and scalability will play a bigger role. An infrastructure dedicated to an e-business strategy will focus more on the security aspects; interoperability with external Internet standards will be key.

- Network operating system infrastructures: Novell, IBM mainframes, OpenVMS, existing directory structure. This information will be used to design the Active Directory schema and to define the source for directory information. Some companies will want to continue using their current directory for the management of user data. Synchronization between heterogeneous directories may then be required in order to publish and update the records in the Active Directory. From a security perspective, a step toward single sign-on may be desired to integrate the various operating systems' security principals.

- Windows NT 4.0 infrastructure: number of domains, their purpose, and administrative model. The NT 4.0 infrastructure and the administrative model will give clues to the current administrative practices and delegation requirements. This information will also form the base for the migration strategy.

- Network infrastructure: DNS, DHCP, WINS, bandwidth between physical locations, user population, network usage, and growth rates. This is critical information for the network elements and site topology designs.

- Systems: DCs, member servers, client systems—their configuration, storage settings, and backup solutions in place. This is information used to determine which systems can be reused. The disaster tolerance aspects and requirements will be gathered here.

- List of installed applications. If some legacy applications require NetBIOS names, then the WINS infrastructure may not be shut down and it could be desirable to review it. Knowing which applications are certified or supported on Windows 2000 helps in defining a migration path for them. Some applications may require a development cycle and therefore spin off a new project.

Some systems may not be able to run Windows 2000 for a number of reasons, as follows:

- Systems may be too old. Intel 486–based CPUs are not supported by Windows 2000.

- Systems are not sized correctly to support a consolidated design. For example, they may not have enough memory or not enough I/O throughput.

- Components such as network adapters or controllers may not be certified to run in a Windows 2000 environment.

- Applications may not be certified or supported in a Windows 2000 environment.

These reasons may impact the migration strategy and may force companies to upgrade their systems or take a particular approach. In this case, some companies prefer to migrate the server infrastructure first if the systems are ready. Migrating a server infrastructure also requires making a choice between migrating account domains or resource domains first. We will review the differences and approaches of migrating resource domains versus account domains in this chapter.

10.3.2   Planning and design phase

The planning and design phase is composed of an analysis of the requirements and a detailed design of the Windows 2000 infrastructure. The analysis evaluates a number of possible solutions for addressing the requirements and provides recommendations for the adoption of a specific technology. The detailed design defines how the selected technology can be applied to address the needs as defined by the requirements. This phase shapes the look of the Windows 2000 infrastructure and designs in detail the various components, such as DNS, forests, group policy objects, OU and administration models, capacity planning and sizing, networking, site topology, and more. The planning and design phase defines the strategies used for migrating objects from the current infrastructure.

10.3.3   Pilot phase

The pilot phase produces a semiproduction environment to prove the concepts defined in the planning and design phase. Generally, these concepts are tested in special proof-of-concept labs during the design phase; however, the pilot phase provides the ability to test the new infrastructure with real users, often disseminated in various physical locations. The pilot phase will test the critical aspects of the new infrastructure, such as new Windows 2000 clients and associated applications as well as server functionality and server-side applications, similar to Exchange 2000. Once the pilot phase is completed, the implementation and migration phase can begin.

10.4   Migration strategies

Which migration strategy will work best for a specific company? Some companies will be concerned that the employees will not see the immediate benefits of the migration, in which case they may prefer to start with the client migration. Some companies, on the other hand, will prefer to upgrade the servers first and perform the client migration later to avoid affecting users before a stable infrastructure is provided. Finally, some companies will run the two migration projects (client and server) in parallel, with independent schedules. Compaq decided to adopt this approach.

Migrating clients also involves migrating the installed applications. While some of these applications are easy to migrate, some may require a development cycle. Microsoft has provided a certification path for Windows 2000 and many ISVs are already porting their applications to Windows 2000. Microsoft is hosting a web a site providing the list of applications tested to run on Windows 2000; this site can be found at *http://www.microsoft.com/windows2000/upgrade/compat/search/software.asp*.

It should also be noted that many companies have home-grown applications, which require development efforts to be migrated.

Migrating the Windows NT 4.0 domains requires selecting between starting with the accounts domains or the resource domains. In any case, it's strongly recommended to start the migration with the smaller or less-important domains first, the rationale being that if a problem occurs, a smaller community will be affected. As experience grows, the larger or critical domains can be migrated.

Migrating the infrastructure has a number of benefits, as follows:

- The foundation is established; Windows 2000 provides a number of benefits to reduce operational costs while increasing performance and reliability over Windows NT infrastructures. The total number of domains is likely to decrease and many servers will be consolidated. The trend in Windows 2000 designs is fewer but larger servers.

- More flexibility. Windows 2000 allows delegation of administration at a very granular level. Flexibility to define policies and disseminate them to a large number of users and computers is important, as is flexibility to easily change these rules by editing group policy objects.

- Adoption of standards allows companies to integrate with their partners in a heterogeneous environment.

- Stronger security by using authentication protocols such as Kerberos. This benefit is not, however, fully implemented while clients are still running Windows NT 4.0.

- Easier trust relationship management. Windows 2000 trusts are transitive.

Migrating the clients will provide the following benefits:

- Users see the advantage of running Windows 2000.

- Greater reliability and performance. Windows 2000 requires far fewer reboots than Windows NT 4.0 and is much more stable.

- New features such as hibernation and plug-and-play. Hibernating is similar to standby, in which it allows for saving power by shutting down system functions such as spinning disks without closing applications. However, hibernation goes further than standby, and the system is completely shut down—that is, the power is turned off. Turning the power back on restores the system state, and applications are found in the same state as they were prior to the hibernate operation.

- Encrypted File System (EFS) to protect the data stored locally on the client system

- Easier user interface

The infrastructure migration can be accomplished using the following two techniques:

1. In-place upgrade

2. Restructuring

The in-place upgrade involves upgrading the existing infrastructure to Windows 2000, while the restructuring technique involves moving or copying the data from one infrastructure to another. Each technique has pros and cons and has implications on the approach taken and the tools used.

In-place upgrade

The in-place upgrade technique involves upgrading every DC, member server, and client in a Windows NT 4.0 domain structure. In other words the domain structure remains unchanged, since each domain is upgraded to Windows 2000. This is probably the quickest path to Windows 2000 and is a recommended approach for small network infrastructures.

Generic steps in an in-place upgrade migration

The in-place upgrade can be broken down into four main steps, as following:

1.   Preparing for the migration

2.   Upgrading the PDC

3.   Upgrading the BDCs

4.   Switching to native mode

Preparing for the migration

Preparing for the migration involves checking that the DCs can run in a Windows 2000 environment. This verification must be performed on both the hardware and the software running on the servers. To verify that the systems can be upgraded, the following questions must be answered:

- Is the server on the hardware compatibility list for Windows 2000? As mentioned, Intel 486–based systens are not supported by Windows 2000.

- Are the peripheral components supported in a Windows 2000 environment? If not, then the systems must be upgraded and the peripherals replaced before the migration can occur.

- Are the drivers for these components certified? If not, there are possibilities that the drivers have not been thoroughly tested, which could lead to a system halt, hang, or the "blue screen of death."

- Are the systems sized correctly? Windows 2000 requires more memory than Windows NT 4.0. The minimum recommended amount of memory for DCs is 256 MB, and 128 MB is the minimum recommended amount for clients.

- Are the applications supported and certified? If not, can they be moved to a member server? Windows NT 4.0 member servers can be members of a Windows 2000 domain.

- Is a DNS infrastructure in place? This is required by Windows 2000. If DNS has not been implemented correctly, the Windows 2000 domain will not function properly.

Some protective actions must be performed before starting the upgrade: An easy protective action is to synchronize the entire domain and shut down one of the BDCs. This DC will remain offline until the upgrade of the PDC and a few BDCs has proved to be successful. If an error occurs during the upgrade phase of the PDC, then the offline BDC can be rebooted and promoted to the PDC role. It's important to note that once DCs have been upgraded to Windows 2000, a downgrade is not possible.

Upgrading the PDC

The in-place upgrade must be initiated on the Primary Domain Controller (PDC). The PDC is the only DC with read/write access to the account database. The reason for starting with the PDC is that when the first DC in a domain is upgraded to Windows 2000 it inherits the domain-wide operation master roles. One of these roles is the PDC emulator. If you start the upgrade with a BDC, you effectively have two PDCs in a domain, which isn't possible.

Once the upgrade of the PDC is performed, a number of advantages become immediately available. These are all related to the fact that the server is now running Windows 2000. This means that administrators can start using Windows 2000 management tools such as the Microsoft Management Console. Administrators can also keep using the Windows NT 4.0 management tools. The PDC emulator acts completely like a Windows NT 4.0 PDC and all the NT 4.0 tools can be used seamlessly. From the perspective of the NT 4.0 BDCs in the domain, the PDC emulator is a Windows 4.0 PDC.

It is strongly recommended that you perform the upgrade on a second BDC shortly after the upgrade of the PDC. This allows two systems to run Windows 2000, and, if something happens to the first DC, the second Windows 2000 DC can become the PDC emulator, thus preserving the upgrade phase and allowing the domain to carry on business operations. Also, in the case where workstations are upgraded to Win2000 Professional first, these Win2000 workstations are able to logon to Windows 2000 domain controllers only when the domain is changed from NT 4 mode to Active Directory mixed mode. The reason is that Win2000 workstations need to use Kerberos as authentication protocol, which is not supported on NT 4 BDCs in an Active Directory mixed mode domain.

The new Windows 2000 DCs in the domain replicate using Active Directory replication. This means that they are replicating in a multimaster fashion. The PDC emulator uses NT 4.0 synchronization to replicate information to the BDCs.

When the NT 4.0 PDC is upgraded to Windows 2000, the domain is transformed into a Windows 2000 domain from the perspective of the PDC, and all Windows 2000 member servers and workstations; however, it remains an NT 4.0 domain from the perspective of the NT 4.0 BDCs and member servers. This mixed environment is called a mixed-mode domain.

Upgrading the BDCs and switching to native mode

Once the PDC has been upgraded to Windows 2000, it is now the turn for the BDCs to be upgraded. You must upgrade all the BDCs to allow the domain to be switched to native mode. This is a one-way operation, which cannot be reversed. The operation is initiated on any Windows 2000 DC and is replicated to all the DCs in the domain. Native mode implies that Windows NT 4.0 BDCs are no longer accepted in the domain. NT 4.0 member servers and clients are, however, accepted in the domain. Therefore, the domain mode affects only the DCs and not the member servers or clients of the domain.

A mixed-mode domain does not have all the features available in Windows 2000. There are a number of restrictions, and this is because BDCs in the domain may not understand or function appropriately using some of the objects that can be generated in a native-mode domain. For example, group nesting is only available in native mode. This is due to the fact that in a mixed-mode domain the PDC emulator would replicate nested groups to BDCs, which wouldn't be able to understand them. Table 10.1 lists the differences between mixed mode and native mode.

Trust relationships in a mixed-mode environment   Trust relationships are used to allow security principals of one domain to access the resources of another domain. Trusts don't grant permissions but simply make security principals stored in trusted domains visible to other domains. Permissions

Table 10.1   *Differences Between Mixed and Native Mode*

Feature	Mixed Mode	Native Mode
Location of security principals	Active Directory for Windows 2000 DCs, SAM database for NT 4.0 BDCs	Active Directory
Scalability beyond 65 KB accounts	No, due to SAM database limitations	Yes
Universal groups (security)	No	Yes
Distribution groups	Yes	Yes

Table 10.1   *Differences Between Mixed and Native Mode (continued)*

Feature	Mixed Mode	Native Mode
Global groups	Yes	Yes
Domain local groups	No	Yes
Local groups	Yes	Yes
Group nesting	No	Yes
Transitive trusts	Yes, with restrictions when using NTLM	Yes
NTLM authentication	Yes	Yes
Kerberos authentication	Yes (for Windows 2000 clients and DCs)	Yes (for Windows 2000 clients)
Management Console	Yes, for Windows 2000 DCs in the domain	Yes
NT 4.0 synchronization	Yes, between the PDC-emulator and the down-level BDCs	No
Active Directory replication	Yes, between Windows 2000 DCs	Yes
Hierarchical organizational unit structure	Yes, for Windows 2000 DCs	Yes
Group policy objects	Yes, for Windows 2000 based servers and clients	Yes, for Windows 2000–based servers and clients
Microsoft Software Installer	Yes, except for Windows 3.11	Yes, except for Windows 3.11
Security Configuration Manager	Yes	Yes
LAN Manager Replication (LMRepl)	Yes, on Windows NT 4.0, based servers; no, on Windows 2000–based servers	Yes, on Windows NT 4.0–based member servers; no, on Windows 2000–based servers
File Replication Service (FRS)	Yes, on Windows 2000–based DCs	Yes, on Windows 2000–based DCs
sIDHistory attribute in security principals	No	Yes
User principal names	No	Yes
NetBIOS names support	Yes	Yes

Figure 10.1
Trust transitivity

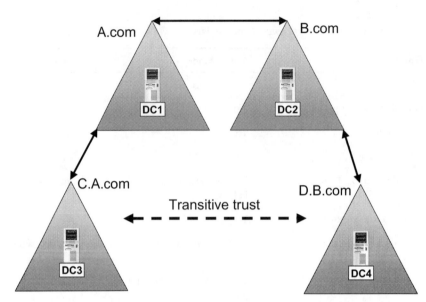

are granted by modifying the ACL of a particular resource. In Windows NT 4.0, trusts were one-way, nontransitive, and explicitly created by administrators. If a trust relationship was not physically available between two domains, then the security principals of one domain were not visible by the other domain. The transitivity characteristic of Windows 2000 trust relationships is independent of the authentication protocol, but it depends on the version of the DC used. Trusts can only be transitive if the trust path between the physically trusted domains is composed of Windows 2000 DC. Figure 10.1 illustrates physical trusts between four domains: A, B, C.A, and D.B.

By transitivity of the physical trusts, C.A trusts and is trusted by D.B. The trust path is verified by following the physical trusts in place from the source domain and the target domain. In some cases, the transitivity is not available. This is the case when a down-level DC is in the trust path. In this case the administrator must create a short-cut trust between two domains not physically trusted. Let's review the different scenarios in more details and see what the solutions are.

Let's assume that we have a forest composed of three domains. The root domain is called *Root*. The *Root* domain has two child domains: *Accounts* and *Resources*. The *Accounts* domain is in mixed-mode domain. This means that in the *Accounts* domain there are potentially down-level BDCs accepting authentication requests. Let's assume that the *Accounts* domain contains a number of workstations running either Windows NT 4.0 Workstation

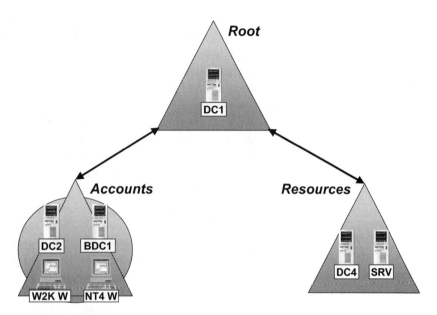

Figure 10.2
Mixed mode domains and trust transitivity

or Windows 2000 Professional. In that domain there are two DCs: One is a Windows 2000 DC with the PDC emulator operation master role, and the second is a Windows NT 4.0 BDC. (See Figure 10.2.)

The second child domain in the forest, *Resources*, is in native mode and contains member servers running Windows 2000.

The physical trust relationships in place are those automatically generated by Windows 2000 when the forest and the domains were put in place. There are two two-way transitive trusts in place: one from the *Root* domain to the *Accounts* domain and one from the *Root* domain to the *Resources* domain. Trust transitivity allows the *Accounts* domain to trust the *Resources* domain and vice versa.

Given this environment, there are three scenarios when users authenticate depending on the client and the DCs used, as follows:

1. A Windows 2000 client authenticates to a Windows 2000 DC. The authentication protocol is Kerberos.

2. A Windows NT 4.0 client authenticates to a Windows 2000 DC. The authentication protocol used is NTLM.

3. A Windows NT 4.0 client authenticates to a Windows NT BDC. In this scenario the authentication protocol used is NTLM.

Let's now assume that a user authenticates in the *Accounts* domain using a Windows 2000 client. As we have seen, the authentication protocol used is Kerberos. During the authentication process, the Key Distribution Center (KDC) running on the Windows 2000 DC provides the client with a Ticket Granting Ticket (TGT). The TGT contains information about the user credentials. This information is encrypted using a special key called the domain master key. Only the Windows 2000 DCs of the authenticating domain know this key. Using the TGT the client can request the DC of its own domain a session key to access resources in the domain. For example, a user requires a session key to access his or her own client system or requires access to a Resource Server in the same domain. The session key is provided to the client, which, in turn, will provide it to the resource system. The resource system will not need to contact the DC as in Windows NT 4.0, since the session key provides the credential information and is protected in such a way that only the DC could have created it and only the resource system can decrypt it. The session key is protected by a secret between the DC and the resource system. Since only the DC and the resource system share the secret, allowing encryption and decryption of the session key, the resource system can trust its content—that is, the credentials of the user. This mechanism provides a secure and fast authentication in a distributed environment. Once the resource system has decrypted the session key, validated the user's credentials, and verified the allowed permissions, it can provide access to the resource to the user.

If the client in the *Accounts* domain attempts to access a resource in a remote resource domain, it will request a session key to a DC in its own domain, the *Accounts* domain. The KDC on the DC in the *Accounts* domain cannot provide a session key to the client, because it is not authoritative for the *Resources* domain and must therefore create a referral request. In order to process the referral, the DC must verify the physical trust relationships in place and will use the closest trust to the target domain for this operation. In our scenario such trust is established between the *Root* domain and the *Accounts* domain. The client then contacts the DC in the *Root* domain to request a session key to the resource server in the *Resources* domain. The KDC on the *Root* domain is not authoritative for the *Resources* domain and will in turn verify the established physical trust relationships. This time, the KDC can create a referral to the *Resources* domain, because a physical trust exists between the *Root* domain and the *Resources* domain. Finally, the contacted DC in the *Resources* domain can provide a session key to allow the client to provide credentials to the resource server and access the resource.

The transitivity provided by transitive trusts is only apparent. Under the hood a physical connection must be established between domains physically

Figure 10.3
*Trust transitivity
referrals*

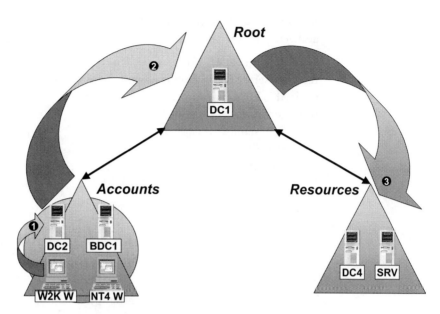

connected by trust relationships, as shown in Figure 10.3. In a forest with multiple domain levels and multiple trees it is recommended that you establish short cut trusts, alleviating the referral process and increasing the authentication speed.

The Kerberos protocol allows a client to access a resource in any domain in the same forest or in physically trusted forests or non–Windows 2000 Kerberos realms. Kerberos realms are security boundaries: A Windows 2000 Kerberos realm is a domain. See Chapter 5 for a more detailed description. This is regardless of the domain mode of the domains involved. It will not, however, allow authentication between a Windows 2000 domain and a trusting Windows NT 4.0 domain. For this Windows 2000 supports the NTLM protocol.

The NTLM protocol is used when either the DC or the client or both are running Windows NT 4.0.

NTLM is a token-based authentication protocol. When using the NTLM protocol, a DC provides the client with a token containing a list of SIDs. These SIDs are the user's own SID and the list of SIDs of the groups in which the user is a member.

When a client requires access to a resource server, this system must verify the credentials of the client by contacting a DC. The DC provides the resource domain with a token containing the user's credentials. After matching the SIDs in the token with the ones stored in the resource ACL and verifying the allowed permissions, access is granted to the client.

When a client requires access to a resource in a remote domain, the resource server must establish a connection to the client's domain. In order to do this a trust relationship must exist between the two domains. In our scenario the *Resources* and *Accounts* domain trust each other using a transitive trust established with the *Root* domain. A trust path will be established from the resource server to the *Accounts* domain. However, because the *Accounts* domain is running in mixed mode, the trust path may be established with either a Windows NT 4.0 DC or a Windows 2000 DC.

If the trust path is established with the Windows 2000 DC, then the transitive trust will allow the DC to provide authentication information to the resource server. This means that even when using NTLM authentication where Windows 2000 DCs are involved, the transitivity of the trusts is validated and the client can access the resource in the remote domain.

However, if the trust path is attempted with a Windows NT 4.0 DC, this DC cannot verify the transitivity of the trust relationship, and access to the resource will be denied. In order to allow access to the resource, administrators must establish an explicit trust between the *Resources* domain and the *Accounts* domain.

To summarize, when a client in a domain requires access to a resource in a different domain trusted via a transitive trust, there are three golden rules, as follows:

1.   If any of the three systems is running Windows NT 4.0, then the authentication protocol used is NTLM.

2.   If one of the two servers runs Windows NT 4.0, then the trust is nontransitive. A shortcut trust is required to allow access to the resource.

3.   In all other cases, the trust is transitive.

Limitations of the SAM database in mixed-mode domains   It is often the goal to consolidate domains in order to reduce physical resources such as DCs. Security principals are stored in the Active Directory and are replicated between all DCs in a domain. Windows 2000 can scale up to a theoretical 4 billion objects (2 at the power of 32), accommodating the requirements for most, if not all, companies. A mixed-mode domain can, however, contain Windows NT 4.0 BDCs. While Windows 2000 DCs will use Active Directory replication to replicate directory information between DCs, Windows NT 4.0 BDCs will contact the PDC to perform Windows

NT 4.0 synchronization. A Windows 2000 DC performs the PDC emulator operation master role. It establishes the connection with the down-level BDCs and synchronizes the data stored in its own database: the Active Directory. The down-level BDCs store security principals in the SAM database, which is still limited to 65 MB even in a mixed-mode Windows 2000 domain. If the amount of data stored in the Active Directory exceeds 65 MB, then the PDC emulator will perform the synchronization with the down-level BDCs in the domain, which will result in exceeding the limitations of the SAM database and potentially making the BDCs unavailable. Therefore, it is important to take into consideration the existence of Windows NT 4.0 BDCs while in the process of consolidating domains. Switching to native mode will remove this limitation, since NT 4.0 BDCs will no longer be accepted in the domain. It is therefore recommended to consolidate domains within the limitation of the SAM database. If the number of security principals resulting in a consolidation effort exceeds the maximum supported size of the SAM database, then it's strongly recommended to wait until the target domain for the consolidation is running in native mode.

Another advantage of switching to native mode is to allow interdomain movements of security principals. This is discussed later in the chapter.

Limitations of LAN Manager Replication Service Windows 2000 servers do not support LAN Manager Replication Service (LMRepl). This could potentially be an issue when upgrading DCs that exported or imported directories via LMRepl. LMRepl provides Windows NT 4.0 servers with the ability to synchronize data by allowing a server to export a directory that will be imported by another server.

Windows 2000 DCs use the File Replication Service (FRS) instead of LMRepl. Every Windows 2000 has a system folder (SYSVOL), which automatically replicates in a multimaster manner with other DCs in the same domain.

A solution to this problem is to use Lbridge.cmd to create a bridge between LMRepl directories and FRS folders. Lbridge.cmd is available from the Windows 2000 resource kit. While this solution duplicates the exported data on a server, it provides a convenient way to maintain the two services during the migration process.

System policy versus group policy objects Windows NT allows you to control and lock down the user's environment on desktops. System policy provides this mechanism. System policy uses registry settings to control desktop settings and system behavior.

Windows 2000 uses a different mechanism, implemented by GPOs. While in theory the mechanisms are similar, GPO provides a more flexible and powerful way to disseminate policy information to users and computers. In addition, GPOs allow disseminating applications. For more information on GPOs, refer to Chapter 7.

System policy files are not compatible with group policy files and must be converted.

In the process of migration, we could have a case where the computer still resides in a Windows NT 4.0 domain while the user account is stored in a Windows 2000 domain. If that is the case and if the computer system must be locked down by a policy, then the system policy for the computer can be processed during the authentication of the user. To perform this operation, the system policy for the computer (NTCONFIG.POL) can be placed in the Netlogon share of the Windows 2000 DC authenticating the user. This is, however, a temporary workaround, which can help while waiting for the client computers to be upgraded. We recommend using it as a temporary solution and migrating the client policies to GPOs.

Windows 2000 clients in a mixed-mode domain   Many companies will migrate client systems to Windows 2000 Professional before migrating the DCs. The reason behind this is that these companies will see immediate benefits and user acceptance by providing them with the ability to run Windows 2000 on their desktops or laptops. Having run Windows 2000 on my laptop since the early Betas of Windows NT 5.0, I never looked back and will recommend it.

Let's assume that before upgrading the DCs, a company proceeds to upgrade all the clients. We now have all the clients running Windows 2000 while the DCs are still running Windows NT 4.0. We have learned that when performing the in-place upgrade on NT 4.0 domains, the PDC will be the first to be upgraded to Windows 2000 and acts as a PDC emulator for the Windows NT 4.0 BDCs. If this operation has been performed after the upgrade of the client workstations, then what will happen is that all the Windows 2000 clients will attempt to perform a Kerberos-based authentication. This is because each client will switch the authentication protocol in LSA. A side effect of this behavior is that if the Windows 2000 KDC becomes unavailable, the clients will fail to authenticate and will not try to use NTLM. All the clients will attempt to connect to a Windows 2000 DC even if there is a closer Windows NT 4.0 BDC available to accept the authentication request. Given that only the PDC emulator will be available to perform and accept such operation, the overall infrastructure may suddenly become very slow and the network may be overwhelmed. The only solution for this problem is to deploy Windows 2000 DCs quickly, after the upgrade of the PDC, or, if at all possible, to postpone the upgrade of the clients until a number of DCs have been upgraded.

Using the same scenario there is another interesting behavior worth noting. This is when the PDC has been upgraded to Windows 2000 and something happens forcing the administrator to abort the upgrade, remove the PDC, and promote a BDC. All the Windows 2000 clients will not be able to authenticate since the Windows 2000 DC has been removed from the domain and an NT 4.0 DC is replacing it. The only solution for this is to remove all the clients from the domain and add them again. In a situation where many clients are deployed, it's strongly recommended to stabilize the Windows 2000 server infrastructure before upgrading the clients.

Pros and cons of an in-place upgrade strategy The in-place upgrade is the fastest path to Windows 2000. There are, however, other benefits associated with it. These benefits are related to the fact that there is no change in the infrastructure as known by the users, as follows:

- Many small companies are likely to want to reuse the same domain name to reduce impact on employees. These impacts are related to the requirement to inform users of the new authentication domain.

- The migration is transparent to users.

- There is no need to use migration tools, since the domain is unchanged and all its security principal SIDs are preserved during an in-place upgrade.

There are, however, some risks in adopting this strategy. These risks are related to the fact that the production domain is being upgraded to Windows 2000. The systems running in the domain may not be able to run correctly in a Windows 2000 environment. There are many parameters to a successful migration, including the following:

- Is the hardware compatible with the Windows 2000 Hardware Compatibility List (HCL)?

- Are the drivers for the peripherals certified to work in a Windows 2000 environment?

- Are the applications supported on Windows 2000? Are they certified?

- What if the upgrade of the PDC fails?

- What if there is a need for an NT 4.0 BDC once the switch to native mode has been made?

- What are the contingency plans in each phase of the migration, and have they been tested?

Addressing each of these questions will certainly help reduce the risk of a poor migration, but, no one can be absolutely sure of the success of the migration until the last user or resource has been migrated. Preparing a contingency plan is going to be crucial. For example, something that could easily be performed to prepare the primary DC for the upgrade is to synchronize the domain, take a BDC, and shut it down. If something happens during the upgrade, the PDC can be removed from the domain, and the BDC can be rebooted and promoted to PDC. Another task worth executing is to upgrade a BDC shortly after the PDC has been upgraded. The Windows 2000 PDC emulator operation master role can easily be transferred from one DC to another provided that they both run Windows 2000 and are part of the same domain.

When multiple domains must be upgraded, it is strongly recommended to start with the smallest of the domains. If something goes wrong, a smaller population of users will be affected, and, as the administrators are performing the migration, they will gain experience for larger and more complex domains.

In all cases we strongly recommend using proven tools tested in a lab and documenting each migration step with an associated tested contingency plan.

10.4.1   Restructuring

Restructuring is a strategy that allows migrating to Windows 2000 by performing one of the following actions:

- An in-place upgrade of the existing Windows NT 4.0 domain structure followed by a restructure of the domains and their objects.

- A direct migration by generating a brand-new forest and copying (cloning) the security principals from the old domains.

This migration technique relies on the ability of the Active Directory to do the following:

- Scale potentially to millions of security principals, hence allowing fewer but larger domains.

- Retain the SIDs belonging to security principals moved from other domains, hence allowing coexistence between migrated domains and down-level trusted or trusting domains.

Probably the biggest advantage of the restructuring technique is the ability to leave the current NT 4.0 environment intact, thus reducing the risk of migrating to Windows 2000.

The current Windows NT 4.0 structure of domains may have been the result of either of the following:

- The limitations of the SAM account database, forcing administrators to create multiple domains for the largest companies.

- The inability of NT 4.0 to delegate administrative management or provide a more granular delegation.

Windows 2000 provides the ability to lift the SAM limitations and allows a very fine delegation of administration. The reasons for hosting multiple domains in a company's Windows 2000 infrastructure are mostly of a political, business, or security nature, or are due to network bandwidth constraints.

During the design phase of a Windows 2000 infrastructure, it is common practice to start with a forest composed of a single domain and then look at valid reasons to split that domain into either child domains or multiple trees. Those reasons, as mentioned, are mostly political, due to a trust between business units; security reasons can be due to the inability to export particular pieces of information outside of a country, and business reasons can include, for example, a conglomerate requiring multiple namespaces.

In all of these cases we are still talking about going from potentially hundreds, if not thousands, of domains to a mere few. Compaq had 1,700 NT 4.0 resource domains.

Eliminating domains provides the instant advantage of having to manage far fewer domain controllers, which reduces the cost of hardware, administration, and troubleshooting for these servers. It also allows an easier and more flexible structure in which to deploy policies and applications.

It is not, however, easy to consolidate the domains of a large company such as Compaq while maintaining a working environment and not affecting daily operations. The reason for this is that such a migration may take months if not years. We did not, after all, shut down every business and put 69,000 people on vacation for 18 months to perform the migration. A different approach was required.

During a restructuring migration while some people have yet to be migrated, some have already been migrated. Some resource domains have been eliminated while others are still up and running and require the SID of the security principals of the former account domains to grant or deny access to resources. This means that if we have an account that has been migrated from a former Windows NT 4.0 account domain to a new Windows 2000 domain, the domains containing the resources of that account may still be running NT 4.0 and not know about the new domain. Not knowing about the new domain means not having the SID from the new domain in the ACL protecting the resources. A user with a new Windows 2000 account may still require access to resources in a Windows NT 4.0 domain. If this user can't access the resources, then the migration strategy is failing in maintaining normal business operations. The goal is to ensure that the migration is as transparent as possible to users. To accomplish this, Windows 2000 has the ability to retain old security principal identifiers from the former NT 4.0 account domains. Old SIDs are stored in the Active Directory as part of a security principal attribute. The attribute is called sIDhistory. The sIDHistory attribute is multivalued and can contain up to 255 SIDs. This attribute is only available if Windows 2000 is running in native mode. This means that if the in-place upgrade technique is used with a Windows NT 4.0 domain, the domain will be in mixed mode; restructuring other domains into this mixed-mode domain while maintaining the SID history will not be possible. The migrated accounts to this mixed domain will not have SID history information.

The sIDHistory attribute allows security principals to be cloned. No, not with DNA samples, but with SID samples. Windows 2000 migration tools are injecting SIDs into the sIDHistory of a Windows 2000 security principal. This allows Windows 2000 users to use their new Windows 2000 accounts, since the authentication process will store the list of SIDs the users are entitled to, including those stored in the SID history, as part of the PAC of a Kerberos ticket or an NTLM token. In other words, this allows a Windows 2000 user to access resources protected with the SID of his or her old NT 4.0 account. This is transparent to the user, who seamlessly continues to access his or her resources once the account has been migrated.

Cloning versus Moving

The clone operation copies the attributes of an object from one domain to a Windows 2000 native-mode domain and populates the SID history of the new object. From a Windows 2000 perspective, the object cloned is a new one, since it receives a new GUID. The GUID will be used to internally identify the object.

The moving operation, on the other hand, is a destructive operation, which creates a new object in the target domain with the GUID of the old object and destroys the old object.

Moving objects has a rather important consequence on the objects in the source domain. If, for example, you need to move a group, then the members of this group must be moved as well. If the group resides in a native-mode domain and contains nested groups, then the nested groups and their members need to be moved as well. This is because the move is a destructive operation, and destroying the group without moving all its members would result in a loss of data. The worst-case scenario occurs when users and groups are so linked together that moving one of them requires moving the entire domain. A way around this constraint is to create parallel groups on the target domain—that is, the users will be moved but not the groups, resulting in a duplication of groups that need to be managed. Another possibility is to transform the groups into a universal group. This is only possible if the source domain is in native mode and has the effect of making the group available in the entire forest. Universal groups are stored in GCs. One last possibility around this constraint is to use the cloning technique for the groups and move the users only.

During a move operation the target domain can be either in mixed or native mode. However, as previously mentioned, the sIDHistory attribute will only be preserved if the target domain is in native mode.

The source domain mode does not matter in either scenario. However, during a move operation, the source and target domains must belong to the same forest.

There are some differences and restrictions depending whether a moving or cloning strategy is adopted. These differences are summarized in Table 10.2.

Restructuring account domains

The restructuring technique differs for account and resource domains. For account domains the generic steps are as follows:

1.   Create a Windows 2000 forest or define the target Windows 2000 native domain

2.   Establish a trust relationship between the former account domain and the Windows 2000 domain.

3.   Global groups cloning

4.   Account cloning

Table 10.2   *Cloning versus Moving*

Feature	Cloning	Moving
Source domain	Windows NT, Windows 2000 from different forest	Windows 2000 domain from same forest. No Windows NT.
Source domain mode	Mixed or native	Mixed or native
Target domain	Windows 2000 from different forest	Windows 2000 from same forest
Target domain mode	Native	Native
Password preserved	Yes, depends on the tool	Yes
Security Principal SID from source domain	Must not exist in target domain and must not be found in the sIDHistory attribute of any object.	Must not exist in a sIDHistory attribute (there can't be a second primary SID)
Object GUID	A new GUID will be generated.	The same GUID will be preserved.
Tools	ADMT, ClonePrincipal, third party based on DsAddSIDHistory API	ADMT, third-party tools supporting DsAddSIDHistory API, MoveTree

Creating a Windows 2000 forest

In a restructuring migration the target domain may exist or may need to be created. If the domain must be created, it's then recommended to perform the necessary planning and design steps to define the purpose and scope of the new domain. Windows 2000 domains cannot be renamed, and the design phase must define the name of the domain and how it coexists in a company's global namespace. Adopting a design without such considerations may lead to a second restructuring phase. Designing a Windows 2000 infrastructure is a step that may take several months for the largest companies.

The restructuring technique requires a native-mode domain to allow the SID history to be populated; therefore, selecting a target domain that is in mixed mode is not an option. Transforming that domain into a native-mode domain is also not something that can be performed lightly. As we saw earlier, it is a one-way operation with a point of no return.

It is in the best interest of users to plan their migration and target domains and avoid multiple restructuring operations in order to "get it right."

Establishing the trust relationships

Before migrating the users and groups, it is necessary to establish the same trust relationships that exist between the resource domains and the former account domains with the new Windows 2000 domains. The Windows 2000 domain will need to be trusted by the resource domains to allow users to access their resources.

This is an operation that may take a long time to perform manually and it can be automated using specific tools. The tools are discussed in a later section.

Cloning the global groups

Once the trust relationships have been established between the resource domain and the target Windows 2000 domain, the global groups can be cloned. The global groups are cloned before the users to allow memberships to be retained during the cloning phase of the users.

Cloning the accounts

Cloning users can be done in an incremental fashion. Some organizations may decide to clone groups of users instead of the entire set. Once all the users and groups have been cloned, it's generally recommended to disable the accounts in the former account domain. This will reduce administrative costs and will help in ascertaining that users are really using the new account domain prior to the shutdown of the Windows NT 4.0 account domain. In some cases, there is a possibility that both the former and the new account can be enabled. However, it's important to note that the profiles for the users will not be the same, and customizations of the old profile may not be accessible by the user when the former account domain is disbanded.

Restructuring resource domains

For resource domains, the migration steps are more complicated, due to the need to clone security principals, which may be stored in shared local groups. These are local groups created on the PDC and are available on BDCs. These shared local groups store information about the domain and require the DC for that domain to authenticate the SID. In this case, it is not possible to eliminate the resource domain before performing additional steps. The main steps of a resource domain migration are as follows:

1.   Establish trusts between the resource domain and the target Windows 2000 domain.

2. If the account domain has not been migrated yet, then additional trust relationships must be established between the new Windows 2000 domain and the Windows NT 4.0 account domain.

3. Clone local and shared local groups

4. If applications are running on BDCs, these systems need to be demoted to member servers. This is an operation that can be performed during the upgrade of Windows 2000 on the system.

5. Move member servers to the Windows 2000 domain.

Establish trust relationships

As with master account domains, resource domains require trust relationships to be established with the target domain. In addition, if the target domain needs to be accessed by accounts stored in other domains, such as Windows NT 4.0 account domains that haven't been migrated yet, trusts must be established between the target Windows 2000 domain and those domains. This technique will allow organizations to adopt different schedules for their migration. Some resource domains may be migrated before the account domains. Establishing these trusts will allow accounts in down-level domains to continue to access migrated resources. Again, tools such as ADMT will allow generating the required trust relationships.

Clone Local and Shared Local Groups

There are two types of local groups: those that have a machine scope and have been created on member servers or workstations and those that have a domain scope and have been created on the PDC. While the former are stored in the SAM database of member servers and workstations, the latter replicate from the PDC to all the BDCs in the domain. Shared local groups require at least the PDC of the domain in which they belong to authenticate and validate their SID. In other words, if shared local groups are cloned to a Windows 2000 domain, the SID history will be populated with the shared local group SID of the source resource domain. This resource domain cannot be eliminated until the SID is tracked and replaced in the new domain. If this operation is not performed and the resource domain is eliminated, then the SID cannot be authenticated—resulting in an access denied when accessing the resource in the new domain. The access denied is produced because the SID cannot be validated and Windows 2000 will assume that the SID is unknown.

To track and replace these types of SIDs, administrators can use the SIDWalker tool available from the Windows 2000 resource kit. SIDWalker will allow administrators to search for resources for a specific SID and replace it with another SID.

Demote DCs

Demoting DCs is not a standard operation in Windows NT. Administrators are required to reinstall the operating system in order to demote a BDC. In Windows 2000, however, promoting a member server to a DC is an operation performed using the Active Directory installation wizard (DCPROMO). Demoting a Windows 2000 DC can also be performed with the Active Directory installation wizard.

Demoting DCs in our restructuring migration context means performing an in-place upgrade of the NT 4.0 BDC. The Windows 2000 installation procedure will detect that the system is a DC and once the system has been upgraded, the wizard will automatically launch the Active Directory installation wizard. During the execution of the Active Directory installation wizard it's possible to cancel the operation. As a result of this, the NT 4.0 domain SAM information is lost, while the new Active Directory data haven't been replicated locally. A SAM database with built-in security principals has been generated and the system is a member of the same domain.

Move member servers

Moving member servers can be performed using Netdom, ADMT, or third-party tools. This operation involves creating computer accounts for member servers in a Windows 2000 domain. Some third-party tools provide the ability to move the data of specific servers in an effort to consolidate shares.

Pros and cons of a restructuring strategy

The restructuring strategy provides the benefit of starting with a brand-new forest. This forest is the ideal one, designed without the limitations of NT 4.0 and with the business and security objectives in mind. Obviously, since this forest is created in parallel with the current infrastructure, there is no risk for the Windows NT 4.0 production domains, since they remain untouched.

However, creating a new infrastructure is not free; there are hidden costs related to managing two infrastructures. There are also additional costs due to the additional hardware. Cloning tools must be tested and while in principle they perform similar functions, they are not the same and do not cost the same.

Coexistence will also be problematic, and migrated users living in the new infrastructure may be required to access resources in the old infrastructure and vice versa. This is the recommended approach for large corporations.

10.5   Migration tools

Migration tools can be categorized relevant to the type and scope of the operation that needs to be performed. Depending on whether we'll be moving an object within a domain of the same forest or between domains of the same or different forests, different tools may be required.

In all cases, it is always possible to write custom scripts based on Active Directory Services Interface (ADSI). ADSI is a set of COM interfaces allowing scripting languages to easily bind to a container and perform management tasks on the objects stored in the container.

10.5.1   ClonePrincipal

ClonePrincipal is a collection of Visual BASIC scripts based on the DsUtil Component Object Model (COM) object. DsUtil can be found in the clonepr.dll dynamic link library. DsUtil provides three main interfaces, as follows:

1. Connect. Allows a script to authenticate and connect to the source and target domains. The bind operation in the source domain must be performed on the primary DC if the domain is running Windows NT 4.0. This operation can be performed on DC on source domains running Windows 2000. It's important to note that the source and target domain must not belong to the same forest. Auditing must be enabled on the target domain.

2. AddSidHistory. Provides the ability to copy SID information from a security principal in the source domain to a new object in the target domain. AddSidHistory populates the SID history attribute of the target object with the SID of the source object.

3. CopyDownlevelUserProperties. Copies all attributes from the object stored in the source domain to the equivalent attributes in the object in the target domain.

ClonePrincipal is an interesting set of samples for those wishing to learn and modify the scripts to provide additional functionality. It is not, however, an adequate tool for migrating large amounts of users and groups.

ClonePrincipal cannot be used between domains of the same forest, and this restricts its use for cloning objects in interforest migrations. A tool recommended for large migrations is Active Directory Migration Tool.

10.5.2   MoveTree and Netdom

MoveTree is a tool that allows migrating OUs, users, and groups between domains of the same forest. MoveTree cannot be used for interforest migrations and cannot be used with Windows NT 4.0 domains. MoveTree will preserve the old security principal SIDs in the SID history of the new security principal objects, will reuse the GUID of the original object, and will preserve the password of the original users. MoveTree cannot, however, be used for migrating computers. For this task, administrators can use Netdom. In addition to migrating computers, Netdom can be used to list and establish trust relationships between Windows 2000 domains and downlevel domains or Kerberos realms.

10.5.3   Active Directory Migration Tool (ADMT)

Active Directory Migration Tool is available for free and was codeveloped by Microsoft and Mission Critical Software. ADMT uses a graphical user interface in the form of an MMC snap-in. ADMT provides all the features of ClonePrincipal but also provides convenient wizards to allow the program to guide the administrator in the choice of options during the migration. In addition, ADMT establishes the necessary trust relationships and can be used for both cloning and moving strategies.

ADMT is also pretty unique among the Microsoft migration tools, since it can migrate user profiles, service accounts, and update ACLs on migrated resources.

10.5.4   Third-party tools

Third-party vendors have developed management tools based on the AddSidHistory API. The most important of these tools are as follows:

- DM/Manager and DM/Consolidator by FastLane Technologies
- Domain Migration Administrator by NetIQ, which also allows migrating the resources, such as shares.
- Bv-Migrate by BindView

Domain Migration Administrator by NetIQ is a cloning tool capable of preserving the original password for security principals. This tool also pro-

vides extensive logging and reporting capabilities as well as security translation on shares and Exchange mailboxes. NetIQ also provides tools for
managing Windows 2000 and Windows NT using a unified console:
Directory and Resource Administrator. This tool uses a set of predefined
rules to enforce Active Directory security and integrity and provides easy
delegation of administration. In terms of management and monitoring
NetIQ offers AppManager, a comprehensive systems and application suite
providing monitoring for Windows 2000 and BackOffice applications such
as SQL, Exchange, IIS, MTS, and more.

FastLane Technologies provides reporting tools, migration tools, and
management tools bundled in the DM/Suite. The DM/Reporter is capable
of impressive reporting and is very useful in the discovery phase of a project.
For example, it can be used to track client and server configurations and
verify the conformance of groups and users given a naming convention.

DM/Manager provides the ability to migrate passwords and can merge
accounts from different sources. This tool is also capable of converting the
ACLs on the shares and can schedule computer membership in the new
domain as well as the reboot. Finally, it is capable of converting a BDC into
either a Windows 2000 DC or member server.

Bv-Migrate from BindView also preserves passwords. This tool is capable of migrating profiles and allows you to model the Active Directory on
top of Windows NT.

Moving objects within a domain

When an object must be moved between containers in the same domain,
such as moving users between organizational units, then the Microsoft
Management Console (MMC) can be used. For example, if a user, group, or
computer must be moved from one OU to another, then the users and
computers snap-in can be used.

Moving objects between domains of the same forest

When moving objects between domains of the same forest, the following
tools can be used:

- Movetree, a tool provided in the Windows 2000 support tool kit, can
  move a tree of objects from one domain to another. For example,
  Movetree can move the objects in an organizational unit, including
  child OUs and their content, to another OU. MoveTree will preserve
  SIDs in the SID history if the target domain is running in native
  mode and will also preserve passwords.

- Active Directory Migration Tool

- Netdom (also available from the support tool kit) can be used to move computers from one domain to another.

Cloning objects between domains of different forest

Between forests, we are using the cloning technique. Cloning is supported by ADMT and by third-party tools. Additionally, the task of enumerating trust relationships and establishing them can be performed by ADMT and Netdom.

10.6 Summary

A migration is not something to take lightly. The most important aspects are understanding the various options and choosing the best strategy that will fit business needs. A successful migration strategy is one that seamlessly migrates users and computers without disrupting business operations. Documenting each step and testing contingency plans will reduce migration risks. Before attempting a migration, it's crucial to understand the current environment and have a well-designed Windows 2000 infrastructure. The migration phase in a Windows 2000 project will define the necessary steps to move from the current environment to the new Windows 2000 infrastructure.

Index